JEWISH CULTURE IN EARLY MODERN EUROPE

To Phil x
Betsy
with love x
affection

3/3
Paul

DAVID B. RUDERMAN
Photo by Tobias Barniske, 2009

JEWISH CULTURE
IN EARLY MODERN EUROPE

ESSAYS IN HONOR OF DAVID B. RUDERMAN

Edited by
Richard I. Cohen, Natalie B. Dohrmann,
Adam Shear, and Elchanan Reiner

HEBREW UNION COLLEGE PRESS
❊ ❊ ❊
UNIVERSITY OF PITTSBURGH PRESS

This publication is made possible with support from the Herbert D. Katz Publication Fund

Published by the University of Pittsburgh Press, Pittsburgh, PA, 15260,
and Hebrew Union College Press, Cincinnati, OH, 45220
Copyright © 2014, Hebrew Union College Press
Manufactured in the United States of America
Printed on acid-free paper
10 9 8 7 6 5 4 3 2 1

Library of Congress Cataloging-in-Publication Data

Jewish Culture in Early Modern Europe: Essays in Honor of David B. Ruderman / edited
by Richard I. Cohen, Natalie B. Dohrmann, Adam Shear, and Elchanan Reiner.
p. cm
Includes bibliographical references and index.
ISBN 978-0-8229-4433-1 (hardcover: alk. paper)
1. Jews—Europe—History—18th century. 2. Jews—Europe—History—17th century. 3.
Jews—Europe—History—16th century. 4. Jews—Civilization. 5. Judaism—Relations. 6.
Civilization, Modern—Jewish influences. 7. Europe—Ethnic relations.
I. Ruderman, David B., honoree. II. Cohen, Richard I., editor. III. Dohrmann, Natalie B.,
editor. IV. Shear, Adam, editor. V. Reiner, Elchanan, editor.
DS135.E82J49 2014
305.892'4040903—dc23   2014008210

CONTENTS

✼ ✼ ✼

II. KNOWLEDGE NETWORKS

III. "JEWS" AND "JUDAISM" IN THE EARLY MODERN EUROPEAN IMAGINATION

ACKNOWLEDGMENTS

❈ ❈ ❈

FROM the beginning, the transatlantic collaboration which made this book possible has been an easy and rewarding partnership. The editors are grateful to colleagues and friends who have helped us prepare this tribute to David Ruderman. Michael Meyer, the distinguished historian and former head of HUC's publication committee, showed immediate interest and involvement in the project, and was instrumental in shepherding it through its initial stages. Rabbi David Ellenson, Chancellor and former President of Hebrew Union College–Jewish Institute of Religion, was extremely supportive of the project. We are also indebted to David Altshuler for his sage advice and guidance in bringing this to fruition. *Im en kemaḥ en torah.* Arthur Kiron, Schottenstein-Jesselson Curator of Judaica Collections at the Katz Center/University of Pennsylvania, has offered valuable input and assistance. Thanks go to Bonnie Blankenship and Etty Lassman for help with the manuscript.

At Hebrew Union College Press, Sonja Rethy and Angela Roskop Erisman have guided the manuscript through the stages of publication with grace and expertise. Many thanks to the director of HUC Press, David H. Aaron, and the director of the University of Pittsburgh Press, Peter Kracht, for making this an inaugural project of their new publishing collaboration. We are grateful to the Klau Library at Hebrew Union College for permission to use the illustration on the cover. We are also deeply grateful for support from the Herbert D. Katz Publication Fund and to the Katz Center for Advanced Judaic Studies at the University of Pennsylvania for making space over the years for the intellectual fellowship that reverberates through these essays.

Sadly, as the book goes to press, our beloved colleague and a remarkable human being, Michael Heyd, passed away. His intellectual contribution to the conversation on the early modern period will be sorely missed. We are pleased that his essay here will enable this dialogue to continue.

Shevat/January 5774/2014, Jerusalem/Philadelphia/Pittsburgh

INTRODUCTION

❈ ❈ ❈

From Venice to Philadelphia—Revisiting the Early Modern

Adam Shear, Richard I. Cohen,
Elchanan Reiner, Natalie B. Dohrmann

IN his introduction to *Early Modern Jewry*, David Ruderman reveals something of his intellectual autobiography by relating to three seventeenth-century figures who inspired him in his scholarly path and had a significant impact on how he conceives of the Early Modern as a distinct era in Jewish history. Each figure is connected in some way to the Italian port of Venice. Though they differ considerably from one another, in their distinctive hybridity Leon Modena, Simone Luzzatto, and Joseph Shlomo Delmedigo were each paradigmatic of the age.

Modena, the enigmatic rabbinic figure, was full of internal contradictions. A man of great learning—restless and creative with no bounds, critical and sharp like a knife, courageous and questioning—he delved into the new and traditional worlds of knowledge that engaged Jewish culture in his day. Modena, as a man of many worlds and interests, a dabbler and an intellectual, holds in his person the vicissitudes and internal conflicts of the early modern intellectual experience.

The second, Simone Luzzatto, while also a Venetian rabbi like Modena, was dramatically different from Modena. Standing in between the Jewish community and the Italian surrounding, Luzzatto sought to lower the walls of the ghetto. His 1638 *Discorso circa il stato de gl'hebrei et in particolar dimoranti nell'inclita città di Venetia* (A discourse on the state of the Jews, particularly those dwelling in the illustrious city of Venice) fused notions of Italian civic thought with emerging concepts of raison d'état. This stirring apologetic for the Jews of Venice forcefully argued that their petty trading, their overall usefulness and, especially, their loyalty to the Republic combined to make a significant contribution to the welfare of the city. In a work that is cited repeatedly in modern discussions on the emancipation of the Jews, Luzzatto enunciated a new political vision for the Jews, one in which they would be integrated more fully, even if not seamlessly, into seventeenth-century society.

The third figure, Delmedigo, charted a course for Jews toward the new sciences of the early modern period. Born in Crete, and of very distant Ashkenazic origin, Delmedigo's identity was no less imbued with Sephardic and Mediterranean roots. He studied medicine in Padua, where he learned astronomy with Galileo, and spent a year in Venice where he encountered both Modena and Luzzatto. Delmedigo was clearly not the sedentary type. He traveled to the Middle East, Eastern Europe, and later to Central Europe, taking with him his conflicting identities and interests, *inter alia*, science and Kabbalah, rabbinism and Karaism, East and West, new books and old manuscripts. Even more than the other two, Delmedigo reflects in his person the cultural image of the period to which this book is dedicated. Despite the fact that these three were individuals on the margins (or perhaps because of it), their restlessness, curiosity, and lust to travel were symptomatic of an age of changing boundaries and kaleidescopic new vistas.

The Talmud tells of a stone in Jerusalem, the so-called stone of claims (*even to'im*). From atop this stone, in this highest city at the navel of the world, a person would announce what they had found, ask one's great questions, and stake one's claims. Ruderman's stone of claims—his intellectual touchstone—has always been Venice. Venice was not just the incidental meeting place of these enigmatic men; it is the metropolis that best emblemizes the Italian world that sparked the intellect and curiosity of David Ruderman. Writing in the late 1980s, he described this Italian Jewish world in the following words:

> In absorbing diverse Jewish and non-Jewish cultural forms and creatively molding them into constantly novel configurations, in patiently tolerating diversity and discord, in channeling ideas and values from one place to another as an entrepôt and clearing house of merchandise, and in allowing individuality to blossom within a framework of communal consensus, Italian Jewry was expressing its own vitality, its own creativity. Perhaps the function of mediating and correlating, of translating one universe of discourse into another, is not so passive, not so unspectacular an achievement… From the perspective of the postmodern world in which we live, one of diverse cultural lifestyles and values where no single ideology reigns supreme but where bitter acrimony and extremism hold sway, the image of Italian Jewry seems refreshingly appealing. Perhaps in its quiet sanity and dignified restraint, in its mutual respect and tolerance for competing and dissenting parties, and in its harmonizing and integrative capacities, can be located not only the essential legacy of Italian Jewish civilization but also its enduring significance for contemporary culture.[1]

In this urban space we find excitement mingled with fear before the emerging world of print; encounters between Christians and Jews, some acerbic others welcoming and inviting; Jews tentatively exiting the secluded experience of the ghetto and embracing the adventure found on untrodden paths; and an explosion of intellectual innovation in science, mysticism, and a range of heretical ideas. Italy—with Venice at the center conceptually and historically—where the Talmud was burnt and Christian scholars integrated Kabbalah into their religious world, has long fascinated Ruderman, and over the course of his career he has sought to tell its complex story through a series of unexpected and wondrous characters, from Abraham Farissol and Abraham Yagel in northern Italy, to figures outside Italy but who embodied the "Italian-ness" described above, like Abraham Tang in London, and most recently Pinḥas Hurwitz in Vilna.[2] Ruderman has crafted in and through them the intricate world of what we might call a Venetian paradigm for understanding Jewish cultural history.

David Ruderman was hardly the first Jewish historian to focus attention on this period, or even on the Jews of Renaissance Italy. But when he began his career in the 1970s, an entire volume devoted to case studies on the dynamics of Jewish culture in early modern Europe would have made little sense to most Jewish and European historians. While social, religious, and intellectual developments among European and Middle Eastern Jews in the period from the expulsion of the Jews from Spain (1492) to the French Revolution (1789) were the subject of many studies—including by scholars as renowned as Gershom Scholem, Jacob Katz, Salo Baron, and Cecil Roth—this span of time was usually understood as the end of the Jewish Middle Ages and rarely conceptualized as a distinctive historical period.[3]

In the last two decades, historians in North America, Europe, and Israel have refined and developed the discussion of a period roughly spanning the three centuries from 1500 to 1800 in Jewish culture and more and more have found a periodization that offers an "early modern" period as a useful heuristic for interpreting historical developments. Demographic, geographic, and technological factors suggest different dynamics in Jewish culture and society than in the period up to the late fifteenth century ("medieval") and different as well from the nineteenth (and "long nineteenth") and twentieth centuries ("modern").[4] Such a view, clearly also reflecting a general historiographical trend in European history away from "Renaissance-Reformation" and "Enlightenment" periods toward a view of the "Early Modern" as a more broadly integrated conceptual frame, has more slowly made its way into synthetic treatments of Jewish history as well.[5] Conversely, increasing progress has been made toward incorporating the Jewish experience into what is sometimes called "general" European history with the complex dynamics of Jewish-Christian cultural interchange in this period of particular interest.[6] The incorporation of the Jewish experience and Jewish-Muslim interchange into the "general" history of the Islamic world is also on-going, enriching broader discussions of the intersections of Europe and the Islamic world.[7]

Periodization, however, is always an aide for historiographical inquiry, and never a determining demarcation of epochs. Where, for example, ought one draw the line between this period and that? Does the Jewish Middle Ages end in 1450? 1492? 1500? Does the Modern enter the stage in 1750? 1772? 1789? 1800? Any decision in these instances is itself an historical interpretation. Still, delineating aspects of continuity and discontinuity across periods and with respect to specific areas of social, religious, political, and intellectual life offers rich opportunities for more precise descriptions of particular aspects of the past. Any synthetic interpretations of a period must depend on a broad base of case specific research.

Arguably the first attempt to explicitly conceptualize the span from the beginning of the sixteenth century to the late eighteenth century as a distinctive period in Jewish history came from the economic and political history *European Jewry in the Age of Mercantilism, 1550–1750,* by Jonathan Israel (1985). Israel attempted to argue for an "early modern" period in Jewish history based primarily on changed economic and political circumstances associated with the gradual return of Jews to Western Europe.[8] In a review of Israel's work published in 1987, Ruderman—a Jewish intellectual historian, then at Yale, and already immersed in his work on the Italian world of figures like Modena, Luzzatto, and Delmedigo— praised the work for its attempt to conceptualize the period, but pointed out its deficiencies in the arena of Jewish cultural and intellectual history.[9] In what might be seen as a belated response to Ruderman and other critics,[10] Israel's preface to the third edition of his work (1997) gestured toward cultural and intellectual factors.[11] Israel could reference a number of studies of early modern Jewish-Christian interactions in the religious and culture sphere (as well as the economic) penned by historians in North America, Israel, and Europe between the mid 1980s and the late 1990s.[12] Jewish-Christian interactions, and changes and developments in Jewish thought and religious life in this period had been studied before, against the backdrop of the Renaissance, the Reformation, the Scientific Revolution, Absolutism, and Enlightenment. However the conceptualization of the period as a distinctive one in Jewish historiography was a new, and growing historiographical development.

Ruderman has played a key part in the advance of an early modern Jewish cultural history. Through his early monographic studies of two northern Italian Jewish intellectuals, Abraham Farissol (c. 1451–c. 1525)[13] and Abraham Yagel (1553–c. 1623), he offered a close reading of the intellectual interests and scholarly agendas of two representative figures contextualized against the backdrop of Renaissance humanism, and late Renaissance interests in science and magic.[14] With these studies, Ruderman joined a small group of scholars, among them Robert Bonfil, Arthur Lesley, and Moshe Idel, who were considering the impact of Renaissance culture on Jewish scholars in new and sophisticated ways that went beyond the Burckhardtean framework of older studies by Cecil Roth and Moshe Shulvass.[15] Ruderman in particular focused on the dynamics and complexities of the interactions of multiple traditions in the intellectual lives of early modern Italian Jews, in his case studies of Farissol and

Yagel and in his work as an editor of two significant collections that set the agenda for the field of Italian Jewish intellectual history for the 1990s and the 2000s.[16]

A full contextualization of Jewish intellectual life in the sixteenth and seventeenth century required an assessment of the role of the Scientific Revolution in Jewish culture—the world of Delmedigo—a relatively understudied subject prior to Ruderman's *Jewish Thought and Scientific Discovery in Early Modern Europe* (1995).[17] Although Jews had played a limited role in the development of the new science, Ruderman suggested that engagement with the natural world and new scientific developments partly shaped Jewish culture and society. In considering these issues, Ruderman moved beyond the sphere of Jewish culture in Italy and past the early seventeenth century, to consider the work of Jewish intellectuals in the Ottoman Empire, early modern Ashkenaz, and England, ranging from the sixteenth through the eighteenth centuries, thus anticipating the theme of mobility and border crossing that so defines his understanding of the era to this day.

Charting the trajectory of Jewish scientific learning brought Ruderman to a new series of studies of Jewish engagement with the Enlightenment, complicating regnant narratives of the Haskalah. In a series of studies of eighteenth-century English Jewish intellectuals, Ruderman has contributed to a broadening of the horizon of eighteenth-century Jewish thought beyond the traditional focus on the German-based Haskalah movement.[18]

From his early studies of Italian Jewish intellectuals to his later work on eighteenth-century English, German, and Polish Jews, Ruderman has placed central emphasis on the individual as the representative or exemplary figure through whose life and career the problems of a period and cultural context are revealed.[19] Whether by design or by serendipity, Ruderman's scholarly trajectory has allowed him to explore the dynamics of cultural and intellectual interactions of early modern Jews with most of the major intellectual trends of early modern Europe, grouped under the heuristic rubrics of "Renaissance," "Scientific Revolution," and "Enlightenment." Arguably the only major area left unexplored by Ruderman is the direct impact of the Protestant and Catholic Reformations on Jewish culture, a field that has received renewed attention in the last decade or so, as can be seen in some of the studies in this volume.[20]

Perhaps not surprisingly, the range of Ruderman's own research and writing increasingly drew him toward a synthetic consideration of the period as whole.[21] In 2010 he published the programmatic *Early Modern Jewry: A New Cultural History*, which lays out what he sees to be the distinctive elements of an "early modern Jewish culture." *Early Modern Jewry* represents the fruit of decades of attempting to synthesize the period in teaching undergraduate and graduate students at the University of Maryland (1974–83), Yale University (1983–94), and the University of Pennsylvania (since 1994).[22]

Without pretending to any kind of comprehensiveness, this volume is an extension of Ruderman's project, contributing a series of telling historical snapshots of the current state of research that forward, refine, and challenge how we understand the early modern period, and spark further conceptualization and inquiry. As such, the editors and the authors offer it as a tribute to David Ruderman for his formative role in the development of this discussion since the mid-1980s, not only in his own scholarship, but also as a teacher and as a program builder and facilitator of scholarly conversation.

Ruderman had already delineated some key elements in early modern Jewish intellectual life in earlier writings, including the key role of print, the significance of networks and mobility among Jewish intellectuals, and the value of extraordinary individuals who served as conceptual diplomats, absorbing and translating so-called external traditions into a Jewish idiom. Interaction between Jewish and Christian cultures, through texts and personal encounters of Jewish and Christian intellectuals, has also been central to Ruderman's understanding of this period. In his 2010 work, Ruderman articulated what he deemed the five defining factors of a Jewish Early Modernity: an "accelerated mobility"; "communal cohesiveness"; a "knowledge explosion"; a "crisis of rabbinic authority"; and a "blurring of religious identities."[23] While acknowledging that this list cannot capture all aspects of early modern Jewish life, Ruderman argued that these were symptomatic and constitutive of a distinct period in the cultural framework of Jewish life lasting roughly from the late fifteenth through the late eighteenth century. The intense and ongoing cultural encounter of Jews and non-Jews throughout this period also suggests ways that this periodization of Jewish culture could be a useful common language linking Jewish history to the dynamics and processes unfolding in early modern European culture in general.

Ruderman's categorical pentaverate proves compelling to several of the authors represented in this volume. Individually, the essays collected are tightly wrought case studies that illuminate aspects of Jewish culture in early modern Europe, whether constructions of Judaism by non-Jews or those on the margins of Jewishness or the interplay of social and intellectual connections between and among Jews. Read as a mosaic, the microstudies present a rich and nuanced portrait of a Jewish culture that is both a contributing member and a product of early modern Europe.

In the first section of this volume, "Realms of Authority: Conflict and Adaptation," we examine the dynamics of the authority structures of the Jewish communities in the aftermath of the seismic expulsions and migrations that reshaped the geographical contours of the Jewish world. This section explores the formation of Jewish communities, Jewish communal autonomy, and cultural representations of leadership. These are traditional concerns of Jewish historiography but require renewed attention for the early modern period against the backdrop of changing geographical/demographic patterns and political arrangements. Expulsion and migration not only led to a mobility that had consequences for Jewish culture, but also for the internal cohesion of now larger transregional Jewish communities (such as the Sephardic Diaspora in the Ottoman empire or the networks of Ashkenazim that stretched across German lands and the Polish-Lithuanian Commonwealth); and in places where Jews from different regions came together (such as northern Italy). These essays also demonstrate the ways that Jewish leaders and intellectuals conceptualized their and their community's places within local, regional, and national polities. The emergence of Sabbatianism and the changes in European politics in the seventeenth and eighteenth centuries only sharpen questions of communal politics and leadership at the end of the period.

Although Jews very much responded to political and religious developments in Christian Europe, a large percentage of early modern Jews lived under Muslim rule, and the experiences of Jews living in the Islamic world need to also be incorporated into the broad historiographical conception of Early Modernity in a global Jewish history. While this volume does not contain essays on developments in the Persian sphere, a number of essays relate to the Ottoman Empire and North Africa and to interconnections and exchanges across the Mediterranean, an important corrective to overly Eurocentric studies. The geographical remapping of a Jewish Early Modernity can contribute a great deal to a better understanding of the integrated economic and cultural landscape of the era for Christians and Muslims alike, and permits a keener awareness of the porous, changing, and context-dependent boundaries dividing the broader cultural, political, economic, and demographic landscape of the epoch.

The impact of expulsions and migrations in the fifteenth century, especially the expulsion from Spain in 1492 and the forced conversion of Jews in Portugal in 1497, has been much discussed and is proposed by many as the natural starting point for consideration of Jewish Early Modernity. By carefully tracing the history of an elite Portuguese exile family and their marriage patterns, Joseph R. Hacker's essay is a case study of the dynamics of social change in the aftermath of expulsions and in the encounter of Jews from distinct communities in new locations. But such encounters did not begin only in 1492, and Elliott Horowitz shows the impact of encounters of Italian Jews from different backgrounds in his analysis of the fifteenth-century rabbi Judah Messer Leon's projections of his authority in central Italy in the social and intellectual arenas. The impact of the later, catastrophic Chmielnicki massacres (1648–49) on family life is the subject of Adam Teller's article, and shows the importance of gender for understanding intersections of family life and communal affairs.

If Horowitz's account of Jewish politics in the career of Messer Leon plays out against a backdrop of internal Jewish communal life, Matt Goldish's essay on Prague maps the way that internal Jewish politics and family rivalries can play out against a broader political canvas. And while the relation to external political events is implicit in the calculations of Goldish's subjects, the studies by Benjamin Fisher and Anne Oravetz Albert on Sephardic political discourse illuminate explicit attempts among key intellectuals in the Spanish and Portuguese community of Amsterdam to put forward *Jewish* political theories. Ruderman and others have stressed that Jewish communal authority and autonomy in this period consolidates and intensifies medieval patterns.[24] Yet while the Amsterdam community is often pointed to as a key example, Fisher's work on the Jewish identification with the Dutch state suggests a proto-modern anticipation of nineteenth-century emancipation-era patterns. At the same time, Albert suggests that Orobio de Castro was reconceptualizing Jewish communal autonomy as Jewish communal sovereignty in a robust defense of rabbinic authority and in dialogue with Christian political thought.

Section II, "Knowledge Networks," collects essays that engage the dynamics of intellectual life in light of demographic, political, and technological change. The advent of print changed the means of communication and reshaped networks of scholarship. While the "meta-halakhic" disciplines[25] of philosophy and Kabbalah had been pursued in the medieval period, early modern publishing (first among several factors) led to new phenomena with unanticipated consequences: the popularization of the Kabbalah, the spread of knowledge in the vernacular, and intellectual engagement with new science.

We begin this section in the fifteenth century, with Talya Fishman's analysis of Profiat Duran's ideas of the possibility of a somatic spiritual engagement with Scripture, a theory that, Fishman suggests, ties together several late medieval Jewish intellectual trends on the eve of major intellectual and cultural change. In his careful study of Joseph Shlomo Delmedigo's interests in atomism in the seventeenth century, Y. Tzvi Langermann also takes up the issue of Jewish intellectual engagement with current philosophical issues. The deep entanglement of both Fishman's and Langermann's subjects with Kabbalah represents one continuity of the late medieval to the early modern. But Kabbalah was far from static, and Langermann shows the developing connections of Lurianic Kabbalah and evolving scientific theories. Yossi Chajes's study of the intersections of Lurianic Kabbalah and the new science through diagrams gives a fascinating look at the kinds of novel intercultural intellectual dynamics that emerged in Early Modernity.

So crucial is print to understanding early modern Jewish intellectual history that Ruderman, in his *Early Modern Jewry,* treats the history of ideas and the history of this ground-breaking technology in tandem under the historiographic rubric "explosion," which suggests its potentially violent, landscape-altering, and unpredictable consequences.[26] Ruderman's reflections there join a growing body of scholarship on the impact of print on Jewish culture in the period,[27] and two essays here expand our understanding of the implications of what was printed for shaping Jewish culture: Moshe Idel focuses on the printing of Kabbalah while Amnon Raz-Krakotzkin traces the printing of works related to or extracted from the Talmud at the time of its burning.

Both Idel and Raz-Krakotzkin show the critical interrelationship between the printing of Hebrew books and the encounters of Jewish scholars with Christians, be they other scholars, printers and publishers, or church censors, expurgators, and inquisitors. Indeed, all the essays in the first two sections concern themselves with Jews who were in one way or another deeply engaged with non-Jewish sources of authority and texts. The third section of the book, "'Jews' and 'Judaism' in the Early Modern European Imagination," focuses a lens explicitly on cultural and intellectual interchange, especially between Jews and Christians, noting the major role of conversos as intermediaries and mediators. The early modern period saw not only an unprecedented level of Christian interest in post-biblical Judaism, it also witnessed the emergence of a large number of Jews, especially exconversos, with an intimate knowledge of Christianity. The constructed images of Jews and Judaism that emerge in this period can hardly be called the product of a "Christian" imagination but rather of a broader *European* imagination.

Giuseppe Mazzotta's study of the intersection of the work of Pico della Mirandola with Jewish thought offers an introduction to this theme. As with Talya Fishman's study of Profiat Duran, Mazzotta's is a case study of a figure, Pico della Mirandola, who was a pioneer of what would become characteristic of Christian scholarship on the Jews—a move from purely (or primarily) polemical motivations to an engagement with Judaism as a new way of thinking about Christianity. Anthony Grafton's examination of Christian discussion and presentation of Hellenistic Judaism is a case example both of the dynamics of that encounter and of what happens in an era of expanding knowledge. Andrew Berns, in a similar vein, looks at instances in which knowledge of the Jewish past was a joint endeavor of Jewish and Christian scholars. Joanna Weinberg's study of the memorialization of Erasmus in both Latin and Hebrew similarly demonstrates how scholarship can transcend boundaries within a republic of letters.

Boundaries were never fully erased as evidenced in Jonathan Karp's study of Luther's ideas about Jews and usury during the Reformation. But various kinds of cultural, intellectual, and social interchange are critical to understanding this period. Debra Kaplan's nuanced study underscores the critical role of converts in the kind of Christian Hebraist activity examined by Berns, Weinberg, and Grafton. Adam Sutcliffe's case study of the converso Miguel de Barrios and his idiosyncratic construction of an identity on the borders of Judaism and Christianity suggests another model—what Sutcliffe calls "conservative hybridity." Of course, border-crossing hybridity had real consequences in some early modern contexts, as Roger Chartier's study of Antônio José Da Silva's encounter with the Inquisition makes clear.

One of the consistent questions about the Early Modern is its relationship to Modernity. If case studies dealing with the fifteenth through the seventeenth centuries permit us to see basic trends and patterns that define early modern Jewish cultural life, what changes or remains the same in the eighteenth century, typically viewed as the key hinge point in the emergence of European—and Jewish—modernity? As in many synthetic interpretations it is sometimes easier to point to the beginning of a series of phenomena than to the end.

Various cultural, intellectual, and social developments arguably make the eighteenth century the key period for the emergence of modern European social and political conditions, including secularization and the rise of the centralized nation state. Recent books on the period have sharpened discussion of the nature of the Enlightenment and secularization. Do developments in this period presage or predict aspects of modern Jewish culture? Do new developments, especially political ones, in the eighteenth century mark the end of the period and the beginning of a new one? Or are the dynamics of Jewish enlightenment and secularization processes continuations of early modern cultural trends? If such trends continue into the eighteenth century, which continue into the nineteenth?

Ruderman ends his *Early Modern Jewry* with the proposal that much of eighteenth-century Jewish cultural history should be seen as continuous with the Early Modern, along with the tantalizing suggestion that some Jewish cultural dynamics in the period of emancipation and industrialization from the late eighteenth century through the nineteenth century might be profitably analyzed for their early modern characteristics.[28] In particular, Ruderman is not convinced that the Haskalah movement represents a break from the early modern in intellectual or cultural terms, a position he has elaborated in a series of essays and oral and written dialogues with Shmuel Feiner and others.[29] For Ruderman, the paradigmatic synthesis and interchange of "Venice" remains alive in places like London, Berlin, Amsterdam, and Prague in the eighteenth century.

The penultimate section of this volume, "The Long Eighteenth Century in an Early Modern Key," examines eighteenth-century Jewish culture as a hinge between the Early Modern and the late. Despite recent rejections of the secularization thesis as a master-theme of modernity, understanding issues of secularization and secularity remain a part of the historiographic conversation.[30] In his essay, Michael Heyd suggests that a general crisis of confidence in the connections between a "secular" human realm and the divine pervaded early eighteenth-century European discussions and that understanding the general crisis could shed light on the Jewish case of modernization.

Yaacob Dweck's study of the Holy Land emissary and bibliophile Ḥayim Yosef Azulai opens a window onto eighteenth-century Hebrew book culture, showing continuity with the previous two centuries, but also the emergence of a new phenomenon that would be critical for nineteenth-century Jewish scholarly activity—the great public and semipublic libraries of Europe. Francesca Bregoli's study of Livorno (in which Azulai also plays a role) likewise depicts a scene in which the upheavals of a secularizing milieu of the Livornese Jewish elite is braided with strong lines of continuity with earlier patterns of patronage and networking.

Such continuities of Early Modern "connectedness" of Jews across time is echoed in space, as can be seen in Andrea Schatz's portrait of Naphtali Herz Wessely and other Enlightenment figures, who were mediators not only between the Jewish past and present but also across geographic boundaries. Present-day Jews could themselves be bridges, which is the role they play in Edward Gibbon's thinking about Jews and Christians of antiquity, as David Katz shows. Katz's essay returns us to the familiar world of the transmission of negative images of Jews, adherence to which early modern Christian Hebraism and Enlightenment discourse on the "other" proves continuous rather than discontinuous.[31]

How to mark clear change—and when it can be observed—in the discourse about the "Jewish question" as well as internal Jewish discussion takes center stage in Shmuel Feiner's essay on Moses Mendelssohn's responses to the critical events in the year 1782. While it would be too simple to take one year as the "beginning" of modernity, Feiner highlights the ways in which most of the key issues in Jewish modernity were adumbrated by state action, public debate, and Jewish responses in one remarkable year. In Sharon Flatto's study of three generations of rabbis from the Landau family of Prague, beginning with Ezekiel Landau, one of the key interlocutors in the debates of the 1780s, we can see the indications of a rapid process of intellectual and cultural modernization at the end of the eighteenth and beginning of the nineteenth centuries. In other realms, however, the years around 1800 do not mark a clear divide between an early modern and a modern Jewish history. Rebecca Kobrin's study of the treatment of Eastern European domestic servants, and the relationship between gender and class stratification among Jews, shows considerable continuity from the seventeenth to the end of the nineteenth century.

Part V, "From the Early Modern to the Late Modern (and Back Again)," follows the traces of the Early Modern that are both etched into and effaced from later eras. Moving from the social to the literary, even an unimpeachably modernist writer like Mendele Moykher Sforim could, as Israel Bartal shows, offer an attempt to return to early modern patterns of language use from the middle of the nineteenth century. While Bartal does not invoke a concept of medievalism, in fact, by reaching to a pre-Haskalah past, Mendele was reaching back to what he would have considered a "medieval" Ashkenazic past. And while we typically think of American Jews as belonging firmly to modern Jewish history, Beth Wenger's essay provocatively situates eighteenth-century American Jews in an early modern context. Her subjects could not foresee a future exceptionalist American Jewish historiography, and she shows how they naturally drew their own lines to Jews elsewhere in the world and back into Jewish history.

Thus Bartal and Wenger, in different ways, offer us reflections on the project of historiography as retelling the past and as connecting to the past in whatever present one finds oneself. They also remind us of the contingencies of periodization. In her essay, Vivian Liska takes up these problems by examining the twentieth-century reception of Rahel Varnhagen, a figure who stands on the precipice of the Early Modern/Modern (or Medieval/Modern) divide. Yosef Kaplan's portrait of an acrimonious exchange over the role of the Jews in premodern Spanish history, as preserved in the writings of and letters between two towering twentieth-century historians offers us a final reflection on the connection binding the work of the historian and the dynamics of modern Jewish culture and politics.

Liska and Kaplan remind us that David Ruderman and all of the writers in this volume operate not in an early modern culture but in a contemporary academic world and a particular series of institutional and political arrangements that cannot but inform scholarship. Ruderman's interlocutors here are in fact his colleagues and students who have relationships with him ranging from decades of close friendship to more recent interactions. While some of the authors here (Cohen, Kaplan, Heyd, Hacker) were educated with Ruderman at the Hebrew University of Jerusalem at a time when the distinctiveness of the early modern period was not part of the Jewish historiographical agenda, his doctoral students from Yale and Penn represented here (Chajes, Flatto, Kobrin, Shear, Kaplan, Bregoli, Dweck, Albert, Berns, Fisher) more or less "grew up" with the notion of an early modern period in Jewish history naturalized and internalized.

Over four decades, Ruderman's Renaissance Jews have found in him a most sympathetic and astute observer who always sought to uncover the context and intellectual setting in which they traveled. His *dramatis personae* were not one-dimensional figures who spent their days studying only the canonical books of Jewish tradition. They moved in many different circles, crossed between Jewish and Christian worlds, dabbled in science and Kabbalah, studied and practiced medicine and the occult, engaged in economics and had a compulsion for gambling, played with allegories and imaginative constructions, and never ceased to redraw the sensitive boundary between loyalty to and identification with Jewish culture and community and the Christian world and thought.

Ruderman's passion does not end with the intellectual figures of the Renaissance. Always attuned to the currents of modern Jewish thought, an interest he cherished long before he became an academic, he has informed his studies of the eighteenth century with extensive knowledge of, and keen insight into, modern science, philosophy, and religion. Dramatically, he has given new life to a group of English-Jewish thinkers, who clearly struggled with their attraction to and rejection of Christianity, and tried to enunciate a position that was never free of the ambiguous identities and religious influences they experienced.

Ruderman the scholar has always also been a teacher, and a devoted one. Not only does he love shepherding bright young minds into serious scholarship, he trains them to challenge and dispute their teachers. His students know that this is his calling, and they have reaped the riches of his knowledge, passion, and support. Whoever has not heard David Ruderman sing the praises of this or that student who will become the future "great" has never heard David Ruderman speak. He takes deep pride in their achievements, even—especially—as they find their own independent voice.

A generous and capacious intellect, Ruderman possesses an unsurpassed ability to bring people together from all backgrounds and traditions to study, learn from each other, grow, and bring new insights to the scholarly world and the general public. He has invested the energy, drive, and vision he brings to scholarship and teaching to the institution of Jewish learning he has directed at the University of Pennsylvania since 1994. The Herbert D. Katz Center for Advanced Judaic Studies has evolved under his leadership into one of the premier centers for advanced studies in the humanities. As one peruses the subjects that have dominated the interests of the Center and the personalities who have participated in its activities, one sees the nature of Ruderman's orientation from the outset. For Ruderman, Jewish studies needs to be studied within the wider web of its contexts, be they geographic, intellectual, thematic, or comparative. The topics on which the Center focused its year-long seminars range from biblical archaeology to contemporary art, with much in between. In turn, the interdisciplinary interaction that became synonymous with the seminar has shaped his own catholic approach to the Early Modern.

And the teaching mission for Ruderman has not been limited to his students. Public lectures, programs that bring congregational rabbis together with academic scholars, and opportunities for members of the Center's board to learn from the Center's fellows all bring to fruition another aspect of his notion of community of learning, in which nonacademics and academics learn together and widen each other's horizons. Professor, rabbi, and former camp counselor merge seamlessly in David as he convenes these scholarly communities year by year at the Center and as he communicates the value of serious learning to a wider public.

It might be an over-determined reading of historiography as biography to relate too closely David's scholarly emphasis on interaction and cultural symbiosis to his own role as a bridge-builder across different academic communities in Israel, Europe, and the United States. But if we can speak of a "Philadelphia" school in Jewish history that has emerged under David's leadership, it would be one that looks a lot like the paradigmatic "Venice" that has characterizes his own scholarship: a view that emphasizes mediations of minority groups and wider cultures, while still giving due weight to the internal dynamics and dynamism of the minority. Indeed, the early modern period—with increasing crossing of boundaries, hybridity, acculturation, and an attractive wider culture even while Jews maintained semi-autonomous communal structures in the Polish-Lithuanian Commonwealth, the Ottoman empire, or the Italian ghettos—seems a particularly fruitful realm of investigation for someone with David's range of interests and commitments. Perhaps we might even say that David has acted in many ways as a model early modern Jewish intellectual who moves seamlessly between the "general" republic of letters, and the particular Jewish conversation.

All this David has accomplished while remaining a modest man who reveres others more than he does himself, inquisitive and down-to-earth, sensitive to the needs, wishes, and goals of others, and a dear friend, colleague, and mentor. Unfortunately we could only bring together a small number of his friends and colleagues to collaborate in this volume. In this project of affection and honor, the contributors have each offered him an aspect of their scholarship that they feel ties them to David. The editors and the authors of the essays here each feel privileged to have been part of David Ruderman's intellectual and social world and look forward to continuing conversation with him for many years to come.

Notes

1. "At the Intersection of Cultures: The Historical Legacy of Italian Jewry," in *Gardens and Ghettos: The Art of Jewish Life in Italy*, ed. V. B. Mann. (Berkeley, Calif., 1989), 21.

2. *A Best-Selling Hebrew Book of the Modern Era: The Book of the Covenant of Pinḥas Hurwitz and Its Remarkable Legacy* (Seattle, forthcoming).

3. See for example, Yosef Kaplan, "The Early Modern Period in the Historiographic Production of Jacob Katz," in *Historiography Reappraised: New Views of Jacob Katz's Oeuvre*, ed. I. Bartal and S. Feiner (Hebrew; Jerusalem, 2008), 19–35.

4. For discussion of the emerging periodization, in addition to Ruderman, *Early Modern Jewry*, see Elisheva Carlebach, "European Jewry in the Early Modern Period, 1492–1750," in *The Oxford Handbook of Jewish Studies*, ed. M. Goodman (Oxford, 2002), 363–75; Adam Shear, "Jews and Judaism in Early Modern Europe," in *The Cambridge Companion to Jewish History, Religion, and Culture*, ed. J. R. Baskin and K. Seeskin (Cambridge, 2010), 140–68. Dean Bell has recently offered a one-volume textbook treatment in *Jews in the Early Modern World* (Lanham, Md., 2007). [Note that the *Cambridge History of Judaism* has a forthcoming volume covering the period 1500–1815, edited by Adam Sutcliffe and Jonathan Karp.]

5. The division of medieval and modern is epitomized in textbook accounts such as H. H. Ben-Sasson et al., *A History of the Jewish People* (Hebrew; Tel Aviv, 1969: English; London, 1976). Even recent surveys such as David Biale, ed., *Cultures of the Jews: A New History* (New York, 2002), split this period between the "medieval" (vol. 2) and the "modern" (vol. 3). In the case of this volume the division is between "Diversities of Diaspora" and "Modern Encounters." Likewise, Raymond P. Scheindlin, in his one-volume *A Short History of the Jewish People from Legendary Times to Modern Statehood* (Oxford, 1998), divides this period differently for different areas of the Jewish world—"medieval" Jewish history in both the Islamic world and in Christian Europe come to an end around 1500; the Jews of the "Ottoman Empire and the Middle East" are then considered in a chapter that spans 1453 to 1948; the Jews of "Western Europe" from 1500 to 1900 are treated in one chapter; while the Jews of Eastern Europe are treated in a chapter that extends from 1770 to 1948.

6. For some discussion, see Debra Kaplan and Magda Teter, "Out of the (Historiographic) Ghetto: Jews and the Reformation," *Sixteenth Century Journal* 40 (2009): 365–93; Anthony Grafton, *Worlds Made by Words: Scholarship and Community in the Modern West* (Cambridge, Mass., 2009), 178–80.

7. Attention to Jews in the Muslim world in the period from circa 1492 to 1800, however, is often presented as a continuation of the medieval or as a prelude to the modern. See, for example, the periodization in the two volumes of primary sources and textbook overviews by Norman A. Stillman, *The Jews of Arab Lands: A History and Sourcebook* (Philadelphia, 1979), which takes the story from the medieval through the nineteenth century, and the overlapping *The Jews of Arab Lands in Modern Times* (Philadelphia, 1991). More recently, see Zion Zohar, ed., *Sephardic and Mizrahi Jewry: From the Golden Age of Spain to Modern Times* (New York, 2005), which places most articles on the early modern period in a section titled: "From Expulsion to the Modern Era: Exile, Decline, and Revival" but includes an article on "early modern Sephardim and blacks" in the section titled "Sephardic Jewry in the Modern Era and Special Topics." In Biale, *Cultures of the Jews*, attention to Jews in the Ottoman Empire, North Africa, and Central Asia in the broad "early modern" period generally occurs in articles devoted to those areas in the third section titled "modern encounters." See also Scheindlin's periodization discussed above. Likewise a distinctive "early modern" period does not emerge in the three volumes edited by Shmuel Ettinger, *Toldot ha-yehudim be-artsot ha-Islam* (Jerusalem, 1981), that has been influential in teaching Jewish history in Israel. Volume 1 of that work published by Merkaz Zalman Shazar is subtitled "The Modern Period up to the Middle of the Nineteenth Century," and begins with the seventeenth century. The connection between a me-

dieval period and a late modern period for Jews in Islamic lands is usually understood through the historiographic lens of "decline"; for analysis, see Daniel Schroeter, "From Sephardi to Oriental: The 'Decline' Theory of Jewish Civilization in the Middle East and North Africa," in *The Jewish Contribution to Civilization: Reassessing an Idea*, ed. J. Cohen and R. I. Cohen (Oxford, 2008), 125–48.

8. Oxford, 1985; a paperback edition was published in 1991; and a third edition appeared in 1997. In the second edition, Israel added a section to his final chapter on aspects of vibrancy of Jewish life in the eighteenth century, changing the title of the chapter from "Decline" to "Decline and Renewal." The republication of his book provides an indication of the growing attention to the time frame as a unique historical period.

9. *Jewish Quarterly Review* 78 (1987): 154–59. Cf. Ruderman's reflections on Israel's work in *Early Modern Jewry*, 207–14.

10. See e.g., John Edwards's comments in the introduction to his survey, *The Jew in Christian Europe, 1400–1700* (London, 1988), wherein he offered his own work focusing on the religious history of Jews and Christians as a kind of corrective to Israel's focus on largely secular factors. Although Natalie Zemon Davis and Peter Burke (among others) had published before Israel, the 1980s and 1990s saw an explosion of work in which cultural approaches to early modern European history became central. For an overview of the "cultural turn," see Lynn Hunt, ed., *The New Cultural History* (Berkeley, Calif., 1989).

11. Israel, *European Jewry*, ix: "If mercantilism was one main branch of the dichotomy of impulses and pressures which transformed European Jewry in the sixteenth and seventeenth centuries, just as important, if my argument is right, was the mounting European spiritual and intellectual crisis, rooted in humanism and the Reformation, which first became fully evident, with far-reaching consequences in the second half of the seventeenth century."

12. It will be impossible to list all the relevant works here. In addition to the works by David Ruderman discussed here, also of importance are the essays of Yosef Kaplan, collected later in his *Alternative Path to Modernity: The Sephardi Diaspora in Western Europe* (Leiden, 2000). For other works from this period, see Giuseppe Veltri, "A Bibliography of Jewish Cultural History in the Early Modern Period," in *Cultural Intermediaries: Jewish Intellectuals in Early Modern Italy*, ed. D. B. Ruderman and G. Veltri (Philadelphia, 2004), 270–86; Joseph Davis, "The Cultural and Intellectual History of Ashkenazic Jews, 1500–1750: A Selective Bibliography and Essay," *Leo Baeck Institute Yearbook 38* (1993): 343–86.

13. *The World of a Renaissance Jew* (Cincinnati, Ohio, 1981).

14. *Kabbalah, Magic, and Science: The Cultural Universe of a Sixteenth-Century Jewish Physician* (Cambridge, Mass., 1988).

15. For references to this literature and an overview of the historiographical developments up to the early 1990s, see Ruderman, "Introduction," in Ruderman, ed., *Essential Papers on Jewish Culture in Renaissance and Baroque Italy* (New York, 1992), 1–39.

16. In addition to *Essential Papers*, see the volume coedited with Veltri, *Cultural Intermediaries*. Also influential in agenda-setting is Ruderman, "The Italian Renaissance and Jewish Thought," in *Renaissance Humanism: Foundations, Forms, and Legacy*, ed. A. Rabil, Jr. (Philadelphia, 1988), 1:382–433.

17. New Haven, Conn., 1995.

18. *Jewish Enlightenment in an English Key* (Princeton, N.J., 2000); *Connecting the Covenants: Judaism and the Search for Christian Identity in Eighteenth-Century England* (Philadelphia, 2007).

19. Ruderman was certainly not alone among early modern Jewish historians in focusing on individual biography as a means of getting at larger issues. Cf. Yosef Hayim Yerushalmi, *From Spanish Court to Italian Ghetto: Isaac Cardoso: A Study in Seventeenth-Century Marranism and Jewish Apologetics* (New York, 1971); Yosef Kaplan, *From Christianity to Judaism: The Story of Isaac Orobio de Castro*, trans. R. Loewe (Oxford, 1989). While some studies of historiography have noted the fall and rise of biography within professional historiography, an examination of the fortunes of biography in

Jewish historiography is a desideratum. It is worth noting that very few of Ruderman's doctoral students wrote intellectual biographies for their dissertations.

20. For surveys of this field, see Kaplan and Teter, "Out of the (Historiographic) Ghetto"; and Miriam Bodian, "The Reformation and the Jews," in *Rethinking European Jewish History*, ed. J. Cohen and M. Rosman (Oxford, 2009), 112–32. Also of note is Dean Phillip Bell and Stephen G. Burnett, eds., *Jews, Judaism, and the Reformation in Sixteenth-Century Germany* (Leiden, 2006). For older studies, see Haim Hillel Ben-Sasson, "Jewish-Christian Disputation in the Setting of Humanism and Reformation in the German Empire," *Harvard Theological Review* 59 (1966): 369–90; Ben-Sasson, "The Reformation in Contemporary Jewish Eyes," *Proceedings of the Israel Academy of Sciences and Humanities* 4.12 (1970): 239–326.

21. His interest in synthesis certainly began much earlier. See e.g., "At the Intersection of Cultures."

22. Ruderman, *Early Modern Jewry*, 227.

23. Ibid., 15–16.

24. See the essays collected in *Kehal Yisrael*, vol. 2, "The Middle Ages and the Early Modern Period," ed. A. Grossman and Y. Kaplan (Hebrew; Jerusalem, 2001); and vol. 3, "The Modern Period," ed. I. Bartal (Hebrew; Jerusalem, 2004). Some material in volume 2 extends to the late modern period, while there is material in volume 3 concerned with the eighteenth century.

25. For this terminology, see Isadore Twersky, "Talmudists, Philosophers, and Kabbalists: The Quest for Spirituality in the Sixteenth Century," in *Jewish Thought in the Sixteenth Century*, ed. B. Cooperman (Cambridge, Mass., 1986), 431–59.

26. On the connection between print and too much information, see Ann Blair, *Too Much to Know: Managing Scholarly Information before the Modern Age* (New Haven, Conn., 2010).

27. In addition to Ruderman in *Early Modern Jewry*, see his "Buchdruck und jüdische Kultur in der Frühen Neuzeit Europas," *Münchner Beiträge zur Jüdischen Geschichte und Kultur* 2 (ed. M. Brenner, 2009): 8–22; and "The People and the Book: Print and the Transformation of Jewish Culture in Early Modern Europe," in *Faithful Narratives: Historians, Religion, and the Challenge of Objectivity*, ed. A. Stark and N. Caputo (Ithaca, N.Y., 2014). For a sample of other work, see Elchanan Reiner, "The Ashkenazi Elite at the Beginning of the Modern Era: Manuscript versus Printed Book," *Polin* 10 (1997): 85–98; Amnon Raz-Krakotzkin, "Print and Jewish Cultural Development," in *Encyclopedia of the Renaissance*, ed. P. Grendler (New York, 1999), 3:344–46.

28. *Early Modern Jewry*, 198–205.

29. See especially their coedited "Schwerpunkt," in *Early Modern Culture and Haskalah: Reconsidering the Borderlines of Modern Jewish History*, in *Jahrbuch des Simon-Dubnow-Instituts* 6 (2007): 17–268.

30. See Shmuel Feiner, *The Origins of Jewish Secularization in Eighteenth-Century Europe*, trans. C. Naor (Philadelphia, 2011); *Shorshe ha-ḥilun* (Tel Aviv, 2010).

31. Cf. Adam Sutcliffe, *Judaism and Enlightenment* (Cambridge, 2003).

JEWISH CULTURE IN EARLY MODERN EUROPE

PART I

REALMS OF AUTHORITY

❈ ❈ ❈

Conflict and Adaptation

CONTINUITY OR CHANGE

❈ ❈ ❈

The Case of Two Prominent Jewish Portuguese Clans in the Ottoman Empire

Joseph R. Hacker

The Hebrew University of Jerusalem

THE fifteenth and early sixteenth centuries were marked by Jewish mass migrations —some willing, some by force.[1] Much movement was from west to east—as from Christian Europe to the Ottoman lands, or from Central to Eastern Europe. These demographic changes are not just visible to historians. At the beginning of the sixteenth century, Rabbi Isaac Abravanel wrote in his commentary on the Book of Ezekiel:

> From then [1464], trials befell the Jewish people and all of the Jews and their off-spring in Savoy [1464–75], Provence [1493], and Piedmont, and in all of Lombardy and the kingdoms of Spain [1492] and Sardinia and Sicily and Russia [1495], and in the lands that the emperor inherited from his father in Ashkenaz [the Holy Roman empire] and Portugal [1497] and Navarre [1498] and in the kingdoms of Naples [1495] and Florence [1495] and in the other countries that expelled the Jews . . . and many thousands of apostates and Conversos were killed, but far more people and populations fled for their lives, some to the land of Islam, but most to the land of the Turk. And in the name of the Lord, I hope that these forty years have come to an end in this year of 5265 [1505], and that the salvation of the Jewish people will henceforth commence.[2]

This observant contemporary statesman witnessed the spate of upheavals and expulsions in the late fifteenth century. In his understanding, these events were part of a process that would lead ultimately to a collective redemption:

> We also witnessed with our own eyes that God aroused the spirit of the kings of countries in the West to expel all of the Jews from their lands . . . in a manner that they went from all corners of the West toward the Land of Israel . . . and in this way they are congregating on the Holy Land.[3]

Processes of mass migration and their associated conditions can lead not only to much turmoil and change in the material and social lives of the migrants, but can also impact their consciousness, their social and religious values, their mood, and their worldview, even if they do not necessarily cause revolutionary and comprehensive changes in their language or culture.[4]

The marriage of one's sons, and particularly the first born, had significant implications for the continuity, inheritance, pedigree, and social standing of the family. The question of marriage custom is then a test case on migration and social change—an opportunity to ask whether the trauma of migration and the context of the Ottoman Empire caused significant alteration in the lifestyle and worldview of the refugees. This essay is a study of marriages arranged by two "pedigreed" families that emigrated from Portugal to the Ottoman Empire at the turn of the sixteenth century. Did they continue to consider lineage an important factor in choosing a spouse, and did they preserve the patriarchal family structure that they maintained in Portugal after their move to the Ottoman Empire? With a few exceptions, the place of the Jewish family among Spanish-Portuguese exiles in the Ottoman Empire remains under-researched.[5] I have chosen these two families because of our ability to reconstruct their family trees, even given the general dearth of notarial and communal documents. A similar lack does not plague Christian sources,[6] as is reflected in the robust scholarship on the Christian family.[7]

From the testimony of a refugee from Iberia who came to the Ottoman Empire, it seems that an immediate change took place in the manner in which the refugees selected marriage partners in their new home, and particularly in the prominence of family pedigree. The most conspicuous testimony attesting to this change is provided by R. Abraham Shamsolo's[8] 1508–9 description of the migration (penned in Lepanto):

> Men arrived without their wives and women without their husbands. And they were beset by poverty and travail and famine and loneliness (Job 30:3), and their cares broke their strength (bBer 58b). And when they recalled the destruction of their homes, the blow was desperate (Jer 15:18), but as each one found himself alone, he sought a helpmate (Gen 2:18). From whatever they chose, they obtained what they needed. And as they assembled, the women encompassed the men (Jer 31:22), and they

courted without respect for each other's lineage, as if it was the same,[9] in their families and their town. And if it was right and proper, the more they were afflicted, the more they multiplied (Ex 1:12), and the desire for pure marriage grew. Each went to his tent, young and old, and both young man and virgin returned to their tents.[10]

Shamsolo testifies to the fact that in the first decades after the arrival of Iberian Jews in the Balkans, new family units were soon created among the refugees. The refugees were no longer particular about differences in social standing or in social ideals that existed before the expulsion, but instead valued the establishment of a new family and a new life as soon as possible. Shamsolo does not explain what brought about the change, but we can deduce from his words that the dispersion caused a weakening of the bonds between far-flung relatives, and may even have altered the manner in which parents evaluated good matches for their children. The passage conveys a sense of urgency to rebuild in the face of what had been destroyed.

However, it appears that only the first generation of exiles made such adjustments; their children and grandchildren soon returned to the practices and social values that were prevalent in the Iberian Peninsula before their exile. At least among those with pedigree, lineage and wealth these values reappear as important factors in marriage considerations. This interest in pedigree is apparent from an ethical admonition of R. Isaac Onkeneira, who was close to the courtiers in Istanbul in the third quarter of the sixteenth century, directed to prominent men. Basing himself on the commentary of R. Isaac Abravanel to tractate *Avot*,[11] he wrote:

> Family. A man is tempted to appreciate his pedigree when everyone rushes to marry
> him. And they offer their daughters with a rich dowry to his sons and take his daugh-
> ters for nothing, and they rise in his presence. All this may render him arrogant and
> he will seek eminence among his friends who excel him in wisdom and deeds, and
> he will walk proudly, seeing himself as the glory of young men and the crown of the
> elderly. Thus he dishonors his ancestors and the glory of the elders of his family who
> earned their reputation through humility and fear of heaven, and he causes those who
> were beloved to be cursed.[12]

Clearly pedigree is highly valued, despite the moral danger such cultural currency threatens. This passage is complicated by the phenomenon of changing status— Onkeneira was also aware that the rich may lose their standing and the poor can rise.[13] Wealth and honor, he says, may be falsely conflated. Beyond wealth alone, he emphasized the role of relatives in one's social standing, and pointed out the power of the extended family in creating a strong and influential position.

> Many relatives make a man proud, for whoever regards him perceives the extent of his
> help and the backing of his friends and supporters. And if any man breaks his word,
> they will all rise against him, fellows who pervert the words of the righteous.[14]

In his work *Tovah tokhahat*, R. Menahem Lonzano, who lived in Istanbul in the second half of the sixteenth century, wrote with sharp irony about the wealthy people around him who try at all cost to establish a pedigree for themselves.

> There are those for whose lineage it is enough to be connected to the Arodi and the 'Eri [Num 26:40–42];
>
> To Shuham the families of Shuham, and to ba'ale Beri'ah or Tslafhad the Hofri [Num 26:42, 28, 45, 33];
>
> To Yerav'am, to Jezebel the mighty, to Ba'asha the son of Achiyah or to Zimri [1 Kgs 16:13, 9–11];
>
> The honor of their lineage covers all of their transgressions and defects, and there is no need of a crown,
>
> And they have proof from Amalek and Esav, the linked sons of Isaac.[15]

The theme of lineage and public life appears without irony in the homilies of R. Joseph Garçon on the securing of public office. Thus, for example, he wrote in a eulogy for R. Samuel Franco in Salonica as early as 1501:

> For men [in public positions] can be saved from troubles in one of three ways: Either (1) because they treat him with respect because he is one of the great sages of the generation who can say that he is the descendant of sages or of kings, and they are therefore reticent before him, and even those who hate him and his enemies give him respect . . . or (2) because he has a large family . . . or (3) because he has great courage and fortitude.[16]

Similar expressions of the central role of lineage in determining a person's potential and a family's standing were also heard in Salonica in the sixteenth century. A scholar from the Uziel clan, Samuel Uziel, on the occasion of his appointment as the rabbi of the community of "exiles" (lit. *kahal kadosh gerush* of Salonica), expresses his awareness that he is no more worthy of the position than other candidates and that his appointment can be attributed to his family pedigree.[17] R. Solomon le-Bet ha-Levi (1532–1600)[18] claims that his lineage is a decisive factor in securing a position as the rabbi in the Portuguese community of exiles from Evora in Salonica. In a treatise that R. Solomon composed as a youth he stresses the significance of his levitical bloodline. In his work, which was written with youthful exuberance, he tries to establish that "estate, wealth, and ancestry" are the heritage of the Levites, as is their right to communal and religious leadership. In his polemic with R. Isaac Abravanel, whose lineage was traced to King David, the issue was not whether blood mattered, but rather whose lineage was more splendid.[19] His grandson, R. Solomon le-Bet ha-Levi "the younger" (1581–1634), described the family of his ancestors in several letters.[20] The picture that emerges from the descriptions is of a Portuguese tribal clan. He emphasizes the dynastic foundation, describing an extended family with many branches, and he speaks with longing of the days of his grandfather when the family was in its glory.

The examples cited above hint that the structure of family life and the social values of affluent and pedigreed families that came to the Ottoman Empire from Spain and Portugal did not change from their previous format in Portugal, even if some of the foundations were shaken and undermined in the early years after expulsion. By tracing the Jewish family to the Ottoman Empire, I am attempting to add to what we already know of parallel phenomenon in Christian Europe.[21] Below I look for evidence of marriage patterns in the family trees of two Portuguese families that emigrated to the Ottoman Empire in the fifteenth and sixteenth centuries.

THE FAMILY TREE OF THE IBN YAḤYA FAMILY IN THE OTTOMAN EMPIRE

The family tree of the Ibn Yaḥya family from Portugal has been reconstructed several times, in nearly all cases based on *Sefer shalshelet ha-kabalah* (The chain of tradition) of R. Gedalya Ibn Yaḥya (Venice, 1587), with additions based on other sources.[22] Recently, an attempt was made to reconstruct the history of the family members in Portugal before the persecutions and their subsequent emigration, based on archival documentation in Portugal,[23] as well as documents on a few family members from the fourteenth century.[24] Variation characterizes these family trees, but one common denominator is the scarce representation of family members from the Ottoman Empire. It is now known that an author's autographic first edition of *Sefer shalshelet ha-kabalah*[25] is noticeably different from the printed text.[26] This manuscript, only recently accessible, shows that the book was written in stages. It includes events up to approximately 1568, while the printed version includes information up to the death of the author in 1587, when the book was published. Moreover, the printed version omits much information from the manuscript relating particularly to the history of the Ibn Yaḥya family. The manuscript, in sum, enables a detailed reconstruction of the Ottoman branches of the family that was previously impossible.[27]

The family trees printed below are based on the manuscript with supplements from the printed work. The data was gathered by Gedalya Ibn Yaḥya, apparently from information that he received from relatives in Salonica during his visit there in 1568.

What can we deduce from these family trees?

1. A significant portion of the Ibn Yaḥya clan, one of the most economically and politically powerful Jewish families in Portugal until the last decade of the fifteenth century, found their way to the Ottoman Empire. In contradiction to what was thought to be the case, this number was apparently larger than the number that went to Italy. Some eastward migration predated the late fifteenth-century persecution.

THE IBN YAḤYA CLAN IN THE OTTOMAN EMPIRE

TABLE 1. Sons of David ibn Yaḥya (Lisbon, d. 1465)

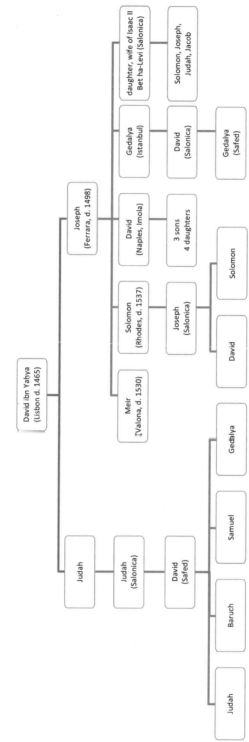

Table 2. Sons of Gedalya ibn Yahya

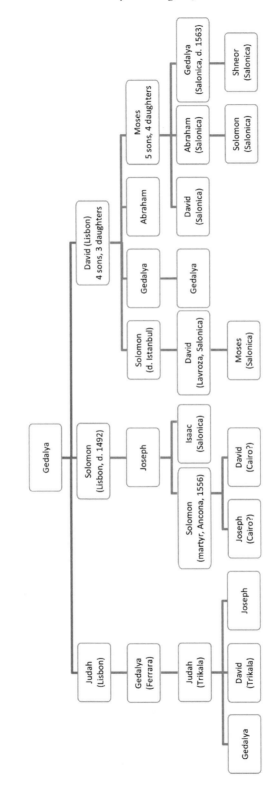

Table 4. Sons of Solomon ibn Yaḥya (Lisbon)

Solomon (Lisbon) — Gedalya (Maiorca) — Solomon (Salonica) — Abraham (Sofia)

Table 3. Sons of David ibn Yaḥya (Constantinople)

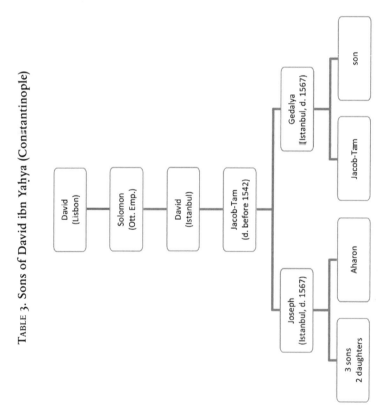

David (Lisbon) — Solomon (Ott. Emp.) — David (Istanbul) — Jacob-Tam (d. before 1542)

Joseph (Istanbul, d. 1567)
— 3 sons 2 daughters
— Aharon

Gedalya (Istanbul, d. 1567)
— Jacob-Tam
— son

TABLE 5. Ibn Yaḥya Families (Salonica)

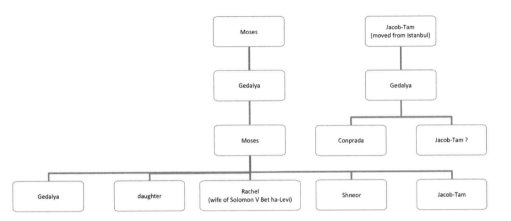

2. Many of the members of the family spread out among central cities in the Ottoman Empire, settling in the large communities of Salonica, Istanbul, and Cairo; others resided in Valona, Trikala, Sofia, and Safed. Some continued to wander from place to place throughout the empire for one or two generations.

3. Connections were maintained between the various branches of the family, both between Italy and the Ottoman Empire, and among the branches that lived in the empire itself. Members of the family had information about distant relatives—not a small matter given the obstacles to communication at that time. They knew at least basic information on location and family status. This strong network is attested to by the visit of Gedalya Ibn Yaḥya to his family in Salonica in 1568.[28] This visit and the information that he gathered in Salonica from the community and his relatives apparently determined his motivation to write the book, even though, according to his words, he began writing in 1556, before the visit.

4. The information that can be garnered about members of the Ibn Yaḥya family and their spouses from the lists of Gedalya and other sources is scant, but it is fascinating that *all* of the information that we have attests to the fact that they married within the family, or with other respected and affluent families from Portugal.[29]

THE FAMILY TREE OF THE BET HA-LEVI FAMILY

The Bet ha-Levi clan was a respected family from Evora, Portugal. They apparently arrived there from Castille, although the date of their arrival is unknown. Many were doctors, and although we do not have documentation attesting to their status and their activities in Portugal, it is clear that they were part of the city's Jewish upper echelon. With the emigration of the expert doctor Maestre Solomon

TABLE 6. The Family Tree of the Bet ha-Levi of Evora

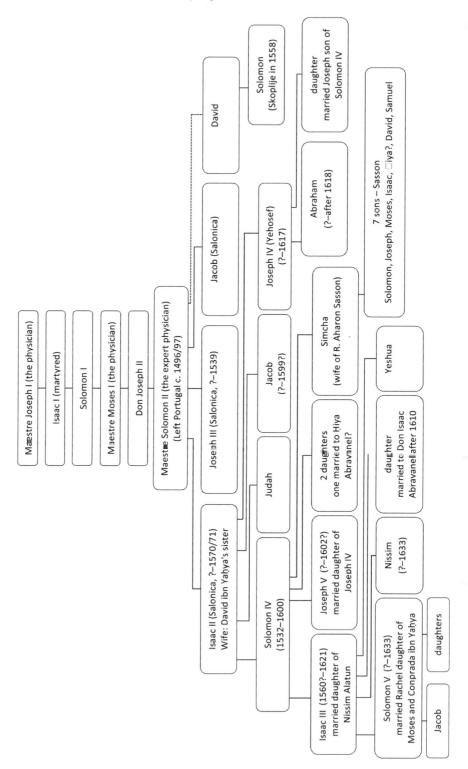

Maestre Joseph I (the physician)

Isaac I (martyred)

Solomon I

Maestre Moses I (the physician)

Don Joseph II

Maestre Solomon II (the expert physician)
(Left Portugal c. 1496/97)

Jacob (Salonica)

David

Solomon
(Skoplije in 1558)

daughter
married Joseph son of
Solomon IV

Joseph III (Salonica, ?–1539)

Joseph IV (Yehosef)
(?–1617)

Abraham
(?–after 1618)

7 sons – Sasson
Solomon, Joseph, Moses, Isaac, □iya?, David, Samuel

Isaac II (Salonica, ?–1570/71)
Wife: David ibn Yahya's sister

Judah

Jacob
(?–1599?)

Simcha
(wife of R. Aharon Sasson)

Solomon IV
(1532–1600)

2 daughters
one married to Hiya
Abravanel?

Yeshua

daughter
married to Don Isaac
Abravanel after 1610

Joseph V (?–1602?)
married daughter of
Joseph IV

Nissim
(?–1633)

Isaac III (1560?–1621)
married daughter of
Nissim Alatun

Solomon V (?–1633)
married Rachel daughter of
Moses and Conprada ibn Yahya

Jacob

daughters

le-Bet ha-Levi from Portugal, his son Isaac leased mines in Sidrokapsi, and became one of the wealthiest members of the Jewish community in Salonica. Data on the family is extant from family correspondence and from books written by R. Solomon le-Bet ha-Levi "the elder," his son Isaac, and his grandson Solomon, "the younger." Unlike the case of the Ibn Yaḥya family, the nature of the sources enables us to access much more information on a large number of the spouses of family members in the sixteenth and early seventeenth centuries. Within this clan, as well, there was frequent written communication between family members, especially at the start of the seventeenth century.

What can we learn from this family tree?

1. At least two members of this family were married to members of the Ibn Yaḥya family: Isaac the son of Solomon (d. 1570–71) married the sister of David Ibn Yaḥya, and Solomon (d. 1633) married Rachel, the daughter of Moses and Conprada Ibn Yaḥya.

2. Apparently, the daughter of Solomon "the elder" married Ḥiya Abravanel, a member of the well-known Abravanel family,[30] and his son Isaac (d. 1621) married the daughter of Nissim Alatun, one of the wealthy Portuguese exiles in Salonica. Alatun's father Don Isaac Alatun and he were heads of the Lisbon community in Salonica.[31] After 1610, one of Isaac's daughters married another son of the Abravanel family, Don Isaac Abravanel.

3. Within the extended family, the daughter of Yehoseph le-Bet ha-Levi (d. 1617) married Joseph, the son of Solomon "the elder" (1532–1600).

A lack of data on other matches does not allow a more detailed analysis. In this family, as well, almost all of the known spouses married well-born members of distinguished Portuguese families or members of the extended family (except for Simcha who married R. Aaron Sasson, one of the greatest sages of Salonica and subsequently Istanbul, who was a student of her father Solomon, and the son of a wealthy family).

CONCLUSION

Even in the face of large scale migration, social and economic upheaval, and encounters with varied groups of Jews, the marriage practices of elite Iberians who immigrated to Ottoman lands did not change. Despite the detailed and colorful testimony of R. Abraham Shamsolo with which I opened this essay, members of leading families in Portugal exiled to the Ottoman Empire maintained old patterns and priorities in matchmaking, as affirmed by several first hand family documents. Encounters with new populations did not alter a preference for marriage within families or to those of similar origins, with a premium placed on lineage, position, and wealth. The changes portended by Shamsolo may have been local or temporary, reflecting only his immediate surroundings in the Balkans and the society in which he lived during the decades immediately following the expulsion. It is not consistent with the picture that one perceives from sources describing the reality in Salonica and Istanbul, particularly among affluent and pedigreed families, among them those with the title "Don."[32] Among these individuals and those around them, those influenced by them, and those that followed them, there was continuity, not revolution, regarding the worldview and values that guided them in selecting a spouse.

This close study raises two avenues for further thought. If the picture drawn characterizes general Jewish society in the Ottoman Empire in the sixteenth century, and not only specific levels within it (which would still need to be proven), it stands to reason that this group preserved other values and practices of their ancestors from the Iberian Peninsula in spite of the radical changes in their circumstances. How far can we trace patterns of cultural preservation, and where can we see evidence of rupture? Second, this essay has addressed the question of transmission but not that of adaptation. To what extent may the apparent continuity between Iberian marriage custom and that practiced in the Ottoman Empire and/or Moslem society be described as an assimilation or adaptation of local practices and mores? Although I know of no research on the considerations in selecting a spouse in Ottoman society at that period, it appears from studies of the Ottoman family in the sixteenth to eighteenth centuries that there is much similarity between the societies in the structures of the patriarchal, multibranched clan. For each it was accepted opinion that it is inappropriate to marry if it entails descent in pedigree.[33] On the other hand, romantic love is not absent from contemporary Ottoman art and literature of the time.[34] Having digested the new documentary evidence on the question of marital filiation, it remains for this material to be inserted in other horizontal studies of Jewish migration across borders.

Notes

1. See Salo W. Baron, *A Social and Religious History of the Jews* 11 (New York, 1967), 192–283; 379–422; David B. Ruderman, *Early Modern Jewry* (Princeton, N.J., 2010), 24–55, 235–44; Joseph R. Hacker, "The Sephardim in the Ottoman Empire in the Sixteenth Century," in *Moreshet Sepharad: The Sephardi Legacy*, ed. H. Beinart (Jerusalem, 1992), 2:109–15; Michel Abitbol, "Juifs d'Afrique du Nord et expulsés d'Espagne après 1492," *Revue de l'histoire des religions* 210.1 (1993): 49–65. See also Benjamin Z. Kedar, "Expulsion as an Issue of World History," *The Journal of World History* 7 (1996): 165–80.

On the movement from the Western Mediterranean to the Eastern shores see: J. R. Hacker, "The Jewish Community of Salonica from the Fifteenth to the Sixteenth Centuries" (Hebrew; Ph.D diss.; Hebrew University, 1978), 191–217; Hacker, "The Links between Spanish Jewry and Palestine, 1391–1492," in *Vision and Conflict in the Holy Land*, ed. R. I. Cohen (Jerusalem, 1985), 118–25, 134–38.

2. Isaac Abravanel, *Commentary to the Latter Prophets* (Pesaro, 1520), on Ezekiel (chap. 20, fol. 114b).

3. Ibid., on Isaiah (chap. 43, fol. 89b). See also his *Ma'ayane ha-Yeshu'ah* (Wells of Salvation) (Ferrara, 1551), fol. 125a–b.

4. Joseph R. Hacker, "Superbe at désespoir: l'existence sociale et spirituelle des Juifs ibériques dans l'Empire ottoman," *Revue Historique* 285 (1991): 261–93; Hacker, "The Responses of the Exiles to the Spanish Expulsion and to the Forced Conversion in Portugal," in *Jews and Conversos at the*

Time of the Expulsion, ed. Y. T. Assis and Y. Kaplan (Hebrew; Jerusalem, 1999), 223–45; Eleazar Gutwirth, "Continuity and Change after 1492," in ibid., 93–108.

5. See, for example, the articles in the following collections: Steven M. Cohen and Paula. E. Hyman, eds., *The Jewish Family: Myth and Reality* (New York, 1986); David Kraemer, ed., *The Jewish Family: Metaphor and Memory* (New York, 1989); Joseph Shatzmiller, ed., *La famille juive au moyen âge: Provence-Languedoc, Provence Historique*, t.XXXVII (Marseille, 1987), fasc. 50, pp. 485–600.

Two important exceptions to the dearth of research in this area are Katz and Ben-Naeh: Jacob Katz, "Marriage and Sexual Life among the Jews at the End of the Middle Ages" (Hebrew), *Zion* 10 (1945): 22–54 (and the modified English version in *Tradition and Crisis: Jewish Society at the End of the Middle Ages*, trans. B. Cooperman [New York, 1993], chaps. 14–15. On the issue of pedigree in Ottoman Jewish society, see: Yaron Ben-Naeh, *Jews in the Realm of the Sultans: Ottoman Jews in the Seventeenth Century* (Tübingen, 2008), index, s.v. "lineage".

6. See, for example, David Herlihy and Christiane Clapisch-Zuber, *Tuscans and Their Families:. A Study of the Florentine Catasto of 1427* (New Haven, Conn., 1985).

7. See, for example, Peter Laslett and Richard Wall, eds., *Household and Family in Past Time* (Cambridge, 1972); Laslett, *The World We Have Lost, Further Explored* (London, 1983); Lawrence Stone, *The Family, Sex and Marriage in England 1500–1800* (London, 1977); Jean Louis Flandrin, *Families in Former Times* (Cambridge, 1979); Natalie Zemon Davis, "Ghosts, Kin and Progeny: Some Features of Family Life in Early Modern France," *Daedalus* 106.2 (1977): 87–114; Stanley Chojnacki, "Dowries and Kinsmen in Early Renaissance Venice," in *Marriage and Fertility. Studies in Interdisciplinary History*, ed. R. I. Rotberg, T. K. Rabb (Princeton, N.J., 1980), 41–70; Rosemary O'Day, *The Family and Family Relationship, 1500–1900* (London, 1994).

On the family in Spain, see: James Casey et al., *La familia en la Espagna mediterránea (siglos xv–xix)* (Barcelona, 1987); David S. Reher, *Perspectives on the Family in Spain, Past and Present* (Oxford, 1997), index: s.v. "lineage"; C. R. Phillips," Family and Community in the Spanish World," in *Between the Middle Ages and Modernity*, ed. C. H. Parker and J. H. Bentley (Lanham, MD., 2007), 71-92; Raymond B. Waddington, "Marriage in Early Modern Europe," *The Sixteenth Century Journal* 34 (2003): 315–18.

8. On Abraham Shamsolo, see Hacker, "Jewish Community of Salonica," appendix 8, 54–55; Hacker, "Sephardim in the Ottoman Empire," 472–73; Abraham David, "A Fragment of a Hebrew Chronicle" (Hebrew), *Aley Sefer* 6–7 (1979): 198–200; Meir Benayahu, "The Sermons of R. Yosef b. Meir Garson as a Source for the History of the Expulsion from Spain and the Sephardi Diaspora" (Hebrew), *Michael* 7 (1981): 199–205.

9. See Maimonides, *The Guide for the Perplexed*, trans. S. Pines (Chicago, 1963), I.73, 3, p. 196.

10. Hacker, "Jewish Community of Salonica," 54–55.

11. See Isaac Abravanel, *Naḥalat Avot* (Venice, 1545, 116a–117b; Jerusalem, 2004, pp. 227–34).

12. Isaac Onkeneira, *Ayuma ka-nidgalot* (Istanbul, 1577), fol. 20b [24b], see also fol. 16b [20b]: "Wealth can make its owners wise and benefit others who marry his daughters, as well"; ibid., fols. 20b–21a [24b–25a]: "And after them their sons rose up and filled their place, and they performed good deeds like the practice and actions of their ancestors, until the family was considered to have a good name and lineage and glorified status. And more so, he responds in his heart and says: I am empty of any of the good qualities that my ancestors possessed, and I benefit from their wealth, prestige, precious things, and honor and respect within the community and the public."

13. See ibid., fol. 28a [32a]: "At times the downtrodden were raised to the heights and wore silk clothing and the dress of authority . . . and the poverty of their youth stood them in good stead in their old age . . . as I wrote in the book of the lineage of Sephardi Jewry . . . that is called *Marot Elohim*"; ibid., fol. 21a [25a]: "And it is a daily occurrence that some of the common people, and even those who were among the important people when they were poor, increase in value and when they become wealthy, they change their values as if the previous ones never existed, and they do

not recognize themselves. And this disease can be found among many types of people, and it is only the few who refrain from it."

14. Ibid., fol. 21a [25a]. His words here, unlike the previous citations, are taken almost word for word from Isaac Abravanel, *Naḥalat Avot,* fol. 117a (Jerusalem and New York, 2004, p. 229).

15. The title of the ninth section of the book *Tovah tokhaḥat* (published in *Shte yadot*, Venice, 1616) is "One who Exalts Himself with a Fictitious Gift, Lacks Hospitality, and Glorifies Himself with his Pedigree" (fol. 133a). The poem cited: ibid., fols 137a–b (Hebrew). Note that many of the examples bear negative connotations. See also, ibid., fol. 147a: "The Article on Pedigree" from the book *Totsa'ot Ḥayim.* Lonzano advises the men in his society to:

> Choose a woman below your rank / For a life that is pleasant and not bitter,
> Take her and let her not take you / Lest you be like a servant sold. (fol. 125a)

16. For a printed version of this passage, from the MS, see Joseph R. Hacker, "On the Intellectual Character and Self-Perception of Spanish Jewry in the Late Fifteenth Century" (Hebrew), *Sefunot* (n.s.) 2; (o.s.) 17 (1983): 88. See also his homilies in manuscript, *Ben Porat Yosef*, British Library, Or. 10.726, Microfilm 8041, in the Institute of Microfilmed Hebrew Manuscripts in the National Library, Jerusalem (IMHM-NL), 229a (Damascus, 1518). Also, cf. there 208b and 227b. Cf. also to Abraham Saba, *Eshkol ha-kofer* (Drohovitz, 2004), 95–96.

17. Columbia University, MS D442 X893, fols. 18a–b (microfilm no. 27224 in the IMHM-NL).

18. Born in Salonica to a wealthy family that originated in Evora, Portugal, he served as a rabbi in Skoplije (Üsküb) from 1568, and from 1571, as a rabbi in Salonica, where he was one of the leading scholars. He died on 27 Av in 1600. See: Isaac S. Emmanuel, *Precious Stones of the Jews of Salonica,* vol. 1 (Hebrew; Jerusalem, 1963), no.407; Joseph R. Hacker, "Israel among the Nations as Described by Solomon le-Beit ha-Levi of Salonika" (Hebrew), *Zion* 34 (1969): 43–89; Hacker, "Despair of Redemption and Messianic Hopes in the Writings of Solomon le-Beit ha-Levi of Salonika" (Hebrew), *Tarbiz* 39 (1970): 195–213.

19. Beyt ha-Levi, manuscript in the British Library, Or.12351 (=Gaster manuscript, no. 36). See my forthcoming book in Hebrew: *Beyt ha-Levi – A Portuguese Jewish Family in Salonica: Letters and Documents,* part 2.

20. See Emmanuel, *Precious Stones,* no. 599; Joseph R. Hacker, "The Links between Salonican Jews and the Community of Safed in the 16th and 17th Centuries," *Shalem* 8, ed. J. R. Hacker (2008): 249–326. The letters appear in Hacker, *Beyt ha-Levi,* parts 4–5 (based on the Kaufman MS, 586/1 KA, microfilm 15013 in the IMHM-NL, and other sources).

21. Conspicuous examples of this phenomenon are the Abravanel and Mendes-Nasi families in Italy. See Renata Segre, "Sephardic Refugees in Ferrara: Two Notable Families," in *Crisis and Creativity in the Sephardic World, 1391–1648,* ed. B. R. Gampel (New York, 1997), 164–85, 327–36. On the Mendes-Nasi family and its members, see Robert Bonfil, "Business, Politics and Philanthropy of the Powerless: Dona Gracia Nasi as Metaphor," *Italia* 21 (2012): 7–41, and sources in n.18. See also the studies by José Alberto Rodrigues da Silva Tavim in *El Presente* 3 (2009): 45–61; *Hispania Judaica* 7 (2010): 211–32; *Jewish History* 25 (2011): 177–81. On the Abravanel family in Italy, see also, for example: Samuel H. Margulies, "La famiglia Abravanel in Italia," *Rivista Israelitica* 3 (1906): 1–19 (repr.); Aron di Leone Leoni, "Nuove notizie sugli *Abravanel*," *Zakhor* 1 (1997): 153–206.

22. Elyakim Carmoly, *Sefer Divre ha-yamim le-bne Yaḥya* (Frankfurt aM, 1850), 4; Carmoly, "Die familie Iachia," *Israelitische Annalen* 2 (1840): 393–94; S. Ochser, "Yaḥya," *The Jewish Encyclopedia* (New York, 1901–06), 12:581–84; Abraham David, "The Historiographical Work of Gedalya Ibn Yaḥya, Author of Shalshelet ha-Kabbalah" (Hebrew; Ph.D. diss.; The Hebrew University, 1976), 4–17, and the family tree there.

23. Maria Jose Pimenta Ferro Tavares, *Los judíos en Portugal,* trans. M. Merlino (Madrid, 1992), 91; see also: Tavares, *Os judeus em Portugal no século XV* (Lisbon, 1982), 235.

24. Elias Lipiner, *Two Portuguese Exiles in Castille: Dom David Negro and Dom Isaac Abravanel* (Jerusalem, 1997), 33–45, 83–101.

25. See Samuel Wiener, *Da'at kedoshim* (St. Petersburg, 1897–98), the chapter dealing with the ban of R. Jacob Pollack, 46–48; Abraham David, "The Spanish Expulsion and the Portuguese Persecution through the Eyes of the Historian R. Gedalya Ibn Yaḥya," *Sefarad* 56 (1996): 47–48.

26. The Ginsburg-Moscow MS 652, microfilm 44117 in the IMHM-NL.

27. On the attempt to reconstruct one branch of the Ibn Yaḥya family in Salonica, based on a variety of sources, see Hacker, "Links between Salonican Jews and the Community of Safed," 269–71. Descriptions and lists of members of the Ibn Yaḥya family can be found on various pages of the printed version: 5b, 39a, 40b, 55a, 57b, 59a–60a, 62b-63a, 65a, 65b–67a, 112a, and 116a; so too in the manuscript version: fols. 62b–63b, 67b, 98a–b, 107b–108a, 113a–115a, 122b–125a, 129 a–b, 133b–134b.

28. See *Sefer shalshelet ha-kabalah*, 43a; 48b ("that I received from the elders of the generation, and particularly in Salonica when I was there in 1568."); 66b. In the list of his books, he says: "The fourth is called *The Ibn Yaḥya Book of Chronicles* . . . which I reworked and completed to a greater degree than that written by our elders, because I acquired new information from my relatives in Salonica and Constantinople and I have written them with a nice introduction to the work that was not there previously. And I began it in the name of Rabbi Judah my son in the year 1556 in Ravenna" (117a). Much has been written on the inauthenticity, the fabrication, and the anecdotal accounting that the author integrated in to his work in describing the past. Though this is not the place to expand on such issues, nevertheless, it is inconceivable that he fabricated contemporary personalities and members of his family, and incorporated them in a book that he published for mass consumption.

29. See in table 1 (the wife of Solomon le-Bet ha-Levi) and in table 5 (the marriage of Moses and Conprada Ibn Yaḥya; Rachel—the wife of Solomon le-Bet ha-Levi "the younger"). See additional data in a manuscript in the Bodlean Library, Oxford, Poc. 74², Neubauer catalogue, no. 1986 (Tam Ibn Yaḥya was the owner of the manuscript and his signature appears on fols. 3a, 103b, and 238b), fol. 2a: "To Rabbi Saadya Longo, may his soul rest in Eden, to the ketubah of my sister, may she be blessed among the women in the tent, who was married to a family member who was not an immediate relative, Moses Ibn Yaḥya, may his soul rest in Eden, and his father's name was Gedalya of blessed memory, he died at a young age, and the name of my father, may his memory be for life in the world to come, was also Gedalya." See also fol. 97b.

30. On the Abravanel family in Salonica and on Ḥiya Abravanel, see: Meir Benayahu, "The House of Abravanel in Saloniki," *Sefunot* 12 (1971–78): 7–67. It also discusses the connections between the family in Italy with the family in Salonica. My interpretation of Solomon Bet ha-Levi's letter to Ḥiya Abravanel differs from that of Benayahu.

31. On Nissim Alatun and the Alatun family in Salonica and Istanbul, see Joseph R. Hacker, "Public Libraries of Hispanic Jewry in the Late Medieval and Early Modern Periods," in *From Sages to Savants: Studies Presented to Avraham Grossman*, ed. J. R. Hacker, Y. Kaplan, B. Z. Kedar (Hebrew; Jerusalem, 2010), 284–86.

32. On the meaning of this title and the changes that it underwent in the seventeenth century, see: Manuel Ferrer-Chivite, "El factor judeo – Converso en el proceso de consolidación del titulo 'Don,'" *Sefarad* 45 (1985): 131–73.

33. See, for example: Alan Duben, "Turkish Families and Households in Historical Perspective," *Journal of Family History* 10 (1985): 75–97; Haim Gerber, "Anthropology and Family History: The Ottoman and Turkish Families," *Journal of Family History* 14 (1989): 409–21; Judith E. Tucker, *In the House of the Law: Gender and Islamic Law in Ottoman Syria and Palestine* (Berkeley, Calif., 1998), 37–77.

34. Walter G. Andrews and Mehmet Kalpakli, *The Age of Beloveds: Love and the Beloved in Early-Modern Ottoman and European Culture and Society* (Durham, N.C., 2005), 163–250.

DON'T MESS WITH MESSER LEON

❋ ❋ ❋

Halakhah and Humanism in Fifteenth-Century Italy

Elliott Horowitz

IN 1455, shortly after arriving in Ancona, in the Marche region on Italy's Adriatic coast, the humanist rabbi and physician Judah Messer Leon boldly sought to make changes in both the ritual practices and intellectual orientation not only of the local Jews, but of those residing a considerable distance away, threatening those who failed to obey his decrees with dire imprecations. The ritual practices were primarily in the realm of female observance, and the intellectual issues related to both philosophy and Kabbalah. This episode has sometimes been misinterpreted as a brazen attempt on the part of the erudite young rabbi to "extend his rabbinic authority over all of Italian Jewry,"[1] or—with specific reference to his proposed alterations in female ritual practice—"to bring about a minor revolution in the life of the Italian Jewish family."[2] More accurate, perhaps, is Cecil Roth's less dramatic assertion that Messer Leon, while residing in Ancona early in his career, "engaged in a number of polemics which attracted a great deal of attention among his contemporaries."[3]

Among those who paid particular attention to Messer Leon's decrees, and especially to the imprecations which accompanied them, was the Florentine rabbi and banker R. Benjamin (Gugliemo) b. Yoab (Dattilo) of Montalcino, who, together with his brother Jehiel/Vitale, had been active as a banker in Florence and the surrounding region since 1438.[4] Shortly before moving to nearby Prato in order to manage a branch of the family bank there, Jehiel commissioned a Florentine scribe to prepare a lavish and finely written *maḥzor* of the Italian rite whose two volumes, together with accompanying illustrations and illuminations, were completed during the summer of 1441.[5] A decade later their nephew Baruch, a son of their brother Solomon, who seems to have remained in Montalcino, completed copying there a Hebrew arithmetic treatise which had been translated from the Arabic.[6]

R. Benjamin, Messer Leon's most vocal opponent during the mid-1450s, who like the former had rabbinic ordination, thus came from a respected Italian Jewish family which had both business and cultural interests. Just as R. Benjamin followed his father into banking so did Messer Leon follow his into medicine, a field in which he had been awarded the degree of "Magister," probably from the University of Padua, where the qualifying examination was normally preceded by six years of study.[7] He was thus known as "Messer Leon," with Leon serving as the Italian equivalent of Judah, just as R. Benjamin's banking name was Gugliemo. Furthermore, his rabbinic learning also came from the Veneto region (probably from Treviso), where Ashkenazic scholars from Mainz had established a yeshiva during the early decades of the fifteenth century.[8]

The two rabbis who clashed in 1455 over Messer Leon's decrees were thus representative of two sub-cultures of Italian Jewry, an older one whose religious traditions were locally rooted and whose worldliness was more commercial than intellectual, and an emerging subculture whose religious traditions came from across the Alps but whose intellectual world reached back to ancient Greece and Rome, to the philosophy of Aristotle and the rhetoric of Cicero. R. Benjamin of Montalcino probably possessed no secular education beyond the level of "the abacus or arithmetic school," which was "the most popular form of secondary education" in early Renaissance Florence, and where "the emphasis was on methods which would be of use in the commercial world, and instruction was conducted entirely in Italian."[9] Messer Leon, by contrast, was a rabbi whose "entire intellectual world," it has been claimed, "was based upon Aristotle and Averroes, Cicero and Quintilian," and who consulted the works of the latter two in their original Latin while composing his *Nofet tsufim* (1475), the first Hebrew work published during its author's lifetime.[10] Although R. Benjamin was a skilled rhetorician in Hebrew, and may also have been Messer Leon's equal in rabbinic learning, he could not have conversed learnedly with the local humanists in Florence. Messer Leon's ability to do so—evidently unique then among Italian rabbis—apparently convinced him that his halakhic opinions therefore carried extra intellectual heft, somewhat like those of Maimonides in the twelfth century.

We can thus understand what one scholar has referred to as the young rabbi's "immense sense of self-worth,"[11] allowing him to address certain alleged failures in both the ritual observance and intellectual orientation of his Italian coreligionists. His efforts in the former realm, outlined in his first letter of 1455, were directed at neighboring communities in the Marche region, as well as those further south in Rome and in the regions of Abruzzi, Apulia, and Campania. In that letter, he instructed married women to change some of their traditional practices with regard to ritual immersion and their manner of preparing for that monthly ritual. In his second letter, written later that year in response to sharp criticisms of the first, especially by R. Benjamin of Montalcino, to the community of Florence and to the Jews in "the surrounding areas of Tuscany" Messer Leon also addressed (what he saw as) dangerous heresies in both the philosophical writings of Gersonides (Levi b. Gershom) and the theology of the kabbalists.[12] In contrast to his ritual rulings, the Ancona rabbi seems not to have directed his theological pronouncements to specific geographical regions but to Italian Jewry more broadly, evidently feeling no need in such matters to avoid treading upon the turf of northern Italy's two dominant halakhic authorities—R. Joseph Colon and R. Judah Minz—neither of whom was philosophically trained. Messer Leon's former teachers in Treviso were probably not overly surprised at his hubristic conduct in 1455, since in his second letter he reported having earlier spoken publicly "in the yeshiva of Treviso, and in some of the German yeshivot" about his reservations regarding certain views on the limits of God's knowledge expressed by Gersonides in his fourteenth-century Torah commentary.[13] In that second letter Messer Leon also attacked the kabbalists for their belief in *sefirot* as intercessors between man and God, a belief which, as a good Aristotelian, he thought dangerously tainted by Platonism.[14]

I

Messer Leon was not, then, attempting to extend his halakhic authority over the entire Italian peninsula. In that realm he respected the authority of his venerable northern colleagues Colon and Minz—one representing French halakhic tradition and the other German. Rather, with youthful impetuousness, he was staking a claim upon a "virgin" territory, south of their orbits of influence to which he was geographically closer. Although he was not seeking to establish himself as Italy's first chief rabbi, he does seem to have been attempting to establish himself as its first Jewish "archbishop," with a self-demarcated diocese stretching south from the Marche communities along the Adriatic to those along the heel of the Italian boot. If Messer Leon's confidence in philosophic matters stemmed from having studied at the University of Padua, his confidence as a halakhist was rooted in having studied with Ashkenazic rabbis, probably in nearby Treviso, to which, as noted above, some of Germany's greatest halakhic scholars had earlier emigrated. These included R. Simon of Nuremberg, who had been a rabbi in Frankfurt before coming south to Italy, and R. Judah (Liva) Landau (d. 1464), who had been a favorite student of the great R. Jacob Moellin (Maharil) in Mainz.[15]

Landau's son Jacob also made his way south from Germany, first to Pavia and then to Naples, where sometime after 1487 he published his *Agur*, probably the second Hebrew work (after *Nofet tsufim*) to be published in the lifetime of its author, and almost certainly the first to include a formal approbation, composed by Messer Leon himself.[16] This has surprised some scholars, since the *Agur* was one of the first halakhic works to incorporate kabbalistic material into its rulings.[17] In his laws of *tefilin,* for example, the younger Landau acknowledged that it was common practice to recite two separate blessings for each of the phylacteries, but cited a number of opinions, including that of the *Zohar,* in favor of a single blessing, expressing surprise "at those ostensibly superior ones who [dare to] disagree with R. Simeon bar Yoḥai," the *Zohar*'s purported author.[18] Jacob Landau had presumably embraced the Kabbalah and its teachings not in his native Germany, but somewhere on his southbound sojourn from Pavia to Naples.

As an example of the impact of Kabbalah in Italy already during the first half of the fifteenth century we may note the aforementioned illustrated *maḥzor,* completed in Florence in 1441 for a member of the Montalcino family, which included a long kabbalistic discourse on the Menorah inserted as a gloss to Psalm 67, the seven verses of which (not including the first introductory one), were linked with the seven branches of the biblical candelabrum, in whose shape the verses were copied out. This was evidently the first such instance of talismanic presentation (with kabbalistic gloss) of that biblical text in an Italian prayer book, although it appears in the Byzantine sphere a century earlier.[19]

It is likely that by the time of the *Agur*'s publication in Naples, where both Messer Leon and his son David (who signed the book's approbation) were then residing, the humanist rabbi had changed his attitude toward the Kabbalah, possibly due to his son's influence.[20] The *Agur*'s publication there should thus be seen in conjunction with the 1492 printing in Naples—while Messer Leon was still alive—of R. Baḥya b. Asher's Torah commentary in its first edition. Had he maintained his opposition, expressed nearly four decades earlier, to the kabbalistic doctrine of the *sefirot,* it is not likely that R. Baḥya's heavily kabbalistic work would have appeared there during his lifetime.[21]

There was, however, another aspect of Landau's *Agur* that dovetailed with Messer Leon's audacious interventions of 1455. This was the willingness to break with the Ashkenazic tradition, in which both were schooled, of regarding local tradition as sacrosanct. In the laws of evening prayer in that late fifteenth-century work Landau addressed a question that had been of particular concern to northern European halakhists for centuries: Could *Ma'ariv* be recited even before the stars were visible, the official time designated by the Mishnah, during the long days of summer? Since the days of Rashi, as Jacob Katz has shown, it had been standard among Franco-German Jewry to recite the evening prayer even before sundown during the summer months—a practice which northern European rabbis not only refused to condemn, but heroically attempted to justify.[22] Landau, however, writing in Naples where the dog days of summer were hotter but mercifully shorter than in the north, sharply criticized those Jews of "Ashkenaz and [northern] Italy who recite the evening prayer during summer . . . more than two hours before the stars come out," asserting further that "this custom has neither root nor branch, but is merely a bad habit . . . based on laziness."[23]

II

Among the issues addressed in Messer Leon's first letter of 1455 was the time of day at which married women were to begin preparing for their monthly immersions. This is ostensibly a minor one, but, together with a related ruling which affected the number of days per month couples were to refrain from intimate contact, one that allowed the Ancona rabbi entrance of a sort into the bedroom chambers of his coreligionists, a significant foothold in his larger strategy of conquest.

In his opinion, which relied heavily on Ashkenazic sources—although it addressed Italian communities in which the presence of Ashkenazim was minimal—these preparations were to begin before dark, thus requiring women to leave their homes before nightfall. Members of the communities, mostly to the south, to which his letter was addressed, were audaciously warned that those failing to conform to its instructions, "would have all the curses written in the Torah" fall upon them. Moreover, they would "be erased from the book of life" and "singled out by the Lord for calamity from all the tribes of Israel," as well as having their names "blotted out from under heaven."[24]

These last words, perhaps more than the rulings themselves, had a strong effect upon Messer Leon's senior Florentine colleague R. Benjamin of Montalcino, who in his sharp, and sometimes sardonic, response to the Jews of Ancona took issue with Messer Leon's expansive sense of authority, by which he allowed himself to act as a "single judge" over adjoining regions, and treating "our land" as if it were "entirely without [rabbinical] anointment and authority."[25] In R. Benjamin's letter he referred facetiously to their rabbi's "great love and compassion for the members of his generation," which he compared to that "of a father for his son and a teacher for his students, reprimanding them with the rod of his mouth (Is 11:4), his lips full of indignation (Is 30:27) . . . hurling venom at them all, large and small."[26] R. Benjamin went on to discuss at length the limited authority conveyed by rabbinical ordination, particularly with regard to its geographical scope, asserting that since talmudic times there had not been a single rabbi who sought "to force the scholars of other cities, by means of maledictions or weaponry, to accept his views in matters of ritual law."[27] Speaking of Messer Leon, whom he did not deign to mention by name, R. Benjamin wrote that "if that trustworthy friend's true aim was for his decrees to be observed, he should have set them on a firm basis by becoming the master of many students from different places," who would then spread his teachings through their sermons or by means of their own students.[28] And again to the Jews of Ancona, to whom he was indignantly returning Messer Leon's letter, he wrote :

> I wonder why your exalted community, after accepting his teachings, did not also establish him, with all due submission, as your king," suggesting that Messer Leon had never been formally appointed as rabbi of Ancona's community, which had merely allowed him to act as a rabbinic authority while supporting himself, it may be presumed, through his work as a Padua-trained physician.[29]

In this respect Messer Leon's status was similar to that of R. Benjamin in Florence, who was also ordained but supporting himself through banking. This helps to explain the latter's remark that "if someone as lowly as myself would make announcements on his own, and curse the many learned scholars who follow Gersonides . . . he would be denounced as a fool deserving of disgrace."[30] Earlier in his letter to Ancona, R. Benjamin had facetiously accused his younger colleague of arrogating to himself more power than had either the Pope (Nicholas V) or the Emperor (Frederick III), "through whom, directly or indirectly, he has received his title 'Messer Leon.'" Both the Pope and the Emperor, he claimed, "scrupulously refrain . . . from enjoining orders and decrees upon the inhabitants of these lands, for these have not been subjugated by them."[31] It would appear that R. Benjamin was alluding to the period of relative tranquility ushered in by the Peace of Lodi (April, 1454) and the creation soon afterward of a defensive league between Florence, Milan, and Venice, who were eventually joined by Naples and the Papacy. The subsequent treaty between these five powers reflected, as one scholar has written, "a recognition of common ideals and common dangers transcending the particularist interests of the several states."[32] The Florentine rabbi, who was presumably aware of Cosimo de'Medici's role in engineering the treaty, may well have hoped for a similar reining in those "particularist interests" among Italian rabbis.

Moreover, as both he and his younger Ancona colleague probably knew, Nicholas V and Frederick III had recently come face to face in Rome when the latter was crowned Emperor of the Holy Roman Empire. Early in his coronation ceremony the new emperor was required to kiss both of the pope's feet, and then later "kissed his foot and right hand" before receiving a kiss from Nicholas "on the right side of his face" in a ceremony that I have elsewhere described as one of "submissive intimacy."[33] Even before the five members of the Italian League had done so, the pope and the emperor formally recognized each other's realms of authority. When Christian rulers were reining in their authority on the Italian peninsula, was it not strange— R. Benjamin seems to have been saying—that a local rabbi was audaciously attempting to expand his own? Although his assertion that Messer Leon's honorific title had been conferred by both the Pope and the Emperor has been accepted at face value by some scholars,[34] it seems rather to have been the banker's way of alluding facetiously (but perhaps also enviously) to his younger colleague's secular learning and prestigious university degree. The Florentine banker, who represented an older Italian world in which influence was gained by attracting students, and rabbis generally issued rulings only when they were first consulted, was justifiably worried by an overeducated newcomer to the scene who was trying to change the rules even before establishing a modicum of seniority.

R. Joseph Colon, by contrast, was concerned primarily with the content of Messer Leon's decrees rather than the question of the latter's attempt to assume authority over distant communities. He acknowledged that the decree requiring ablution preparations to begin before dark was supported by a host of medieval sources, adding that "indeed this is our practice." But he stressed that there was an alternate tradition reaching back to R. Aḥai Gaon, in eighth-century Mesopotamia, and continuing through such prominent Mediterranean scholars as R. Isaac Alfasi, Maimonides, and R. Solomon ibn Adret of Barcelona, which ruled that it was preferable to begin such preparations at night. "How then has your heart driven you," he challenged Messer Leon, "to threaten with excommunication those [women] who follow R. Aḥai and the rabbis who agree with him, since even his opponents agree that it is permissible [though not preferable] for women to cleanse themselves at night?" Colon asserted that not only should women who began their preparations after dark not be excommunicated, "but they should not even be criticized, if that indeed is the local custom."[35]

If the point of Messer Leon's first letter was to show the communities of central and southern Italy that there was a new sheriff in the region, who would critically examine their practices (and those of their wives) in the most intimate areas of ritual observance, the point of the second was to demonstrate that he could also save Italy's northern communities from grave theological errors. It is important to stress, however, that although the young rabbi had brazenly resorted to the rabbinic *ḥerem* (ban) in his letter concerning ritual immersion, his second letter, concerning the errors of Gersonides and the kabbalists, merely criticized specific theological views, but stopped short—as not all scholars have realized—of imposing an actual ban on any of his works.[36] What, in fact, explains his choice of those two subjects as a means of establishing his credentials as an arbiter in matters of Jewish belief?

It would appear that he was influenced by the great Spanish rabbi Isaac b. Sheshet Perfet (Ribash, d. 1408), who was born in Barcelona but settled in North Africa after the anti-Jewish riots of 1391. Two of R. Isaac's responsa (first published only in 1546) dealt with the very theological issues concerning which Messer Leon saw fit to warn his Italian coreligionists. One, written in response to a query concerning the nature of "Greek wisdom" prohibited in the Talmud,[37] referred to the errors of Gersonides, whom the Spanish rabbi described as having been "a great scholar of the Talmud who composed a fine commentary on the Pentateuch and Prophets, and followed the [philosophical] path of Maimonides." Unlike the latter, however, Gersonides allowed himself to be steered by Greek wisdom "far away from the way of truth . . . in a number of matters, such as God's knowledge of the future."[38] In another R. Isaac dealt critically with some of the core beliefs of the kabbalists, especially the doctrine of the *sefirot,* testifying that his late teacher R. Perez b. Isaac ha-Kohen "would not speak of, or recognize, those *sefirot.*" He also reported hearing from R. Perez that the latter's own teacher, the tosafist R. Samson of Chinon (d. 1330), would say that he prayed "in the manner of that child," by which he understood that the French rabbi had "intended to counteract the opinion of the kabbalists, who sometimes pray to one *sefirah* and sometimes to another."[39]

Messer Leon seems to have chosen the topics concerning which his Italian coreligionists allegedly needed to be protected from error less on the basis of their actual reading habits—Gersonides' Commentary on the Pentateuch, for example, was published only some two decades later [40]—than due to a strong need to assert himself as their supreme theological authority. For that purpose he could almost arbitrarily lift two topics from the responsa of a Spanish-born rabbi who had been dead for decades. A century later, when those responsa were available in print, such "borrowing" would likely have been detected. But in the mid-fifteenth century, when manuscript copies were often incomplete, he could—and evidently did—get away with it.

Notes

1. Moses A. Shulvass, *The Jews in the World of the Renaissance,* trans. E. I. Kose (Leiden, 1973 [1955]), 77; echoed by Hava Tirosh-Rothschild, *Between Worlds: The Life and Thought of Rabbi David ben Judah Messer Leon* (Albany, N.Y., 1991), 26–27. See also Shulvass's earlier article, "The Disputes of Messer Leon with His Contemporaries and His Attempts to Exert His Authority on the Jews of Italy" (Hebrew), *Zion* 12 (1947): 17–23, reprinted in idem, *Bi-tsevat ha-dorot* (Tel Aviv, 1960).

2. Robert Bonfil, *Rabbis and Jewish Communities in Renaissance Italy,* trans. J. Chipman (Oxford, 1990 [1979]), 259. Bonfil, it should be noted, postulated a copyist's error allowing him to postdate Messer Leon's "revolutionary" efforts by two decades, to 1475. See ibid., 258, n. 181. See also Bonfil's introduction to the facsimile edition of Messer Leon's *Sefer nofet tsufim* (Jerusalem, 1981), 16, as well as the comments of Tirosh-Rothschild, *Between Worlds,* 250, n. 77, whose doubts I share. By contrast, Joseph Hacker implicitly accepts Bonfil's late dating. See Joseph R. Hacker, "Sixteenth-Century Internal Censorship of Hebrew Books," in *The Hebrew Book in Early Modern Italy,* ed. J. R. Hacker and A. Shear (Philadelphia, 2011), 111.

3. Cecil Roth, *The Jews in the Renaissance* (Philadelphia, 1959), 312.

4. Umberto Cassuto, *Gli ebrei a Firenze nell'età del rinascimento* (Florence, 1918), 245–46.

5. George Margoliouth, "A Florentine Service-Book at the British Museum," *JQR* (o.s.) 16 (1904), 73–74. As Margoliouth noted, the manuscript was sold by Jehiel (in Florence) some two decades later. See also Margoliouth, *Catalogue of the Hebrew and Samaritan Manuscripts in the British Museum* 2 (London, 1905), 218–28 (nos. 626–27).

6. Benjamin Richler, ed., *Hebrew Manuscripts in the Vatican Library* (Vatican City, 2008), 342 (no. 396). See also Cassuto, *Gli ebrei,* 247, n. 14.

7. Later, in 1469, Messer Leon was granted the supreme academic degree of Doctor of Philosophy and Medicine, which he subsequently awarded to two other Jews. See Daniel Carpi, "Notes on the Life of Rabbi Judah Messer Leon," in *Studi sull'ebraismo italiano in memoria di Cecil Roth,* ed. E. Toaff (Rome, 1975), 44–45. On his father Jehiel as a physician see Tirosh-Rothschild, *Between Worlds,* 25.

8. Israel J. Yuval, *Scholars in Their Time: The Religious Leadership of German Jewry in the Late Middle Ages* (Hebrew; Jerusalem, 1988), 108, 183, 231, 256

9. Robert Black, "Florence," in *The Renaissance in National Context,* ed. R. Porter and M. Teich (Cambridge, 1992), 35. This is not necessarily to suggest that Benjamin of Montalcino attended such a school, but that the private instruction he received—beyond his extensive Jewish education —mirrored that of such schools.

10. Bonfil, *Rabbis and Jewish Communities,* 271. On *Nofet tsufim* see Bonfil's aforementioned introduction to the facsimile edition, as well as Abraham Melammed, "Rhetoric and Philosophy in *Nofet tsufim* by R. Judah Messer Leon" (Hebrew), *Italia* 1.2 (1978): 7–39. On Messer Leon's "cultural ideal of an all-inclusive view of the Torah," see David B. Ruderman, *Early Modern Jewry: A New Cultural History* (Princeton, N.J., 2010), 120–21, 198.

11. Tirosh-Rothschild, *Between Worlds,* 27.

12. Messer Leon's first letter, together with responses by R. Benjamin of Montalcino and others, was published by David Frankel in *Divre rivot ba-she'arim* (Husiatyn, 1902) from a manuscript later destroyed during World War I. The second letter appears in a parallel manuscript, from which it was later published by Simha Assaf, "From the Treasures of the Jerusalem Library," *Minha le-David . . . Kovets Maamarim . . . R. David Yellin* (Hebrew; Jerusalem, 1935), 226–28 (reprinted in idem, *Mekorot u-mehkarim be-toldot Yisrael* [Jerusalem, 1946], 218–29). It is only from the second letter that we know to which communities the first was sent. See also See H. Rosenberg, "Alcuni cenni biografici e letterati della comunità israelitica di Ancona," *Saggio degli scritti in lingua ebraica degli Ecc.mi Rabbini Vivanti e Tedeschi* (Casale Monferrato, 1932), xxv. In contrast to Rosenberg and some subsequent scholars I believe that only the second and third of Messer Leon's letters were sent to Florence, and that the garbled passage at the end of the first letter (Frankel, *Divre rivot,* 2) was mistakenly placed there by the printers.

13. Assaf, "From the Treasures," 226–27. On Gersonides and his views on the limits of divine knowledge see Colette Sirat, *A History of Jewish Philosophy in the Middle Ages* (Cambridge, 1985), 282–308. On his discussion of this question in his Torah commentary see also Amos Funkenstein, "Gersonides' Biblical Commentary: Science, History, and Providence," in *Studies on Gersonides,* ed. G. Freudenthal (Leiden, 1992), 308. Messer Leon was hardly the first rabbi to take issue with Gersonides' views on divine knowledge. See especially Charles H. Manekin, "On the Limited-Omniscience Interpretation of Gersonides' Theory of Divine Knowledge," in *Perspectives on Jewish Thought and Mysticism,* ed. A. Ivry et al. (Amsterdam, 1998), 135–70.

14. On Messser Leon's Aristotelianism and that of Padua's university see Melammed, "Rhetoric and Philosophy," 12–14; Bonfil, *Rabbis and Jewish Communities,* 271; Tirosh-Rothschild, *Between Worlds,* 26, 29, 250–51.

15. See Yuval, *Scholars in Their Time.*

16. David W. Amram, *The Makers of Hebrew Books in Italy* (Philadelphia, 1909), 66, 68.

17. See for example, Tirosh-Rothschild, *Between Worlds,* 268–69, n. 108.

18. *Sefer he-agur ha-shalem,* ed. M. Herschler (Jerusalem, 1960), 22b.

19. Margoliouth, "A Florentine Service-Book," 80–81. For the Byzantine precedent see Efraim Gottlieb, "Menorah: In the Kabbalah," *Encyclopaedia Judaica* 11:1367; Richler, *Hebrew Manuscripts in the Vatican,* 152–53 (no. 214).

20. See Amram, *Makers of Hebrew Books,* 66; Tirosh-Rothschild, *Between Worlds,* 52. On his son David's fusion of "rabbinic Judaism, medieval scholasticism, and Kabbalah," see ibid., 184–87.

21. On the early editions of R. Bahya's commentary see Efraim Gottlieb, *The Kabbalah in the Writings of R. Bahya ben Asher Ibn Halawa* (Hebrew; Jerusalem, 1970), 9. On its use as a "safe" kabbalistic text in sixteenth-century Italy, prior to the *Zohar*'s publication, see Elliott Horowitz, "Speaking of the Dead: The Emergence of the Eulogy among Italian Jewry of the Sixteenth Century," in *Preachers of the Italian Ghetto,* ed. D. Ruderman (Berkeley, Calif., 1992), 142–43.

22. Jacob Katz, "'Alternations in the Time of Evening Service': An Example of the Interrelationship between Religious Custom, Halacha, and their Social Background" (Hebrew), *Zion* 35 (1970): 35–60, republished in idem, *Halakhah and Kabbalah* (Hebrew; Jerusalem, 1984), 175–200.

23. Herschler, *Sefer he-agur,* 63a; Katz, *Halakhah and Kabbalah,* 193–95.

24. *Divre rivot,* 1–2. For the latter two curses, see Dt 29:20–21.

25. *Divre rivot,* 3.

26. Ibid.

27. Ibid.

28. Ibid., 5. See also Bonfil, *Rabbis and Jewish Communities,* 46–47.

29. *Divre rivot,* 7. See also Bonfil, *Rabbis and Jewish Communities,* 171–72, who stresses "the absence of any mention of a community-appointed rabbi in Ancona" until the seventeenth century.

30. Ibid.

31. Ibid. Contrast Robert Bonfil, *Jewish Life in Renaissance Italy,* trans. A. Oldcorn (Berkeley, Calif., 1994), 184.

32. C. M. Ady, "Florence and Northern Italy, 1414–1492," in *The Cambridge Medieval History* 8, ed. J. B. Bury, C. W. Previte-Orton, Z. N. Brooke (Cambridge, 1936), 214–15, and more recently David Nicholas, *The Transformation of Europe: 1300–1600* (London, 1999), 46; Christopher F. Black, *Early Modern Italy: A Social History* (London, 2001), 7.

33. For the description of the ceremony, see Elliott Horowitz, "Between Submission and Intimacy: Hand and Foot Kissing among Jews and Christians in Early Modern Europe," in *"Interstizi": Culture ebraico-cristiane . . . dal medioevo all'et'a moderna,* ed. U. Israel, R. Jütte, R. C. Mueller (Rome, 2010), 340, and the sources cited there.

34. See, for example, Carpi, "Notes on the Life," 42–43, Bonfil, *Jewish Life,* 184.

35. Quotations of Colon from Joseph Colon, *New Responsa and Decisions,* ed. E. D. Pines (2nd ed.; Jerusalem, 1984), no. 49. See also Jeffrey R. Woolf, "The Authority of Custom in the Responsa of R. Joseph Colon (Maharik)" (Hebrew), *Diné Yisrael* 19 (1997–98): 43.

36. See, for example, Carpi, "Notes on the Life," 40–44; David B. Ruderman, *The World of a Renaissance Jew: The Life and Thought of Abraham ben Mordecai Farissol* (Cincinnati, Ohio, 1981), 113. This claim is based largely on the later testimony of R. David Messer Leon (in a text published by Moritz Steinschneider in *Hebräische Bibliographie* 8 [1865], 64–65) that his father had imposed a long-lasting ban "throughout all of Italy" on reading the Torah commentary of Gersonides. Bonfil (introduction to the facsimile edition, 11, n. 10), while not doubting that an actual ban was issued by Messer Leon, nonetheless questions his son's testimony that it had been promulgated "throughout Italy." Tirosh-Rothschild (*Between Worlds,* 250, n. 74) suggests similarly that "the son may have exaggerated the impact of the ban in order to magnify his father's political power." However, a careful reading of Messer Leon's second letter (which was not known to Steinschneider) should lead us to question his son's later testimony concerning the very existence of a ban on the commentary by Gersonides.

37. See *bSot* 49b; *bBM* 82b, *bMen* 64b.

38. *Responsa of Isaac bar Sheshet,* 2 vols, ed. D. Metzger (Hebrew; Jerusalem, 1993), no. 45. For a critique of Gersonides see also no. 118. The first responsum was noted by Manekin, "On the Limited-Omniscience Interpretation," 136.

39. *Responsa of Isaac bar Sheshet,* no. 157. For a translation of the entire responsum (by Ephraim Kanarfogel) see J. David Bleich, ed., *With Perfect Faith: The Foundations of Jewish Belief* (Jersey City, N.J., 1983), 257–58. See also Louis Jacobs, *Theology in the Responsa* (London, 1975), 83.

40. The commentary's date of publication is given by Joseph Hacker as "around 1474–75." See Hacker, "Sixteenth-Century Jewish Internal Censorship," 111. Of course I do not quite agree with his assertion there that Messer Leon "tried to prohibit the study of Gersonides' commentary . . . shortly after its print in Mantua . . . by threatening excommunication." One immediate consequence of the work's publication would seem to be Jehiel of Teramo's willingness to include his manuscript copy in a bulk sale of a Torah scroll and several other manuscripts, all for eighty ducats, which took place on 14 Sivan 1476 (May 28). See Benjamin Richler, ed., *Hebrew Manuscripts in the Biblioteca Palatina in Parma* (Jerusalem, 2001), 117 (no. 609).

JEWS AND HABSBURGS IN PRAGUE AND REGENSBURG

On the Political and Cultural Significance of Solomon Molkho's Relics

Matt Goldish
The Ohio State University

THE transfer of the "contact relics"[1] of the martyr Solomon Molkho from Regensburg to Prague around the early 1540s was a minor event with great symbolic implications. While it is unlikely that anyone involved intended the significance of the transfer to be so far-reaching, it would ultimately convey several profound messages. Foremost among these was the bid of the Horowitz family to present a new European Jewish map in which Prague was at the center while Germany and its Jewish leaders were in rapid decline. The transfer also symbolized the dominance of the Horowitzes in Prague, their connection to the tradition of Kabbalah, their power to protect the Jews through political influence, and finally, the capacity of the Jews to maintain their dignity in an iconographic war waged by the Regensburg Christians.

The figure later known as Solomon Molkho was born to a converso family in Portugal around 1500 and christened Diogo Pires. In his middle twenties, Pires came into contact with the messianic adventurer David Reubeni, who set his imagination on fire. Pires, convinced of his own role in the unfolding messianic drama, circumcised himself, declared himself a Jew, and departed for the Ottoman Empire, where he adopted the Jewish and messianically-charged name Solomon Molkho. There he studied classic Jewish texts and Kabbalah with great intensity. After an astonishingly short time his preaching drew large crowds. Molkho went to Italy, despite the great danger to himself as a "relapsed" converso, and preached the imminent arrival of the messiah. He sought and obtained an audience with Pope Clement VII, who was very taken with Molkho and actively protected him from the Inquisition.

In 1530 Molkho met up once again with David Reubeni. The two approached the Holy Roman Emperor, Charles V, in a bid to enlist his support for their messianic mission. They were received by Charles at the Imperial Diet at Regensburg (Ratisbon). The official representative of the empire's Jews, Josel of Rosheim, fearing the backlash against the Jewish community that might result from this adventure, publicly dissociated himself from the two men and left the city. Unlike the pope, Charles showed no sympathy. He had Molkho sent to Mantua where he was burned at the stake as a heretic. Reubeni was sent to Spain where he languished in an Inquisition prison until his death a few years later.[2]

After his death, Molkho's flag (or flags), mantle, and small tallit were taken from Regensburg to Prague for display at the new Pinkas Synagogue that was then being built by the Horowitz family. Nothing is known about precisely when this occurred or the details of the transfer.[3] The mantle and flag are still extant in the Prague Jewish Museum, while the tallit has disappeared. Some contemporary eyewitnesses describe these articles and their ritual display. One is Rabbi Yom Tob Lipmann Heller, author of *Tosafot Yom Tob,* who saw them in the next generation and spoke of them in his *Divre hamudot:*

> Here in the holy congregation of Prague, in the Pinkas Synagogue, there is an *arbach kanfot* [four corners; i.e. a small tallit] made of yellow silk the color of egg yolk, and the fringes on it are also of yellow silk the color of egg yolk. It was brought here from Regensburg, and it belonged to the holy rabbi Shlomoh Molkho of blessed memory. There are, furthermore, two flags of his as well as his mantle, called a "kittel."[4]

A later account from the Sabbatean period gives more details, not all of them correct:

> There in Prague, almost two hundred years ago, had been a holy man, R. Solomon Molkho. In the holy congregation of Prague there are various synagogues, one of which is called *Knesseth Minhah.* In that synagogue, inside the wall near the holy ark, rest the garments of this holy man—his mantle, kittel and *arba' kanfot* . . . Only the *arba' kanfot* are not on display, for there were Holy Names woven into it in silk.[5]

What was the larger context of the decision to bring these objects to Prague and display them in the Pinkas Synagogue? What did they signify?

THE POLITICS OF POWER

At the end of the fifteenth century, an obscure family from the village of Horoviče in Bohemia, thereafter known as the Horowitz or Munk family, moved to Prague.[6] The Horowitz family patriarch, Isaiah ben Moses ha-Levi (d. 1517), had seven sons, including Aaron Meshullam Zalman (1470–1545), who became a leading figure in the Prague Jewish community. While it is difficult to generalize about an entire family, especially one as enormous and diverse as the Horowitzes, there are certain characteristics that appear among them repeatedly in the sixteenth to eighteenth centuries. The Horowitzes were powerful leaders who liked their autonomy; they were scholars, with a particular affinity for the Kabbalah; and they were often wealthy.

Aaron Meshullam exhibited these traits particularly strongly. He was enormously wealthy, though the source of this wealth is not clear. He had such important connections at both the Bohemian and Habsburg courts that he might well be considered the first great Ashkenazi court Jew. He maintained a particularly close tie with the Burggrave (Keeper of the Castle), Lev of Rožmitál, who represented the king any time the latter was absent, and was thus the most powerful noble in the country.[7] Aaron Meshullam used these contacts to intercede on behalf of the Jewish community on numerous occasions. At the same time, however, he presided over the Jewish community with a heavy hand. A printer who had a falling-out with Isaiah and Aaron Meshullam lamented that one could never hope to prevail against their power. Needless to say, the Horowitzes were deeply resented by many in their community despite the protection they were able to provide through their connections.

This intracommunal tension came to a head in 1524 when community leaders assessed the Horowitzes for what the latter felt was too high a share of the Jews' taxes. Aaron Meshullam sued the leaders and a settlement had to be negotiated by the mayor of Prague. While he may have come to a draw in the battle, Aaron Meshullam had no intention of losing the war. His next move was an appeal directly to King Ludwig II of Bohemia for backing. In 1525 the king confirmed the broadest privileges for the Horowitz family: they would hold the offices of both chief rabbi and elder of the congregation in perpetuity. There was nothing anyone could do about this controlling maneuver.

Not surprisingly, the tension between the Horowitz faction and the rest of Prague's Jewish leaders did not abate. In 1531 someone denounced Aaron Meshullam to the government and he was arraigned before the Imperial Court of Justice on the charge of conducting business that would harm the crown. While he was exonerated, the city, as well as the Jewish community was left in an uproar. In 1534, Seligmann Horowitz, Aaron Meshullam's brother, struck a respected rabbi, Joshua Alschul, making matters yet worse. Finally, in 1535, when the argument had spread far beyond Prague, the representative of German Jewry, Josel of Rosheim, was invited to Prague to intercede. This was the same Josel whom we encountered previously running away from the meeting between Emperor Charles V and Reubeni and Molkho. Josel's solution to the Prague standoff was to create a twenty-three–point charter for redistribution of power in the community. This charter did not take into account the privileges bestowed on the Horowitzes by King Ludwig ten years earlier.[8]

Aaron Meshullam was furious with the idea that a foreign Jew had been invited to meddle in the affairs of his community and was attempting to sap his power. The wording in Josel's account of what happened next is somewhat obscure but the general sense is quite clear:

> While I was still at table [celebrating the formulation of the new charter] the spike-
> nard sent forth its odor [Song 1:12]. For the Horowitz man and his confederate by the
> name of Shabba"t Ta"Sh [Shabbatai Sheftel Horowitz] arose to deliver me into the
> hands of murderers, and I was forced to stand at the fortress in the city of Prague
> three times in mortal danger.[9]

Apparently the Horowitzes denounced Josel to the authorities for involving himself
in Bohemian affairs and interfering with royal edicts. This was a charge that might
well have cost Josel his life. Josel was called before the Burggrave at the castle and
had to plead hard for his case. He claimed that it was his extensive support from the
community—meaning the anti-Horowitz factions—that got him freed.

At the time of the events just described, around 1535, the Horowitz family was
completing the rebuilding and expansion of the Pinkas Synagogue, an ancient structure that lay on the family's property. The Pinkas Synagogue was now a private
institution, which represented the Horowitz family's challenge to the old guard of
communal power in Prague. It was, at the same time, a venerable ancient place
of worship and a beautiful new structure designed by the famed and fashionable Prague architect, Benedikt Rejt. As the building was concluded, the relics of
Solomon Molkho were brought in and put on display.

Josel of Rosheim was the representative of the conservative, traditional German
Jewish community, in which capacity he had deliberately and publicly dissociated
himself from Solomon Molkho. To him Molkho represented a threat to the already
equivocal security of the Jews in those lands. What more tangible symbol could the
Horowitz family find to express its antipathy to Josel, his power base, his politics,
and what they perceived as his cowardice and failure, than the relics of Solomon
Molkho? Molkho had indeed been killed in sanctification of the Divine Name on
a mission for which Josel had failed to support him, just as Josel failed to support
the justice of the Horowitz claims in Prague. The Horowitzes, in contrast, were a
growing power in a burgeoning community.

This, then, is one layer of the relics' symbolism.

THE POLITICS OF PLACE

The very fact that there was no Jewish community in Regensburg when Reubeni
and Molkho arrived there might also have been attributed by the Horowitz family
to another "failing" of Josel.

The people of Regensburg had long clamored for the expulsion of the Jews. In
1476 the virulently anti-Jewish preacher Peter Schwarz (Negri) succeeded in having
all the Jews' property confiscated. Soon thereafter, seventeen Regensburg Jews were
arrested in connection with the Trent ritual murder accusation. Another preacher,
Balthasar Hubmeier (later executed as an Anabaptist) pursued a new round of accusations against the Jews for usury and blasphemy, and demanded their expulsion.
He was followed by many others. Only the vigorous protection of King Frederick

III and Emperor Maximilian prevented the Jews' demise. Finally, when Maximilian died in 1519, the burghers took advantage of the interregnum to carry out a complete expulsion of Regensburg Jewry and Josel could do nothing to prevent it.[10]

The roughly 800 Jews (between 5 and 10 percent of the population) of this most ancient and important Bavarian community were forced to leave. Their beloved ancient synagogue was immediately destroyed, replaced with a church dedicated to the Virgin Mary. Thus, when David Reubeni and Solomon Molkho came to the Imperial Diet in Regensburg in 1530 there were no other Jews there.

Hana Volavková, in her wonderful 1955 book on the Pinkas Synagogue, points out in explicit detail that the architecture and almemor (pulpit) of the Pinkas Synagogue were deliberately modeled on the destroyed synagogue of Regensburg. The Molkho relics, she says, complete the connection between Molkho, Regensburg, and the Pinkas Synagogue. "Thus Aaron Meshulam Horovic's decision to erect a larger and more splendid synagogue in the place of the old one was his response to the destruction of the Regensburg Synagogue."[11] Volavková, then, makes an explicit and documented case for Aaron Meshullam Horowitz's intention to create the Pinkas Synagogue as a memorial to the synagogue, Jewry, and tragedies of Regensburg. She unequivocally places the importation of Molkho's relics into that framework.

There are several other dimensions to this symbolism. Regensburg represented, in many ways, the glory and the subsequent decline of the German Jewish community. Its Jews had been protected by a royal power, but, like almost all of German Jewry, they ended up marginalized and then expelled at the end of the Middle Ages.[12] The German Jewish establishment, represented in this case by Josel, no longer had the capacity to defend German Jewry from this rising tide.

The Horowitzes were building a new power base further east. Not only were they amazingly successful at amassing wealth and creating vibrant Jewish institutions in Prague, they also had the political clout to counteract the expulsion decrees and accusations that arose periodically. When Bohemia and Moravia came under Habsburg rule in 1526 Emperor Ferdinand almost immediately confirmed the standing privileges of Prague's Jewish community and pledged that it would not be expelled. But Aaron Meshullam's influence extended as well to local city officials and nobles who held a great deal of the power in Bohemia. This combination was very rare among Jewish leaders and communities during that age, and was also a source of considerable political power.[13]

Thus Prague under the Habsburg rulers and the influence of the Horowitz family in the Jewish community was positioned to assume the leading role and provide a level of security that could no longer belong to German Jewry. The Horowitzes, with their *kloiz*—their rebuilt Pinkas Synagogue—and their extensive Prague-based networks, were ready to create a new Jewish center that would displace the old centers of Ashkenazi Jewish leadership and learning in Germany. The transfer of Solomon Molkho's relics from the destroyed old center in Regensburg to the vibrant new center in Prague was a form of supersession, of passing the torch to the new world of Jewish life.

This shift in the Jewish community is particularly interesting because it parallels developments in the larger world of European politics. As the Habsburg Empire expanded in the 1520s, absorbing Hungary, Bohemia, and Moravia, it faced enormous challenges, particularly from the Ottomans. After the first Turkish siege of the city in 1529, the old seat of imperial power in Vienna appeared no longer to be viable. Were it not for an outbreak of disease and an early winter, the walled city would almost certainly have been lost. At this time Emperor Ferdinand moved himself and many resources northward, away from Austria and Germany and into Bohemia and Moravia. He vastly expanded the Prague castle, laying the groundwork for what would eventually be the Imperial seat there at the time of Rudolf II at the end of the sixteenth century. Indeed, it must have appeared to many—possibly including the Horowitzes—that the shift of the Imperial center to Prague was occurring already in the 1530s. Thus, the coalescence of Horowitz power in the Prague Jewish community, symbolized by the Pinkas Synagogue with Molkho's relics in it, coincided with a shift of Habsburg interest eastward into Prague. This was surely no accident. The wily Aaron Meshullam positioned himself so that the ascent of his family and community would rise with the tide of the new Bohemian government and centrality of Prague in the empire.

THE POLITICS OF PERSONAGES

What else did Solomon Molkho represent that the Horowitzes were so anxious to appropriate?

Molkho was a victim of persecution and a martyr in multiple contexts. He was a converso from Portugal whose return to Judaism made him a target of the Inquisition. Thus he represents the victims of Iberian anti-Jewish bigotry. Later, in Italy, he was pursued by the papal Inquisition, though ironically, he was protected by the pope himself. Molkho was also a victim of Charles V's anti-Jewish sensibilities. Charles had Molkho sent back to the Italian Inquisition for execution. The fact that this decision was made at the diet in Regensburg, where the Jews had been accused of ritual murder and other atrocities, and whence they were expelled just a decade earlier, added another level to Molkho's representation of Jewish suffering. Thus Molkho symbolically ties together three of the most virulent anti-Jewish trends of the late Middle Ages: baseless ritual charges against Jews; expulsions from most of Western Europe; and Inquisitions. His relics were the very emblem of Jewish travail in Christendom.

A second facet of Molkho's image was his status as a mystic. This was important and powerful for the Horowitz family. Molkho had studied with great Spanish kabbalists, such as Ḥakham Joseph Taitazak, in Salonica and Constantinople. His sermons, most of them preached in Italy, were full of mystical symbols and allusions. Perhaps the most potent piece of this legacy was the final act of his career in

Regensburg. Regensburg had for centuries been a center of German Jewish life and learning. It was also the home of the antecedents of Kabbalah, the *Haside Ashkenaz,* or German Pietists, in the twelfth and thirteenth centuries. By coming to Regensburg, Molkho symbolized the return of Jewish mysticism to one of its birthplaces. By his martyrdom he symbolized the final realization of the heavy martyrological strands in the writings of the *Haside Ashkenaz,* and the snuffing out of the mystic's life at the hands of Christian persecutors.[14] We might add, following the work of Moshe Idel, that Molkho was a sort of magician as well, a characteristic which also ties him to the tradition of the German Pietists.[15] Once again, then, the arrival of Molkho's relics in Prague represented a legacy to which the Horowitzes wished to attach themselves, and for which they could hope to offer better security than had Germany.

A third facet of Molkho's image was his status as a prospective messiah. I am not entirely sure what to make of this symbolism and the Horowitzes' relationship to it. Perhaps they hoped to bring this legacy to their home in Prague as well, but this becomes somewhat problematic. Failed messiahs are not often a welcome part of Jewish heritage.[16] I tend to think that this aspect of Molkho's persona was played down, not just by the Horowitzes, but by the entire generation that witnessed his martyrdom. They preferred to remember him as a holy figure, a mystic, and a victim of persecution rather than a messianic disappointment.[17]

THE POLITICS OF PORTRAYAL

In addition to Molkho's image, his contact relics themselves carry an entire set of symbolisms. They are not usually the source of miracles and healing in the way Christian relics are. In this sense they are truly *Jewish* relics; their significance is in what they represent rather than in what they do. This is true of Molkho's relics even as they (or at least the tallit) embody magical codes.

Let us consider the items for a moment as icons. The *talit katan* is a highly personal object, already full of symbolism, to which Molkho had added his own set of potent meanings. I will not enter further into the possible significance of the colors and symbols he appended because Idel has dealt with the topic at length.[18] Molkho's *talit katan* represented his creativity and power as a kabbalist and magician who possessed occult knowledge.

The flag is also a symbol of power. Prague Jewry had a special history with flags, dating from the thirteenth century.[19] For Reubeni and Molkho, flags represented a new Jewish military spirit. While the mission they promoted, to use mystical and physical means to battle the Ottomans, was never realized, the message of Jewish power and activism fit the Horowitzes's image very well. Aaron Meshullam Horowitz was one of a tiny group of Jews who wielded real power in early sixteenth-century Europe. Not only could he usually bend the Jewish community to his will, but he could influence both the provincial and imperial governments to protect the Jews, even when that was an unpopular position. Aaron Meshullam's affairs were known to kings and emperors. He could well identify with Molkho's spirit of renewed

Jewish participation in the great events of the day. The mantle goes with the flag as a symbol of leadership.

What is perhaps more important than the objects themselves is the very idea of saving, displaying, and venerating material objects connected with a Jewish martyr. Relics are a typically Christian expression of piety. Christian relics were sometimes clothes or personal objects, but often they were the actual bones of a person, something Judaism would not sanction. While Pinchas Giller and Yoni Garb have written about the veneration of saints and their grave sites among sixteenth-century kabbalists in terms of relics, I think this is a separate phenomenon.[20] The veneration of relics in medieval Judaism appears to have been extremely rare until the Molkho case and again in the later stages of the Sabbatean movement.[21] Oddly, among the Christians there was a widespread legend that the Jews of Regensburg had lived there since ancient times and had venerated a relic of one of the tablets of the law with which Moses had descended from Mount Sinai.[22] So, two rare phenomena adumbrate the transfer of the Molkho relics: a Jewish relic in Regensburg and a Jewish flag in Prague.

If we look to the Christian world as the influence that brought Jews to honor Molkho's relics, we run into an enigma. It was precisely at the period of Molkho's execution and the arrival of his relics in Prague that the entire institution of relics, reliquaries, and icons was under direct attack, both by Martin Luther and the Protestants, and by internal Catholic reformers like Erasmus.[23] What, then, might be the significance of relics suddenly appearing at this time and place?

Regensburg is again the key. In his book *Jewish Icons,* Richard I. Cohen discusses the etchings of the Regensburg synagogue created by the artist Albrecht Altdorfer, who was one of the proponents of its destruction. Cohen explains that these were intended as mementos to be sold to pilgrims after the synagogue was burned down and a shrine to Schöne Maria was erected in its place:

> Altdorfer enterprisingly promoted the memory of the Jewish expulsion from Regensburg by creating a representative image of its destroyed synagogue. All of these works adopted a new iconographic discourse for the polemic with Judaism, turning away to a great extent from the symbolic, medieval depictions of Jews and Judaism.[24]

There is more. In their frenzy to destroy the synagogue, the townspeople brought the roof down upon a master stonemason named Jacob Kern. He recovered from his injuries in what was taken as a miraculous manner, and with that, the shrine to Schöne Maria became a hugely popular pilgrimage site. More miracles were reported. A woodcut of ecstatic pilgrims at the new shrine by the artist Michael Ostendorfer was circulated. The iconographic significance of the site's transformation from a blasphemous synagogue to a purified venue of miraculous providence was exploited to the full. Such Marian devotion at the places of destroyed synagogues was an established pattern.[25] The shrine and cult at Regensburg were the focus of a backlash against the Reformers and the Catholic Humanists who wished to do away with practices like these—practices that seemed to represent all the problematic medieval Catholic tendencies toward magic and idolatry. These Reformers and Humanists were the same people who, during the first two decades of the Reformation era, appeared to many Christians to be "Judaizers."[26]

With all this in mind we can look at the Horowitz's project as part of what Harris Lenowitz has called *Iconomachia*—an icon war.[27] If the Christian triumphalist position was moving toward a "new iconographic discourse" as Cohen puts it, the Jews too would represent their devotion in more tangible forms. Thus, both the Pinkas Synagogue, built as a memorial to the Regensburg Synagogue, and the importation of Molkho's relics, constitute a form of Jewish response in kind to the Christian assault on Jewish existence in Western Europe. If the German Christians destroyed the synagogue in Regensburg, the Bohemian Jews would rebuild it in Prague. If the German Christians commenced an iconographic attack against Jewry, the Bohemian Jews would counter with their own triumphalist iconography.

Once again, this development in the Jewish quarter of Prague paralleled developments in the city and palace. Emperor Ferdinand I was one of several pretenders to the Czech throne when his brother-in-law, Louis, was killed in battle with the Ottomans in 1526. The nobles opposed his election, but they were eventually convinced to agree. Ferdinand, then, was, like Aaron Meshullam Horowitz, a powerful but fairly new leader in Prague. He was thus anxious to prove his dedication to the rule and glory of Bohemia. He greatly expanded the royal palace in Renaissance style—incidentally, using the same architect who rebuilt the Pinkas Synagogue. Ferdinand also established the Habsburg tradition of collecting. His collections included coins, medals, ancient inscriptions, art, jewels, insignia, and arms. The famous *Kunstkammer* of Rudolf's time began with Ferdinand.[28]

We might thus look at the relics of Molkho not only as religious objects, but also as a sort of Jewish *Kunstkammer,* a small collection of interesting objects that would bring attention and interest to their owners.

CONCLUSION

The relics of Solomon Molkho arrived in Prague at a pivotal moment in many respects. They carried with them an enormous weight of political symbolism that reflected the sunset of German Jewry and the rise of the East. The relics also symbolized the situation of their sponsor, Aaron Meshullam Horowitz, his position in the community, and the Horowitz's position in the city of Prague. At the same time they fit into a larger historical context that included the commencement of Habsburg rule in Bohemia, the expulsion of the Jews from most of Western Europe, and the beginning of the Protestant Reformation. While I cannot claim that the Horowitzes were aware of all these implications as they unfolded, they were all operating, and they all help provide the underlying meaning of the relics' arrival in Prague.

Notes

1. The term is that of Caroline Walker Bynum, who divides Holy Matter into four categories: animated images, relics, contact relics, and *dauerwunder* (lasting Eucharistic miracles.) See Bynum, *Christian Materiality: An Essay on Religion in Late Medieval Europe* (New York, 2011), 136–39. Note that one of Bynum's examples of contact relics (p. 137) is from the Schöne Maria in Regensburg, the significance of which will be clear presently.

2. On Molkho see A. Z. Aescoly, *Sipur David ha-Reubeni* (Jerusalem, 1940); Aescoly, *Jewish Messianic Movements* (Hebrew; 2nd ed.; Jerusalem, 1987), chap. 6; Harris Lenowitz, *The Jewish Messiahs, from the Galilee to Crown Heights* (Oxford, 1998), chap. 5; *Jewish Travellers in the Middle Ages,* ed. E. N. Adler ([1930]; repr., New York, 1987), 251–328.

3. The Christian theologian J. A. Widmannstadt reports seeing the flag in Regensburg in 1541. A. Z. Aescoly suggests that it must have been in the possession of Jews, some of whom clearly lived in the region at that time. See Aescoly, *Messianic Movements,* 433. Widmannstadt may have been in Regensburg for the colloquy held there in April of 1541 in which Catholic and Protestant theologians attempted to bring the Church back into unity.

4. H. K., *Hilkhot tsitsit,* 25. Rachel Greenblatt pointed out to me that Heller was married into the Horowitz family.

5. Moshe Idel, "Shlomo Molkho as Magician" (Hebrew) *Sefunot* (n.s.) 3 [=18] (1985): 208–09.

6. All this is from Chava Fraenkel-Goldschmidt, *The Historical Writings of Joseph of Rosheim* (Leiden, 2006), 219–26; Selma Stern, *Josel of Rosheim* (Philadelphia, 1965), 143–45; and Hana Volavková, *The Pinkas Synagogue* (Prague, 1955), 54–58.

7. See Hugh LeCaine Agnew, *The Czechs and the Lands of the Bohemian Crown* (Stanford, Calif., 2004), 57.

8. See n. 6.

9. Fraenkel-Goldschmidt, *Historical Writings,* 327; modified by me based on the text in the Hebrew edition, 299.

10. See Elisheva Carlebach, "Between History and Myth: The Regensburg Expulsion in Josel of Rosheim's *Sefer ha-Mikneh,*" in *Jewish History and Jewish Memory: Essays in Honor of Yosef Hayim Yerushalmi,* ed. E. Carlebach, J. M. Efron, and D. N. Myers (Waltham, Mass., 1998), 40–53; Raphael Straus, *Regensburg and Ausburg,* trans. F. N. Gerson (Philadelphia, 1939), 146–62; Heiko A. Oberman, *The Roots of Anti-Semitism in the Age of Renaissance and Reformation* (Philadelphia, 1984), chap. 10.

11. Volavková, *The Pinkas Synagogue,* 58–60.

12. On European expulsions see Jonathan I. Israel, *European Jewry in the Age of Mercantilism,* (3rd ed.; London, 1998).

13. The ability of the Horowitzes to maintain relations with royal, noble, and local powers suggests a possible challenge to the thesis of Yosef Hayim Yerushalmi, *The Lisbon Massacre of 1506 and the Royal Image in the Shebet Yehudah* (Cincinnati, Ohio, 1976), chap. 3, that Jews develop relationships specifically with the highest power in the land—usually the royal power—for their self-protection.

14. On the medieval German Pietists see e.g., Gershom Scholem, *Major Trends in Jewish Mysticism* (New York, 1948), third lecture; Ivan Marcus, ed., *The Religious and Social Ideas of the Jewish Pietists in Medieval Germany* (Jerusalem, 1986); Joseph Dan, *Ashkenazi Hasidism in the History of Jewish Thought,* 3 vols. (Hebrew; Tel-Aviv, 1990); idem, *Studies in Ashkenazi-Hasidic Literature* (Hebrew; Ramat-Gan, 1975); Joseph Hacker, ed., *The Social and Spiritual World of the German Pietists* (Hebrew; Jerusalem, 1968). On martyrdom among the German Pietists see e.g., Joseph Dan, "The View of Sanctification of the Divine Name in the Philosophical Literature of the German Pietists," in *Holy War and Martyrology* (Hebrew; Jerusalem, 1967), 121–29; Elliot Wolfson, "Martyrdom, Eroticism, and Asceticism in Twelfth-Century Ashkenazi Piety," in *Jews and Christians in Twelfth-Century Europe,* ed. M. A. Signer and J. Van Engen (Notre Dame, Ind., 2001), 171–220.

15. Idel, "Molkho as Magician."

16. On this problem see Matt Goldish, "The Salvation of Jesus and Jewish Messiahs," in *Jesus among the Jews: Representation and Thought,* ed. N. Stahl (Oxford, 2012), 108–10.

17. This effect can be seen in several of the remembrances of Molkho quoted in Aescoly, *Messianic Movements,* 427–34.

18. Idel, "Molkho as Magician," 208–13.

19. *Encyclopaedia Judaica* (Jerusalem, 1971) 6:1336 (s.v. "Flag"). Rachel Greenblatt has suggested that the later display of banners in the Meisel and Altneuschul synagogues of Prague was modeled on the display of Molkho's flag.

20. Pinchas Giller, "Recovering the Sanctity of the Galilee: The Veneration of Sacred Relics in Classical Kabbalah," *Journal of Jewish Thought and Philosophy* 4.1 (1994): 147–69; Jonathan Garb, "The Cult of the Saints in Lurianic Kabbalah," *JQR* 98.2 (2008): 203–29. The concept of the saint is closely tied, of course, to the adoration of relics. See also Robert L. Cohn, "Sainthood on the Periphery: The Case of Judaism," in *Sainthood: Its Manifestations in World Religions,* ed. R. Kieckhefer and G. D. Bond (Berkeley, Calif., 1988), 43–68; Josef W. Meri, *The Cult of Saints among Muslims and Jews in Medieval Syria* (Oxford, 2002).

21. See Jacob Frank, *Words of the Lord* (*Dicta*) (Lenowitz ed.: http://www.languages.utah.edu/kabbalah/protected/dicta_frank_lenowitz.pdf) #834; Bezalel Naor, *Post-Sabbatian Sabbatianism* (Spring Valley, N.Y., 1999), chap. 17. Note that some of the Sabbatean relics came from Prague.

22. See Carlebach, "Between History and Myth," 49, n. 7; Isaak Meyer, *Zur Geschichte der Juden in Regensburg* (Berlin, 1913), 22–23.

23. See Richard I. Cohen, *Jewish Icons: Art and Society in Modern Europe* (Berkeley, Calif., 1998), 22–24; Bynum, *Christian Materiality;* Hans Beltung, *Likeness and Presence: A History of the Image Before the Era of Art* (Chicago, 1994).

24. Cohen, *Jewish Icons,* 24.

25. Allyson E. Creasman, "The Virgin Mary against the Jews: Anti-Jewish Polemic in the Pilgrimage to the Schöne Maria of Regensburg, 1519–1525," *Sixteenth Century Journal* 33.4 (2002): 963–80. See also Belting, *Likeness and Presence,* 453–57.

26. On destroyed synagogues being converted into churches in this period, with extensive discussion of Regensburg, see J. M. Minty, "*Judengasse* to Christian Quarter: The Phenomenon of the Converted Synagogue in the Late Medieval and Early Modern Holy Roman Empire," in *Popular Religion in Germany and Central Europe, 1400–1800,* ed. B. Scribner and T. Johnson (New York, 1996), 58–86. On Reformers as "Judaizers" see e.g. Louis Israel Newman, *Jewish Influence on Christian Reform Movements* (New York, 1925), book 3 and book 4 sections 1–2.

27. Harris Lenowitz, "Iconomachia!" *Duchowosc zydowska w Polsce* (2000): 197–218.

28. See Eliška Fučiková, "Prague Castle under Rudolf II, His Predecessors and Successors," in *Rudolf II and Prague: The Court and the City,* ed. E. Fučiková et al. (London, 1997), 2–7.

JEWISH WOMEN IN THE WAKE OF THE CHMIELNICKI UPRISING

❊ ❊ ❊

Gzeires Taḥ-Tat as a Gendered Experience

Adam Teller
Brown University

THE experience of destruction and disaster has formed the subject not only for a huge body of Jewish literature in a wide range of genres, but also for a great deal of modern research. Starting from the pious impulse to repent in the face of suffering and to memorialize the dead, and ending with the secular desire to reconstruct and explain the events and feelings of the past, the experience of massacre and martyrdom has played—and continues to play—a central role in Jewish cultural creation.[1] Moreover, as modern scholarship has shown, female figures have held prominent positions within that body of literature. In the book of Lamentations, for example, post-destruction Jerusalem is characterized as "Bat Zion" (the daughter of Zion)— a once beautiful woman, now ravaged and abandoned.[2] The tragic, but heroic, figure of Hannah and her seven sons, first used to describe the religious persecutions of the Hellenistic age, was picked up and reused in talmudic and then medieval writing.[3] Perhaps the best known example of this phenomenon may be seen in the chronicles written following the First Crusade, where women were described as playing a dominant role in the defiant Jewish response to the armies of Christ.[4]

This literary formation, in both its general and gendered aspects, raises a number of important questions. Its gendered nature is particularly intriguing. Post-biblical Jewish culture has tended to memorialize catastrophe through the medium of martyrological prayer, a predominantly male, not to say rabbinic genre.[5] The names mentioned tend to be those of the great scholars, with even whole communities being mourned mostly for the death of the rabbis who were murdered there.[6]

Despite this male and rabbinic focus, the chronicles do devote a certain amount of attention to the fate of Jewish women in times of catastrophe. With certain notable exceptions, the treatment is largely typological and symbolic in nature, emphasizing the shocking nature of the atrocities perpetrated on the women.[7] This might seem to suggest that, in some ways at least, women's suffering in times of disaster may have been somehow more intense than that of men. However, it is not at all clear whether this is an expression of the fact that women and men did indeed experience explosions of anti-Jewish violence in different ways or whether it simply represents gendered attitudes on the part of the authors who viewed female suffering differently from that of men.[8]

Looking at this literature in slightly broader terms, the question arises as to how it is that, while Jewish culture pays such great attention to the murdered victims, it passes over—almost in silence—the experiences of the survivors. This is perhaps exemplified by the fact that it is really only with the recent work of Jeremy Cohen that the Crusade chronicles have been recognized as a form of survivor literature.[9] Another crucial Jewish experience, which accompanied all the disasters, has fared little better in the Jewish communal memory. It is very hard indeed to find references in traditional Jewish texts to the processes of rebuilding shattered lives and shattered communities in the wake of violence and destruction, even though this is undoubtedly the skill which has allowed Jewish society to survive as long as it has in the face of persecution.[10] Since women must inevitably have played a prominent role in the processes of reconstruction, this approach too has tended to minimize the place of women in Jewish collective memory.

In order to correct, to a certain extent at least, this "writing out" of women from Jewish history, I should here like to begin to reconsider the roles of Jewish women in one period of persecution and destruction. I shall do this by looking at their experiences during and after one of the most significant outbreaks of anti-Jewish violence in pre-Holocaust Jewish history—that led by the Cossack and Tatar forces in the Ukraine as part of the 1648 Chmielnicki uprising (commonly known in Jewish literature as *Gzeires Taḥ-Tat*).[11] On the basis of testimonies preserved in the contemporary responsa literature, as well as seventeenth-century chronicles, letters, and autobiographical fragments from introductions to rabbinic texts, I shall attempt to look briefly at the following phenomena: violence against women, issues of forced conversion, some aspects of women's experiences as captives and slaves, the reconstruction of family life, and the allocation of communal resources to help indigent women in the 1650s. Since the source base is fragmentary, my conclusions will be far from comprehensive.[12] Despite this, they might help sketch out at least a preliminary outline of ways in which at least one period of terrible violence and suffering affected Jewish women, as well as some of the strategies they adopted to overcome their suffering.

Perhaps the clearest descriptions of women's experience during this period of violence can be found in the Hebrew chronicles. All the chroniclers make great play of sexual violence against women as a major motif in their descriptions.[13] While it would be hard to imagine that rape would not have taken place on a large scale during the uprising, the emphasis laid on it in these texts suggests that the descriptions also had a symbolic role to play. Portrayals of rape seem to have been used by the chroniclers to represent the defilement not just of Jewish women, but of Jewish society as a whole by its attackers. In similar fashion, graphic—horrifying—descriptions of attacks on pregnant women and their fetuses served this dual purpose of reportage and symbolic portrayal.[14]

Some of the stories, however, had a more realistic ring to them. The chronicle, *Tza'ar bat rabim* (Widespread anguish), tells the tale of a pregnant Jewish mother who went into labor during the attack on Niemirów in June 1648. Fearing for her life, she turned to her non-Jewish neighbor, a woman, for help. The story does not end happily: religious and ethnic hatred overcame any sense of female solidarity; the neighbor called in her husband, who then murdered the Jewess.[15] Nonetheless, it is rare indeed that the stories about Jewish women in the chronicles descend from unbelievable bestiality to such believable dimensions. Perhaps the only other cases are two tales of Jewish maidens who preferred martyrdom to forced marriage with Cossacks. These stories, told in the chronicles *Tzok ha-'itim* (Troubled times) and *Yeven metsulah* (Deep mire), do seem to have been retellings of stories known before the uprising.[16] However, since they portrayed Jewish women as willing martyrs, they fit into the literary genre of Jewish female heroism in time of disaster, which seems to have recommended them to the authors. It is worth noting that neither girl in the stories was given a name, which further emphasizes that these portrayals of Jewish women's suffering were first and foremost symbolic in nature and not any attempt to describe real experiences undergone by Jewish women.[17]

Clearly, however, not all Jewish women in 1648 were pregnant and most avoided rape. Flight was the best option. Many families, as they became aware of the impending disaster, fled, first disposing of whatever valuables they could not take with them (two popular options were burying them or giving them to non-Jewish neighbors for safe keeping).[18] Though the descriptions always mention the male head of the family as organizing the escape, this would seem to be a stereotypical presentation. In times of crisis, women, too could sometimes take control. Dawidowa Nimizikowa from Dubno seems to have organized not only her flight from the town in the face of the Cossack forces in 1648, but also the lawsuit she brought on her return against the Ukrainian burgher whom she accused of stealing the goods she had left behind with him.[19]

The chronicler Natan Notte Hanover, often a very sharp-eyed observer, sensitive to women's roles in the tragedy, presents his own eyewitness account of the Jews' flight from Zasław in stereotypically male terms:

Those who did not possess a horse and cart, even though they had sufficient money to buy them, would not wait, but took wife and children by the hand and fled on foot, leaving all his belongings in his house. Those who had a horse and cart, full with goods, books, or belongings, would throw them out at a tavern and give them to the keeper . . . [When desperation set in] some cast away everything: horse and cart and all that was in it, and with only wife and children fled for their lives into the woods. Many women and men who had led their children by the hands, released them when this panic seized them, and ran for their lives into the woods.[20]

It was at this moment, when the family broke up and even husbands and wives were separated, that the experiences of men and women in flight could take quite different paths. This did not always expose the women to greater danger than the men. The reason for this was that, alongside the Cossack forces, the Tatar army (Islamic marauders who lived in the Crimea and made their living by capturing and selling slaves) were much more interested in taking women captives alive. Jewish men were routinely put to death while women were taken and sold as slaves.[21] In one case heard in the Constantinople Bet Din in the 1650s, a young Jewish man told how he was rescued from death by being dressed up as a girl and taken into captivity.[22]

Another danger which lay in wait for Jewish refugees was that of forced conversion. The chronicles, for the most part, lay more emphasis on women's conversion than on men's (though they acknowledge that this happened, too). Once again, this would seem to have had symbolic significance for the chroniclers. Describing women's conversion seems to have been another way of showing how Jewish society was defiled. Of course, this also raises the question whether single women refugees were, in fact, more exposed to conversionary pressures than men. There are no statistical sources to help find an answer to this question, and anecdotal evidence from court records mentions just as many male converts as female. On the other hand, there is some evidence that women (and children, too) were victims of forced conversion in greater numbers than men. Thus, when the nephew of one of the great rabbinical victims of the uprising, Rabbi Yeḥiel Michel of Niemirów, added his own introduction to his uncle's book, *Shivre luḥot* (Fragments of the tablets), he described the phenomenon of forced conversion during the uprising in the following terms: "And when the Jews do not want to repent and weep in the synagogues . . . then, for their sins, they are forced to weep in enemy hands under all kinds of torture . . . as we have heard from those who have returned from captivity and the tens of thousands of women and children who were defiled among the gentiles."[23]

In distinguishing between the men who return from captivity and the women and children who have been defiled, this text might also seem to suggest that, having once been taken captive and been suspected of converting, it was harder for women to find their way back to Judaism and Jewish society.[24] This was certainly the situation in a case heard by one of the leading Ashkenazic rabbis of the day, David ben Shmuel Ha-Levi, himself a refugee in Moravia, in 1650.[25] Against much legal precedent he ruled that a Jewish student who had heard that his wife had been captured and forced to convert by the Tatars would be allowed to remarry on the basis of rumor alone.[26] The story of Sarah, a Jewish refugee child taken in by a convent, who eventually escaped and ended up marrying Shabtai Zvi, is also suggestive in this regard, hinting as it does that even if they did return to Judaism, such women converts were not to be trusted.[27]

Issues of the integrity of the Jewish family became highly significant in the wake of the uprising. Once children had become separated from their parents, it became extremely difficult to determine to whom they belonged, which opened up the possibility that, later in life, they might unwittingly enter into forbidden marriages with close relatives. The Rabbinical authorities ordered each family to give their children special name-tags with their parents' names to circumvent this problem.[28] The Lithuanian Council of 1650 pronounced a ban on weddings between refugees and other victims of the violence unless proof of identity could be provided.[29] This issue seems to have continued to trouble Jewish society into later decades. In his ethical will, Shabtai Horowitz suggested that anyone who had lived through the uprising make a special effort to draw up a family tree in order to prove their own, and their children's, family background.[30]

Of course, it was not only children that were separated from their families; wives lost contact with their husbands. In wartime conditions, where some Jews were fleeing northward to Belarus and Lithuania, while others were being taken in slave caravans southwards toward the Crimea and Istanbul, discovering the fate of a lost partner was no easy matter. Testimonies found in the responsa literature attest to a lively correspondence, particularly in the Ottoman Empire where peaceful conditions allowed letters to reach intended recipients relatively safely, with requests for information about the fate of lost spouses.[31] Refugees and travelers passing through a community would be questioned and asked to give a deposition before the Bet Din as to whatever information they might have concerning survivors and victims (particularly spouses and relatives of local inhabitants).[32] Another method was to send an emissary to discover, and even save, surviving family members. This is described in the introduction to *Shivre luhot,* though it ended badly for both emissary and survivors in Niemirów—no one made it out alive.[33]

An interesting case of this sort took place in Cairo. A group of Polish Jewish women, presumably redeemed on the slave market there, hired an emissary to return to Eastern Europe, find their husbands, and bring them bills of divorce. He actually managed to pull off this astounding feat, and returned to Cairo with the requisite documents. So amazing was his success, however, that the local Bet Din actually doubted the veracity of the documents involved, leaving the women still in fear of being unable to remarry.[34] This case points up another of the gender differences of the refugee experience. Once a Jewish woman found herself such a long way from home, returning must have been an extremely daunting prospect. It was not impossible—Rabbi Menaḥem Krochmal tells of a Jewish woman enslaved in Jassy who returned to Lublin in the early 1650s[35]—but for the women in Cairo, at least, it must have seemed preferable to start new lives in their new environment than to take on the dangers of traveling back to Eastern Europe.[36]

The Cairo case raises another crucial issue facing Jewish women refugees, that of determining their husband's death in order to allow them to start a new family. If this proved impossible, then the prospect of becoming an *aguna*,[37] being forced to live a solitary life without husband or family, loomed. Though the rabbinic authorities often claimed that they tended toward leniency in such cases, the extremely unsettled conditions of the time and the difficulty of finding good eyewitnesses (which became harder the further away you were from eastern Europe) may have led some rabbis to take a stricter view. This dilemma is summed up in a story told by Jacob Emden about his grandparents. His grandmother, Nehama, had fled to Moravia during the uprising, and lost contact with her husband, Ya'akov. Witnesses arrived at her community giving clear testimony as to his death. On this basis, Rabbi Joshua Heschel, himself a refugee from Kraków, ruled that she could remarry. She refused to do so, and was proved right a few months later when her husband turned up safe and sound. Emden concludes "and from then on, that rabbi did not want to free any *aguna* . . . of whom there were many in those times of war . . . and being afraid of causing sin, he took it upon himself not to rule in favor of wives who had no husbands."[38]

There are no statistical records to give an indication to what extent the male rabbinical establishment was willing to rule leniently in cases of *agunot*. Additionally, though the cases in the responsa literature do not demonstrate a uniformly lenient approach, this may be an issue of genre. The vast majority of cases which could be solved quickly and leniently on the spot would not need to have been posed by letter to the great rabbinical authorities. They would have dealt only with the more difficult and dubious ones, in which harsher rulings would have been, in the nature of things, more prevalent.

As the violence died away, the process of reconstructing some kind of life began. This was done in such a wide range of contexts and situations that it is almost impossible to generalize. However, it should come as no surprise that Jewish women played a range of roles in this process. In the Belorussian towns, such as Pińsk and Słuck, to which many Ukrainian Jewish refugees fled, the urban authorities complained in the 1650s that many Jewish women were taking to the streets to sell baked goods.[39] Though no reason is given for this phenomenon, baking was perhaps one of the few skills that female refugees, particularly widows, could exploit in order to make a living.[40] In cases where widows returned to their previous homes and businesses, they could, if they had the strength of will, take them over themselves in place of their dead husbands. Jenta Leyzerowa of Dubno, for example, on returning home in 1649, laid successful claim to her late husband's property, worth the significant sum of 500 złp.[41]

However, as Moshe Rosman has argued, widowhood was not an easy option for

Jewish women, many of whom seem to have found particular difficulty in making a living on their own.[42] The enormous concern over the *aguna* issue in the responsa literature is a clear sign that many Jewish widows were anxious—if not desperate —to remarry. The straits to which widows might descend are illustrated by the situation in the Ashkenazic Jewish community of Jerusalem in the early 1650s. When the war in Eastern Europe led to the drying up of donations from Poland-Lithuania, the community sank into poverty. As usual in such a situation, the poor and the women were hit hardest; a non-Jewish observer wrote "of 700 widows and poor Jews there, about 400 have been famished."[43] Clearly, the women felt that they were not receiving their fair share of communal resources, since they banded together and sent an emissary back to Europe to raise money for them. He was given a special letter, written in Yiddish by the Ashkenazic women of Jerusalem and addressed to the Ashkenazic Jewish women in Germany and Poland. The German and Polish Jewish women were asked to make special women-to-women donations and to have them sent back to Jerusalem separately from the money meant for the men. This was presumably to ensure that it would actually reach them and not be diverted to other people by male *gabaim* (treasurers).[44] How successful this particular initiative was is not clear, but it did not lead to the establishment of any permanent kind of female philanthropic system. What it does suggest quite strongly, however, is that indigent Jewish women in these times of crisis may have had a harder time than men in obtaining communal resources to help them. With such dangers lurking, remarriage would clearly have been a much better option.

※ ※ ※

The suffering of the Jews during and after the Chmielnicki uprising of 1648 had some clearly gendered aspects. During the violence itself, women seem to have had a greater chance of survival since they fetched a better price on the slave market; there is evidence that many male captives were simply killed without compunction because it was not financially worthwhile to hold on to them. On the other hand, physical violence against women often had a sexual component, which, beyond the physical and psychological damage, also imparted to the victim the social stigma of defilement and impurity. Women who had converted to Christianity either under duress or as a means of survival also faced greater difficulties than men in trying to go back to their former lives. Jewish law, could be and often was, interpreted as imposing stricter criteria for allowing returning women converts back into the fold than men. Beyond showing that it was significantly more difficult for women to recover from this kind of disaster, these phenomena also suggest that male attitudes toward women's experience were culturally determined. In turn, this would seem to indicate that the written sources surviving from the period reflect this viewpoint and so cannot be read as simply transparent expressions of what happened to women.

For Jewish refugees, particularly those who found themselves far from home in the Ottoman Empire, the considerations involved in physically returning home were gendered in nature, too. The dangers facing a single woman on the long sea and land voyage back to Eastern Europe must have deterred many women, who preferred to stay put and try to start a new life, even with all the problems in proving their widowhood. In one case, at least, this led to a group of women in Cairo taking matters into their own hands in an attempt to sort out their status. Female agency can also be seen in the case of the Jewish women of Jerusalem, who tried to establish their own fundraising apparatus to ensure reasonable access to communal resources. It should be noted, however, that though extremely suggestive, neither of these initiatives seems to have had any long-term consequences.

The same should perhaps not be said of the Jewish women remaining in Eastern Europe, who (presumably out of dire necessity) began to take a more active role in economic life. Though Jewish women's economic activity was a phenomenon known before the Chmielnicki uprising, the processes of reconstruction seem to have intensified female Jewish agency in the marketplace.

Little of this experience seems to have found its way into the Jewish collective memory of the events. There were a number of reasons for this. First and foremost, Jewish martyrological prayer left little space for women, focusing almost exclusively on rabbinic figures. The experiences of flight and reconstruction, so crucial in the course of Jewish history, also had no place in this literature. Even in the historical chronicles, these issues were barely touched upon, which further tended to marginalize women's experience. To modern eyes, however, both women's experience and the processes of social reconstruction are topics worthy of serious historical consideration. In this light, it becomes almost impossible to understand the Jews' experience of persecution and destruction without examining the experiences of Jewish women. This includes both those caught up in the violence, and those who survived to begin the process of reconstructing their own, their family's, and their community's lives—often confronting difficulties greater than those facing Jewish men.

Notes

1. On this, see: Alan Mintz, *Hurban: Responses to Catastrophe in Hebrew Literature* (Syracuse N.Y., 1996); David Roskies, *Against the Apocalypse: Responses to Catastrophe in Modern Jewish Culture* (Cambridge, Mass., 1984).

2. Mintz, *Hurban,* 22–42.

3. Gerson D. Cohen, "Hannah and Her Seven Sons in Hebrew Literature," in *Studies in the Variety of Rabbinic Cultures* (Philadelphia, 1991), 39–60.

4. Shoshanna Gershenzon and Jane Litman, "The Bloody 'Hands of Compassionate Women': Portrayals of Heroic Women in the Hebrew Crusade Chronicles," in *Crisis & Reaction: The Hero in Jewish History,* ed. M. Mor (Omaha, Neb., 1995), 73–91.

5. Complete lists of victims, including women, are to be found in the communal *memorbücher,* which were often recited on local memorial days. However, much more influential in creating the Jewish communal memory were the memorial (*El male' rahamim;* =God, full of mercy)

prayers, which were widely recited and copied from community to community. See: Yosef Hayim Yerushalmi, *Zakhor: Jewish History and Jewish Memory* (Seattle, Wash., 1982), 27–52.

6. For a collection of such prayers from the seventeenth century, see Nahum Wahrmann, *Mekorot le-toldot gezerot taḥ ve-tat: Tefilot u-sliḥot le-20 Sivan* (Jerusalem, 1949).

7. And, in the crusade chronicles, also by the women.

8. See Gershenzon and Litman, "The Bloody Hands."

9. Jeremy Cohen, *Sanctifying the Name of God: Jewish Martyrs and Jewish Memories of the First Crusade* (Philadelphia, 2004).

10. Though this concept was central to Simon Dubnow's historiographical outlook, through which he portrayed the course of Jewish history in the Diaspora as a process of cultural centers that rose and fell in turn, Dubnow himself actually paid little attention to the processes of rebuilding after disaster. See his *Weltgeschichte der jüdischen Volkes*, 1–9 (Berlin, 1925–29). On Dubnow's historical outlook, see David Engel, "Ketivat toledot Yisrael 'al pi Dubnov: Ben ha-mekomi la-universali," *Zion* 77 (2012): 307–15; Anke Hilbrenner, "Simon Dubnov's Master Narrative and the Construction of a Jewish Collective Memory in the Russian Empire," *Ab Imperio* 4 (2003): 143–64; Reuven Michael, *Ha-ketiva ha-historit ha-yehudit mi-ha-renesans 'ad ha-'et ha-ḥadashah* (Jerusalem, 1993), 366–423.

11. A comprehensive survey of the historiography dealing with these events is to be found in Yo'el Raba, *Ben zikaron le-hakhḥashah: Gezerot 408 ve–409 bi-reshimot bne ha-zeman u-ve-re ḥi ha-ketivah ha-historit* (Tel Aviv, 1994). English translation: Joel Raba, *Between Remembrance and Denial: The Fate of the Jews in the Wars of the Polish Commonwealth during the Mid-Seventeenth Century as Shown in Contemporary Writings and Historical Research* (Boulder, Colo., 1995). For an attempt to estimate the Jewish loss of life in this period, see Shaul Stampfer, "What Actually Happened to the Jews of Ukraine in 1648," *Jewish History* 17 (2003): 207–27.

12. The most extensive collection of sources can be found in Ḥaim Yonah Gurland, *Le-korot ha-gezerot 'al Yisrael*, 1–7 (Przemyśl-Kraków-Odessa, 1887–92; reprinted in one volume, Jerusalem 1972). Of the chronicles, only Natan Notte Hanover, *Yeven metsulah* (Venice, 1653) is not reprinted by Gurland. Bibliographical details of each chronicle will be given when it is mentioned in the text.

13. The terrible descriptions of female martyrdom found in the Hebrew crusade chronicles find no echo in this literature. In fact, the massacres of 1096 in general are not mentioned. This is exemplified most clearly by the fact that when contemporaries set the date for a memorial day for the massacres, it referred back to a blood libel in Blois in 1171 rather than the events at the time of the crusades. See: Yerushalmi, *Zakhor*, 48–52.

14. On this, see: Natalia Yakovenko, "The Events of 1648–1649: Contemporary Events and the Problem of Verification," *Jewish History* 17 (2003): 165–78.

15. Avraham ben Shmuel Ashkenazi, "Tsa'ar bat rabim," in Y. Gurland, *Le-Korot ha-gezerot 'al Yisrael* 2 (Kraków, 1889), 11–19, esp. 13.

16. I deal with this issue in an unpublished paper, "Wanda and the Jewish Maidens: Contacts between Polish and Jewish Culture in the Sixteenth and Seventeenth Centuries."

17. Adam Teller, "The Jewish Literary Responses to the Events of 1648–1649 and the Creation of a Polish-Jewish Consciousness," in *Culture Front: Eastern European Jews and Their Culture*, ed. B. Nathans and G. Safran (Philadelphia, 2008), 28–31.

18. For a description of this, as reported for the community of Ostróg, see Meir of Szczebrzeszyn, *Tsok ha-'itim* (Kraków, 1650), 5b. Cf. Mordechai Nadav, *The Jews of Pinsk, 1506 to 1880*, trans. M. Rosman and F. Tropper (Stanford, Calif., 2008), 146–56.

19. Moshe Rosman, "Dubno in the Wake of Khmel'nyts'kyi," *Jewish History* 17 (2003): 249.

20. Hanover, *Yeven metsulah*, 5a–b. The translation is my own.

21. On Tatar slavery, see Dariusz Kołodziejczyk, "Slave Hunting and Slave Redemption as a Business Enterprise: The Northern Black Sea Region in the Sixteenth to Seventeenth Centuries,"

Oriente Moderno 25 (2006): 149–59; Michael Kizilov, "Slave Trade in the Early Modern Crimea from the Perspective of Christian, Moslem, and Jewish Sources," *Journal of Early Modern History* 11 (2007): 1–31; Alan Fisher, *The Crimean Tatars* (Stanford, Calif., 1987), 26–39. On the differing fates of men and women in Tatar captivity during 1648, see Shmuel Garmizan, *Sefer mishpete tsedek* (Jerusalem, 1945), 170–71, no. 107.

22. Moshe Benvenishti, *Sefer pne Moshe,* 2 (Constantinople, 1671), 215b, no. 112.

23. Yehiel Mikhel mi-Nemirov, *Shivre luhot* (Warsaw, 1911), 18.

24. This does not seem to have been a new phenomenon in the early modern period. See the discussion of the fate of women captives taken during the crusades in Yvonne Friedman, *Encounter between Enemies: Captivity and Ransom in the Latin Kingdom of Jerusalem* (Leiden, 2002), 181–86.

25. Shmu'el ben David Ha-Levi (1586–1667) had served as Rabbi of Ostróg before the uprising made him a refugee. He was author of the highly influential commentary on the Shulhan 'arukh, *Ture zahav,* first published in 1646.

26. It should be noted, however, that this case caused a polemic among rabbis in Moravia. The former rabbi of Kraków, Gershon Ashkenazi, then serving as a rabbi of Prostějov in Moravia, followed David ben Shmu'el, while the rabbi of Mikoluv, Menahem Krochmal, opposed him. For documentation, see Menahem ben Avraham Krochman, *She'elot u-tshuvot tsemah tsedek* (Amsterdam, 1675), no. 70. This case is discussed (from different perspectives) in Yehezk'el Fram, "Takdim hilkhati she-'eno ra'uy li-shemo," in *'Al pi ha-be'er: Mehkarim ba-hagut yehudit u-ba-mahshevet ha-halakhah mugashim le-Ya'akov Blidshtein,* ed. O. Erlich et al. (Be'er Sheva, 2008), 401–12; Tami Salmon-Mack, "Shvuyah be-tah-tat: Ha-konflikt ha-dati, haminhagi ve-ha-'enoshi," in *Mehkarim be-toldot 'Ashkenaz: Sefer li-khvod Yitzhak (Eric) Zimmer,* ed. G. Bacon et al. (Ramat Gan, 2008), 265–76. See also the story of Jacob Emden's grandmother, below.

27. The text of a folk-tale retelling one version of this story is to be found in Gurland, *Le-korot ha-gzerot,* 5 (Kraków, 1891), 36. For a fuller discussion, see Gershom Scholem, *Sabbatai Sevi: The Mystical Messiah, 1626–1676* (Princeton, N.J., 1973), 191–97; Matt Goldish, *The Sabbatean Prophets* (Cambridge, Mass., 2004), 89–97.

28. Yisrael Halperin, ed., *Pinkas va'ad arba' aratsot* (Jerusalem, 1945), 79, no. 209.

29. Shimon Dubnow, ed., *Pinkas medinat Lita* (Berlin, 1925), 102, no. 462.

30. Quoted in *Pinkas va'ad arba' 'aratsot,* 79.

31. E.g. *Sefer mishpete tsedek,* no. 107; Moshe Shilton, *She'elot u-tshuvot Bne Moshe* (Istanbul, 1712), 50a, no. 25.

32. Ibid., 49a, no. 22; 73 a–b, no. 33.

33. *Shivre luhot,* 9.

34. Mordechai Ha-Levi, *Sefer darkhe no'am* (Venice, 1697), Even Ha-'ezer, no. 5. A partial translation of this source is to be found in Matt Goldish, ed., *Jewish Questions: Responsa on Sephardic Life in the Early Modern Period* (Princeton, N.J., 2008), 66–67.

35. *She'elot u-tshuvot tsemah tsedek,* no. 70.

36. This was in addition to the fact that a returning Jewish woman would have to overcome the social stigma of being suspected of having been raped or forcibly converted during her captivity. Though *halakhah* holds that a woman cannot be condemned for this, Jewish society tended to take a different view and interpreted the law in that light. See above and Mordechai Friedman, *Jewish Marriage in Palestine: A Cairo Geniza Study,* 2 (Tel Aviv, 1981), 266–73; Friedman, "Ribui nashim be-mismakhe ha-genizah," *Tarbiz* 40.3 (1971): 346–56.

37. That is, a woman whose husband has disappeared or deserted her. According to Jewish law, such a person may not remarry until she obtains a legally valid document of divorce or can prove his death.

38. Jacob Emden, *Megilat sefer,* ed. D. Cahana (Warsaw, 1897), 5–7.

39. Archiwum Główne Akt Dawnych we Warszawie, Archiwum Radziwiłłowie, XXIII, 133 plik

1, p. 49; Nadav, *The Jews of Pinsk,* 188. Jewish women's economic activity in the marketplace was by no means new in this period, though it seems to have intensified in the later seventeenth and eighteenth centuries. See Moshe Rosman, "Lihyot 'ishah yehudiyah be-Polin-Lita' be-re'shit ha'et ha-hadashah," in *Kiyum ve-shever: Yehude Polin le-dorotehem,* II, ed. I. Gutman and I. Bartal (Jerusalem, 2001), 415–34; Adam Teller, *Kesef, koah ve-hashpa'ah: Ha-yehudim be-'ahuzot bet Radzhivil ba-Lita' ba-me'ah ha-18* (Jerusalem, 2006), 210–16.

40. Cf. Hanover's description of the fate of Jewish women captured by the Tatars: "The Tatars took many captive, torturing the women and maidens and raping the women in front of their husbands. They took the maidens and beautiful women as servants and *bakers* [my emphasis, A.T.], and some as wives and mistresses." See *Yeven metsulah,* 2b. The problems Jewish women refugees faced in making a living are also reflected in the legend concerning the sister of the great rabbi, Shabtai Ha-kohen, who ended up as a refugee and, unwittingly, worked as her brother's servant. This legend has only survived in a late retelling. See M. ben Yehezk'el, *Sefer ha-ma'asiyot,* 3 (Tel Aviv, 1961), 273–78. I should like to thank Prof. Haya Bar-Itzhak for bringing this fascinating source to my attention.

41. Central State Historical Archive of Ukraine, Kiev, Fond 33 Opis I File 6, p. 61. Quoted in Rosman, "Dubno," 250.

42. Rosman, "Lihyot 'ishah yehudiyah," 426–28.

43. Published in Cecil Roth, "The Jews of Jerusalem in the Seventeenth Century: An English Account," *Miscellanies of the Jewish Historical Society of England* 2 (London, 1935): 99–104.

44. Avraham Ya'ari, *Shluhe 'Erets Yisrael* I (Jerusalem, 1997), 276–77.

FOR GOD AND COUNTRY

⌘ ⌘ ⌘

Jewish Identity and the State in Seventeenth-Century Amsterdam

Benjamin Fisher
Towson University

Though within this great republic we represent only a very small part, in the love and affection that we hold for Your Majesty we are very large. So much so that we are not inferior to anyone else . . . we no longer hold Spain and Portugal, but Holland, to be our *patria*. Not the kings of Castile or Portugal do we recognize as our *Senhores*, but the most noble States [General] and Your Highness . . . we are obliged to expose ourselves to all dangers on behalf of the Almighty God: we shall do the same with great and generous spirit for the health and prosperity of Your Highness, and the illustrious States [General], when it will be necessary to prove it, and the times demand it.[1]

—Menasseh Ben Israel, *Gratulaçao* (Amsterdam, 1642)

WITH a grand flourish bordering on hyperbole, Menasseh Ben Israel lavished praise on Prince Frederick Henry, his son William II, and Queen Henrietta Maria of England on the occasion of their visit to Amsterdam's Portuguese Jewish synagogue on May 22, 1642, and extolled the deep sense of commitment and belonging that he and his coreligionists felt to the United Provinces, the society that had offered them refuge beyond the reach of the Inquisition. Menasseh insisted that Portuguese Jews were not just devoted to their new homeland, but that their devotion was equal—at least—to that of any Dutch Christian; he affirmed that the Netherlands had become the Jewish *patria*, or *Vaderlant*;[2] he announced to the leaders of the Dutch state that he and his coreligionists were even willing to "expose ourselves to all dangers" on behalf of Prince Frederick and the States General; and Menasseh directly equated Jewish obligations to God and country, the dangers that Jews were obliged to risk on behalf of their God, and those that they were required to risk on behalf of their state.[3] Menasseh's dramatic statements are not without precedent. His Venetian colleague Simone Luzzatto similarly presents the Jews of the *Serenissima* as being an integral component of their society and eager to bear arms in defense of the republic.[4] Nevertheless, the extreme loyalty and identification with the state expressed in these passages were highly atypical in the context of early modern Jewish political thought, and deserve greater attention in the literature than they have so far received.

50

Yosef Kaplan, invoking the passage quoted above, has suggested that a growing identification with the Dutch state can be observed during the middle and
late decades of the seventeenth century, and Miriam Bodian has argued that the
Portuguese Jews were more "Europeanized" than other Jews as a result of having
lived as Catholics in the Iberian Peninsula, which enabled them to "feel at ease"
among the Dutch in unique ways.[5] Yet there is currently little understanding of what
it meant for a Portuguese Jew to embrace the political ideals of Dutch society, and
to weave its myths, prejudices, and values into a construction of Jewish identity.
This paper, building on Kaplan's and Bodian's observations, explores the ways in
which certain Portuguese Jews articulated this profound sense of belonging to the
European state in which they had chosen to live, their adoptive Fatherland. Part
1 investigates Menasseh Ben Israel's *Gratulação,* the printed version of his address
to Prince Frederick, as well as the introduction to his *Conciliador* (vol. 2), a biblical
commentary published the previous year. These texts illustrate how Menasseh drew
upon central symbols of Dutch culture in order to create a sense that the Jewish community was a genuine component of the *Vaderlant* cherished by Dutch Christians and
Jews alike. At the same time, the Portuguese Jewish community was as committed to
the biases and prejudices of Dutch society as its ideals and founding myths. Other
leading figures in the community expressed this sense of belonging in a different
and more negative way, by writing vicious critiques attacking the political fringe of
the United Provinces that Dutch Christians and Jews saw as a serious threat to the
public good, peace, and order of society. Therefore, parts 2 and 3 of this essay explore Saul Levi Morteira's criticism of "Libertines" and Quakers, two groups viewed
with deep suspicion and hostility by his Dutch Christian contemporaries. Delivered
within his *Tratado da verdade da lei de Moisés* (Treatise on the truth of the law of
Moses), Morteira's hostility toward Quakers and Libertines enabled him to position
the Portuguese Jewish community within the political mainstream of Dutch society.[6]
Together, the writings of Menasseh and Morteira enable us to see a Jewish community that viewed certain Dutch ideals as its own, identified with its history and myths,
saw its enemies as its own enemies, and embraced its biases and prejudices.

BETWEEN AUTONOMY AND INTEGRATION
IN EARLY MODERN EUROPE

Studies of early modern Jewish communal organization, including David
Ruderman's recent synthesis, have emphasized the increasingly sophisticated structures that Jewish communities established between the late fifteenth and eighteenth
centuries in order to govern their internal affairs. Despite myriad variations and
differences, Ruderman observes that "the early modern period represented a culmination of Jewish communal development everywhere across the Diaspora, emerging
both because of the initiatives of strong Jewish leaders as well as the relatively toler-
ant policies of governments that recognized a certain political and economic utility
in their continued existence."[7] In different ways, the Mahamad of Amsterdam, the

Council of Four Lands, the German *Landjudenschaften*, the mercantile elites of the Venetian ghetto, and the Jewish courts and autonomous *kehalim* of the Ottoman Empire were linked by a common phenomenon—a greater and more robust degree of communal cohesion than was typical of medieval Jewish communities.[8] Sometimes this wide scope of Jewish self-rule sparked concern among Christian observers.[9] In Venice, certain Christians fulminated against the wide-ranging civil and religious powers claimed by residents of the ghetto, which they construed as rendering the Jewish community a "state within a state," and as being detrimental to the sovereignty of the Christian authorities.[10] Among Jews, this level of autonomy was often celebrated. In Amsterdam, as Miriam Bodian and Anne Oravetz Albert have shown, Portuguese Jews enthusiastically created a vision of their community as constituting a *republica* apart, a separate nation not unlike other European states.[11]

However, even as Jewish communal autonomy reached an unparalleled level of sophistication, some Jews were beginning to contemplate a drastically different form of Jewish identity. They envisioned Jews as integral components of the broader societies in which they lived, intimately connected with the welfare and political ideals of their Christian neighbors. Jews, in this vision, were part of the very fabric through which European society was constructed. One of the most well-known examples of this new perspective on Jewish identity can be found in writings of seventeenth-century Venetian rabbi Simone Luzzatto, author of the *Discorso circa il stato de gl'Hebrei* (Venice, 1638). In Luzzatto's view, Jews did not constitute an independent political entity; the *Natione Hebrea* was in fact "incapable in its present state of any political government."[12] While Jews were unsuitable for independent political activity, Luzzatto was equally adamant that Jews be "counted among the integral elements of the general population."[13] He believed that Jews made invaluable contributions to the Venetian Republic through their trade and wealth, and insisted that members of his community were so devoted to the Venetian Republic that "the Jewish people . . . wish to be as able to wield arms and spill their own blood as [they are] ready in the provision of money in the service of the *Serenissima Republica*."[14] Throughout the *Discorso*, Luzzatto is careful to craft his arguments in a way that would appeal to his Venetian audience. He addressed issues of particular concern to Venetian authorities, such as the supposed waning of the republic's commerce due to the withdrawal of native merchants from overseas trade.[15] Ever conscious of the Catholic sensibilities of his audience, he affirmed that "it is certain that the *Natione Hebrea* is in some of its laws more similar to the Roman Church more than to their [Protestants'] opinions. The Jews hold that Sacred Scripture is in many places unintelligible without the light of traditions," and they emphasize the value of free will and good acts in the eyes of God.[16]

Like Luzzatto, Menasseh Ben Israel and Saul Levi Morteira began to identify with the symbols, ideals, and prejudices of the broader state in which they lived, and to see these as their own. However, whereas Luzzatto crafted his arguments for the sensibilities of his Catholic Venetian readers, study of Menasseh's and Morteira's writings reveals how they asserted a strong sense of belonging within a Dutch Protestant setting. Exploring their work promises to enrich our understanding of the political vocabulary adopted by Jews in different settings to articulate a strong feeling of identification and belonging to the state in which they lived.

MENASSEH BEN ISRAEL AND THE BATAVIAN MYTH

Perhaps no Jew felt more at home in the northern Low Countries than Menasseh Ben Israel. Beginning in the winter of 1640, a remarkable series of events began to unfold that left a deep impression upon Menasseh: in a war of secession, Portugal attempted to assert its independence from Spain; King João IV and the House of Braganza ascended to the Portuguese throne; and in short order a truce would be signed between the United Provinces and Portugal.[17] Commenting on these events in the opening pages of the *Conciliador* (vol. 2), Menasseh remarked that with "King João IV returned to his natural and hereditary kingdom, unjustly possessed until now by another, ending the ancient hatred [between Portugal and the Netherlands], the desired peace will follow." Menasseh was doubly excited about the prospect for improved Dutch-Portuguese relations, "being Portuguese with a Batavian spirit."[18] Although this memorable statement has been described as a rhetorical strategy that should not be understood as reflecting genuine political sentiments and "convictions about affiliation,"[19] Menasseh had a number of potential reasons for being quite "pleased" about this turn of events, both as a "Lusitano," and as someone with a "Batavian" spirit.

As a member of the Portuguese Diaspora, it is easy to imagine why these events struck a chord with Menasseh. Menasseh and other exconversos may have hoped that the ascendancy of King João IV would lead to an easing of Inquisitorial pressure in Portugal, since the Inquisition was one of the few Portuguese organizations to support the Spanish in the conflict, and because the activities of the Inquisition crescendoed in two waves between 1584 and 1640, following Spain's annexation of Portugal. And although Menasseh delivered his address early in the rebellion, he may have known that Jacob Curiel was already serving as a munitions supplier and diplomat on behalf of the Portuguese Crown.[20] From an economic perspective, Menasseh may have hoped that the impending truce between Portugal and the United Provinces would lead to financial benefits for members of the Portuguese Jewish community living in Amsterdam.[21] Menasseh described himself not only as being Portuguese, but also as having the "spirit" of a Batavian. Although is not immediately apparent what he meant, Menasseh's identification with the "Batavian spirit" was a deliberate and calculated rhetorical manoeuvre designed to convey a specific message about how he viewed the relationship between Portuguese Jews and Dutch society. It was designed to convey a sense of belonging, a sense of being at home in the Netherlands, almost as if he were a native subject.

The conception of mythic ancestry in the ancient, freedom-loving Batavians who rebelled against the Romans played a central role in the national imagination of Menasseh's Christian contemporaries, and in the political nationalism that was fuelled by the revolt against Spain. The scholarship of Ivo Schöffer, Simon Schama, and others has demonstrated that the Batavian myth was a ubiquitous feature of sixteenth- and seventeenth-century Dutch culture.[22] Prior to the revolt, rival Dutch chroniclers and humanists contested the geographic location of the Batavii in a struggle of local patriotisms, scouring classical texts in order to locate the Batavian heartland in different corners of the northern Low Countries.[23] Following the rebellion against Spain, classical scholarship on the Batavii accentuated the supposed political and cultural values of the ancient Germanic tribe. Hugo Grotius's depiction of the Batavians revealed precedents for the ideals that animated the rebellion: the demurral of the Batavians to pay tribute to Rome, and their steadfast resistance to tyranny made the Batavii obvious heroes to the late sixteenth-century Dutch. Grotius discovered that the Batavii were governed by popular assemblies that bore an uncanny resemblance to the States General of his own day, that these assemblies were free to gather irrespective of whether they were summoned by a count, and that no foreigner could be appointed to positions of authority.[24] While the political, linguistic, and geographic characteristics of this *Vaderlant* were deeply contested, Batavian imagery provided an important unifying touchstone that helped give coherence to the idea of a Dutch nation with particular values that were deeply rooted in the soil of the Netherlands.

The aspiration for freedom and hatred of tyranny that the Dutch associated with themselves and the ancient Batavians resonated strongly with Menasseh. In the *Gratulaçao* he celebrated the victories of Dutch society against the "cruel tyrannies of Spain," which he saw as being akin to the glorious rebellion of the high priest Mattathias and Judah Maccabee against the "tyrannies and oppression of the cruel Antiochus Epiphanes." Through armed rebellion, the ancient Judeans "regained the liberty of their beloved homeland," just as the House of Orange had now achieved prosperity and "happy and general tranquility" in "Batavia."[25] Animosity toward Spain and the desire for freedom were sentiments that Menasseh and his community knew all too well. As Menasseh reminded his listeners, they too had been "deprived of our liberty and dispossessed of our property," and had fled to the Netherlands where "we live, we are defended, and together with all others we enjoy free settlement in these lands."[26] The narratives that Menasseh invoked in this address were rooted in Jewish traditions as well as Christian Scriptures, and were thus calibrated to appeal to the sensibilities of both communities, a goal that dovetailed closely with Menasseh's desire to stress the commonalities shared by Portuguese Jews and Dutch Christians. Menasseh may also have wished to subtly emphasize his own community's connection to an ancient, freedom-loving rebellion that took place even before the Batavian revolt so celebrated by the Dutch. He may have hoped to convey the idea that present-day Jews were as "Batavian" in spirit as their Dutch Christian contemporaries.

When Menasseh invoked the imagery of the Batavii in the *Gratulaçao* and

Conciliador and insisted that, while Portuguese by birth, he was Batavian in spirit, was Menasseh merely playing to the sensibilities of his Dutch listeners? Was he merely adding another layer to the flourish and flattery that he hoped would result in a reward of patronage and support for his move from Amsterdam to Dutch Brazil?[27] Or should we take Menasseh's self-characterization more seriously? If we read Menasseh's statements about "spiritual" Batavian identity against the background of the voluminous discussion of the Batavii in Dutch society at this time, it becomes apparent that both Menasseh and Dutch humanist scholars were playing a similar game. Claiming Batavian ancestry was never just about the genetic link; it was about connecting with the supposed culture and values of the ancient Germanic tribe. Just as Cornelius Aurelius, Gerardus Geldenhauer, and others had sought to press claims of genetic descent from the Batavii in order to position their kin as the heirs to the laudable values and ethics of the Germanic tribe, so too Menasseh's efforts to claim spiritual affiliation with the Batavii were intended to stress the congruity between the ideals of his own community, the ancient Batavii, and the modern Dutch. Being "Batavian" for Menasseh and his Dutch Christian contemporaries meant (at least in part) a deep identification with the resistance to tyranny associated with the ancient Batavians, and exemplified by the success of the Dutch rebellion and the escape of the conversos from the Inquisition.

AT THE MARGINS OF DUTCH SOCIETY— MORTEIRA AND THE LIBERTINES

Menasseh's *Gratulaçao* was delivered before an audience of his coreligionists and European nobility. The listeners were eminently respectable members of Dutch and Jewish society. Yet in articulating a Jewish political identity that meshed with the values of Dutch society, leading Jewish figures looked to the periphery as well as the center. They measured their political position in the Netherlands against the political posture of radical Christian religious movements viewed as subversive and threatening by the Dutch majority. And in aligning themselves against these groups, the politics of the Portuguese Jewish community were depicted as being firmly compatible with the outlook of Dutch municipal and state authorities. Saul Levi Morteira's *Tratado da verdade da lei de Moisés* offers a fascinating window into how Amsterdam's Portuguese Jews reflected on—and contested—the political vision of movements on the fringes of Dutch society. One particular group attracted Morteira's attention from the very outset, and appears prominently in the introduction to his work. Remarking upon the arguments that certain Christians made against the ongoing relevance of the Old Testament, in response to Jewish allegations against the divinity of the Gospels, Morteira counters that "denying the Law of Moses is not the same as denying the Gospels, since when the foundation crumbles, so does the house. And denying the Law of Moses is nothing less than confessing oneself a *libertino*, without Law or divine precepts, since these proceed from no other source."[28]

Who were these "Libertines," and why was Morteira concerned to raise the spectre of their challenge to society in the opening passages of his major treatise? Did he have in mind subversive figures from within his own community, or were his eyes set on radical Christian movements within the Netherlands? Given Morteira's status as a leading rabbi of the Portuguese Jewish community who had witnessed several of the most famous episodes challenging the authority of the rabbis and Mahamad, it is natural to consider the possibility that Morteira had heterodox members of the Portuguese Jewish community in mind. Morteira associated the *libertinos* with a deep disregard for the authority of Scripture, antinomian tendencies, and opposition to political and religious discipline, and we do not need to dig deeply in order to discover Jewish figures that fit some of these characteristics. Might he have had in mind individuals like Uriel da Costa, who came to wonder "whether the Law of Moses ought to be accounted the Law of God, seeing that there were many arguments which seemed to persuade or rather determine the contrary," and who ultimately "came to be fully of opinion that it was nothing but a human invention like many other systems in the world and that Moses was not the writer?"[29] Benedict Spinoza, too, may fit the mold of Morteira's *libertinos*, especially in light of antinomian conclusions he drew about the relevance of Law of Moses. "I realized," Spinoza writes, "that the Laws revealed by God to Moses were nothing but the decrees of the historical Hebrew state alone, and accordingly that no one needed to adopt them but the Hebrews, and even they were only bound by them so long as their state survived."[30]

Nevertheless, there are strong reasons to think that Morteira's polemic against the *libertinos* was not entirely restricted to "domestic" targets within the Jewish community. While rabbinic and medieval Jewish literature offered Morteira an extensive vocabulary for describing someone who rejected the law and rabbinic authority,[31] he instead opted to employ a term, *libertino*, that had little Jewish precedent, but which resonated powerfully within Dutch society. The term *libertinos* was not uncommon in translations and commentaries on classical literature, and on the Bible itself during the sixteenth century, as an adjective describing the state of having been freed from slavery or being descended from former slaves.[32] However, in the 1540s John Calvin used the term in a way it had never previously been employed. In two treatises published in 1544 and 1545, Calvin used the term to describe a variety of groups who adopted "spiritual" interpretations of the Old and New Testaments that undermined his ecclesiastical, theological, and moral vision for society. Calvin's "Libertines" were accused of subverting the Trinity, divorcing Christ from the Father and the Holy Spirit,[33] and reducing Christ to a mere model for spiritual reflection, whose Passion, crucifixion, and death had no actual impact on the spiritual state of mankind. Calvin accused the Libertines of regarding Scripture as mere "fables,"[34] mocking the Word of God to the point where their beliefs were synonymous with atheism. All of these subversive, heterodox ideas advanced by the *libertinos* threatened to introduce "a confusion into the world that overturns all civil government, order, and human decency."[35] The anger that Calvin vented against the *libertinos* in the mid-sixteenth century was in response to specific queries from the Low Countries, and indeed conflict between Calvin's successors and those who were, allegedly, "men without faith, without law, and without religion" continued into the seventeenth century.[36]

Why was Morteira, a leading rabbi in the Portuguese Jewish community, concerned to condemn the *libertinos,* a group seen as especially threatening to Christian authorities? There are a number of potential explanations, all of which are compatible with one another. One possibility is that Morteira truly had subversive members of his own community in mind, but in critiquing them decided to employ an explicitly Protestant idiom that he had internalized. Another possibility is that Morteira and the leaders of the Dutch Reformed Church faced similar challenges in enforcing strict standards of belief and behavior, and thus were attuned to similar types of subversive political and religious groups. Just as the Dutch Reformed Church had consistently struggled with Libertines, Remonstrants, Arminians, and others who rejected its vision of confessional orthodoxy and discipline, the Portuguese Jewish community struggled with exconversos who established separate prayer houses, visited the so-called "lands of idolatry," and disregarded the authority of the Mahamad.[37] A third possibility, explored below, is that Morteira identified strongly with the political mainstream of Dutch society. In a context where it was becoming possible for Jews to imagine themselves as part of the fabric of the Dutch Republic, they were as eager to condemn those who questioned or subverted the laws and values of the state as they were prepared to embrace its ideals and myths. Morteira's commitment to the leadership of the Dutch state led him to see its enemies as his own. Nowhere is this alignment more evident than in an encounter between Morteira and an anonymous Quaker that took place even as Morteira was in the midst of compiling his massive treatise.

AT THE MARGINS OF DUTCH SOCIETY—
MORTEIRA AND THE QUAKERS

Morteira's angry confrontation with a Quaker in Amsterdam illustrates the degree to which he was concerned about radical Christian movements in the Netherlands and the challenges they presented against Dutch authorities. Morteira describes the confrontation in chapter 47 of the *Tratado* after surveying the articles of faith that Maimonides presents in the Mishneh Torah's "Book of Knowledge"—belief in the unity of God, acknowledgment of God as the Prime Cause, and acceptance that God must be worshiped, revered, honored, and loved. Respect, worship, honor, love, and devotion to God are clearly, for Morteira and his Christian neighbours, a *sine qua non* of the religious and social order.[38] However, Morteira was concerned that certain Christian movements took these principles to a conclusion that was perhaps logical, but also extreme: "They assert, teach, and profess that nobody except God is to be honored; nobody else is to be feared, except God; nobody is to be recognized as superior, except for God . . . And they do not see that with this they deny all of the respect and honor that is due to the kings, governors, and magistrates."[39] The identity of these "impudent" and "presumptive" men is made apparent almost immediately:

> This sect arose not long ago in our times, those who are called Quakers, who, following this hypocrisy, will under no circumstances hail nor call anyone "master." And it was a few days ago that I was before a member of this sect (which I did not know) saying a certain proposition, speaking about the lords the magistrates: "The lords are our judges." He reprehended me with anger, saying: "there is nobody who is our judge, except for God." And I, knowing the temperament of the man, did not wish to respond to such madness.[40]

Shocked at the political implications of this statement, and the volatile disposition of his interlocutor, Morteira extricated himself from a political discussion in which he wanted no part. The Quaker he encountered espoused a political position so extreme that there was little room for, or point to, further discussion. Morteira cited this Quaker as offering indisputable proof of how certain religious movements espoused doctrines that "confounded all order," all "good governance," and *todo policia*—a phrase that in the seventeenth century denoted all of the laws established in cities and republics in order to maintain the social order. The political implications of Quaker religious perspectives, in Morteira's view, threatened to "place the world in a miserable confusion."[41]

Morteira was very careful to emphasize that the extreme political position of the Quakers was repugnant to members of his own community, as much as it was to civil magistrates in the United Provinces. On the one hand, he draws parallels between the Quakers of his own day and the biblical followers of Korah who rebelled against Moses, protesting that "All the congregation are holy, every one of them, and the Lord is among them. So why then do you exalt yourselves above the assembly of the Lord?" In Morteira's view, Korah's polemic against stratified authority within his community aligned perfectly with the Quaker view that it was forbidden to recognize the authority of the municipal and state authorities in the Netherlands. On the other hand, Morteira (always an assiduous reader of Calvin's writings) pointed to passages in the *Institutes of the Christian Religion* that showed his perspective to be perfectly in line with doctrines held by the Dutch Reformed Church.[42] Here, Calvin emphasizes that "[t]hose who desire to usher in anarchy object that, although in antiquity kings and judges ruled over ignorant folk, yet that servile kind of governing is wholly incompatible today with the perfection which Christ brought with his gospel." Arguing against these figures, Calvin stresses that "where David urges all kings and rulers to kiss the Son of God [Ps 2:12], he does not bid them lay aside their authority and retire to private life." The benefits of civil rule for Calvin are clearest in 1 Timothy 2:2, where Paul states that "prayers be offered for kings in public assembly . . . that we may lead a peaceful life under them with all godliness and honesty."[43] Morteira—and Menasseh Ben Israel—could readily concur with these sentiments. Prayers for the government were a deeply traditional element of the Jewish liturgy with precedents in biblical, rabbinic, and medieval sources, and the welfare of the Portuguese Jewish community in Amsterdam most certainly depended on the favour of the rulers who governed the city and the States General. Indeed, it is for this very reason that Menasseh Ben Israel was so eager to invoke the symbols of Dutch patriotism in his presentation of Dutch Jewish political identity, and why Morteira was so eager to distance himself from religious and political postures that the mainstream in Dutch society viewed as corrosive to the religious, political, and moral order. Together, although from very different directions, Morteira and Menasseh conveyed a political image of Jewish society that conformed to the ideals, myths, and prejudices of the Dutch society in which they lived.

CONCLUSION

As uncommon as it may be to find seventeenth-century Jews in Western Europe speaking about European states as their *Vaderlant*, aspiring to participate in the defense of their homelands, or marshalling the arguments of Protestant theologians against radical Christian movements, many of the sentiments that Menasseh and Morteira expressed did become much more common in Jewish society beginning in the mid-eighteenth century. During this period, Jews in the Habsburg Empire, France, and other contexts grappled with questions about Jewish loyalty to the state, integration of Jews into the social fabric of broader non-Jewish society, and the ability of Jews to contribute to the state through military service. The Jews of Habsburg Trieste proclaimed their patriotism and loyalty to the state at public events, emphasized these values in their educational curriculum, and welcomed legislation mandating Jewish military service in the empire.[44] The Jews of mid-eighteenth century France accentuated their patriotic sentiments for the *patrie* in public festivities marking important events, liturgical texts honoring the royal family, and public opposition against foreign and domestic enemies of the state. They invoked traditions of kingship central to French society to assert their status as equal subjects, and to demonstrate that Jewish society was an integral element of the French state.[45] The Enlightenment debates and absolutist policy that drove these discussions lie in a time and territory a distant world away from that of the Portuguese Jews of seventeenth-century Amsterdam. Even within the context of their own times, Menasseh and Morteira were atypical in their identification with Dutch myths, symbols, and prejudices. Yet despite their anomaly, and indeed because of it, these examples of Jewish commitment to the state and its leaders are important. Menasseh's invocation of the Batavian myth, and Morteira's attacks against Libertines and Quakers, capture a historical moment when this type of thinking was in its infancy. They lived in a time and place that enabled the Jewish political imagination to travel down new and unexpected roads.

Notes

1. Menasseh Ben Israel, *Gratulaçao de Menasseh Ben Israel em nome de sua naçaõ, ao celsissimo Principe de Orange . . . Recitada em Amsterdama, aos XXII. de Mayo 5402* (Amsterdam, 1642). Regarding this frequently quoted passage from the *Gratulaçao,* see Yosef Kaplan, "The Jews in the Republic until about 1750: Religious, Cultural, and Social Life," in *The History of the Jews in the Netherlands,* ed. J. C. H. Blom et al. (Oxford, 2002), 160–61; and Miriam Bodian, *Hebrews of the Portuguese Nation: Conversos and Community in Early Modern Amsterdam* (Bloomington, Ind., 1999), 67–68.

2. Menasseh Ben Israel describes the Netherlands as the Dutch *patria* in the *Gratulaçao,* and as the *Vaderlant* in the Dutch version of this text.

3. Menasseh may not have been the only Portuguese Jew in Amsterdam to make the equation between the risks Jews were obliged to undertake on behalf of their God, and on behalf of their state. His colleague Saul Levi Morteira insisted that "it is necessary to know as well that giving one's life for the public affairs (*pelo publico*) follows the same rules and limits as giving it on behalf of God . . . for just as it is necessary to give the life of the body to God in order to maintain the integrity of the soul from offending his divine majesty . . . so too . . . it is a deed of much perfection and worthy of great praise . . . for someone to give their life in order to save many lives that are in danger of being lost." Saul Levi Morteira, *Tratado da verdade da lei de Moisés. Escrito pelo seu próprio punho em Português em Amsterdao, 1659–1660. Edicao facsimilada e leitura do Autógrafo (1659),* ed. H. P. Salomon (Coimbra, 1988), 613. Note, however, that Morteira's use of the word *publico* is ambiguous, and it is difficult to determine whether he refers to a Jewish or Christian context. With Menasseh's statement, there is no such ambiguity.

4. Luzzatto, *Discorso circa il stato de gl'Hebrei et in particular dimoranti nell'inclita Città di Venetia* (Venice, 1638), 32v.

5. Kaplan, "The Jews of the Republic until about 1750," 160–61; and Bodian, *Hebrews of the Portuguese Nation,* 66.

6. On Saul Levi Morteira specifically, see the recent study by Marc Saperstein, *Exile in Amsterdam: Saul Levi Morteira's Sermons to a Congregation of "New Jews"* (Cincinnati, Ohio, 2005) and the introduction in H. P. Salomon's facsimile edition of the *Tratado.* On Morteira's relationship with radical Christian movements in the Netherlands, see Henry Méchoulan, "Morteira et Spinoza au carrefour du socinianisme," *Revue des Études Juives* 135.1–3 (1976): 51–65; and Benjamin Fisher, "Opening the Eyes of the *Novos Reformados:* Rabbi Saul Levi Morteira, Radical Christianity, and the Jewish Reclamation of Jesus, 1620–1660," *Studia Rosenthaliana* 44 (2012): 117–48.

7. David B. Ruderman, *Early Modern Jewry: A New Cultural History* (Princeton, N.J., 2010), 96.

8. Ibid., 57–98.

9. Ibid., 77.

10. David Malkiel, "The Tenuous Thread: A Venetian Lawyer's Apology for Jewish Self-Government in the Seventeenth-Century," *AJS Review* 12.2 (1987): 223–50. The earliest manifestation of this statement dates to the early 1630s, although the concept became most prominent later in the eighteenth century. See Benjamin Ravid, "'A Republic Separate from All Other Government': Jewish Autonomy in the Seventeenth Century," in *Thought and Action: Essays in Memory of Simon Rawidowicz on the Twenty-Fifth Anniversary of His Death,* ed. A. Greenbaum and A. Ivry (Hebrew; Tel Aviv, 1983), 53–76; and Jacob Katz, "A State within a State: The History of an Anti-Semitic Slogan," *Proceedings of the Israel Academy of Sciences and Humanities* 4 (1971): 29–58.

11. Miriam Bodian, "Biblical Hebrews and the Rhetoric of Republicanism," *AJS Review* 22.2 (1997): 199–221; Anne Oravetz Albert, "Post-Sabbatian Politics: Reflections on Governance among the Spanish and Portuguese Jews of Amsterdam" (Ph.D. diss.; University of Pennsylvania, 2008).

12. Luzzatto, *Discorso,* 38v–38r.

13. Ibid., 7r. Regarding Luzzatto, see Benjamin Ravid, *Economics and Toleration in Seventeenth-Century Venice: The Background and Context of the Discorso of Simone Luzzatto* (Jerusalem, 1978); Abraham Melamed, "Simone Luzzatto on Tacitus: Apologetica and Ragione di Stato," in *Studies in Medieval Jewish History and Literature*, ed. I. Twersky (Cambridge, 1984), 2:143–70; David B. Ruderman, *Jewish Thought and Scientific Discovery in Early Modern Europe* (New Haven, Conn., 1995), 153–85; and Giuseppe Veltri, *Renaissance Philosophy in Jewish Garb: Foundations and Challenges in Judaism on the Eve of Modernity* (Boston, 2009), 195–224.

14. Simone Luzzatto, *Discorso*, 32v. Menasseh's conviction about Jewish readiness to run risks on behalf of the non-Jewish state closely resembles Luzzatto's assertions in this passage. As Benjamin Ravid has demonstrated, Menasseh copied whole passages of the *Discorso* within his *Humble Addresses*. See Ravid, "'How Profitable the Nation of the Jews Are': The Humble Addresses of Menasseh ben Israel and the *Discorso* of Simone Luzzatto," in *Mystics, Philosophers, and Politicians: Essays in Jewish Intellectual History in Honor of Alexander Altmann*, ed. J. Reinharz and D. Swetschinski (Durham, N.C., 1982), 159–80.

15. Ravid, *Economics and Toleration*, 57–63.

16. Luzzatto, *Discorso*, 91v–91r.

17. Jonathan Israel, "Duarte Nunes da Costa (Jacob Curiel) of Hamburg, Sephardi Nobleman and Communal Leader," in *Empires and Entrepots: The Dutch, the Spanish Monarchy, and the Jews*, ed. J. Israel (London, 1990), 333–54; and Jonathan Israel, "Dutch Sephardi Jewry, Millenarian Politics, and Brazil (1640–1654)," in *Sceptics, Millenarians, and Jews*, ed. D. S. Katz and J. Israel (New York, 1990), 85.

18. Menasseh Ben Israel, *Segunda parte del Conciliador, Epistola Dedicatoria* [unpaginated]. It was in fact not uncommon for members of the Portuguese Jewish community to celebrate news of these events with what has been described as "genuine zeal." See Israel, "Duarte Nunes da Costa (Jacob Curiel)," 342, and Israel, "Dutch Sephardi Jewry, Millenarian Politics, and Brazil," 85.

19. Bodian, *Hebrews of the Portuguese Nation*, 67–68 and 183, n. 67.

20. Israel, "Duarte Nunes da Costa (Jacob Curiel)," 342; Regarding the ebb and flow of Inquisitorial activity in Spain and Portugal, see Daniel Swetschinsky, *Reluctant Cosmopolitans: The Portuguese Jews of Seventeenth-Century Amsterdam* (London, 2000), 70–75.

21. Israel, "Duarte Nunes da Costa (Jacob Curiel)." Duarte lived in Hamburg but conducted significant trade with Amsterdam, using the nearby Hanseatic port as a convenient way to circumvent the embargo on trade between Portugal and the Netherlands. The impending peace between the two states would reduce the impetus for this type of manoeuvre.

22. I. Schöffer, "The Batavian Myth during the Sixteenth and Seventeenth Centuries," in *Britain and the Netherlands*, ed. J. S. Bromley and E. H. Kossmann, vol. 5 (The Hague, 1975), 78–101; and Simon Schama, *The Embarrassment of Riches: An Interpretation of Dutch Culture in the Golden Age* (New York, 1987), 51–95.

23. Schöffer, "The Batavian Myth," 81.

24. Schama, *Embarrassment of Riches*, 75–77.

25. Quoted from the translation in Theodor Dunkelgrün, "'Neerlands Israel'—Political Theology, Christian Hebraism, Biblical Antiquarianism, and Historical Myth," in *Myth in History, History in Myth*, ed. L. Cruz and W. Frijhoff (Leiden, 2009), 225–26. See also Henry Méchoulan, "À propos de la visite de Frédéric-Henri, Prince d'Orange, à la synagogue d'Amsterdam," *Lias* 5.1 (1978): 81–86.

26. Menasseh Ben Israel, *Gratulaçao*, 5.

27. Noah Rosenbloom, "Discreet Theological Polemics in Menasseh Ben Israel's Conciliador," *Proceedings of the American Academy for Jewish Research* 58 (1992): 152–53.

28. Saul Levi Morteira, *Tratado*, 3–7.

29. Uriel da Costa, *Examination of Pharisaic Traditions. Supplemented by Semuel da Silva's Treatise on the Immortality of the Soul*, trans. and ed. H. P. Salomon and I. S. D. Sassoon (New York, 1993), 557–58.

30. Spinoza, *Theological-Political Treatise*, ed. J. Israel, trans. J. Israel and M. Silverthorne (New York, 2007), 9.

31. For instance, see the discussion of *minim* (heretics) and epicureans in bRH 17a, and their association with denial of the Torah. Maimonides' *Mishneh Torah* deprives the *kofer ba-Torah,* one who denies the Torah, of any share in the world to come, and describes the *kofer* as one who contests the divinely revealed status of any element of Scripture or the Oral Law. Joseph Albo identifies anyone denying one of his six cardinal beliefs necessary for the existence and authority of the Torah as a heretic. However, none of these terms appear in the *Tratado*. Moses ben Maimon, *Mishneh Torah*, ed. Y. Kafah (Kiryat Ono, 1984), 605–12; Joseph Albo, *Sefer ha-'ikkarim. Book of Principles*, ed. I. Husik (Philadelphia, 1946), 7 and 181–86.

32. J. C. Margolin, "Libertins, Libertinisme et 'Libertinage' au XVIe siècle," in *Aspects du Libertinisme au XVIe siècle*, ed. M. Bataillon (Paris, 1974), 1–4.

33. John Calvin, *Contre la secte phantastique et furieuse des libertines*, in Benjamin Wirt Farley, ed. *Treatises against the Anabaptists and against the Libertines* (Grand Rapids, Mich., 1982), 259–60.

34. John Calvin, *Contre la secte phantastique et furieuse des libertines,* 221.

35. Ibid., 192.

36. Benjamin Kaplan, *Calvinists and Libertines: Confession and Community in Utrecht* (Oxford, 1995).

37. Yosef Kaplan, "The Social Functions of the Ḥerem," in his *An Alternative Path to Modernity. The Sephardi Diaspora in Western Europe* (Leiden, 2000), 108–42; Jonathan Israel, *The Dutch Republic: Its Rise, Greatness, and Fall* (Oxford, 1995), 361–67, 422–31, 660–61.

38. Maimonides, *Mishneh Torah*, 94–104.

39. Morteira, *Tratado*, 601.

40. Ibid., 603.

41. Ibid.

42. Ibid. Morteira's reference to the *Institutes* is mistaken. In the Portuguese version of the *Tratado* he erroneously cites *Institutes* IV.2.5 instead of IV.20.5, "Against the Christian denial or rejection of the magistracy." Morteira cites Calvin's writings throughout the *Tratado*. See for example references to Calvin's *Institutes of the Christian Religion* and *Commentary on the Harmony of the Three Evangelists: Matthew, Mark, and Luke* in Morteira, *Tratado*, 139–41 and 264.

43. John Calvin, *Institutes of the Christian Religion*, ed. J. T. McNeill, trans. F. L. Battles (Philadelphia, 1960): 2:1490–91.

44. Lois Dubin, *The Port Jews of Habsburg Trieste: Absolutist Politics and Enlightenment Culture* (Stanford, Calif., 1999), 95–151.

45. Ronald Schechter, *Obstinate Hebrews: Representations of Jews in France, 1715–1815* (Berkeley, Calif, 2003), 110–48.

"A CIVIL DEATH"

❈ ❈ ❈

Sovereignty and the Jewish Republic in an
Early Modern Treatment of Genesis 49:10

Anne Oravetz Albert
University of Pennsylvania

PREDICTING that "the sceptre shall not depart from Judah, nor a lawgiver from between his feet, until Shiloh come,"[1] Genesis 49:10 is usually understood as foretelling the continuity of Jewish rule until the messianic age. In addition to the polemical challenge posed by this apparent confirmation of Christian supersessionist claims, the disparity between the promise and historical reality has required Jews to account for the exile in some fundamental way. In his examination of medieval polemics, Amos Funkenstein identified three types of Jewish response: missionary, cathartic, and soteriological.[2] All of these theological and historical explanations acknowledge or even embrace the exile as an incontrovertible fact, and emphasize the present abject dispersion of the known Jewish world, whether they take comfort in the prospect of their eventual restoration, seek hidden Jewish states in the Khazar kingdom or beyond the Sambatyon, or celebrate the lost political glory of ancient Jews.

A fourth type of response to this polemical—and existential—challenge was to deny that the scepter had yet departed from Judah, in essence arguing that Jewish sovereignty persisted in the Diaspora. Funkenstein's implication is that such a claim was quite incongruous in the European Middle Ages, where no amount of juridical independence or strong communal leadership could efface the stark conditions of Jewish vulnerability vis-à-vis Christian monarchs, or the increasing determination of Christians to make their theological claim to superiority manifest in social and political conditions.[3] By the latter half of the seventeenth century, however, the transformations of the early modern period were being enacted in both non-Jewish and Jewish politics, and Isaac Orobio de Castro (1620–1687)[4] put forward just such an argument. As a midlife immigrant to the Spanish and Portuguese Jewish community of Amsterdam, and formerly a well-connected *converso*, Orobio was privy to the political and religious debates of early modern Europe in addition to being an heir to the Sephardi intellectual tradition. In his major polemical work, *Prevenciones divinas contra la vana idolatria de las gentes*,[5] Orobio picked up on his Christian contemporaries' interest in the ancient "republic of the Hebrews" along with evolving views of sovereignty and the rule of law in order to depict a scepter of sorts in the hands of present day Jews.

Indeed, the new interpretation hinges on the characterization of the scepter. In a move that parallels the shift from life under the monarchies of Iberia and France to the new circumstances in Amsterdam, Orobio emphasizes that the *shevet* (scepter) in Genesis 49:10 need not represent kingship, but rather any form of "rule" (*mando* in Orobio's Spanish), in this case, the rule of lawgivers and judges. In one striking passage, he locates this rule in the hands of judges, i.e., rabbis, who possess absolute, God-given authority in a distinctly governmental sense:

> The doctors of the law . . . have so much authority over the people, conceded by God himself in the law . . . that it is not lawful for anyone to repudiate their decrees . . . These same doctors . . . are absolute judges of the people throughout the world, not only in what pertains to ceremonial rules and legal precepts, but also in all civil and criminal law.[6]

The implication that rabbis governed politically as well as religiously presents Jewish communities as entities that parallel the states that surround them, but does not necessarily indicate sovereignty. Orobio takes the argument farther, however, by indicating that the Jewish rule of law constitutes the *shevet* precisely because it was not limited or contingent. The crux of the matter is whether or not Jews have ultimate authority, not just any authority; indeed, Orobio reports that Christian polemicists "allege that our scribes, or legal judges, don't have rule or jurisdiction anywhere, because they cannot punish with corporal punishment,"[7] engaging a common definition of supreme authority as the right to take the life of a subject. Orobio then argues for a kind of stateless sovereignty by claiming that excommunication—which was, in reality, the most extreme tool of law enforcement within his community—was its equivalent. To wit, "excommunication . . . is a civil death."[8]

The connection between excommunication (*ḥerem*) and death does not come from thin air. One infrequently-used term for the ban, *shamta*, is explained in a talmudic passage as being derived from the words *sham* and *mata*, and therefore meaning "there is death."[9] However, this is not a central concept in rabbinic treatments of the ban; nor does *shamta* appear in the records of the Amsterdam Sephardim, which tended to use the term *ḥerem*.[10] Instead, Orobio may have arrived at the connection through his knowledge of Christian treatments of Jewish politics. The great Dutch Hebraist Hugo Grotius had defined Jewish excommunication as the equivalent of the death penalty in his *De imperio summarum potestatum circa sacra* (published posthumously in 1647), stating that *shamta* is the highest degree of excommunication, reserved for those who would have received the death penalty before Jews lost the right to impose it.[11] Orobio turned this link between the ban and the death penalty on its head in order to emphasize the authority still held by Jews instead of that which had been taken away.

Such a reversal was typical of Orobio. The *Prevenciones* is devoted in its entirety to the refutation of Christian supersessionism, based on the idea that God had anticipated gentile arguments and seeded scripture with the exegetical ammunition required to overcome them.[12] Orobio was particularly suited to such a project because of his Christian education and self-image as a politico. Before coming to Judaism, he had enjoyed social and professional contacts with members of the Spanish and French nobility who were both politically and intellectually influential and *au courant*.[13] After his arrival in Amsterdam in 1662, this vocation was folded into his strong sense of Jewish particularity, as he claimed an equivalent position for himself among the elite of his new community, and made a name for himself as a debater and defender of Judaism.[14]

From the outset, his mindset differed from that of many of his predecessors in the converso Diaspora who had addressed exile by turning the *shevet* into a rod, staff, or cane that was to continually accompany Judah's descendants. Solomon ibn Verga's *Sefer shevet Yehudah*, for example, gave a long litany of the trials suffered by Jews throughout history.[15] Ibn Verga (1460–1554) granted this suffering a central place in Jewish identity, explaining the title of his work as a play on the term *shevet*: Judah, who once ruled, now suffers for his sins, flogged by the staff of the almighty.[16] A similar emphasis on Jewish suffering was displayed by Samuel Usque in his *Consolaçam as tribulaçoens de Israel* (1553),[17] when he explained these trials as fulfilling biblical predictions, and looked forward to their end in the time of messianic redemption. Continuing along the path from the expulsion to seventeenth-century Amsterdam, another lachrymose interpretation was offered by Elijah Montalto (d. 1616), a former Portuguese converso who attended the court of Louis XIII after leaving Iberia. His interpretation put an even stronger point on the matter: according to him, not only is the *shevet* a rod of punishment, but the "lawgiver" in the passage represents laws, statutes, and tribunals (such as the Inquisition) that were instituted to persecute Jews.[18] He also emphasized that this was only temporary, explaining that when *shevet* is read as "scepter," the verse promises that the monarchy will return to King David's line in messianic days.[19]

A generation younger than Montalto, Saul Levi Morteira (1596–1660) first arrived in Amsterdam in the early years of its Sephardi settlement, when he accompanied the body of the deceased Montalto from France for burial.[20] As the congregation grew, he became its senior rabbi even though he was not himself of Sephardi descent, and passed down an interpretation nearly identical to that of Montalto, explaining that the passage about the staff (*vara*) of Judah "shows us the punishment, whipping, and bloodshed that [Judah's] sons would have to bear until the coming of that Prince of Peace."[21] The image of present-day Jews continues to be as a dispersed and suffering nation.

In contrast, a student of Morteira's, Menasseh ben Israel (1604–1657), emphasized the hope for restoration promised in Gen 49:10, without dwelling on exilic tribulations. Among the first students to be educated from childhood in the new Jewish schools of Amsterdam, Menasseh had a sunnier view of the conditions of Jewish life. He took pride in his relations with high-ranking members of the Christian intellectual and political elite, and in what he called the "nobility" of the Jewish nation, as he worked to obtain residency rights and religious freedom for Jews in England.[22] In a 1655 work, he linked Gen 49:10 with Usque's well-known suggestion that dispersion was key to Jewish survival:

> if they were all under one prince, he could destroy all of them . . . but since they are spread out, when one banishes them from his lands, another recognizes and accepts them. God promised this when he said, "The staff (or cane) will not depart from Judah (or from the Jews) until the Messiah comes."[23]

Menasseh interpreted *shevet* as a cane or walking stick that supported the Jews through their wandering, suggesting promise rather than injustice.[24] Nevertheless, his interpretation of the scepter of Judah, and of Jewish political status in general, was still based on an assumption of powerlessness, with political glory transposed to the ancient past or messianic future.

Less than twenty years later, Orobio's interpretation shifted the enjoyment of political power to his own times, reflecting a major change of perspective on Jewish status in the Diaspora. The novelty of his view is clarified through a contrast with the work of Isaac Abravanel (1437–1508), which in some ways anticipated it.[25] Like Orobio, Abravanel moved away from the image of "royal Jews,"[26] as he formulated a theory of biblical republicanism, and suggested that the biblical Israelites could be analogous to Europeans in their politics. In his treatment of Gen 49:10, Abravanel, expanding on Rashi, already suggested that Jews had not lost the *shevet*, since it represented the various forms of rule that would be continually possessed by a few members of Judah's line in each generation from the great exilarchs to latter-day Jewish scholars and beyond.[27] However, Abravanel did not even approach Orobio's bold assertion of sovereignty and favorable evaluation of Jewish status in the Diaspora. He presented Jewish rule as greatly attenuated, emphasizing only the continuity of the dynastic line that would eventually give rise to the restored Jewish monarch to end the exile. Orobio, in contrast, specifically notes that the prophecy does not require the *shevet* to remain in the hands of Judah's heirs, but rather in the hands of those who serve a Jewish republic or polity.[28]

If Abravanel's innovation was to recast biblical Jewish politics as republican-

ism, that of Orobio's generation was to cast the present-day community as a republic. Miriam Bodian cites several instances in which contemporaries of Orobio
referred to their communities in such terms, a step that Abravanel had not taken.[29]
My own research has further shown that the treatment of the community as a polity, characterized by the same political dynamics as other polities, was pervasive
in the Amsterdam of Orobio's time.[30] In their communal discourse, "religion" and
"politics" were explicit categories of behavior that would ideally work in harmony in
a well-rounded republic,[31] and Orobio includes both in his account of Jewish rule.
Less than a decade later, his contemporary in Italy and fellow former converso, Isaac
Cardoso, gave a contrasting view:

> It means that the staff of dominion will not be taken away from the Jews until the
> coming of the Messiah: they will always maintain rule (*mando*), and be self-governed
> by their sages in their rites, ceremonies, weddings, burials, festivals, and traditions,
> all in conformity with the law with which God entrusted us. The verse does not say
> crown, but rather staff, which indicates some dominion, and the word scribe refers to
> the sages who decree and sentence according to Scripture.[32]

Like Abravanel and Orobio, Cardoso specified that the scepter need not represent
kingship, and that the rule it represents may be ascribed to rabbis. But Cardoso
limited their rule to the religious realm in no uncertain terms, whereas Orobio wrote
that the rabbinic judges had authority "not only in what pertains to ceremonial rules
and legal precepts, but also in all civil and criminal law," as quoted above. (This is
not the place to take up the question of whether these treatments of Jewish legal
jurisdiction are related to Spinoza's comments in the *Theological-Political Treatise* published less than a decade earlier, regarding the ceremonial and political aspects of
Jewish law.)

To be sure, there are problems with Orobio's vision of a Jewish republic in which
rabbis, as lawgivers and judges, have sovereign jurisdiction over both civil and religious affairs. Not the least is the relationship of such Jewish rule to the sovereignty
of the state. When he introduces the notion of the "civil death" penalty, Orobio
distinguishes between the "power of the king or lord to punish subjects"—which
is not currently possessed by Jewish communities, since they are not run by kings
or lords—and the power of legal officials to "punish transgressors with spiritual
punishment."[33] This plainly contradicts his other comments, that the same officials
indisputably ruled on affairs of civil and criminal law, unless the "spiritual punishment" is understood broadly as any punishment specific to Judaism, since Jewish
law includes both governmental (civil and criminal) and spiritual (ritual, ethical,
and theological) content. He also notes that where the actual power to punish has
been taken away, the legal "office" or "dignity" remains, by which he seems to mean
that rabbis possess the *de jure* right to rule in this manner, even if they are *de facto*
prevented from doing so.[34] Even so, if sovereignty may be characterized as "supreme
authority within a territory,"[35] Orobio is forced to transmute Jewish territory to a

"spiritual" plane in order to retain the sense of supremacy, and he does not fully consider the competing claim of sovereignty held by the Christian ruler. He also ignores the claim of authority on the part of Jewish lay leaders. Amsterdam was, in reality, governed by the *Mahamad,* a council of laymen who owed very little obeisance to the rabbis they employed, as was common in late–seventeenth-century Europe.[36]

Although Orobio's image of a sovereign Jewish republic governed by legal and religious scholars was counterfactual, it was not random. It closely matched the image of the Jewish republic that was so celebrated in contemporary political thought. His treatment of the scepter echoes that found in one of the most influential works of political Hebraism, Petrus Cunaeus's *De Republica Hebraeorum* (1617, and reprinted throughout the century): "For my own part, I think that the scepter can only represent sovereign power, namely that which lies in the very republic itself."[37] Many Christian writers used the models of ancient Jewish government to justify their views on the relationship between civil and ecclesiastical power, or between religious and political aims of the state. Grotius's discussion of the meaning of Jewish excommunication (cited above), for example, comes in support of his view that civil and religious power ought to be concentrated in the same hands, on the model of the ancient Israelite polity and Babylonian exilarchs.[38] Hobbes makes a similar claim that biblical Jewish leaders held civil and ecclesiastical power concurrently: "whosoever had the Soveraignty of the Common-wealth amongst the Jews, the same had also the Supreme Authority in matters of God's externall worship."[39] John Selden spent the last years of his life writing "an attack on ecclesiastical power, and a demonstration that the Sanhedrim [*sic*] had possessed all religious rights including the right to excommunicate."[40] Through Orobio, we may perceive Hebraist ideas, themselves gleaned from earlier Jewish sources, seeping back into a completely different Jewish context, as he and his peers exhibited tensions over the respective roles of rabbis and lay leaders that paralleled such debates in wider political context.

This observation begs the question of how new Orobio's attitude actually was. As an interpretation of Gen 49:10, it clearly diverges from the ones that had been offered by his immediate predecessors, and contrasts with the medieval ones highlighted by Funkenstein. However, this set of gloomy views on an opaque scriptural passage does not animate the entirety of exilic politics. Some, like David Biale, would emphasize the extent to which powerlessness and exile were actively rejected in medieval thought, rather than justified.[41] Many medieval writers traced the authority of rabbis and communal leaders back to the era of Jewish sovereignty, seeing such power as a substitute for, if not equivalent to, actual sovereign rule.[42] Furthermore, Menachem Lorberbaum has revealed how some medieval Spanish Jews began to treat the community as a polity with a sphere of collective activity not limited to the religious. In fact, in a passage that is likely to have served as a source for the early modern commentators, Moses Nahmanides (1194–1270) specifically connected the community's right to impose the *ḥerem* with the ancient Jewish right to impose capital punishment.[43] In other words, the fact that Orobio—and others in Amsterdam at that time—were thinking politically about the community and treating the ḥerem as a central symbol of Jewish communal power is not in itself new.

But tracing communal authority back to sovereign rulers is different from claiming ongoing sovereignty; and calling the ḥerem a substitute for the death penalty is different from calling it a "civil death penalty." The fact that Nahmanides and other medieval rabbis opened a space for treating the community as a polity is, as Lorberbaum suggests, significant, but primarily in intracommunal terms—they addressed questions of communal governance rather than communal status. When Orobio, on the other hand, introduces this material into a discussion of a text as central to Jewish identity as Gen 49:10, it becomes a reevaluation of the nature of the Diaspora and of relations with the non-Jewish world. I would argue that this was precisely his intention in his treatment of the scepter of Judah.

The difference lies not only with Orobio. The political landscape had changed so as to make Jewish sovereignty both more necessary and more impossible to justify. In a medieval Europe made up of corporate polities, a number of "courts"— mercantile, seigneurial, etc.—possessed independent jurisdictions for which the authority was not necessarily seen as derivative of the king's, even though it may have been delimited by royal mandate.[44] Each was understood to constitute its own separate rule without threatening the sovereignty of the kingdom, and juridically independent Jewish communities fit easily into this scene. Even in the sixteenth century, in Abravanel's time and beyond, these arrangements were still in place and mainly *ad hoc,* without yet being eroded or subjected to extensive theoretical treatment. Perhaps because of that, it was clear enough to everyone that Jewish autonomy need not be seen as a threat.

By Orobio's time, sovereignty itself was coming under scrutiny. Jean Bodin's treatment set the stage in requiring sovereignty to be unitary, and subsequent thinkers puzzled over where exactly to locate the sovereignty in mixed constitutions.[45] The insistence that civil and ecclesiastical power be concentrated together that is found in the quotations from Hobbes, Selden, and Grotius above is evidence of increasing discomfort with powers that might compete with a central one. In this context, as it was less and less possible for rule to be contingent or limited, Jewish semi-autonomy was less and less tenable, and we can see the roots of the view that a Jewish community was problematic as a "state within a state."[46] At this stage, though, as a polemicist faced with the all-or-nothing choice of sovereign rule or no rule, Orobio was still able to choose the former. Absurd though such a claim might be on the face of it, the idea that a Jewish community was sovereign was an elegant solution to the problem, and one that suited the proud and politically savvy Sephardim in Amsterdam.

In a way, this moment can be characterized as an intermediate stage between contrasting dualities of Jewish life. If most medieval Jews accepted their national subjugation to other peoples as an incontrovertible (if temporary) fact, they seem to have taken their separateness, both political and religious, just as much for granted.

Modernity would erase both the subjugation and the separation in political terms, but draw a new line between politics and religion in Jewish life. The in-between period reveals both medieval holdovers and forerunners of modernity, but it was more than just a period of slippage from one to the other. Its sometimes strange combination of impulses and assumptions constituted a unique context which could run counter to both medieval and modern ways of being. Orobio's polemical innovation, untenable as it was, took medieval Jewish corporate status to its extreme, paradoxically by assimilating political trends that anticipated modernity.

Notes

1. King James Version.

2. Amos Funkenstein, "Basic Types of Christian Anti-Jewish Polemics in the Later Middle Ages," *Viator* 2 (1971): 373–82. Later he added a fourth type, the "sacrificial" explanation found mainly in Maimonides' conception of Israel as a *korban 'ola*. Amos Funkenstein, *Perceptions of Jewish History* (Berkeley, Calif., 1993), 206.

3. The view that the second half of the Middle Ages presented a distinct and negative change in Jewish-Christian relations is neatly summarized in David Berger, *From Crusades to Blood Libels to Expulsions: Some New Approaches to Medieval Antisemitism* (New York, 1997). Funkenstein noted in passing that these responses predominated until the early modern period.

4. On Orobio, see primarily Yosef Kaplan, *From Christianity to Judaism: The Story of Isaac Orobio De Castro*, trans. R. Loewe (New York, 1989).

5. Isaac Orobio de Castro, *Prevenciones divinas contra la vana idolatria de las gentes* (Hs. Ros 631). The precise date of composition is not known, but Kaplan has shown that it was probably written between 1668 and 1672 (Kaplan, *From Christianity to Judaism: The Story of Isaac Orobio De Castro*, 244). See ibid., 243–49 on the *Prevenciones divinas* in particular, and 235–62 on his polemical work in general.

6. Orobio, *Prevenciones divinas*, 74.

7. Ibid.

8. Ibid., 73–74.

9. *bMK* 17a.

10. A discussion of the usage of the various rabbinic terms for the ban—*nidui, nezifah, herem*, and of course *shamta*—is found in Yosef Kaplan, *An Alternative Path to Modernity: The Sephardi Diaspora in Western Europe* (Leiden, 2000), 128–29.

11. Hugo Grotius, *De Imperio Summarum Potestatum Circa Sacra. Critical Edition with Introduction, English Translation and Commentary by Harm-Jan Van Dam*, 2 vols. (Leiden, 2001), 1:395 (9, 2). See Eric Nelson, *The Hebrew Republic: Jewish Sources and the Transformation of European Political Thought* (Cambridge, Mass., 2010), 102. Moses Nahmanides was probably Grotius's source; see below.

12. Book 2, chapters 15–18.

13. Kaplan, *From Christianity to Judaism*, 64–67 and 103–5.

14. Ibid., 235–307.

15. First published in Hebrew in Adrianople, Turkey, c. 1554; Spanish (1640) and Latin (1651) translations were published in Amsterdam.

16. Solomon Ibn Verga, *La vara de yehudah (Sefer Sebet Yehudah)*, trans. M. J. Cano (Barcelona, 1991), 21.

17. Samuel Usque, *Samuel Usque's Consolation for the Tribulations of Israel*, trans. M. Cohen (2nd ed.; Philadelphia, 1977).

18. Eliah Montalto, *Libro feito plo ilustrissimo Haham Eliau Montalto de G.M. / Em que mostra a*

verdade de diversos textos e cazos, que alegaõ as gentilidadez para confirmar suas sectas [Commentary on Isaiah 53], (Hs. Ros 76) 43–45.

19. Ibid., 47–48.

20. On Morteira, see Marc Saperstein, *Exile in Amsterdam: Saul Levi Morteira's Sermons to a Congregation of "New Jews"* (Cincinnati, Ohio, 2005).

21. Saul Levi Morteira, *Obstaculos y opociciones contra la religion [chris]tiana en Amsterdam* (Hs EH 48 D 3), 76–78.

22. See, among others, Antonio José Saraiva, "Menasseh Ben Israel and His World," in *Menasseh Ben Israel and His World,* ed. Y. Kaplan, H. Méchoulan, and R. Popkin (Leiden, 1989); David S. Katz, *Philo-Semitism and the Readmission of the Jews to England, 1603–1655* (Oxford, 1982); Aaron Katchen, "Menasseh Ben Israel the Apologist and the Christian Study of Maimonides' *Mishneh Torah,*" in *Jewish Thought in the Seventeenth Century,* ed. I. Twersky and B. Septimus (Cambridge, Mass., 1987), 201–20; and Benjamin Ravid, "'How Profitable the Nation of the Jewes Are': The 'Humble Addresses' of Menasseh Ben Israel and The 'Discorso' of Simone Luzzatto," in *Mystics, Philosophers, and Politicians: Essays in Jewish Intellectual History in Honor of Alexander Altmann,* ed. J. Reinharz and D. Swetschinski (Durham, N.C., 1982), 159–80.

23. Menasseh ben Israel, *'Even Yeqarah. Piedra Gloriosa O De La Estatua De Nebuchadnesar* (Amsterdam, 1655), 72–73. Usque did not connect this "consolation" with Genesis 49:10. Usque, *Consolation,* 227.

24. A similar attitude to exile is present in his *Hope of Israel*, with the expectation that the lost tribes were awaiting discovery in the New World. Henry Méchoulan and Gérard Nahon, eds., *Menasseh ben Israel: The Hope of Israel. The English Translation by Moses Wall, 1652* (Oxford, 1987).

25. On Abravanel's life, thought, and influence, see Benjamin Netanyahu, *Don Isaac Abravanel: Statesman and Philosopher,* 5th, revised and updated ed. (Ithaca, N.Y., 1998); Seymour Feldman, *Philosophy in a Time of Crisis: Don Isaac Abravanel, Defender of the Faith* (London, 2003); and Eric Lawee, *Isaac Abarbanel's Stance toward Tradition: Defense, Dissent, and Dialogue* (Albany, N.Y., 2001).

26. I am referring to the previous self-image as "royal Jews" with a particular relationship to monarchy, exemplified especially in Ibn Verga's *Shevet yehudah* and Emanuel Aboab's *Nomologia* (Amsterdam, 1629). See Yosef Yerushalmi, *The Lisbon Massacre of 1506 and the Royal Image in the Shebet Yehudah* (Cincinnati, Ohio, 1976); and Eleazar Gutwirth, "The Expulsion from Spain and Jewish Historiography," in *Jewish History; Essays in Honour of Chimen Abramsky,* ed. A. Rapoport-Albert and S. Zipperstein (London, 1988), 141–61.

27. Isaac Abravanel, *Perush ha-Torah* (Jerusalem, 1997), 1:766–70. It appears that Orobio encountered Jewish sources mainly in translation, and a summary of Abravanel's interpretation had been published in Spanish translation by Menasseh. Menasseh ben Israel, *Conciliador o de la conveniencia de los lugares de la S. escriptura que repugnantes entre si Parecen* (Amsterdam, 1632–1651), 124–25.

28. "Whether [the judges] are members of this tribe or another, they must uphold the office in service of the tribe of Judah. This is like any king who has a council to judge the people, just as it happens now in the political kingdoms of Europe: even when the judges are not natives [of his kingdom], but rather come from other nations, no one would say that the tribunal is not [the king's], because it is still under his dominion." Orobio de Castro, *Prevenciones divinas,* 71.

29. Miriam Bodian, "Biblical Hebrews and the Rhetoric of Republicanism: Seventeenth-Century Portuguese Jews on the Jewish Community," *AJS Review* 22.2 (1997): 199–221; Bodian, "The Biblical 'Jewish Republic' and the Dutch 'New Israel' in Seventeenth-Century Dutch Thought," *Hebraic Political Studies* 1.2 (2006): 186–202.

30. Anne Oravetz Albert, "Post-Sabbatian Politics: Reflections on Governance among the Spanish and Portuguese Jews of Amsterdam, 1665–1683" (Ph.D. diss.; University of Pennsylvania, 2008).

31. Albert, "Post-Sabbatian Politics," 99–139.

32. Isaac Cardoso, *Las excelencias de los Hebreos* (Amsterdam, 1679), 22.

33. Orobio, *Prevenciones divinas,* 74

34. Elsewhere in his treatment of Genesis 49:10, Orobio discusses at length the idea that Jews still possess the *right* to the scepter (though not the scepter itself) because its removal was illegal, a discussion that seems to be informed by Bossuet and Cano. His discussion of Genesis 49:10 is the longest and most involved elaboration of any single topic within his *Prevenciones.* The discussion offers several different and sometimes contradictory arguments, as Orobio covers all his polemical bases, but he displays a preference for explanations according to which the scepter is retained in some way.

35. Dan Philpott, "Sovereignty," http://plato.stanford.edu/archives/sum2010/entries/sovereignty/.

36. See David Ruderman's discussion of the historiography on laicization and the decline in the status of the rabbinate, *Early Modern Jewry: A New Cultural History* (Princeton, N.J., 2010), 57–98.

37. Petrus Cunaeus, *The Hebrew Republic,* trans. P. Wyetzner (Jerusalem, 2006), 39–40.

38. Nelson, *The Hebrew Republic,* 102–4.

39. Hobbes, *Leviathan,* ed. R. Tuck (Cambridge, 1996), 331.

40. Richard Tuck, "Grotius and Selden," in *The Cambridge History of Political Thought 1450–1700,* ed. J. H. Burns (Cambridge, 1991), 529.

41. David Biale, *Power and Powerlessness in Jewish History* (New York, 1987), 38.

42. Biale, *Power and Powerlessness,* 43–53. See also Michael Walzer, Menachem Lorberbaum, and Noam J. Zohar, eds., *The Jewish Political Tradition,* vol. 1: *Authority* (New Haven, Conn., 2000).

43. Nahmanides also mentioned *shamta* in this connection. Nahmanides, "Mishpat ha-ḥerem," in *Ḥidushe ha-Ramban,* ed. M. Hershler (Jerusalem, 1970), 281–304. See Menachem Lorberbaum, *Politics and the Limits of Law: Secularizing the Political in Medieval Jewish Thought* (Stanford, Calif., 2001), 108.

44. Harold J. Berman, *Law and Revolution* (Cambridge, Mass., 1983), 215–21, discussed in Lorberbaum, *Politics and the Limits of Law,* 98.

45. Julian Franklin, "Sovereignty and the Mixed Constitution: Bodin and His Critics" in *The Cambridge History of Political Thought 1450–1700,* 298–328.

46. Jacob Katz, "A State within a State—the History of an Anti-Semitic Slogan," in *Zur Assimilation und Emanzipation der Juden* (Darmstadt, 1982), 124–53.

PART II

KNOWLEDGE NETWORKS

❈ ❈ ❈

THE HEBREW BIBLE AND THE SENSES
IN LATE MEDIEVAL SPAIN

❊ ❊ ❊

Talya Fishman

University of Pennsylvania

IN her groundbreaking study of the writings of Profiat Duran (1350–1415), Maud Kozodoy draws attention to the Torah-centered ideology of this forcibly-baptized Catalan Jew and notes that it enabled conversos (like the author himself) to affirm their Jewishness.[1] Duran's identification of "the craft of Torah" as the *only* curricular approach that could lead to life's ultimate goal reflected certain realities of converso life, observed Kozodoy.[2] Whereas a baptized individual could not have participated in Jewish study circles focusing on Talmud, philosophy, or Kabbalah (which Duran portrays as competing disciplines on the Jewish cultural landscape),[3] conversos retained access to Scripture. Even those who could not understand the meaning of the words might still have been able to sound out the Hebrew.[4]

Informed by her work and by that of others,[5] this essay will reexamine Duran's seemingly dissonant claims about the locus of Torah's power, and the ways in which that power could be accessed and used. Duran's biblical grammar, *Ma'aseh efod* (Work of the priestly breastplate) is an analytical tool, an aid to the intellectual comprehension of Torah. Yet in the preface to that work, Duran claims that the power of Torah is accessible through somatic, rather than cognitive, engagement, and that the locus of that power is the scriptural artifact. These are conspicuously discordant claims. If Duran believed that mere vocal or visual engagement with the material text of

Torah could attract the divine effluence, why would he have composed an aid to comprehending Torah's content?[6]

For want of space, this attempt to reconstruct the unity of Duran's worldview can only nod to three of the broader contexts in which it should be situated. The author's melange of claims reflects a well-attested moment in the history of science when medieval rationalists simultaneously privileged empirical observation, and yet clung to inherited metaphysical teachings.[7] Duran's perspectives also evoke the interpenetration of philosophy and Kabbalah in Jewish thought of the fourteenth and fifteenth centuries.[8] Lastly, the methodological assumptions of this study place it in dialogue with works on pre-modern Jewish thought that emphasize the historical contingency of terms like "rationalism," "science," and "occult."[9]

❊ ❊ ❊

Like thousands of other Jews, Duran—also known as Isaac ben Moses Halevi, "Efodi,"[10] and Honoratus de Bonafide—converted to Catholicism during Spain's anti-Jewish riots of 1391.[11] In the years before the onset of the Inquisition (1478), the Disputation of Tortosa (1413–14) and the implementation of restrictive laws (1412) fanned by Vincent Ferrer's incendiary anti-Jewish preachings, Duran, as a Christian, produced several Hebrew works that were intended to improve the lot of his beleaguered compatriots—Jews and conversos alike.[12] His anti-Christian polemics of 1395 to 1397, 'Al tehi ka-avotekha (Be not like your fathers) and Kelimat ha-goyim (Shame of the gentiles),[13] were militant contributions to this project, but his biblical grammar, appearing at a highly charged moment, was designed to aid in a different way. Ma'aseh efod was composed in 1403, the year that was to mark the end of exile (galut), according to the widely-known calculations of Nahmanides, Spanish Jewry's towering scholar of the thirteenth century.[14] Because Duran regarded Scripture as "the proximate cause of the Nation's existence and survival in this long galut,"[15] he intended for his own composition, an aid to Hebrew Bible study, to serve as a catalyst of redemption.

Duran's unique reading of Jewish history highlights the salvific powers of Scripture. Intervals of national vitality are understood as ones in which Jews had intensely engaged Torah, and times of national crisis are portrayed as ones in which Torah had been neglected.[16] He claims, for example, that the felicitous return to Zion and reestablishment of the Temple following the Babylonian Exile were coterminous with the activity of the biblical scribes (sofrim) and with the creation of Masorah, the corpus of tradition that preserves Scripture's precision. By the same token, the Temple's destruction and the period of decline that immediately preceded it are portrayed as having occurred in an era when Jews turned away from Bible to study other subjects. Duran strikingly frames the first 1200 years of the post-70 dispersion as a period of calm. Jews found favor in the eyes of their neighbors during this interval, he claims, because the works they composed enhanced access to Torah and intensified divine protection. Mishnah and Talmud helped to clarify biblical legislation, while writings by Babylonian geonim and by Spanish, French, and Ashkenazi scholars focused on Scripture.[17] In his own time, he laments, the signs of divine Providence are palpably absent. Contemporary Jews suffer, claims Duran, because they "terminate their days" studying the Talmud, a notoriously difficult work. Jewish neglect of Torah is the cause of the national crisis in his time.[18]

In setting forth his remarks on the power of Torah, Duran takes pains to distinguish his own perspective from those of two discrete groups of Jews, one that operates with faulty metaphysical assumptions, and another that is epistemologically misguided. Jews who imagine that rote performance of biblical commandments is efficacious, even when unaccompanied by intellectual and spiritual intention, constitute the first mistaken group. As Kozodoy noted, Duran's insistence on intention as the key to sacramental efficacy abetted his larger project in two ways. He was able to deflect blame from the conversos (who did not perform the commandments at all) by assigning culpability for the nation's crisis to unconverted Jews whose religious performance lacked proper intent.[19] Moreover, Kozodoy observed, conversos could find comfort in a theological perspective that enabled them to view their own—mechanical—performance of Christian rite as "an empty action," devoid of religious meaning and efficacy.[20]

But if Duran's critique of this mistaken perspective was self-serving, it was also consistent with his understanding of the cosmos and its structure. According to Duran's metaphysics—a pastiche of Aristotelian and Neoplatonic notions[21]—all entities within the cosmos experience the flow (or effluence) of God's power because all are situated on the Chain of Being. The nearer an entity is to the Source itself, the stronger its experience of divinity. To put it in other words, the number of intermediaries (emtsaim) that separate an entity from God affects that entity's experience of Providence (whether strong or weak). Distance from God also determines the channel through which an entity engages the divine effluence. Entities closest to the Source, like angels and celestial orbs, experience the divine flow intellectually because they are nonmaterial.[22] The same is true of Torah's content. This is why students of Scripture's teachings can only "tap into" the divine effluence through intellectual engagement.[23] Duran's metaphysics inform his insistence that performance of the Torah's commandments are only efficacious when accompanied by proper cognitive intention. He makes this point by contrasting the power of medicine with the power of the commandments: "the action of medical drugs is natural, while biblical deeds [i.e., performed commandments] are activated by intellect and thought."[24]

The same metaphysical scheme explains why Duran regards the mentally laborious pursuit of biblical grammar as an activity possessing redemptive potential. Acquired through rational analysis and disciplined study, grammar is the entryway to the study of Tanakh, and in this sense, the portal to ultimate felicity.

> the summum bonum will be apprehended through engagement with Torah and through
> the intensified investigation and probing of it, and of the prophetic books. And the

starting point and cause of their comprehension is the comprehension of the truth of the Hebrew language, which is the Sacred Tongue, and knowledge of variations in the uses of [its] verbs, nouns and adjectives.[25]

According to Duran's metaphysical scheme, entities like humans, animals, vegetation, and minerals do not experience the divine effluence through the unmediated intellectual pathway reserved for the nonmaterial. Instead, their experience of divine power is mediated through the pathway of *nature,* channeled by the constellations.[26] Though never explicitly stated, it is this assumption that lies behind the assertion that a devotee's somatic engagement of Torah, qua artifact, strengthens the flow of divine effluence. After all, whether the material text of Torah takes the form of a scroll or of a codex, it is a composite of natural products including leather, sinews, vegetable or mineral-based ink, and wood. Each technology involved in manufacturing the artifact—flaying, dehairing, liming, soaking, stretching, stitching, scraping, shaving, buffing, cutting, line tracing, and writing, to mention only those involved in parchment preparation—demands the artisan's strenuous involvement with products of nature. And because each of these products has its proper place on the Chain of Being, each, in its own measure, is a node of the divine effluence. For this reason, one who would strengthen this flow, and experience Providence more intensely, may do so by engaging the *text* of Scripture (as opposed to its *content*) in manners that befit a composite of nature, by engaging the artifact in manners that are sensory (rather than intellectual).

Duran not only mentions, but recommends, two ways in which one may engage Torah (*la'asok ba-Torah*) using the senses. One is to audibly pronounce the words of Scripture, even without comprehension.[27] Commenting on the scriptural phrase enjoining perpetual engagement with Torah—"And you shall utter it day and night" (Josh 1:8)—Duran distinguishes quite explicitly between vocalization (*hagaha*) and reading with understanding:

> It is wondrous that it said, "and you shall utter it" (*ve-hagita bo*). For mere utterance (*hagaha*), that is, calling it out [without comprehension], is of that which leads to this *proprium* (i.e., *segulah*). And even more so if, along with this, there is good comprehension (of Scripture's meaning).[28]

One who can intellectually comprehend Torah's content can draw the divine effluence with greater intensity, given the absence of intermediaries. But one unable to do so is in no way barred from the efficacious activity of spiritual exertion. Expanding on this point, Duran juxtaposes his own perspective with that expressed by Maimonides in *Guide for the Perplexed*, III.51. Duran normally defended the twelfth-century master, but in this case, he disagrees with Maimonides' identification of silent meditation as the only way for humans to connect with God, and calls, instead, for engagement of Torah through the senses.

He [Maimonides] set down as a condition . . . the rectification of intention and the emptying [of the mind] of thought, for this is the true worship that is fitting for God, as it says "You shall love the Lord your God with all your heart" (Dt 6:5). But I say that engagement, and the mere utterance and reading of them [i.e., words of Scripture without comprehension] is also some part of this worship, and of that which assists in drawing the Divine influence and Providence—by means of the *proprium* adhering to them (*ba-segulah deveka ba-hem*). For this too is of God's will.[29]

Relying once more on the comparison of medicine's power with the power of Torah, Duran notes that gazing on the Torah is also efficacious:

And [this is] like the medical drugs: some of them are activated when taken with food and drink, and some are activated through touch, and some through smell—and also by looking, as is the case with the spectacle lens[30] for those with distorted vision. Such is the matter with this sanctuarized Scripture (*ha-mikra ha-mekudash ha-zeh*). For the facets of the actions that are drawn from its *proprium* change.[31] And it, too, is active, in some manner, when gazed upon, and (through) reading and utterance.[32]

Many earlier (and contemporaneous) Jews had ascribed theurgic powers to Torah,[33] but Duran differs from them in that his perspective is not rooted in mysticism. As he sees it, somatic engagement with Torah can attract the divine effluence through natural, and not supernatural, processes.[34]

Duran's commitment to the explanatory value (what we might call, the scientific utility) of observing natural processes is evident in his harsh epistemological critique of the philosophers. This group, according to Duran, engages in:

mere supposition and overflowing thought (*sevara u-mahshava goveret*), fine for the credulous who live by their faith [cf. Hab 2:4], without seeking proof . . . [M]erely spoken words lacking any reality outside of the soul . . . [T]he craft of dialectic[35] [is one] in which you don't look for agreement between that which is sensed and that which is pictured in the soul, but instead, force reality to accord with opinions . . . For [i.e., whereas] the intellect, by its nature, can neither incline toward, nor concede to any of this.[36]

Philosophers do not advance true understanding of the world, claims Duran, because they limit their inquiries to matters of logic, and thus perpetuate received teachings that lack sensory corroboration. "For with all their investigations, the philosophers would not be able to apprehend the form of the tiniest plant, or of any of the other existents."[37] Duran not only regards empirical observation as the *essential* epistemological pathway, he is also of the opinion that its explanatory potential has yet to be fully realized. True, he notes, the therapeutic efficacy of medicines and of eyeglasses are not understood by people living in his time. Yet the present stage of ignorance does not imply that these aids work outside of the natural framework![38] Whether he intended the word *nisayon* to denote "experience" or "experiment," Duran seems to hold out hopes for future breakthroughs in the understanding of natural processes:

> The powers of the existents, and their *propria,* were also not apprehended through dialectic and logic, and there is nothing about them that the intellect can discern. Rather, whatever is known of them is known via experience/experiment (*nisayon*) and the senses. And then, [i.e., later] perhaps, a rational explanation can be ascribed to them.[39]

❈ ❈ ❈

Ma'aseh efod's preface contains two sets of guidelines for engaging Torah through the senses. One is Duran's microtreatise on memory enhancement; this literary unit, the first of its kind in Jewish literature,[40] reflects ancient and medieval understandings of memory as a physiological process triggered by somatic experience. Most of the fifteen recommendations on Duran's list are designed to accomplish one or more of the following tasks: intensify the individual's powers of concentration; render more indelible the image to be stored in memory; ensure proper storage of the datum, or facilitate its swift retrieval from storage.[41]

Duran's other set of instructions for engaging Torah through the senses takes the form of a guided contemplative practice. The devotee should start by noting the structural equivalence between the tripartite Tanakh [consisting of *Torah, Nevi'im* and *Ketuvim*] and the tripartite Temple. The former, writes Duran,

> is equivalent in its *propria* (*be-segulotav*) to the Temple . . . its earliest division was into three parts—as was the case in the Temple. For it [i.e., the Temple] had a *Sanctum Sanctorum,* the site of the ark and Torah scroll; and the Sanctuary, site of the table and candelabrum and the golden altar; and the Courtyard or Hall, containing the sacrificial altar.[42]

These parallels are not accidental, Duran intimates, for both material objects—the textual artifact of Hebrew Bible and the Temple—have been proximate causes of Providence. Both, moreover, have served as agents of expiation/atonement (*kaparah*) for the Jewish people.[43] Indeed, notes Duran, the respective roles of Tanakh and Temple have at times converged. As long as the Temple stood, it housed the Torah. But, since the Temple's destruction, the Tanakh has functioned as a surrogate Temple, or, in the words of the prophet Ezekiel (2:16), as a *mikdash me'at,* a "micro-sanctuary." Throughout his preface to *Ma'aseh efod,* Duran eschews the conventional term "sacred Scripture" (*sefer ha-kodesh* or *ha-sefer ha-kadosh*) and instead refers to Tanakh as *ha-sefer ha-mekudash* (i.e., the sanctuarized Scripture). He notes with approval the practice of referring to Tanakh codices by the term *Mikdashya* (i.e., God's Temple).[44]

Having established the correspondences between the triadic structures of Temple and Tanakh, Duran prescibes an exertionary task. The contemplating devotee must now bring to mind a third, cosmic, triad:[45]

Its [the Tanakh's] tripartite division parallels the division of the Temple, and thus calls it to mind. And this, in its entirety, is a simulacrum (*mashal ve-dimyon*) of the three parts of existence which are: the world of the intellect for the God of Israel and the holy angels; and the celestial world and those pure material bodies, and this lower world, world of generation and of loss.[46]

In this brief passage, Duran indicates quite explicitly how the physical artifact of Tanakh might be used as a site of recollective collation[47] and as a springboard to facilitate ascent through increasing levels of abstraction. The spiritual gymnast starts by sensorily engaging the scriptural text, a material object that is present, and then calls to mind the Temple, a material object that is absent. Using this mental image as a launching pad, s/he ultimately conjures the realm that is devoid of all materiality, the Source of all. When understood in light of Duran's metaphysics, this contemplative praxis need not only be seen as one that alters the consciousness of the devotee, but as one that links the material with the spiritual, intensifying the divine effluence and hastening redemption.

⌦ ⌦ ⌦

Duran's strategy for "instrumentalizing" Tanakh sheds new light on a cultural phenomenon that has long engaged historians of Jewish art.[48] For around a millennium, Jews had produced no depictions of either the Temple of Solomon or of the portable Sanctuary. This changed in the late 1200s; between the late thirteenth century and the end of the fourteenth, more than twenty Hebrew Bible manuscripts were produced in Spain and Provence, each containing lavish illuminations of the Temple or Sanctuary, and of its implements. These illustrations appear at the beginning of the Bible codices in question, often in multiple folio carpet pages.[49] Most scholarship on this cultural phenomenon understands these as images of messianic import, affirmations of Jewish belief in the imminent redemption.

Duran's guided meditation adds a new dimension to this explanation. It provides evidence that images of the Temple (or Sanctuary) vessels in Hebrew Bible codices of this time and place did not simply inspire; they were utilized in performance. Individuals with access to one of these magnificent tomes (mentioned explicitly by Duran),[50] and who were familiar with this contemplative practice, or with others,[51] used these graphics quite purposefully, in order to alter their own spiritual realities—and perhaps that of the Jewish nation as a whole.

Notes

1. See Maud Kozodoy, "A Study of the Life and Works of Profiat Duran." (Ph.D. diss.; Jewish Theological Seminary, 2006).

2. *Ma'aseh efod,* ed. Y. Friedlander and J. Kohn (Vienna, 1865), 10. Henceforth *ME.*

3. Though articulated in a tendentious context, this three-fold typology has been taken as an accurate map of curricular predilections in Duran's time. See, e.g., Yosef H. Yerushalmi, *Zakhor: Jewish History and Jewish Memory* (Seattle, Wash., 1982), 52.

4. Kozodoy, "Study," 203–04, 327.

5. The following is not an exhaustive list: Kalman Bland, "Medieval Jewish Aethetics: Maimonides, Body and Scripture in Profiat Duran," *Journal of the History of Ideas* 54 (1993): 553–59; Bland, *The Artless Jew* (Princeton, N.J., 2000), 82–91; Dov Rappel, "Hakdamat *Sefer ma'aseh efod* le-Profiat Duran," *Sinai* 100 (1987): 749–95; Josef Stern, "Meaning and Language," in *Cambridge History of Jewish Philosophy*, ed., S. Nadler and T. Rudavsky (Cambridge, 2009), 245–53; Isadore Twersky, "Religion and Law," in *Religion in a Religious Age*, ed. S. D. Goitein (Cambridge, Mass., 1974), 69–82; Irene Zwiep, "Jewish Scholarship and Christian Tradition in Late-Medieval Catalonia: Profiat Duran on the Art of Memory," in *Hebrew Scholarship and the Medieval World*, ed. N. de Lange (Cambridge, 2001), 224–39.

6. On Duran's concept of the divine effluence (*shefa'*), see Kozodoy, "Study," 265. The tension between these perspectives is noted by Rappel, "Hakdamat," 750–51, and by Kozodoy, "Study," 287. On the location of charisma outside the scholastic realm, see Michael Swartz, *Scholastic Magic* (Princeton, N.J., 1996), 205, 220; 225–26.

7. Katherine Tachau, "Logic's God and the Natural Order in Late Medieval Oxford: The Teaching of Robert Holcot," *Annals of Science* 53 (1996): 235–67, esp. 238.

8. The literature on this is vast, and growing. Among the many relevant writings, see Ze'ev Harvey, "Yesodot kabaliyim be-*Sefer or ha-shem* le-Rav Hasdai Crescas," *Meḥkere Yerushalayim Bi-Maḥshevet Yisrael* 2 (1983): 75–109; Shaul Regev, "Ha-maḥshava ha-ratsionalit-mistit be-hagut ha-yehudit ba-me'ah ha-15," *Meḥkere Yerushalayim be-maḥshevet Yisrael* 5 (1986): 155–89; Dov Schwartz, "Maga'im ben pilosofya le-mistikah yehudit be-reshit ha-me'ah ha-15," *Da'at* 29 (1992): 41–67; Hava Tirosh-Samuelson, "Philosophy and Kabbalah: 1200–1600," in *The Cambridge Companion to Medieval Jewish Philosophy*, ed. D. H. Frank and O. Leaman (Cambridge, 2003), 218–57

9. See for example, David Ruderman, *The World of a Renaissance Jew: The Life and Thought of Abraham ben Mordecai Farissol* (Cincinnati, Ohio, 1981), 119–30; Ruderman, *Kabbalah, Magic and Science: The Cultural Universe of a Sixteenth-Century Jewish Physician* (Cambridge, Mass.,1988), 1–3; Ruderman, *Jewish Thought and Scientific Discovery in Early Modern Europe.* (New Haven, Conn., 1995), *passim*. On the revaluation of vocabulary that facilitated the transition from medieval to modern worldviews, see Amos Funkenstein, *Theology and the Scientific Imagination from the Middle Ages to the Seventeenth Century* (Princeton, N.J., 1986). On the anachronistic tendency (often associated with Pierre Duhem) to identify as "science" only those intellectual phenomena which would warrant that label in the researcher's own time, see Tachau, "Logic's God," 235–36, and John Murdoch, "Pierre Duhem and the History of Late Medieval Science and Philosophy in the Latin West," in *Gli stui di filosofia medievale fra otto e novecento,* ed. A. Maieru (Rome, 1991), 253–302.

10. On the significance of the name "Efodi," see Kozodoy, "Study," 48–49.

11. Though Duran's apostasy was first noted in Richard Emery, "New Light on Profayt Duran 'The Efodi,'" *JQR* 58.4 (1967/68): 328–37, some doubts remained. In an as yet unpublished article, Maud Kozodoy points to definitive proof of Duran's apostasy, drawn from a Hebrew letter sent by the Christian Hebraist, Marco Lippomano, to the Jew Crescas Meir in 1420. The letter appears in G. Busi and S. Campanini, "Marco Lippomano and Crescas Meir: A Humanistic Dispute in Hebrew," in *Una Manna Buona per Mantova: Man Tov le-Man Tova,* ed. M. Perani (Mantua, 2004), 185.

12. On the assumption that Duran wrote for knowledgeable readers of Hebrew, see Daniel Lasker, "Popular Polemics and Philosophical Truth in the Medieval Jewish Critique of Christianity," *Journal of Jewish Thought and Philosophy* 8 (1999): 252–53; Kozodoy, "Study," 131.

13. Jeremy Cohen, "Profiat Duran's *The Reproach of the Gentiles* and the Development of Christian Anti-Jewish Polemic," in *Shlomo Simonsohn Jubilee Volume,* ed. D. Caspi, et al. (Tel Aviv, 1993), 71–84; Eleazar Gutwirth, "History and Apologetics in Fifteenth-Century Hispanic Jewish Thought," *Helmantica* 35 (1984): 231–42 ; David Berger, "On the Uses of History in Medieval Jewish Polemic against Christianity: The Search for the Historical Jesus," in *Jewish History and Jewish Memory: Essays*

in Honor of Yosef Hayim Yerushalmi, ed. E. Carlebach, J. M. Efron, and D. N. Myers, (Hanover, N.H., 1998), 25–39. Among the works by Daniel Lasker that discuss Duran's anti-Christian polemics, see "The Jewish Philosophical Critique of Transubstantiation," in *Mystics, Philosophers and Politicians,* ed. J. Reinharz and D. Swetchinski (Durham, N.C., 1982), 99–118.

14. Ramban, *Sefer ha-ge'ulah,* in *Kitve Rabi Moshe ben Naḥman,* ed. H. D. Chavel (Jerusalem, 1963), 2: 291. Baḥya ben Asher transmits this same date in *Kad ha-kemaḥ* (Warsaw, 1870), 23d. An examination of Nahmanides' end-time calculations in light of those produced by Christian millenarians in the Crown of Aragon appears in Nina Caputo, *Nahmanides in Catalonia* (Notre Dame, Ind., 2007), chap. 4.

15. *ME,* 11.

16. *ME,* 11, 13–15.

17. *ME,* 14. On late medieval Sephardi writings that portray diaspora as a place where Jews enjoyed providential protection, see Talya Fishman, "Changing Early Modern Discourse about Christianity," in *The Lion Shall Roar: Leon Modena and His World,* ed. D. Malkiel (Jerusalem, 2002), 169–71.

18. *ME,* 13–14. On the critique of "talmudocentrism" as part of a larger cultural development, see Talya Fishman, *Becoming the People of the Talmud: Oral Torah as Written Tradition in Medieval Jewish Cultures* (Philadelphia, 2011), chap. 5.

19. Kozodoy, "Study," 118.

20. The term appears in *ME,* 2. See Kozodoy, "Study," 147, 149–50. See also, Eric Lawee, "The Path to Felicity: Teachings and Tensions in *Even Shetiyyah* of Abraham ben Judah, Disciple of Hasdai Crescas," *Medieval Studies* 59 (1997): 209.

21. Kozodoy, "Study," 190, 200.

22. This is explained in the Introduction to *Ḥeshev ha-efod,* Duran's astronomical and calendrical work of 1395, which appears (in Hebrew) in the German section of *ME,* 43. See Kozodoy, "Study," 160–63, 165; 231–33; 238.

23. See Kozodoy, "Study," 239–41, and *ME,* 160.

24. *ME,* 3.

25. *ME,* 16.

26. See Kozodoy, "Study," 265.

27. On *segulah,* see ibid., 287–93.

28. *ME,* 10.

29. *ME,* 13.

30. The term used by Duran for corrective lens is "*mareh ha-tsiniyit.*" Kalman Bland considered this term in "Medieval Jewish Aesthetics," 547, n. 57.

31. This is a tentative translation, which does not account for the fact that the word *mithalef* is in the singular.

32. *ME,* 13.

33. Early rabbinic traditions portrayed Torah study as an experiential recreation of revelation. A range of Jewish mystical writings identifies the Torah (and Torah study) as possessing the power to summon God's presence supernaturally. See, for example, Moshe Idel, "Tefisat ha-Torah be-sifrut ha-hekhalot ve-gilguleha ba-kabalah," *Meḥkere Yerushalayim be-maḥshevet Yisrael* (1981): 23–84; Elliot Wolfson, "The Mystical Significance of Torah Study in German Pietism," *JQR* 84.1 (1993/94): 43–78; Wolfson, *Through a Speculum That Shines* (Princeton, N.J., 1994), 156–58.

34. See Kozodoy, "Study," 181, 186.

35. Like the more commonly encountered *ḥokhmat ha-dibur,* Duran's term, *ḥokhmat ha-devarim,* also means "craft of speech." Both the term "logic," and the Arabic, *al-mantiq,* are etymologically related to the term for spoken word. See M. Breuer, "Min'u bnekhem min ha-higayon," in *Mikhtam le-David (Memorial Volume for R. David Ochs),* ed. Y. Gilat and E. Stern (Ramat Gan, 1978), 241–42.

36. *ME,* 13.

37. Ibid.

38. *ME*, 14.

39. *ME*, 13.

40. Its appearance should be linked to the rediscovery of Aristotle's *De Memoria et Reminiscentia* in the thirteenth century. (See Mary Carruthers, *The Book of Memory* [Cambridge, 1990], 101, 150–53.) Renewed Christian interest in memory training was manifest in the composition of commentaries (by Albertus Magnus and Thomas Aquinas, among others) while Jewish interest can be seen, directly, in Efodi's pioneering Hebrew composition, and, less directly, in the growing prominence of Jewish scribal arts.

41. *ME*, 18–25.

42. *ME*, 11.

43. "Just as the Temple was the cause of the *Shekhina*'s perpetual sojourn among Israelites [Ex 25:8/Lev 26:11], so this sacred book, which is the cause of divine supervision/providence of this nation . . . is the cause of its existence, survival and success." *ME*, 11.

44. *ME*, 11–12. The phrase comes from Ex 32:16. On the use of *mikdashya* to refer to a Tanakh codex, see Yitzḥak Ben Zvi, "Mikdashya ha-Yerushalmi ve-khitve ha-Torah she-be-vate ha-kneset ha-Karaiyim be-Kushta u-ve-Mitsrayim," *Kiryat Sefer* 32 (1956/57): 366–74, esp. 366, n. 1. See also, Naftali Wieder, "Sanctuary as Metaphor for Scripture," *Journal of Jewish Studies* 8 (1957): 165–75; Joseph Gutmann, "The Messianic Temple in Spanish Hebrew Manuscripts," in *The Temple of Solomon,* ed. Gutmann (Missoula, Mont. 1977), p. 132.

45. This tripartite mapping of the cosmos would have been well known to medieval Jews. See, for example, Maimonides, *Mishneh Torah, Hil. Yesode ha-Torah* 2:3.

46. *ME*, 11.

47. See Carruthers, *Book of Memory*.

48. The following is not meant to be exhaustive: David Kaufmann, "Zur Geschichte der jüdischen Handschrift Illustration," *Gesammelte Schriften* (Frankfurt aM, 1915), 3:178–79; Cecil Roth, "Jewish Antecedents of Christian Art," *Journal of Warburg and Courtauld Institutes* 16 (1953): 25–26; Thérèse Metzger, "Les Objets du Culte, le Sanctuaire du Desert et le Temple de Jerusalem, dans les Bibles hebraïques mediévales enluminées, en Orient et en Espagne," *John Rylands Library Bulletin* 52 (1969/70), 397–436 (Pt. 1), and *John Rylands Library Bulletin* 53 (1970/71); 169–209 (Pt. 2); Gutmann, "The Messianic Temple," 125–45; Evelyn Cohen, "Decoration of Medieval Manuscripts," in *A Sign and A Witness,* ed. L. Gold (New York, 1988), 47–60; Gabrielle Sed-Rajna, "Hebrew Illuminated Manuscripts from the Iberian Peninsula," in *Convivencia: Jews, Muslims, and Christians in Medieval Spain,* ed. V. Mann, J. Dodds, T. Glick (exh. cat.; New York, 1992), 133–55; Elisheva Revel-Neher, *Le temoignage de l'absence: Les objets du culte du sanctuaire à Byzance et dans l'art juif du XIe au XVe siècles* (Paris, 1998); Eva Frojmovic, "Messianic Politics in Re-Christianized Spain: Images of the Sanctuary in Hebrew Bible Manuscripts," in *Imaging the Self, Imagining the Other,* ed. Froimovic (Leiden, 2002), 91–128; Katrin Kogman-Appel, *Jewish Book Art between Islam and Christianity* (Leiden, 2004).

49. A list of the Bible manuscripts with frontispieces featuring images of Sanctuary vessels appears in Frojmovic, "Messianic Politics," 125–27.

50. On wealthy people holding these codices in their storerooms, see *ME*, 20. And see guidelines 6 and 12 of Duran's microtreatise on memory. On book adornment as a graphic reaffirmation of the metaphorical value of the enclosed texts as *thesaurii,* i.e, treasure houses of memory, see Carruthers, *Book of Memory,* 41.

51. When juxtaposed with images of the multiwalled city of Jericho in a number of medieval Hebrew manuscripts, images of the Temple and its implements may well have been used to facilitate a contemplative practice (with a known medieval Christian analogue) of ascending from the earthly Jerusalem to the heavenly Jerusalem. I hope to discuss this, among other exertionary mental praxes undertaken by medieval Jews in a monograph.

PRINTING KABBALAH IN
SIXTEENTH-CENTURY ITALY

❊ ❊ ❊

Moshe Idel

The Hebrew University of Jerusalem

KABBALISTIC EXOTERICISM AND THE
EMERGENCE OF CHRISTIAN KABBALAH

FROM the end of the fifteenth century, kabbalistic books and ideas spread widely. This was the result of three different processes: the Italian intellectual ambiance in Florence was newly receptive to Jewish views; Spanish kabbalists now dispersed throughout the Mediterranean brought their books with them to new centers; and, last but not least, the printing of kabbalistic books led to their broad dissemination. Printing contributed substantially to the propagation of those cultural developments, which included the emergence of Christian Kabbalah in Northern Italy, enabling its dissemination beyond the small circle of scholars around the Medicis in Florence. Printing also insured the dissemination of kabbalistic traditions.

During this same period two conceptions of Jewish Kabbalah can be identified, one esoteric and the other exoteric, stemming from the different ways kabbalists studied this lore. In Spain, and following the Expulsion in the Ottoman Empire, Kabbalah was taught in talmudic academies (*yeshivot*) and transmitted both in written and oral form.[1] In late fifteenth-century Italy, prior to the arrival of Jews from the Iberian Peninsula, those interested in Kabbalah studied it exclusively from manuscripts, without the guidance of an authoritative mentor.[2] The absence of an oral tradition that could be guardedly transmitted from teacher to student contributed to the open nature of this study among the Italian kabbalists.

While it is not clear what inspired Jewish figures to discuss matters of Kabbalah openly with Christians, Christian motivation for such conversations was more apparent. The early Florentine Platonists were fascinated by ancient theologies, among them, the ancient theological doctrines of the Jews. A more traditional—missionizing—attitude toward Jews also nourished this novel interest in Kabbalah. Interestingly enough, the first individuals to print substantial quantities of kabbalistic material were Christians—Giovanni Pico della Mirandola, Paulus Riccius, Johann Reuchlin, Augustino Giustiniani, Egidio da Viterbo, Francesco Giorgi Veneto, and William Postel. Their printings preceded, in most cases, the first substantial Jewish printing of books on Kabbalah.[3]

Perusing early Christian kabbalistic books one finds theories that presumably stem from earlier Hebrew texts now lost.[4] Moreover, in at least two cases, passages from earlier Hebrew works are found embedded in Christian books. Two such examples are Hebrew quotes from Abraham Abulafia's *Sefer ge'ulah,* found in Flavius Mithridates's Latin translation still in manuscript,[5] and three Hebrew quotes from Abulafia printed in Augustino Giustiniani's *Polyglota,* only two of which are identifiable in Abulafia's extant books.[6] Likewise, some excerpts from a largely lost commentary on the Psalms by the late thirteenth-century R. Isaac ibn Sahulah was printed in the *Polyglota.*[7]

When the first Spanish kabbalists arrived in Italy,[8] Christian Kabbalah had already taken its first steps. Some Spanish converts (such as Abner of Burgos, Pedro de la Caballeria, and Paulus de Heredia) had already produced Christological interpretations of kabbalistic themes[9]—and de Heredia, who was active at the end of his life in Italy was especially well-acquainted with kabbalistic texts, and probably also forged some passages or short treatises.[10] At the end of the fifteenth century, R. Abraham Farissol, who reliably described the intellectual life in Renaissance Italy, was acquainted with other kabbalistic forgeries produced by converts in Spain.[11] Another convert, Flavius Mithridates, a native of Sicily,[12] although hardly known in Spain, translated a huge collection of Jewish kabbalistic writings for Pico della Mirandola in Italy.[13] Pico printed his *Conclusiones* in Italy based on Mithridates's translations, as did other converted Jews who were acquainted with kabbalistic concepts.[14] Some of them were of Ashkenazic origin, while Mithridates was a Sicilian. Figures like Yohanan Alemanno or Elijah del Medigo cooperated with Pico, although they remained observant Jews.[15] This was indeed a unique phenomenon; the particularistic and esoteric Kabbalah that had emerged in Spain now encountered a much more cosmopolitan setting in late fifteenth-century Northern Italy.[16]

Nevertheless, this Christian appropriation of the Kabbalah, which was deeply related to the philosophical understanding of the Kabbalah that emerged in Italy, was not mentioned in the contemporaneous writings of the Spanish kabbalists living in Italy. This silence is surprising and significant since later Italian and Spanish kabbalists living in Palestine openly reacted to the emergence of the Christian Kabbalah by the mid-sixteenth century. Notwithstanding this initial Jewish reticence to speak about the Christian Kabbalah, the many affinities between Jewish and Christian mystical sources composed in late fifteenth-century Italy were already well-known by contemporaneous Jews and Christians alike.[17]

For most Spanish Jewish kabbalists, until Moses Cordovero's more popular writings appeared in the sixteenth century, Kabbalah remained an esoteric lore to be studied by the Jewish elite. Though an awareness of such a view lingers in many Christian texts as far as the nature of the Jewish Kabbalah is concerned, for Christian intellectuals secrecy was not a crucial issue. Unhampered by an esoteric ethos, treatises on Christian Kabbalah were published sometimes as soon as they were written. For example, Pico published his kabbalistic theses in 1486 and a short time afterwards Reuchlin published his two kabbalistic works. A series of other Christian kabbalistic texts and Jewish discussions of Kabbalah appeared before the middle of the sixteenth century, decades before Jewish kabbalists dared to print their texts,[18] among them: the *Polyglota on the Psalms* compiled by Augustino Giustiniani (including several kabbalistic passages authored by R. Isaac ibn Avi Sahulah and Abraham Abulafia in their Hebrew original and in Latin translation); Francesco Giorgio Veneto's *De harmonia mundi,* Cornelius Agrippa of Nettesheim's *De occulta philosophia,* and William Postel's *Commentary on Sefer yetsirah.* All of these works greatly contributed to the dissemination of some of the most important kabbalistic views in Western Europe.[19] Postel's Latin translation of *Sefer yetsirah,* for example, was printed in Paris in 1552, ten years before the printing of the Hebrew text of this fundamental book with some commentaries by Jews in Mantua. This tension between Spanish Jewish reticence and Christian openness in Italy was a decisive factor in the ultimate decision by some Italian Jews to eventually go public and publish what they considered to be the authentic Kabbalah.

PRINTING KABBALAH BY JEWS

The printing of Christian Kabbalah thus had broad repercussions on Jewish kabbalistic publishing, some of which I have discussed elsewhere.[20] In this essay, I would like to focus on certain characteristics of the kabbalistic books published by Jews in sixteenth-century Italy. Some preliminary quantitative remarks are necessary. During the sixteenth century, the number of kabbalistic books in print was quite small compared to other Jewish literatures. Depending upon how we define a kabbalistic book, we may speak about several dozen books out of many hundreds. The vast majority of these printed kabbalistic books reflected the medieval tradition, primarily the Spanish one. Abraham Abulafia's books, however, did not play a significant role among them nor did books by Jewish Italian kabbalists during the Renaissance. On the other hand, Abulafia's opus is much better represented in the Latin translations of Mithridates and others, and in the excerpts of Augustino Giustiniani and Francesco Giorgio Veneto. The dominant role of Spanish Kabbalah in Jewish books published in the sixteenth century consistently followed an earlier confrontation between it and the Italian Kabbalah which ultimately privileged the Spanish tradition.[21] I refer specifically to an early list of kabbalistic works compiled by a major Spanish Kabbalist in Italy that enumerates both those books that he recommended and those that he found deleterious. This list parallels precisely the kabbalistic books that were eventually printed in Italy during the sixteenth century. R. Yehudah Ḥayyat wrote in his introduction to his commentary on *Sefer ma'arekhet ha-elohut*:

> These are the books that you shall approach (*tikrav 'elehem*): *Sefer yetsirah*, attributed (*ha-mekhuneh*) to R. Akiva, blessed be his memory; *Sefer ha-bahir*, attributed to R. Nehuniyah ben ha-Qanah, should be "a crown to your head"[22]; the book of the *Zohar* "should not depart from your mouth"[23]; and the books of R. Joseph Gikatilla and those of R. [Moshe ben] Shem Tov de Leon, you "shall tie them about thy neck"[24]; and the secrets of Nahmanides, "should be written upon the tablet of your heart"[25]; and the books of R. Menahem Recanati, "thou shall bind them for a sign upon thy arm"[26]; and *Sefer ma'arekhet ha-elohut* with my present commentary, "shall be as frontlets between thy eyes" and then you will be successful in your ways and then you will be illuminated.[27]

It is significant that the list of the recommended books faithfully reflects the kabbalistic sources which informed most of the discussion between R. Yehudah Ḥayyat and R. Joseph Alqastiel in their correspondence with each other.[28] With the exception of the works of Menahem Recanati, written in Italy, but replete with excerpts from books composed in Spain, and Abulafia's numerous books written in Italy and Sicily, all the above books reflect Spanish Kabbalah. On the other hand, Ḥayyat deplores the dissemination and study of kabbalistic books of Italian provenance:

> The words of the divine Sage, R. Isaac ibn Latif, blessed be his memory, the author of *Sefer [sha'ar] ha-shamayim*, and [*Tsurat*] *ha-'olam and tseror ha-mor* and *Sefer ginze ha-melekh*, are more precious than gems; but insofar as his words concern the science of Kabbalah, one of his feet is within while the other without [Kabbalah]. Consequently, you should see only a small part of them, but not see all of them. And if God will tell me to do it, I shall distinguish the fine from the coarse flour.[29]

The last sentence is crucial for understanding the entire point of Ḥayyat's discussion. He wished to distinguish between the proper and improper writings passing for Kabbalah in different Jewish circles. Despite his disapproval, ibn Latif's books were still cited by the Italian kabbalist Yohanan Alemanno and one of them even influenced Pico della Mirandola.[30]

Moreover, in the same introduction Ḥayyat admits that he has seen "many books" of Abulafia which were studied in Italy, but he refers explicitly to only three of them: *Sefer or ha-sekhel, Sefer ḥaye ha-'olam ha-ba,'* and to one of Abulafia's commentaries on the *Guide of the Perplexed*. The founder of the ecstatic school of Kabbalah is described by Ḥayyat, *inter alia,* as "mad," and his books are "replete with imaginary things and fakes invented by his heart."[31] Unlike Nahmanides' secrets, which represent the quintessence of kabbalistic secrecy and should be engraved on the heart and only transmitted orally, for Ḥayyat, Abulafia's Kabbalah is a figment of the author's imagination. Indeed, the confrontation between Abulafia and Nahmanides' main successor in Spain, the Rashba (Shlomo ben Aderet [1235–1310]) was known to Ḥayyat.[32] Ḥayyat also attacked an anonymous commentary on the book *Ma'arekhet ha-elohut,* printed as *Perush zulati* by R. Reuven Tsarfati, a kabbalist active in Italy.[33] This commentary was strongly influenced by Abulafia's thought, and it is the single treatise that related to ecstatic Kabbalah in a significant manner which was printed during the sixteenth century, albeit in a shortened form. Last on Ḥayyat's index of unworthy kabbalistic books is the fourteenth-century R. Shmuel ibn Motot, a Castilian thinker with kabbalistic propensities. The "pernicious" kabbalistic books are precisely those which had a strong impact on R. Yohanan Alemanno, the Italian contemporary of Ḥayyat. Alemanno also compiled a list of recommended books, in which three of the names criticized by Ḥayyat play a prominent and positive role.[34]

Ḥayyat's list of endorsements of theosophical Spanish Kabbalah and his disapproval of Italian and ecstatic Kabbalah need to be compared with the actual record of printing of kabbalistic books in the century that followed. Speaking retrospectively, this list may be seen as an unintended but de facto program for the publication of kabbalistic books in sixteenth-century Italy. First and foremost, Ḥayyat's book, the commentary on *Ma'arekhet ha-elohut,* from whose preface we quoted, was printed twice in 1558, in Ferrara and Mantua. The books of R. Menaham Recanati were printed much earlier; his most important work, the *Commentary on the Pentateuch,* in Venice in 1523 and again in 1545. However, the kabbalistic author who was printed more than any other in the sixteenth century was R. Joseph ben Abraham Gikatilla. His two main books, *Sha'are tsedek* (Riva de Trento, 1561) and *Sha'are orah* (Mantua and Riva de Trento, 1561), were printed relatively early, and a short text of his was printed in each of the three collections to be described below. However, his ideas were also disseminated by numerous and important citations and reverberations found in the works of R. Baḥya ben Asher, R. Menaham Recanati, R. Shem Tov ben Shem Tov and R. Meir ibn Gabbai, all of which were printed during the sixteenth century. In 1562 *Sefer yetsirah* was printed in Mantua accompanied by some of its theosophical commentaries. R. Moshe de Leon's writings were not printed in Italy in the sixteenth century. However, one of them, *Sefer ha-nefesh ha-ḥakhamah* was printed in Basel in 1608.

The three main kabbalistic books from mid-sixteenth-century Italy that were not mentioned in Ḥayyat's recommended list were R. Shem Tov ben Shem Tov's *Sefer ha-emunot* (Ferrara, 1556),[35] R. Meir ibn Gabbai's *Derekh emunah* (Padua, 1563) and his more famous *Sefer 'avodat ha-kodesh* (Venice, 1567). All three works reflect rather faithfully the theosophical-theurgical Kabbalah typical of Spain. Together with the printing of Ḥayyat's *Minhat yehudah,* the publication of ibn Gabbai's books showcases the immense success of Spanish Kabbalah in the very stronghold of Italian Jewish culture.[36]

This Sephardi propensity is no less obvious when we see the impact of the two commentaries on the Pentateuch, which contain a substantial amount of kabbalistic material: R. Baḥya ben Asher's (Venice, 1524, 1544, 1546; Riva de Trento, 1559, Venice 1566.) and R. Abraham Saba's (Venice 1523, 1567). The impact of these commentaries can be seen in a series of kabbalistic commentaries on the Pentateuch compiled in Italy in the mid-sixteenth century apparently by R. Shlomo ben Yehudah de Blanes (which is still extant in some manuscripts).[37]

Thus, the Italian Jewish printers' neglect of Abraham Abulafia's numerous books, of Yohanan Alemanno's voluminous writings, of R. Abraham de Balmes's commentary on the ten sefirot, of R. Berakhiel ben Meshullam Qafman's *Lev adam,* and Leone Ebreo's philosophical best-seller *Dialoghi d'amore,* illustrates the axial change Italian kabbalistic thought underwent during the sixteenth century, thus perpetuating an Italian tradition of absorbing and prioritizing kabbalistic material coming first from the West, especially Spain, and later from the Ottoman Empire and Safed in the East.

To be sure, I do not assume that Ḥayyat's list constituted a formal program of action for printing kabbalistic books in Italy during the sixteenth century. Though some of the Jewish Italian printers may have been acquainted with his recommendations, especially R. Isaac de Lattes who also printed Ḥayyat's book in the Ferrara edition and the *Zohar* in the Mantua edition, one can assume neither that the list shaped the printers' agenda, nor that Ḥayyat was even interested in printing kabbalistic books. Ḥayyat and another Spanish Kabbalist active in Italy after the expulsion, R. Joseph ibn Shraga, and perhaps also R. Joseph Alqastiel, contributed to a shift to more mythical forms of primarily Spanish Kabbalah among Italian Kabbalists whose basic predilection had been, before the expulsion, much more philosophical, as we have mentioned. Suffice it to look at the content of the numerous manuscripts copied in the early sixteenth century by and for the wealthy kabbalist R. Yehiel Nissim of Pisa in order to perceive the substantial change generated by the arrival of the Spanish kabbalists after the expulsion. The printers' choices mirror this change as well. Ḥayyat's attitude reflects the beginning of an attempt to resist the more universalistic leanings of pre-Expulsion Italian kabbalists, and with them the tendencies and predilections found in early Christian Kabbalah. This might explain one of the main reasons why Abulafia was hardly printed in the sixteenth century.

Looking at the content of three later collections of kabbalistic writings printed in Italy between the mid-sixteenth and early seventeenth century, one can trace not only the particular interest of sixteenth-century publishers but also that of some scribes who earlier copied kabbalistic manuscripts in Italy. *Likute shikhehah u-fe'ah* was printed in 1556 in Ferrara by R. Abraham ben Yehudah Elimelekh. It consists of lengthy extracts from R. Ezra of Gerona's *Commentary on the Talmudic Legends,*[38] several pages from Abraham Abulafia's commentary on the secrets of the *Guide of the Perplexed* entitled *Sitre Torah* composed in 1280 in Capua, but printed anonymously,[39] short treatises, one dealing with the *Secret of Bath-Sheva*, authored by R. Joseph Gikatilla,[40] another written by a certain R. Joseph ben Ḥayim,[41] as well as a short anonymous text, apparently written by R. Joseph ibn Shraga, an expelled kabbalist who migrated to Italy.[42] Thus, the vast majority of the material printed in this collection stems from Spanish forms of Kabbalah written between the early thirteenth to mid-fourteenth century.

In 1601, a collection of esoterically oriented treatises was printed in Venice under the title *Arze Levanon*. In addition to some mystical midrashic texts and some elements of Hekhalot literature, the gist of the book consists of three longer kabbalistic writings: R. Jacob ben Sheshet's *Sefer ha-emunah ve-ha-bitahon*, attributed here to Nahmanides,[43] R. Joseph Gikatilla's *Sefer ha-nikud*,[44] and his *Sod ha-ḥashmal*, an excerpt from his commentary on Ezekiel's account of the chariot.[45] Only a very short excerpt, half a page, presumably related to ecstatic Kabbalah, and dealing with various techniques of gematria, appears in this collection.[46]

Another substantial collection of kabbalistic texts, *Hekhal ha-shem*, was printed in Venice by R. Yehiel ben Israel Luria Ashkenazi, sometime between 1594 and 1604. It consists of some medieval Spanish kabbalistic treatises, like R. Joseph Gikatilla's kabbalistic secrets, R. Shem Tov ibn Ga'on's preface to his *Keter shem tov*, and a much longer tractate *Sefer ha-shem*, written by a certain R. Moshe,[47] but also much more updated kabbalistic developments, like R. Shimeon ibn Lavi's famous poem Bar Yoḥai,[48] and some Safedian kabbalistic material (such as a short treatise of Moses Cordovero on metempsychosis and shorter Lurianic commentaries).[49] Nothing in this collection reflects the interests of Renaissance Italian Jewish kabbalists, and not a single page by such a kabbalist was printed in it. This may be also related to the Polish background of the printer, a man of Ashkenazic origin.

Finally, one needs to consider the context of the printing of Kabbalah in Venice. In 1587, R. Moshe Cordovero's popular booklet *Or ne'erav* was published there, followed a year later by his *Tomer Devorah*. Both works represent a serious attempt by the publisher to disseminate the writings of this major kabbalist, inspiring several of Cordovero's students to follow suit.

These books and collections represent trends in classical Spanish Kabbalah and its offshoots in Safed, but do not include Jewish books dealing with Kabbalah written during the Renaissance in Italy, confirming the conspicuous domination of Spanish Kabbalah in Italy after 1492, at least insofar as the politics of printing is concerned. This development did not erase more philosophically-oriented Italian Kabbalah, but relegated it to the periphery. This development may help us better understand developments in contemporary Safed, the major kabbalistic center that similarly relied heavily on Spanish forms of Kabbalah, especially the *Zohar*.

In the mid-sixteenth century, when the Kabbalah blossomed in Safed, creating the most dramatic development in that lore since the late thirteenth century, the main task of the kabbalists in Italy became the preservation and publication of earlier kabbalistic books while integrating them into the new conceptual theories of Safedian Kabbalah among the followers of Luria and Cordovero. Initially, the printing of earlier kabbalistic texts in Italy resulted in relatively little alteration to their intellectual content. But Safed did seem to have sparked conceptual developments as well as the rapid dissemination of printed kabbalistic texts.

This new environment to disseminate the works of the Kabbalah is the background behind the printing of the *Zohar*. The printing of this chef d'oeuvre stirred bitter controversy among some Italian Jewish authorities.[50] The Italian Jewish printers R. Isaac de Lattes and his son-in-law R. Meshullam of St. Angelo presented their decision to print it as part of a messianic effort to spread its secrets, and thereby prepare for the coming of the Messiah. This messianic pretext was at times accepted by modern scholarship as the real, or at least the main motive, for the printing of the *Zohar*.[51] However, these two kabbalists closely involved in the printing of the *Zohar*, themselves authors of other kabbalistic writings, were not known as messianic activists, nor were their opponents accused of anti-messianic views. Influenced rather by Yohanan Alemanno's exoteric Kabbalah, the printers copied some of his voluminous treatises and carefully studied them.[52] On the other hand they did neglect the publication of esoteric kabbalistic books from Spain, the super commentaries on Nahmanides, and the writings of R. David ben Yehudah he-Ḥasid. Their printing decisions not to publish such works present a fascinating contrast to the importance these same works held among contemporary kabbalists in Safed. Presumably the esoteric bent of Nahmanides' school contributed something to the reticence concerning printing the *Zohar*, as Joseph Hacker has shown.[53] In any case, to attribute messianic expectations and propaganda as the catalyst of the printing of the *Zohar*, as Isaiah Tishby once argued, appears unfounded.[54] Instead, we may adopt the statement of a contemporary kabbalist, who formulated the affair as follows: "The printing of the *Zohar* was for us a remedy for the loss of the Talmud."[55]

The printing of kabbalistic books written by a contemporary Italian kabbalist only begins at the end of the sixteenth century with the publication of the writings of R. Menahem Azariah of Fano. This prodigious and prolific thinker became an authority in matters of Kabbalah, an expert and disseminator of Safedian kabbalistic ideas whose status was unparalleled by any of his Italian contemporaries.[56] Yet, the substance of his writings appears to me to represent mere elaborations upon the Safedian Kabbalah in its Cordoverian and Lurianic forms, with only minor additions that may be traced to his Italian background. In general, the last third of the sixteenth century in Italy witnesses, in matters of Kabbalah, a turn from the West to the East. If by the West we refer to the Kabbalah composed in the Iberian Peninsula or by exiles who left it and printed mainly in the second third of the sixteenth century, by the last third of the century Safedian Kabbalah of the East and its reverberations especially in the form of Fano's writings became the most prominent form of printed Kabbalah. As in the first two thirds of this century, when almost no Italian kabbalist saw his books in print, so too in the last third, Italian kabbalists, like

Abraham Yagel,[57] were unsuccessful in printing their writings. Whereas Italy had generated many of the most important publications of Christian Kabbalah, Jewish Italian Kabbalah remained mostly in manuscript. Thus insofar as Italian kabbalistic printing served as a cultural agent, it did so by disseminating the intellectual products created by kabbalists stemming from Spain and later Safed.[58]

SOME CONCLUSIONS

The exoteric nature of Kabbalah produced on Italian soil—Jewish and Christian—was indubitably influential on the printing of the Kabbalah. However, the actual books printed by Jews reflect the victory of Spanish Kabbalah in Italy. Though the Italian kabbalist R. Menahem Recanati's book was printed as early as 1523, most of the kabbalistic books were printed between 1556 and 1566, in the aftermath of the burning of the Talmud in 1553. This acceleration in the printing of kabbalistic books precisely in the years immediately following the lack of available important Hebrew books occasioned by the flames of the Holy See is significant and needs to be emphasized more in accounts of the publication of the *Zohar*.

For different reasons, an exoteric turn in promoting kabbalistic doctrine is evident in the writings of R. Moshe Cordovero and his disciples. Cordovero's prodigious literary activity also flourished during the decade from 1556 to 1566. This turn, represented by the printing of his two books mentioned above, together with the printing of the *Zohar* in Italy, and the dissemination of Kabbalah among Christians are all parallel phenomena that characterize the dissemination of kabbalistic books and ideas in the second third of the sixteenth century. However, while this exoteric trend remained unchallenged in Italy for at least two generations, the situation in Safed was different. R. Isaac Luria's circle insisted on stringent instructions for secrecy.[59] Luria's teachings were carefully reserved for a few select kabbalists and jealously kept from the eyes of curious scholars long after his death. Although some Lurianic treatises made their way to Italy and Greece,[60] the largest part of the kabbalistic corpus in the possession of R. Ḥayim Vital remained unknown, and in very many cases, incomprehensible to the wider public for several decades. Luria and Vital attempted to return to Nahmanides' form of esotericism, and Vital explicitly invoked one of the passages of the Geronese master to justify his secrecy.[61]

However, the passion of the kabbalists and the power of print could not be stopped. Italian kabbalists sent Lurianic treatises from Safed to Italy, and by the end of the sixteenth century, one of Luria's students, R. Israel Sarug, made his way to Venice to teach Kabbalah.[62] Neither the unequalled authority of Luria among kabbalists and non-kabbalists nor the zeal of Vital to keep those Lurianic books secret could prevent this material from reaching the eyes of outsiders. R. Yeḥiel Ashkenazi, apparently related to Luria, printed short Lurianic treatises in his *Hekhal ha-shem*, as noted above. R. Ḥayim Vital's brother, R. Moshe, so a tradition argues, allowed a curious and rich kabbalist, R. Joshua bin Nun of Safed, to copy Lurianic treatises in manuscripts while Vital himself was ill in 1587.[63] R. Moshe granted this privilege for a nice bribe, fifty guldens. Indeed, as R. Isaac Sagi Nahor put it, "the written thing has no master," or according to another possible reading, it has no closet.[64] Isaac Sagi-Nahor and Isaac Luria formulated traditionalist rhetoric and perhaps also practices to keep secrets hidden. However, the cultural processes they attempted to neutralize were too powerful and the interest in these secrets was too keen. Without a doubt printing was a leading factor in unveiling this new hidden lore.

Notes

1. See Joseph R. Hacker, "On the Intellectual Character and Self-Perception of Spanish Jewry in the Late Fifteenth Century" (Hebrew), *Sefunot* 17, (n.s.) 2 (1983): 52–56.

2. And, in at least one instance—that of R. David Messer Leon—against the will of his father, who was also his teacher. Cf. Solomon Schechter, "Notes sur Messer David Leon," *Revue des Études Juives* 24 (1892): 121; Hava Tirosh-Rothschild, *Between Worlds: The Life and Thought of Rabbi David ben Judah Messer Leon* (Albany, N.Y., 1991).

3. See Moshe Idel, "Particularism and Universalism in Kabbalah, 1480–1650," in *Essential Papers on Jewish Culture in Renaissance and Baroque Italy*, ed. D. B. Ruderman (New York, 1992), 324–44. On the printing of the Jewish book in the sixteenth century see Joseph R. Hacker and Adam Shear, eds., *The Hebrew Book in Early Modern Italy* (Philadelphia, 2011).

4. See, e.g., Idel, "Il mondo degli angeli in forma umana," *La Rassegna Mensile di Israel* 63.1 (1997): 73–75.

5. Those quotes were not included in Raphael Kohen, *Rabbi Abraham Abulafia ben Samuel, Liber Redemptionis* (Jerusalem, 2001).

6. See M. Idel, "A Unique Manuscript of an Untitled Treatise of Abraham Abulafia in Biblioteca Laurentiana Medicea," *Kabbalah* 17 (2008): 27–28.

7. Genoa, 1516, e.g., the excerpt included alongside Psalm 49.

8. See M. Idel, "Encounters between Spanish and Italian Kabbalists in the Generation of the Expulsion," in *Crisis and Creativity in the Sephardic World*, ed. B. R. Gampel (New York, 1997), 189–222.

9. See Gershom Scholem, "Considerations sur l'histoire des débuts de la Kabbale chrétienne," in *Kabbalistes Chrétiens,* ed A. Faivre and F. Tristan (Paris, 1979), 31–36. On the latter, see François Secret, "L'Ensis Pauli de Paulus de Heredia," *Sefarad* 26 (1966): 79–102, 254–71.

10. Scholem, "Considerations," 31–32; Secret, "L'Ensis," 86–89.

11. Scholem, "Considerations," 36–38; David B. Ruderman, *The World of a Renaissance Jew: The Life and Thought of Abraham ben Mordecai Farissol* (Cincinnati, Ohio, 1981), 47–51.

12. It should also be mentioned that de Heredia had visited Sicily, accounting, in my opinion, for his acquaintance with Abulafia's kabbalistic thought. See Secret, "L'Ensis," 100.

13. See Chaim Wirszubski, *Pico della Mirandola's Encounter with Jewish Mysticism* (Cambridge, Mass., 1989).

14. See Ruderman, *The World of a Renaissance Jew*, 43–47.

15. On del Medigo's relationship to Pico see Bohdan Kieszkowski, "Les rapports entre Elie del Medigo et Pico de la Mirandole," *Rinascimento* 4 (1964): 58–61.

16. See Idel, "Particularism and Universalism."

17. See Ruderman, "Hope against Hope," and David Ruderman, "The Italian Renaissance and Jewish Thought," in *Renaissance Humanism: Foundations, Forms, and Legacy*, 3 vols.; ed. A. Rabil, Jr. (Philadelphia, 1988), I: 405–12.

18. See Idel, "Particularism and Universalism."

19. See Frances Amelia Yates, *The Occult Philosophy in the Elizabethan Age* (London, 1979), 189–90; Wilhelm Schmidt-Biggemann, *Philosophia Perennis, Historische Umrisse abendländischer Spiritualität in*

Antike, Mittelalter und Früher Neuzeit (Frankfurt aM, 1998); Schmidt-Biggemann, "Christian Kabbala: Joseph Gikatilla (1247–1305), Johannes Reuchlin (1455–1522), Paulus Riccius (d. 1541), and Jacob Boehme (1575–1624)," in *The Language of Adam, Die Sprache Adams,* ed. A. Coudert (Wiesbaden, 1999), 81–121.

20. See Moshe Idel, *Absorbing Perfections: Kabbalah and Interpretation* (New Haven, Conn., 2002), 461–65.

21. See Idel "Encounters."

22. Exodus Rabbah 19.8.

23. Josh 1:8.

24. Prov 6:21.

25. Prov 3:3; 7:3.

26. Deut 6:7.

27. *Minhat Yehudah* (Mantua, 1558), fols. 3b–4a.

28. See the books quoted in the text edited by Gershom Scholem, "To the Knowledge of Kabbalah on the Eve of the Expulsion" (Hebrew), *Tarbiz* 24 (1955): 167–206, and the reference to three commentaries on Nahmanides' kabbalistic secrets and some folios from the book of the *Zohar* in an epistle of R. Isaac Mor Hayim, a Sephardi kabbalist, who visited Italy before the expulsion from Spain, to R. Isaac of Pisa. From the context it is clear that the Italian kabbalist did not possess these writings. See Yael Nadav, "An Epistle of the Qabbalist R. Isaac Mar Hayim Concerning the Doctrine of 'Supernal Lights'" (Hebrew), *Tarbiz* 26 (1957): 458.

29. *Minhat Yehudah*, fol. 3b.

30. See Moshe Idel, "The Study Program of Yohanan Alemanno" (Hebrew), *Tarbiz* 48 (1979): 309–10, n. 64; Idel, "The Throne and the Seven-Branched Candlestick: Pico della Mirandola's Hebrew Source," *Journal of the Warburg and Courtauld Institutes* 40 (1977): 290–92.

31. *Minhat Yehudah*, fol. 3b.

32. See Moshe Idel, "R. Shlomo ibn Adret and Abraham Abulafia: For the History of a Neglected Polemic," in *Atara L'Haim, Studies in the Talmud and Medieval Rabbinic Literature in Honor of Professor Haim Zalman Dimitrovsky,* ed. D. Boyarin et al. (Hebrew; Jerusalem, 2000), 235–51.

33. See Ephraim Gottlieb, *Studies in Kabbalistic Literature*, ed. J. Hacker (Hebrew; Tel Aviv, 1976), 357–69.

34. Idel, "The Study Program," 329–330.

35. On this book, see Meir Benayahu, "A Source about the Exiles from Spain in Portugal and Their Departure to Saloniki after the Decree of 1506" (Hebrew), *Sefunot* (o.s.) 11 (1971/78): 236–44 and Menahem Schmelzer, "Hebrew Manuscripts and Printed Books among the Sephardim before and after the Expulsion," in *Crisis and Creativity*, 262.

36. In this context the printing in 1566 in Venice, of R. Moshe Galante's *Mafteahha-Zohar,* a helpful key to the study of the book of the *Zohar*, needs to be mentioned.

37. See M. Idel, "R. David ben Yehudah he-Hasid's Translation to the Zohar" (Hebrew), *'Ale Sefer* 8 (1980): 96–98.

38. Fols. 1a–20b. On the precise content of those folios see Isaiah Tishby, *Commentarius in Aggadot, auctores R. Azriel Geronensi* (Hebrew; Jerusalem, 1945), 12.

39. See fols. 23a–35b.

40. Fols. 37a–38b. On fol. 39a there are some short discussions dealing with the rationale of the commandments by the same kabbalist.

41. See fols. 21a–23b; On this obscure kabbalist see M. Idel, *Kabbalah: New Perspectives* (New Haven, Conn., 1988), 350, n. 333.

42. Ibn Shraga's text has been printed on fols. 39b–40a. On this text, see Gershom Scholem, "The Author of the Forged Sohar [*sic*] Fragment in the Time of Rabbi Abraham Ha-Levy . . ."

(Hebrew), *Kiryat Sefer* 8 (1931/1932): 262–65, and Isaiah Tishby, *Messianism in the Time of the Expulsion from Spain and Portugal* (Hebrew; Jerusalem, 1985), 131–49.

43. Fols. 7a–32b.

44. Fols. 33a–40a. On this treatise and its different versions see Gottlieb, in *Studies*, 99–105.

45. Fols. 40b–42a.

46. See fol. 47b.

47. See Gershom Scholem, "Ha-'im ḥiber R. Moshe de Leon 'et *Sefer ha-Shem?*" *Kiryat Sefer* 1 (1924/25): 45–52. See now Michal Oron, ed., *Sefer ha-Shem, Attributed to R. Moses de Leon* (Los Angeles, 2010).

48. Fols. 44b–45a. See Boaz Huss, *Sockets of Fine Gold: The Kabbalah of Rabbi Shim'on ibn Lavi* (Hebrew; Jerusalem, 2000), 23.

49. See, respectively, fol. 36a–37b, and fols. 44ab, 46b–47a. This printer also published in Venice in 1601 the entire work of another main Safedian mystic and a disciple of Cordovero, R. Eleazar Azikri's *Sefer ḥaredim.*

50. See Isaiah Tishby, *Studies in Kabbalah and Its Branches* (Hebrew, Jerusalem, 1982), 1:79–130; Joseph Hacker, "A New Epistle from the Polemic Concerning the Publication of the Zohar in Italy," in *Massu'ot: Studies in Kabbalistic Literature and Jewish Philosophy in Memory of Prof. Ephraim Gottlieb*, ed. M. Oron and A. Goldreich (Hebrew; Jerusalem, 1994), 120–30, who updated the pertinent bibliography on the topic.

51. Tishby, *Studies*, 127–30.

52. See Idel, "Major Currents in Italian Kabbalah," in *Essential Papers*, 347–48.

53. Hacker, "A New Epistle," 127–30. The anonymous author of the document he cited relies on one of Rashba's responsa.

54. See Idel, *Kabbalah: New Perspectives*, 257, Idel, "Major Currents," 244, 248–249, and Hacker, "A New Epistle," 126 and n. 27.

55. See David Tamar, "On the Printing of the Zohar," reprinted in his *Studies in the History of the Jewish People in Eretz Israel and in Italy* (Hebrew; Jerusalem, 1972), 164–65.

56. See Joseph Avivi, "Rabbi Menaḥem Azariah of Fano's Writings in Matter of Kabbalah" (Hebrew), *Sefunot* (n.s.) 19.4 (1989): 347–76; Reuven Bonfil, "New Information on Rabbi Menaḥem Azariah da Fano and His Age," in *Studies in the History of Jewish Society in the Middle Ages and in the Modern Period. Presented to Professor Jacob Katz*, ed. I. Etkes and Y. Salmon (Hebrew; Jerusalem, 1980), 103–04; Bonfil, "Halakhah, Kabbalah, and Society: Some Insights into Rabbi Menaḥem Azariah da Fano's Inner World," in *Jewish Thought in the Seventeenth Century*, ed. I. Twersky and B. Septimus (Cambridge, Mass., 1987), 39–61.

57. David Ruderman, *Kabbalah, Magic, and Science: The Cultural Universe of a Sixteenth-Century Jewish Physician* (Cambridge, Mass., 1988).

58. See also Zeev Gries, *The Book as the Agent of Culture, between 1700–1900* (Hebrew; Tel Aviv, 2002).

59. See Gershom Scholem, "A Document by the Disciples of Isaac Luria" (Hebrew), *Zion* 5 (1940): 133–60; Idel, *Absorbing Perfections*, 461–67.

60. See Joseph Avivi, "The Writings of Rabbi Isaac Luria in Italy before 1620" (Hebrew), *'Ale Sefer* 11 (1984): 91–130.

61. See *Shevaḥ ḥokhmat ha-kabalah*, printed in *Sha'ar ha-gilgulim* (Premislany, rpr. 1975), fol. 26cd.

62. Ronit Meroz, "R. Israel Sarug, the Student of Luria? A Reconsideration of the Question" (Hebrew), *Da'at* 28 (1992): 41–50; Meroz, "The School of Sarug, A New History" (Hebrew), *Shalem* 7 (2002), 151–93.

63. See Scholem, *Major Trends*, 253, 256–57, according to the story preserved by R. Shlomo Dresnitz in R. Yashar of Kandia, *Ta'alumot ḥokhmah* (Basel, 1629), fol. 46.

64. See Daniel Abrams, *Kabbalistic Manuscripts and Textual Theory* (Jerusalem, 2011), 90–91, n. 252.

PERSECUTION AND THE ART OF PRINTING

❈ ❈ ❈

Hebrew Books in Italy in the 1550s

Amnon Raz-Krakotzkin
Ben-Gurion University of the Negev

IN his seminal *Early Modern Jewry*, David Ruderman surveys the role of the printed book in shaping early modern Jewish culture.[1] He begins with the publication of the *Shulḥan 'arukh*, suggesting that its writing, publication, and later expurgation represent an outstanding manifestation of print consciousness, and accordingly, marks a crucial moment in the Jewish transition to modernity. In this essay I would like to follow Ruderman's cue and expand on my own previous work on this topic,[2] to propose that the two decades before the publication of the *Shulḥan 'arukh* in 1565 represent a fundamental period in the history of Hebrew print and Hebrew culture.

About twenty years before the publication of the *Shulḥan 'arukh* in Venice, the Mishnah was published in 1546, also in Venice. By 1553, with the burning of the Talmud, the Venetian Hebrew printing industry was shut down, only to resume in 1565, the year of the publication of the *Shulḥan 'arukh*. When the Venetian firms were shuttered, Hebrew printing had to find other locations. As a result, many of the books to be discussed here were printed in shops established in other places, like Sabbioneta, Ferrara, Mantua, Cremona, and Riva di Trento.

In 1559, the same year in which the last burning of the Talmud took place in Cremona, two editions of the Mishnah were printed in different locations, the first in Riva di Trento, sponsored by Cardinal Cristoforo Madruzzo, the Prince-Bishop of nearby Trent, where a few years later the third session of the Council of Trent

(1562–63) dedicated a formative discussion to the methods of control over the print industry. The second began in Sabbioneta in the print shop of Tuvia (Tobias) Foa. The publication of this edition was completed four years later in Mantua. Different in form and size, these two editions are nearly identical in terms of text and content. Both include the commentaries of Maimonides and R. Obadia of Bertinoro, the latter published for the first time a decade earlier and from then on included in most editions of the Mishnah. Another edition of the Mishnah was printed in 1560, also in Riva di Trento.

The brief span separating the burning of the Talmud with the printings of the Mishnah tells us that the Church distinguished clearly between the two works. To my knowledge, there is no extant Catholic statement of explicit recognition or toleration of the Mishnah. Still, its licit publication in a time of heightened Christian awareness of Jewish religious books is telling. Despite the fact that in burning a Talmud, the Mishnah is consumed as well, the Mishnah was evidently tolerated as an independent text. The act of burning might be viewed as one of purification, whereby the "authentic" was distinguished from the "demonic" and "blasphemous." In precisely this same period the Mishnah attained a new and revolutionary status in the Jewish world, playing a crucial role in the cultural revival that took place in Safed and elsewhere in the mid-sixteenth century. Though this process happened independently, the publication of the Mishnah as a separate text, not embedded in the Talmud, marks a critical moment in the history of Jewish culture and religion and Jewish modernity. To date, historians who analyze the condemnation and burning of the Talmud, or those who deal with the history of the Hebrew book, have not paid attention to the concurrence of these events.[3]

The Mishnah was not the only major composition published between 1553 and 1559. The period is significant in the history of Hebrew printing, and witnesses the printing of several canonical Jewish books, some of them for the first time. Among them were the kabbalistic *Zohar*, the *Bet Yosef* by R. Yosef Karo that anticipates the soon-to-come *Shulḥan 'arukh*, and editions of the midrashic anthology *'En Ya'akov*. Thus during the very years surrounding the burning of the Talmud, nearly the entire Hebrew canon (in form and content) was printed, including much "talmudic" literature extracted from the Talmud or built on it, constituting what could be considered the cornerstones of "the Jewish library" as we know it today.

By viewing the 1550s and early 1560s as a prism through which to examine the interrelations between printing, burnings, censorship, and cultural developments, I am not suggesting any simple causal links between these dimensions, such as, for example, that the printing of the *Zohar* or *Shulḥan 'arukh* was directly caused by the Talmud burnings, or framing specific cultural developments as the immediate result of the printing of this or that text. Such linear analyses must remain tenuous at best. The historical dynamics at play are more complicated, and only by looking at a range of aspects together can we understand printing in its larger context. What I argue is that both the burnings and the publications mark, in two diametrically opposite ways, the rise of a new awareness of the opportunities and implications embedded in the invention of print.

In many ways, this period represents a third formative period in the history of Hebrew printing, following the activities of the Soncino printers in the late fifteenth and early sixteenth centuries, and the unique project of Daniel Bomberg, who established his print shop in Venice in 1516 and over four decades printed approximately two hundred compositions in Hebrew. In Bomberg's wake in Venice and the smaller cities where Hebrew printing reemerged in the 1550s, we see a series of entrepreneurs, printers, and editors whose explicit intention was to preserve the standards and layouts of his editions. Among them were editors previously employed by Bomberg. Indeed, as Isaiah Sonne and Meir Benayahu have pointed out, most of the products of the Conti press in Cremona were reproductions of the Venetian editions.[4] Nevertheless, innovations do emerge in this period; during the period of the burnings, professionalization of the editing process evolved, new tools such as indices and references were integrated into printed editions, and official external surveillance and the practice of "expurgation" were first introduced. The printing professionals were well aware of their innovative role. This is clear from the title and colophon of R. Isaac of Corbeil's *Amude golah* (Pillars of exile), printed in Cremona in 1556:

> The holy new work was undertaken in order to be of aid to the public. In comparison with the earlier edition, our edition is renovated and supplemented by recent and earlier notes as well as by references to biblical verses and talmudic passages, indicating in what chapter and in what leaf the latter are to be found.[5]

As Sonne commented, "the striking feature of this title is the special emphasis laid upon the innovations and supplements introduced by the editor. . . . Moreover, the editor paid special attention to the establishment of a correct text, using, as he states, seven manuscripts, so that to a certain extent the edition can be considered as a critical one." Sonne directs us to recognize the novel self-awareness of the editors that became part of the process of publication.[6]

The productions emerging from the Conti press in Cremona in particular evidence this new stage in the history of Hebrew printing. Working under the threat of the burning and within an atmosphere of increasing pressure, the press internalized the restrictions of the Church, and for the first time initiated a prepublication censorship. Books that were published there from 1557 carried the official permission of the censors.[7] Sonne observed that editions that were more carefully censored were also more professionally and carefully edited.[8]

THE BURNING OF THE TALMUD

None of the above is meant to downplay the implications of the burnings and the continuous prohibitions on the publishing of the Talmud—each event remains crucial in the development of Jewish publishing for generations to come.[9] Indeed, looking backward, the prohibition, condemnation, and burning of the Talmud in the sixteenth century can be seen as a chain in a series of burnings that began in thirteenth-century Paris.[10] But we should also notice the significant difference determined by the sixteenth century context. Kenneth Stow, who provided an illuminating analysis of papal anti-Jewish policy, argued that the measures taken by the Church against the Jews and their books expressed a shift from its traditional policy, and should be understood within the framework of Paul IV's messianic desire to bring about the conversion of the Jews.[11] Christians remained ambivalent about the project of converting the Jews, but following Stow we should recognize the new dimension implied by the burnings of the sixteenth century. It is important to note that the Talmud that was burnt was itself a new object; most of the copies that were set to fire were printed volumes. The content was ancient, but the product itself, the printed Talmud, and mainly the full Talmud, was new. The first stage in designing the printed page of the Talmud was presented in the tractates issued by Gershom Soncino, who inserted the major talmudic commentaries (Rashi and the Tosafot) on the pages of the Talmud itself.[12] But it was Bomberg who began the most important stage by publishing the entire Talmud and determining the talmudic page layout and its pagination. As was argued by Elchanan Reiner, the publication of the *full Talmud* produced a new kind of composition. Until then the focus of learning was the singular *sugya* (passage), but the publication of the entire Talmud immediately generated new ways of learning that focused on the Talmud as a text.[13]

This process reached its culmination only a few years before the burning. Between 1548 and 1551 Marco Antonio Giustinian published what has become the standard of all further editions. In this edition we can clearly see a growing awareness of print and editorial innovation that emerges in publications of this period. Though based on Bomberg's previous editions, the editor Yehoshua Boaz added crucial tools, such as *Masoret ha-talmud* (for talmudic and tosafist sources), *'En mishpat* and *Ner mitsva* (for literature of codification), and *Torah or* (for biblical quotes). By making these additions he showcases the advantages of the printing press over the manuscript.[14] Reiner showed that these improvements came as a response to the needs of the diverse students and readers who emerged after the appearance of Bomberg's full editions.[15] Thus, we should remember that the standard Talmud was created only six years before its consignment to the flames.

No less important is the number of copies that were burnt. For comparison, no conclusive estimate for the number of manuscripts burnt in Paris is available, though Salo Baron suggests 12,000.[16] Yet even the number of 1,200, mentioned by R. Hillel of Verona a few decades after the burning, seems very large, considering the number of manuscripts of the Talmud at that period. The burnings of the sixteenth century came after the publication of five editions of the full Talmud, preceded by a significant number of individual tractates. Although we cannot know the exact number of copies of each edition—with many assuming around 1500—or exactly how many remained in Italian cities rather than being distributed to other places, we can assume that thousands of copies of Talmud tractates were extant in Italy by 1550. The quantity of books is important to appreciate the significance of the events, and the anxiety of the church created by the large distribution of the Talmud. The burnings that took place in central places in the Italian cities must have been spectacular events.

Nonetheless, the burning did not prevent the Talmud from remaining a main source of authority for the Jews. Moreover, as Reiner argues, the time of the Italian conflagrations is the same time that the Talmud reached its place as the core of study in Poland. Giustiniani's edition was even designed according to the needs of the Polish yeshivot.[17]

PRINTING THE MISHNAH

The Mishnah was not published for the first time in 1559–60, but its publication in such striking proximity to the burnings of the Talmud is significant. The Mishnah, together with a Hebrew translation of Maimonides' commentary, was first printed in 1492 in Naples, followed by a probably limited edition in 1515 in Pesaro. An important stage in the shaping of the standard version and form of the Mishnah took place in Venice in the 1540s, when two editions were printed. The first, based on the text of the Naples edition but with many corrections of errors of the earlier printing, was published by Giustiniani (1546–47), during the preparation for the later publication of the Babylonian Talmud.[18] A year later (1548–49) the Mishnah was published by Meir Parenzo in the Venetian printing press of Antonio Querini, which included for the first time the commentary of R. Obadiah of Bertinoro. This would become standard in most later editions. Hence, this Venetian edition should be seen as the model of all future editions of the Mishnah. Accordingly, the 1559 editions themselves should be seen as a confirmation and hence canonization of the previous Venetian editions.

These two publications demonstrate simultaneously a new stage in the history of printing, and the dramatic shift in the reception of the Mishnah as an independent composition. As Yaakov Sussman proved in a seminal essay, the Mishnah as a distinctive composition had hardly any existence in most of the Jewish world, particularly in the Ashkenazi domain, from at least the end of the geonic period.[19] Full mishnaic manuscripts numbered only three, all from medieval Italy, and may say something about the persistence of a Byzantine tradition. Moreover, aside from Maimonides' commentary of the Mishnah, the only other pre–fifteenth-century commentary is that of R. Samson of Sens who covered only those tractates to which there was no Bavli.[20] Several references, mainly from the fifteenth century, to the study of the Mishnah as a separate text exist in Spanish circles. Indeed, as Saul Lieberman demonstrated, "the Mishna was not published in writing" but was known through oral transmission from the Tanna (repeater, reciter) to his disciples, a fact worthy of consideration when dealing with the absence of manuscripts.[21] Nonetheless, it seems that the Mishnah had hardly any independent status during the Middle Ages, a far cry from its role in Jewish culture in the sixteenth century.[22] The very publication of five editions of the composition in little over a decade demonstrates the growing popularity of the Mishnah.

A case in point was what transpired in Safed. Founded on the memory of the tannaim, and the link to the Mishnah and the *Zohar* (to be discussed below), Safed witnessed traditions of learning and ritualistic reciting of the Mishnah that had a fundamental role in the shaping of the self-perception of many of its prominent figures—R. Yosef Karo, R. Moshe ben Makhir and others.[23] The Mishnah was revealed to R. Yosef Karo during his work on his comprehensive legal projects. R. Yosef Ashkenazi (Ha-Tana, of Safed) renewed rituals of reciting and chanting individual mishnayot, and revised the text of the Mishnah (perhaps one of the Venetian editions), according to ancient manuscripts. This reached its most elaborate form with the arrival of R. Yitzḥak Luria Ashkenazi (Ha-Ari) and the emergence of Lurianic Kabbalah. The importance of the Mishnah was also emphasized by a contemporary, R. Judah Loew ben Bezalel (Maharal of Prague), who ruled that a serious learning of the Mishnah as a separate book was to precede the study of the Talmud.

The commentary of R. Obadia of Bertinoro (1440–ca. 1530), who immigrated to Jerusalem in the early decades of the sixteenth century, is perhaps an early manifestation of this new mishnaic consciousness. His commentary was written after the advent of the printing press, and maybe with the intention that it would be printed. Following the publications of the Mishnah several commentaries appeared, e.g., that of Yitsḥak Gabbai and Yom Tov Lipmann Heller, later included in most editions. Yet, it was not printing itself that generated the new status of the Mishnah; rather, printing responded to an existing need and provided the tools for the Mishnah's future role in Jewish culture, its dispersion, and its new role in learning and ritual. In these rituals and practices, we see interestingly, that printing facilitated a renewal of the orality of tannaitic culture.[24]

THE MISHNAH AND THE *ZOHAR*

In the same years, 1558–60, the *Zohar* (and previously other sections of zoharic literature) was published for the first time, and also in two editions, Mantua (three volumes, 1558–60) and Cremona (one volume, 1559). Unlike the printing of the Mishnah, the publication of the *Zohar* has received significant scholarly attention. So while the publication of the *Zohar* generated an intense debate, that of the Mishnah was accepted as natural although in fact it was no less revolutionary.

There are obvious differences between the two compositions. Unlike the case of the Mishnah, the two editions of the *Zohar* were not identical. In spite of differences between several textual traditions of the Mishnah, the compilation of the mishnaic text was ancient. On the other hand, as Daniel Abrams has shown and Boaz Huss has conclusively proven, the *Zohar* only became a "book" through its publication.[25] The very idea of the "Book of Zohar" did not exist previously. Print was crucial for its canonization and formation as an integral entity. As Huss showed, the printings of the *Zohar* can be seen as a crucial stage in the gradual creation of a relatively standard edition.

Notwithstanding these differences, we should remember that the *Zohar* was, like the Mishnah, considered a tannaitic composition. Therefore, it is from some angles misleading to separate the discussion of these two compositions. The publication of the *Zohar* was not only permitted, but encouraged by Christian scholars. To a certain extent, it could be seen as a common project of Jews and Christians, the latter who considered it as an authoritative manifestation of Divine revelation and a crucial source of knowledge for the understanding of Christianity.[26] Such enthusiasm did not accompany the publication of the Mishnah, although this project was also a product of collaboration.

One of the enthusiastic supporters of the publication of the *Zohar* was the biblical scholar and Hebraist Sisto of Siena. Sisto, who was also the major figure in the campaign against the Talmud in Cremona, proudly claimed to have rescued 2000 copies of the *Zohar*.[27] Shifra Baruchson has challenged this number, but the important fact is Sisto's proud claim, which shows his sense of the stark distinction between the *Zohar* and the Talmud.[28] He may or may not have also encouraged the publication of the Mishnah, but it is improbable that he had no knowledge of it. In both cases his intention was to advance the conversion of the Jews, but in his attitude to these seminal Jewish texts, he demonstrated two seemingly contradictory aspects of the Christian Hebraist discourse: recognition (and even embrace) and condemnation.

THE REVELATION OF THE MISHNAH AND THE CODIFICATION OF THE LAW—R. YOSEF KARO

Unlike the Mishnah and the *Zohar*, the compositions of R. Yosef Karo were composed during this period. So while his efforts are the conclusion of a long process, the origins of which go back to the twelfth century with the appearance of Maimonides' codification, the *Mishneh torah*, from the start, Karo possessed a deep awareness of the implications and advantages of print. According to Karo's mystical diary (*Magid mesharim*), the Mishnah was revealed to him and directed him in his studies as he composed the *Bet Yosef* and the *Shulḥan 'arukh*.[29] Karo's project is therefore another example, or manifestation, of what we may call a "Mishnah consciousness." His commitment to the Mishnah did not come to replace the Talmud, but acted as a guide in reading the entire Jewish tradition, from the Talmud to the later halakhic literature.

The burning of the Talmud extended the *Bet Yosef*'s role, as it contained a substantive number of quotations from the banned composition, and was thus perceived as an invaluable source of talmudic knowledge. Evidently, this was not the intention of the author and not the reason for its immediate reception as an ultimate authority. In fact, Karo began writing this work already in 1522, when he resided in Adrianople,[30] and the first two volumes printed in Venice and Sabbioneta in the years 1551 and 1553, respectively, precede the burnings. After the decree against the Talmud, its publication was interrupted, only to be completed several years later; the last two volumes were published in Sabbioneta and Cremona in 1558 and 1559 respectively.

The *Shulḥan 'arukh* was composed in Safed over a period of four years (1555–59), and while far away from the Italian cities in which the Talmud was burnt, its composition was certainly impacted by the violent measures and new restrictions. Unlike the *Bet Yosef*, it does not include the entire halakhic apparatus, but brings the conclusions and exact decisions concerning each of the commandments. The *Shulḥan 'arukh* instantly became a best seller, and since its first publication it has been recognized as the authoritative presentation of Jewish law.[31]

The *Shulḥan 'arukh* embodies many aspects associated with the advent of print, such as unification, distribution, the rise of new codes, new communities of readers, and the standardization of textual traditions and praxis. Karo was an obvious, albeit exceptional example, of "a new author," who was well aware of the advantages and restrictions of print. The explicit purpose of the book was popularization—namely to make the law available to both scholars and lay people—and the author was well aware that it would be quickly disseminated throughout the Jewish world, and hoped that it would bring unification and consensus.

The first edition of the *Shulḥan 'arukh* appeared in 1565, a year after the publication of the *Index of Trent* (1564), which significantly reduced the number of prohibited books and also introduced a system of permanent surveillance based on the principle of expurgation, the removal or revision of certain paragraphs as a condition for a book's publication. The *Shulḥan 'arukh* was therefore one of the first Hebrew books to be revised *before* publication. The work that reflected the reshaping of Jewish tradition appeared at the same time and in the same context in which Catholic boundaries and ecclesiastical institutions were also being shaped.

The concurrence of the arrival of the *Shulḥan 'arukh* manuscript to the Venetian printing press (Di Gara) and the introduction of censorship should not be seen as merely coincidental: both were part and parcel of the same process associated with the professionalization of publication. Moreover, the publication of the *Shulḥan* was delayed for several years. It was compiled in four years (1555–59; in each of which Karo completed one volume), but was published only several years later.[32] We have no evidence concerning the reason for this delay, but one conjecture is that the temporary closure of the Venetian Hebrew printing houses was partially responsible. We may assume that Karo believed that explicit permission from the Catholic authorities would prevent any further objection.

The act of unification in the codification, was, however, also an act of division, as shortly after its appearance R. Moshe Isserles (the ReMa) published the *Mapa* (Table Cloth) to the *Shulḥan 'arukh* (Set Table). An interpretation and supplement to the *Shulḥan*, the *Mapa* also challenged Karo's claim to universal authority by introducing Ashkenazi traditions and customs that differed from the *Shulḥan*'s Sephardic tradition. But, as Reiner demonstrated, it was Isserles who established the status of the *Shulḥan 'arukh* as the authoritative text. In most editions since 1574, the *Shulḥan* has been printed with the *Mapa*, thus creating an interesting tension that was realized on the printed page.[33]

To complete this short survey, mention should be made of the republication of Ibn Habib's *'En Ya'akov* as another venue for making talmudic material available in the aftermath of the burnings. The collection of talmudic aggadot was compiled by Ibn Habib following the Spanish expulsion, and was first published in Salonica in 1516. He presented this project as a completion to the literature of codification and stated that "Alfasi and later codifiers took upon themselves the task of assembling and conveying in clear and understandable manner all the halakhot. It is also important to gather the aggadot in which the profound thoughts of our sages are concealed."[34] It was published again in Venice in 1546, and then condemned and burned together with the Talmud. But later its publication was permitted, and it was republished in 1566, under the title *'En Yisrael*. The imposed title change can be read as a new status of the Jews: not the Chosen People (Jacob), but an ethnic group with its special code, Israel.

CONCLUSION

Needless to say this presentation is partial, as it could only concentrate on a few of the dozens of works printed during this period in Venice and then elsewhere. Yet, the outline may contribute to our understanding of the cultural meaning to be found in the selection of titles and their editions during the period surrounding the burning of the printed Talmud. The main titles, perceived as representative of the traditional Jewish canon, were published for the first time in this period, and thus should be seen tied to the beginning of Modernity. The publication of the Mishnah during the time of the burnings of the Talmud is a critical case in point that may enrich our understanding of the cultural development of the period. Moreover, we have alluded to the growing distinction made by Christians between the Mishnah and the Talmud, which later became crucial in reshaping Jewish discourse. On many occasions this distinction served attempts to refute the authority of the Talmud, and among extreme secularist approaches, which did not make such a distinction, to undermine talmudic literature altogether.[35]

Notes

1. David B. Ruderman, *Early Modern Jewry: A New Cultural History* (Princeton, N.J., 2010).

2. Amnon Raz-Krakotzkin, "Legislation, Messianism, and Censorship: Printing the Shulkhan Aruch as the Beginning of Modernity," in *Tov Elem: Memory, Community, and Gender in Jewish Communities in the Middle Ages and in the Beginning of the New Age: Articles in Honor of Reuven Bonfil*, ed. E. Baumgarten, R. Weinstein, and A. Raz-Krakotzkin (Hebrew; Jerusalem, 2011), 306–35. An earlier, English version was printed as "From Safed to Venice: The Shulhan Arukh and the Censor," in *Tradition, Heterodoxy and Religious Culture: Judaism and Christianity in the Early Modern Period*, ed. C. Goodblatt and H. Kreisel (Beer Sheva, 2007), 91–115. See also Yaacob Dweck, "What is a Jewish Book?" *AJS Review* 34.2 (2010): 367–75.

3. Judith Thomanek's analysis of the postpublication censorship of a copy of Riva di Trento's edition (1558–59), helped to highlight this disjunctive moment. Judith Thomanek, "'Dies ist die *Mishna* des Giuseppe Salvador Ottolenghi': Zu Druck, Besitzer, Zensor und Zensur eines hebräischen Buches aus dem 16. Jahrhundert," in *Zwischen Zenzur und Selbstbesinnung: Christliche Rezeptionen des Judentums*, ed. C. Böttrich, J. Thomanek and T. Willi (Frankfurt aM, 2009), 93–123. Some of the ideas elaborated here were first presented as a lecture in Greifswald, later published as "Printing, Burning and Censorship: Hebrew Books in Italy in the 1550s," *Judaica: Beiträge zum Verstehen des Judentums* 66.1 (2010): 1–13. I would like to thank Dr. Thomanek and Prof. Thomas Willi for the opportunity to discuss these issues.

4. Isaiah Sonne, "Expurgation of Hebrew Books: The Work of Jewish Scholars," *Bulletin of the New York Public Library* 46 (1942): 993–96; Meir Benayahu, *Hebrew Printing in Cremona: Its History and Bibliography* (Hebrew, Jerusalem, 1971).

5. As quoted in Sonne, "Expurgation," 999.

6. See Roger Chartier, *The Order of Books: Readers, Authors, and Libraries in Europe between the Fourteenth and Eighteenth Centuries*, trans. L. G. Cochrane (Stanford, Calif., 1994).

7. Chartier, *The Order of Books*, 74–86; Sonne, "Expurgation," 994–95.

8. Sonne, "Expurgation," 994–95.

9. Fernando Bravo López, "Continuity and Change in Anti-Jewish Prejudice: The Transmission of the Anti-Talmudic Texts of Sixtus of Siena," *Patterns of Prejudice* 45.3 (2011): 225–40.

10. See Solomon Grayzel, "The Talmud and the Medieval Papacy," in *Essays in Honor of Solomon B. Freehof*, ed. W. Jacob et al. (Pittsburgh, 1964), 20–45; Jeremy Cohen, *The Friars and the Jews: The Evolution of Medieval Anti-Judaism* (Ithaca, N.Y., 1982); Robert Chazan, "The Condemnation of the Talmud Reconsidered (1239–1248)," *Proceedings of the American Academy for Jewish Research* 55 (1988): 11–30. On the exact date of the burning, see recently Paul Lawrence Rose, "When was the Talmud Burnt at Paris? A Critical Examination of the Christian and Jewish Sources and a New Dating: June 1241," *Journal of Jewish Studies* 62.2 (2011): 324–37.

11. Kenneth R. Stow, *Catholic Thought and Papal Jewry Policy, 1555–1593* (New York, 1977).

12. Marvin J. Heller, *Printing the Talmud: A History of the Earliest Printed Editions of the Talmud* (Brooklyn, 1992); Raphael Nathan Neta Rabinowitz, *An Essay on the Printing of the Talmud* (Hebrew; Munich, 1877), 9–37; Elisheva Carlebach, "The Status of the Talmud in Early Modern Europe," in *Printing the Talmud: From Bomberg to Schottenstein*, ed. S. Liberman Mintz and G. M. Goldstein (New York, 2005), 81.

13. Elchanan Reiner, "The Printed Talmud: A Project of Modern Jewish Culture," unpublished lecture.

14. Edward Fram, "In the Margins of the Text: Changes in the Page of the Talmud," Mintz and Goldstein, *Printing the Talmud*, 91–96.

15. Reiner, "The Printed Talmud."

16. Salo W. Baron, *A Social and Religious History of the Jews* (New York, 1970), 9:270, n. 10. Baron based his conclusion on the descriptions of twenty-four wagonloads of books. See Cohen, *The Friars*, 64, n. 23.

17. Elchanan Reiner, "Transformations in the Polish and Ashkenazi *Yeshivot* during the Sixteenth and Seventeenth Centuries and the Dispute over *Pilpul*," in *Ke-Minhag Ashkenaz u-Polin: Sefer Yovel le-Khone Shmeruk*, ed. I. Bartal, C. Turniansky, and E. Mendelsohn (Hebrew; Jerusalem, 1993), 9–80.

18. The printers of Naples were aware of the errors, occasioned by the use of a manuscript of Maimonides' commentary, where at times the mishnaic text was replaced by the Hebrew translation of Maimonides' Arabic formulations. In these cases Parenzi in Venice used the mishnaic text that existed in the Bavli. See Jacob N. Epstein, *Introduction to the Mishnaic Text* (Hebrew; Jerusalem, 2000 [1948]), 2:1275–80.

19. Yaakov Sussman, "Manuscripts and Text Traditions of the Mishnah" (Hebrew), *World Congress of Jewish Studies* 7 (*Studies in the Talmud, Halacha and Midrash*) (1981): 215–50.

20. Paradoxically, this tendency grew in the first stages of print. While in most manuscripts, the entire chapter of the Mishnah was placed at the head of the chapter in the Talmud, Soncino placed the text of the Mishnah before each talmudic chapter. See Carlebach, "The Status of the Talmud," 81.

21. Saul Lieberman, "The Publication of the Mishna," in Lieberman, *Hellenism in Jewish Palestine* (New York, 1962), 83–99.

22. On the revolution in the status and significance of the Mishnah, see Aaron Ahrend, "*Mishna* Study and Study Groups in Modern Times" (Hebrew), *Jewish Studies, An Internet Journal* 3 (2004): 19–53.

23. R. J. Zwi Werblowsky, *Joseph Karo. Lawyer and Mystic* (London, 1962); Ronit Meroz, "The Circle of R. Moshe ben Makhir and Its Regulations" (Hebrew), *Pe'amim* 31 (1987): 40–71.

24. See Haviva Pedaya, *Nachmanides: Cyclical Time and Holy Text* (Hebrew; Tel Aviv, 2003).

25. Boaz Huss, *The Radiance of the Sky: Chapters in the Reception History of the Zohar and the Construction of Its Symbolic Value* (Hebrew; Jerusalem, 2008). See also Huss, "Sefer ha-Zohar as a Canonical, Sacred and Holy Text: Changing Perspectives on the Book of Splendor between the Thirteenth and the Eighteenth Centuries," *Journal of Jewish Thought and Philosophy* 7 (1998): 257–307. See also Daniel Abrams, "The Invention of the Zohar as a Book: On the Assumptions and the Expectations of the Kabbalists and Modern Scholars," *Kabbalah: Journal for the Study of Jewish Mystical Texts* 19 (2004): 7–142.

26. Huss, *The Radiance*, 236–41. François Secret, *Les Kabbalistes chrétiens de la Renaissance* (Paris, 1964).

27. On Sisto da Siena, see Fausto Parente, "Alcune osservazioni preliminari per una biografia di Sisto Senese: Fu realmente Sisto un Ebreo convertito?," in *Gli ebrei in Italia tra Rinascimento e Età barocca* (Rome, 1986), 211–31; Parente, "Quelques contributions à propos de la biographie de Sixte de Sienne et de sa (prétendue) culture juive," in *Les Églises et le Talmud. Ce que les Chrétiens savaient du judaïsme (XVIe-XIXe siècles)*, ed. D. Tollet (Paris, 2006), 57–94. Parente proved unequivocally that the claim that Sisto was a convert was unfounded.

28. Benayahu, *Hebrew Printing*, 201. Shifra Baruchson-Arbib, *Books and Readers: The Reading Interests of Italian Jews at the Close of the Renaissance* (Hebrew; Ramat Gan, 1993), 41.

29. Werblowsky, *Joseph Karo*. For an analysis of Karo's messianic approach and its expression in his legal project see Rachel Elior, "R. Joseph Karo and R. Israel Ba'al Shem Tov: Mystical Metamorphosis, Kabbalistic Inspiration and Spiritual Internalization" (Hebrew), *Tarbiz* 65 (1996): 671–709, Mor Altshuler, "Prophecy and Maggidism in the Life and Writing of R. Joseph Karo," *Frankfurter judaistische Beiträge* 33 (2006): 81–110.

30. According to his testimony at the end of the last volume, *ḥoshen mishpat* (Sabbioneta, 1558).

31. For a more detailed discussion see Raz-Krakotzkin, "Legislation."

32. Reuven Margaliot, "The First Prints of the *Shulchan Aruch*," in *Rabbi Yosef Karo: Insights and Studies in the Mishnah of the Maran of the Shulchan Aruch*, ed. Y. Raphael (Hebrew; Jerusalem, 1969), 89–100; Meir Benayahu, *R. Yosef Beḥiri* (Hebrew; Jerusalem, 1991).

33. Elchanan Reiner, "The Ashkenazi Élite at the Beginning of the Modern Era: Manuscript versus Printed Book," *Polin* 10 (1997): 85–98.

34. Quoted in Marvin J. Heller, *The Sixteenth Century Hebrew Book: An Abridged Thesaurus* (Leiden, 2004), 93. On Ibn Habib's work and its reception, see Marjorie Lehman, *The En Yaaqov: Jacob Ibn Habib's Search for Faith in the Talmudic Corpus* (Detroit, 2012).

35. One area not covered directly in this essay is the important relationship between print and the place of the Mishnah in Christian Hebraism. The frequent citation of the Mishnah by

these Hebraists, who, to my knowledge, did not distinguish from the Talmud, leads me to think that they may have been working from printed Mishnayot, not the entire Talmud. For related discussions, compare: my "Legislation;" other important studies which bear on this discussion are Theodor Dunkelgrün, "The Multiplicity of Scripture: The Confluence of Textual Traditions in the Making of the Antwerp Polyglot Bible" (Ph.D. diss.; University of Chicago, 2012), 147, n. 55; A. Kuyt and E. G. L. Schrijver, "Translating the Mishnah in the Northern Netherlands: A Tentative Bibliographie Raisonnée," in *History and Form: Dutch Studies in the Mishnah*, ed. A. Kuyt and N. A. Van Uchelen (Amsterdam, 1988), 1–42; Chanan Gafni, *The Mishnah's Plain Sense: A Study of Modern Talmudic Scholarship* (Hebrew; Tel Aviv, 2011).

KABBALAH AND THE DIAGRAMMATIC PHASE
OF THE SCIENTIFIC REVOLUTION

❈ ❈ ❈

J. H. (Yossi) Chajes
University of Haifa

Ich schau in diesen reinen Zügen
Die wirkende Natur vor meiner Seele liegen.
—Goethe, *Faust*

IN what follows, I would like to consider the interplay of Lurianic Kabbalah and early modern science from a fresh perspective. Lurianism, long portrayed in the historiography as the *ne plus ultra* of arcane obscurantism, has come to be regarded by today's scholars as a distinctively early modern lore in which individuality, embodiment, and even a quasi-scientific orientation are palpably present.[1] Moreover, scholars now accept that the pioneers of the scientific revolution—natural philosophers rather than scientists in the modern sense[2]—were no less deeply engaged by matters of religion and the occult, Lurianism included.

I begin with a pair of premises not sufficiently clear to scholars working on the Lurianic Kabbalah-science question. Firstly, whenever one works on Lurianic Kabbalah, it is vital that one distinguish between different internal (Jewish) stages in its history. There is Luria's thought (which itself has been stratified in the historiography);[3] its (re)presentations by Vital and other students;[4] and its reception and the reformulations and representations of subsequent generations. Secondly, when one works on topics in the history of science, it is vital that one be clear about what "science" meant in the particular place and time under scrutiny. Sophisticated practitioners of the history of science have long since abandoned an ahistoric, essentialized notion of science in favor of an approach that takes as its objective to disclose the ways in which science has been variously constructed through discursive practices in their socio-political contexts.[5] In short, the term "science" is a historical variable rather than a constant, and must be treated as such. To further complicate matters, the period of the emergence and reception history of Lurianism in its first long century, roughly from the mid-sixteenth to the late seventeenth centuries, coincides with perhaps the most dramatic, dazzling, and often baffling period in the history of western science. Neither Lurianism nor science meant in 1570 what they would in 1700; when we explore their interplay from an historical perspective (rather than from a strictly phenomenological one), precision with regard to each variable is vital to the avoidance of specious and anachronistic arguments as well as to the facilitation of fresh insights.

With that methodological preface out of the way, we turn to the big question of this essay: Why *did* so many scientific "revolutionaries" take an interest in Lurianic Kabbalah? After all, Lurianism, like astrophysics, is utterly incomprehensible to all but the rarest of initiates. In 1975, Allison Coudert, having recently finished her Ph.D. under Francis Yates, published her first article, "A Cambridge Platonist's Kabbalist Nightmare."[6] In this article she proposed a thesis that has been at the heart of her work ever since: Francis Mercury van Helmont (1614–98) and Baron Christian Knorr von Rosenroth (1638–89)—as well as to varying extents seventeenth-century natural philosophers who knew them or their work, from Henry More (1614–87) and Joseph Glanvill (1636–80), to Gottfried Wilhelm Leibniz (1646–1716) and Isaac Newton (1642–1727)—took a keen interest in Lurianic Kabbalah *because of its optimistic character.*[7] In Coudert's reckoning, Luria's doctrine taught universal salvation, as it was based on the premise of God's supreme attributes being love and goodness. Moreover, salvation would be achieved not by divine grace but by collective human effort—*tikkun* (repair). Lurianism thus supplied the perfect ethos for the scientific revolution, empowering humanity in the quest for progress.

Coudert's "optimism thesis" seems to have emerged from her reading of these seventeenth-century figures in light of (her reading of) Scholem.[8] I would like to explore an alternative (perhaps additional) explanation: natural philosophers of the seventeenth century were drawn to Lurianism out of a perception of its complementary kinship to their own pansophical project. Moreover, this perception was not merely a function of wishful thinking or projection; discursive practices characteristic of Lurianism, verbal as well as pictorial, were closely related to those deployed by natural philosophers. These were anything but static fields; yet their striking proximity is further evinced in the parallel developments in natural philosophical and Lurianic discursive practices between the mid-sixteenth and late seventeenth centuries.

Before increasing the historical resolution too much, however, I would like to make a few germane generalizations.

DIVINITY OBJECTIVIZED

Despite the great variety of literary styles and genres in kabbalistic literature, matters of divinity were generally presented with scarcely a reference to the subjective experience of the mystic—in stark contrast to the norm in Christian mysticism.[9] As Yehuda Liebes argued some twenty years ago, this general characteristic was amplified in the mythic (rather than symbolic) Lurianic Kabbalah, by which Liebes meant that its discourse of the divine was 1:1, precise, and objective.[10] More than any form of Kabbalah that had preceded it, Lurianic objectivism allowed for the possibility of knowing and describing all of reality, spiritual and material, with the unabashed precision that was precisely the aspiration of contemporary natural philosophers.

ANOTHER GENERALIZATION: NOT TOO JEWISH

Much kabbalistic literature is devoted to biblical exegesis, speculation regarding the reasons for the commandments, and performative-ritual activity. It is inextricably bound up with Judaism, and yes, with Jews. Lurianic literature is no exception. But neither all of Kabbalah nor all of Lurianism was of equal interest, let alone accessibility, to Christian readers. I would suggest that the most important works of Kabbalah for natural philosophers were precisely those that were most *judentumrein*. The authoritative voices of these objectifying texts do not seek legitimation in the precedents of biblical or rabbinic literature; invocations of such are rare features of *Sefer yetsirah,* the zoharic *Idrot,* or the Lurianic *'Ets ḥayim* and its parallels. They present a Book of God as universal as three-dimensional space.[11]

These texts could, therefore, be divorced with relative ease from Jewish particularism and read in a universal key. According to Paolo Rossi,

> In the "pansophic ideal" which dominated seventeenth-century culture there was an insistence both on the necessity of possessing total knowledge, and on the existence of a single law, key or language which would enable one to read the alphabet impressed by the Creator in material things. For the pansophists the real world and the world of knowledge formed a unified and harmonious whole and shared an identical structure.[12]

'Ets ḥayim exemplified such a view of reality as unified in a consistent structural principle.

COMPATIBLE LACUNAE

But it is possible to be more precise. As we consider characteristics of particular expressions of Lurianism in light of characteristics of natural philosophy in the first phase of the scientific revolution, we can do more than point to similarities. We can point to differences. Indeed, in this instance, I would suggest that a key difference between the "totalizing" universal discourse of *'Ets ḥayim* and that of seventeenth-century natural philosophers may have made its assimilation easier than would have been the case had they been more alike. Roni Weinstein's recent work has laudably made the case for reading Lurianism in the early modern European Christian context.[13] Amidst his enthusiasm for a good cause, however, Weinstein has not always been careful to distinguish the cultural context of mid-sixteenth century Palestine from late seventeenth-century Italy, or between Luria's "Lurianism" and its reception history; he has also focused on similarity (at times in rather forced readings) to the exclusion of difference and what can be learned from it.

Pansophism is a case in point. Truly, both Lurianism and early modern natural philosophers aspire to a comprehensive, seamless knowledge of reality, top to bottom as it were. Putting aside for the moment the question of whether Luria was a precocious pansophist, how was Lurianic pansophism distinct? Weinstein presents Luria's pansophism, which he treats under the rubric of "encyclopedism," as all-inclusive—from the infinity of *En Sof* through the divine worlds, to the material world, and down to the lowest realms of the demonic. This may be true enough, but it is no less true that along this vast spectrum there are vast disparities when it comes to real attention and interest. Luria, and it is fair to say most of his kabbalistic predecessors and subsequent expositors, had little interest in pursuing knowledge of the material world "for its own sake," nor in advancing this knowledge by any of the various means being pursued by his naturalist contemporaries. We look in vain for the kabbalistic polymath who was equally attentive to all aspects of reality, material and spiritual.[14] Ḥayim Vital's astronomical treatise, *Sefer ha-tekhunah,* seems typical of its genre—no interest in advancing science, but merely in teaching the astronomy an educated Jew would need to calculate his calendar.[15] This is not to say that *Sefer ha-tekhunah* did not take its place on the spectrum of Vital's works devoted to describing how everything worked. Indeed, this celestial primer sat adjacent to his treatments of how the divine worked—quite literally, as a number of extant fragmentary manuscripts of the work are bound alongside his Lurianic treatise *Sha'ar ha-hakdamot.*[16] Vital's alchemical-magical manuscript, recently published for the first time, can, in turn, be seen as occupying the next spot on the spectrum, in its earthly, this-worldly practical orientation.[17]

The eclectic and ambitious intellectual agendas of leading early modern natural philosophers, on the other hand, could and did include extensive forays into esoterica and matters of divinity; the "Book of God" was studied with avid interest alongside the "Book of Nature."[18] I cannot therefore quite say that the Lurianic lacuna with regard to the Book of Nature was matched by a seventeenth-century natural philosophy lacuna with regard to the Book of God. What I would suggest, however, is that the Book of God as represented in Lurianism was, at the very least discursively and, as we shall soon see, visually as well as verbally, well-matched to sit alongside the Book of Nature as it was being conceived in the early, or to use James Franklin's term, "diagrammatic" phase of the scientific revolution. Indeed, in the expressions of Lurianism that reached seventeenth-century Christians via Rosenroth's *Kabbala denudata,* the divine world was represented with geometrical precision, to exacting specifications, in excruciating detail. They had to love it.

But perhaps no less significant was the lack of real interest in the Book of Nature in Lurianic pansophism. This gap in the spectrum, this *difference,* made for easier assimilation. There was no rival kabbalistic Book of Nature that came as a package deal with their Book of God that had to be countered or suppressed.

"PYTHAGOREAN CABALA"[26]

Having made passing reference to the early diagrammatic phase of the scientific revolution, let us unpack that designation as an entrée to a consideration of what my recent work on kabbalistic diagrams might contribute to a history of the interplay between Kabbalah and science in the early modern period. First, we should define the term: a diagram "is *a picture, in which one is intended to perform inference* about the thing pictured, by mentally following around the parts of the diagram."[19] Second, we should note its significance, as emphasized by Franklin: if the later phase of the Scientific Revolution was *algebraic,* the earlier one was *diagrammatic.* This may be seen though innumerable examples, from Descartes' (1596–1650) conviction that science could be forwarded by ignoring all properties of matter except the purely geometrical; to Leibniz's (1646–1716) comment that geometrical diagrams were "the most useful of characters" for recognizing, discovering, or proving . . . truth;"[20] to Spinoza's (1632–77) attempt to develop ethics *more geometrico* (in the [deductive] manner of geometry), an attempt indicative of a conviction that geometry was the key to much more than mathematics. In short, in Franklin's whiggish formulation, reasoning with diagrams in the Middle Ages and Renaissance "trained Europeans to think adequately to do science."[21]

Meanwhile, the conflation of Kabbalah and Pythagoreanism (and of course Platonism) had long been axiomatic amongst Christians. It figures centrally in the writings of Johannes Reuchlin (1455–1522) and persisted in the minds of sixteenth-century figures including Giordano Bruno (1548–1600) and John Dee (1527–1608/9).[22] In 1698, Leibniz expressed his admiration for van Helmont by composing an epitaph describing him as one "who joined together the wealth of various arts and sciences. Through him Pythagoras and the sacred Cabala were reborn."[23] Even when figures such as Henry More or Isaac Newton were critical of the Kabbalah, their critiques bear witness to such a perception; so too must be understood the contemporary "charge" that Spinoza was in fact a kabbalist.[24]

Such an identification could only be consolidated, and to some extent vindicated, when Kabbalah shifted from the eros of the *Zohar* to the anatomical architecture of *'Ets ḥayim.*[25] Or should we say the astronomy of *'Ets ḥayim?* As Vital himself writes in the book, the structure of the *sefirot,* in their endless concentric circles, may be pictured "in the manner of the pictures of the spheres as found in astronomical treatises." (*'Al derekh temunat ha-galgalim ka-nizkar be-sifre tokhniim.*)[26]

It is striking that what have been called *"the* two sciences" of the mid-sixteenth century, anatomy and astronomy, are so palpably central to the discourse of 'Ets ḥayim. Significantly for our current discussion, however, the two rely on very different modes of visualization and representation.[27] Anatomy's "rhetoric of reality" uses "recognizable visual signals of uncompromising naturalism"; in astronomy, representing the heavens as they appear to the unaided eye would be pointless. Astronomy requires the representation of things that cannot literally be seen: "the orbs that enclose the paths of the planets, the points that mark the centers around which they turn, or the circles that map out the invisible spheres." Astronomy's "'rhetoric of irrefutable precision,' [was] conveyed by tables of figures and flat geometrical diagrams."[28]

Although much of the verbal rhetoric of 'Ets ḥayim is anatomical, anatomical conventions of visual representation were *not* deployed by kabbalists. Lurianic divinity shared the invisibility no less than the perfect, dynamically sentient circularity of the astronomical sky. It should hardly surprise us, then, to find astronomical-style diagrams in the earliest Lurianic works, just as they had been deployed in the works of earlier kabbalists.[29]

It should be noted that diagrams of concentric spheres were supplemented by, and later integrated within, more complex graphical presentations that deployed two other conventional modes of medieval scientific diagramming: *arbores* and *tabulae.* The former were typically deployed to classify and analytically divide wholes into their constitute parts; the latter to summarize large bodies of information. *Arbores* and *tabulae* survived and indeed thrived in early modern science, as may be observed in the revival of the Lullian image of the tree of sciences in the works of Francis Bacon and René Descartes.[30] Tables were indispensable ordering and presentation devices. They could also be versatile tools deployed to express something as ineffable as infinity; here too the figures of mathematicians and astronomers converge with those of kabbalists.[31] Finally, the innumerable acrostics in the Lurianic Book of God could only have heightened the sense that it was written in some kind of Euclidean language.

Until approximately the mid-seventeenth century, Lurianic diagrams were very much like those in medieval works of natural philosophy; they served to illustrate "specific arguments set forth by some segment—perhaps of only a few lines—of text." (p. 288) Thus there are a handful of verbal cues in the Vitalian corpus to illustrative diagrams that form an integral part of the presentation. Thus, to use the most widespread example, early in the exposition of the emanatory scheme of creation, Vital concludes a section of his discussion with some version of "and we will draw its form here like this" or "just like this." The detail diagrams that follow—in which a series of concentric circles are penetrated from above by a channel—are a ubiquitous feature of manuscripts and subsequent printed editions of the various receptions of Vitalian-Lurianic cosmogony[32] (fig. 1). More ambitious "synoptic" diagrams of Lurianic cosmology may have been attempted by Vital, as may be inferred by the references in subsequent generations to his "*daf ha-tsiyur,*" which at this point is not

FIGURE 1. "Detail" diagram. From Ḥayim Vital, *Sefer ha-drushim*, X893 K11, Hebrew Manuscripts Collection, Rare Book & Manuscript Library, Columbia University in the City of New York, 15v. This manuscript was copied c 1600 and contains comments by R. Menachem de Lonzano.

extant. It is likely, however, that such a synoptic diagram resembled the drawing in R. Menachem deLonzano's (1550–1626) manuscript rather than any of the ramified exemplars of a later provenance (fig. 2).[33]

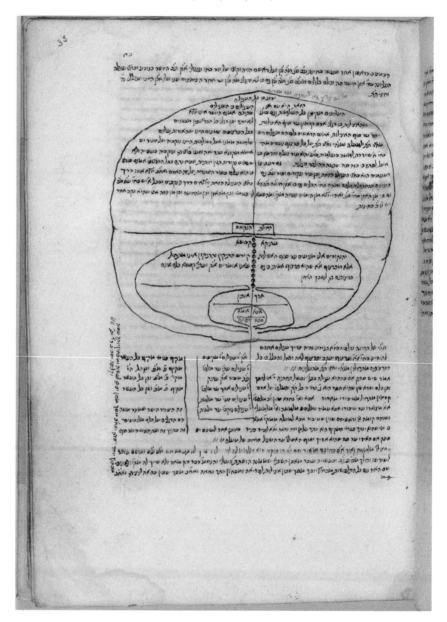

FIGURE 2. "Synoptic" diagram. From Ḥayim Vital, *Sefer ha-drushim*, X893 K11, Hebrew Manuscripts Collection, Rare Book & Manuscript Library, Columbia University in the City of New York, 33r.

Indeed, preliminary results of my research on Vital's particularly mechanistic presentation of Lurianic cosmology, *Otsrot ḥayim,* seem to point to an increasing supplementation with diagrams in the seventeenth and eighteenth centuries to manuscripts that were originally quite sparsely illustrated. The more ambitious attempts to represent Lurianic cosmology diagrammatically in large scrolls (as well as in codices with fold-out illustrations) begin only in the mid-seventeenth century. These are the great *Ilanot, arbores* that can run many meters in length and stretch nearly a meter wide, associated with R. Meir Poppers (1624–62) and R. Nathan Nata Hammerschlag (active 1680s–1690s). From the sporadic and modest medieval-style concentric circles that seem to have been Vital's preferred visual idiom to the proliferation of detail and synoptic diagramming from the mid-seventeenth century onward, the diagramming of Lurianism would thus appear to have marched in step with trends in natural philosophy.

The pansophical differential complementarity I described above is plain to see in these attempts to diagram the whole. The impressively large synoptic diagrams like Oxford Hebrew MS 1949 (which, as an exemplar of a family of *ilanot* scrolls of fifteenth-century Italian provenance, is pre-Lurianic), or Hammerschlag's *Ilan de-Adam Kadmon*[34] treat the divine world(s) in great detail (diagrammatically the Lurianic manuscript much more so). Such diagrams often include a schematic representation of the spheres that revolve around the earth; many conclude with a mapping of demonic, sub-terrestrial realms. There is never, however, significant investment made in the treatment of the sublunar or even the celestial spheres. These maps are of the divine, albeit fashioned in a manner bespeaking the presumption that the divine was susceptible to cartographical conquest.

IN THE END, AESTHETICS

One last salient feature to consider in this context is aesthetics. When kabbalistic lore is diagrammed, it looks very little like the images we come across in the first places someone like me runs to look—the memory palaces or emblems so magnificently analyzed by Frances Yates, Lina Bolzoni, and Mary Carruthers.[35] It does, however, look very much like the diagrams in early modern editions of Euclid or Sacrobosco, and in the new works of Galileo, Kepler, and Copernicus. That Lurianism was a form of esotericism that did not cultivate the emblematic visual representation of other contemporary forms of esotericism may have ultimately lent it a modern aesthetic uniquely appealing to a vanguard like Kepler. Kepler was determined to liberate science from the imaginative polyvalence of the emblematic image.[36] Tellingly, Kepler also perceived the Kabbalah in geometrical rather than emblematic terms, as evinced in his noting that he had "planned a little work, Geometric Kabbalah, which is about the ideas of natural things in geometry."[37]

It may be that kabbalistic diagrams, in particular the more ambitious *arbores*, were perceived as more important by Christian than Jewish kabbalists. At the very least they may have felt fewer compunctions about going public with visual representations of the divine. Guillaume Postel (1510–81) refers in his work to *ilanot* as a distinct genre of Hebraica.[38] It is hard to think of a Jewish writer (including modern scholars) who has adopted such a generic classification. We also know that elaborate *ilanot* of Renaissance Italian provenance were commissioned or copied at great expense by patrons among whom were members of the illustrious Medici family.[39] A beautifully colorful parchment scroll now in Oxford was copied by Yaakov Hevron, aka Scottish Hebraist James Hepburn.[40]

The most ambitious and influential example is to be found in Rosenroth's *Kabbala denudata,* the work Coudert has argued was so significant "for understanding the emergence of modern thought."[41] Rosenroth published comprehensive *ilanot* nearly two centuries before Jews would begin to publish increasingly anemic versions of similar material. The significance of the diagrams in Rosenroth's presentation seems to have been appreciated by his readers. Thus, for example, Henry More's *Opera Omnia* includes his own version of Figure XV of *Kabbala denudata.*

And another interesting example: recently I discovered a note from Johann Benedict Carpzov II (1639–99), a former student of Johannes Buxtorf II's in Basel, and professor of Oriental languages at Leipzig from 1668.[42] In this note, addressed to the pious Lutheran hymn composer Johann Jakob Schütz (1640–90), Carpzov explains that the recondite speculations of the Kabbalah have been all but impenetrable in the past, not only to Christians but to Jewish rabbis. Why? "Because most of them do not know anything about its Cabbalistic tree, which is the foundation of the whole doctrine." Carpzov continues by noting that Theodoricus Hackspan (1607–59) wrote in his *Miscellanea sacra* that he had given up on his plan to provide an explicated kabbalistic tree because of the great difficulty of the subject matter (p.453). Recently, however, Carpzov reassures Schütz that "a highly illustrious man [i.e., Rosenroth] has undertaken it in a really heroic way, that Christians could not even have dared hope for." A reader of *Kabbala denudata* today would be unlikely to regard the explicated *ilanot* diagrams as Rosenroth's most heroic accomplishment, but that is precisely the opinion of his learned contemporary Carpzov. What made the diagrammatic explication so impressive to Carpzov? And what led Rosenroth to pursue such an unprecedented and elaborate presentation of diagrammatic *ilanot*? I would suggest that Rosenroth's diagrammatic presentation of the Kabbalah was an expression of his perception that this "Book of God" could be seamlessly incorporated into the pansophic project of contemporary natural philosophy, or, in the retrospective terms suggested by Franklin, into the diagrammatic phase of the Scientific Revolution.

What early modern natural philosophers knew of Lurianism they knew from Knorr. Rosenroth's diagrammatic representation of Lurianism constitutes a juncture where the parallel evolving discourses of Lurianism and early modern natural philosophy converged, en route to a meeting with the makers of modernity if not modernity itself.

POSTSCRIPT: AN AESTHETIC ASIDE

Understanding that the conventions of astronomical representation were consciously adopted by exponents of Lurianism may explain an aesthetic enigma: why

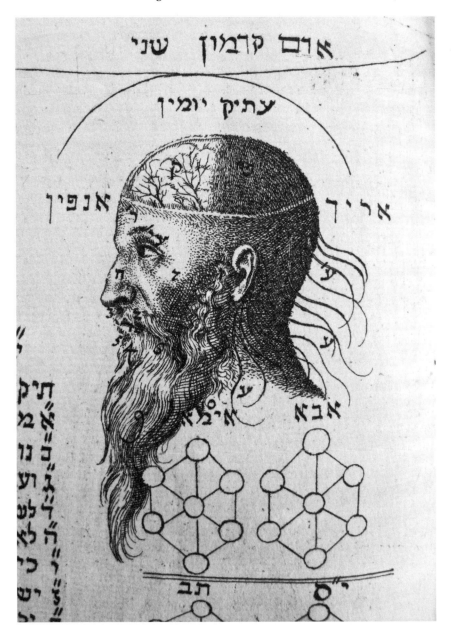

FIGURE 3. Detail from figure 12 of Christian Knorr von Rosenroth, *Kabbala denudata*, vol. 2 (1678) (unpaginated fold-out diagram).

would someone with access to Johann Christoph Sartorius, an artist-engraver of real distinction who embellished the frontispiece of *Kabbala denudata* with an emblematic image of subtle complexity,[43] present diagrammatic representations of Lurianism with hardly an attempt to improve upon them? There is the one tease—the lovely engraving of the head of *Adam Kadmon II* (fig.3)—but no more.

This head, presented in profile, likely owes its origins to precedents ranging from "wind diagrams" illustrating manuscripts of Isador of Seville's *De rerum natura* to more complex later expressions including Andrea Bacci's *Ordo universi et humanarum scientiarum prima monumenta*. Steffen Siegel has recently emphasized the central place of the head in early modern visual representations of world pictures;[44] Rosenroth may have found this an opportune moment in his diagrammatic presentation to incorporate this venerable albeit rapidly transforming tradition of cosmological representation.[45] Yet the more the *ilanot* are appreciated as implementations of the economical "aesthetic of the unseeable" typical of astronomy, the more Rosenroth's foray into veridical representation seems the exception that proves the rule.

Heads indeed recur in *ilanot* diagrams, including elsewhere in the materials quite faithfully copied for inclusion by Rosenroth. With the exception of the Hammerschlag *ilan* and the much later Shantuch *ilanot,* the heads of Jewish *ilanot* are, however, crudely if suggestively geometrical rather than figurative. In some sense the geometrical suggestion may even be viewed as an apt representation of the underlying presumption of identity between cosmic and anatomical structures.[46]

Notes

1. The Catholic resonances of Lurianism have also been suggested by early modernists beginning with David Ruderman. See David B. Ruderman, "Hope against Hope: Jewish and Christian Messianic Expectations in the Late Middle Ages," in *Essential Papers on Jewish Culture in Renaissance and Baroque Italy*, ed. D. B. Ruderman (New York, 1992), 299–323. The most comprehensive attempt to read Lurianism in light of European early modern cultural history is Roni Weinstein, *Kabbalah and Jewish Modernity* (Tel Aviv, 2011). For earlier, ahistorical, but nevertheless relevant readings of this corpus, see Joseph Dan, "Kabbalat ha-Ari: Between Myth and Science," in *Meḥkere Yerushalayim be-maḥshevet Yisrael* 10, ed. R. Elior, and Y. Liebes (Jerusalem, 1992): 9–36; and in the same volume, Karl E. Grözinger, "Principles and Aims in Lurianic Cosmology" (Hebrew), 37–46.

2. Unlike the "sciences" that later replaced it, "natural philosophy was unified by its search for a better understanding of God—of divine creation (in natural historical disciplines) and divine laws (in the mathematized disciplines)." See Ann Blair, "Natural Philosophy," in *The Cambridge History of Science*, vol. 3: *Early Modern Science*, ed. K. Park, and L. Daston (Cambridge, 2006), 403.

3. See Ronit Meroz, *"Geula be-Torat ha-Ari"* (Jerusalem, 1988); Joseph Avivi, *Binyan Ariel* (Hebrew; Jerusalem, 1987). For a comprehensive attempt to recover Luria's own thought amidst a bibliographical thicket, see Avivi's *Kabalat ha-Ari*, 3 vols. (Jerusalem, 2008).

4. Ronit Meroz, "Faithful Transmission versus Innovation: Luria and His Disciples," in *Gershom Scholem's Major Trends in Jewish Mysticism 50 Years After: Proceedings of the Sixth International Conference on the History of Jewish Mysticism*, ed. P. Schäfer and J. Dan (Tübingen, 1993), 257–74.

5. For a consideration of the "constructivist" approach to the history of science, see Jan Golinski, *Making Natural Knowledge: Constructivism and the History of Science* (Cambridge, 1998).

6. Allison P. Coudert, "A Cambridge Platonist's Kabbalist Nightmare," *Journal of the History of Ideas* 35 (1975): 633–52.

7. See especially Allison P. Coudert, *Leibniz and the Kabbalah* (Dordrect, 1995); Coudert, *The*

Impact of the Kabbalah in the 17th Century: The Life and Thought of Francis Mercury Van Helmot, 1614–1698 (Leiden, 1999).

8. It should be noted that Coudert's reading of Scholem-on-Luria is somewhat idiosyncratic. Coudert's later work includes references to the revisionist work of Moshe Idel. Idel's revisionism does not seem to have had a significant impact on Coudert's perception of Lurianism, however.

9. Gershom Scholem, *Major Trends in Jewish Mysticism* (New York, 1961), 15–16.

10. Yehuda Liebes, "Myth vs. Symbol in the Zohar and in Lurianic Kabbalah," in *Essential Papers on Kabbalah*, ed. L. Fine (New York, 1995), 212–42.

11. Of course even the kabbalistic works that seem minimally integrated with classical Judaism were written in Hebrew or Aramaic, and, in that sense, are indelibly Jewish. So we find in a 1688 letter from Leibniz to Gerhardt Molanus (1633–1722), "the Cabala of the Jews is a certain kind of more lofty metaphysic, which, diverted of its covering of words, reveals certain very splendid matters." Coudert, *Leibniz and the Kabbalah*, 48. In another letter, Leibniz refers to *Kabbala denudata* as a book "on the kabbalistic science of the Jews," ibid., 55. Although Coudert argues that Leibniz "'rationalizes' the mythology of the Kabbalah," my observations here, building upon Leibniz's very different understanding of mythology vis-a-vis Lurianism, would suggest that Leibniz's task would not have been as difficult as Coudert imagined. For her assertion, see ibid., 59. Cf. p. 88 regarding Leibniz's rationalization of metaphors used by van Helmont. On John Dee's "nearly asemitic" writings on Kabbalah, see Karen De León-Jones, "John Dee and the Kabbalah," in *John Dee: Interdisciplinary Studies in English Renaissance Thought*, ed. S. Clucas (Dordrecht, 2006), 143–58.

12. Paolo Rossi, *Logic and the Art of Memory: The Quest for a Universal Language*, trans. S. Clucas, (Chicago, 2000). 38.

13. Weinstein, *Kabbalah and Jewish Modernity.*

14. See, for example, David B. Ruderman, "Judaism to 1700," in *The History of Science and Religion in the Western Tradition: An Encyclopedia*, ed. G. B. Ferngren, et al. (New York, 2000), 240.

15. Unfortunately no complete manuscript is extant of this work. The published version and most manuscripts preserve only the first section.

16. See, e.g., MS Benayahu 132 (F72312); New York—M. Lehmann 8 (F23183); Moscow—Russian State Library, MS Guenzburg 251 (F27955). Dr. Eliezer Baumgarten brought to my attention another interesting juxtaposition of astronomical and kabbalistic discussions and diagrams in Abraham Azulai's *Hesed le-Avraham* (Amsterdam, 1685), 9b-11b, 28b-29b.

17. Ḥayim Vital, *Sefer ha-pe'ulot* (Modi'in Illit, 2009).

18. See, e.g., Richard H. Popkin, "The Religious Background of Seventeenth-Century Philosophy," *Journal of the History of Philosophy* 25.1 (1987): 35–50. On the Book of Nature, see Allen G. Debus and Michael T. Walton, eds., *Reading the Book of Nature: The Other Side of the Scientific Revolution* (Kirksville, Mo., 1998).

19. My emphasis in the quote. James Franklin, "Diagrammatic Reasoning and Modelling in the Imagination: The Secret Weapons of the Scientific Revolution," in *1543 and All That: Image and Word, Change and Continuity in the Proto-Scientific Revolution*, ed. G. Freeland and A. Corones (Dordrecht, 2000). 55. The proliferation of diagrams in medieval scientific literature probably owes something to Roger Bacon's (c.1214–94) claim that through figures in geometry we learn *per experientiam* [through experience]. John Emery Murdoch, *Album of Science: Antiquity and the Middle Ages* (New York, 1984), 113.

20. Richard W. Serjeantson, "Proof and Persuasion," in *Cambridge History of Science*, vol. 3 (Cambridge, 2006). 168.

21. Franklin, "Diagrammatic Reasoning and Modelling," 75. Cf. Amos Funkenstein, *Theology and the Scientific Imagination from the Middle Ages to the Seventeenth Century* (Princeton, N.J., 1989), 6.

22. On John Dee's equation of Pythagoreanism and Kabbalah, see De León-Jones, "John Dee and the Kabbalah."

23. Coudert, *Leibniz and the Kabbalah*, 12.

24. See, e.g., James E. Force, and Richard Henry Popkin, *Newton and Religion: Context, Nature, and Influence* (Dordrecht, 1999); Popkin, "Spinoza, 'Neoplatonist Kabbalist'?" in *Neoplatonism and Jewish Thought,* ed. L. E. Goodman (Albany, N.Y., 1992), 387–409. The passage is cited in Weinstein, *Kabbalah and Jewish Modernity*, 63–64.

25. On the eros of the *Zohar*, see Yehuda Liebes, "Zohar and Eros" (Hebrew), *Alpayim* 9 (1994): 67–119. For the comparison, see Liebes, "Myth vs. Symbol."

26. In his pioneering work on visual Kabbalah, Giulio Busi evinces keen awareness of the significance of astronomical (and astrological) illustration for an understanding of the history of kabbalistic diagrams. Although Busi's work deals chiefly with pre-Lurianic materials, in treating Lurianism he incisively notes "Il sistema teosofico elaborato da Vital ha il respiro di un'ambiziosa astronomia mistica e, in effetti, le sue sequenze di figure luminose e di *sefirot* possono essere viste come costellazioni del cosmo intelligibile." See Giulio Busi, *Qabbalah visiva* (Torino, 2005). 397. On earlier connections between astronomy and kabbalistic thought and diagrams, see also 72–74, 95, 102–103, 133–36, 195–96 (Moon=*Malkhut!*). The passage here cited is adduced in Weinstein, *Kabbalah and Jewish Modernity*, 63–64.

27. See Martin Kemp, "Vision and Visualisation in the Illustration of Anatomy and Astronomy From Leonardo to Galileo," in *1543 and All That*, 17–51.

28. Ibid., 19–20.

29. For a brief survey of astronomical iconography, see Sabine Krifka, "Zur Ikonographie der Astronomie," in *Erkenntnis, Erfindung, Konstruktion: Studien zur Bildgeschichte von Naturwissenschaften und Technik vom 16. zum 19. Jahrhundert*, ed. H. Holländer (Berlin, 2000), 409–48.

30. Rossi, *Logic and the Art of Memory*, 37. For a study of Lull's *arbor elementalis* in terms of sacred geometry, see Charles Lohr, "Mathematics and the Divine: Ramon Lull," in *Mathematics and the Divine: A Historical Study*, ed. L. Bergmans and T. Koetsier (Amsterdam, 2005), 213–28.

31. See the examples in John Emery Murdoch, *Album of Science: Antiquity and the Middle Ages,* 159. Cf. Jewish Theological Seminary MS S431 for an example of a kabbalistic diagram of infinity that, at least in external appearances, is strikingly similar. The inferential mathematical annotation of the Latin diagram from Richard Swineshead's *Liber calculationum* has no parallel in the Hebrew manuscript.

32. The difference of opinion with regard to the channel's degree of penetration is reflected in different graphical representations in various manuscripts. In this context I might note that the fascinating question of the hermeneutical status of these visual materials is the subject of another essay currently in preparation.

33. The National Library of Israel, Jerusalem MS Heb. 28°7991, 10a.

34. For online access to this *Ilan*, go to: http://opacplus.bsb-muenchen.de/search?oclcno= 643070081 (accessed August 8, 2013).

35. See, e.g., Frances Amelia Yates, *The Art of Memory* (Chicago, 1966); Lina Bolzoni, *The Gallery of Memory: Literary and Iconographic Models in the Age of the Printing Press*, trans. J. Parzen (Toronto, 2001); Mary Carruthers, *The Craft of Thought: Meditation, Rhetoric, and the Making of Images, 400–1200* (Cambridge, 2000).

36. The geometrical regularities of Keplerian diagrams were central to Kepler's attempt to develop exact scientific representations of the motions of the universe. See Raz Chen-Morris, "From Emblems to Diagrams: Kepler's New Pictorial Language of Scientific Representation," *Renaissance Quarterly* 62.1 (2009): 134–70.

37. See Judith Veronica Field, *Kepler's Geometrical Cosmology* (Chicago, 1988).

38. Judith Weiss was kind enough to bring this to my attention.

39. Edward L. Goldberg, *Jews and Magic in Medici Florence: The Secret World of Benedetto Blanis* (Toronto, 2011).

40. See Anthony Grafton, and Joanna Weinberg, *"I have always loved the Holy Tongue": Isaac Casaubon, the Jews, and a Forgotten Chapter in Renaissance Scholarship*, (Cambridge, Mass., 2011), 83–86.

41. Coudert, *The Impact of the Kabbalah in the 17th Century*, xv. Coudert continues by arguing that within *Kabbala denudata* "one can find the basis for the faith in science, belief in progress, and commitment to religious toleration characteristic of the best aspects of western culture," xv. Although in this essay I am specifically engaging with Coudert's thesis, a significant body of scholarship on *Kabbala denudata* has emerged in recent years. See, e.g., Andreas B. Kilcher, "Die *Kabbala Denudata* in Text und Kontext," in *Die Kabbala Denudata: Text und Kontext: Akten der 15. Tagung der Christian Knorr von Rosenroth-Gesellschaft, Morgen-Glantz* (Bern, 2006), 9–14. In the same volume see also Andreas B. Kilcher, "Verhüllung und Enthüllung des Geheimnisses: Die *Kabbala Denudata* im Okkultismus der Moderne," 343–83; Yossef Schwartz, "Kabbala als Atheismus: Die Kabbala Denudata und die religiösen Krise des 17. Jahrhunderts," *Morgen-Glantz: Zeitschrift der Christian Knorr von Rosenroth-Gesellschaft* 16 (2006): 259–84.

42. I am grateful to Yossef Schwartz for encouraging me to make the trip to Wolfenbüttel, and to Sven Limbeck of the Herzog August Bibliothek for his invaluable assistance. The note, MS 157.1 Extrav. 42 R & V, may be viewed at http://diglib.hab.de/wdb.php?dir=mss/157-1-extrav (accessed August 8, 2013).

43. Rosemarie Zeller, "Der Paratext der Kabbala Denudata. Die Vermittlung von jüdischer und christlicher Weisheit," *Morgen-Glantz* 7 (1997): 141–69.

44. Steffen Siegel, "Kosmos und Kopf: die Sichtbarkeit des Weltbildes," in *Die Welt als Bild: Interdisziplinäre Beiträge zur Visualität von Weltbildern*, ed. C. Markschies und J. Zachhuber (Berlin, 2008), 113–42.

45. The sixteen fold-out diagram plates published by Rosenroth present some five distinct *ilanot*, each with its own provenance. As this article goes to press, I am exploring the hypothesis that figures 8–12, including the "representational" head, were conceived by Rosenroth himself and subsequently copied by Jews. I hope to publish a more thorough treatment of the Rosenroth diagram collection in the near future.

46. Van Helmont's *Alphabet of Nature* is also worth considering in this context, asserting as it does an identity between the shapes of the Hebrew letters, the anatomy of the human head, and the building blocks of the universe. See Allison Coudert and Taylor Corse, eds., *The Alphabet of Nature* (Leiden, 2007).

YOSEF SHLOMO DELMEDIGO'S
ENGAGEMENT WITH ATOMISM

❂ ❂ ❂

Some Further Explorations into a Knotty Problem

Y. Tzvi Langermann
Bar-Ilan University

YOSEF Shlomo Delmedigo (1591–1655), often referred to by his acronym, Yashar of Candia, flaunted his knowledge on just about every topic below (and above) the sun. His disquisitions are of interest in many ways for the history of Hebrew literature, and for the history of science and ideas within, and, occasionally, beyond the Jewish communities of Europe and the Middle East as well. Moreover, his art of writing and the way his creations were brought to print illuminate important aspects of Jewish cultural history.

My original and modest goal in preparing this essay was to locate Yashar's engagement with atomism within the history of that theory, and the examination of Yashar's atomism remains the main focus. However, Yashar's interest in atomism is intimately connected to his interpretation of the Kabbalah—mostly Lurianic Kabbalah, by modern definitions, but also non-Lurianic and even (by some accounts) pseudo-Lurianic. When one turns to the reception history of Lurianic Kabbalah, in order to see how Yashar's discussions fit into the history of Kabbalah, one discovers that Yashar is one of the key sources for this history. In other words, taking a stance on Yashar's atomism will inevitably require making some statement about his role in the dissemination of the Kabbalah.

I make two major arguments in the course of the essay: (1) The atomism that Yashar endorses, or, at least, introduces at times into his disquisitions without distancing himself from it, is part and and parcel (no pun intended) of the atomistic, or corpuscular, theories that had wide currency in seventeenth-century Europe. His atomism differs from the medieval Islamic (including Karaite) variety in some significant points, and there is no reason to stress a linkage to the thought of Giordano Bruno, though some connection cannot be ruled out. (2) Yashar brings in atomism in the course of his exposition of Kabbalah, giving the impression that Kabbalah is a different expression of a scientific theory. This would indicate a positive view of the Kabbalah on Yashar's part and a shift from the opinion he expresses in some of his early writings, where he denigrates it as magic. (The denigration is his express judgment, not mine.) However, a close reading of several passages in the texts that I shall discuss reveals some subtle but, I think, unmistakable hints that, when all is said and done, Yashar, even at the later stages of his thought, held very much a negative opinion.

To complicate matters further, Yashar's discussion of language, the Hebrew language in particular and its system of writing, as indeed also his suggestive side remarks on magic and trickery, all of which bear upon his discussion of atomism, will also connect to his view of the Kabbalah. Though I am not a historian of the Kabbalah, if the topic that I have chosen requires me to delve into that particular field, I will not shy away, and I will present here, with all due caution and modesty, what my own diggings have revealed.

In order to carry out this project in an organized fashion, I will proceed as follows:

1. I will limit my attention almost exclusively to a single essay by Yashar (though ascribed to someone else; more on this later), which, as shall become clear, is the most telling one for my topic.
2. I will first display, very concisely, the results of my investigations into Yashar's atomism, its historical context and some interesting features of the way it is presented.
3. I will then turn to other aspects of the problem, especially the role of letters, and other kabbalistic and non-kabbalistic aspects of his exposition.

We are almost through with the preliminaries. Before proceeding, I should first state that, from my point of view, atomism is a theory of matter. Whereas even staunch continuists must acknowledge an atomistic presence in the theory of time (the now or the instant) and in geometry (the point), with regard to the theory of matter there is a clear choice between the view that matter is endlessly divisible (in theory at least) and the atomistic claim that it is not.[1]

A short summary of research on Yashar's engagement with atomism is in order. Two scholars have weighed in to date. Isaac Barzilay maintains that Yashar appealed to atomism in order to rationalize the Kabbalah; in so doing he found it to be "only a new garb for the ancient views of the atomists."[2] Moshe Idel advances the hypothesis that Yashar is presenting an adequate explanation of at least one aspect of the

Kabbalah of Israel Sarug (a kabbalist who came to Italy from Safed, claiming to have been a student of Luria himself), namely the emergence of letters from points.[3] Idel adds "that for him [Yashar] atomism was neither a comprehensive philosophical doctrine nor a way to interpret Kabbalah in its entirety. Atomism appears almost exclusively when dealing with one particular issue: the emergence of letters from points."[4]

It seems to me that Yashar explicates—though he does not necessarily adopt it personally—a physics wherein the letters, whose role is crucial in kabbalistic theory, function as atoms. At least in part, his reason for connecting the Kabbalah to atomism was in order to make it intellectually respectable. In this regard I agree with Barzilay, who, however, contributed nothing toward the contextualization of Yashar's atomism within seventeenth-century thought. As for Idel, I certainly appreciate his insights. Yashar may be presenting a faithful exposition of Sarugian Kabbalah, and that in turn may betray some link to (small parts of) Bruno's thought. However, there is much more than that to Yashar's engagement with atomism, as I shall show.

I. KOAH YHWH—THE POWER OF GOD

The essay that I have chosen for close examination, "Koah YHWH" (The Power of God [PG]), is included in the volume *Novelot hokhmah*.[5] That volume is a collection of texts, and as such its organization is a vestige of the hand-written medieval codices. Most of the texts comprising *Novelot hokhmah* purport to be written by Yashar but brought to press, against his will, by his student, Shmu'el Ashkenazi, who garnished the texts with notes (*hagahot*). No historical person by this name has been identified, and the consensus of scholars, which I join, for the purposes of this essay at least, is that Yashar is the true author.[6]

Only one manuscript of *Novelot hokhmah*, MS Moscow, Russian State Library, Guenzburg 266 (F 47622 at Institute of Microfilmed Hebrew Manuscripts in Jerusalem), may antedate the printing; however, "Power of God" is not included in this codex.[7] It is found in another, later copy of *Novelot hokhmah*, MS Jerusalem, Mossad haRav Kook 791 (IMHM F 26424), ff. 114–76. The PG was reprinted in *Likute ha-shas,* a collection of Lurianic and Sarugian texts (Livorno, 5545).

Is "Power of God" an authentic writing of Yashar or a pseudepigraph? This is not an easy question to answer. A pseudepigraph is usually a writing for which the true author invents a different name for himself. The case of *Novelot hokhmah* is far more complex. Assuming that Yashar is the true author, he assigns to himself a secondary role, as the author of unpublished materials that are brought to press against his will by his student Ashkenazi, and duly annotated and interpreted by the fictional disciple. But "Power of God" is different still: it is presented not as a work by Yashar, but as something written by Ashkenazi himself, based on the teachings of Yashar. Barzilay has observed that this move is meant to place even more authorial distance between Yashar and the tract "in which the philosophication of the Cabbalah reaches its highest degree."[8] There is even more—an essay at the beginning of the volume presents in vivid detail a story, presumably concocted by Yashar's imagination, of Ashkenazi's adventures in bringing the book to press.

The cast of characters does not end with Ashkenazi. "Power of God" was written in a single night, in response to the request of an unnamed individual—in my view, another convenient fiction—for an explanation of a statement attributed to Ḥayim Calabresi, that is, Ḥayim Vital, in "Limude atsilut." (Later on, as part of his explication of the passage, Yashar ascribes "Limude atsilut" to Luria. The current consensus assigns that work to Sarug, who is not mentioned by name in the texts dealing with atomism; Yashar does mention his name in a few other places.) The very same passage is cited in one of the numbered "leaves" that are included at the end of *Novelot ḥokhmah* as an appendix. There, as in "Power of God," the elaboration on the short passage involves a heavy dose of atomism. But I anticipate; let me return to the question of authorship. Yashar has constructed an elaborate literary disguise for his atomistic exposition of a kabbalistic text. I shall return to this a bit later on.

II. YASHAR AND SEVENTEENTH-CENTURY ATOMISM

Yashar of course cites Democritus, the patron saint of just about all atomistic theories since antiquity. This is not particularly helpful for placing Yashar in historical context. Extremely well read in a variety of languages, a migrant from one intellectual center to another throughout the eastern Mediterranean as well eastern and northern Europe, and knowledgeable in just about every field, Yashar's writings are filled with references and citations. Simply cataloguing these, as is often the scholarly practice, will not necessarily lead to an accurate assessment of the historical nexus within which Yashar discusses any given issue. In the case under study here, two mild statements, to my knowledge not yet noticed in published studies, allow us to locate Yashar more precisely within contemporaneous atomistic speculations. In particular, they show how different his atomism was from that presented at length in two medieval, and hostile sources to which he had access as well: Maimonides' *Guide of the Perplexed* and *'Ets ḥayim* by the Karaite Aron the Younger of Nicomedia.[9]

The first of these is Yashar's unambiguous declaration that there is no vacuum. After endorsing the Aristotelian definition of place (in the course explicating the very un-Aristotelian Lurianic concept of *tsimtsum*) as the outer limit of the body, Yashar, continuing his Aristotelian line of thought, declares that the vacuum does not exist. "As a result of the *tsimtsum*, and from the left-over light that remained within the measure,[10] *for there is no vacuum*, points were generated, which are like the atoms [literally: "individual essences"] that the ancient philosophers Empedocles, Democritus, Anaxagoras and the like assumed to be the material principles created by [or: from?] God."[11]

In classical and Islamic physics, atomism and the vacuum went hand in hand.

However, in Yashar's epoch, the view that atoms moved in some sort of plenum was widespread, perhaps even dominant, even though atomists continued to formally align themselves with Democritus. Sebastian Basso, now considered one of the leading exponents of atomism in the seventeenth century, allows for a plenum filled with a (Stoic-like) pneuma.[12] Basso is not alone; and medieval thinkers such as John Wyclif "anticipated" this position.[13]

Bruno too denied the vacuum. His atoms ("ensouled monads") move in a spirit that has been characterized as a combination of Stoic pneuma and Platonic anima mundi.[14] Though Yashar and Bruno have in common the rejection of the vacuum, this fact does not necessarily reveal any meaningful connection between the two thinkers. Note in particular that, as far as I can see, unlike Bruno, Yashar says nothing about what fills space, or whether it is infinite. On the other hand, it is significant that Vital explicitly states that tsimtsum resulted in a vacuum, what he calls *avir panuy ve-rekani*.[15]

The second hint may be even more useful in locating Yashar historically. It is his remark on the gradations of corpuscular bodies, what he calls "larger parts" that are formed out of the atoms. I take this to refer not to individual atoms but to aggregates, that is, corpuscles or molecules. (PG, f. 181a) The remark occurs in the context of a discussion of yet another issue widely debated in his time. Yashar argues that individual components do not change when mixed, and hence they can be separated, as into two metals or wine and water. However, even when they cannot be completely separated, one must agree that they remain separate, since Aristotle has said that bodies cannot interpenetrate.[16] Following upon this, Yashar refers to the gradations (second, third, fourth, fifth, and beyond) of these aggregates, according to their size. These ideas—the notion of molecule, which Basso is credited by some with anticipating, as well as their gradations—are found in Basso's work too.[17] The compound ultimately formed by atoms and their aggregates takes its label (i.e., fluid or hot) from the preponderant element (of the four classical elements) in its makeup. This too conforms to a trend among seventeenth-century atomists.[18]

Mention must also be made of some additional features of Yashar's atomism that I have as yet been unable to connect to other thinkers of the period:

1. A possible reference to microscopic organisms in PG f.181. Following upon a cursory mention of Aristotle's rejection of atomism (but implying that Plato does allow for it), Yashar tells the reader, "don't be amazed [or: befuddled] by this" and then mentions microscopic organisms, each of which must have many tiny organs within. Therefore, they must be made up of bodies "that are not divisible on account of their small size; several hundred organs would not suffice for all of those [biological] activities." It is not clear to me whether Yashar intends that they are indivisible, as an atomist would say, or merely that they are indistinguishable.[19] His seemingly favorable references to atomism notwithstanding, it is not clear to me how fully or consistently Yashar is committed to that doctrine.

2. A reference to atomistic "powers" that serve as building blocks or typeset (see the following section on the significance of printing) for the cosmos, along with the letters. Primary powers are indivisible, just like atoms. The world was created out of the primary powers; their number is the same as the number of letters in the Torah. (PG, f.181b) I have found no corresponding discussion in the physics of the period.

III. OTHER KABBALISTIC AND NONKABBALISTIC ASPECTS

A. Printing

Letter mysticism is an ancient phenomenon. The invention of printing opened up for it new vistas. Medieval kabbalists spoke about how the combinations and permutations of the same letters gave rise to different things. Now one could observe how the very same type could be reset in order to produce books on different subjects. In the first analogy that he draws, Yashar observes that when printers remove type, the product compounded out of the type—a book on logic, for example—is destroyed, but the letters are not. And they can be arranged anew to print a book on physics or theology.[20] It is the order and arrangement of the indivisible and indestructible units of type that give character to the finished product. Again like Basso, Yashar holds that atoms or minima retain their properties even when in combination.[21]

When God wished to destroy Sodom, he put together the four letters, *kaf, lamed, yod, heh,* which spell out the Hebrew word for "destruction," just as a king would put together letters when writing or printing a decree (PG, 181b). When God disconnects the letters, the action stops. Before *tsimtsum,* all the letters were "together within his essence (*atsmuto*)." The letters were then indistinct, they could not be separated or combined, and so it was impossible to do anything.

Yashar was familiar not only with printing but with some very different systems of writing that had already found expression in print. He was aware that the Chinese and Japanese had preceded the Europeans in the invention of printing, and that their ideographs were very different from the letters used in western alphabets. He refers to printing in China and Japan, which serves as an illustration of writing or printing with words that are not formed out of separate letters, thus:

> We have learned that the art of printing was known for about a millennium in China and Japan before it was found in Europe. Books in the sciences of medicine and astronomy have been brought to Amsterdam, along with pictures [illustrations?] from there. We have learned that they have there a Book of Elements in geometry, but not arranged as in Euclid. We saw that they do not have separate letters in their printing, but rather complete words. Thus, when they want to write "straight line" for example, they take one piece [block or type], which contains "line," and another piece, that has "straight." (202b)

Yashar discusses the strengths and weaknesses of this system, and finds that the latter are more weighty. It is for this reason that God chose to use the "European"—that is Yashar's term—system for the letters used in creation, a striking remark, indeed. Rather than insisting on the superiority of Hebrew over all other languages, Yashar opts for the superiority of European writing systems over those of the Far East.[22]

B. Kabbalah and Magic

I find three powerful hints that, for all of his efforts at making the kabbalistic doctrine appear intellectually respectable, Yashar still considers the Kabbalah to be a form of magic in the negative sense of hoodwinking and trickery.[23]

First, there is the question posed by the fictional interlocutor, to whose answer "Power of God" is entirely devoted. The interlocutor remarks that the kabbalistic doctrine of creation by letters recalls the claim of the pyromantics ("the magicians and sorcerers by means of fire, who are called pyrosmantim [sic]"), that when the "corporeal" flame moves and the coals hiss, letters are produced that are unlike the "corporeal" letters, communicating with whoever merits understanding them, i.e., the fortunetellers who understand this science (PG, 201a–b). This is a serious accusation, and one might expect Yashar (through the authorial disguise he uses in this essay) to refute it, showing clearly how the kabbalistic theory is *not* pyromantics. But he does nothing of the sort.

The second hint is found at the very beginning of the reply to this query. Yashar begins modestly with a confession that these topics are beyond his expertise. However, he has been "conjured" into replying—the Hebrew *hergaztani le-ha'alot* is a clear allusion to the prophet Samuel's exclamation at En Dor (1 Sam 28:15). Indeed, this passage suggests an explanation why Yashar chose "Samuel" for a pseudonym—he has been conjured up to explain Lurianic Kabbalah! Luria was also surnamed Ashkenazi. So it may just be the case that in this tract, Shmuel Ashkenazi is not just Yashar's amanuensis—he is the spirit of Luria himself. In any case, the necromantic allusion is strikingly clear.

Finally, the notion that the same letters can be used to produce a variety of objects suggests to Yashar parlor magic by means of paper folding: "But the deceivers fold the very same [piece of] paper, making forms of animals, birds, ships, and various instruments; but the material is always the very same. So also is the case with the letters" (PG, 204a). Unfortunately, I have not been able to find any information about paper-folding as a form of entertainment in Yashar's time.

In sum, then, my highly focused study of one of Yashar's later works has led me to the same conclusion reached by Leon Modena, who knew Yashar personally: "He [Delmedigo] fashions himself as defending the wisdom of the Kabbalah and defending it, but his intention is to degrade it with all his might."[24] My conclusions with regard to Yashar's attitude toward the Kabbalah are necessarily tentative, seeing as they are based upon a single text. But with that stricture in mind, I stand by them nonetheless.

C. Anagrams and Other Graphic Manipulations

The cosmology of "Power of God" is grounded in the belief that the Hebrew alphabet, and the words formed from it, uniquely provide the tools for divine creation and governance. This view of the Hebrew language was widespread among non-Jews at the time (in no small way due to the Kabbalah).[25] Yashar, however, draws mainly from the halakhic literature, rather than the Kabbalah, in order to substantiate this doctrine in the PG's preface. There is no cause for wonder that Yashar's exposition on this particular point of view remains entirely within the Jewish tradition. However, I am struck by Yashar's indications that the same manipulations are operative with other alphabets as well. For example, he displays some technical terms of this art—Greek in origin, as he says, but his transcriptions betray some contamination from Romance languages.

For example, the most evident, or easiest to detect, manipulation is the rearrangement of the same letters to produce entirely different meanings (or events, or objects). Yashar calls this technique "the equalization (*shivuy*) of the letters," but he knows two more names for it. The Roke'aḥ (R. Eliezer of Worms, early Ashkenazi, pre-zoharic mystic) called it "the explicated [=manifest, *mevu'ar*] gate" but it also has a name "in Greek, anagramtismus" (PG, 204a). Anagrams were used in Yashar's time to convey scientific discoveries. In fact, Yashar's teacher at Padua, Galileo Galilei, famously encrypted a discovery in an anagram that he sent to Kepler.[26] Anagrams were used to conceal the name of the author in Italian printings of the seventeenth century.[27] Yashar is very likely to have known, then, that it was not just the Hebrew alphabet that had this property.

Similarly, when mentioning the use of initial or final letters of the words in a sentence to spell out a new word, *nutrikon* in Hebrew, Yashar cites the "Greek" equivalent, spelled *vrakhigraphia* in the printing. Yashar clearly has in mind *brachographia*, or *brevigraphia*, that is, shorthand. Giving the Greek equivalent may well be just another instance of Yashar's flaunting his knowledge. Nonetheless, it may also hint that the techniques work in all "European" languages, and not just in Hebrew.

CONCLUSIONS

Yashar's atomism, especially his denial of the vacuum and his recognition of corpuscles or molecules, is clearly in line with seventeenth-century trends. His letter atomism takes into account the technology of printing as well as the new acquaintance with languages of the Far East. It is particularly significant that Yashar claims superiority, not for Hebrew in particular, but for "European" languages as a group. As for his attitude toward the Kabbalah, I am of the opinion that Yashar went to great lengths to make Lurianic Kabbalah respectable by showing in a variety of ways how Lurianic theory, especially letter atomism, resonates with many contemporary scientific teachings and technological innovations. Nonetheless, he hints along the way that a spirit has been conjured against its will to give this explanation, and that the Kabbalah remains inextricably linked with forms of trickery.

Notes

1. I will cite a few general studies on the history of atomism that the reader may consult for background. The fundamental study remains Kurd Lasswitz, *Geschichte der Atomistik vom Mittelalter bis Newton* (Hildesheim, 1894). Shlomo Pines, *Studies in Islamic Atomism* (Jerusalem, 1997, an updated English version of a monograph published in German in 1936) is a thorough survey not only of Kalam atomism, but also of Greek, Roman, and Indian texts. Finally, for later developments, see *Atomism in Late Medieval Philosophy and Theology*, ed. C. Grellard and A. Robert (Leiden, 2009).

2. Isaac Barzilay, *Yoseph Shlomo Delmedigo (Yashar of Candia): His Life, Works, and Times* (Leiden, 1974), 296.

3. Moshe Idel, "Differing Conceptions of Kabbala in the Early 17th Century," in *Jewish Thought in the Seventeenth Century*, ed. I. Twersky and B. Septimus (Cambridge, Mass., 1987), 187. Idel has misinterpreted Barzilay's remarks about "total failure and disappointment," by which judgment Barzilay referred to Yashar's "search for 'solutions' to the great problems of creation and existence, for which he took refuge in the Cabalah," rather than Yashar's interpretation of a specific kabbalistic doctrine, as Idel implies.

4. Idel, "Differing Conceptions of Kabbala in the Early 17th Century," 187.

5. The contents of *Novelot ḥokhmah* (Basel, 1631), also known as volume two of *Taʿalumot ḥokhmah*, are surveyed in detail by Barzilay, *Yoseph Shlomo Delmedigo*, 108–15. The recalcitrant problem of the volume's authorship will be discussed presently.

6. The various views concerning the authorship are reviewed in detail by Barzilay, *Yoseph Shlomo Delmedigo*, 116–21. Idel, as indeed all writers after Barzilay, treat Yashar as the author of the texts and do not take up the question of authorship.

7. The manuscript is in an Italian hand of the seventeenth century, according to the online catalogue of the Institute of Microfilmed Hebrew Manuscripts, and was "probably" copied from the printed version, Basel 5389, scil. Hannover 5389–5391. The composition of this codex, similar but not identical to other codices printed by Yashar or in his name is of interest for the transition from manuscript to print culture.

8. Barzilay, VI 21.

9. Those two books are mentioned in *Noveloth ḥokhmah*, fol. 56a. Maimonides' thorough refutation of the Kalam and its atomism is well-known. Though some of the early Karaites were atomists, Aron, the writer named by Yashar, was not; see Daniel J. Lasker, *From Judah Hadassi to Elijah Bashyatchi: Studies in Late Medieval Karaite Philosophy* (Leiden, 2008), 76.

10. *Ba-shiʿur*. This may be a shorthand for *Shiʿur komah*. However, in Yashar's understanding of the Lurianic creation process, as elaborated in particular in the third "leaf" appended to *Novelot ḥokhmah*, *shiʿur*, and also *Shiʿur komah*, refer to the computation or estimation by *En sof* of the area or volume appropriate for the creation of the material world. As such it relates to the following words, all of which are important in the exposition in the third "leaf": *Hokhmah ha-shiʿur*, "geometry," or "the science of measure"; *shiʿer bi-atsmo*, "estimated"; *godel ha-ʿolam ha-meshuʿar ba-sekhel*, "the size of the world as estimated in the intellect." Note also that in PG the technical term for the "left-over light," *reshimo*, does not appear, though it is found in the third "leaf."

11. *Novelot ḥokhmah*, 180b (PG, we recall, is appended to *Novelot ḥokhmah*, with continuous pagination). Note that the theories of Democritus and Anaxagoras are not identical, though Yashar seems to think that they are.

12. On Basso (or Basson, in the French spelling), see the exhaustive study of Christoph Lüthy, "Thoughts and Circumstances of Sébastien Basson," *Early Science and Medicine* 2 (1997): 1–73. The

point that, contrary to much historical writing, ancient Stoics as well as some early modern thinkers did not regard atoms and plena as incompatible, was forcefully made earlier by Peter Barker and Bernard R. Goldstein, "Is Seventeenth-Century Physics Indebted to the Stoics?" *Centaurus* 27 (1984): 148–64, 150.

13. On Wyclif, see Emily Michael, "John Wyclif's Atomism," in *Atomism in Late Medieval Philosophy*, 183–220.

14. See the end of n. 3 on Lüthy, "Thoughts and Circumstances of Sébastien Basson," 5, citing Bruno, *De triplici minimo*, 10: "Nobis vacuum simpliciter cum atomis non sufficit; certam quippe oportet esse materiam, qua conglutinentur." Bruno is not totally consistent in his pronouncements; see Dorothea Waley Singer, "The Cosmology of Giordano Bruno (1548–1600)," *Isis* 33.2 (1941): 187–96, 194.

15. Ḥayim Vital, *'Ets ḥayim,* vol. 1 (Jerusalem, 1910), 22.

16. On this debate in the seventeenth century, see Lüthy, "Thoughts and Circumstances of Sébastien Basson," 12. Yashar takes as his example the "dust of the spice peddlars," Hebrew *avkat rohel* (Song of Songs 3:6).

17. Lüthy, "Thoughts and Circumstances of Sébastien Basson," 14, dissents from the applause Basso receives for anticipating molecular theory, e.g., by H. H. Kubbinga, "Les premieres theories 'moléculaires': Isaac Beeckman (1620) et Sébastien Basson (1621)," *Revue de l'histoire des sciences* 37 (1984): 215–33.

18. Lüthy, "Thoughts and Circumstances of Sébastien Basson," 5: "They [seventeenth century thinkers] mended its [Epicurean atomism's] perceived shortcomings by introducing God into the model and by identifying the atoms with the traditional four elements."

19. Biology played a role in early modern atomistic theories, but I have not found any argument similar to that given by Yashar in the studies that I have seen; see, e.g., Kubbinga, "Les premieres theories 'moléculaires.'" For further reading I recommend in particular Richard T. W. Arthur, *Animal Generation and Substance in Sennert and Leibniz*, published online at http://www.humanities. mcmaster.ca/~rarthur/papers/AnimalGenLeibSenn.pdf (visited January 8, 2012).

20. PG, 201b; passage translated by Barzilay, 295.

21. Lüthy, "Thoughts and Circumstances of Sébastien Basson," 12.

22. PG, 202b; partial translation of the same passage in Barzilay, 295. On the Chinese translation of Euclid, see P. M. Engelfried, *Euclid in China* (Leiden, 1998).

23. Chapter 16 of Barzilay is devoted to Yashar's attitude (better yet, attitudes) toward the Kabbalah; the end of the chapter (pp. 255–59) describes his attack on wonder-working.

24. I cite the translation in the new book of Yaacob Dweck, *The Scandal of Kabbalah: Leon Modena, Jewish Mysticism, Early Modern Venice* (Princeton, N.J., 2011), 134. Modena is referring here to *Ta'alumot ḥokhmah,* an earlier writing by Yashar.

25. There is a good deal of literature on this phenomenon; I refer the reader to Umberto Eco, *The Search for the Perfect Language* (Oxford, 1995).

26. Stillman Drake, *Galileo at Work* (Chicago, 1978), 163. Just how common this practice was is controversial; see Ernan McMullin, "Openness and Secrecy in Science: Some Notes on Early History," *Science, Technology, & Human Values* 10 (1985): 14–23.

27. Phyllis Dearborn Massar, "Valerio Spada, Seventeenth-Century Florentine Calligrapher and Draughtsman," *Master Drawings* 19.3 (1981): 251–75, 253.

PART III

"JEWS" AND "JUDAISM" IN THE EARLY MODERN EUROPEAN IMAGINATION

❊ ❊ ❊

THE THEATER OF CREATION AND RE-CREATION

❈ ❈ ❈

Giuseppe Mazzotta

Yale University

THIS paper will examine some philosophical reflections on the theater by some lead-ing Renaissance thinkers and will pay special attention to two plays, *La Mandragola* (The Mandrake Root) by Machiavelli (1525) and *Il Negromante* (The Necromancer) by Ariosto (1528). Within this general context I will seek to explore the elusive question of the relation between these two major authors of the Italian sixteenth century. Each is known for harboring reservations about (as well as fascination for) the other. Their reservations were part of what I would call their "silent dialogue," by which I also mean that it is understandable that no large-scale study exists on their complex intellectual relationship. I will sketch here the alternative routes they took in confronting the crisis of their times and envisioning the sort of future direction they wanted to impart to Renaissance culture. Thinking about their sharply diver-gent outlooks together allows us to grasp some of the debates that characterize the history of sixteenth-century thought.[1]

There are many large issues—the question of power, the role of aesthetics in political life, judgments about history and ethical values—that they both addressed with the self-conscious awareness of their differing viewpoints. A primary area where Machiavelli and Ariosto imaginatively met and engaged with the other was the the-ater. Plays such as *La Mandragola* and *Il Negromante* disclose, plainly enough, their shared knowledge of the classical tradition (Plautus and Terence) and their common openness to Aristotelian doctrines dealing with both the shape of tragedies and the debates about comedies available in contemporary commentaries on the *Poetics.*

The plays on which this paper focuses belong to the genre of comedies, and even at a hasty glance they both disclose Machiavelli's and Ariosto's shared recognition of the theater as an art-form uniquely equipped to unveil the dissembling that envelopes the experiences of everyday living. In effect, neither playwright saw his theatrical works, in spite of their occasional ironic disavowals, as pieces of simple entertainment. Quite to the contrary, both of them saw the theater as a political place in the broadest sense of the term, the ground where social and moral values are debated and where the possible beginnings of a future history can be imagined. That both of them vied for a sort of special recognition by asking that their respective plays be performed in the presence of Pope Leo X in Rome (a privilege granted to Machiavelli but not to Ariosto) signals their conviction of the importance of their respective works and, one infers, of the specific readings they presented of the chaos hovering over their historical times. But to what extent did the theater, as a new form of public debate, reveal questions that philosophical tracts never did?

The question raised here draws *La Mandragola* and *Il Negromante* within the speculative horizon of a metatheater, but it is not an arbitrary question. The medieval debates on the immorality of the stage had been resolved by figures such as Hugh of St. Victor, who in his *Didascalicon* (II, 20) legitimized the value of the "science of spectacles." From the end of the fifteenth century on a renewed interest in the theater as a metaphor for a new philosophical discourse emerges. Figures such as Pico, Vives, and Giulio Camillo had grasped the metaphysical potential inherent in the theater and had made it the metaphoric shrine of various speculative aims.[2] The political/philosophical power of Poliziano's *Fabula di Orfeo*, which can be called the first text of modern theater, had stirred theoreticians and playwrights alike to integrate "perspectival" principles of art, that is, new ways of perception that had been theorized by Alberti, with the theater.[3]

The theatrical metaphor undergirds Pico's oration, "On the Dignity of Man." As is known, the piece defines man as an unbounded, free entity that occupies an intermediate place in the cosmos, between the angels up on high and the animals down low (that is, he contains the double composite in himself). In standing apart from the fixed, necessary laws of the universal order, and contemplating the architecture of creation—conceived as "quasi mundana scena," the theatre of the world—man is the spectator, a role requiring the consciousness of a viewpoint or perspective. Another structural detail in Pico's treatise evokes the theatrical metaphor shaping it. The oration casts the peculiar mimetic powers of man through the figure of the chameleon. Deprived of any defining essence, man, like a chameleon, is an actor capable of becoming everything he touches.[4]

Pico's implied imaginative link between metaphysics and the theater possibly rests on the etymology of "theater." From the Greek *theasthai*, to look at, it suggests a place for viewing or the "spectare" (from the Latin *specere*, to look at). Thanks to the intellectual contemplation (*theoria*) by humans, they can penetrate the depths of being and look beyond the illusions spread over the harmonious economy of the cosmos. This insight governing Pico's Oration reappears in *Fabula de homine* (A Fable about Man), written by Juan Luis Vives (1492–1540), a Spanish humanist and con-verso, in 1518.[5] The "fable," in the sense of an imaginary account of the initial event of creation in man's history, introduces what can be called the theater of philosophy, both in the sense that it stages the classical philosophical dialogues on the nature of man and because it traces the metaphysics of man's fate. The *Fabula de homine* tells the story of man's creation by the gods. The locus of this event, which is also where man and the gods originally meet, is not the biblical garden but the theater. Man's creation occurs when Jupiter yields to a request by Apollo. The gods are bored by the old dramas staged for their entertainment at their feasts and banquets. They de-mand new forms of amusement. In a sign of Vives's consciousness of the newfangled culture of "regular plays," Jupiter complies by conjuring into being, like an extempo-raneous artist, first an amphitheater and then a man as an actor who will perform on the amphitheater of the cosmos. The fable of the divine origin of the theater is thus born, and it is a variant of Livy's claim that the Roman theater was first founded to propitiate the gods at the time of a plague.

At stake is the creation of man, simultaneous with the creation of the theater. Like the theater, man is indeed "a fable and a play," but, in a reversal of Pico's sense of the cosmos as a spectacle in which man is the awe-struck spectator, for Vives the gods are man's spectators. Vives also makes a crucial reference to Plato's *Laws* (803–4), where we are told that man is a toy in the hands of the gods. Plato deploys the ludic metaphor to evoke what can be called the ethics of play (sacrificing to the gods, the pursuit of peaceful activities etc.). Vives's philosophical tale brings into the light the point in Aristotle's *Poetics* where the mimetic arts are said to rest on man's innately imitative nature (*Poetics* 1448b). Whereas for Pico indeterminate man himself, capa-ble, like a chameleon, of playing all parts and free from all determinations, produces boundary-setting experiences, for Vives, man, whom the gods restrict to a subordi-nate role, is, thanks to his chameleonic mimicry, always at the edge of transgressing the plan the gods fashioned for him.

A different dimension of the significance of the theater emerges in a text by Giulio Camillo, *L'Idea del Theatro*. At its heart lies what can be called a metaphysics of production. God is the Maker of both the spiritual and the material world (p. 63). The motif picks up Pico's *Heptaplus* (VI, 4)[6] in which production is the essential action of the divinity or creation. Like *Heptaplus*, which is the narrative of the seven days of Genesis and stages a genuine theater of education by drawing on Plato, Aristotle, and the Kabbalah to retrieve the vestiges of the wisdom of God, *L'Idea del Theatro* comes forth as a vast syncretic compilation. It rests on the theme of Solomon's seven pillars of wisdom and on the seven planets, arranged in ascending order from the moon to Saturn, that govern the chain of cause and effect. Through this formal structure, Camillo digs into ancient knowledge, esoteric and exoteric—

the Jewish Kabbalah, the *Pimander*, the occult traditions of magic, Greek and Roman philosophers all the way down to Petrarch, and Renaissance mythographers (such as Conti and Cartari)—to explain the principles of divine "order" for the education of the mind and the making of oneself.

Camillo's description of the ascent of the mind is figured through classical myths —Prometheus, Pasiphae, the Gorgons etc. But he is not another mythographic compiler, no more than he is a slavish follower of Pico. If *Heptaplus* stages an interpretive journey into the hidden meaning of the "beginning" in Genesis's account of Creation, Camillo reverses the order of knowledge. He posits the divine as the ground or point of departure of all existence and maps the ascent of the mind toward the productive liberal and mechanic arts. The high peak is associated with the human arts which, though recently discovered, stand for the power of the modern world of knowledge. In the highest seventh rank of the theater he drafts, where all the arts are represented, Camillo places Prometheus as the overseer of the noble arts. His theft of the fire violated Jupiter's order, but paradoxically his transgression made man partake of the divine, since to know the gods is tantamount to want to share in their knowledge. By redefining the myth of Prometheus and casting him as the emblematic hero of the arts of modernity, Camillo reveals his awareness of the danger inherent in his conception: man's art might eclipse the power of the gods. It can be said that Prometheus is the mask of Camillo himself. A friend of painters, such as Titian, and architects, such as Serlio and Palladio, Camillo turns his mind to the human re-creation of the divine order—the "fabrica" or workshop of the higher and lower worlds (p. 51). The theater he drafts is nothing less than the theater of the world modeled on Plato's *Republic* (p. 83) and asks to be read as the architecture of a utopian dream.

A prefiguration of this extraordinary series of philosophical reflections on the theater is found in the plays of Ariosto and Machiavelli, who conceive of the theater as a force capable of bringing into focus and rethinking the historical realities of their times. *Il Negromante*, written in the wake of the Sack of Rome by Charles V (1527), evokes the disintegration of the very myth of the Renaissance and the emergence of the modern world.[7] Ariosto begins his play with a nod in the direction of Politian and of the Renaissance myth of language. The "Prologue" evokes the mythical figures of Orpheus and Amphion, the poets who by the power of the word and song moved stones and built the cities of Thebes and Troy. Ironically, they are cities with a tragic fate, destined to end up in, respectively, a moral catastrophe and utter destruction. The two cities introduce the place where his play is located, Cremona, during the Carnival season. The ritual of revelry and masking hints at the serious concern by Ariosto, modernity's crisis. Its distinctive trait is one of generalized dislocation and dissembling, when, as in the theater, things are not what they seem and all reality is reduced to its deceptive appearance.

The dislocation, as the emblem of modernity, is at first identifiable as a question of topography, a being out of place, but it soon it emerges as the very condition of all reality. The initial two scenes of Act I cast the city of Cremona as a strange and yet familiar site where ancient bonds of family and social interaction are interwoven with unaccountable and unknowable happenings. At the start, one character, Margarita, goes visiting an old friend, Lavinia. In the following scene, that begins emblematically with an old man, Lippo, a stranger in Cremona looking for an address, we witness a chance encounter of two old Florentine friends (Lippo and Fabio). From their conversation, some light is shed on what, in reality, is a labyrinthine configuration of characters and situations. Fazio is an *émigré* who has moved away from Florence to escape the heavy taxation imposed by his city. Lippo, on the other hand, is on a mission to Cremona to collect some money for a Florentine creditor. Against this background of political displacement the plot unfolds along more dramatic lines in which family blood ties seem to be set aside.

We are told of a young man, Cinzio, who has been adopted by the wealthiest man in town, Massimo, and who has secretly married a beautiful young woman, Lavinia, who in turn has been adopted by Fazio. The marriage has to be kept secret because Massimo had made a deal to have Cinzio marry Emilia, the daughter of another wealthy citizen of Cremona, Abondio. Out of love for his secret wife Lavinia, Cinzio simulates impotence with Emilia. On the face of it, the magic of money frames, determines, and displaces the classical and philosophical understanding of magic. It is as if, with sharp realism, Ariosto unveils the new mercantile values that have undercut the theories of Renaissance magic or "black art." The comedy's tile, *Il Negromante*, in point of fact, describes a form of magic with its occult power to create apparitions of ghosts and to discover hidden knowledge, through divination (Greek *manteia*) and signs available by conjuring up the spirits of the dead (Greek *necros*).

In Act II, the play shifts to questioning the reality of magic. It turns to the enigmatic figure of the Necromancer himself, whose name is Iachelino and who is variously known as the "Astrologer" and the "Physicist." Iachelino moves center stage, sought by the other characters because he supposedly can provide a cure for Cinzio's apparent impotence. We find out that he is the archetypal figure of displacement: he goes by different names (John and Peter), he pretends to come now from Greece, now from Africa, he is rumored to have all secret knowledge, and he professes to be "a philosopher, alchemist, physician, astrologer, *magus,* and exorcist" (II, i). In reality, he is a Jew, who was among the 200,000 Jews expelled from Spain in 1492 (II, i). Paradoxically, though displaced and bent on sheltering his secret identity to the point of being openly evasive about it, he acts as a centripetal presence in the play.

As a figure who has escaped a potentially tragic history, Iachelino encompasses and echoes a critical time in Italian history, and Ariosto evokes it in his "Prologue." His is the time when Swiss and German mercenaries fight for France or Spain on Italian soil. Through his necromancer, Ariosto stages the community of strangers, refugees, Florentine bankers and business men who have provisionally convened in the city of Cremona and who will soon vanish from the scene. But the figure of necromancer also embodies Ariosto's own Janus-faced intellectual predicament vis-à-vis the modern epoch. Like Ariosto, who writes his play to make visible the fractured world of Italy vulnerable to invaders and the inadequacies of Renaissance culture to confront the crisis, of which the façade of economic values are the symptom, Iachelino stands for what can be called the double aspect of modernity, the displacement that in turn demands the quest for new ordering principles of political life and for finding a way to retrieve the whole of knowledge.

As stated above, Ariosto is not alone in the consciousness of a crisis enveloping his times. The other author who stubbornly seeks a restoration of culture to overcome the feared eclipse of the Renaissance is Machiavelli. The route Machiavelli takes in his *Mandragola* leads him to concerns and depths that are left unexplored by *Il Negromante*. Many are the points of contact between the two plays. For one, Machiavelli's title also alludes to the magic arts, to a love potion that would increase fertility available in an aphrodisiac plant, the "mandrake root." Furthermore, both texts focus on a political/moral existence of a community, Florence and Cremona. And both reflect on the nature of a "place." Cremona is a sort of utopian place, or a nonplace, which actually lacks governing institutions. Neither Church nor State controls the goings on in that city. *La Mandragola,* on the other hand, is centered in the defined, bounded political community of Machiavelli's native Florence, at a time when a precarious morality rules and a clergyman, such as Friar Timoteo, embodies the moral disarray of the Church.

In the "Prologue" to *La Mandragola,* Machiavelli calls his play a "piece of entertainment," a sort of playground for the free exercise of his imagination. We quickly discover that the pastime he produces is a form of *serio ludere,* and his care is for the future of his city. Unlike Ariosto's Cremona, Florence emerges as a world held together in place by shared historical memories, a common language, a common religion, and the characters' productive social interactions. And just as Ariosto alludes to the precise localities in Cremona (I,ii), so Machiavelli draws the urban configuration of his city as the principals are introduced: at one side, on the "piazza" or the gathering space, there stands the house of the doctor of laws; at the other is the "Street of Love" with Friar Timoteo's Church across from it, and Callimaco, the merchant who comes to Florence attracted by the legend of Lucretia's great beauty. In this delimited space of a concrete, historical city, we encounter Nicia, the foolish husband of Lucretia, and Ligurio, who conceives a plan to get the two lovers, Lucretia and Callimaco, together. And he does so by involving Friar Timoteo, Callimaco, Nicia himself, and Lucretia' own mother.

The primary goal of both Machiavelli and Ariosto in thinking about place (as well as time and action) defines their concern with the nature of the virtual place we call the theater. They wish to observe the dramatic requirements of the principle of the three unities theorized by the neo-Aristotelian sixteenth century commentators on Aristotle's *Poetics*, such as Vida (1527), Daniello (1536) and the slightly later Robortello and Castelvetro, all the way to Minturno and Tasso, namely that situations and characters, being in their proper place, gain in verisimilitude and intelligibility. For Ariosto, who conjures mostly expatriates as characters, it is not clear that the understanding of what human beings are can hang on their place in the city. His desire to go beyond the pedantries over the proper formal structure of a comedy finds confirmation in Machiavelli's procedure. For all the topographical concreteness about "place" in *La Mandragola*, the play stages its own version of the characters' total displacement.

Machiavelli understands displacement as the very mode of language, action, and history and he intertwines "place" and "displacement" in the awareness that one cannot think of one without the other. Most of the characters are displaced especially when they think that they are rooted in place. I have alluded to Callimaco, who, bewitched by the legend of Lucretia's beauty, goes from Paris to Florence to possess her. Nicia, on the other hand, is one who foolishly thinks he is rooted in Florence as his familiar and thus real place. He never uses words which are not Florentine, and he clings to commonplaces of his vernacular in the comical illusion that only the empirically palpable is real. But he is unaware of what is going on between Callimaco and Lucretia.

The most radical experience of displacement the play enacts is both historical and linguistic: the theater, the fictive place of colliding viewpoints, replaces the role of the Church within the community. We will not be surprised when almost a century later Shakespeare, in, for instance, *The Winter's Tale* (but similar threads can be untangled in *Hamlet*, *Othello*, and others) digs into the frozen area of proximity between theology and politics and invests the theater with magical, miraculous properties of statues coming alive. In *La Mandragola,* church and theater, the world of the sacred and the world of the profane, stand in a relation of complicity and convergence. Fra Timoteo stands in his church and he makes the church the locale where he can persuade Lucretia to accept Callimaco's advances. Timoteo even decides to take part in the expedition that would favor Callimaco going to bed with Lucretia.

In effect, the play becomes in Machiavelli's handling the occasion to reflect on the theater's aura, its charismatic power to bring characters together and produce magic out of the ordinary experiences of reality. His conclusion is that to restore the culture of his time, we must come back to the sources of the sacred. Ironically, then, Machiavelli, the skeptical political thinker of modernity, produces, thanks to his reflections on the theater, a metaphysics of nature and the consequent announcement of an event to come, the birth of a child for old Nicia and for Lucretia.

On the other hand, Ariosto's *Il Negromante* ends on an overtly humanistic note. By the end of the play, Iachelino's legendary knowledge emerges as the knowledge of the circle of the liberal arts. Ariosto has Iachelino exemplify the magic of language, which as Shakespeare and Calderon will later understand, coincides with the magic of the theater. Iachelino is given the last word as he asserts the value of the liberal education in the persuasion that the secret magic for a possible reconstruction of the Renaissance lies in the retrieval of the culture of the Humanists.

There is, nonetheless, an ironic twist to the play's seemingly happy ending: the city of Cremona is for Ariosto the theater, a virtual space that reduces all characters to mere appearances, as if on a stage. The metaphor of the theater strips layers off any realistic hope that the reintegration of the culture triumphant till the end of the fifteenth century will be achieved. What survives, so Iachelino exemplifies, is the magic of words, which, as Shakespeare and Calderon understood, is nothing less than the magic of the theater with its ongoing performances and its unavoidable vanishing acts. It can be said that both Ariosto and Machiavelli grasped the double aspect of the Renaissance—the thrust forward and its disappointments that had probably escaped the optimism of Pico, Vives, and Camillo.

Notes

1. I have traced some aspects of the oblique conversation, held at a distance, as it were, in which Machiavelli and Ariosto were engaged in "Ariosto and Machiavelli: Real Worlds/Imaginary Worlds," in *Cosmopoiesis: The Renaissance Experiment* (Toronto, 2001), 25–51.

2. The conceit about the theater as the metaphor of life is obviously old. Cf. John of Salisbury's "Totus mundud agit histrionem" (*Policraticus* 3, 8, 25–26) which was taken over by Shakespeare's Globe Theater (1599). The conceit appears in Dante's picture of the Heavenly Jerusalem, both a city and an amphitheater (*Paradiso* 30, 129–37). The notion of the cosmos as a theater where all the entities of creation are engaged in a musical performance lies also at the heart of St. Francis's "Canticle of All Created Things."

3. The link between Renaissance art theories, elaborated in the wake of Alberti's *Della Pittura*, and Renaissance theater has recently been explored in a striking way by Kristin Phillips Court, *Perfect Genre: Drama and Painting in Renaissance Italy* (Burlington, Vt., 2011).

4. I am quoting from Pico della Mirandola, "Oration on the Dignity of Man," in *The Renaissance Philosophy of Man,* ed. E. Cassirer et al. (Chicago, 1956), 223–54.

5. The text can be found in *The Renaissance Philosophy of Man,* 385–93.

6. On the knot of questions I raise in the following paragraph cf. David B. Ruderman, *Kabbalah, Magic, and Science: The Cultural University of a Sixteenth-Century Jewish Physician* (Cambridge, Mass., 1988).

7. I am quoting from *The Necromancer/Il Negromante* in *The Comedies of Ariosto*, trans. and ed. E. M. Beame and L. G. Sbrocchi (Chicago, 1975), 99–158.

WEEPING OVER ERASMUS IN HEBREW AND LATIN

❈ ❈ ❈

Joanna Weinberg
University of Oxford

THE constant flow of studies on Erasmus, his life, works, and fortune bears eloquent witness to the abiding role of his contributions to religion and scholarship. There is not one aspect of Erasmus's voluminous writings, from the adages to the works on the Christian life, education, the editions of Greek and Latin texts, or on how to pronounce Latin and Greek, that has not been studied in minute detail by scholars of all descriptions. My paper will add to the glut of Erasmian studies, focusing on a text which appears ephemeral. On closer examination, however, it could be claimed to be something more than a curiosity, since it provides us with a snapshot of Christian Hebraic scholarship set within the framework of the complex and conflict-ridden world in which Erasmus lived and died.

The starting-point of my tale is a Hebrew eulogy written for Erasmus by the Protestant Hebraist Sebastian Münster. News of Erasmus's death provoked a sustained outpouring of grief by friends and admirers. Several volumes of eulogies, epitaphs, and lamentations were published in Basel, Paris, Antwerp, and Louvain, many of which were reprinted in the first volume of Le Clerc's edition of Erasmus's *Opera omnia* (1703).[1] Descriptions of the first collection of obituaries, edited in 1536 by Boniface Amerbach, printed by Froben in Basel (February, 1537), and republished in Paris the very same year, usually overlook the last rather conspicuous piece in

145

the volume, the Hebrew eulogy facing the last page of Latin epitaphs.[2] The simple heading is not disguised in Hebrew characters; rather, it bears the Latin name of the author, Sebastianus Munsterus.[3] It is doubtful whether Erasmus himself would have been able to read this particular obituary. As he himself admitted in a letter to John Colet dated 1504, "I began my study of Hebrew, but abandoned it, put off by the strangeness of this language and persuaded that life and the human mind do not permit one to devote time equally to so many things."[4] In later life, however, he certainly did not reject the importance of the language: "I myself now in my forty-ninth year return when I can to Hebrew which I formerly sampled in some fashion; there is nothing which the human mind cannot do if there is the will and the desire."[5] An evident ambivalence and sometimes downright distaste lurks in all Erasmus's pronouncements about Hebrew, which evidently he never mastered.[6] The Amerbach brothers came to his assistance on matters Hebraic, as did Johannes Oecolampadius, who fell out of favor when Erasmus was later accused of egregious errors in Hebrew.[7] It would seem that in the case of Hebrew, Erasmus's philological needs were served by a surrogate in the form of Jerome or contemporary colleagues.[8] Nevertheless, it was Erasmus who had promoted the trilingual ideal. It must therefore be supposed that he would not have objected to, but may even have welcomed, Sebastian Münster's Hebrew dedication to his memory.

During the sixteenth century, literary epitaphs in Hebrew—which seem to have originated in Italy among Jews—and other commemorative texts often studded the printed volumes dedicated to the memory of distinguished Christian scholars or rulers.[9] As a renowned Hebraist and Christian representative of the talented grammarian and poet Elijah Levita, Münster had either been commissioned or offered his services for the sake of honoring the deceased in Hebrew. The scholarly community of Basel, amongst whom for some time he lived, taught, and worked for the printers, were the recipients of his Hebraic learning. He composed a Hebrew heading in Jewish fashion for the tombstone of the printer Johann Froben which was printed in a revised edition of two of Erasmus's works.[10] He also penned a long verse epitaph—it is long despite his own assertion in the second line of the poem: "I Munsterus will write here in brief (*bekotser*)"—for the reformer Johannes Oecolampadius, Erasmus's Hebrew assistant.[11] This poem has more literary merit than Münster's prose epitaph for Erasmus, a rather awkward composition, hardly a fitting memorial to the humanist who set such great store by proper use of language.[12]

Münster's offering to Erasmus's memory is constructed predominantly as a "laudatio" (like most eulogies of this type) with a prefatory brief invocation to scholars that constitutes a kind of "lamentatio." Certain commonplaces and motifs, which adorn many of the Latin obituaries in the Froben volume, appear here in a Hebrew garb. Erasmus—so the eulogizer writes—combined religious devotion and scholarly brilliance which earned him a universal reputation; his amazing intellectual powers were founded on the true faith; he believed steadfastly in the Messiah our redeemer. His piety and study of theology and the humanities outshone that of all his contemporaries. In old age he continued his studies with as much and even greater vitality and success. He was loved by God and humans (*ahuv l'elohim ve-livne ha-adam*). (This last expression could possibly be read as Münster's deliberate inversion or adaptation of the saying from *mAvot* [6.1], "He is called *ahuv*, one that loves God and loves humans, that makes glad both God and humans.") His posthumous reputation is ensured by his books and writings, indeed he will never cease to be the teacher of humanity.[13] He has earned an illustrious name and likewise his homeland Ashkenaz [Germany] basks in his glory. "For many years there was nobody comparable to him among the people of God."[14]

At this juncture in the panegyric Münster introduces an alien phrase which disturbs the flow of this commemoration of a Christian life: "The Holy one blessed be He instilled him with the heart of a sage and filled him with the spirit of wisdom and knowledge." The Holy one blessed be He, the common rabbinic epithet for God, introduces a phrase which virtually in its entirety is taken from Exodus 31:3 (and other parallels) in which God tells Moses of his choice of Bezalel as architect of the tabernacle: "The Lord spoke to Moses, 'See, I have singled out by name Bezalel son of Uri . . . I have instilled him with a divine spirit of skill, ability and knowledge in every kind of craft.'" Bezalel's was a divinely ordained task. Likewise, we are being told, Erasmus's great gifts of scholarship are inherently divine and divinely inspired. Such hyperboles are, as Karl Enenkel has shown, a conspicuous feature in the Latin texts that are replete with references to the divine Erasmus, whose authority as the exemplary humanist is of heavenly origin.[15]

Münster's eulogy continues on the divine sphere with another verbatim quotation from the Hebrew Bible, God's announcement in Isaiah 42:13, "I will make darkness light and crooked things straight." By means of biblical imagery, Münster is now ascribing divine powers to Erasmus—he is the savior of humanity. Although he does not develop this theme, the message is clear and may be extracted from the other more elaborate obituaries where Erasmus is said to have defeated barbarism and to have restored the sacred books to their pristine glory.

The brief biography comes to a close with a description of Erasmus's afterlife: "After seventy-two years of life among humans the Creator delivered him from mortal life, and placed him in the Garden of Eden with the other righteous and special individuals."[16] The imagery used by Münster suggests that he is consciously adapting some biblical and rabbinic expressions. In Genesis 2:15 God puts Adam in the Garden of Eden, and in tractate *Ta'anit* of the Babylonian Talmud (31a): "In the days to come, the Holy One Blessed be He will hold a chorus for the righteous and he will sit in their midst in the Garden of Eden." Erasmus is chosen by God and is with God.[17] The obituary is sealed by the date of Erasmus's death according to Jewish convention: "in anno mundi 297, in the month of Av [with a slip of the year—5297 instead of 5296] in the reign of his Majesty, the Roman Emperor Charles V, may his glory be exalted."[18] Here, too, Münster uses an abbreviation י"רה commonly used in rabbinic texts.

So much for Münster's *In memoriam Erasmi*, which does bear affinity to several other eulogies printed in the same volume. It was overlooked by modern scholars, but not by Münster's contemporaries. A Latin rendition of the eulogy was produced by Georg Witzel (Georgius Wicelius[19]) and included in his work *Conquestio de calamitoso in praesens rerum Christianarum statu* (Lament about the present terrible state of Christianity) published in Leipzig in 1538.[20] Not only did Witzel consider the text worth translating with a few glosses, but he also supplied a note to the reader which, as will be shown, complicates the story further.

Georg Witzel, prolific author of more than 120 books, was born in Vacha, and studied in Erfurt in 1516 to 1517.[21] In 1521 he was ordained as a priest. Later he married without permission and was compelled to resign his position in Vacha. He moved to Eisenach and became an assistant to Jacob Strauss. As a convert to Lutheranism he then received a parish north of Wittenberg, where he studied Hebrew and the Church Fathers. His Hebrew teacher was the convert Antonius Margaritha, notorious for his *Der gantz Jüdisch Glaub* (The entire Jewish faith; 1530), a vicious representation of his erstwhile religion. It would appear that Witzel and Margaritha met each other during the Lutheran phase of their lives in Niemegt bei Belzig near Wittenberg. The relationship between the two scholars is engraved in a handwritten note on a copy of Antonius Margaritha's Hebrew Psalter (Leipzig, 1533) which proudly announces "Antonius Margaritha Hebrew teacher of G. Wicelius."[22] But Witzel rejected Luther and returned to Eisleben as a Catholic preacher, and in 1538, Duke George of Saxony employed him as a consultant in the cause of religious reconciliation. Witzel's task was to formulate a statement that could be the basis of new religious discourse. His reform program, which tried to forge a middle road between papal and Lutheran extremes, favoured a return to the simplicity of the apostolic Church,[23] a position which earned him the epithet "Papist" or "humanist" by the Lutherans and "Lutheran" by the Catholics. Until his death in 1573, Witzel continued to believe that concord could be achieved. In 1534 he made a German translation of Erasmus's Psalms commentary entitled *De sarcienda ecclesiae concordia* (On mending the unity of the Church) which as Erika Rummel has shown, was published without preface or commentary, but supposedly intended as a tribute to Erasmus. He regarded himself as an Erasmian, but judging from Erasmus's failure to respond to two of his letters it would seem that Erasmus had no desire to keep Witzel's company or to get involved in his struggle against the Lutherans.[24] Indeed, according to Rummel, he cannot be regarded as an Erasmian and never espoused the idea of accommodation. For our purposes here, what is important is Witzel's own self-image as a follower of Erasmus.

Witzel's literary production was not restricted to matters of religious belief and practice. Among his numerous writings are two small treatises on the Hebrew language.[25] In both tracts Witzel mentions some of the renowned Hebraists of his time, singling out Münster for special praise.[26] In his *Oration in Praise of the Hebrew Language* Witzel graphically describes the heavenly reward which awaits the Hebraist, literally, "the one who crosses over."[27] Such a person, Witzel assures us, is ensured a speedy transition to the future life where he will find himself in the academy of the prophets and other "Bibliographi," scribes, or authors of the Hagiographa. Such dedication to the holy tongue reappears some years later in another small treatise entitled *Idiomata quaedam linguae sanctae in Scripturis veteris Testamenti observata* (Some idioms of the Holy Tongue discerned in the Old Testament Scriptures) (Mainz, 1543). This is an original work. Using his knowledge of the Vulgate, Greek and Latin literature, and German, Witzel examines how biblical Hebrew idioms are translated into other languages.[28]

Clearly then Hebrew played an important role in Witzel's religious life. He never seems to have had any aspirations to study rabbinic literature although on one occasion he refers to his astonishment at being shown all the numerous volumes of the Talmud.[29] In his quest to learn Hebrew, Witzel appears to have sought out Jews and apparently came across a good cross-section of the community ranging from downright imposters to a rather better kind, a certain "Slomo," and a "Nephtalim Islebianus" with his assistant Jehuda who taught him literature. He describes how he deliberately avoided theological debate with his instructors, not wishing to suffer the frustration of "throwing pearls before swine."[30] In 1543, during his stay in Prague, however, Witzel became embroiled in discussions with Jews, an experience which led him to denounce them in no uncertain terms.[31]

Long before these experiences had alienated Witzel from Jews and their traditions, he had read Münster's Hebrew piece which impressed him more than the other "little gems" (*gemmulae*) of the collection printed by Froben.[32] The admiration was not generated by aesthetic but rather by religio-political considerations. Witzel's devotion to Erasmus's memory and his religious commitment to fight Lutheranism had stimulated him to undertake the translation. For Witzel, Münster's testimonial for Erasmus was particularly compelling by virtue of being written by a schismatic.[33] His own recognition of Erasmus's divine gift only underlined the behavior of certain Lutherans who had hated Erasmus during his lifetime, and continued to vent their spleen on him now that he was dead. In Witzel's terms their behavior was exceptional because it did not follow the rule that envy should become "silent after death," an allusion to Ovid's *Amores* (1, 15, 39), also quoted in Erasmus's *Adagia*. Their reaction to the magnificent commemoration of Erasmus's death was to sully his memory with false accusations. The accusations that Witzel enumerates are the usual ones: Erasmus was impious, and he did not know Scripture for he did not possess the spirit.[34] Worse still, Witzel exclaims, they allege that this exemplary person was no different from or even inferior to the Lombards, Thomas, Albertus, Scotus, the Hugos and other followers of Aristotelian theology.[35] It was this state of affairs that had prompted Witzel to produce a Latin rendering of the beautiful testimony penned by the outstanding polymath Sebastian. He admits that allowances have to be made for Münster's "native" Hebraisms; after all, he remained a steadfast adherent to the truth. This statement of Witzel requires comment. Ostensibly he is referring to the actual eulogy in which Münster occasionally lapses into rabbinic idiom. But there is also a more general point to his mild criticism. In his Hebrew obituary of

Münster, Oswald Schreckenfuchs gives us an insight, albeit not an impartial one, into his master's life of devoted study.[36] He argues that Münster had performed a very great service for Christians by editing and translating Hebrew texts. But he also notes that his teacher had suffered for these activities earning the denigratory epithet of "judaiser." According to Schreckenfuchs, Münster wrote his dialogue between a Christian and an "arrogant Jew"—an anti-Jewish polemic—in order to deflect criticism of his learned devotion to Jewish literature. Witzel seems to have been familiar with these allegations and therefore took pains both to acknowledge Münster's "native" knowledge of Hebrew and to insist on his religious integrity.

Witzel's address to the reader then moves from polemics to philology with a gesture to conventional apologetics. The Latin translation necessarily loses the charm (*gratia*) of the original, but it is required since very few people know the "alien language." There may be an echo here of Adage 826. Discussing the proverb "Wickedness proceeds from the wicked," (1 Sam 24:14) Erasmus states, "If a proverb is transferred into a foreign language, its charm (*gratia*) is greatly diminished."[37]

From philology Witzel progresses to rhetoric and to the early Fathers. He had wanted to write a monody, but Friedrich Nausea had already produced one such tribute.[38] Witzel confers the highest praise on Nausea's *Monodia*, comparing it to Gregory of Nazianzus's panegyric on St. Basil, a text that describes the benevolent relationship between master and disciple. Gregory's rather longer oration had received universal approbation for its powerful rhetoric and beauty.[39] In his analogy between the two funeral orations, Witzel seems to be implicitly forging a connection between Basil and Erasmus. Given Erasmus's own predilection for Basil—he had edited the *editio princeps* of part of Basil's works, and had commended Basil's simple and natural style—such an analogy conferred Erasmus with the highest accolade he himself would value. Witzel concludes this preface with the plea that underpins the mood of all the mourners: "It is a crime for any scholar to remain silent in the face of such a momentous disaster for the Republic [of letters]."[40]

A *mispad*—this is how Witzel describes Münster's eulogy. Biblical Hebrew requires the word *misped* (lament), as in Genesis 50:10, or else he could have used the rabbinic term *hesped* (eulogy).[41] My task here is not to point out errors which do occur in his rendition, usually on account of misreading the root of the verbs used by Münster. Rather, what is of interest, reading between the jagged lines, is Witzel's mode of translating and interpreting the text. Here, as in his German translation of Erasmus's work discussed above, Witzel molds his rendition according to his own religious notions.

As shown above, Münster's description of Erasmus as beloved of God and humans is a conscious adaptation of a passage from tractate *Avot*. In his marginal gloss on the text Witzel suggests that "beloved" is an allusion to the meaning of Erasmus's name in Greek (*erasmios*).[42] It was indeed the name Erasmus adopted in full knowledge of its meaning when he had begun to make progress in Greek in 1503.[43] Whether it was Münster's authorial intention to pun on Erasmus name, I cannot say for certain.

Witzel's gloss does engage the reader with the man Erasmus rather than with a somewhat abstract notion of the deceased.

Yet clearly another agenda informs Witzels's glosses, namely a desire to Christianize Münster's text. Münster writes "all his trust was in the Messiah our redeemer," Witzel translates "ad CHRISTUM Redemptorem contulit." The capital letters used in this context enhance the Christian message. Similarly, Münster uses the expression "there was none like him among the people of the Lord," a common Hebrew phrase that seems to allude in particular to 1 Sam 10:24, where Samuel addresses the people concerning their future king, Saul, whom "the Lord has chosen for there is none like him among all the people." In his marginal gloss Witzel points the reader to the New Testament and to the use of the same idiom in Matthew 11:11 in which Jesus states, "Verily I say unto you: Among them that are born of women there has not risen anyone greater than John the Baptist." The climax of the eulogy offers a vision of Erasmus seated among the righteous in Paradise. Münster's choice of vocabulary suggested certain possible Hebrew parallels. Witzel had something else in mind and his gloss refers the reader to Jesus's words to the malefactor in Luke 23 (v. 43), "Verily I say unto thee, Today shall thou be with me in paradise." By giving Münster's few rabbinisms a good Christian gloss Witzel's purpose is quite clear. There is to be no ambiguity about Erasmus—he belongs to the context of Christian, not Old Testament or Jewish, salvation history.

From the beginning of the sixteenth century onwards all manner of literary artifice was used in order to commemorate marriages, deaths and other events of public significance. As Money and Olszowy have shown, the purpose of this type of literary endeavor was to exhibit learning (which explains the presence of both Hebrew and Greek in the sixteenth-century collections) as well as to create an outlet for expressing emotions.[44] (Yet Erasmus himself encouraged the suppression and concealment of any great grief of the spirit.[45]) In addition, these *Festschriften* and memorial volumes could serve political and religious ends. This is all true in the case of the volumes published in response to the death of Erasmus. There is no question that Münster was showing off his prowess in Hebrew, and there is no reason to doubt that he was also genuinely mourning the passing of Erasmus. But as I hope to have shown, his short tribute triggered a very particular reaction from a theologian and scholar. Witzel admired Münster, but he was also a colleague. Münster coopted him to write the description of Buchonia and its capital Fulda in the third part of his *Cosmographia*.[46] Once again religious boundaries were transcended; in this case, for the sake of scholarship. But Witzel also used Münster for his religious mission, and his Latin rendition was supposed to help disseminate a picture of the true Erasmus.

Each scholar had and has his or her own notion of Erasmus. It is telling that in his obituary of Münster, Oswald Schreckenfuchs also brings Erasmus into the picture. In Hebrew he relates, "Then God raised a wonderful prince and instilled his heart with the intellectual powers to fathom all wisdom—his name, Erasmus of Rotterdam, blessed be his memory—and I swear that he was the only one to inspire

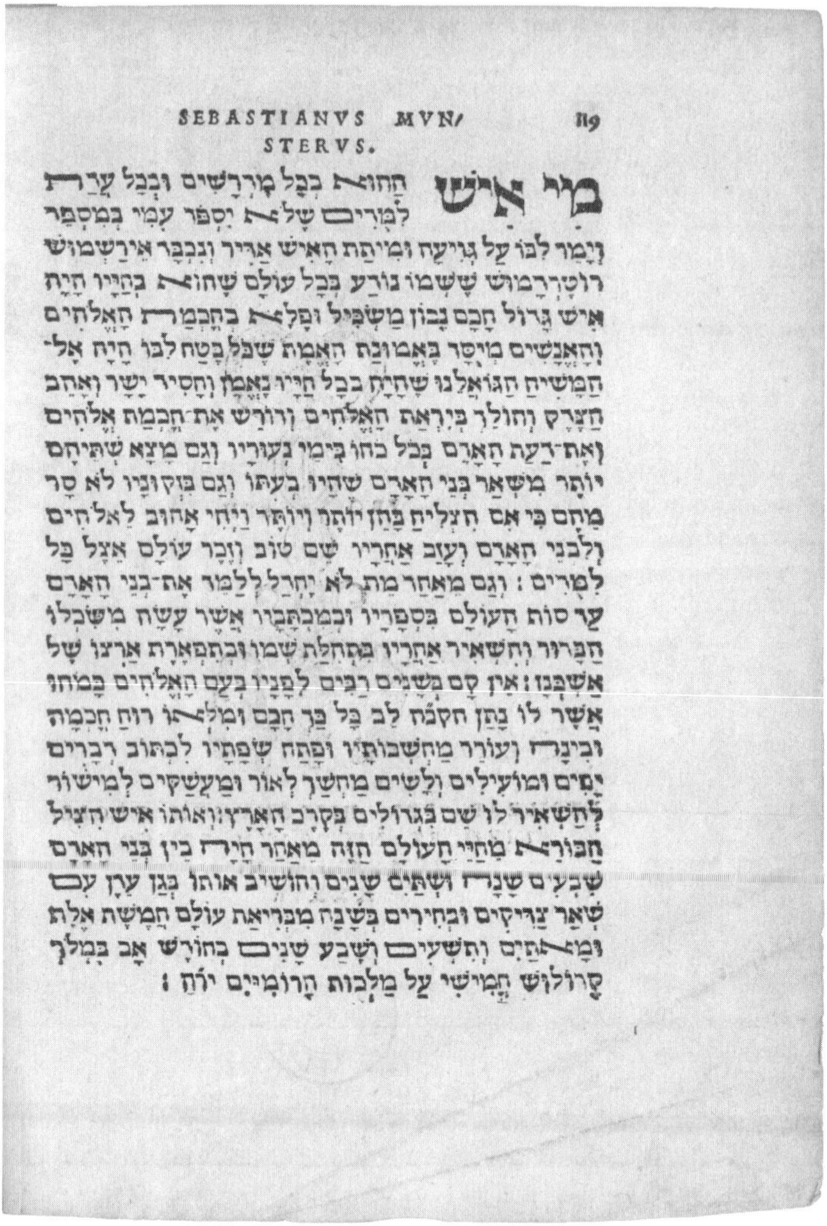

מִי אִישׁ הֶחָפֵץ בְּכָל מֶרְחַשִׁים וּבְכָל עֲרָרֶת
לְמֹרִים שֶׁלֹּא יְסַפֵּר עִמִּי בְּמִסְפַּר
וְיָמֹר לִבּוֹ עַל גְּרִיעָה וּמִיתַת הָאִישׁ אַדִּיר וְנִכְבָּר אֵירַשְׁמוּשׁ
רוֹטְרְדַמוּשׁ שֶׁשְּׁמוֹ נוֹדַע בְּכָל עוֹלָם שֶׁהוּא בְּחַיָּיו הָיָה
אִישׁ גָּדוֹל חָכָם נָבוֹן מַשְׂכִּיל וּפֶלֶא בְּחָכְמַת הָאֱלֹהִים
וְהָאֲנָשִׁים מְיַסֵּר בְּאֵמוּנַת הָאֱמֶת שֶׁפֵּל בָּטַח לִבּוֹ אֶל
הַמָּשִׁיחַ הַגּוֹאֲלֵנוּ שֶׁחַח בְּכָל חַיָּיו נֶאֱמָן וְהָסִיר יָשָׁר וְאָהַב
הַצֶּדֶק וְחוֹלֵך בְּיִרְאַת הָאֱלֹהִים וְדוֹרֵשׁ אֶת חָכְמַת אֱלֹהִים
וְאֶת דַּעַת הָאָרֶם בְּכָל כֹּחוֹ בְּיָמִי נְעוּרָיו וְגַם מָצָא שְׂפָתֵיהֶם
יוֹתֵר מִשְּׁאָר בְּנֵי הָאָרֶם שֶׁהָיוּ בְּעִתּוֹ וְגַם בּוּקְוָיו לֹא סָר
מַחַס כִּי אִם תִּצְלִיחַ בָּהֶן יוֹתָרְ וְיוֹתֵר וַיְהִי אָהוּב לָאֱלֹהִים
וְלִבְנֵי הָאָרֶם וְעָזַב אַחֲרָיו שֵׁם טוֹב וְזֵכֶר עוֹלָם אֵצֶל כָּל
לְמֹרִים : וְגַם מֵאַחַר מֹת לֹא יֶחְרַל לְלַמֵּר אֶת בְּנֵי הָאָרֶם
עַר סוֹת הָעוֹלָם בִּסְפָרָיו וּבְמִבְחַבֶּרָיו אֲשֶׁר עָשָׂה מִשְּׂכְלוֹ
חַבָּרוּר וְהִשְׁאִיר אַחֲרָיו בִּתְחִלַּת שְׁמוֹ וּבְתַמְאֶרֶת אַרְצוֹ שֶׁל
אַשְׁכְּנָזוּ : אֵין קָם מִשֵּׁנִים רַבִּים לְפָנָיו בָּעָם הָאֱלֹהִים בָּמְחֵנוּ
אֲשֶׁר לוֹ נָתַן חִקְנֹת לֵב בְּל בַּר חָכָם וּמִלֵּא־וּ רוּחַ חָכְמָה
וּבִינָרֶ וְעוֹרֵר מַחְשְׁבוֹתָיו וּפָתַח שְׂפָתָיו לִכְתוֹב רְבָרִים
יָמִים וּמוֹעִילִים וְלֵשִׂים מַחֲשַׁרְ לְאוֹר וּמַעֲשָׂקִים לְמִישׁוֹר
לְהַשְׁאִיר לוֹ שֵׁם בִּגְרוּלִים בְּקֶרֶב הָאָרֶץ וַאוֹתוֹ אִישׁ הִצִּיל
חַבּוּרֵ־א מַחַיֵּי תַעֲלוֹם הַזֶּה מֵאַחַר חַיָּרֹ בֵּין בְּנֵי הָאָרֶם
שְׁבְעִ־ם שָׁנָרֶ וּשְׁתַּיִם שָׁנִים וְחוֹשִׁיב אוֹתוֹ בְּגַן עֵרֶן עִם
שְׁאַר צַדִּיקִים וּבְחִירִים בְּשָׁבַח מִבְּרִיאַת עוֹלָם חֲמֵשֶׁת אֶלֶת
וּמַ־אָתַיִם וְתִשְׁעִים וְשֶׁבַע שָׁנִים בַּחוֹרֵשׁ אָב בְּמֶלֶךְ
סָרוֹלוֹשׁ חֲמִישִׁי עַל מַלְכוּת הָרוֹמִיִּם יֹרֹחַ ‖

FIGURE 1. Sebastian Münster's eulogy for Erasmus (Basel, 1537).

the Germans (Ashkenazim) with love of scholarship."[47] Despite himself Erasmus was also appropriated by Hebrew scholars, complicating the already complicated *persona* that is Erasmus.

Notes

1. Le Clerc's edition of Erasmus's complete works, *Des Erasmi Roterodami Opera Omnia*, 10 vols. (Leiden, 1703–6), does not include the Hebrew obituary.

2. The volume has two parts: *Catalogi duo operum Des. Erasmi Roterodami ab ipso conscripti et digesti*. Amerbach, one of the three administrators of Erasmus's estate, writes that this catalogue of Erasmus's works produced by Erasmus himself was partly meant to prevent incorrect attribution of works to Erasmus. The second part or appendix is entitled *Epitaphiorum ac Tumulorum libellus quibus mors Erasmi defletur cum elegantissima Germani Brixii epistola ad clarissimum virum D. Gul. Bellaium Langaeum* (Basel, 1537). On reactions to Erasmus's death see Bruce Mansfield, *Phoenix of His Age: Interpretations of Erasmus c1550–1750* (Toronto, 1979) and Karl Enenkel, "Epitaphs on Erasmus and Self-Definition of the Republic of Letters," *Erasmus of Rotterdam Society Yearbook* 21 (2001): 14–29.

3. *Epitaphiorum . . . libellus*, 119. Joseph Prijs, *Die Basler Hebräischen Drucke (1492–1866)* (Olten und Freiburg I. Br., 1964), 76, refers to Witzel's Latin translation of Münster's obituary discussed in the second half of this paper.

4. *Opus Epistolarum Des. Erasmi Roterodami*, ed. P. S. Allen (Oxford, 1906), 1, 405,ll. 36–38. On Erasmus's knowledge of Hebrew, see Leon E. Halkin, "Érasme et les langues," *Revue des langues vivantes* 6 (1969): 563–79. See also Basil Hall, "Erasmus: Biblical Scholar and Catholic Reformer," in his *Humanists and Protestants, 1500–1900* (Edinburgh, 1990), 63–64; Shimon Markish, *Erasmus and the Jews* (Chicago, 1986), ch.6, 112–41; Dominic Baker-Smith, *Introduction to Exposition of the Psalms* (Toronto, 1997), xlvii–lvi.

5. Preface to the New Testament *Methodus*, ll. 97–100.

6. In *De recta latini graecique sermonis pronunciatione dialogus*, in *Opera omnia* (Amsterdam, 1969), 1:4, 32, he states that Hebrew should not form part of the essential curriculum for the young— Hebrew should be left to theologians and Jews, to prevent the child imbibing "some Judaism with his alphabet."

7. *Opus Epistolarum Des. Erasmi Roterdami*, 2:77.

8. On Erasmus's biblical commentaries see Erica Rummel, "The Textual and Hermeneutic Work of Desiderius Erasmus of Rotterdam," in *Hebrew Bible/Old Testament*, ed. M. Sæbø (Göttingen, 2008), 219–21.

9. On literary epitaphs in Hebrew, see the forthcoming article of Michela Andreatta, "Collecting Hebrew Epitaphs in the Early Modern Age: The Christian Hebraist as Antiquarian" in *Jewish Texts and Their Readers in Early Modern Europe*, ed. S. Mandelbrote and J. Weinberg (Leiden, 2014).

10. On this revised edition of *De recta latini Graecique sermonis pronuntatione and Ciceronianus* (Basel, 1530) see Judith Rice Henderson, "Language, Race and Church Reform: Erasmus' *De recta Latini Graecique sermonis pronunciatione dialogus* and *Ciceronianus*," "*Renaissance and Reformation* 30.2 (2006): 3–41. One of the new additions of the edition was Münster's Hebrew text printed among other memorial poems and epitaphs for Froben (Basel, 1530), 444: "Sebastiani Munsteri in eundem hebraice."

זאת המצבה חוצבה לזכר החשוב יוחנן פרובאניות הדופס בזלי שנפטר בשם טוב ונקבר
פה ביום ב' לה" כסליו בשנת חמשת אלפים רפ"ה מבריאת עולם

(This inscription was sculpted in memory of the esteemed Johann Frobenius the Basel printer who died with good repute and was buried here on Monday, 5 Kislev 5285 aera mundi).

11. Münster's epitaph was printed in DD. *Ioannis Oecolampadii et Huldrichi Zvinglii epistolarum libri quatuor* (Basel, 1536), sig. θ3 recto. He makes a Hebrew play on Oecolampadius's name בית לפידי.

12. See appendix.

13. A similar sentiment is expressed by Paulus Volzius in his letter to Beatus Rhenanus published in the same volume: "The one consolation for everybody that relieves the pain is that al-

though he is physically dead, his spirit lives forever teaching through his books (*libris*) which like children (*liberis*) survive him" (*Epitaphiorum libellus,* 93).

14. Erasmus, *Epitaphiorum libellus,* 119,11.13–14.

15. Karl Enenkel, "Epitaphs on Erasmus and the Self-Definition of the Republic of Letters," *Erasmus of Rotterdam Society Yearbook* 21 (2001): 14–29. Cf. Nausea's *Monodia* H3 verso where Erasmus is compared to Basil as depicted by Gregory Naziazenus.

16. There has been much speculation about the date of Erasmus's birth, but I have not come across any reference to 72. The conventional birth date is 1466 which would suggest that he was seventy when he died in 1536. See Harry Vredeveld "The Age of Erasmus and the Year of His Birth," *Renaissance Quarterly* 46.4 (1993): 754–809.

17. Latin writers celebrate Erasmus's heavenly life in a similar fashion. See, for example, Johann Witz (Sapidus), for example, who described Erasmus sanctified and seated in good company—that of St Paul and St Jerome (*Epitaphia,* "Erasmus, sive Apotheosis Erasmi, Joanne Sapido autore," 96–108, esp. 99–100).

18. Prijs (*Die Basler Hebräischen Drucke,* 76) points out this error. It may be that Münster confused the date of Erasmus's death with the year of publication.

19. He also wrote under the pseudonym Agricola Phagus.

20. The rendition and its preface to the reader also contained some short Latin poems by Witzel, Joannes Rubecanus, and Joannes Gigas Thuringus.

21. On Witzel, see Ralph Keen,"The Fathers in Counter-Reformation Theology in the pre-Tridentine period," in *The Reception of the Church Fathers in the West: From the Carolingians to the Maurists,* 2 vols., ed. I. Backus (Leiden, 1997), 2:701–43, and Keen, "The Early Church as a Model of Religious Unity in the Sixteenth Century: Georg Cassander and Georg Witzel," in *Conciliation and Confession: The Struggle for Unity in the Age of Reform, 1516–1648,* ed. H. P. Louthan and R. C. Zachman (Notre Dame, Ind., 2004), 106–33.

22. See Barbara Henze, *Aus Liebe zur Kirche Reform: Die Bemühungen Georg Witzels (1501–1573) und die Kircheneinheit* (Münster, 1995), 15, n. 105. The copy is in the Freiburg University library, sig. L 4030.

23. This is formulated in his *Typus ecclesiae prioris* which was reprinted many times.

24. Erika Rummel, "Erasmus and the Restoration of Unity in the Church," in *Conciliation and Confession,* 67–70, and Rummel, *The Confessionalization of Humanism in Reformation Germany* (Oxford, 2000), 138–44.

25. For a list of his writings see Gregor Richter, *Die Schriften Wizels bibliographisch bearbeitet* (Fulda,1913) which comprises a catalogue of Witzel's writings made by Johann Quenters Erben in the year of Witzel's death, and Henze, *Aus Liebe zur Kirche Reform,* 306–411.

26. *Oratio in laudem hebraicae linguae* printed in *Homiliae duae de ecclesiae mysteriis* (Leipzig, 1534 and separately in Leipzig, 1538). It was republished by Hermann von der Hardt in *Programma . . .* Helmstadt, 1704: *Programma,* Sig. D 4 recto. Münster is also mentioned in similarly laudatory terms in Witzel's *Idiomata linguae sanctae* (Mainz, 1543), 3r.

27. Witzel, *Oratio in laudem Hebraicae linguae,* sig. B 5 recto.

28. It should be noted, however, that his examples are not given either in Hebrew characters or in transliteration.

29. Witzel, *Idiomata linguae sanctae,* 3r: "When I stayed in Bamberg for some days last year . . . Paulus Nedeccarus showed me all the books of the Talmud. I was amazed at the sight of such bulk." This innocent and apparently nonjudgmental reaction to a first viewing of the Talmud is exceptional for a Christian scholar of this period.

30. Witzel, *Conquestio de calamitoso in praesens rerum Christianarum statu* (Leipzig, 1538), sig. E iv recto.

31. Witzel describes these experiences in the introduction to *Disputatio Christianorum et*

Iudaeorum olim Romae habita coram Imperatore Constantino (Mainz, 1544). 13v–14r. See F. Secret, "Notes sur les hébraisants chrétiens," *REJ* 124.1 (1965): 159–62.

32. Witzel, *Conquestio.* The reader's note is at the end of the work sig. E iii verso–E iv recto and the translation of Münster's text on sig. E iv verso–F recto.

33. Witzel, *Lament,* E iii verso.

34. An allusion to the debate over free will. In *Hyperaspistes,* Erasmus responds to the charges of impiety by claiming the authority of tradition in support of the doctrine of free will.

35. This seems to echo Erasmus's own comment in his Dedication to his Paraphrase on the Epistle of St James where he speaks of his acceptance or not of the interpretations of Thomas, Hugo, and the other scholastic theologians.

36. Oswald Schreckenfuchs, *Ma'amar Kinah: Oratio funebris de obitu . . . Sebastiani Munsteri* (Basel, 1533), sig. ג 2v–3r.

37. *Adagiorum chlias prima,* in *Opera Omnia Desiderii Erasmi Roterodami,* II, 2 (Amsterdam, 1998), 350. Here Erasmus provides the Hebrew text without transliteration. Hebrew words are found sporadically in other works such as in his *In Praise of Folly.* The Cologne edition of 1526 edited under Erasmus's supervision contains Gerardus Listrius's somewhat idosyncratic annotations attempting to gloss the Hebrew words (e.g. 304) or to provide more illustrations in Hebrew (e.g. 231).

38. Schreckenfuchs, *Ma'amar Kinah,* sig. G2 recto–I recto. Nausea also describes Erasmus as "Germanus."

39. Erasmus did not translate Gregory Nazianzenus's works, but wrote a preface to Wilibald Pirkheimer's translation of thirty orations of Gregory including his panegyric on Basil. Erasmus's preface is mostly a eulogy to his friend Pirkheimer, but he speaks of Gregory's Isocratean style and sublime theology which had deterred him from translating the works.

40. Witzel, *Conquestio,* sig. E iv recto.

41. Witzel, *Conquestio,* 80v–81r.

42. Witzel, *Conquestio,* sig. F verso.

43. See Beatus Rhenanus's letter to Charles V of June 1540 printed in the Basel edition of Erasmus's *Opera omnia* (Basel, 1538–40), 1:70–71.

44. David K Money and Judith Olszowy, "Hebrew Commemorative Poetry in Cambridge, 1564–1763," *Transactions of the Cambridge Bibliographical Society* 10.5 (1995): 549–76.

45. Erasmus, *De conscribendis epistolis* (1522), 433.

46. *Cosmographiae universalis lib. VI,* (Basel, 1550), 705–7. On Münster's appeal to scholars, cities, and princes for help with his monumental enterprise see Matthew Mclean, *The Cosmographia of Sebastian Münster. Describing the World in the Reformation* (Aldershot, 2007), 156–62.

47. Schreckenfuchs, *Ma'amar Kinah,* sig. ג2 recto.

"FAIR MEASURES FROM OUR REGION"

❊ ❊ ❊

The Study of Jewish Antiquities in Renaissance Italy

Andrew Berns

University of South Carolina

THE Jews of Renaissance Italy displayed an acute interest in the material culture of the ancient and late antique Jewish past. One manifestation of that interest is a flurry of compositions that concern weights, measures, and coinage from the biblical and talmudic periods. The number of texts that have survived, the breadth of their compass, and the consistency of their style present a new phenomenon to the historian. From their medieval forbears, Renaissance Jews inherited an interest in numismatics that was episodic, undisciplined, and polyglot. In the sixteenth century they formed that interest into an intellectual preoccupation that ran parallel to, and received inspiration from, a passion for the study of classical antiquities that affected many sectors of Italian culture and society, Jewish as well as Christian.

Renaissance Jews were not, strictly speaking, innovators in this regard; they inherited a concern with the proper understanding of technical terminology in Judaism's canonical texts from medieval scholars. In the middle of the nineteenth century, Leopold Zunz demonstrated that a number of medieval Jews investigated ancient weights and measures.[1] There were two medieval authorities who wrote in sustained fashion on these topics: Joseph Ibn Aknin (d. ca. 1220), and Estori HaParhi (d. 1337). Ibn Aknin was born in Barcelona but spent most of his life in Fez. He wrote a treatise in Arabic that was translated into Hebrew as *Ma'amar al ha-midot veha-mish-*

kalot (Exposition on Measures and Weights).[2] HaParḥi penned a lengthy work on the geography and antiquities of the Land of Israel that contains a chapter on coinage, weights, and measures.[3] Maimonides (d. 1204), too, scattered observations on this issue throughout his commentaries and treatises.[4] Two common denominators underlie these twelfth- and thirteenth-century writings: a tendency to rely on Hebrew or Aramaic equivalents for ancient values, and the related absence of one single, internationally recognized currency into which biblical and talmudic figures could be rendered. Occasionally Ibn Aknin, HaParḥi, and Maimonides did give Arabic or Spanish equivalents for Hebrew terms; Ibn Aknin used three different languages to translate talmudic currencies, Arabic, Provençal, and French.[5] More frequently, however, medieval writers resorted to other Hebrew words to explain the values and measures about which they wrote.[6] Such intramural calculation may have given their readers a rough sense of the volume of a *kor* or the weight of a *shekel*, but it was less effective at summoning in their readers' minds a clear image of ancient measures that they could understand in contemporary terms. In the Renaissance things were different; texts and collections proliferated that sought to display ancient coinage in its full splendor.[7] From the fifteenth century on coins had a ubiquitous presence in princely and ducal collections, in paintings, and in various sorts of writings. And the study of them was undertaken to help students and connoisseurs develop a more accurate and visually sophisticated appreciation of the ancient world.[8] Such a detailed understanding of the ancient world was more than just a fashion; it constituted a form of commentary on classical texts.

If only a few medieval Jews wrote about coins, weights, and measures in a sustained fashion, more Renaissance Jews did so. Ibn Yaḥya's *Shalshelet ha-kabalah*, printed in 1587, contains an important investigation (*derashah*) on coins. In that work Ibn Yaḥya mentions his teacher Ovadiah Sforno, with whom he studied in Bologna. Sforno taught him about numismatics, and Ibn Yaḥya states that he saw among Sforno's papers some notes that rendered talmudic coinage into contemporary values.[9] Several of those notes are preserved in Ibn Yaḥya's book, and even more may be found in a manuscript in Cambridge University Library, along with additional observations on the same topic by Isaac HaCohen. That manuscript will be the focus of this essay.[10] Besides Ibn Yaḥya's composition and the Cambridge manuscript miscellany there are other examples of this trend. For instance, at the turn of the seventeenth century Abraham Portaleone dedicated a chapter in his encyclopedia of biblical antiquities, *Shilte ha-giborim*, to coins, weights and measures.[11] If we shift our gaze to Christian writings about Jewish coinage even broader vistas open. Scholars such as Guillaume Budé, Benito Arias Montano, William Peacham, and, later Blasio Ugolini, wrote about and collected writings on Jewish antiquities, particularly coins.[12] In Jewish culture this flourishing of interest in numismatics took place not only in specific monographs devoted to the subject, as was the case with Christian scholars, but in book chapters (Ibn Yaḥya, Abraham Portaleone), personal letters (Ovadiah Sforno), and casual jottings (Ovadiah Sforno and Isaac HaCohen). The diversity of genres in which Renaissance Jews wrote about numismatics testifies to the broad diffusion of interest in that topic.

A number of factors help explain this rather sudden and energetic profusion of writings on Jewish antiquities, especially numismatics. In the middle of the sixteenth century several works by medieval Jewish thinkers were printed on Italian presses either for the first time, or in enlarged, improved editions. Among them were those of Maimonides and HaParḥi.[13] Though both thinkers had been read in manuscript for several hundred years before the spread of printing on the Italian peninsula, the printed publication of such books stimulated a renewed study of those texts.[14] Another potential cause of this interest in numismatics is the emergence and diffusion of a new, more favorable attitude toward money in the fifteenth century. Jacques Le Goff has shown that while Church authorities in the Middle Ages condemned money, saw it as despicable, and viewed wealth as suspect, humanists such as Francesco Barbaro, Leonardo Bruni, Poggio Bracciolini, and Leon Battista Alberti helped change European perceptions of money.[15] They did so at the same time that a new series of compositions on ancient coinage emerged, both Greco-Roman and Hebrew.

But more important than the printed publication of medieval works, or a new view of money promulgated by a few humanists, was a widespread fascination in Europe at this time with numismatics.[16] In the early sixteenth century, Thomas More wrote to a Flemish antiquities dealer and extolled the historical value of coin-collecting. Several of Titian's paintings around the middle of the century depict the Venetian antiques collector Jacopo Strada proudly displaying coins.[17] In the 1550s and 1560s the Spanish cleric Antonio Augustín exchanged a series of letters on coins with the Italian antiquarian Fulvio Orsini.[18] Later, in 1571, Augustín published his *Dialogos de las medallas*, which was translated into Italian in 1592 by Dionigi Ottaviano Sada and achieved considerable notoriety as a ground-breaking work in numismatic methodology. As Peter Miller, John Cunnally, Francis Haskell, and Roberto Weiss have all shown, the study of antiquities was a conspicuous feature of Renaissance intellectual life, and numismatics constituted a serious subset of it.[19]

In Italy this energy for antiquities was powered by geography and archeology; the soil that Renaissance Italians walked on and occasionally excavated teemed with material remains of the ancient past. The art historian Leonard Barkan dubbed Rome of the fifteenth and sixteenth centuries "a gigantic archaeological playground."[20] Nearer to the dawn of the Renaissance Petrarch described in his *Familiar Letters* (completed in 1359) how "often there came to me in Rome a vine digger, holding in his hands an ancient jewel or a golden Latin coin, sometimes scratched by the hard edge of a hoe, urging me either to buy it or to identify the heroic faces inscribed on them."[21] In the Renaissance, collectors and scholars pioneered a new attitude toward antiquity. In contrast to views in the Middle Ages, which valued the tangible remains of the ancient world largely because they were attractive or useful, fifteenth- and sixteenth-century scholars cherished them because they were ancient.[22]

Historians of Jewish intellectual and cultural history have made only passing mention of Renaissance Jews' interest in antiquarian subjects.[23] Similarly, historiography on the Italian Renaissance in general has not properly acknowledged the prevalence of Jewish interest in their own cultural history—an interest that developed in step with the antiquarian researches of their Christian neighbors. The Hebrew manuscript I focus on in this study consists of a single crabbed folio sheet, written in a small, Italian hand of the late sixteenth century. A Cambridge University scholar has identified the codex in which it is found as a supercommentary on Rashi by Ovadiah ben Abraham of Bertinoro, the famous interpreter of the Mishnah. The colophon indicates that the work was copied by Judah ben Samuel da Fermo, and completed on 13 Sivan 5296 (according to the Jewish custom of assigning dates from the creation of the world) or June 20, 1536. The bibliographer's thorough description of the manuscript includes this observation: "the fly-leaves at the commencement contain interesting notes in which R 'Obadyah Sforno's, R. Yitzchaq Kohen's and an anonymous owner's own calculations of coins, weights, and measures mentioned in the Talmud (and some also of those in the Bible) are given."[24] The work is difficult to date, but given that Ibn Yaḥya's *Shalshelet ha-kabalah* is mentioned, we may presume that these notes were recorded after 1587. The manuscript is a miniature miscellany. Rather than representing Bertinoro's own researches into the modern equivalents of ancient coins, weights, and measures, the text collects and distills the numismatic and metrological work of several prominent Jewish scholars active in Italy in the later fifteenth and sixteenth centuries.

In an undated letter, Ovadiah Sforno, who served as head of the Jewish academy (*rosh yeshiva*) in Bologna, wrote about talmudic coins. At the beginning of the letter he recollected that "being in Rome with my colleagues, [in order] to find out the truth about the coins of the Talmud," he intended "to compare them to the currency of Romagna," a region in north-central Italy that was at that time part of the papal states.[25] The notes preserved in the Cambridge manuscript add that Sforno wished to provide a "practical accounting (*ḥeshbon asui*)" of ancient currencies. As an educator and leader of a Jewish academy, the "practical" aims of such an accounting are clear: Sforno wished his students to have a more precise knowledge of the Talmud. That knowledge included awareness of its material culture and economic language, expressed in the vernacular with which his students were familiar. Sforno's close working relationship with prominent Christian scholars in Bologna, where he lived, taught, and practiced medicine from 1527 until his death in 1550, may have stimulated his interest in rendering talmudic values into contemporary Italian ones.[26] Although Sforno's complete work on coins has been lost, sections of it are preserved in the Cambridge manuscript.

In both Sforno's and HaCohen's jottings, talmudic coins are routinely translated into Italian currency. Solid measurements, on the other hand, lack a reliable vernacular standard. Sixteenth-century Italians such as Sforno, HaCohen, and Ibn Yaḥya could rely upon international standards of coinage, those struck and disseminated by the Venetian government and that of the papal states. They could not, however, rely on an accepted standard for liquid and solid measurements.

Sforno's work, for example, lists eleven types of currencies mentioned in the Bible and Talmud, including the *isar, pundion, me'ah, drachmon, dinar,* and *kikar.* Of these, all but one are explained in terms of their contemporary Italian values. For example, Sforno writes that "the *isar* is equivalent to four measures, two *quattrini.*"[27] A *quattrino* was a coin of very limited value that circulated widely in late Medieval and Renaissance Italy.[28] Besides the *quattrino,* Sforno uses other Italian coins to explain the value of talmudic ones, including the *bagattino* and the *giulio.* And there are many other examples.[29] As we have seen, medieval scholars such as Moses Maimonides and Estori HaParhi linked biblical and talmudic coins to a wide variety of coinages from disparate geographical areas. Sforno, by contrast, could use popular Italian currencies to assign standard values to the ancient coins he studied.

The next author included in the Cambridge miscellany is Isaac HaCohen of Mantua. HaCohen's selection reads remarkably like Sforno's, more like a list than a piece of formal prose. Unlike Sforno, however, Isaac HaCohen deals not only with coins but also units of liquid and solid measurement. In the first section on coins, neatly marked off by the scribe with a thick black line, HaCohen only uses one contemporary currency, the Venetian Ducat.[30] HaCohen writes that "the *me'ah* is [worth] two *pundion* [sic: *pundionin*], and three *me'ot* are worth half a *dinar,* that is, the weight of one ducat." Continuing on, HaCohen adds that "one *me'ah* is three ducats, the *me'ah* is [worth] sixteen measures according to the Venetian ducat." In a similar vein, HaCohen suggests that the *isar* is worth four measures and it is equivalent in weight to "one quarter of a ducat," and, in a sort of extraneous mathematical exercise, he calculates that the "measures of twelve *isarin* are worth the weight of thirty one ducats."[31] For HaCohen the Venetian ducat is a powerful tool in his project to reconstruct the value of talmudic coinage.

The economic historian Carlo Cipolla insists that in the later fifteenth century the Venetian ducat "represented the international currency *par excellence.*"[32] Given how often HaCohen refers to the ducat, it is clear that it was an important currency in his time. More to the point, HaCohen's equivalences of biblical and talmudic quantities to contemporary ones remain consistent because he is able to use a single modern currency. Even if Cipolla exaggerates the prestige of the ducat in the Renaissance, to Isaac ha-Cohen, the ducat is the most useful economic standard against which to measure the values of ancient coins.

The remaining sections of HaCohen's work are devoted to explaining units of solid measurement. It is significant that in these passages no contemporary Italian or European units are given. Rather than finding modern equivalents for ancient terms, the author builds an internal system of corresponding ratios using only Hebraic measurements. Here is an example of the wording of one such passage: "the *kav* is 4 *login* and 24 *betsim.* The *se'ah* is 400 *kavin* and 144 *betsim.* The *log* is 4 *revi'iot* and 400 *betsim.*"[33] The tone and content of the passage speak for themselves—Isaac HaCohen constructs a functional system of talmudic equivalences without reference to any outside quantity.

This feature of the Cambridge manuscript miscellany—that talmudic coins are matched to contemporary Italian equivalents while solid measurements are rendered only using internal, Hebrew referents—has parallels in other Hebrew compositions from the Renaissance. The work of Isaac Abravanel, a fifteenth-century biblical commentator and political advisor to a host of Iberian and Italian rulers, displays this same tendency.[34] Abravanel, like HaCohen, used Italian terms to explain monetary currency. However, when faced with solid measurements in the Bible, his otherwise unified explanations fragment into a set of discrete terms.[35]

Italian Renaissance scholarship on ancient Jewish numismatics and metrology differs significantly from the medieval forms it inherited. In the case of coinage, the diversity of terms that people like Moses Maimonides and Estori HaParhi used to describe ancient measurements give way to a geographically delineated and internationally accepted standard of measurement, that of early modern Italy. Because of these standardized units of measurement, readers of these Renaissance works were able to identify with and understand more immediately the quotidian life of the biblical and talmudic worlds.

The novel form of exposition undertaken by Isaac HaCohen and Ovadiah Sforno, with its consistent reference to non-Jewish weights and measures, indicates not only their dissatisfaction with the way medieval authorities treated ancient Jewish material culture, but their own full immersion in contemporary Italian culture. In his exposition on coins and measures Gedaliah Ibn Yahya quoted a series of medieval scholars who gave only Hebrew equivalents for standards of measurement: Rashi, Ibn Ezra, Nahmanides and Gersonides all used Hebrew rather than Arabic or Romance language terminology in their commentaries.[36] Ibn Yahya even went so far as to state explicitly that rendering ancient quantities in modern languages would assist his readers' efforts to conceptualize the texts they were studying. "I shall set before you coins and measures," Ibn Yahya intoned, and "arrange them according to Italian coins and measures, according to my ability, so that their understanding will be clear before you."[37] Of all the measurements of Italy those of the Emilian city of Bologna were the most relevant to Ibn Yahya. Ibn Yahya had been a pupil at Sforno's academy in Bologna. While there he recalled having seen Sforno's notes: "when I was at the academy in Bologna of the exalted Rabbi Ovadiah Sforno, may his memory be a blessing, I saw among his papers and novellae (ḥidushim) these things."[38] "These things" were a list of equivalences—a similar, but not identical, version of which is copied on the fly leaf of the Cambridge manuscript. But Ibn Yahya learned something else in Bologna besides the teachings of his master. He became accustomed to relying on Bolognese standards of measurements. Discussing the revi'it, a unit of liquid measure, Ibn Yahya pronounced the "Bolognese measure" to be the proper one in identifying the revi'it.[39]

As we have seen, in the middle decades of the sixteenth century a small constellation of scholars in central and northern Italy took an active interest in the material culture, particularly the coinage, of ancient and late antique Jewish civilization. That they did so is evidence of the pervasive mania for archeological discovery and close study of the material remains of the past that swept across the Italian peninsula at the time. That mania affected Jews as much as it did Christians. Given that Sforno wrote to his brother about his search for coins, composed an ephemeral composition giving their values, and transmitted those remarks to Ibn Yaḥya—and likely other students in his academy we do not know of—it was deemed pedagogically effective, and not simply fashionable, to encourage students to think of ancient values as concrete realities rather than abstractions.

To students scrutinizing the legal practices of late antique society, as Sforno's pupils would have done, having a proper appreciation for the amounts of money involved in civil suits and other transactions was invaluable not only for numismatic purposes but for monetary and devotional ones as well. Of all the medieval authorities that Ibn Yaḥya cites in his essay on measures only one renders a Hebrew coin into an internationally acknowledged currency—the Venetian Ducat. Ibn Yaḥya notes, as an aside, that he "saw in the glosses of the writer Mordechai [ben Hillel HaCohen] at the end of [the tractate] *Ketubot* [that he renders the *peruta*] in terms of Venetian ducats."[40] It is more than a coincidence that Mordechai (or perhaps the sixteenth-century Italian printers who published his work) chose to use the Ducat when explaining what a *peruta* was worth. The *peruta* was a standard currency that appeared in many antique legal texts. It also featured prominently in Jewish marriage contracts from the period since, according to Jewish law, a *peruta* represented the minimum requisite value of the object used to effectuate matrimony.[41] Given the ubiquity of the *peruta,* and its continued presence in juridical texts such as marriage contracts, it is understandable that a medieval commentator—and his Renaissance readers—would take an active interest in its real value.

The connection between money and law had a long pedigree by the Renaissance, stretching back to Aristotle in the *Nicomachean Ethics.* The sixteenth-century numismatist Antonio Agustín observed, in the first of his dialogues on medals, that the study of law and the study of money were closely connected. "The etymology that Aristotle gives in his [Nicomachean] Ethics for the word *nomisma* [i.e., money]," Agustín writes, "is that it derives from *nomos,* which in the Greek language means law."[42] The Spanish numismatist went on to paraphrase Aristotle, who remarked that money bears an etymological affinity to law because "it exists not by nature but by convention (*nomos*) and it is in our power to change its value and to render it worthless."[43] For Sforno and his disciples, the values of ancient coins were more than an antiquarian concern; a proper understanding of law and history depended on deep knowledge of such matters.

To Renaissance scholars and collectors, familiarity with ancient coins enabled them to have a closer relationship to the classical world.[44] As early as 1528 Castiglione, in his *Libro del Cortegiano,* remarked that a prince ought to have good knowledge of "ancient and modern statues, vases, buildings, medals, coins and other such things."[45] But such acquaintance with coins entailed more than merely lending a patina of culture to wealthy collectors or heirs apparent to European thrones; early modern Europeans were aware of a distinction between collecting precious stones or porcelain, for example, and coins.[46] The former objects were, as the seventeenth-century French scholar Charles Patin put it, about "*divertissement;*" coins, by contrast, embodied physical instantiation of real knowledge about the past.[47] Some sixteenth-century monographs, such as Guillaume Budé's *De asse et partibus eius libri V,* explicitly aimed to facilitate more historically sensitive readings of classical texts. As Thomas More wrote to Budé, "if anyone will turn his eyes to what you have written and give it careful and continued attention, he will find that the light you have thrown upon your subject brings the dead past to life again."[48] The dead past, of course, included the ancient Jewish past. And it was not only Jews who had an avid interest in illuminating it. Henry Peacham, in his *Compleat Gentleman,* included a chapter entitled "of antiquities," which is mainly about coins. In the midst of a long list comparing values of Latin, Greek, and Hebrew coins, Peacham noted that "Abraham bought the Field, Cave, and Trees of Machpelah for 400 shekels, that is for 50l. sterl. Moses made the golden Candlesticke with his seven Lamps, Snuffers, and Snuffe-dishes of a Talent of Pure Gold, that is five thousand two hundred fiftie pounds sterlin." In case the significance of these equivalences was lost on his readers, Peacham made it plain: "by this time you may perceive that without this money-learning, you must be forced to balke the most materiall passages of ancient History."[49]

A fear of missing the most significant passages of ancient history was what drove Sforno to "go down" to Rome "with some colleagues . . . determined to find the truth about coins in the Talmud."[50] And it also drove Sforno and Isaac HaCohen to set down their thoughts about translating talmudic weights and measures. The clear interest that fifteenth- and sixteenth-century Italian Jewish scholars displayed in numismatic and economic research, as well as the way they carried out that research, signals a subtle passage from the Middle Ages to the Renaissance. In the cases presented here, that passage was characterized by intensified scrutiny of the *realia* of the Talmud, reference to contemporary Italian systems of weight and measurement, and desire that their students could understand—and implement—the requirements of Judaism's legal traditions.

It was not until the nineteenth century that investigators of the remote Jewish past produced comprehensive works detailing the values of ancient coins.[51] However, the evidence presented here proposes that the beginnings of modern critical study of biblical and talmudic material culture, including coins, weights, and measures, may be found in the bustling marketplaces of Bologna and the exchange fairs of Renaissance Rome, rather than in the subdued halls of the rabbinical academies and German universities of the nineteenth-century *Wissenschaft des Judentums.*

Appendix

Cambridge University Library MS Add 395 133

אמר הגאון כמהרר עבדיה ספורנו ז"ל בה[יותי] ברומה עם חברי [ועמדנו][1]

למצא האמת ממטבעות התלמוד ולהביאם למטבע רומנייא לחשבון עשוי

פרוטה חצי שעורה א' בגטינו

איסר ד' שעורות[2] ב' קווטריני

פונדיון ח' שעורות א' ביוקו

מעה והוא הדרכמון י"ו שעורות ב' ביוקי

דינר והוא זוז צ"ו שעורות י"ב ביוקי וחצי

שקל והוא מחצית השקל ק"ד שעורות כ"ה ביוקי

סלע שס"ח שעורות ה' יוליאי

דרכמון ב' סלעים עשרה יוליאי

דינר זהב כ"ה דינרים כסף הם ג' סקודי א' יוליאו ב' ביוקי

מנה ד' דינרי זהב או כ"ה סלעים או ק' דינרי כסף י"ב סקודי ה' יוליאי

ככר היא ג' אלפים סלעים שהם אלף ת"ק סקודי

ככר זהב הם לפי החשבון הנ"ל ל"ז סלעים וחמש מאות סקודי

אמנם מצאתי כתוב שהוא י"ב אלפים סקודי אך לפי החשבון אינו

יען אם דינר זהב הוא כ"ה דינרי כסף ככר זהב יהיה כ"ש[3] כ"ב

שו,ט לפי החשבון הוא ל"ז סקודי ת"ק אמנם זה החשבון שהוא א' דינר

הוא כ"ה דינרי [כ]סף בהיות שהזהב אינו שוה לפי האמת כי אם אלפים

יותר מהכסף [ע]ל זה כתוב בספר הקבלה ליחייא ז"ל דף פ"ט ע"א[4]

מכמהרר יצחק כהן ז"ל מויתרבו

הסלע הוא ד' דינרים והוא משקל א' אונקיה שעורות

הדינר הוא ו' מעות והוא משקל רביע אונקיה צ"ו שערות

המעה הוא ב' פונדיון וג' מעות שהם חצי דינר הן משקל א' דוקאטו

וא' מעה הוא שליש דוקאטו המיעה י"ו שעורות הדוקאטו ונצ'יאנו לפי

---

1. Following Ibn Yahya's *Shalshelet ha-kabalah*. See below, note 3.
2. In this manuscript the scribe, following Ibn Yahya, uses the plural שעורות instead of the more common שעורין.
3. Here the calculation does not compute.
4. See Ibn Yahya, *Shalshelet ha-kabalah* (Venice, 1587), 89r.

החשבון הוא משקל מ"ח שעורות

הפונדיון הוא ב' איסרין הפונדיון הוא משקל ששית הדוקאטו ח' שעור[ות]

האיסר הוא ד' שעורות והוא משקל א' רביע הדוקאטו א"כ האיסר הוא ד'

שעורות י"ב איסרין הוא משקל א' דוקאטו האיסר הוא חצי קואטו יען

הדוקאטו שהוא שמינית באונקיה הוא ו' קואטי

הכור הוא י' איפות ד' אלפים ש"כ ביצים

האיפה היא ג' סאין תל"ב ביצים

הקב הוא ד' לוגין כ"ד ביצים

הסיאה הוא ו' קבין קמ"ד ביצים

הלוג ד' רביעיות ו' ביצים

הרביעית א' ביצה וחצי

הבצה היא ו' גרוגרות

ג' ביצים הם סעודה אחת

עשירי[ת] האיפה הוא מ"ג ביצים וחומש ביצה

כי האיפה ל"ב ביצים ועשירית ת"לב הוא מ"ג וחומש והוא העומר והוא

שיעור חלה נמצא שיש בעומר מזון י"ד סעודות ב' חמישי סעודה שהוא

לתך חצי כור והכור שלש סאין

סעודה היא ג' ביצים א"כ מ"כב ביצים הם י"ד סעודות [נ]שאר בעומר א' ביצה וחומש

ביצה שהן ו' חומשי ביצה שארי ג' ביצים הם סעודה אחת והם

ט"ו חומשי ביצה וכל חומש סעודה הוא ג' חומשי ביצה א"כ ו' חומשי ביצה

הם ב' חומשי סעודה א"כ יש בעומר י"ד סעודות וב' חומשי סעודה

הקורטוב הוא א' איסר בלוג א"כ הלוג הוא ס"ד קורטוב הרביעית

הוא י"ד קורטובים והיא א' ביצה וחצי א"כ א' ביצה י' קורטובים וב' שלישי

קורטוב

Notes

1. Leopold Zunz, "Münzkunde," in Zunz, *Zur Geschichte und Literatur* (Berlin, 1845), 535–64.

2. Published in *Ginse nistarot* 3 (1872): 185–200. For a description see Elhanan Reiner, "Between Ashkenaz and Jerusalem: Ashkenazic Scholars in the Land of Israel after the 'Black Death'" (Hebrew), *Shalem* 4 (1984): 27–62, 54.

3. Estori HaParhi, *Kaftor va-ferah* (Berlin, 1852), chap. 16.

4. Zunz, "Münzkunde," 535.

5. Ibid., 536.

6. Ibn Aknin, "Ma'amar al ha-midot veha-mishkalot," in *Ginze nistarot* 3 (1872): 186, 190.

7. John Cunnally, *Images of the Illustrious: the Numismatic Presence in the Renaissance* (Princeton, N.J., 1999).

8. Francis Haskell, *History and Its Images: Art and the Interpretation of the Past* (New Haven, Conn., 1993).

9. Ibn Yahya, *Shalshelet ha-kabalah* (1587; Jerusalem, 1961), 207.

10. Cambridge MS Add 395.

11. Abraham Portaleone, *Shilte ha-giborim* (Mantua, 1612), chap. 72. See also Gianfranco Miletto, *Glauben und Wissen im Zeitalter der Reformation: der salomonische Tempel bei Abraham ben David Portaleone (1542–1612)* (Berlin, 2004), 198–205.

12. Guillame Budé, *De asse et partibus eius Libri V* (Paris, 1514); Benito Arias Montano, *Thubal-Cain sive de mensuris sacris liber* (Antwerp, 1572); William Peacham, *The Compleat Gentleman* (London, 1634); Blasio Ugolini, *Thesaurus antiquitatum sacrarum*, 34 vols. (Venice, 1744–69).

13. *Kaftor va-ferah* was first printed at Venice in 1549.

14. In general see Joseph R. Hacker and Adam Shear, eds., *The Hebrew Book in Early Modern Italy* (Philadelphia, 2011); Yaacob Dweck, *The Scandal of Kabbalah: Leon Modena, Jewish Mysticism, Early Modern Venice* (Princeton, N.J., 2011); Amnon Raz-Krakotzkin, *The Censor, the Editor, and the Text: the Catholic Church and the Shaping of the Jewish Canon in the Sixteenth Century*, trans. J. Feldman (Philadelphia, 2007).

15. Jacques Le Goff, *Le moyen age et l'argent* (Paris, 2010), 209–19. Medieval antecedents to Renaissance interest in numismatics among Christians include Nicole Orseme (d. 1382). See Hendrik Mäkler, "Nicolas Oresme und Gabriel Biel zur Geltheorie im Späten Mittelalter," *Scripta Mercaturae: Zeitschrift für Wirtschafts- und Sozialgeschichte* 37.1 (2003): 56–94.

16. M. H. Crawford, C. R. Ligota, and J. B. Trapp, eds., *Medals and Coins from Budé to Mommsen* (London 1990); P. Berghaus, ed., *Numismatische Literatur 1500–1864: die Entwicklung der Methoden einer Wissenschaft* (Wiesbaden, 1995).

17. Haskell, *History and Its Images,* 14–16.

18. "Lettere italiane di Antonio Agostini Arcivescovo di Tarracona a Fulvio Orsini," in Antonio Augustín, *Opera Omnia*, 8 vols. (Lucca, 1772), 7:231–63.

19. Peter N. Miller, *Peiresc's Europe: Learning and Virtue in the Seventeenth Century* (New Haven, Conn., 2000); John Cunnally, *Images of the Illustrious;* Haskell, *History and Its Images*; Roberto Weiss, *The Renaissance Discovery of Classical Antiquity* (New York, 1969).

20. Leonard Barkan, *Unearthing the Past: Archaeology and Aesthetics in the Making of Renaissance Culture* (New Haven, Conn., 1999), 29.

21. Ibid., 1.

22. Roberto Weiss, *The Renaissance Discovery of Classical Antiquity* (New York, 1969).

23. Moses Shulvass, *The Jews in the World of the Renaissance* (1973); Shulvass, "The Knowledge of Antiquity among the Italian Jews of the Renaissance," *Proceedings of the American Academy of Jewish Research* 18 (1948/49): 291–300; Alessandro Guetta, "Avraham Portaleone, le scientifique repenti," in

Torah et science: Perspectives historiques et théoriques. Études offertes à Charles Touati, ed. G. Freudenthal, J.-P. Rothschild, G. Dahan (Paris, 2001), 213–27; Miletto, *Glauben und Wissen.*

24. S. M. Schiller-Szinessy, *Catalogue of the Hebrew Manuscripts Preserved in the University Library, Cambridge,* 2 vols. (Cambridge, 1876), 1:68–70. See also Stefan C. Reif, *Hebrew Manuscripts at Cambridge University Library: A Description and Introduction* (Cambridge, 1997), 104–5.

25. Ze'ev Gottlieb, ed., *Kitve Rabbi Ovadiah Sforno* (Jerusalem, 1983), 519–20. Many of Sforno's letters were composed to his younger brother Hananel. We do not know who the addressee of this letter was. See Gottlieb, *Kitve Rabbi Ovadiah Sforno,* 10.

26. Saverio Campanini, "Un intellettuale ebreo del rinascimento: 'Ovadyah Sforno a Bologna e i suoi rapporti con i cristiani," in *Verso l'epilogo di una convivenza,* ed. M. G. Muzzarelli (Florence, 1996), 99–128.

27. Cambridge MS Add 395.

28. Carlo M. Cipolla, *Money, Prices, and Civilization in the Mediterranean World: Fifth to Seventeenth Century* (Princeton, N.J., 1956), 35–36. Other works on Italian coins in this period include E. Bernareggi, *Monete d'oro con ritratto del rinascimento italiano, 1450–1515* (Milan, 1954) and G. Praj, "La moneta piemontese ai tempi di Vittorio Amedeo I e Carlo Emanuele II," *Bollettino storico-bibliografico subalpino* 40 (1938): 221–327, which focuses especially on the *scudo.*

29. The *giulio,* or *yulio,* as pronounced in Hebrew, was, like the *quattrino,* also popular in Romagna. Sforno observes that the *selah,* a generic biblical and mishnaic term often the equivalent to one sacred or two common *shekels,* was worth approximately five *yuli* in modern terms. Sforno's *giulio* refers to the *grosso papale* or *carlino*—a silver coin of Pope Julius II, who reigned from 1503 to 1513. To cite one final example, Sforno mentions the currency *scudo* four times in this text, and uses it to explain the values of the golden *dinar,* the *maneh,* the *kikar,* and the golden *kikar.* The *scudo* was ubiquitous in early sixteenth-century Italy, and came onto the peninsula from France in the fourteenth century, where Philip IV of Valois (1328–1350) first minted it. In the sixteenth century alone, there were *scudi papali, scudi ossidionale di Mantova, scudi della galera,* and *scudi della croce.* It is difficult, if not impossible, to be absolutely certain about which type of *scudo* Sforno had in mind. What is key for our purposes is the fact that Sforno consistently used it alongside the *giulio,* the *buco,* and the *cavatrino* to find values for a wide variety of ancient Jewish coins.

30. On the ubiquity and diversity of the ducat in the sixteenth century see Fernand Braudel, *The Mediterranean and the Mediterranean World in the Age of Philip II,* 2 vols. (New York, 1966) 2: 42, n. 333.

31. All quotations in this paragraph are from Cambridge MS Add 395.

32. Cipolla, *Money, Prices, and Civilization,* 21.

33. Cambridge MS Add 395.

34. On Abravanel see Benzion Netanyahu, *Don Isaac Abravanel: Statesman & Philosopher* (Philadelphia, 1953); Eric Lawee, *Isaac Abravanel's Stance toward Tradition: Defense, Dissent, and Dialogue* (Albany, N.Y., 2001); and, most recently Cedric Cohen Skalli, ed. and trans., *Isaac Abravanel: Letters* (Berlin, 2007).

35. Compare Abravanel's commentary to 1 Kgs 6, where he renders the *kikar* in terms of Venetian ducats, to his work on 1 Kgs 5:2, which mentions the unit of solid measurement *kor.* Abravanel equates the *kor* to a series of Castillian, Portuguese, and Neapolitan quantities.

36. Ibn Yaḥya, *Shalshelet ha-kabalah,* 207–8.

37. Ibid., 207.

38. Ibid., 209.

39. Ibid., 210.

40. Ibid. Mordechai (d. 1298) wrote commentaries on a number of talmudic tractates which were included in the rear of printed Talmuds from that of Soncino onward. As the manuscript

tradition of Mordechai's works is unstable, we cannot be sure if he, as opposed to early Italian printers, used the term "ducat."

41. See the texts presented in Liliane Grassi and Vittore Colorni, eds., *Kettubot italiane: antichi contratti nuziali ebraici miniati* (Milan, 1984). The *peruta* was worth approximately ¼ of an *isar.*

42. Antonio Agustín, *Dialoghi intorno alle medaglie inscrittioni et altre antichita* (Rome, 1592), 2.

43. Aristotle, *Nicomachean Ethics,* trans. R. Crisp (Cambridge, 2000), book 5, 1133a.

44. Giuseppe Olmi, *Inventario del mondo: catalogazione della natura e luoghi del sapere nella prima età moderna* (Bologna, 1992), 169–70.

45. Castiglione, "Il libro del Cortegiano," in *Opere di Baldassare Castiglione, Giovanni della Casas, Benevenuto Cellini,* ed. C. Cordié (Milan, 1960), 86. Quoted in Miletto, *Glauben und Wissen,* 202.

46. Antoine Schnapper, *Le géant, la licorne, la tulipe: collection françaises au XVIIe siècle,* 2 vols. (Paris, 1988), 1:137.

47. Charles Patin, *Introduction à l'Histoire par la connaisance des Médailles* (Paris, 1665), 121–22. Cited in Schnapper, *Le géant, la licorne, la tulipe,* 137.

48. Thomas Stapleton, *The Life and Illustrious Martyrdom of Sir Thomas More* [first published 1588], trans. P. E. Hallet (1928), ed. E. E. Reynolds (Bronx, 1966), 48.

49. Peacham, *Compleat Gentleman,* 122–23.

50. Cambridge MS; also quoted in Ibn Yaḥya, *Shalshelet ha-kabalah,* 209.

51. Zunz, "Münzkunde"; Simcha Ejges, *Geld im Talmud: Versuch einer systematischen Darstellung der wirtschaftlichen Geldtheorie und–praxis nach talmudischen Quellen* (Giessen, 1930).

CHRISTIAN HEBRAISM AND THE REDISCOVERY OF HELLENISTIC JUDAISM

❊ ❊ ❊

Anthony Grafton

Princeton University

WHAT was Christian Hebraism? Who practiced it? What did they study? The standard answers to all of these questions are clear. From the mid-fifteenth century onwards, printing made Jewish books available, and debates about the text and interpretation of the Bible showed that knowledge of Hebrew might be vital for Christian theology and exegesis. Christian society showed little tolerance for actual Jews, who were expelled from Castile and Aragon, forced into ghettos, made to surrender their copies of the Talmud in Italy, and even accused of ritual murder. Prominent scholars always denied that Jews or Jewish learning had anything to offer the Christian world. Yet interest in the traditions of Jewish learning spread. Christians learned from Jews and converts, drew up Hebrew and Aramaic grammars and dictionaries, edited and translated Hebrew texts, and studied Jewish traditions, from the Kabbalah to the Talmud.[1]

The attitudes of Christians toward Jewish ritual and scholarship often remained strikingly negative, even when they collaborated with Jewish scholars, as Paul Fagius did with Elijah Levita.[2] The most vivid accounts of Jewish life and customs, often written by converts, also showed little sympathy for the world they described.[3] Still, by the late sixteenth century, institutions of learning across both Catholic and Protestant Europe sponsored the formal teaching of Hebrew, Aramaic, and even Yiddish texts, and many of the most original scholars used Jewish sources as eagerly as Greek and Latin ones.[4] Even thinkers who were not profound students of Hebrew took Jewish texts and scholarship into account. Jean Bodin, for example, included the Sanhedrin in his comparative study of forms of government and drew on the help of Jean Mercier and others in order to study the talmudic passages that described it.[5] Most scholars would identify the large and varied set of projects that engaged so many scholars as Christian Hebraism, and treat Bodin as one of the still larger group of learned men who took an interest in the Hebraists' work and applied it in new fields outside the tradition.

For all its richness, this account misses some of the most original forms of early modern scholarship on the Jews. Consider the case of Joseph Scaliger (1540–1609), the most legendary polymath of his polymathic age. He taught himself Hebrew, by his own account, in the 1560s, inspired by the charismatic Orientalist Guillaume Postel, with whom he briefly shared lodgings in Paris. He conversed with Jews, especially, it seems, during a memorable visit to the Avignon ghetto not long before he left France for the Low Countries in 1593. He studied the Jewish tradition of calendrical writing; collected references to the calendar from the Talmud and assembled them; wrote in Hebrew to the Samaritans in the hope that they might have ancient books about which he had read in the Bible; assembled a formidable collection of Jewish books; and read the Talmud for half a year, late in life, with a converted Jew from Poland, Philippus Ferdinandus. And he took a serious interest in some of the questions that mattered most to Christian Hebraists, for example, the origins and status of the Masoretic text of the Old Testament. In 1606 he argued, against the great Hebraist Johann Buxtorf, that the *Zohar* could not provide evidence to show that the Hebrew vowel points were ancient, since it was itself a relatively recent text. True, Scaliger never drew up a Hebrew grammar or edited books of the Bible for use by students. Though he made regular use of passages from the Babylonian Talmud, his first modern biographer, Jacob Bernays, noted the serious mistakes that marred his work.[6] Nonetheless. Scaliger accomplished enough in the study of Judaism that no serious account of Christian Hebraism in the Renaissance would omit his name or fail to give some account of what he accomplished.[7]

In some ways, though, Scaliger's most decisive intervention into Jewish studies took place in a realm of Greek rather than Hebrew texts, and in an area that canonical accounts of Christian Hebraism do not discuss. Early in the 1590s, he wrote at length to a friend, Gilbert Seguin, who had lent him a copy of the works of Philo. Scaliger began in the metaphorical key of friendship, describing Philo as an old acquaintance whom he had wrongly dropped:

> Heartfelt thanks for Philo, who used to be an intimate acquaintance of mine. But I received him today, not as if he were a foreigner, but as an old friend. For a century seems to have passed since I last paid him a call. And though he could complain about my negligence, I would rather contract a new friendship with him than fail to return to his good graces. So I'll do it, and pinch a few hours from my working time for him.[8]

Almost immediately, though, Scaliger ceased apologizing for the bad manners that had led to his dropping Philo in the past and began to gossip about him in a dramatic new way: "I can tell you something about him that may surprise you. He was completely ignorant of Hebrew—and so much so that even Christian beginners, to say nothing of the Jews, can challenge him. You'll be surprised. But I'm not surprised."[9] Philo's ignorance, it seemed, was not his own fault, but symptomatic of something larger. He had been a particular kind of Jew—one found in Alexandria and elsewhere—who had used the Greek text of the Septuagint as his Bible:

> For that is what the Alexandrian Jews and the other Hellenists were like. Their name set them off from the Jewish Hebraists, who read their Bibles in the synagogue in Hebrew and Aramaic. But those Alexandrians read only the Greek text that is still extent, and that Philo himself and other Jews pretend was translated by seventy Jerusalemite Jews at the command of Ptolemy.[10]

Scaliger went on to note that he could explicate passages in chapters 6 and 11 of Acts in which the term "Hellenists" appeared, because he had access to material that had been quite unknown to previous commentators on the New Testament, "since it is rather recondite; and perhaps if they hear it, they will either not believe it, or reject it."[11]

In another, undated letter, written later than this one, Scaliger expanded on what he had first told Seguin about the Septuagint and the stories of its miraculous origins.[12] The tale of the seventy translators, Scaliger insisted, was originally a Jewish invention, on which the Christians had embroidered. Ptolemy, he believed, had forced the Jews to write their contracts in Greek and to date them from his accession. They ascribed the Greek Bible as well to the king who had forced them to use that language. In fact, though, the evidence of other ancient Jewish versions proved that this claim was false.

> If this were true, it would be necessary that the other paraphrases of the Bible—Aramaic, Persian, Arabic—that they use nowadays were composed at the orders of a king. It's absurd even to think this. Therefore the Greek paraphrase of the Seventy translators was composed not at the orders of [Ptolemy] Philadelphus, but to serve the needs of the Jews. For they knew little Hebrew, since the kings forced them to speak and write Greek.[13]

Like the ancient Aramaic Targumim and other Jewish versions, the Septuagint had come into being as a practical aid to understanding the Bible. It was created, more likely by one translator than by seventy, to serve the needs of Jews who could not follow the Hebrew text when it was read aloud in synagogues. Unlike the Targumim, however, the Septuagint was a terrible translation, "mendosissima et falsissima," and the Latin Vulgate that derived from it was even worse.[14] Though Scaliger did not develop this point for some years, it became a central argument of his last great work, the *Thesaurus temporum* of 1606, where it would provoke what became an almost endless series of debates, often inspired by problems in chronology.[15]

In his notes on the New Testament, finally, Scaliger expanded on these arguments. Following Josephus, previous Christian scholars had divided the Jews of Palestine in the time of Jesus into Pharisees, Sadducees, and Essenes.[16] Scaliger, by contrast, used his Semitic evidence to argue that the division between Hellenists and Hebraists revealed in Acts actually pointed to the divisions of the Jewish world in the time of the Second Temple, which he recast in a new tripartite form. The extant Targum Onkelos and Targum Yerushalmi, he argued, had been used by the Jews of Babylon and Israel respectively. As for the Septuagint, it too was made for use in synagogues—Greek ones.

> It is to be noted that the Jews had one capital for their religion and ritual, Jerusalem. But the three capitals of the Jewish polity were Jerusalem, Babylon and Alexandria. There were two diasporas: the Asian, to which Peter wrote, and the European, which is mentioned in John 7:35 . . . The capital of the Asian diaspora was Babylon, and the Jews there used the Aramaic paraphrase of Onkelos, as they still do, in their synagogues. Peter wrote to them from their capital, Babylon. The capital of the European diaspora was Alexandria. Those Jews had a temple as large as those at Jerusalem, and used the Greek paraphrase of the 70. That is why they were called Hellenists in Acts 6:1 and 11:20 . . . The third form of polity was made up of the Jews who belonged to the capital at Jerusalem, who are called Hebrews in that same chapter 6, to set them apart from the ones called Hellenists. They used the Jerusalem paraphrase that is still extant today.[17]

This passage was not published in full in Scaliger's lifetime. However, he included his discovery that Philo was ignorant of Hebrew and his gloss on the Hellenists in Acts in the second edition of his massive work on chronology, the *De emendatione temporum*.[18] Reading the copy of the book that Scaliger sent him, Isaac Casaubon was fascinated by his arguments, though he thought there might be more to be said about Philo.[19] The full text came out soon after Scaliger died, and he extended its arguments in his *Thesaurus temporum*.

In this, his last massive book, Scaliger publicly denounced the letter of Aristeas as a fake and Philo as an ignoramus. He also cited further texts that had not previously been used by Christian scholars in connection with the Septuagint. Most important, Scaliger made clear—as neither his predecessors nor he himself had done in the past—the full implications of his discoveries. The Hellenists, he now explained, "read only the Greek Bible in their synagogues throughout all of Egypt, Greece, and Italy. For every thousand Jews, barely one could be found who read Hebrew."[20] For the first time since antiquity, a scholar showed that ancient Judaism had included an enormous Greek-speaking diaspora, the members of which continued to be Jews but largely abandoned Hebrew and Aramaic, even in the synagogue—a massive, lost Jewish world that the Jews themselves had forgotten. This thesis has provoked generations of scholarship and debate. Arnaldo Momigliano was Scaliger's heir when he wrote, "there was a distinctive brand of Hellenism which was Jewish Hellenism. There were entire communities which, even though they considered themselves Jews and practiced the Jewish religion, spoke Greek, thought in Greek and knew hardly any Hebrew or Aramaic. For at least seven or eight centuries, Greek remained the alternative cultural language of the Jews."[21] These vital facts—nowadays part of the common knowledge of the learned—came back to light only when Scaliger shone his torch on the primary sources. Did this rediscovery of a forgotten chapter in the history of Judaism form part of Christian Hebraism as an enterprise?

The best way to answer the question is to look, one by one, at Scaliger's arguments. Scaliger insisted to Seguin that he was the first interpreter of the New Testament to grasp that the noun "Hellenists" in Acts 6 and 11 referred to Jews who spoke Greek. In fact, commentators had long since made this point. In a 1527 addition to his note on Acts 6:1, Erasmus argued that the term "Hellenists" referred to Jews born among the Greeks, who simply used the language of their birthplace.[22] François Vatable and other authoritative commentators followed Erasmus's lead. Scaliger added to what earlier commentators had said by pointing out that the Jewish Hellenists had read their Bibles in Greek in the synagogue. Yet he went too far in one crucial respect. The verb *hellēnizein,* "to speak or act like a Greek," did not apply only to Jews who did so, as Scaliger thought, but to members of any non-Greek people.[23] And Scaliger's pupil Daniel Heinsius went even farther off the track when he argued that the New Testament was written in a "lingua Hellenistica," a Greek transformed by the presence of many Semiticisms, as Claude Saumaise would show in a detailed refutation.[24] We seem to be, at most, on the borders of the territory that the Christian Hebraists cultivated.

When Scaliger raised the question of Philo's knowledge of Hebrew, as Joanna Weinberg has shown, he was also less iconoclastic than he thought, but in this case he remained within the larger traditions of Christian Hebraism.[25] True, Christian scholars from Eusebius and Jerome down to Sigismundus Gelenius and David Hoeschel in Scaliger's own day had admired Philo's profound learning. They enthusiastically praised both his mastery of the Bible and his ability to explicate it allegorically in terms of Platonic philosophy. Far from worrying about Philo's relation to Jewish traditions, Christians had traditionally treated him as one of their own, or almost one of them. But the rise of Christian biblical scholarship brought new questions with it. The scholarly Augustinian Agostino Steuco, who would eventually rule the Vatican Library, used the weapons of philology to defend the traditions of the Church against the criticisms of Valla and Erasmus. As early as 1529, he drew up a detailed review of the various texts of the Old Testament.[26] Philo, Steuco noted, took Gen 2:6 as reading "But there went up a spring (πηγή) from the earth," as the Septuagint did, rather than "a mist (אֵד)," with the Hebrew. He concluded that the ancient Jewish writer "seems not to have known his own letters, as is clear both from many other passages and especially from this one . . . He certainly seems not to have read the Hebrew text. For as he had an excellent command of Greek, thus perhaps he did not know Hebrew at all. He thought very highly of the Septuagint, even though it clearly contains many errors."[27] Philo's testimony could not give the Septuagint authority because he had not been competent to assess it.

Christian Hebraism often involved collaboration or discussion between Jews and Christians. Steuco's brief treatment helped to stimulate the Ferrarese Jewish scholar Azariah de' Rossi to deal with Philo's knowledge of languages in a far more exhaustive—and far more provocative—way, in his *The Light of the Eyes* of 1575.[28] Here as elsewhere Azariah brought Christian and Jewish traditions into a productive collision, in a way no Christian could have done. After exhaustive study of Philo's works, which he read in Latin, and close comparison of his opinions with rabbinical tradition, de' Rossi concluded that Philo "grew up in the Greek world and despite all his wisdom and fluency in their language never saw nor knew the actual original text of Torah. It was not just a question of the holy tongue, but he was even ignorant of Aramaic, the language that was widely used in the land of Israel."[29] Yet he also decided that Philo had observed the law, and praised the profundity and beauty of some of his ideas. In the end, he told his readers, "I shall call him neither Rav nor sage . . . Whenever he is mentioned in these chapters, it will not be as an intimate member of my people, but as any other sage of the world to whom a hearing will be given when he makes general statements and has no vested interest in the subject."[30] Scaliger confided his criticisms of Philo to Seguin with all the zest of a schoolboy seizing his chance to be the first to spread slander about a friend. He could do so only because in this, as in other cases, his knowledge of the existing tradition was incomplete. When Scaliger proclaimed his priority in denouncing Philo's ignorance —as when he insisted that he was the first Christian who dared to announce that Jesus was not born on December 25—he revealed chiefly that he knew the Christian Hebraist tradition less well than we do.[31]

At their core, however, Scaliger's arguments about Hellenistic Judaism rested on another body of material: the Targumim and the Septuagint itself, and on the historical parallel he drew between them. Scaliger held that the Greek translation, like the Aramaic ones, derived not from the command of an Egyptian king but from the needs of an Egyptian Jewish community. Like the Jews of Babylon and Palestine, who spoke Aramaic, those of Egypt, who spoke Greek, needed a translation in order to follow a public reading of the Hebrew Scriptures. As Scaliger investigated the ancient Jews' use of Greek and their views of translation, he pursued topics that had interested earlier Christian Hebraists, whose work he may well have known.

Almost half a century before Scaliger, the Italian Hebraist Angelo Canini, whom Scaliger admired, had published a short but penetrating treatment of Semitic words and phrases in the New Testament.[32] In the course of this work, Canini discussed a famous passage of the Palestinian Talmud, which deals with the *shema'*:

Rabbi Levi the son of Hazota [Hazia] went up to Caesarea, and he heard those who recited the *shema'* in Greek. He wanted to forbid them to do this. When Rav Yose . . . had heard this, he became angry and said, "Whoever does not know how to recite it in Hebrew, shall he not recite it? By reciting it in the language that he understands, thus he fulfills his obligations (*y. Sot.* 7.1 21b)."[33]

After mentioning Yose's name, Canini rightly remarked that he "was of greater authority" than the other rabbi. Evidently, then, the rabbis accepted that Jews could pronounce their holiest prayer—the prayer they revered, Canini remarked, as Christians revered the Lord's Prayer—in Greek.[34] Canini found support in this exchange for his rejection of the Kabbalistic view that the Hebrew language harbored special mysteries—mysteries that a Christian must master in order to read the Bible with full understanding.[35] Like Canini and other sixteenth-century philologists, Rav Yose had seen all languages as equal.

Another semitic scholar, Andreas Masius, covered related ground in his 1574 *Iosuae imperatoris historia.* To illuminate the origins of the Septuagint, he cited not only the Greek accounts of Aristeas and others, but also a rabbinical source, *Masekhet Soferim* 1, 7–8.[36] And to illustrate what he took as the rabbis' superstitious view of translations, he quoted another now-famous passage from Babylonian Talmud *Megillah* 3a. According to this text, an earthquake followed Jonathan ben Uzziel's creation of the Targum to the prophets. A heavenly voice then demanded, "Who are these who have revealed my Mystery to man?" Jonathan replied: "It is I who have revealed Thy secrets to mankind. It is fully known to you that I have not done this for my own honor or for the honor of my father's house, but for Thy honor I have done it, that dissension may not increase in Israel."[37] Both Canini and Masius made clear, in other words, that rabbinical tradition did not unequivocally condemn prayer or study of the Bible conducted in languages other than Hebrew. Still, neither Canini nor Masius anticipated Scaliger's bold and comprehensive treatment of the languages—and divisions—of the ancient Jews. Even if Scaliger was aware of the hints offered by their work, he extended and generalized them.

One specialist in Hebrew studies whom Scaliger knew well, finally, may have made the same discovery independently, and perhaps helped to shape Scaliger's later theories. Like Scaliger, Joannes Drusius, who taught at Leiden and at Franeker, insisted that theologians must know Hebrew if they hoped to interpret the Bible, and argued that their ignorance often led them astray.[38] Like Scaliger, he held that the extant text of the Septuagint showed "great incompetence in the Hebrew language"—though instead of attacking the legend of its creation, he argued that it must be a different work.[39] And like Scaliger, he took a deep interest in the multiple forms that Judaism took in the Second Temple period—the question that led to his notorious and intricate controversy with the Jesuit Hebraist Nicolaus Serarius.[40] Not long after Scaliger described his thoughts about the Hellenists to Seguin, he discussed the text of Ecclesiasticus with Drusius, and then corresponded with him about it. Both agreed that it had been first composed in Hebrew by Jesus Sirach and then translated into Greek by the author's grandson.[41] Questions about ancient Jews and their mastery of Greek fascinated Drusius, and he and Scaliger may well have chewed them over after Scaliger came to Leiden in 1593. But the evidence known to me at present suggests that Scaliger reached his fundamental insight independently, though his later discussions with Drusius very likely helped him to develop it further.[42]

Scaliger's approach differed from earlier ones, finally, in one fundamental—and unfortunate—way. In the discourse on the Letter of Aristeas that he inserted into his *Thesaurus temporum,* he argued, at length, that the work was a forgery, and, as a forgery, typical of its Jewish creators. "Who," he asked rhetorically, "is not acquainted with the fabrications of the Jews?"[43] Humphrey Hody and some other, later scholars adopted not only Scaliger's arguments but also his prejudices, which did much to shape the later study of Hellenistic Judaism.[44] In the mid-nineteenth century, Bernays's pupil Jacob Freudenthal, later a great authority on Spinoza, denounced Scaliger for labeling all Jews as mendacious. It was "incomprehensible," he argued, "that . . . men like Scaliger would invoke the nature of the Jewish people as a whole to explain the deceptive writings of Jewish Hellenists."[45]

Yet Scaliger's vision of the Hellenists was not entirely shaped by the conventional prejudices against the Jews that he shared with most Christians, and probably most Christian Hebraists. In the years around 1600, he and his friend Isaac Casaubon dedicated themselves to exposing forgeries. Casaubon, as is well known, subjected one particularly notorious fake, the Hermetic Corpus, to a dazzling public anatomy in his 1614 *Exercitationes* on the *Annales* of Cesare Baronio. Though Casaubon analyzed this text in detail only after Scaliger's death, he notified his friend as early as 1603 of his view that it was a fake.[46] Scaliger, for his part, denounced many ancient forgers, including Jewish ones, in a 1605 letter to Casaubon. He dismissed Aristeas as a "spurious effort, forged by the Hellenistic Jews," and he denounced (Pseudo-) Hecataeus, a Greek who had composed an ethnography of the Jews, because "it is clear from Origen that the same Hellenists forged him as well, in very ancient times."[47]

But Scaliger also railed against those "monsters," the spurious accounts of the Trojan War ascribed to Dictys and Dares, which pagans had created.[48] He showed his greatest animus, in fact, when it came to the ancient Christians: "Did they consider the word of God so powerless that they thought the kingdom of Christ had to be furthered by lies?"[49] The "pseudo-Sibylline oracles, which the Christians used against the pagans, though they were a product of the Christian workshop and were not to be found in pagan libraries," irritated him just as much as Aristeas and Hecataeus.[50] Scaliger's animus against the Hellenists reflected part—though not all—of what he felt about the Jews. But it also reflected a general sense that members of many ancient peoples had done their best to falsify the textual and historical record, a sense that became more acute as Scaliger and Casaubon found themselves embroiled in bitter controversies with Catholic scholars about the history of the early Christian church, and questions about which texts were genuine took on a new ideological urgency.[51] Scaliger, like many Christian Hebraists, studied the Jews in part to improve his mastery of Christian tradition. Paradoxically, his anger at the deceptions of early Christians—themselves users of the Septuagint—flavored his approach to the Jews who had created it and then veiled its origins in historical fantasy.

Nothing Scaliger wrote about Jews, ancient or modern, was more consequential than the discussions he devoted to the Hellenists. The scholarly fires that he set continue to burn, and sharp disagreement persists about the origins of the Septuagint and the nature of Hellenistic Jewish culture.[52] Closer to Scaliger's own time, his history of Hellenistic Judaism became a crucial part of the larger seventeenth-century vision of the ancient world, a vision of nations and cultures in contact, across linguistic and cultural barriers, which in many respects represents the ancient world much more as scholarship now constructs it than did the purely classical antiquity conjured up by eighteenth-century Neo-Hellenists and nineteenth-century historicists. It was almost an ancient Republic of Letters. This vision came into being because Scaliger, and others, brought classical, Christian, and Hebraic scholarship into fruitful contact.[53] The rediscovery of the Hellenists may not form part of the story of Christian Hebraism. But it was one of the most sweeping transformations in Christian scholarship devoted to the Jews. It seems possible that it would be more productive to see Christian Hebraism itself as part of that second, broader set of terms.[54]

Notes

1. See, e.g., Stephen Burnett, *From Christian Hebraism to Jewish Studies: Johannes Buxtorf (1564–1629) and Hebrew Learning in the Seventeenth Century* (Leiden, 1996); Burnett, *Christian Hebraism in the Reformation Era (1500–1660): Authors, Books, and the Transmission of Jewish Learning* (Leiden, 2012); Allison Coudert and Jeffrey Shoulson, eds., *Hebraica Veritas?: Christian Hebraists and the Study of Judaism in Early Modern Europe* (Philadelphia, 2004); Albert van der Heide, *Hebraica veritas: Christopher Plantin and the Christian Hebraists* (Antwerp, 2008). Much remains to be learned, especially about the debt of Renaissance Christian Hebraists to their medieval predecessors. For aspects of this complex story see Judith Olszowy-Schlanger, "Robert Wakefield and the Medieval Background of Hebrew Scholarship in Renaissance England," in *Hebrew to Latin, Latin to Hebrew: The Mirroring of Two Cultures in the Age of Humanism*, ed. G. Busi (Berlin, 2006), 61–87; Piet van Boxel and Sabine Arndt, eds., *Crossing Borders: Hebrew Manuscripts as a Meeting-Place of Cultures* (Oxford, 2009); and C. Philipp E. Nothaft, *Dating the Passion: The Life of Jesus and the Emergence of Scientific Chronology (200–1600)* (Leiden, 2012).

2. Jerome Friedman, *The Most Ancient Testimony: Sixteenth-Century Christian-Hebraica in the Age of Renaissance Nostalgia* (Athens, Ohio, 1983).

3. Ronnie Po-chia Hsia, "Christian Ethnographies of Jews in Early Modern Germany," in *The Expulsion of the Jews: 1492 and After*, ed. R. Waddington and A. Williamson (New York, 1994), 223–36; Yaacov Deutsch, "Polemical Ethnographies: Descriptions of Yom Kippur in the Writings of Christian Hebraists and Jewish Converts to Christianity in Early Modern Europe," in *Hebraica Veritas*, 202–32; and Deutsch, *Judaism in Christian Eyes: Ethnographic Descriptions of Jews and Judaism in*

Early Modern Europe (New York, 2012); Maria Diemling, "Anthonius Margarita and his 'Der Gantz Jüdisch Glaub,'" in *Jews, Judaism and the Reformation in Early Modern Germany*, ed. D. P. Bell and S. Burnett (Leiden, 2006), 303–33.

4. See Aya Elyada, "Protestant Scholars and Yiddish Studies in Early Modern Europe," *Past & Present* 203 (2009): 69–98, and Elyada, *A Goy Who Speaks Yiddish: Christians and the Jewish Language in Early Modern Germany* (Stanford, Calif., 2012).

5. Jacob Guttmann, *Jean Bodin in seinen Beziehungen zum Judentum* (Breslau, 1906).

6. Jacob Bernays, *Joseph Justus Scaliger* (Berlin, 1855), 124.

7. See in general Willem den Boer, "Joseph Scaliger en de Joden," in *Bestuurders en geleerden*, ed. S. Groenveld et al. (Amsterdam, 1985), 65–74; *"All my Books in Foreign Tongues": Scaliger's Oriental Legacy in Leiden, 1609–2009. Catalogue of an Exhibition on the Quatercentenary of Scaliger's Death, 21 January 2009*, ed. A. Vrolijk et al. (Leiden, 2009); Anthony Grafton, *Joseph Scaliger: A Study in the History of Classical Scholarship*, 2 vols. (Oxford, 1983–93) and Anthony Grafton and Joanna Weinberg, *"I Have Always Loved the Holy Tongue": Isaac Casaubon, the Jews, and a Forgotten Chapter in Renaissance Scholarship* (Cambridge, Mass., 2011).

8. Scaliger to Gilbert Seguin, November 11 [1590–92]; *The Correspondence of Joseph Scaliger*, 8 vols., ed. Paul Botley and Dirk van Miert. (Geneva, 2012), 2:133.

9. Ibid.

10. Ibid.

11. Ibid.

12. On the origins and development of this legend see Abraham Wasserstein and David Wasserstein, *The Legend of the Septuagint: From Classical Antiquity to Today* (Cambridge, 2006); and Tessa Rajak, *Translation and Survival: The Greek Bible of the Ancient Jewish Diaspora* (Oxford, 2009), chap. 1.

13. Scaliger to Seguin, between November 11, 1590 and June 1593, *The Correspondence of Joseph Scaliger*, 2:136.

14. Ibid., 2:137.

15. For the development of Septuagint scholarship in early modern Europe see J .C. H. Lebram, "Ein Streit um die Hebräische Bibel und die Septuaginta," in *Leiden University in the Seventeenth Century*, ed. Th. H. Lunsingh Scheurleer and G H M Posthumus Meyjes (Leiden, 1975), 20–63; Scott Mandelbrote, "English Scholarship and the Greek Text of the Old Testament, 1620–1720: The Impact of Codex Alexandrinus," in *Scripture and Scholarship in Early Modern England*, ed A. Hessayon and N. Keene (Aldershot, 2006), 74–93; and *Isaac Vossius (1618–1689): Between Science and Scholarship*, ed. D. van Miert and E. Jorink (Leiden, 2012).

16. Grafton and Weinberg, *"I Have Always Loved the Holy Tongue,"* 189–90.

17. Joseph Scaliger, "Notae in Novum Testamentum," *Novi Testamenti libri omnes* (London, 1622), sig. A2 6 verso.

18. Joseph Scaliger, *Opus de emendatione temporum*, 2d ed. (Leiden, 1598), 143 and 406.

19. Casaubon's copy of the book is now Eton College Library Gg.2.7. See his note on the verso of the title page, his copious underlining on 143, and his note on 503.

20. Joseph Scaliger, "Animadversiones in chronologica Eusebii," in *Thesaurus temporum* (Leiden: 1606), 124. The new texts Scaliger cited included the description of darkness covering the world because of the translation of the Bible in *Megilat Ta'anit* (Wasserstein and Wasserstein, *The Legend of the Septuagint,* 81) the description of R. Eleazar ben R. Zadok's purchase of what had been a synagogue of the Alexandrians from *y. Megilah* 73; Tertullian's description in *Apologeticus* 18.9: "Sed et Iudaei palam lectitant"; and, unfortunately, the travel account of Benjamin of Tudela, into which Scaliger misread a reference to a twelfth-century community of Hellenists at Alexandria (Grafton, *Scaliger*, 2:418–19).

21. Arnaldo Momigliano, *The Classical Foundations of Modern Historiography* (Berkeley, Calif., 1990), 25; also quoted by Rajak, *Translation and Survival*, 217.

22. Erasmus, *Paraphrase on Acts,* ed. J. Bateman, trans. and ann. R. Sider (Toronto, 1995), 46, 200–201, 225, 238. His exegesis, here as elsewhere, followed a suggestion in the interlinear gloss (ibid., 201, 225).

23. For these texts see Luciano Canfora, *Ellenismo* (Rome, 1987), 86–87.

24. Ibid., 87–88.

25. See Joanna Weinberg, "The Quest for Philo in Sixteenth-Century Jewish Historiography," in *Jewish History: Essays in Honour of Chimen Abramsky,* ed. A. Rapoport-Albert and S. Zipperstein (London, 1988), 163–187, and Charles Touati, "Judaïsme talmudique et rabbinique: La découverte par le judaïsme de la Renaissance de Flavius Josèphe et de Philon le Juif," *Annuaire École Pratique des Hautes Études, Ve section: Sciences Religieuses,* 97 (1988–89): 214–17.

26. On Steuco's scholarship and its polemical uses see Ronald Delph, "Valla Grammaticus, Agostino Steuco, and the Donation of Constantine," *Journal of the History of Ideas* 57.1 (1996): 55–77.

27. Agostino Steuco, *Veteris testamenti ad veritatem Hebraicam recognitio* (Lyons, 1531), 80.

28. For de'Rossi's use of Steuco see *The Light of the Eyes,* ed. and trans. J. Weinberg (New Haven, Conn., 2001), xl–xli and 128.

29. Ibid., 129.

30. Ibid., 159.

31. Carl Philipp Emanuel Nothaft, "From Sukkot to Saturnalia: The Attack on Christmas in Sixteenth-Century Chronological Scholarship," *Journal of the History of Ideas* 72 (2011): 503–22.

32. See Joanna Weinberg, "A Hebraic Approach to the New Testament," in *History of Scholarship: A Selection of Papers from the Seminar on the History of Scholarship Held Annually at the Warburg Institute,* ed. C. Ligota and J. L. Quantin (Oxford, 2006), 238–47.

33. Angelo Canini, "Loci aliquot Novi Testamenti cum Hebraeorum originibus collati atque historice explicati," in Canini, *Institutiones linguae Syriacae, Assyriacae atque Thalmudicae, una cum Aethiopicae atque Arabicae collatione. Addita est ad calcem Novi Testamenti multorum locorum historica enarratio* (Paris, 1554), 12–13. Hazota is the form used by Canini.

34. Ibid., 13: "Rab Ioses (qui nempe maiore erat authoritate) . . ." See Weinberg, "A Hebraic Approach to the New Testament," 244–45. For the Talmud passage and its context see Lee Levine, "The Jewish Community at Caesarea in Late Antiquity," in *Caesarea Papers: Straton's Tower, Herod's Harbour, and Roman and Byzantine Caesarea,* ed. R. L. Vann (Ann Arbor, Mich., 1992), 268–73.

35. Canini, *Institutiones,* 12. See Weinberg, "A Hebraic Approach to the New Testament," 245.

36. *Iosuae imperatoris historia,* ed. A. Masius (Antwerp, 1574), 1:118. On this and the other rabbinical testimonia see Giuseppe Veltri, *Eine Tora für den König Talmai: Untersuchungen zum Übersetzungsverständnis in der jüdisch-hellenistischen und rabbinischen Literatur* (Tübingen, 1994), and Wasserstein and Wasserstein, *The Legend of the Septuagint,* 51–83.

37. Masius, *Iosuae,* 1:120.

38. Joannes Drusius, *Observationum libri xii* (Antwerp, 1584), 2:20, 52.

39. Ibid., 6:9, 132–33. See also Drusius to Thomas Bodley, n.d., in his *De quaesitis per epistolam* (Franeker, 1595), 40–41, where his discussion presupposes the general validity of the story of the LXX.

40. See J. C. H. Lebram, "De Hasidaeis. Over Joodse studiën in het oude Leiden," in *Voordrachten Faculteitendag 1980* (Leiden, 1980), 21–31; Johannes van den Berg, "Proto-Protestants? The Image of the Karaites as a Mirror of the Catholic-Protestant Controversy of the Seventeenth Century," in *Jewish-Christian Relations in the Seventeenth Century,* ed. E. van der Wall and J. van den Berg (Dordrecht, 1988), 33–50, reprinted in his *Religious Currents and Cross-Currents: Essays on Early Modern Protestantism and the Protestant Enlightenment,* ed. Jan de Bruijn et al. (Leiden, 1999), 43–55; Francis

Schmidt, "The Hasidaeans and the Ancient Jewish 'Sects': A Seventeenth-Century Controversy," in *Sects and Sectarianism in Jewish History*, ed. S. Stern (Leiden, 2011), 187–203.

41. Drusius to Scaliger, n.d. (1594, before October 1), in *De quaesitis*, 18–20 = Scaliger, *Correspondence*, ed. Botley and van Miert, 2:434–36; Scaliger to Drusius, October 1, 1594; ibid., 2:440–41; Drusius to Scaliger, n.d., (after October 1, 1594–early 1595), in *De quaesitis*, 215–16 = Scaliger, *Correspondence*, ed. Botley and van Miert, 2:442–43. The first letter refers explicitly to a conversation.

42. Drusius discussed the Hellenistae mentioned in Acts 6 and 11 in his *Annotationum in totum Jesu Christi Testamentum sive Praeteritorum libri decem* (Franeker, 1612), 166–67, 177. He described them, as Scaliger did, as Jews who "read Greek Bibles in their synagogues and knew Greek, using a particular dialect known as Hellenistic," and referred the reader to Scaliger's discussions in the *Thesaurus temporum* (166). Cf. Canfora, *Ellenismo*, 87.

43. Scaliger, "Animadversiones in chronologica Eusebii," 123–24, at 124: "Quis nescit Iudaeorum commenta?"

44. Rajak, *Translation and Survival*, 38–39.

45. Jacob Freudenthal, *Alexander Polyhistor und die von ihm erhaltenen Reste judäischer und samaritanischer Geschichtswerke* (Breslau, 1874–75), 194.

46. Grafton and Weinberg, "*I Have Always Loved the Holy Tongue*," 30–42.

47. Scaliger to Casaubon, November 9, 1605, edited by Botley and van Miert.

48. Ibid.

49. Ibid.

50. Ibid.

51. See Grafton and Weinberg, "*I Have Always Loved the Holy Tongue*," 164–230.

52. See esp. Rajak, *Translation and Survival*.

53. See, e.g., G. J. Toomer, *John Selden: A Life in Scholarship*, 2 vols. (Oxford, 2009).

54. This essay owes a special conceptual debt to two of David Ruderman's books: *Jewish Enlightenment in an English Key: Anglo-Jewry's Construction of Modern Jewish Thought* (Princeton, N.J., 2000) and *Connecting the Covenants: Judaism and the Search for Christian Identity in Eighteenth-Century England* (Philadelphia, 2007). Warm thanks also to Theo Dunkelgrün, Henk Jan de Jonge, Scott Mandelbrote, Peter Miller, Piet van Boxel, and Joanna Weinberg for many discussions of related problems.

JEWS, NOBILITY, AND USURY IN LUTHER'S EUROPE

❈ ❈ ❈

Jonathan Karp

Binghamton University,
State University of New York

THE second half of the sixteenth century inaugurated a period of renewed economic dynamism in much of European Jewish life. According to Jonathan Israel's influential if ironic characterization, the expulsions of the preceding century had resituated Jews in a constellation of locales that enabled them to create far-flung trading networks, ones that well fit new and vital trends in global commerce. These networks linked the Ottoman Eastern Mediterranean via overland trade routes to Northern Italy and, via ocean-going routes, to Italian ports like Venice, Spalato (the Venetian controlled Dalmatian port), Ancona, and Livorno. Many New Christians, sincere and otherwise, maintained commercial ties with former coreligionists, enabling merchant communities living in Italian ports to trade with their counterparts in Iberian entrepôts, with New Christian communities in western France, Antwerp and parts of the New World, and (by the seventeenth century) with Jewish communities in Amsterdam and Hamburg.[1]

This depiction of a veritable golden age of Jewish mercantile prowess centers principally on Sephardic commerce; nevertheless, a more modest Ashkenazic corollary has sometimes been claimed for the Jews of Eastern Europe. Polish Jewry became increasingly significant to the economic life of Eastern Poland and Lithuania in this period as Jewish colonists began to settle in Lithuanian and Ukrainian territories that the Polish state had recently subsumed. By the seventeenth century Jews had become commercial agents and managerial middlemen of the Polish nobility. Some scholars have even suggested (if not demonstrated) that the trade of the Sephardim in ports dotting Europe's Atlantic coast was linked with the Baltic grain trade, in which Jews played a role, through Hamburg and Amsterdam, which thereby established connections between Sephardic and Ashkenazic commercial networks.[2] Even if these linkages appear tenuous, the historical speculations underlying them reflect a perception among historians that the various Jewries of the early modern period had become newly interconnected in vital ways, not least in their economic ties.[3]

If there is one Jewish population that seems to stand apart in this hopeful story, it is the Jews of German lands. By 1550 Jews there were reeling from two centuries of local expulsions and mounting economic restrictions. German Jewry of the sixteenth century is generally seen as suffering severe demographic decline, intellectual stagnation, and economic constriction. And while this portrait has recently been subject to criticism, no historian would claim that German Jewish communities in this period displayed vigor comparable to their sister communities.[4] As is often the case, however, the recorded perceptions of contemporary non-Jews at times seem to reflect the very opposite of this reality. In addition to the familiar medieval motifs of Jews as ritual murderers, sorcerers, and magicians, we find in contemporary German-language writings a new emphasis on the Jews' worldly power, their deployment of commerce and moneylending to exploit and enervate Christians, their undue influence with governmental authorities, and most of all, their unholy alliance with the German nobility.[5] The anti-Jewish literature of this period is far from uniform. Indeed, some critics of the Jews displayed a keen awareness of their destitution. Nevertheless, even these more realistic observers exhibit a preoccupation with Jewish ties to the powerful noble estate. The question is why this motif appears so prominently and pervasively, and what its consequences might be.

The writings of Martin Luther on Jews provide a rich point of entry to this topic. Among the best-known (and most infamous) anti-Jewish writings of the sixteenth century, Luther's attitudes to Jews have been subject to copious analysis, both because of his singular historical importance and due to their somewhat perplexing nature. Their tone appears to shift radically, violently and—in the eyes of many readers—inexplicably over the course of his career.[6] These shifts are certainly on display also with regard to one of the few motifs of Luther's Jewish writings that has not received adequate attention: his analogies between nobles and Jews. This theme is fully aired in his two most famous, and seemingly antithetical, writings on Jews: the 1523 *That Jesus Christ was Born a Jew* (*Dass Jesus Christus ein geborner Jude sei*) and his 1543 screed, *On the Jews and Their Lies* (*Von den Juden und ihren Lügen*). Whereas the former partly endorses Jewish recalcitrance—at least against the hitherto monopolistic Roman Christianity ("If I had been a Jew and had seen such dolts and blockheads govern and teach the Christian faith, I would sooner have become a hog than a Christian")—the latter insists that Jews are willfully blind and stubbornly fixated on worldly lordship ("If God were to give me no other Messiah than such as the Jews wish and hope for, I would much, much rather be a sow than a human being").[7] Whereas in the early essay Luther chides Christians for their cruel mistreatment of Jews, in the latter one he takes Christian authorities to task for tolerating and indulging Jews. While in 1523 he emphasizes Jews' tribal relation to Christ, in 1543 he insists that Jews have acted to forfeit their claim to the patrimony of biblical Hebrews. Finally, whereas in the 1523 *That Jesus Christ was Born a Jew*, Luther excuses Jewish usury on the grounds that it was self-servingly imposed upon Jews by Christians, in the 1543 *On the Jews and Their Lies* he identifies usury as, in a sense, the proper villainous profession of the Jews, and an activity in keeping with their misanthropic and exploitative natures.[8]

In addition to seeking out attitudinal continuities between the earlier and later writings of Luther on Jews (usually aimed at demonstrating a more consistent measure of underlying hostility than is apparent on the surface), scholars have been at pains to show that Luther's ideas about Jews are far from novel. For instance, there is nothing particularly new in Luther's suggestion, in his statement of 1523, that Jews will respond more favorably to the milk of Christian kindness than to the vinegar of revenge, nor is there much that is innovative in his recommendation there of a tactical gradualism (first show the Jews why Jesus is their messiah rather than alienate them off the bat with the difficult claim that he is also the son of God). Like the denunciatory paranoia of his later diatribe, this soft approach to Jews embraced by Luther in 1523 has ample medieval precedent.[9]

Still, this skepticism about Luther's uniqueness or the disjunctive quality of his Jewish writings misses an essential point. What is thematically new—and more to the point, pronouncedly Protestant—in the earlier writing is Luther's self-conscious back-to-scripture emphasis on the Pauline doctrine from *Romans* identifying Jews as "from the lineage of Christ" (*von dem Geblut Christi*). And what is striking and original in the later diatribe is his rejection of this very doctrine, not as factually false, but as essentially meaningless in light of Luther's doctrine of *sola fide*.

In *That Jesus Christ was Born a Jew* Luther makes much of the Jews' unique and elevated tribal status, their lineage and high birth. They are indeed the children of the promise: "Although the gospel has been proclaimed to all the world, yet He committed the Holy Scriptures, that is, the law and the prophets, to no nation except the Jews, as Paul says in Romans 3:2 and Psalm 147:19–20." Luther recalls that, to this very day, God "has not dealt thus with any other nation." In a clear demonstration of Luther's wish to return in the matter of Jews to authentic Pauline principles, he relies heavily on Romans 9:4–5, where the Apostle paraphrases the sui generis blessings and honors afforded to the Hebrews, "to whom pertaineth the adoption, and the glory, and the covenants, and the giving of the law, and the service of God, and the promises."[10] Consequently, as the sole relations to and remnants of the family of Christ, Jews in Luther's portrayal are veritable blue bloods and aristocrats whose anticipated conversion retains a unique status. Hence, "the Jews are closer to Christ than are we" (*so gehoren je die Juden Christo naher zu, den wir*).[11] Yet here Luther is careful to include a quiet caveat to the praise: "if we can boast of flesh and blood" (*wenn man sich des Bluts und Fleischs ruhmen sollt*)."[12] Luther thus qualifies his exaltation of Jewish descent with a subtle reminder that he is speaking primarily in fleshly terms.

This almost parenthetical thread (this "as it were" or "so to speak") of the 1523 text becomes the full-blown rationale of the text from 1543, wherein the Jews' pretensions to nobility are precisely what constitute their fatal flaw of pride. "There is one thing about which they boast and pride themselves beyond measure, and that is their descent from the foremost people on earth, from Abraham, Sarah, Isaac, Rebecca, Jacob, and from the twelve patriarchs, and thus from the holy people of Israel."[13] Quoting the exact same verse that he had cited in 1523 (Rom 9:4–5), in which Paul extols the Jews' holy patrimony, Luther now lambasts them precisely for claiming to be "the only noble people on earth" (*allein edle Menschen auf Erden*) in comparison with which the rest of mankind are *arme würme*, "poor worms," "not of that high and noble blood, linage, birth, and descent."[14]

We recall that the renewed emphasis on Pauline themes had been a Reformation hallmark of the 1523 *That Jesus Christ was Born a Jew*. The same can be said of *On the Jews and Their Lies* written two decades later, but now to dramatically different ends. If previously in Luther's writings the Jews' biblical lineage stood in their favor, here it is merely a source of vainglory. Luther excoriates Jews for boasting in their prayers of the very chosenness he had previously professed to admire:

> to strut before God and boast about being so noble, so exalted, and so rich (*wie es so Eddel, Hoch, Reich*) compared to other people—that is devilish arrogance (*teuflische Hoffart*), *since every birth according to the flesh is condemned before him without exception* (*alle Geburt nach dem Fleisch gar zu gleich verdampt ist*).[15]

Lineage is thus of no avail, high birth of no spiritual worth, without at the same time a different and second birth consequent upon the faith that comes through engagement with Scripture.

> Oh, what do we poor muck-worms (*Armen drecksekte*), maggots, stench and filth presume to boast of before him who is the God and Creator of heaven and earth, who made us out of dirt and out of nothing! . . . All that we are and have comes from his grace and rich mercy.[16]

Exactly why Luther seemed to express admiration for the Jews' noble likeness in the earlier text and only admonishment in the later remains to be scrutinized. First, however, it is important to emphasize that Luther's deployment of the noble analogy in discussing Jews is not merely rhetorical or metaphorical. The lordly behavior of which he accuses the Jews in 1543 relates both to their liturgy, which he claims celebrates their exaltation above common mankind, *and* to their usury, which grants them economic mastery over the lowly German. "They let us work in the sweat of our brow to earn money and property while they sit behind the stove, idle away the time, fart and roast pears . . . They mock and deride us because we work and let them play the role of lazy squires . . . They are our masters and we are their servants, with our property, our sweat, and our labor (*mit unserm eigen gut, schweis und arbeit*)."[17] It is, moreover, not just that the audacious Jews act like and adopt the lifestyle of lazy squires, but rather that their lordly misbehavior is enabled, claims Luther, by the *actual* German nobility's misgovernment. "Princes and lords (*Fürsten und Herrn*) you must not and cannot protect them unless you wish to become participants in all their abominations."[18] If the German nobility responds that employing Jews as creditors is "useful to the state" (in the manner of emerging *raison d'état* and proto-mercantilist arguments), Luther continues, they must be reminded that the state's first obligation is to protect its humble Christian subjects, in this case from their usurious exploitation by infidels.

We should be careful not to imagine that Luther's critique was merely a social one cloaked in religious garb. Rather, this is a religious critique for which social elements comprise much of the fabric. By 1543 Luther had strongly hedged the doctrine of contemporary Jewry's relation to ancient Hebrews or the family of Christ, even if merely in terms of flesh and blood. On the contrary, consanguinity with the family of Christ was always only a theological construct, Luther makes clear, since its very facticity has now been negated by Jewry's perfidy. Luther's dissociation of modern Jews from ancient Hebrews even adduces as a quasi-theological concept the all-too-worldly doctrine of *servi camerae,* "chamber serfdom" (the medieval notion that Jews are the property of the crown and, in its imperial guise, subject to being pawned for taxation purposes to local princes and *Hochadel*). The role Jews play as agents of *Herrschaft* is one predetermined, so to speak, by their rejection of God. According to Luther, when Pilate asked the Jews if they really wanted him to crucify their king (i.e., Christ), they replied, "We have no king but Caesar!" This, Luther insists, marked a decisive self-abrogation of Jews' covenantal loyalty to God and a shift of their allegiance to Caesar instead (whose successor is the Catholic Holy Roman Emperor). But ironically, this shift meant that the very Mosaic law that the Jews cite to justify their usury toward Christians—Deuteronomy 23.20 ("Unto a stranger thou mayest lend upon usury")—is invalid, since the Jews now belong to Caesar alone and (at least so long as they reside in Germany) no longer to the Mosaic covenant itself. The bond of servitude to Caesar that Jews willfully chose marks their fall from favored to degraded status.[19]

Unfortunately, concludes Luther, in our own day the emperor, princes, and lords defy divine intentions by making Jews instruments of their own fiscal exploitation, foisting their usury upon a helpless population in order to then exorbitantly tax this ill-gotten wealth. Luther would single out for censure Joachim II, Elector of Brandenburg, King Ferdinand of Bohemia, and Counts Philip and Hans George of Mansfeld, but he also admonished the territorial lords (*Schutzherren*) in general and, of course, the Emperor especially for this greedy indulgence of the Jews. This sinister bargain must cease, Luther insists, and his arguments toward that end constitute one of the principal aims of *On the Jews and Their Lies.*[20]

Luther's two major essays on Jews are particularly brilliant for their reworking of older stereotypes, both positive and negative, to fit Protestant theology—an endeavor for which analogies between Jews and nobility provide the fulcrum. Nevertheless, the motif linking Jews and nobles transcended religious denomination in sixteenth-century Germany. Luther's great Catholic antagonist, for instance, Johannes Eck, in his 1541 *Ains Judenbüchlins verlegung*, inveighed not merely against Jewish usury but even more pointedly against the Jews' noble patrons. Eck's book, which endorsed without qualification the blood libel officially rejected by the Roman Church, was as anti-Jewish a text as any written during the century. Yet Eck—who far more than Luther accepted the legitimacy of limited (5 percent) interest rates on consumption loans—did not blame Jews primarily for charging excessive interest. Rather, in his view it was the princes and lords who bore the greater responsibility. Their lust for tax revenue, according to Eck, was what made possible Jewish usury in the first place; therefore, the nobles, at least as much as the Jews, should be obligated to make financial restitution to their subjects.[21]

Eck had something else in common with his nemesis Luther: namely, the prescription that Jews be compelled to abandon usury and work with their hands. The goal was not "productivization" in the manner of nineteenth-century formulae for Jewish occupational restructuring, or even the removal of Jewish usury as a source of social tension with Christian populations (which had been the aim of rhetorical demands by such medieval kings as Edward I and Louis IX that Jews take up agriculture in place of moneylending).[22] Eck's aim, rather, was essentially religious. Eck postulated that usury is a principal obstacle to the (voluntary) conversion of the Jews. This is because it gives the nobility an incentive to maintain a distinct Jewish population, one able to perform financial services that Christians theologically cannot.[23] This, we might add, was a long-existing irony of Jewish policy, in which the Church generally favored efforts to convert the majority of Jews while the crown had a vested interest (through the taxation of Jewish lending) in opposing mass conversion. But by the sixteenth century a number of writers in Northern and Eastern Europe seemed prepared to denounce this contradiction and propose to eliminate it by weaning Jews from usury. The only way this could be accomplished, they believed, was by breaking the noble/Jew alliance.[24]

An impressive number of prominent sixteenth-century authors, such as the reformers Martin Bucer and Ulrich Zwingli, harped upon this theme. Zwingli's 1523 *Auslegung der Schlußreden* is not altogether insensitive to the compulsory character of Jews' activity as economic agents of the nobility. Nevertheless, Zwingli's favored solution to the problem of noble exploitation was to expel the Jewish population.[25] Bucer, for his part, withheld even this modicum of sympathy; where Jews could not be expelled they must be shorn of their usurious professions and confined instead to occupations demanding the most demeaning forms of physical labor, such as the cleaning of sewers and the disposal of carcasses. Naturally, the intention of such demands was not to valorize physical work but rather to punish and degrade Jews, with the hope that some of them might convert.[26]

On the other hand, one discerns hints of a reformist agenda in the prescriptions of several other contemporary commentators. Few were more attuned to the economic dilemmas of Jews than the triumvirate of sixteenth-century converts, Antonius Margaritha, Johannes Pfefferkorn, and Victor von Carben. No longer able to draw sustenance from the kinds of livelihoods available to Jews (however meager), converts lacked ready access to Christian ones as well, whether due to lack of skills or guild exclusion.[27] That they often had to depend upon charitable support to eke out a living (Luther himself struggled for years to support the former Jew, "Bernard the convert"[28]) only deepened their animosity toward the usury permitted to former co-religionists. Just as important, in their view noble support for Jewish usury, along with the absence of meaningful provisions for supporting converts and channeling them into virtuous "Christian" trades, served as a mighty obstacle to mass conversion.[29]

These converts were among the pioneers of a new type of realistic literature on Jews, one that focused on Jewish customs, prayers, and folkways. Although intended largely to expose the depravity of Jewish life and its anti-Christian animus, these descriptions were also generally presented in a realistic fashion. This has caused some modern scholars to define the genre they created as a primitive form of Jewish ethnography (a term first applied by Ronnie Hsia and later modified by Yaakov Deutsch as "polemical ethnography").[30] These authors were at pains to expose the degraded, indeed, debased conditions afflicting Jewish communities as just deserts no doubt for their sins against Christ and Christians, but also as a reflection of the internal harm caused by Jewish dependence on moneylending. Usury functioned as a major source of Jewish economic strife because it led to intense internal competition for clients, provoked Christian retribution, prompted exorbitant noble taxation, and led ultimately to expulsion and dislocation. Margaritha's *Der gantz Jüdisch Glaub,* a work that directly influenced Luther's *On the Jews and Their Lies,* contains recollections of the harsh character of Jewish economic life found in the author's childhood home of Ratisbon, rent by factionalism and economic strife, and can be read, in part, as a call to Jewish social reform via conversion to Christianity.[31]

That something appeared dreadfully wrong with the Jewish economy in sixteenth-century Germany should not have been surprising, given the periodic waves of expulsions over the preceding two centuries. If there was anything like a medieval golden age of German-Jewish finance, it was long over by the sixteenth century.[32] It had been replaced with a much-reduced Jewish population even more dependent on the protection of the nobles, not in return for loaning them money, but rather for extracting on their behalf the surplus wealth of the poor: peasants, artisans, commoners —indeed, all those who could be described by the label the common man (*der gemeine Mann*). This virtuous but defenseless class was, in the eyes of Pfefferkorn and others, the victim not only of the Jew's high interest rates, but of the imperial courts that enforced exorbitant debt penalties against defaulters and of the notorious *Hehlerrecht* (law of stolen goods) that indemnified Jewish lenders against the illegal purchase of stolen pledges and mandated full compensation to the pawnbroker for their return. Both institutions were widely viewed as contrary to general legal norms, through "fixed" courts in the first instance and the application of legal double standards in the second. And in both cases such patent injustices reflected the collusion of princely and imperial authority with Jews.

The Jews' alleged crimes were therefore ones befitting not Shylocks or Rothschilds but rather the petty racketeers of a far-flung criminal enterprise otherwise known as the Holy Roman Empire. That in this construction Jews served as convenient scapegoats seems evident even from the vantage point of Martin Luther. As we have seen, his *On the Jews and Their Lies* is typically juxtaposed with his earlier missionary tract of 1523, *That Jesus Christ was Born a Jew.* But perhaps an equally telling comparison would be his nearly contemporaneous writings from the 1525 Peasants War. In Luther's initial commentary on that burgeoning conflict, he admonished the lords, "who do nothing but cheat and rob the people so that you can lead a life of luxury and extravagance," to "stop your raging and obstinate tyranny and not deal unreasonably with the peasants." However, in the face of peasant violence, abetted by Anabaptist preaching, Luther soon shifted gears, coming to the defense of the nobility and condemning the peasants to enjoy the same "sharp mercy" (*scharffe barmherzigkeit*) he would later recommend for Jews. As is well known, Luther ultimately sided with the nobility as divinely sanctioned authority (and often as Protestant protectors of Luther himself). Having made peace with the noble estate, a move that allowed for the continued spread of his reforms, Luther's suppressed hostility to these "obstinate tyrants" eventually resurfaced as a call to arms against a *counterfeit* Jewish nobility, which operated on the real nobility's vicarious behalf. If the Jews symbolize the misrule of the German (and especially the Catholic) nobility, then attacking them has the virtue of presenting a soft target for an otherwise dangerous social critique.[33] That Luther's analogizing of Jews to "lazy squires" is laughable, given the decimation and virtual bankruptcy of the Jewish population of the time, does not diminish its symbolic, not to mention psychic, impact.

In actuality, Jewish usury was a petty and minor economic affair in Luther's day. As Robert Birley notes, "the sixteenth century constituted a transitional period between Jewish predominance in moneylending in the later Middle Ages and the rise of the court Jew in the seventeenth century, and so a low point in Jewish financial activity."[34] It is not too much to say that the disjuncture between this humble reality and widespread perception of Jewish economic potency, although a common discrepancy in the history of anti-Semitism, derived its plausibility from the Jews' ever greater dependency on the imperial nobility. As expelled Jewish populations fanned out into the countryside or sought haven on noble estates, their services as petty lenders and pawnbrokers brought them into increasing contact with the so-called *gemeine Mann*.[35] That Jews could do little themselves to alter this reality is apparent from the comments of the great Jewish intercessor (or *shtadlan*), Josel of Rosheim, who enjoyed the favor of successive emperors. Under compulsion to respond to the numerous critiques of authors like Margaritha and von Carben, Josel prepared a remarkable proposal (*Artikel und Ordnung*), in connection with the 1530 Augsburg Diet, to curb alleged abuses by Jews in their moneylending and pawn-brokerage. There Josel condemned such familiar tricks as hidden interest charges (*bedeckten wucher*), adding interest charges to the loan principal, reckoning inter-est half- or quarter-yearly, lending to minors, and forcibly collecting (i.e., through imperial courts) debts from heirs and widows. By censuring and preventing such activities, claimed Josel, "the poor will not be exploited and will be able to maintain themselves side by side with the rest of mankind" [*damit der arm nit zu ubersezen und einer be idem andern sein leibisnarung durchainander handlin*]. In addition to curbing these abuses through fines imposed by the Jewish community, Josel sought to limit the resort of creditors to imperial courts and even appeared to renounce altogether key aspects of the traditional *Hehlerrecht*, the aforementioned law of stolen goods.[36]

Yet despite these concessions to the critics, Josel did not believe that Jews could survive exile without relying on moneylending as their mainstay. Instead of de-nouncing the fiscal alliance with princes and nobility, Josel reaffirmed its divine sanction. Fortunately, he concluded, "God gives the great rulers such intelligence that they also understand the Holy Scriptures [i.e., its provisions on legitimate usu-ry], and therefore, they protect us from our enemies and do not hearken to all the venomous clamor against us. The greater the ruler, the greater the grace with which God endows them, and the [greater] their benevolence toward all."[37]

Yet Josel was wrong in his assumptions about the permanence of Jewish money-lending. The critique of usury, the demands for its elimination by various regional Diets, and the ongoing expulsions, had the cumulative effect of shifting the Jewish population away from the cities and dispersing them in small numbers into the countryside. This was a process that began in the fifteenth century, at the latest, and continued apace through the decades following the Thirty Years War. Pawnbroker-age provided a bridge from moneylending back to commerce, since it supplied Jews with a stock of commodities for trade. And while moneylending by no means dis-appeared, it would increasingly become a sideline for many rural and itinerant Jews engaged in peddling, dealing in old clothes, cattle-trading, the raising of livestock, and related activities—the stereotypical undertakings of Central European Jews well into the nineteenth century.

At the same time, the relative shift of Jews out of moneylending did not have the result expected by Pfefferkorn, Margaritha, or Eck. Jews' religious allegiances were not conditioned upon their concentration in a single occupational field. The Jews' increasingly more ramified occupational structure (while still overwhelmingly commercial), moreover, did not preclude a reconstitution of their alliance with the nobility. On the contrary, the activities of the seventeenth- and eighteenth-century Court Jews partly depended upon these rural trading endeavors. Although strained and subject to vehement criticism, the relationship of central European Jews and nobles would endure and occasionally blossom until it was finally shattered—like so much else—by the upheaval of the French Revolution. This may explain why in the aftermath of the French Revolution the kinds of criticisms so powerfully expressed by Luther would resonate again in the writings of Fichte and other German critics of the *ancien regime.*[38]

Notes

1. Jonathan Israel, *Diasporas within a Diaspora: Jews, Crypto-Jews and the World Maritime Empires (1540–1740)* (Leiden, 2002).

2. Jonathan Israel, *European Jewry in the Age of Mercantilism* (Oxford, 1991), 26–31.

3. This is an important theme of David Ruderman's, *Early Modern Jewry: A New Cultural History* (Princeton, N.J., 2010), chap. 1.

4. For a recent corrective, see Debra Kaplan and Magda Teter, "Out of the (Historiographic) Ghetto: European Jews and Reformation Narratives," *Sixteenth Century Journal* 40.2 (2009): 369–94; for a review of some of the recent literature, see Jonathan Karp, "Jews, Hebraism, and the Reformation World," in *Reformation* 12 (2007): 177–90.

5. Although it focuses on a slightly later period, I emphasize these same themes in my "Antisemitism in the Age of Mercantilism," in *Antisemitism: A History*, ed. A. S. Lindemann and R. S. Levy (Oxford, 2010), 94–106.

6. See most recently, Eric W. Gritsch, *Martin Luther's Anti-Semitism: Against his Better Judgment* (Grand Rapids, Mich., 2012).

7. *Luther's Works*, vol. 47, ed. F. Sherman, trans. M. H. Bertram (Philadelphia, 1971), 292.

8. The literature on Luther's attitude to Judaism is considerable. For a collection of primary texts and a selected German bibliography up to 1982, see Walther Bienert, *Martin Luther und die Juden* (Frankfurt aM, 1982). See also the works cited in Thomas Kaufmann, "Luther and the Jews," in *Jews, Judaism, and the Reformation in Sixteenth-Century Germany*, ed. D. P. Bell and S. Burnett (Leiden, 2006), 69–104.

9. Miriam Bodian, "The Reformation and the Jews," in *Rethinking European Jewish History*, ed. J. Cohen and M. Rosman (Oxford, 2008), 112–32.

10. *Luther's Works*, vol. 45, ed. W. Brandt (Philadelphia, 1962).

11. As Martin Brecht, the author of the most exhaustive Luther biography to date, notes: "Luther once stated that he admired—indeed loved—the Jewish people. Their great men were superior to the church fathers of the Christians. Christ was the flower that grew from the beautiful plant of this people." Martin Brecht, *Martin Luther: The Preservation of the Church, 1532–1546*, trans. J. L. Schaff (Minneapolis, Minn., 1999), Kindle edition.

12. *Dr. Martin Luther's sämmtliche Werke: Reformationshistorische und polemische deutsche Schriften*, vol. 29, ed. J. G. Plochmann (Erlangen, 1848), 48.

13. *Luther's Works*, 47:140. *Martin Luthers Werke*, 53 (Weimar, 1920), 419.

14. Ibid.

15. *Luther's Works*, 47:143; *Martin Luthers Werke*, 53:421–22, my emphasis.

16. *Luther's Works*, 47:144; *Martin Luthers Werke*, 53:423.

17. *Luther's Works*, 47:266. *Martin Luthers Werke*, 53:521.

18. *Luther's Works*, 47:270; *Martin Luthers Werke*, 53:524.

19. *Luther's Works*, 47:270–71; *Martin Luthers Werke*, 53:525.

20. *Luther's Works*, 47:272–73; *Martin Luthers Werke*, 53:525; Brecht, *Martin Luther: The Preservation of the Church, 1532–1546*, Kindle edition. It should be noted that even the Luther of *That Jesus Christ*

was Born a Jew did not recognize the right of Jews to practice usury on the basis of their "tribal brotherhood," to employ Benjamin Nelson's phrase. Luther consistently opposed most lending at interest (with a small number of exceptions) and insisted on the Jews' obligation to observe the prohibition not just with regard to their coreligionists but toward Christians as well, since they were required to obey the law of the land like all other subjects. See Martin Brecht, *Martin Luther: Shaping and Defining the Reformation, 1521–1532,* trans. J. L. Schaaf (Minneapolis, Minn., 1990), Kindle edition. In fact, Jews' practice of usury was not only biblically sanctioned (according to traditional interpretation) but also authorized by the charters under which they lived, hence the law of the land. For the most recent works on Jews and medieval usury, see Joseph Shatzmiller, *Shylock Reconsidered: Jews, Moneylending, and Medieval Society* (Berkeley, Calif., 1990); and Michael Toch, *The Economic History of European Jews: Late Antiquity and Early Middle Ages* (Leiden, 2013). Arguing for the continuity of usury as the central motif in images of Jewish economic life, see Derek Penslar, *Shylock's Children: Economics and Jewish Identity in Modern Europe* (Berkeley, Calif., 2001); and Jerry Z. Muller, *Capitalism and the Jews* (Princeton, N.J., 2010), esp. chap. 2.

21. See Robert Birely, "The Catholic Reform, Jews, and Judaism in Sixteenth-Century Germany," in *Jews, Judaism, and the Reformation,* 253.

22. On these episodes, see William Chester Jordan, *The French Monarchy and the Jews: From Philip Augustus to the Last Capetians* (Philadelphia, 1989); James William Parkes, *The Jew in the Medieval Community: A Study of His Political and Economic Situation* (New York, 1976).

23. And theoretically, since in practice many moneylenders were Christians. Still, even if they outnumbered Jews, the latter proved especially useful and accommodating to noble patrons.

24. Hans-Martin Kirn, *Das Bild vom Juden im Deutschland des frühen 16. Jahrhunderts* (Tübingen, 1989); Magda Teter, *Jews and Heretics in Catholic Poland: A Beleaguered Church in the Post-Reformation Era* (New York, 2006), 89–97.

25. Hans-Martin Kirn, "Ulrich Zwingli, The Jews, and Judaism," in *Jews, Judaism, and the Reformation,* 171–95.

26. R. Gerald Hobbs, "Bucer, the Jews, and Judaism," in *Jews, Judaism, and the Reformation,* 165. See also *The Historical Writings of Joseph of Rosheim: Leader of Jewry in Early Modern Germany,* ed. and trans. C. Fraenkel-Goldschmidt, trans. from Hebrew by N. Schendowich; English edition ed. A. Shear (Leiden, 2006).

27. Kirn, *Das Bild vom Juden,* 63, 73.

28. Martin Brecht, *Martin Luther: The Preservation of the Church,* Kindle edition.

29. R. Po-chia Hsia, "The Usurious Jew: Economic Structure and Religious Representations in an Anti-Semitic Discourse," in *In and Out of the Ghetto: Jewish-Gentile Relations in Late Medieval and Early Modern Germany,* ed. R. Po-chia Hsia and H. Lehmann (Cambridge, 1995), 170–72.

30. R. Po-chia Hsia, "Christian Ethnographies of Jews in Early Modern Germany," in *The Expulsion of the Jews: 1492 and After,* ed. R. B. Waddington and A. H. Williamson (New York, 1994), 223–35; Yaakov Deutsch, "Polemical Ethnographies: Descriptions of Yom Kippur in the Writings of Christian Hebraists and Jewish Converts to Christianity in Early Modern Europe," in *Hebraica Veritas? Christian Hebraists and the Study of Judaism in Early Modern Europe,* ed. A. Coudert and J. Shoulson (Philadelphia, 2004), 203–33; Yaakov Deutsch, *Judaism in Christian Eyes: Ethnographic Descriptions of Jews and Judaism in Early Modern Europe,* trans. A. Aronsky (New York, 2011).

31. See Elisheva Carlebach, "Between History and Myth: The Regensberg Expulsion in Josel of Rosheim's *Sefer ha-miknah,*" in *Jewish History and Jewish Memory: Essays in Honor of Yosef Hayim Yerushalmi,* ed. E. Carlebach, J. M. Efron, and D. N. Myers (Hanover, NH, 1998), 42–43.

32. See Michael Toch, "Der jüdische Geldhandel in der Wirtschaft des deutschen Spätmittelalters: Nürnberg 1350–1499," in Toch, *Peasants and Jews in Medieval Germany: Studies in Cultural, Social, and Economic History* (Aldershot, UK, 2003).

33. I do not mean to suggest that Luther favored any kind of leveling in the social sphere to

match that of the spiritual. On the contrary, his attitude to the divisions of estates and their social distinctions and wealth were conventional and conservative. Each estate has its place and function. But the abuse and misdirection of these constitute a deadly serious affront to divine rule. See Hans-Jürgen Prien, *Luthers Wirtschaftsethik* (Göttingen, 1992), 162–70.

34. Robert Birley, "The Catholic Reform, Jews, and Judaism in Sixteenth-Century Germany," in *Jews, Judaism, and the Reformation*, 266.

35. On this in the Alsace region, see the superb recent study of Debra Kaplan, *Beyond Expulsion: Jews, Christians, and Reformation Strasbourg* (Stanford, Calif., 2011), Kindle edition. By showing important continuities between pre- and post-expulsion Strasbourg Jewry, especially in the economic sphere (where Jews continued to trade in the city and sometimes to provide substantial loans) Kaplan provides a valuable corrective to the scholarly trend reflected here.

36. *The Historical Writings of Joseph of Rosheim*, 377–87. It may have been the last of these items, the partial renunciation of the *Hehlerrecht,* that inspired Selma Stern to label the *Artikel und Ordnung* "the first large-scale attempt within their own group to purge the life of the Jews, to improve their deteriorating social and economic position, and to help them adjust to the changing social and economic conditions under which they lived." Selma Stern, *Josel of Rosheim: Commander of Jewry in the Holy Roman Empire of the German Nation*, trans. G. Hirschler (Philadelphia, 1965), 119. While thought-provoking, this assessment is no doubt too generous since Josel appears to have been attempting to protect Jews' concentration in moneylending by curbing its worst abuses, and ineffectively at that. On Josel's effort to appease the Strasbourg magistrates through similar reforms, see Kaplan, *Beyond Expulsion*, chap. 4.

37. Quoted in Salo W. Baron, *A Social and Religious History of the Jews*, vol. 13 (New York, 1970).

38. On this process, see Jonathan Karp, *The Politics of Jewish Commerce: Economic Thought and Emancipation in Europe, 1638–1848* (Cambridge, 2008), 135–200.

"ADOPT THIS PERSON SO TOTALLY BORN AGAIN"

❂ ❂ ❂

Elias Schadeus and the Conversion of the Jews

Debra Kaplan
Yeshiva University

"THE Hebrew language," preached Elias Schadeus, "is the oldest, first [and] holiest, and is of the highest importance for the promotion of the true religion."[1] Schadeus made this statement in the third of a three-part sermon preached at the Strasbourg cathedral on the fifteenth, seventeenth, and eighteenth Sundays after Trinity Sunday in 1592. It is a classic depiction of *Hebraica veritas*—Christian use of Hebrew and Judaica aimed expressly at affirming the truth of Christianity. Such Christian Hebraism has been categorized by David Ruderman as part of the knowledge explosion that was characteristic of early modern life, with Hebraists as boundary-crossers who brought knowledge of Judaica to the Western Christian tradition.[2]

Hebraists did not only cross textual boundaries. Whether in print shops or through private lessons and correspondence, Christian Hebraism led to interactions between live Jewish and Christian intellectuals.[3] Schadeus's career expands our understanding of the interpersonal relations between Hebraists and Jews. Having dedicated much of his career to proselytizing local Jews in the Holy Roman Empire, Schadeus is notable not in the scope of his Hebraism, but in his missionary activities, through which he presented Hebraism to both lay Protestants and Jews. To do so, he used techniques that had been successful in spreading the Protestant Reformation. An analysis of how this elite local churchman sought to marshal both Jewish and Christian laypeople in his mission to convert the Jews affords a glimpse into a particular and understudied type of Jewish-Christian interaction. In addition, a comparison of Schadeus's program with the recorded experience of one of the women he baptized reveals the deep dissonance between his plans and the very real fissures that separated lay Jews and Christians in German-speaking lands.

Born in Saxony in 1541, Schadeus moved to Strasbourg, then a Protestant city.[4] He married in 1570 and, one year later, purchased citizenship rights. After becoming a citizen, Schadeus was elected deacon of the parish church St. Aurelia's; six years later, he became the pastor at Old St. Peter's parish. His clerical career in Strasbourg flourished as he served as the preacher at the cathedral from 1581 until his death in 1593. Schadeus also served as a professor of both Hebrew and theology at the university.[5] Like most of his colleagues of his generation, Schadeus focused on producing materials on Hebrew grammar for his theology students.[6] Yet, alongside these pedagogical texts, he published what may be considered his magnum opus—his *Mysterium,* a volume comprising various projects he had undertaken, all of which centered on his main goal: actively converting the Jews.

Mysterium is a patchwork of Schadeus's writings. In some versions, such as the one I examined, it was published in the same volume as his Judeo-German translation of portions of the New Testament.[7] One half of the codex was printed in Latin characters and the other in Hebrew ones; Schadeus is known for his printing press, which used both. When reading the codex from left to right, the text begins with a German preface, followed by the three aforementioned German sermons that Schadeus had preached at the cathedral. Next, Schadeus included excerpts from the respective writings of Bernard of Clairvaux and Martin Luther; a copy of a supplication he had made to Strasbourg's magistrates; a brief summary of the Hebrew alphabet, written in German; and a German letter to the Jews, containing ten arguments demonstrating that Jesus was the messiah. This same letter, published in Judeo-German, served as the preface to the other half of the codex when one read the volume from right to left. To this, Schadeus appended sections of both the Old and New Testaments in Judeo-German.[8] The biblical selections were aimed at convincing Jewish readers of the truth of Christianity. The title page of the codex when one opened the volume from right to left was printed in both Judeo-German and German, and was strategically entitled *Hamisha: Das ist funff Bücher des Newen Testaments,* not so subtly evoking a parallel to the Pentateuch that would be apparent to every Jewish reader.

As the two titles, the content, and the languages in which *Mysterium* was penned demonstrate, the book was explicitly aimed at two different audiences.[9] Schadeus intended his book for both Jewish and Christian readers, writing that he hoped that "both Christians, and especially preachers who interact with Jews, and Jews themselves can find this [book] useful and of service."[10] The dual audience reflected Schadeus's oft-repeated mantra that the Hebrew language had two interrelated purposes. First, it was essential "for the preservation and propagation" of Christianity.[11] Schadeus placed the Hebrew language squarely in the context of Lutheran tradition, tracing its use from Adam through the patriarchs, other biblical figures, the apostles, and medieval and Protestant Hebraists.[12] Second, Hebrew was also "especially" important for the "inspiration and conversion" of the Jews.[13] This was not only because the Jews used Hebrew, but also because of Schadeus's conviction that Hebrew and Judaica verified Christianity, and thus had the power to convince the Jews of the truth.

Schadeus's belief that Hebrew was relevant both for Christians and for the Jews he hoped would become Christians found expression in his approach to securing Jewish conversion. Schadeus directed his program at both Jews and Christians, using his studies of the Bible to convince the Jews of the truth of Christianity and also to encourage Christian investment and involvement in procuring Jewish converts. In order to outline the different pieces of his plan as found throughout his writings, I will categorize the program into three parts: attempts to convince and educate Jews; activities within his own parish, intended to foster a community into which Jews would wish to convert; and concrete steps suggested to political authorities, designed to support his program.

Schadeus's printed works served as his main vehicle for convincing Jews of the truth of Christianity. The arguments he presented to demonstrate the validity of Christianity were far from innovative. Schadeus recycled familiar polemics, such as those pointing to the Davidic lineage recorded in Matthew, the *'alma* passage in Isaiah 7:14, and the references to *Shiloh* in Genesis 49:10. Yet his technique of printing a vernacular version of those arguments along with relevant passages from both the Old and New Testaments was something new, beginning in the early modern period.[14] Schadeus explained that using Hebrew characters was essential for reaching a Jewish audience:

> The Jews use no language other than Hebrew in their spiritual and political matters, and also in their households, [even] where they can already speak the language of the lands where they live—especially [in] Germany, but also [in] Italy, Bohemia, Poland, Lithuania, and far and wide. . . . Out of thousands of printed or [hand]written books, [they] do not read one in Latin or another language, but only Hebrew, or German written in Hebrew characters.[15]

That Schadeus was keenly aware of the power of the vernacular can be seen elsewhere in the *Mysterium*. Schadeus noted that he printed his sermons, which discussed the Christian obligation to convert Jews and which were aimed at a Christian audience, in German, "for those who do not yet understand the Hebrew."[16] Perhaps more interesting is his assertion that his technique of printing missionary materials in the vernacular could be exported to the Muslim world as well. Schadeus suggested that since the Qur'an contained references in which "Mohammed himself" extolled the virtues of the patriarchs and of early Christians, printing relevant Christian material in Turkish or Arabic could lead to the conversion of the Muslims.[17] That Schadeus saw the potential to expand this strategy beyond Europe testifies to the increased geographic and cultural awareness that permeated Europe at the dawn of the seventeenth century in the wake of exploration, print, and the expansion of the Ottoman Empire.

For Schadeus, the portions of the Gospel which he translated into Judeo-German in his *Mysterium* were essential for reeducating the Jews about Christianity. He advocated that all copies of *Toldot Yeshu*, the Jewish counter-history to the Gospels, be collected and burned.[18] Instead, he hoped that Jews would study the New Testament directly in their schools, and suggested that this could be done with the oversight (or force) of relevant political authorities. Schadeus explained that using a version of the New Testament in Hebrew, or in Hebrew characters—one readily available in Schadeus's *Mysterium*—was essential for successfully teaching the Jews.[19]

Although those sections of *Mysterium* were accessible to anyone who read Judeo-German, Schadeus suggested specifically targeting Jewish youth, whom he saw as more open to missionary activity.[20] Archival records from Strasbourg demonstrate that he practiced what he preached, for Schadeus baptized two young adults. Strasbourg itself did not have Jewish residents, as its Jews had been expelled in 1391, readmitted again only in 1791. Yet Jews entered the city on a daily basis, engaging in trade, money lending, and conversations (even on matters religious) with their Protestant neighbors.[21] On July 25, 1581, Schadeus presided over the baptism of an eighteen-year-old Jewish girl, the daughter of a Jew from Niedershofen, who was christened Susanna.[22] Several months later, on September 28, he baptized a Jewish boy, Josheyl bar Mardochei, as Michael Christenn.[23]

We do not have data on how these two Jewish adolescents, likely residents from neighboring Alsatian villages, met Schadeus.[24] Strasbourg's Protestant clerics did frequent the countryside to preach.[25] Before their respective baptisms, both Josheyl and Susanna had resided at Schadeus's house, Josheyl for a few weeks, and Susanna for six months. During that time Schadeus educated them about Christianity. Living with him in Strasbourg also shielded them from the influence of the rural Jewish community, whose members would have undoubtedly tried to stop their conversion and bring them back to their respective villages.

The baptism of Jews was a significant theological and ritual event, and, not surprisingly, Schadeus baptized these two Jews in his own parish church, Old St. Peter's. They were then assigned prominent godparents. Josheyl's godparents included a former *Meister* of the city, a member of the city council, and a female relative of Johannes Pappus, one of the most noted theologians of the city.[26] Susanna's godparents included members of Strasbourg's patriciate.[27] Christians had long chosen godparents as a way to create beneficial and strategic social ties for a child.[28] Schadeus strategically connected recent converts from Judaism with patrons of wealth and persuasion, seeking to ease the converts' transition into their new Christian environment. There were practical aspects to such patronage as well. Susanna served as a domestic servant in her godfather's home for ten years after her conversion, where she received shelter and income.[29]

Schadeus's attempt to foster receptivity to converts in his parish was theological as well, for he claimed that the Bible obligated Christians to actively convert Jews. Interpreting the word "Israel" throughout scripture as referring to *Verus Israel,* or Christianity, Schadeus maintained that biblical references to the Jews as Israel promised that the Jews would become Israel, namely, Christians.[30] Such verses thereby not only prophesied that Jews would convert, but mandated that Christians *actively* work to transform Jewish blindness into Christian truth. At the conclusion of his third sermon, he expressed his hope that "we, out of Christian love and enthusiasm, each one according to his standing and [his] means, will demand to help" the Jews escape their "blindness."[31]

Schadeus aimed to spread this message to a wide Christian audience. To achieve that goal, he first preached about Jewish conversion at Strasbourg's cathedral. In these sermons, he expounded on the biblical obligation of Christians to convert Jews, and shared some aspects of his program for doing so. Moreover, Schadeus expanded his reach to Christians beyond Strasbourg by printing these sermons. Noting that with his *Mysterium,* "any other intelligent Christian . . . has enough to persuade a Jew," Schadeus explained that other preachers and even lay Christians who could not "yet" read Hebrew would be equipped to take on the task of securing Jewish converts.[32] To that end, he dedicated *Mysterium* to various Lutheran princes from the house of Brandenburg whom he hoped would help implement his vision of converting the Jews.[33]

Protestant readers now had a text that elaborated on ten reasons for Jews to convert, biblical selections from both the Old and New Testaments written in the Jewish vernacular, and a preface that outlined the value of each biblical excerpt. They were also armed with the letter in Judeo-German, which they could potentially share with Jewish readers if they so chose. In addition, Schadeus included a brief German section which discussed the Hebrew *aleph bet.* The goal of this section was to teach Christians "enough of an introduction" to reading Judeo-German.[34] These few folios focus on phonetic recognition of letters, presented through a chart transliterating each Hebrew character into the parallel German one. In addition, Schadeus listed a few words in Yiddish that had Hebrew, rather than German roots, such as *leḥem* or *goyim,* to help Christians understand how contemporary Jews spoke.[35] While the actual utility of this section for lay Christians interested in procuring converts is dubious, his aim was to provide non-Hebrew readers with rudimentary skills in conversing with Jews and in helping them read through the biblical texts. Conversely, the Judeo-German version expanded on some Christian terms to help in cases where Jewish readers might "need interpretation."[36]

Alongside the tools that he provided to Christians, Schadeus recommended that Christians pray together "enthusiastically" for Jewish conversion at church on Christian holidays.[37] With their oral format, these prayers, conducted in the vernacular and timed when attendance was bound to be highest, had great potential to engage a broad audience, for through them even illiterate lay Christians could learn about and become invested in Jewish conversion.

It is striking that the various aspects of Schadeus's missionary program built on strategies that had been successful in spreading the Protestant Reformation. In many German cities, including Schadeus's Strasbourg, the spread of reform among the laity was facilitated by their exposure to printed vernacular bibles and to sermons delivered in the vernacular.[38] Prayers and educational material such as catechisms were designed to help forge confessional unity.[39] The imagery of the early decades of the Reformation included young Christians confronting the old; perhaps Schadeus similarly sought to solicit young Jews who might show their elders the "true" meaning of the Bible.[40]

It is highly likely that Schadeus consciously employed these techniques, as he was well-aware of the results they had achieved in spreading Lutheranism. Half of the audience he sought to reach with his *Mysterium* was Lutheran; they were thus already familiar with these types of materials. Because Schadeus saw converting the Jews as an essential part of the Lutheran faith, it is all the more probable that he built on those tools that had been employed effectively by his confession, using print, sermons, prayer, and the targeting of youth to expand his mission. Schadeus was firmly convinced that these techniques would be successful among Jews. Moreover, he expressed the desire that other missionaries use these techniques to spread Lutheran truth in the Muslim world.

While Schadeus was not the first Hebraist to make use of Judeo-German as a missionary tool, he seems to have been the only sixteenth-century figure to target both Jewish and Protestant audiences.[41] Schadeus's tactical use of Judeo-German was clearly motivated by the work of Paul Fagius, a former Hebraist and theologian at Strasbourg, who had already produced a Judeo-German Hebrew Bible.[42] Schadeus also likely had access to Sebastian Münster's Aramaic dictionary, which had Yiddish glosses, for a copy of it had been owned by an earlier Hebraist professor in Strasbourg, Johannes Pappus.[43] But above all, Schadeus was inspired by Luther, explicitly interpreting his own actions in light of Luther's teachings.

For example, when advocating for specific policies toward Jews, Schadeus explicitly mentioned Luther's 1523 treatise *That Jesus Christ Was Born a Jew*.[44] Schadeus insisted on treating Jews kindly, and urged refraining from violence against them. To that end, he appended one of Bernard of Clairvaux's letters urging Christians to refrain from violence against Jews during the Second Crusade to his own arguments in *Mysterium;* this text was followed by excerpts from Luther's 1523 treatise.[45] Schadeus noted that events such as the 1338 Armleder massacres and the violence in Strasbourg in 1349 at the time of the Black Death were counterproductive to encouraging Jewish conversion.[46]

Like Luther, Schadeus also deemed it essential to give Jews training and jobs in fields other than usury. He recommended that they be taught agriculture, crafts, trade and business, claiming that Jews were capable of these professions. To prove this contention, Schadeus pointed both to biblical examples and to contemporary travel literature which described Jews engaged in crafts in Cairo, Constantinople, and Jerusalem. When advising political authorities to follow his advice, Schadeus invoked Luther's similar recommendations, thus situating his program as part of a Lutheran tradition.[47]

Interestingly, Schadeus also acknowledged Luther's "later" writings that advocated dealing harshly with the Jews, explicitly referencing *Against the Sabbatarians, On the Jews and their Lies*, and *Von Schem Mephoras*.[48] Schadeus maintained that these later writings reflected Luther's policy toward Jews should their conversion prove impossible, and argued that *That Jesus Christ was Born a Jew* remained Luther's ideal position; cruel measures should only be imposed as a last resort. Having reinterpreted Luther's position in this light, he then contrasted himself with Luther. Schadeus contended that unlike Luther, he *had* been successful in securing Jewish conversion, pointing to his successful conversion of the Jewess Susanna. Having achieved success where Luther had not, Schadeus urged the political authorities to follow his recommendations (which he claimed were identical with Luther's wishes) to educate the Jews in new professions.[49]

Schadeus went beyond Luther in his advocacy for creating a climate into which Jews could be seamlessly integrated. Ten years after Susanna's baptism, Schadeus approached the magistrates of Strasbourg to intercede on her behalf. About to get married, Susanna had almost nothing in the way of property. Schadeus asked that the magistrates award her the status of *Stadtkind*, a ward of the city, which would confer upon her the rights of citizenship.[50] Wards of the city were provided with a stipend of twenty *Gulden*, with which they could begin to work in the city. This sum, which Schadeus volunteered to pay out of his own pocket, would buy Susanna the right to work at a craft in Strasbourg. This had important practical ramifications for the couple wishing to wed. The man whom Susanna wished to marry had been born in Wurtemburg, and was affiliated with the joiner guild in Strasbourg. Likely a traveling journeyman, he stood to benefit from his marriage to Susanna were she to be granted the status of *Stadtkind*. The rights of work and citizenship that she would gain could serve as a dowry, enabling him to establish himself as a formal resident and a master in the guild.[51]

Schadeus explained that upon her baptism, Susanna "was required to abandon her people, father, mother, friends, also nourishment and heritage."[52] With this, he likened her to other *Stadtkinder*, orphans who were placed under municipal care in the wake of the Reformation.[53] In the preface to *Mysterium*, Schadeus advocated extending the status of *Stadtkinder* to all converts. Using biblical examples in which converts and strangers were welcomed into a community, he insisted that providing the Jews with a set place in society was essential to their integration into Christian life. Moreover, Schadeus once again made use of a parallel to the Muslim world, arguing that:

> [It] is also customary under the Turks, that those individuals [who] come from other peoples, and accept the religion and enter into a place where their profession is

performed, should become accepted equally in the community of all civic rights and freedoms.[54]

Schadeus's comparisons to conditions in Muslim lands again reflect the increasing information that Europeans had about other parts of the world. He applied his awareness of travel literature, of parts of the Qur'an, and of the status of new converts to Islam to urge support for his program, casting himself as a strategic thinker who wished to employ new forms of knowledge and technology to spread the message of Christianity.[55] As a Hebraist, Schadeus believed in the power that language had in conveying religious truth. He was simultaneously sensitive to the success that innovations such as print and the use of the vernacular in preaching, education, and prayer had had in spreading religious doctrine.

Despite his enthusiasm for securing converts worldwide, Schadeus had limited success in his endeavors. Whether the magistracy conferred the status of *Stadtkind* upon Susanna is unknown. However, the circumstances which led Schadeus to advocate before the magistrates on her behalf speak volumes as to the dissonance between Schadeus's vision and contemporary reality. Ten years after her baptism, Susanna was living life as the poor of society did. Like other members of that class, Susanna served as a domestic servant; according to Schadeus, "other than her clothing, [she] brings together nothing more than that which her godfather and godmother and other good-hearted and Christian people have relieved her."[56] Far from being ushered into a receptive Christian society, and despite the prominence of her godparents, this formerly Jewish woman had almost no property, and had waited a relatively long time to find a spouse.

A decade after her baptism, Schadeus still found it necessary to remark that Susanna "behaved both in her service and in the neighborhood, making herself known, that her Christian and merciful change was [out of] complete love."[57] Apparently, suspicions about the sincerity of her conversion still needed to be addressed. That Christians often continued to view converted Jews in light of their former Judaism has been well-established for this time period; even those who converted and entered the priesthood were referred to as Jews in a derogatory manner.[58] Susanna was no different. Schadeus urged the magistrates to "adopt this person [who is] so totally born again," seeking to counter any resistance to the city's "adoption" of Susanna by personally defraying the cost:

> I will provide the endowment in its entirety, so that nothing is repugnant or work against this, even though she wants the twenty *Gulden* for the beginning of her craft, through which other poor Christian wards of Your Honor are recognized.[59]

By differentiating her from other poor wards of the city, Schadeus undermined his own argument in which he had likened Susanna to an orphan, as she, too, no longer had a family to provide her with a dowry. Such differentiation was necessary because even ten years after her conversion, Susanna was still seen as a former Jewess, different from orphaned women who had been born as Christians.

Thus, despite his best attempts, Schadeus's hopes that the Christian laity would eagerly embrace his program were not met. Local Christians did not readily accept Jewish converts. While we have no further data on Josheyl's experience, Strasbourg's archives record the prejudice experienced by another convert from Judaism to Christianity several decades later.[60] Given the lack of any data to the contrary in Strasbourg and beyond, and the multiple examples of the difficulties facing converts in their new faith, it is safe to assume that Josheyl, too, was not easily integrated into his new community.[61]

Other Hebraists and preachers both in Strasbourg and beyond similarly did not build on Schadeus's Judeo-German program. While later Hebraists, such as Johann Christoph Wagenseil, were successful at promoting Yiddish as a tool for missionary work among their disciples, Schadeus was unable to find or to create a Christian audience for his missionary plan.[62]

Schadeus's optimism that his approach would speak to Jews was similarly unfounded. Not only did he only succeed in converting two Jews, Schadeus was woefully unfamiliar with what arguments might seem attractive to most Jews who might read his work. Among his ten points designed to convince Jews of the truth of Christianity was the assertion that:

> Also in this time, many Jews have adopted the Christian faith, not only poor and unlearned from among them, as some would like to say, that it was done out of poverty or lack of knowledge. [But] also and especially many highly learned men, pious in Judaism.[63]

Schadeus continued by listing several converts, including Antonius Margaritha, Victor von Carben, and Ludovico Carreto. These converts were notorious, and were loathed by the Jewish community, particularly in the Holy Roman Empire.[64] Writers such as Josel of Rosheim and Yosef ha-Kohen blamed such converts, sometimes by name, for the misfortunes of Jews in the sixteenth century.[65] Converts were deemed responsible for ritual murder accusations, expulsions, and the burning of the Talmud in Rome. While such Jewish reports pinning blame on the converts often cannot be verified historically, they are highly indicative of the Jewish attitude toward these *meshumadim*.[66] By citing the actions of men who were so deeply reviled as role models for Jews to emulate, Schadeus simply displayed his deep ignorance of the people he sought to baptize; for Jewish communal leaders, these men were not role models, but the cause of contemporary Jewish tribulations.

Thus, although Schadeus's mission was built to involve lay Protestants and Jews, his attempts failed in both communities. For him, Hebrew seemed the perfect meeting ground: intrinsic to Christian truth, it was also a language that Jews used, making it a seemingly ideal way for Jews to connect with the Christian community Schadeus hoped they would join. While the tactics of vernacular sermons and printed materials, and the specific targeting of youth had been successful when used by his predecessors to spread Protestant reform among Christians, they proved ineffective in bridging Lutheranism and Judaism. Lay Christians and Jews were for the most part removed from Hebraism and its goals. They also shared with one another a profound mistrust of those who converted. The vision of this sixteenth-century elite Hebraist cleric was too far removed from the attitudes of both Jewish and Christian laypeople, rendering Schadeus's program dissonant for non-Christians and for Christians who were not Hebraists alike.

Notes

1. Schadeus, *Mysterium*, Sermon 3. Title quote from Elias Schadeus, *Mysterium. Das ist Geheimnis S. Pauli Rom. am II. Von Bekehrung der Juden. Ausgelegt und geprediget zu Strassburg im Munster durch M. Eliam Schadeum Ecclisiastem und Professorem. Sampt anderem gleiches Inhalts nutzlichen Materien. So dan auch einem gewisseen Bericht von der Juden Teutsche-Hebreischen Schrift* (Strasbourg, 1592), Supplication. All translations are my own. Because *Mysterium* is unpaginated, I have indicated the section from which I have quoted. My translation of the supplication can be found at http://www.earlymodern. org/citation.php?citKey=52&docKey=e (accessed January 24, 2012).

2. David Ruderman, *Early Modern Jewry: A New Cultural History* (Princeton, N.J., 2010), 111–20.

3. For examples, see Alison Coudert and Jeffrey Shoulson, eds., *Hebraica Veritas?: Christian Hebraists and the Study of Judaism in Early Modern Europe* (Philadelphia, 2004).

4. Salo Baron erroneously claims that Schadeus was himself a convert from Judaism. No data or biographical material support this claim. See Salo Baron, *A Social and Religious History of the Jews*, 18 vols. (New York, 1952–1983), 13:240.

5. Oscar Berger-Levrault, *Annales des professeurs des académies et universités alsaciennes, 1523–1871* (Nancy, 1892), 111; Marie-Joseph Bopp, *Die evangelischen Geistlichen und Theologen in Elsaß und Lothringen von der Reformation bis zur Gegenwart* (Neustadt a.d. Aisch, 1959); Wilhelm Horning, *Magister Elias Schadäus, Pfarrer an der Alt-St.-Peterkirche, Professor der Theologie und Münsterprediger zu Straßburg. Beitrag zur Geschichte der lutherischen Judenmission in Strassburg (16. Jahrhundert)* (Leipzig, 1892); Edouard Sitzmann, *Dictionnaire de biographie des hommes célèbres de l'Alsace depuis les temps les plus reculés jusqu'à nos jours*, 2 vols. (Rixheim, 1909), 2:657; *Nouveau dictionnaire de biographie alsacienne*, 48 vols. (Strasbourg, 1982–2006), 33: 3387–88.

6. Schadeus, *Oratio de linguae sanctae origine, progresivi et varia fortuna, ad nostrum usque saeculum* (Strasbourg, 1591). See also Debra Kaplan, *Beyond Expulsion: Jews, Christians, and Reformation Strasbourg* (Stanford, Calif., 2011), 134–43.

7. In some editions these were published as two separate volumes.

8. These included Luke, John, Acts, Hebrew and Romans, as well as excerpts from Malachi 3 and 4; Zachariah 9, 11, and 12; Isaiah 41 and 53; and Psalms 22 and 110.

9. This is the case even for the editions in which the Judeo-German New Testament was not included, as *Mysterium* included a letter written to Jews as well as an instruction manual for Christians on reading Judeo-German.

10. Schadeus, *Mysterium*, Sermon 3.

11. Ibid., Preface.

12. Schadeus, *Oratio*.

13. Schadeus, *Mysterium*, Sermon 3.

14. On Christian missionaries' use of Yiddish, see Aya Elyada, *A Goy Who Speaks Yiddish: Christians and the Jewish Language in Early Modern Germany* (Stanford, Calif., 2012), 22–38.

15. Schadeus, *Mysterium,* Sermon 3.

16. Ibid., Preface.

17. Ibid., Sermon 3.

18. This predates Wagenseil's publication of the text. Schadeus undoubtedly knew of it from Luther's writings, or possibly from Wolfgang Capito, who reported to Josel of Rosheim that he had obtained a manuscript of the text. See Archives Municipales de Strasbourg (AMS) III/174/23.

19. Schadeus, *Mysterium,* Sermon 3.

20. Ibid., Preface.

21. Kaplan, *Beyond Expulsion.*

22. AMS, *Kirchenbuch,* Alt Sankt Peterskirche, Taufen.

23. Ibid.

24. Archival references from fifty-eight years earlier refer to a Jacob of Niedershofen. See AMS III/174/21, 86–87.

25. Such visits began at the start of the Reformation, and continued to be mandated in the late sixteenth century. For an example of the latter, see *KirchenOrdnung, wie es mit der Lehre Göttliches Worts und den Ceremonien auch mit anderen dazü nothwendigen Sachen in der kirchen zü Straßburg bißher gehalten worden und fürohin mit verleihung Göttlicher Gnade gehalten werden soll* (Strassburg, 1603.)

26. AMS, *Kirchenbuch,* Alt Sankt Peterskirche, Taufen; Jacques Hatt, *Liste des Membres du Grande Senat de Strasbourg: des Stettmeisters, des Ammeisters, des Conseils des XXI et XV du XIIIe siècle à 1789* (Strasbourg, 1963).

27. AMS, *Kirchenbuch,* Alt Sankt Peterskirche, Taufen; Schadeus, *Mysterium,* Supplication.

28. Bernhard Jussen, *Spiritual Kinship as Social Practice: Godparenthood and Adoption in the Early Middle Ages,* trans. P. Selwyn (Cranbury, 2000).

29. Schadeus, *Mysterium,* Supplication.

30. Ibid., Sermon 1.

31. Ibid., Sermon 3.

32. Ibid.

33. Ibid., Preface.

34. Ibid., Bericht.

35. If one compares the ten point letter in German with the one in Judeo-German, words with Hebrew or Aramaic origins are further translated in the German version.

36. Schadeus, *Mysterium,* Judeo-German Preface; Bericht.

37. Ibid., Sermon 3.

38. Miriam Usher Chrisman, *Conflicting Visions of Reform: German Lay Propaganda Pamphlets, 1519–1530* (Boston, 1996), 162; Robert W. Scribner, "Oral Culture and the Diffusion of Reformation Ideas," in his *Popular Culture and Popular Movements in the German Reformation* (London, 1987), 49–69.

39. Miriam Usher Chrisman, *Lay Culture, Learned Culture: Books and Social Change in Strasbourg, 1480–1599* (New Haven, Conn., 1982).

40. Natalie Zemon Davis, "The Reasons of Misrule: Youth Groups and Charivaris in Sixteenth-Century France," in her *Society and Culture in Early Modern France* (4th ed.; Stanford, Calif., 1975), 122.

41. Before Schadeus, the convert Paul Helicz had published a Yiddish New Testament, which did not seem to have influenced Schadeus. Elyada, *A Goy Who Speaks Yiddish,* 24.

42. On Fagius's Judeo-German Bible, see Elyada, *A Goy Who Speaks Yiddish,* 25–26. On Schadeus and Fagius, see the otherwise unidentified statement cited in Gérard E. Weil, *Élie Lévita: Humaniste Et Massorete (1469–1549)* (Leiden, 1963), 151.

43. On Münster and his dictionary, see Elyada, *A Goy Who Speaks Yiddish,* 69, especially nn. 17

and 18. For Pappus's book collection, see Stephen Burnett, "Christian Aramaism: The Birth and Growth of Aramaic Scholarship in the Sixteenth Century," in *Seeking Out the Wisdom of the Ancients: Essays Offered to Honor Michael V. Fox on the Occasion of His Sixty-Fifth Birthday*, ed. R. L. Troxel, K. G. Friebel, and D. R. Magary (Winona Lake, Ind., 2005), 436.

44. Martin Luther, *Das Jesu Christi ist ein Geborner Jud*, in *D. Martin Luthers Werke. Kritische Gesamtausgabe* (WA) (Weimar, 1883 ff.), 11:314–36.

45. For an English version of this letter, see Robert Chazan, *Church, State, and Jew in the Middle Ages* (West Orange, N.J., 1980), 104–105.

46. Schadeus, *Mysterium*, Sermon 3.

47. Ibid.

48. Martin Luther, *Wider die Sabbather. an einem guten Freund*, WA 50: 312–77; idem., *Von der Juden und iren Lügen*, WA 53: 417–552; idem., *Von Schem Mephoras und von Geschlecht Christi*, WA 53: 579–648.

49. Schadeus, *Mysterium*, Sermon 3.

50. Ibid., Supplication.

51. On guilds, marriage, and immigration, see James R. Farr, *Artisans in Europe, 1300–1914* (Cambridge, 2000), 147–48.

52. Schadeus, *Mysterium*, Supplication.

53. See Thomas Max Safley, *Children of the Laboring Poor: Expectation and Experience among the Orphans of Early Modern Augsburg* (Leiden, 2005).

54. Schadeus, *Mysterium*, Supplication.

55. Schadeus's use of standards in the Muslim world may be an early example of Christian bible scholars' interest in Arab lands as relevant for understanding Christian truth. This was discussed in a lecture by Elliott Horowitz, "Middle Eastern Travel and Biblical Interpretation," Center for Advanced Judaic Studies, Philadelphia, November 9, 2011.

56. Schadeus, *Mysterium*, Supplication.

57. Ibid.

58. See the case of Stephan Isaac, as discussed in Elisheva Carlebach, *Divided Souls: Converts from Judaism in Germany, 1500–1750* (New Haven, Conn., 2001), 61–62.

59. Schadeus, *Mysterium*, Supplication.

60. AMS V, 39, 40.

61. Carlebach, *Divided Souls.*

62. Elyada, *A Goy Who Speaks Yiddish*, 26.

63. Schadeus, *Mysterium*, Beweissung.

64. See Hava Fraenkel-Goldschmidt, "On the Periphery of Jewish Society: Jewish Converts to Christianity in Germany During the Reformation," in *Culture and Society in Medieval Jewry: Studies Dedicated to the Memory of Haim Hillel Ben Sasson*, ed. M. Ben Sasson, R. Bonfil, and J. Hacker (Hebrew; Jerusalem, 1989), 623–54; Carlebach, *Divided Souls*, 23.

65. Hava Fraenkel-Goldschmidt, ed., *Sefer ha-Miknah*, (Jerusalem, 1970); Robert Bonfil, "Who was the Apostate Ludovico Carreto?" in *Exile and Diaspora: Studies in the History of the Jewish People Presented to Professor Haim Beinart on the Occasion of his Seventieth Birthday*, ed. A. Mirsky, A. Grossman and Y. Kaplan (Hebrew; Jerusalem, 1989), 437–42

66. Elisheva Carlebach, "Between History and Myth: The Regensburg Expulsion in Josel of Rosheim's Sefer ha-Miknah," in *Jewish History and Jewish Memory: Essays in Honor of Yosef Hayim Yerushalmi*, ed. E. Carlebach, J. M. Efron, and D. N. Myers (Hanover, N.H., 1998), 40–53.

THE CONSERVATIVE HYBRIDITY OF
MIGUEL DE BARRIOS

✼ ✼ ✼

Adam Sutcliffe
King's College London

CULTURAL border-crossing has long fascinated historians of early modern European Jewry. The softening of the boundaries separating Jews from Christians has, since the pioneering work of Jacob Katz, been recognized as a key hallmark of early modern Jewish history, while the nature of the innermost loyalties and identities of those Jews of this period who—whether under pressure from the Iberian Inquisitions or as Sabbatean or Frankist heretics—abandoned their outward affiliation with Judaism has been the focus of extended historiographical controversy.[1] The final core chapter of David Ruderman's bold interpretive survey of early modern Jewry is titled "Mingled Identities," and he identifies the blurring of boundaries, both within the Jewish community and between Jews and Christians, as the strongest linking theme between all five of his key elements of the early modern Jewish experience. Increased mobility, more sophisticated communal structures, the "knowledge explosion" unleashed by print, the undermining of rabbinical authority, and a "blurring of religious identities" were all, he argues, generative of "a variety of new options for Jewish self-definition and for representing Jewish civilization to the non-Jewish world."[2] Ruderman here eloquently synthesizes and builds upon the consensus that has emerged among historians that the distinctiveness of this period of Jewish history, and the incipient modernity embedded within it, seems most crucially to be located in the transformation of the border zones between Jewish and Christian culture.

Early modern Sephardim, in the long seventeenth century in particular, were boundary-crossers *par excellence*. Widely scattered in a Diaspora that was religiously variegated (encompassing committed Jews, convinced Christians, and crypto-Jews of various hues) but bound together by strong ethnic and familial ties that transcended these differences, the Sephardim were able to sustain long-distance trade across the imperial and confessional divides of the period more successfully than any other trading group.[3] But does this combination of cultural malleability and economic flourishing mark the Sephardim as precociously "modern"? They certainly figured prominently, as Richard Popkin and others have noted, in the intellectual upheavals associated with the rise of philosophical scepticism in the seventeenth century.[4] Extending this association further, Yirmiyahu Yovel has recently argued that the Marranos of Spain and Portugal anticipated modernity by forming a unique "other" within Iberian society. Sustaining a Jewish consciousness alongside their outwardly Christian existence, these Jews were, according to him, the first to develop the complex split identity that provided the vital, unsettling impetus to modern creativity. First in the Iberian peninsula and then in Diaspora, Yovel argues, the early modern Sephardim prefigured Western modernity and opened up its possibilities to others.[5]

The concentration of contrasting cultural influences was nowhere more intense than within the Sephardic community of Golden Age Amsterdam. Migrant Marranos here, psychically stamped by the Catholicism of the Iberian peninsula and in some cases also steeped in the Aristotelianism of Spanish universities, sought to establish a normative Jewish community while negotiating a very different type of encounter with Dutch Protestantism, spiced with the philosophical challenge of Cartesianism. This relatively small community, at most a few thousand strong, was notably fractious. Spinoza, Amsterdam's most famous dissident, has, since his death in 1677, been widely seen as a harbinger of modernity—a perspective elaborated at length by Yovel in his earlier work as well as, most recently, by Jonathan Israel.[6] How widespread, though, was such intellectual restlessness among the Amsterdam Sephardim? Daniel Swetschinski has typified them as "reluctant cosmopolitans," highlighting the surprising absence of any traces of psychic trauma or even of practical difficulty as they combined Jewish religious and community life with seizing the economic and cultural opportunities that Amsterdam offered them, forging their own "patchwork culture" with its Iberian, Dutch and Jewish elements.[7] The boundaries of the Jewish world were blurred in other northern Sephardic centers such as Hamburg and London, as well as in Amsterdam, by a significant number of "semi-Jews," as Yosef Kaplan has called them, culturally and linguistically part of the community but eschewing religious affiliation.[8] Their presence highlighted the disaggregation of religious and ethnic identity within the northern Sephardic Diaspora. However, far from being self-consciously modern, these communities were bound together by practical ties of language and commerce, reinforced by a heightened consciousness of blood lineage that has its roots in the Spanish preoccupation with *limpieza di sangre*. Religious disaffiliation was also not unique to the Sephardim: scholars of seventeenth-century Dutch Christianity have also noted significant levels of religious indifference and of confessional flux.[9]

The unselfconscious integration of contrasting cultural identities into the practices of an individual life is particularly vivid in the case of the dramatist and poet-historian Miguel, or Daniel Levi, de Barrios. Best known for his stylized history of Sephardic Amsterdam, *Triumpho del govierno popular, y de la Antiguidad Holandesa* (Amsterdam, 1683–84), Barrios straddled two worlds, combining laureate status in Amsterdam with a crypto-Jewish existence in Brussels. It is tempting to see him, following Yovel's paradigm, as a quintessentially modern Marrano, creatively melding his sense of Jewish pride with his Iberian identification and commitment to the high baroque style of Spanish letters.[10] This fusion, however, was in important respects deeply conservative. Barrios's literary style was rigorously traditional in its adherence to the stylized norms of the Spanish Golden Age, which he deployed to reinforce and celebrate a very hierarchical, quasi-aristocratic understanding of the social structure of Sephardic Amsterdam. Rather than looking forward to a future of increasing social and cultural fluidity, Barrios's particular hybridity was firmly coupled to traditions and hierarchies of the past. An exploration of his life and writing defamiliarizes the world of the Amsterdam Sephardim, and throws into question the widespread tendency to project the origins of our own modernity onto them.

※ ※ ※

Born near Córdoba in 1635, Barrios left Spain with his family as an adolescent, arriving in Italy in 1650. He joined the Jewish community, and was circumcised in Livorno, and in 1660 traveled briefly to the Caribbean, with the apparent intent to settle there. His name first appears in the Amsterdam community records in 1663. However, before arriving in Amsterdam he resided in Brussels for a spell, where he remained a frequent presence until the early 1670s, when he settled permanently in Amsterdam. In Brussels he was known by his birth name, Miguel, and lived as an outward Christian, holding the rank of captain in the Spanish army. In this period he lived what at first glance seems to have been a double life, with two names, two religious identities, and also two literary audiences. To use David Graizbord's term, he was a classic example of a "cultural commuter."[11] His most significant collections of poetry, *Flor de Apolo* (1665) and *Coro de las Musas* (1672), were both published in Brussels, and he enjoyed the literary patronage of a number of influential non-converso Christians in the Hispanic world, such as Francisco de Melo, the Portuguese ambassador in London. Even after settling in Amsterdam as a professing Jew he continued in some contexts to use his Spanish name and military title, apparently until his death in 1701.[12]

Simultaneously a Spanish patriot and a proud Jew, Barrios combined allegiance to the enforcers and to the victims of the Inquisition. There is no sign, however, that these identifications, so flagrantly contradictory from our perspective, were experienced as such by him, or caused him any inner turmoil or tension. Given his visibility as an author and the even greater prominence of his patrons, it seems extremely unlikely that it would have been a secret, either in Brussels or in Amsterdam, that Barrios straddled both Jewish and non-Jewish worlds. In 1686 he published a collection of admiring poems and letters lauding the King of Spain, Charles II—not in Brussels (though this city was falsely given on the volume's title page, in order to be acceptable to Christian readers) but in Amsterdam, as part of a broader collection dedicated to Manuel de Belmonte, one of the most prosperous Sephardim in the city, and the representative there of the Spanish Crown.[13] Barrios was by no means unique in his fusion of loyalties, and his writings did not simply give expression to his personal sense of self as both a Jew and an exiled Spaniard, saturated in the literary traditions of Iberia. They reflected, in a notably intense form, the seemingly contradictory but nonetheless experientially coherent cultural identity of much of the Dutch Sephardic elite of his generation, particularly those born in Spain or the Spanish Netherlands or with close personal ties there.

As a professional writer, often struggling to make money by his pen, Barrios was beholden to the tastes of his patrons. In the 1670s he circumvented the censorship of his works by the Amsterdam Mahamad, which objected to their incorporation of Christian metaphors, by publishing in Antwerp instead. By the end of this decade, however, the patronage of the Spanish and crypto-Jewish elite in the Southern Netherlands was no longer sustaining him, and he was forced to turn to the Amsterdam community for financial support. This led him to tailor his poetry to the religious and aesthetic preferences of the leaders of the Amsterdam Sephardim, whose "aristocratic tastes," according to Daniel Swetschinski, "were becoming more and more pronounced."[14] The impact of this patronage is particularly apparent in the tone and content of his *Triumpho del govierno popular*. This opuscular work—a collection of free-standing essays, many of them partially poetic in form, which recount the history of the Amsterdam Sephardic community and its various associations and institutions—is strongly imbued with a spirit of laudatory commemoration. The *Triumpho* is today a very rare text, and surviving copies vary slightly in their contents and ordering, which sometimes appear somewhat haphazard.[15] It is dedicated to the six community *parnasim*, whom Barrios fawningly lauds in an extended allegory, praising each day of the week as representative of one of them, and the Sabbath as the day of "el muy Noble Gabay."[16] Around the time of the completion of the *Triumpho* his financial predicament was so bad that he was considering moving to London, and he includes a poem dedicated to the *Kahal Kados* of that city, praising its virtues and lamenting his own suffering and impoverishment.[17] The presence of this paean within the volume clearly signalled that Barrios's pen was available for the service of multiple patrons. The explicit visibility of relationships of patronage in shaping Barrios's writings was, indeed, an important aspect of their literary texture as highly controlled and stylized articulations of emotion, erudition, commemoration and praise.

Barrios has been described as "the most baroque" of the leading seventeenth-century Marrano poets. Following the revered poetic model of Luis de Góngora, he was a flamboyant exponent of the techniques of *culturalismo*, the self-conscious use of classical allusion and metaphorical imagery, and *conceptismo*, the witty and intellectually agile juxtaposition of ideas and themes.[18] These aesthetic tropes were not purely decorative; they were also poetic devices to imbue linguistic artifice with intellectual significance, philosophical gravitas, and memorability. Barrios's ornately baroque poetics thus furnished his semi-historical panegyrics with a deeper matrix of cultural meaning. The *agudeza* (poetic wit) that he demonstrated, and the elaborate allegorical symbolism that he marshalled, enabled his readers to experience the *Triumpho* not simply as a record of events, and also not simply as an aesthetic artifice. By fusing these elements so closely together he produced a work that, for his intended readership at least, bathed the history and institutions of the Amsterdam community in an aura of grandeur, moral weight, and literary-historical significance. The taste for high literary Spanish among the Sephardic patricians of Amsterdam reinforced the connection of this elite to the time-honoured hierarchies and high cultural status with which this poetic and dramatic language was associated.

This literary burnishing of the activities of the Sephardic elite is most striking in Barrios's writing on the rich associational life of the community. Most prestigious among these were the literary academies founded by Manuel de Belmonte: first the *Academia de los Sitibundos* (Academy of the Thirsty, 1676), and later the *Academia de los Floridos* (Academy of the Flowering, 1685). These associations brought together intellectuals such as Orobio de Castro, as well as leading entrepreneurial merchants and aristocrats, to engage in light-hearted discussion of pseudo-philosophical topics. The format of the academies was a direct imitation of Spanish literary societies. They were most fundamentally shaped by the sponsorship of Belmonte, for whom they provided a forum in which to demonstrate his aristocratic munificence and sophistication. The secular topics discussed at the academies were, like those broached in much of Barrios's poetry, mildly frowned upon by community's religious establishment. However, they were not seriously transgressive. In cultural terms the academies reinforced both the Iberian tastes and the elevated status of the moneyed elite: Daniel Swetschinski has aptly described them as emblematic of the "aristocratization" of the Sephardic community.[19] Barrios was a participant in these academies, and also wrote about both of them.[20]

Much of the *Triumpho* is devoted to the many voluntary associations of the community. Barrios describes in detail no fewer than fifteen *Sacras Hermandades* (sacred fraternities), including five academic associations—the yeshivot—and five charitable organizations.[21] For each association he typically provides a brief history and a description of its activities, followed by a laudatory poetic roll call of membership, sometimes also listing former members or distinguishing those who have been no-table benefactors. Five confraternities are, in addition to this, celebrated dramatically in brief allegorical plays, which are printed in the *Triumpho* along with their stage directions. These dramas follow the model of the sacred theatre of the Spanish Counter-Reformation, of which the leading exponent was Calderón. The figure of the law (*la ley*) appears personified in all five plays; often the Jewish people are sim-ilarly personified, as is an antagonist figure associated with Christianity, as well as various virtues and the confraternity itself. The only scholar to study these dramas closely, Julia Rebollo Lieberman, has found evidence that they were performed at associational gatherings, with the members themselves perhaps taking the various parts.[22]

At first sight it seems paradoxical, or even perverse, that Barrios should adopt a literary form so closely associated with Catholic theological assertiveness in order to celebrate the nobility and religiosity of the confraternities of Sephardic Amsterdam. These dramas, however, served a number of functions. While giving expression to the Jewish pride and religious knowledge of their honorees (hidden biblical allu-sions are ubiquitous in the plays), they also enabled the Sephardim to reassert their proximity to the Spanish literary and dramatic tradition.[23] These associations were themselves hybrid in inspiration. Their welfare activities, often intertwined with an emphasis on religious study, served to reassert and sustain a sense of connection to normative Jewish observance and community among their members. However, they also had a more informal social function as gatherings for aesthetic appreciation and discussion—again following the Iberian model of literary academies.[24] Barrios's plays delicately fused these Jewish and Iberian elements, preserving the revered lit-erary forms of baroque Spanish drama but filling them with Jewish content. Despite this innovative integration, however, their overall tone was highly conservative. Barrios's dramas harked back to old-fashioned Iberian rhetorics of moral tradition and classical decorum, ritualistically flattering their status-conscious audience.

Barrios's play in honor of *Ḥonen Dalim* ("He who pities the poor": an association that aided widows and the sick) opens with a morally edifying dialogue between Israel ("a frail old man, dressed very simply") and the Holy Law ("dressed in furs, with a garland of flowers").[25] This is followed by the presentation of the history of *Ḥonen Dalim,* and a brief paean to each of its leading members, through the voices of two allegorical figures representing revelation (*anuncio*) and mercy (*socorro*).[26] His "harmonious dialogue" dedicated to *Maskil el Dal* (Enlightener of the poor) is loosely similar, combining abstract poetic moralization with praise for the membership of the association, a brief account of its history, and a more detailed description of its current activities. (Barrios tells us that the brotherhood was divided into two groups: the *politicos*, or supporting members, and the "*hermanos eruditos.*" the erudite, who would meet each Sunday to discuss and resolve an intellectual problem posed to them by the younger students of the *rosh* [teacher].)[27] This drama also includes an extended rendition of De Barrios's semi-mythical account of the original arrival of

the Sephardim in Amsterdam, when, he relates, a secret Yom Kippur service was at
first mistaken by the Amsterdam authorities as a Catholic service. Once the officials
realized the truth, however, all was harmony:

> Esto dijo el Hebreo esclarecido,
> al Cónclave de Astrea prevenido,
> que hallando resplandores solamente
> de Papística no, de Hebrea Gente,
> que por Misericordia soberana
> segura está de la Justicia humana
> el Judaísmo en Ámsterdam permite,
> porque el Dios de Israel la felicite,
> y la libre, de Furias belicosas
> en campañas floridas, y espumosas.[28]

(One of the Jews explained everything to the investigating Astraean conclave [the
Amsterdam authorities, here associated with the Greek goddess of Justice], which, on
discovering the shining truth, that these were not Papists, but of the Hebrew race,
was, in divine mercy, sure in human justice; Judaism was permitted in Amsterdam, as
the God of Israel smiled on his people, and freed it from warlike violence and intricate
and stormy campaigns of persecution.)

The *Triumpho* is one of our most important sources for the history of the Amsterdam
community, and historians have rightly been concerned to scrutinize its accuracy. Wilhemina Pieterse has shown that the *Triumpho* is, in general, fairly accurate,
though decreasingly so for the earlier decades of the Amsterdam settlement. Focusing
on this account of the foundation of the community, however, H. P. Salomon has
convincingly argued that Barrios consciously diverged from the available evidence
in order to exaggerate the degree to which the first settlers in the 1590s were committed to return to Judaism.[29] As a piece of historiography Barrios's work is clearly
useful, though it must be approached with caution. Stylistically and intellectually,
though, it recounts the past in a formulaic fashion, never failing to genuflect respect-
fully to past and present worthies, and bathing recent generations in a reassuringly
steady glow of moral uprightness, harmony and grandeur.[30]

What, though, was Barrios's relationship to the political culture that surrounded
him in the Dutch Republic? Miriam Bodian has attempted to situate the *Triumpho del
govierno popular* in the context of late seventeenth-century Dutch republican thought.
While acknowledging that his political thought is confused and in places contradictory, Bodian argues that Barrios strove to present the "popular government" of the
Amsterdam community as a form of republican democracy—an autonomous, con-
sensually governed polity, in harmony with the political spirit of the Law of Moses,
and also with the republican tradition of the city of Amsterdam.[31] It is certainly the
case that Barrios appreciatively celebrated the political freedoms enjoyed by the

Sephardim in the Dutch Republic. As Bodian observes, he uses the term "popular government" primarily to refer to the autonomy of the Jewish community, which he contrasts to the oppression they experienced under Spanish rule (a memory they shared, of course, with the Dutch).[32] Barrios may also have imbibed some sense of the intense identification by the Dutch of their own republican polity with the biblically ordained structures of the "Republic of the Hebrews," which was a central *topos* of seventeenth-century European political thought.[33] His limited incorporation of this Dutch discourse into the *Triumpho* enabled him to establish a commonality between the Sephardim and the Dutch, and to emphasize his community's appreciative sense of belonging in Amsterdam. The overall political tone of the *Triumpho*, however, is highly respectful of hierarchy, and its cultural tone thoroughly Hispanic. Barrios was only in the most superficial sense a republican; his celebration of "popular government" was fleeting and derivative, and must be set against the deferential conservatism that more broadly suffuses his work.

❧ ❧ ❧

Yirmiyahu Yovel casts Barrios as a tortured individual, in his later life unhappily "imprisoned" in Amsterdam.[34] There is, however, no clear evidence for this claim. It seems at least equally plausible to regard Barrios's hybrid sense of self—as both Iberian and Jewish, and both an exiled subject of the Spanish King and an extoller of communal freedoms in Amsterdam—as a personally successful endeavor, experienced by him, as far as we can discern, as coherent, comfortable and dignified. Following David Graizbord's reassertion, borrowing the phrase from Jaime Contreras, of the importance of the "low and pedestrian" in interpreting the lives, choices and conversions of early modern converso Jews, attention to the economic options and pressures of patronage faced by Barrios would seem to provide a relatively straightforward explanation for his complex and mobile self-presentation, without recourse to intricate psychological speculation.[35] Fluidity of identity was certainly a hallmark of the early modern Sephardic Diaspora, even more pronounced outside Europe, in Atlantic locales such as Senegambia, where Sephardim often moved back and forth between Jewish and Christian outward identities, or in Dutch Brazil, where there was a great deal of fluidity between formal and informal modes of Jewish expression and affiliation. In these settings also, though, it is striking how relatively unproblematically these complexities of identity were accommodated and accepted.[36]

This flexibility of identity and ease of cultural border-crossing was not, however, unique or original to the Sephardim. In Senegambia the multiple or sequential adoption of different cultural identities was an established local African tradition, to which the New Christian Portuguese traders readily adjusted.[37] The case of sixteenth-century Muslim geographer and traveler al-Hassan al-Wazzan, or Leo Africanus, to whom Natalie Zemon Davis has devoted a masterly study, is a noteworthy early example in a different context of what she has termed a "braided" early modern life.[38]

The Sephardic Diaspora, meanwhile, which in the seventeenth century was so hospitable to braided or mobile identities, was by the early eighteenth century in cultural and economic decline. The strong sense of blood lineage as a bond that transcended differences of outward religious expression was increasingly undermined by the local assimilation of Sephardic elites on both sides of the Atlantic, and by the decline of arranged marriages, which in the Sephardic heyday had consolidated and connected the wealth of the Diaspora but which were subverted by the new romantic values of Enlightenment individualism.[39] In his suggestive account of the origins of modern selfhood, Dror Wahrman has argued that fixity of identity, not fluidity, is the key hallmark of the modern era. Focusing on the British context, he regards the 1780s as the crucial decade of transition, when the shock of seeing the King's subjects in North America redefine themselves as independent Americans jolted the metropolitan British out of their relish for identitarian flux and play, and into a long era of cultural rigidity that endured until the recent advent of postmodernity.[40] The factors that enabled the particular type of Sephardic hybridity of which Barrios is a notable exemplar had already waned much earlier in the eighteenth century. When situated in a broad comparative context, however, this notably mobile Sephardic identity can be seen as a part of a larger, distinctively early modern matrix of self-presentation and self-understanding.

The case of Miguel de Barrios's cultural fusions and boundary-crossings, then, disrupts rather than reinforces any simple narrative of the precocious emergence and linear development of Jewish modernity. The ability of the early modern Sephardic Diaspora to accommodate diverse and ambiguous forms of religious expression was closely connected to its strong sense of ethnic superiority, derived from deeply conservative Iberian notions of purity of blood. Barrios's elite patrons were particularly attached to these notions, and commissioned his ornately baroque writings above all because this literary idiom most powerfully imbued its subject matter with an aura of grandeur and a respect for hierarchy. Miguel de Barrios was, then, both an example and an exponent of "conservative hybridity," a formulation that appears almost oxymoronic to us but which captures the combination of eclecticism and traditionalism that felt very natural in the world he inhabited and chronicled. The imaginative challenge that understanding his mentality and milieu poses to our twenty-first century minds is a potent reminder of the distinctiveness of early modern Jewish history, and of the importance of studying it.[41]

Notes

1. Jacob Katz, *Exclusiveness and Tolerance: Studies in Jewish-Gentile Relations in Medieval and Modern Times* (Oxford, 1961). For a summary of the debates on conversos see David L. Graizbord, *Souls in Dispute: Converso Identities in Iberia and the Jewish Diaspora 1580–1700* (Philadelphia, 2004), 8–16.

2. David Ruderman, *Early Modern Jewry: A New Cultural History* (Princeton, N.J., 2010), 14–18.

3. Jonathan I. Israel, "Jews and Crypto-Jews in the Atlantic World System," in *Atlantic Diasporas: Jews, Conversos and Crypto-Jews in the Age of Mercantilism, 1500–1800*, ed. R. L. Kagan and P. D.

Morgan (Baltimore, Md., 2009), 3–17; *Diasporas within a Diaspora: Jews, Crypto-Jews and the World Maritime Empires (1540–1740)* (Leiden, 2002), esp. 2–5.

4. Richard Popkin, *The History of Scepticism from Savonarola to Bayle* (Oxford: Oxford University Press, 1979); David S. Katz and Jonathan I. Israel, eds., *Sceptics, Millenarians and Jews* (Leiden, 1990).

5. Yirmiyahu Yovel, *The Other Within: The Marranos* (Princeton, N.J., 2009), esp. 337–58.

6. Yirmiyahu Yovel, *Spinoza and Other Heretics: The Marrano of Reason* (Princeton, N.J., 1989); Jonathan I. Israel, *Enlightenment Contested: Philosophy, Modernity, and the Emancipation of Man, 1670–1752* (Oxford, 2006), esp. 43–51.

7. Daniel Swetschinski, *Reluctant Cosmopolitans: The Portuguese Jews of Seventeenth-Century Amsterdam* (London, 2000), 278–318.

8. Yosef Kaplan, "The Jewish Profile of the Spanish-Portuguese Community of London During the Seventeenth Century," in his *An Alternative Path to Modernity: The Sephardi Diaspora in Western Europe* (Leiden, 2000), 155–67.

9. Leszek Kolakowski, *Chrétiens sans église* (Paris, 1969); Benjamin J. Kaplan, "'Remnants of the Papal Yoke': Apathy and Opposition in the Dutch Reformation," *Sixteenth Century Journal* 25 (1994): 653–69.

10. Yovel, *Other Within*, 327–28.

11. Graizbord, *Souls in Dispute*, 64–104.

12. For biographical information on Barrios see Kenneth R. Scholberg, "Miguel de Barrios and the Amsterdam Sephardic Community," *Jewish Quarterly Review* 53.1 (1962): 120–59; Timothy Oelman, *Marrano Poets of the Seventeenth Century* (London, 1982), 219–21; Wihemina C. Pieterse, *Daniel Levi de Barrios als Geschiedschrijver van de Portugees-Israelitische Gemeente te Amsterdam in zijn "Triumpho del Govierno Popular"* (Amsterdam, 1968), 15–30; Swetschinski, *Reluctant Cosmopolitans*, 243–49.

13. Miguel de Barrios, *Bello Monte de Helicona* ("Brussels" [Amsterdam], 1686). On this work see Harm den Boer, "Literature, Politics, Economy: The Spanish and Portuguese Literature of the Sephardic Jews of Amsterdam," in *The Mediterranean and the Jews: Society, Culture and Economy in Early Modern Times*, ed. E. Horowitz and M. Orfali (Ramat-Gan, 2001), 101–11.

14. Swetschinski, *Reluctant Cosmopolitans*, 248.

15. For a comparison of the various copies see Pieterse, *Daniel Levi de Barrios*, 31–35.

16. Daniel Levi de Barrios, *Triumpho del govierno popular, y de la Antiguidad Holandesa* (Amsterdam, 1683), 50–56. I have used a microfilm of the copy held by the Biblioteca Rosenthaliana, call number 19G12, which is included in the microfilm series *Sephardic Editions 1550–1820,* ed. Harm den Boer (Leiden: IDC, 2002) (microfilms J-262–265).

17. Barrios, *Triumpho*, 123–26.

18. Oelman, *Marrano Poets*, 29–31, 221.

19. Swetschinski, *Reluctant Cosmopolitans*, 299–302.

20. Barrios's text on the *Sitibundos*, his *Relación de los Poetas y Escritores Españoles de la Nácion Judayca Amstelodama*, is included in the Montezinos Library copy of the *Triumpho*, and is reprinted in M. Kayserling, "Une Histoire de la littérature juive de Daniel Levi de Barrios," *Revue des Études Juives* 18 (1899): 276–89. See also Scholberg, "Miguel de Barrios and the Amsterdam Sephardic Community," 141–45.

21. See Barrios, *Triumpho*, 339–40, for his tabular listing.

22. Julia Rebollo Lieberman, *El teatro alegórico de Miguel (Daniel Levi) de Barrios* (Newark, Del., 1996), 52–92. This volume also includes a critical edition of these five plays.

23. See Miriam Bodian, *Hebrews of the Portuguese Nation: Conversos and Community in Early Modern Amsterdam* (Bloomington, Ind., 1997), 93–94; Harm den Boer, *La literatura sefardí de Amsterdam* (Alcalá de Henares, 1995).

24. See Lieberman, *El teatro alegórico*, 35–6.

25. Barrios, *Triumpho*, 217. Also in Lieberman, *El teatro alegórico*, 109.

26. Ibid., 226–32; Lieberman, *El teatro alegórico*, 121–26.

27. Ibid., 279–300; Lieberman, *El teatro alegórico*, 152–54.

28. Ibid., 290–91; Lieberman, *El teatro alegórico*, 147.

29. Pieterse, *Daniel Levi de Barrios*, esp. 133–36; H. P. Salomon, "Myth or Anti-Myth? The Oldest Account Concerning the Origin of Portuguese Judaism at Amsterdam," *LIAS* 16 (1989): 275–316.

30. See Adam Sutcliffe, "Mémoire et identité dans la culture sépharade hollandaise du XVIIe siècle: *Triumpho del Govierno Popular* de Miguel de Barrios (1683)" in *Itinéraires sépharades*, ed. E. Benbassa (Paris, 2010), 169–80.

31. Miriam Bodian, "Biblical Hebrews and the Rhetoric of Republicanism: Seventeenth-Century Portuguese Jews on the Jewish Community," *AJS Review* 22 (1997): 199–221.

32. Ibid., 217.

33. See Adam Sutcliffe, "The Philosemitic Moment? Judaism and Republicanism in Seventeenth-Century European Thought," in *Philosemitism in History*, ed. J. Karp and A. Sutcliffe (Cambridge, 2011), 67–92; Lea Campos Boralevi, "Classical Foundation Myths of European Republicanism: The Jewish Commonwealth," in *Republicanism: A Shared European Heritage*, ed. M. van Gelderen and Q. Skinner (Cambridge, 2002), 1:247–61; Eric Nelson, *The Hebrew Republic: Jewish Sources and the Transformation of European Political Thought* (Cambridge, Mass., 2010).

34. Yovel, *Other Within*, 326.

35. Graizbord, *Souls in Dispute*, 12–13.

36. Peter Mark and José da Silva Horta, "Catholics, Jews and Muslims in Early Seventeenth Century Guiné," in *Atlantic Diasporas*, ed. Kagan and Morgan, 170–94; Bruno Feitler, "Jews and New Christians in Dutch Brazil," in *Atlantic Diasporas*, 123–51.

37. Mark and Horta, "Catholics, Jews and Muslims," 186–87.

38. Natalie Zemon Davis, *Trickster Travels: A Sixteenth-Century Muslim between Worlds* (New York, 2006).

39. Israel, *Diasporas*, 567–84; Yosef Kaplan, "Moral Panic in the Eighteenth Century Sephardi Community of Amsterdam: The Threat of Eros," in his *Alternative Path*, 280–300.

40. Dror Wahrman, *The Making of the Modern Self: Identity and Culture in Eighteenth-Century England* (New Haven, Conn., 2004).

41. David Ruderman, "Why Periodization Matters: On Early Modern Jewish Culture and Haskalah," in *Simon Dubnow Institute Yearbook* 6: *Early Modern Culture and Haskalah: Reconsidering the Borderlines of Modern Jewish History*, ed. D. Ruderman and S. Feiner (2007): 23–32.

LE *DON QUICHOTTE* D'ANTÔNIO JOSÉ DA SILVA, LES MARIONNETTES DU BAIRRO ALTO ET LES PRISONS DE L'INQUISITION

❈ ❈ ❈

Roger Chartier

École des Hautes Études en Sciences Sociales, Collège de France and the University of Pennsylvania

EN 1733 les marionnettes du Théâtre du Bairro Alto de Lisbonne représentèrent une pièce nouvelle: la *Vida do grande Dom Quixote de la Mancha e do gordo Sancho Pança*. Elle était la première œuvre théâtrale d'un auteur encore inconnu: Antônio José da Silva. En 1996, le réalisateur brésilien Jom Tob Azoulay a consacré un film intitulé *O Judeu* à la vie tragique du dramaturge, né à Rio dans une famille de juifs conversos et condamné au bûcher par le tribunal de l'Inquisition lisboète en 1739. Il y propose la reconstitution de deux scènes de la pièce telle que, peut-être, les donnaient à voir les marionnettes de Lisbonne.[1] Dans la première, le chevalier errant et son écuyer rencontrent la compagnie théâtrale de Angulo el Malo, en chemin pour donner une représentation de l'*"auto sacramental," Las cortes de la muerte,* durant les fêtes du Corpus Christi. Dans la seconde, Sancho, gouverneur de l'ile des Lézards, la "Ilha de los Lagartos" (chez Cervantès l'île de Barataria), commente l'allégorie de la Justice qui louche et agit à tort et à travers. Cet dernier extrait indique bien l'écart entre l'adaptation d'Antônio José da Silva et le texte de *Don Quichotte:* le Sancho de Cervantès, s'il rend bien (ou mal) la justice, n'explique nulle part pourquoi elle est représentée les yeux bandés et se trouve dotée d'un glaive. De plus, le cinéaste a laissé libre cours à son imagination et s'est écarté du texte de la pièce: à la fin de son commentaire, son Sancho fait mine de sodomiser la Justice, une hardiesse qui aurait été tout à fait impossible dans la Lisbonne de 1733.

La première attribution de la *Vida de Dom Quixote* de 1733 à Antônio José da Silva date de 1741, soit deux ans après la mort sur le bûcher du dramaturge. On la rencontre dans la *Bibliotheca Lusitana* de Diogo Barbosa Machado qui indique dans son premier tome, à la page 303: "Antonio Joseph da Silva né à Rio de Janeiro fils de João Mendes da Silva et de Lourença Coutinho. Il étudia le Droit Civil à l'Université de Coimbra puis il s'installa à Lisbonne où il exerçait l'office d'Avocat pour les causes judiciaires. Il eut du génie pour la Poésie Comique."[2]

"Il eut de génie pour la Poésie Comique": la *Bibliotheca* mentionne donc six de ses *comédias* qui furent représentées avec les "applaudissements des spectateurs": trois titres sont donnés comme ayant été imprimées, *Labirinto de Creta* en 1736, *Variedades de Proteu* et *Guerras do Alecrim e Manjerona* en 1737, et trois autres sont suivis par les deux lettres M. S., c'est-à-dire qu'elles sont demeurées en manuscrit: *Anfitrião ou Júpiter e Alcmena, Vida do grande Dom Quixote de la Mancha* et *Precipício de Faetonte.*

En 1744, ces six œuvres sont publiés dans un volume intitulé *Theatro cômico portuguez,* accompagnées de deux autres: *Esopaiada ou Vida de Esopo* et *Os Encantos de Medéia* qui dateraient respectivement de 1734 et 1735.[3] Le nom de l'auteur n'apparaît pas sur la page de titre mais il est aisément déchiffrable dans le poème acrostiche qui termine la préface adressée *ao leitor desapaixonado,* au lecteur sans passions ou sans préjugés. Lues verticalement, les première lettres des premiers mots des vingt vers des deux *décimas* finales indiquent: ANTONIO JOSEPH DA SILVA.

Qui était Antônio José da Silva en 1733? Nous pouvons suivre précisément sa vie tourmentée et son destin malheureux grâce aux deux magnifiques livres de Nathan Wachtel, *La Foi du souvenir* et *La Logique des bûchers.*[4] Il était né en 1705 à Rio de Janeiro dans une famille de *cristãos novos,* de juifs portugais convertis par force au christianisme après 1497 et installé au Brésil sans doute aux commencements du 17e siècle. En 1711, ses deux parents et une partie importante de sa famille furent dénoncés à l'Inquisition comme pratiquant des rites judaïques: jeûnes rituels, interdits alimentaires, port de vêtements propres le samedi. Tous furent transportés à Lisbonne où Antônio José arriva avec ses deux frères Balthazar et André. Incarcérés, son père João et sa mère Lourença confessèrent leur retour au judaïsme. Le 9 juillet 1713, lors d'un autodafé, ils furent "réconciliés" avec l'Eglise et condamnés à la confiscation de leurs biens et au port de l'*hábito penitencial* les dimanches et jours de fête.

Cette première rencontre avec le tribunal de l'Inquisition lisboète ne fut pas la dernière. En 1726, une cousine d'Antônio, Brites Coutinho fut dénoncée à l'Inquisition par son fiancé, Luis Terra Soares, étudiant en droit canon à Coimbra, qui était peut-être lui-même en partie "nouveau chrétien" et craignait pour sa propre vie. Antônio José fut arrêté avec sa mère, sa tante Isabel Cardoso Coutinho, ses deux frères et plusieurs cousins. Il confessa son retour à la "loi mosaïque," dénonça d'autres parents, mais non pas sa mère et, pour ce refus, il fut torturé. Meurtri par la question, il ne put signer son acte d'abjuration "pour ne pouvoir signer pour cause de torture." Il fut "réconcilié" avec l'Eglise lors de l'autodafé du 13 octobre 1726 et condamné à la confiscation de ses biens, à l'*hábito pénitencal* et à recevoir une instruction chrétienne.[5]

Demeurant à Lisbonne, Antônio José, qui était avocat comme son père, entreprit une carrière littéraire. Il composa non seulement les huit *óperas* publiés dans l'ouvrage publié en 1744 qui désigne ainsi ses *comédias* mais aussi deux poèmes publiés en 1736 avec son propre nom dans deux anthologies qui attestent ses liens avec la cour de João V et ses relations avec des membres de l'élite aristocratique. Le premier poème, paru dans le recueil *Acentos Saudadosos das Musas Portuguesas,* est une *Glosa* au Sonnet de Luiz de Camões dans lequel le Portugal exprime son sentiment devant la mort de sa très belle Infante D. Francisca. Le second poème est un *Romance héroïco* à la louange de João Cardoso da Costa dont les poèmes sont réunis dans ce volume intitulé *Musa Pueril.* La réédition de la *Bibliotheca Lusitana* en 1759 attribue également à Antônio José da Silva une *comedia de santo* en castillan, *El Prodigio de Amarante San Gonçalo,* écrite en 1735 ou 1737,[6] qui serait une preuve donnée par le dramaturge de l'authenticité de son abjuration, et une *Sarzuela Epithalamica* composée pour le mariage du fils de João V et de la fille de Philippe V d'Espagne.[7]

Ces liens avec les puissants ne protégèrent pas Antônio José d'une seconde arrestation par l'Inquisition. En 1737, il fut incarcéré avec son épouse, Leonor Maria de Carvalho, et sa mère après la dénonciation de son frère André et de sa famille comme "judaïsants" par un nouveau chrétien réconcilié qu'ils avaient accueilli. Emprisonné durant deux années, alors même qu'était représenté au Théâtre du Bairro Alto son dernier opéra, *O Precipício de Faetonte,* Antônio José fut lui-même précipité dans un précipice. Il nia toutes les accusations portées contre lui, mais il fut perdu par les rapports des espions qui l'épièrent par les trous ménagés dans les murs de sa cellule, puis ceux des "moutons" qui y furent introduits. Ils affirmèrent qu'il observait les jeûnes du judaïsme, qu'il n'effectuait pas correctement les gestes chrétiens et qu'il s'était moqué des prières de l'un de ses compagnons de cellule. Les témoignages en sa faveur de trois Dominicains et d'un Augustin qui le dirent bon chrétien n'empêchèrent pas qu'il fut "déclaré coupable, négatif, obstiné et relaps du crime d'hérésie et d'apostasie et qu'il fut hérétique apostat de Notre Sainte Foi Catholique." Remis au bras séculier, il fut étranglé puis brulé (ce qui se disait *queimar de garrote* et était considéré comme une grâce de l'Inquisition) à la suite de l'autodafé du 16 octobre 1739 dans lequel sa femme, sa mère, son frère, sa belle-sœur et sa tante furent, une nouvelle fois, "réconciliés" avec l'Eglise malgré le risque que certains couraient d'être tenus pour relaps.[8]

Avant l'examen des possibles relations tissées entre ce destin marqué par les persécutions et les œuvres d'Antonio José da Silva, en particulier sa *Vida do grande dom Quixote* composée après son premier procès, la torture et sa condamnation, l'étude de deux scènes de la première partie de l'opéra permet de comprendre comment le dramaturge s'était emparé du texte de Cervantès pour en faire du théâtre.[9] Il s'agit des huitième et neuvième scènes de l'œuvre dans lesquelles don Quichotte et Sancho voyagent au Parnasse pour satisfaire la demande de la muse Calliope qui a demandé l'aide du chevalier errant pour combattre les mauvais et méchants poètes ligués contre Apollon. La dernière scène de ce premier acte ou première partie montre la bataille gagnée par don Quichotte contre les *poetazinhos* et s'achève avec l'air burlesque de Sancho: "Puisque ma chanson / sera un braiement, / je donne le ton, / Hi han! Hi han! han!"[10]

Dans le *Don Quichotte* de Cervantès, on ne trouve aucune "poétomachie" semblable au combat mis sur la scène par Antônio José da Silva, et don Quichotte n'y visite pas le Parnasse. Mais le dramaturge connaissait bien son Cervantès et c'est dans une autre œuvre qu'il puise son invention théâtrale: *El viaje del Parnasso* publié à Madrid en 1614.[11] Il s'agit d'un poème de plus de trois mille vers qui narre le voyage de Cervantès au Parnasse et la bataille de livres entre les bons et les mauvais poètes. L'œuvre appartient au genre des "voyages au Parnasse" et imite explicitement le *Viaggio in Parnasso* publié par Cesare Caporali en 1582.[12] Cette imitation permettait à Cervantès, tout à la fois, une satire des poètes de son temps, une parodie burlesque de la mythologie, et une autobiographie déguisée.[13]

Antônio José da Silva s'empare du poème cervantin avec subtilité. Dans son opéra, don Quichotte rencontre Calliope, et non Mercure comme le fait celui de Cervantès, ce qui ouvre la série de trois arias chantés par les Muses, Calliope d'abord, puis Euterpe et Terpsichore. Le voyage jusqu'au Parnasse s'effectue en volant sur un nuage, et non pas en bateau, ce qui autorise un effet scénique plus spectaculaire. Le dramaturge portugais introduit également dans la situation des traits comiques qui jouent avec l'illusion théâtrale et la *suspension of disbelief* requise par la fiction. Lorsque Calliope apparaît à don Quichotte, celui-ci déclare: "Souveraine nymphe, / Echarpe d'Iris de cet horizon. / Qui déchirant les nues diaphanes . . . / Montre ta divinité." Mais Sancho rompt l'enchantement et double chaque exclamation de son maître par de plus prosaïques remarques: "Nymphe souveraine. / Arc-en-ciel de cet horizon. / Qui déchirant les nuages en carton-pâte . . . / Montres ta vetustité."

C'est ce même procédé qui attribue au Sancho de da Silva le rôle "brechtien" de destruction de l'illusion. Ainsi dans la septième scène de la première partie, alors que pour don Quichotte la grotte de Montesinos est une merveille: "Vois-tu, Sancho, cet admirable palais? Vois-tu ces colonnes doriques et corinthiennes? Regarde-moi ces jaspes? Que t'en semble?"—son écuyer le ramène à la réalité, et au théâtre: "J'ai l'impression que tout cela est peint sur des planches en bois de pin." Et dans la première scène de la seconde partie de la pièce, à Sancho qui lui demande: "Sais-tu bien où nous sommes?" "Je le sais parfaitement. Au Théâtre du Bairro Alto."

Antônio José da Silva démontre son génie théâtral en condensant la bataille entre les deux armées poétiques telle que la narre, longuement, Cervantès. L'inventaire détaillé des armes poétiques de destruction massive qui occupe les 361 vers du chapitre 7 du *Viaje al Parnasso* est drastiquement abrégé par Sancho qui décrit ainsi l'armée des mauvais poètes: "Ne voyez-vous point leur armée, de dix mille romances, quatre mille sonnets, deux cent dizains, quatre-vingt madrigaux, et leur escadron de satires volantes en salve de silves." Le dramaturge déplace aussi certains motifs du poème: à la blessure à la main de Mercure, atteint par "une satire licencieuse / de style aigu, mais pas très sain" est substituée celle de Sancho: "Au secours, j'ai un sonnet en rimes pointues qui me traverse de part en part."

Antônio José transforme les textes cervantins, tant celui de *Don Quichotte* que celui du *Viaje al Parnasso,* pour répondre à deux exigences de la pièce qu'il écrivait pour le Théâtre du Bairro Alto. D'une part, elle devait accueillir des parties chantées, dont le nombre s'accrut dans ses opéras ultérieurs, pour atteindre trente et une dans *Labirinto de Creta* en 1736 et trente-deux dans *O Precipício de Faetonte* en 1738. Le compositeur de la musique et des airs de la *Vida do grande Dom Quixote* n'est pas connu, mais on sait que da Silva collabora avec Antônio Teixeira pour *Os Encantos de Medeia, As Variedades de Proteu* et les *Guerras do Alecrim e Manjerona*—et peut-être également pour *Anfitrião* et *Labirinto de Creta*.[14] D'autre part, sa pièce devait aussi tirer profit des libertés permises par un théâtre de marionnettes et donner à voir aux spectateurs émerveillés de spectaculaires jeux de scène. Antônio José da Silva sut surmonter toutes ces difficultés avec ingéniosité, comme le prouvent les sept autres pièces que lui commanda ou qu'accepta le Théâtre du Bairro Alto entre 1734 et 1738.

Est-il possible de comprendre certaines des inventions dramatiques ou poétiques d'Antônio José da Silva comme des traces de sa propre expérience de *converso,* toujours suspecté par l'Inquisition et brutalement traité lors du procès de 1726? C'est ce qu'a soutenu toute une tradition brésilienne qui a fait du dramaturge un martyr de la liberté de croyance, une victime du fanatisme catholique et un héros des droits de la colonie, violés par la domination de la métropole. La construction d'Antônio José comme héros et martyr commence en 1838 avec la "tragédie romantique" de Domingos Gonçalves de Magalhães intitulée *Antônio José ou O poeta e a Inquisição*[15]; elle se poursuit en 1866 avec le roman de Camilo Castelo Branco, *O Judeu,* paru en 1866[16] et elle s'incarne au 20e siècle dans la *narrativa dramática* du dramaturge portugais Bernardo Santareno, *O Judeu*[17] et dans le film de Jom Tob Azoulay qui porte le même titre.[18]

Les souffrances d'Antônio José da Silva ont-elles laissé des traces dans ses pièces? Machado de Assis ne le pensait pas et il séparait le jugement sur les œuvres du dramaturge de l'émotion produite par son destin tragique. Comme il l'écrit dans son article "Antônio José," repris dans son recueil *Relíquias de Casa Velha:* "La pitié n'est certainement pas déterminante pour la critique, et tel ou tel mauvais poète, succombant à une grande injustice sociale peut inspirer la compassion et émousser l'analyse. Ce n'est pas le cas d'Antônio José: il mériterait que nous l'étudions pour lui seul, même sans les circonstances tragiques qui entourent son nom."[19] Machado de Assis dénie ainsi toute intention dénonciatrice ou tragique aux *comédias* d'Antônio José da Silva, écrites seulement dans le but de faire rire, y compris en recourant aux ressources du *baixo-cômico.* Pour lui, "malgré les traces et souvenirs de ce premier acte de l'Inquisition [la condamnation de 1726], malgré le spectacle de ce que souffraient les siens, les opéras d'Antônio José transmettent la saveur d'une jeunesse imperturbablement heureuse, une facétie grossière et pétulante, comme le lui demandait le goût du parterre, et ils ne manifestent aucune présence du tragique épisode."[20]

C'est cette même distance entre la vie et les œuvres qui se retrouve dans la thèse de José Oliveira Barata, soutenue à Coimbra, et édité en deux volumes en 1983 et 1985 sous le titre *António José da Silva: Criação e realidade.*[21] Dans un texte en français, qui sert de préface à la traduction de quatre pièces d'Antônio José da Silva (dont celle de la *Vida do grande Dom Quixote de la Mancha* que nous citons), l'auteur pourfend ce qu'il désigne comme une "sorte de nouvelle scolastique": "Etant donné que le Juif fut une victime de l'Inquisition, ses œuvres ne pourront que refléter l'animosité de l'homme contre ses féroces persécuteurs. Donc, en lisant l'œuvre superficiellement, beaucoup croient percevoir les indices de la révolte de l'écrivain contre une institution oppressive."[22] Trois arguments sont opposés à une semblable lecture: d'une part, il n'est fait aucune référence aux pièces de théâtre dans les accusations de l'Inquisition et c'est le même Inquisiteur général, le cardinal Nuno da Cunha, qui a signé la condamnation d'Antônio José en 1739 et qui a accordé la *licença* pour la publication de ses *comédias* en 1744; d'autre part, la prudence exigeait une forte autocensure de la part du dramaturge et interdisait tout propos subversif; enfin, ses compositions sont toutes des réécritures parodiques d'œuvres ou d'histoires existantes, sauf *Guerras do Alecrim e Manjerona*, ce qui les inscrit dans la tradition théâtrale, et non dans l'expérience vécue.

Plus récemment, Nathan Wachtel et Roberto Paulo Pereira ont défendu l'idée qu'il était peut-être nécessaire de réviser cette révision. Dans sa magistrale étude des conversos condamnés comme judaïsant par l'Inquisition lisboète, Wachtel indique à propos d'Antônio José da Silva dont il a reconstitué minutieusement l'incarcération, le procès et le supplice entre 1737 et 1739: "un ensemble d'arguments raisonnables permet de bien soutenir la thèse selon laquelle Antônio José aurait été condamné en raison des idées subversives que son théâtre répandait dans le public."[23] Pour lui, le genre satirique n'est aucunement exclusif de la critique sociale, même si celle-ci doit s'énoncer sur un mode comique et même si l'auteur doit s'effacer derrière les propos burlesques de ses personnages. Mais, affirme Wachtel, "reste que l'on peut extraire des pièces du "Juif" nombre de citations qui, replacées dans leur contexte historique, paraissent témoigner d'une rare témérité, jusqu'à faire allusion à son expérience des geôles inquisitoriales."[24] Pereira avance pour sa part, dans sa préface à l'édition portugaise de quatre *comédias* de da Silva, le caractère autobiographique de certains passages des pièces (en particulier *Anfitrião*) et la violence inhabituelle de la satire des institutions et de la société du temps.[25]

Pour trancher entre ces différents jugements, il faut donc retourner au texte. Et, tout d'abord, aux scènes de la *Vida do grande Dom Quixote de la Mancha* où Sancho rend la justice et en commente l'allégorie. Respectant les nécessités dramatiques et fidèle au procédé de la condensation textuelle, da Silva réduit à trois principes les multiples avertissements donnés par don Quichotte à Sancho avant que celui-ci ne prenne possession de son île. Le premier est celui qui exige la justice: "Sancho, aie bien à l'esprit que tu vas gouverner: rappelle-toi que dois toujours avoir devant les yeux la Justice." L'injonction est prise littéralement par Sancho qui réplique: "Oui, seigneur, je vais demander qu'on m'en fasse le portrait, et je le mettrai devant mes yeux," ce qui annonce le commentaire qui ouvre la quatrième scène de la seconde partie. Les deux autres commandements du chevalier errant sont: "Ne te laisse pas corrompre par des présents" et "Aimer Dieu, et ton prochain comme toi-même."

L'explication de l'allégorie de la Justice est une invention d'Antônio José da Silva, totalement absente de *Don Quichotte*. Pour Sancho, la Justice "n'est qu'une peinture" "une figure nécessaire sur terre pour faire peur aux grands personnes, comme le croquemitaine pour faire peur aux enfants." Il détaille ensuite la signification de chacun des attributs d'une telle "figure": elle est "habillée vêtue comme dans les tragédies, car toute justice finit tragiquement," elle a les yeux bandés "parce qu'on dit qu'elle était bigleuse," elle a un glaive dans la main "parce qu'elle agira en tous sens, c'est-à-dire à tort et à travers" et elle tient une balance dont "le fléau n'est guère fiable." Peinture ou allégorie, la Justice n'a pas plus de réalité que le croquemitaine, ou Dulcinée du Toboso.

Les cas jugés par Sancho dans la *comédia* sont tous différents de ceux tranchés par le Sancho de Cervantès. Tous soulignent l'iniquité, la cruauté ou la corruption de la justice ainsi rendue. A un homme qui réclame justice, Sancho donne une image de la justice, *pintada*, car, dit-il "il n'y a d'autre justice sur cette île qu'une justice en effigie." A une femme dénonçant l'homme qui l'a séduite et qui refuse de l'épouser malgré les promesses de mariage qu'il lui a faites, Sancho inflige un châtiment cruel: "que l'on mette cette femme en prison avec une chaîne au cou et des boulets au pied, bien prise aux fers, jusqu'à ce que revienne l'homme avec lequel elle veut se marier." Et quand Sancho doit condamner son propre âne, coupable d'avoir frappé un homme, il déclare en aparté: "ce que je pourrai faire c'est empêcher l'exécution de la sentence."

Dans le monde du *Dom Quixote* d'Antônio José da Silva, la justice n'existe pas. Elle est un leurre, une illusion, une tromperie. Comment comprendre cette réécriture du texte de Cervantès qui en force les effets? En premier lieu, elle permet des parodies cocasses de la rhétorique judiciaire. Ainsi, avec les références burlesques aux juristes et aux codes juridiques. Ainsi, également, l'imitation ridicule des sentences des tribunaux, comme celle par laquelle Sancho prononce la condamnation de son âne. Pour certains, ces facéties inscrites dans la tradition théâtrale, moqueuse depuis toujours des juges et des médecins, devraient interdire de comprendre de manière biographique la satire de la justice présente dans la pièce. C'est ainsi que Machado de Assis indique que "même en admettant que l'allégorie de la Justice dans la *Vida de Dom Quixote* soit un résumé des plaintes du poète (supposition fragile), la vérité est que les événements de la vie d'Antônio José n'influencèrent pas et ne diminuèrent la force originale de son talent, pas plus qu'ils ne modifièrent sa nature qui était fort éloignée de l'hypocondrie."[26]

Plus récemment, pourtant, Paulo Roberto Pereira a souligné la violence de cette satire d'une justice corrompue et Nathan Wachtel a proposé de donner un fondement biographique aux deux motifs essentiels des pièces du "Juif": la métamorphose et le labyrinthe. Les deux auteurs font retour à une scène d'*Anfitrião*, déjà commentée par Machado de Assis et José Oliveira Barata, mais dans des interprétations qui la séparaient de toute référence à la vie de son auteur.[27] Dans la sixième scène de la seconde partie d'*Anfitrião*, Saramago, le valet d'Amphitryon, est incarcéré dans la prison du Limoeiro avec trois autres prisonniers. Pour lui extorquer de l'argent, ceux-ci le torturent avec la même technique que celle employée par l'Inquisition: le *polé,* ou supplice de l'estrapade, dans lequel le supplicié est attaché par des cordes et soulevé jusqu'au plafond de la salle de torture. Avant de commencer le supplice, un des hommes demande à Saramago: "Pourquoi as-tu été arrêté ?" "Pour rien" répond le valet qui, plus tard, déclare à ses bourreaux: "Quelles libertés peut-il exprimer celui qui n'en a pas?"

Emprisonné dans la même prison, Amphitryon dit son infortune dans un récitatif suivi d'un aria. Dans le récitatif, il déclare:

> Tyrannique destin, étoile rude, / qui néfaste diffuse avec une lumière opaque / une si cruelle rigueur sur un innocent! / Quel délit ai-je commis, pour que je sente cette chaine très rude / dans les horreurs d'une prison pénible, / dans le triste et lugubre logis où / habite la confusion et demeure l'effroi? / Mais si par hasard, despote, étoile impie, / L'absence de faute est une faute, alors je suis coupable; / mais si ma faute n'est pas une faute, / pourquoi me dérobez-vous avec impiété / le crédit, l'épouse et la liberté?

"Mais si ma faute n'est pas une faute, / pourquoi me dérobez-vous avec impiété / le crédit, l'épouse et la liberté?" Ce n'est sans doute pas forcer les textes que de lire dans cette scène un écho des souffrances endurées dans une prison et sous une torture semblables à celle de l'Inquisition et, également, la dénonciation d'une violence injuste, qui conduit au bûcher les accusés d'un crime qui n'en est un que dans les obsessions de leurs juges.

L'étude de la *Vida do grande Dom Quixote de la Mancha* d'Antônio José da Silva lie ainsi trois histoires: l'histoire des adaptations théâtrales de la seconde partie de *Don Quichotte,* l'histoire d'une pratique théâtrale souvent négligée, celle du théâtre de marionnettes, situé entre le divertissement populaire et l'opéra, et l'histoire d'un dramaturge, trois fois confronté à l'Inquisition et qui a vécu la douloureuse condition des conversos pris entre leurs croyances intimes et les permanentes suspicions des Inquisiteurs. Le destin tragique d'Antônio José da Silva offre ainsi un cas limite pour affronter la question de la relation entre les expériences vécues et les œuvres elles-mêmes—une question particulièrement aiguë et difficile pour des pièces composées en un temps où l'écriture dramatique demeure largement dépendante d'histoires déjà là, de motifs traditionnels et de formules qui n'ont rien d'original. Est-il pour autant impossible de trouver dans des textes appuyés sur ces pratiques communes les traces de souffrances à la fois singulières et partagées?

Notes

1. Job Tom Azoulay, *O Judeu,* Film, 35mm, Dolby-Stereo, 85 min. Coproduction Brésil-Portugal: Animatógrafo, Tatu Filmes, Metrofilme, A & B Produções, 1996. Cf. la critique de Stephen Holden, " A Jew Trapped in Portuguese Terror," *New York Times,* January 8, 1997.

2. Diogo Barbosa Machado, *Bibliotheca Lusitana Historica, Critica e Cronologica,* tome 1 (Lisbonne, 1741), 303.

3. *Theatro Comico Portuguez ou Collecçaõ das Operas Portuguezas* (Lisbonne, 1744), 2 tomes. La *Vida do grande Dom Quixote de la Mancha* est la première pièce du premier tome.

4. Nathan Wachtel, *La Foi du souvenir. Labyrinthes marranes* (Paris, 2001), 298–318, et Wachtel, *La Logique des bûchers* (Paris, 2009), 84–98; 128–41.

5. Sur le procès de 1726, voir Claude-Henri Frèches, *António José da Silva et l'Inquisition* (Paris, 1982), 25–42 ; L'"Abjuração em forma," que Antônio José da Silva ne put signer est traduite et reproduite, ibid., 41–42.

6. La *comedia* est attribuée à Antônio José da Silva dans ses deux éditions modernes: António José da Silva, *El prodigio de Amarante,* ed. C.-H. Frèches (Lisbonne,1967), et idem, *O Judeu em cena. El prodigio de Amarante / O prodígio de Amarante,* ed. A. Dines et V. Eleutério (São Paulo, 2005).

7. Diogo Barbosa Machado, *Bibliotheca Lusitana Historica, Critica e Cronologica,* tome 4 (Lisbonne, 1759), Suplemento p. 41. Sur les œuvres attribuées à Antônio José da Silva, cf. Juliet Perkins, *A Critical Study and Translation of António José da Silva's Cretan Labyrinth* (Lewiston, N.Y., 2004), 28–38.

8. Sur ce second procès, cf. Frèches, *António et l'Inquisition,* 49–167; Wachtel, *La Foi,* 300–313, et le "Traslado do processo feito pela Inquizição de Lisboa contra Antonio Jozé da Silva Poeta Brazileiro," in *Revista Trimensal do Instituto Histórico e Geographico Brazileiro,* tomo 59. parte 1 (1º et 2º trimestres) (Rio de Janeiro, 1896), 5–261 (reproduit sur le site http//:www.fclar.unesp.br/ centrosdeestudos/ojudeu/processo).

9. Nous citons le texte de la pièce dans l'édition suivante: Antônio José da Silva, *As Comédias de Antônio José, o Judeu,* ed. P. R. Perreira (São Paulo, 2007)—*Vida do grande D. Quixote de la Mancha e do gordo Sancho Pança,* 77–148; et dans *António José da Silva, "O Judeu" (dit " Le Juif "),* ed. P. Léglise-Costa et trad. M.-H. Piwnik (Montpellier, 2000)—*Vie du grand don Quichotte de la Manche et du gros Sancho Pança,* 23–76. Cette traduction a été reprise dans *António José da Silva, Vie du grand dom Quichotte et du gros Sancho Pança,* dans *L'avant-scène théâtre,* numéro 1243, 1ᵉʳ mai 2008.

10. Ainsi traduit par Marie-Hélène Piwnik dont nous suivons la traduction dans nos citations.

11. Miguel de Cervantes Saavedra, *Viage del Parnaso* (Madrid, 1614); Réédité dans Miguel de Cervantes, *Poesías Completas, I. Viaje del Parnaso y Adjunta al Paranaso,* ed. V. Gaos (Madrid, 1973).

12. Cesare Caporali, *Il viaggio in Parnaso,* in *Raccolta di alcune rime piacevoli* (Pérouse, 1582). Sur ce poème, voir Norberto Cacciaglia, *Il viaggio di Parnaso di Cesare Caporali* (Pérouse, 1993).

13. Jean Canavaggio, "La dimensión autobiográfica del *Viaje del Parnaso," Bulletin of the Cervantes Society of America* 1.1–2 (1981): 29–41.

14. Perkins, *A Critical Study,* 47–56.

15. Domingos José Gonçalves de Magalhães, *Antônio José ou o poeta e a Inquisição* dans *Tragédias,* ed. M. Alves de Lima (São Paulo, 2005[1838]). Cf. également André Luís Gomes, *Marcas de nascença. A contribuição de Gonçalves de Magalhães para o teatro brasileiro* (São Paulo, 2004).

16. Camilo Castelo Branco, *O Judeu. Romance histórico* (Porto, 1866). Le livre est ainsi dédié: "A la Mémoire d'Antonio José da Silva, Ecrivain Portugais, Assassiné sur les bûchers du Saint Office à Lisbonne."

17. Bernardo Santareno, *O Judeu. Narrativa dramática em três actos* (Lisbonne, 1966).

18. Dans une autre intention, mais avec la même relation entre le destin d'Antônio José da Silva et ses œuvres, il faut lire (ce que nous n'avons pu faire) le drame historique en yiddish d'Alter Kacyzne, *Dem yidns opere,* écrit à Varsovie en 1937 mais non publiée avant sa mort en 1941. Voir

Alter Kacyzne, *Gezamlte Shriftn* I (Tel Aviv, 1967), avec la première œuvre théâtrale de Kacyzne, représentée en 1925, *Dukus,* consacré au comte Walentyn Potocki, supposément converti au judaïsme et brûlé à Vilno en 1749 comme Abraham ben Abraham.

19. Machado de Assis, "Antônio José," in idem, *Relíquias de Casa Velha,* ed. A. de Gama Kury (Rio de Janeiro, 1990), 113–25 (citation p. 114, notre traduction).

20. Ibid., 124.

21. José Oliveira Barata, *António José da Silva: criação e realidade,* 2 tomes (Coimbra, 1985).

22. José Oliveira da Silva, "Préface," *António José da Silva, "O Judeu,"* 12.

23. Wachtel, *La Foi,* 313.

24. Ibid.

25. Paulo Roberto Pereira, "Dramaturgia e Inquisição," in da Silva, *As Comédias de Antônio José,* 30 et 34.

26. Machado de Assis, "Antônio José" in de Assis, *Relíquias de Casa Velha,* 124.

27. Antônio José da Silva, *Anfitrião ou Júpiter e Alcmena,* in Antônio José, *As Comédias de Antônio José,* 317–19. Traduction française de Marie Claire Vromans, *Amphytrion ou Jupiter et Alcmène,* in António José, *"O Judeu" (dit "Le Juif"),* 201–2.

PART IV

THE LONG EIGHTEENTH CENTURY
IN AN EARLY MODERN KEY

❈ ❈ ❈

THE COLLAPSE OF JACOB'S LADDERS?

❈ ❈ ❈

A Suggested Perspective on the Problem of Secularization on the Eve of the Enlightenment

Michael Heyd

The Hebrew University of Jerusalem

THERE is hardly a more significant historical phenomenon in modern times than the so-called process of secularization. The very nature of this process, even its existence as an historical "entity," has been the subject of heated debates among historians, sociologists and students of religion, especially in the past twenty five years or so.[1] Quite a few scholars have cast doubt on the so-called "secularization thesis," and even its supporters no longer see secularization as one homogeneous linear process common to various societies.[2] Nor is it clear any longer that "secularization" is an essential part of "modernization" at all (modernization itself being a highly problematic concept). Compounding the question of secularization is the problem of defining, conceptually and temporally, an "age of faith" in comparison to which a process of "secularization" may be discerned. This is especially relevant to the early modern period.[3] Beyond the growing differentiation and increasing autonomy of spheres of human activity (economic life, politics, international relations and of course, scientific pursuits), can one indeed talk about "secularization" before the late eighteenth century? Furthermore, are not the terms "secular" and "secularization" themselves predicated upon a religious, specifically *Christian*, world view, which has traditionally distinguished between the religious and the secular, between this world and the world beyond?[4]

David Ruderman, for one, is careful to avoid the term in most of his work dealing with the period before 1800, including his latest grand synthesis of the cultural history of early modern Jewry.[5] The present essay, however, will attempt to present a sense of "secularization" appropriate for at least Christian history of the late seventeenth and early eighteenth centuries, and perhaps Jewish history as well. At the same time, it will indicate the dialectical relationship between these monotheistic traditions and the phenomena of "secularization," a relationship which may highlight the problems, as well as the significance, of the idea itself.

In place of the more common progressive elements of secularization such as the rise of the modern state, capitalist consumer economy, and modern science, in this essay I focus primarily on negative factors at play in pre-Enlightenment secularization—those contributing to the loss of credibility of traditional Christianity and Judaism. I shall take my cue from the notion developed by Karl Jaspers, Benjamin Schwartz, and Shmuel Eisenstadt of a "soteriological bridge." The central problem of the monotheistic religions, and of "post-Axial age" civilizations in general, according to this theory, has been the symbolic and institutional means that bridge the gap between this world and a transcendental reality.[6] Rather than a "bridge," though, I prefer the biblical metaphor of Jacob's ladder, which implies a difference between "high" and "low" and also raises the question of the steps leading up to heavens (and of the "angels" going up and down). While traditionally a mystical metaphor,[7] I will try and adopt it here as a heuristic historical-anthropological one.

My argument will be that in the course of the second half of the seventeenth century and the early eighteenth there developed a serious crisis in the symbolic and institutional "ladders" connecting this world, the *saeculum,* and the divine world beyond. This crisis involved either the breakdown of some of the rungs in that ladder, or the tendency to destroy the ladder itself, collapsing the distance between this world and the transcendental source of meaning. Among the ladders leading upward from humanity to God, the first and most evident one is that of ritual and practice. Needless to say, it was precisely this ladder which, in Western Christianity, was the focus of unending controversies since the Reformation. Which were the legitimate sacraments, how effective were they, and how should they be interpreted? In the course of the sixteenth and seventeenth centuries it became increasingly clear that no consensus could be achieved over these questions, neither in the *Respublica Christiana* in general, nor even within each state, society, or community. Consequently, there were more and more voices in the Protestant world claiming (especially in England) that issues of ritual and religious practice were things "indifferent" (*adiaphora*). By reference to the Protestant principle of *sola fide,* it was increasingly argued in the seventeenth century that Christianity was a matter of faith rather than practice. The ritualistic or "practical" ladder thus gradually lost for Protestants its soteriological significance. Concomitantly, daily behavior came to be judged according to secular moral norms, rather than religious ones.[8]

This was not the case, of course, in the Roman Catholic Church (where "secularization" developed indeed outside the Church and to a large extent, against it), and even less so in Judaism where religious practice, and *halakhah,* had traditionally been the principal upward "ladder" leading the Jew to God. The question whether in the late seventeenth and early eighteenth century there was in fact any significant decline in halakhic practice in comparison to previous periods is hotly debated. Yet, for myself, I find the data lately gathered by Shmuel Feiner on the side of decline with respect to Western European Jewry compelling and persuasive.[9] Crucial, in my view, is the fact that a growing laxity toward the observance of Jewish law could be publically admitted and debated in the early modern period, whether or not norms had dramatically shifted. On the other hand, the antinomian tendencies within the Sabbatean movement, to which I shall return below, indicate, in their turn, a crisis of the "ritualistic" and practical ladder within Jewish society.

The second ladder is *institutional.* Is there any human institution which can mediate between this world and the transcendent? Once again, the Reformation had clearly witnessed a crucial break within Western Christian society. In the Middle Ages it was accepted that "outside the Church there was no salvation" (*nulla salus extra ecclesiam*); the Reformation undermined this maxim, not just by divesting the monopoly of the Roman Catholic Church over the distribution of divine Grace (*gratia dei*), but also in emphasizing the Augustinian distinction between the visible and the invisible Church. Moreover, the division within Western Christianity soon led to a multiplicity not only of "churches" but of sects as well. By the middle of the seventeenth century it became clear that this was an irreversible process. Neither did the attempt at "confessionalization" (that is, linking each religious confession with the framework of the emerging centralized states, especially in the German principalities) succeed.[10] The growing number of "Christians without a church"[11] (especially, but not exclusively, in the Netherlands) and the increased emphasis on religious individualism by the late seventeenth century (a development of a potential that existed in Protestantism, especially in Lutheranism, from the beginning), indicate the gradual decline, from the end of the seventeenth century, of the institution as ladder linking the human realm to the divine.

Within Judaism, there was no institution equivalent to the Church. Still, rabbis performed a similar role at least as spiritual guides and legal and ritual arbiters. Once again, the extent to which the authority of the rabbinate declined by the late seventeenth century and in the course of the eighteenth is a complex and open question which the present writer is by no means competent to judge. Indeed, as in the case of Christian society, one should beware of assuming abrupt, revolutionary changes in the transition from traditional Jewish society to a "modern" one.[12] Nevertheless, it seems that the status and prestige of the rabbinate on the eve of the Enlightenment is a highly pertinent subject in view of the rise of the Sabbatean movement on the one hand, and the indications of a decline in halakhic practice on the other.[13]

A third ladder, related to some extent to the former, may be termed sociological. Is there a human community which has a privileged position vis-à-vis the divine? In Judaism this is pretty clear; the People of Israel constitutes a sort of a bridge between this world and the transcendental one. The idea of an elect nation had been prevalent in Christian Europe in the sixteenth and the seventeenth centuries, partly, perhaps, because of the decline in the prestige of the institutional churches, and partly as the result of the emerging nation-states.[14] In the eighteenth and nineteenth centuries, however, the elect collective will gradually be conceived in secular terms, providing, as is well-known, the basis of modern nationalism. This is one example where the ladder itself became "secularized," ironically under the very inspiration of the Bible!

Connected to this idea are the numerous millenarian and messianic movements of the age, both Christian and Jewish, which are perhaps the most dramatic of heaven-earth connectors in the early modern period. Messianism and millenarianism are based on the fundamental idea that history itself is sort of a ladder to the transcendent realm. The idea is of course a biblical and Jewish one. Once again, a seed of "secularization," perhaps the most crucial one, existed within biblical tradition itself, for "saeculum" originally means, indeed, primarily "history." Yet, in post-Augustinian Christianity (as in rabbinic Judaism), the soteriological role of history was pushed to the background,[15] and the Christian idea of a Millennium was softened by allegorical interpretation. In the late Middle Ages, however, and especially after the Reformation, millennial expectations reemerge, first among the radical sects, and, by the late sixteenth century and early seventeenth, among some of the more established Protestant Churches as well.[16] While traditional scholarship tends to view 1660 as the date after which these movements declined, more recent studies demonstrate that such tendencies by no means disappear in the second half of the seventeenth century or even the beginning of the eighteenth.[17] Furthermore, in the course of the eighteenth century, the idea of an "election" was becoming more "secular," stressing political and social relevance over the salvific. After the French Revolution, history was no longer just a bridge to a transcendental source of meaning. From being a manifestation of heavenly Providence, secular history became itself the ultimate judge, the final criterion by which modern ideological movements could be judged.[18]

Yet, the most obvious ladder, at least from a modern perspective, concerns the way to reach and understand God. If God is indeed transcendent, how can human beings recognize him at all? How can man in this world know the truth that saves him but which is yet beyond him? How can he/she know the norms according to which he/she has to act and behave in order to reach salvation? The answer of the three monotheistic religions has been primarily, of course, by the sacred *text*. Nevertheless, as is well-known, the reliance on Scripture as a clear and unambiguous source of religious truth proved increasingly problematic in the course of the religious controversies following the Reformation. Furthermore, the focus on Scripture was to lead in the seventeenth century to growing critical attitudes toward its reliability, primarily among Roman Catholics like Richard Simon (not to mention Spinoza, the Jew) but also among Protestants.

Linked with this issue was a specifically epistemological question: which were the human faculties capable of recognizing the transcendental religious truth? Was *human reason* capable of such recognition? A qualified positive response was given already by some of the Church Fathers (under the influence of classical philosophy), and again by the Kalam in medieval Islam, by Sa'adia Gaon, Maimonides, and their followers in Judaism, and by Thomas Aquinas and his Scholastic followers in the thirteenth and fourteenth centuries. The opponents of these "rationalist" thinkers stressed, by contrast, the absolute (or even exclusive) need to rely on *faith* (*fides*), an attitude also adopted by Luther and Calvin. By the late sixteenth century, however, we witness a resurgence of scholastic and rationalist approaches, primarily among Roman Catholics (Suarez), but increasingly (though once again, with significant qualifications) by Protestant theologians as well.[19] In the late seventeenth century, and in the course of the eighteenth, reliance on human reason (now in its modern Cartesian or Newtonian sense) as a bridge to salutary transcendental truth will become increasingly predominant in both the Catholic and Protestant worlds, not least in response to the various enthusiasts, mystics and prophesiers who claimed to *circumvent* the traditional reliance on Scripture by relying on direct divine inspiration.[20]

The growing dependence on human reason testifies to a measure of "secularization" of the epistemological ladder, and hence, of religion itself. The traditionally delicate balance between limited but communicable and confirmable human means, and the ineffable leaps of faith—a balance which had been an essential constituent of the epistemological ladder to religious truth—was thus destabilized in favor of its extremes: rationalist theology on the one hand, or enthusiastic, pietistic, and later revivalist, religion on the other.[21] These alternatives each tended to narrow the distance between the transcendental God and the human faculties of cognition, if not to collapse it altogether.

Finally, the most important dimension of Jacob's ladder was, especially in Christian theology, the *ontological* one. Christianity offered a most ingenious solution to the monotheistic problem we have outlined above. First of all, it posited Christ not just as a messiah, but also as (the Son of) God. The doctrine of the Incarnation comes to solve the problem of the transcendental gap between God and humanity. Furthermore, Orthodox christological doctrine in the Western Church, formulated definitely and officially by the Council of Chalcedon (451 C.E.), declared Christ to be one Person, with two Natures (substances), a divine one and a human one. He was consubstantial (ὁμοούσιος/homoousios) with the Father in Godhead and consubstantial with us in manhood. The christological doctrine had been itself predicated upon the trinitarian one, concluded at the Council of Nicaea (325), which saw God as one substance but manifested in three persons: God the father, the son and the Holy Ghost.[22] Significantly, the Reformation (except for some of its more radical and extreme sects) did not undermine trinitarian and christological doctrines. The sixteenth and seventeenth centuries, however, produced several thinkers and religious movements critical of traditional theology. The mediating role of Christ

was not necessarily rejected, but his metaphysical status and divine nature was eroded. Such voices and movements were usually labeled "Unitarian" or "Socinian" (after
Lelio Sozzini [Socinius], and especially, his nephew Fausto Sozzini, or Sicinus, the
Italian founders of a Unitarian sect which had a significant following especially in
Poland, Lithuania and Transylvania).[23] These ideas entered the intellectual mainstream by the late seventeenth century, with thinkers like Newton and Locke being
accused of Socinian leanings.[24] This timing coincided with the decline in the credibility of Aristotelian and Scholastic philosophy which had long provided the crucial
terminology for the Trinitarian and Christological doctrines ("substance," "consubstantial," "physis" or "nature," "persona" etc.). Thus, the theological underpinnings of
this most traditional ontological bridge between the transcendental and the human
were seriously weakened.

Within some Protestant communities at least, the concept of the trinity as a
meaningful paradigm became attenuated owing to the gradual decline in the importance of the doctrine (and experience) of Original Sin.[25] Because sin was increasingly
conceived as an evil inclination rather than as inherited guilt, there was less of an
urgency for Christ's atoning self-sacrifice.[26]

The decline in the theological prominence of Original Sin among many
Protestant intellectuals and theologians from the late seventeenth century onwards
points to some of the positive factors underlying "secularization." Clearly, increasing
confidence in human reason, largely the result of the New Philosophy and the New
Science as formulated and synthesized especially by Newton, had contributed to
a growing sense that man could be master of his own destiny, morally as well as
physically. Yet, while positive, one should be careful not to understand such "secularization" in a positivistic manner. Most intellectuals in the eighteenth century, including those usually identified with the Enlightenment, remained good Christians.
Furthermore, the eighteenth century was a period of numerous movements of religious revival—Pietism in the German-speaking world, Methodism in the English-
speaking world, the so-called Great Awakening in North America, and of course,
Hasidism in East European Jewry.

"Secularization" in the early modern period does not necessarily mean a decline in
religious belief, nor even a decline in religious fervor. Rather, in this essay I suggest
that the most important and profound sense in which one can talk about "secularization" in that period—besides the traditional meanings of the secularization of
Church property (and ecclesiastical social functions), the differentiation of spheres,
and the growing role of the secular State—is in the *loss of social consensus concerning
the ladders linking this world and the transcendental source of meaning*. Such ladders, or
links, by no means disappeared, but they no longer retained the *public* role they had
previously held. In this respect, the revivalist movements of the eighteenth century,
shifting the emphasis from the "objective" to the "subjective" realm of religious consciousness, experience and practice, only substantiate my argument. Furthermore,
those ladders which still retained public standing (like Providence in history or

in nature) became themselves increasingly "secular." In certain realms, the distance between Heaven and Earth either collapsed or became so tenuous as to be functionally meaningless. The social and political establishment, for its part, turned to such secular principles as reason, "nature," "natural law," contract, utility, etc., in order to legitimize the public order. In all these respects, the roots of "secularization," with all the problematic and paradoxical connotations of the term, reside in the early modern period.

Notes

1. The scholarly literature on this topic has become very extensive in the last two decades. For a convenient and balanced collection of essays articulating this debate, see, William H. Swatos, Jr. and Daniel V. A. Olson, *The Secularization Debate* (Lanham, Md., 2000).

2. For succinct formulation of the "secularization thesis" see Olivier Tschannen, "The Secularization Paradigm: A Systematization," *Journal for the Scientific Study of Religion* 3 (1991): 395–415. For revised formulations of the thesis, see Frank J. Lechner, "A Case against Secularization: A Rebuttal," *Social Forces* 69.4 (1991): 1103–19, and D. Yamane, "Secularization on Trial: In Defense of a Neo-Secularization Paradigm," *Journal for the Scientific Study of Religion* 36 (1997): 109–22. For early critics of that thesis see Peter F. Glasner, *The Sociology of Secularisation: A Critique of a Concept* (London, 1977); Rodney Stark and William S. Bainbridge, *A Theory of Religion* (New York, 1987). A sharp rebuttal of the secularization thesis may be found in Rodney Stark, "Secularization R.I.P." in *The Secularization Debate,* mentioned above. A recent influential study which brings the concept of secularization back into early modern European history is Charles Taylor, *A Secular Age* (Cambridge, Mass., 2007).

3. For very cogent remarks on this topic see Jonathan Sheehan, "When was Disenchantment? History and the Secular Age," in *Varieties of Secularism in a Secular Age,* ed., M. Warner, J. Van Antwerpen, C. Calhoun (Cambridge, Mass., 2010), 217–42. This collection of articles is essentially a critique of Taylor's *A Secular Age.* The idea of the Middle Ages as an "age of faith" was famously problematized by Jean Delumeau, *Le Catholicisme entre Luther et Voltaire* (Paris, 1971).

4. Sheehan, "When was Disenchantment?," 240–42.

5. David B. Ruderman, *Early Modern Jewry: A New Cultural History* (Princeton, N.J., 2010). Ruderman mentions the term only in connection with a critique of Jonathan Israel's work (206–13, especially 211–12), and in connection with his critique of the notion of "modernization" as an appropriate perspective through which to see the early modern period (216). I should stress, however, that I agree in principle with Ruderman's overall aim to give the "Early Modern Period" its specific characteristics (in Jewish history too), while avoiding any "reifications" of such chronological identities. Yet, I would claim that "secularization," in *some* of its denotations, is very much a part of these characteristics, surely in Christian Europe, but perhaps also in some Jewish communities as well.

6. Karl Jaspers, *Vom Urspruch und Ziel der Geschichte* (Zurich, 1919), translated into English, *The Origin and Goal of History* (New Haven, Conn., 1953); Benjamin Schwartz, "The Age of Transcendence," in *Wisdom Revelation and Doubt: Perspectives on the First Millennium B.C.* (Boston, 1975); Shmuel N. Eisenstadt, *The Origins and Diversity of Axial Age Civilizations* (Albany, N.Y., 1986).

7. On the ladder as a mystical metaphor in the Muslim and Jewish traditions see Alexander Altman, "The Ladder of Ascension," in *Studies in Mysticism and Religion Presented to Gershom G. Scholem* (Jerusalem, 1967), 1–32. I am grateful to Professor Rachel Elior for directing my attention to this classic article. It is important to stress, however, that in the Islamic and (probably under its influence) Jewish mystical and philosophical traditions, the ladder is a figural way for the *individual* to reach God, whereas I suggest to use it in an anthropological and historical sense for the collectivity

as well as the individual, and not necessarily in a mystical sense. For the same metaphor in a Christian context see the article by David C. Steinmetz, "Luther and the Ascent of Jacob's Ladder," *Church History* 55 (1986): 179–92.

8. An early study which has turned the attention of historians to this development, though from a somewhat negative theological perspective, is C. F. Allison, *The Rise of Moralism: The Proclamation of the Gospel from Hooker to Baxter* (London, 1966). Subsequent historiography in the past half century has clearly confirmed and amplified this view, not only with respect to England.

9. Shmuel Feiner, *The Origins of Jewish Secularization in 18th-Century Europe,* trans. C. Naor (Philadelphia, 2011), especially chaps. 1–2.

10. On Confessionalism see the classical studies: Wolfgang Reinhard "Gegenreformation als Modernisierung? Proleg zu einer Theorie des konfessionellen Zeitalters," *Archiv für Reformationsgeschichte* 68 (1977): 226–52; Heinz Schilling, "Die Konfessionalisierung im Reich," *Historische Zeitschrift* 246.1 (1988): 1–45. And see more recently, *Confessionalization in Europe, 1555–1700: Essays in Honor and Memory of Bodo Nischan,* ed. J. M. Headley, H. J. Hillerbrand and A. J. Papalas (Aldershot, 2004).

11. See the classical book by Leszec Kolakowski, *Chrétiens sans Église: La Conscience religieuse et le lien confessionnel au XVII siècle,* trans. A. Posner (Paris, 1969).

12. For references to the decline of the authority of the rabbinate, principally in Germany, but also in Poland to some extent, see Azriel Shohet, *Beginning of the Haskalah among German Jewry* (Hebrew; Jerusalem, 1960), 92–105; Jonathan Israel, *European Jewry in the Age of Mercantilism 1650–1750* (London, 1998), 153–57, 214–15. They refer to the growing influence of the secular authorities and absolutist princes in internal Jewish judicial matters and in the process of nominating rabbis, to the widespread phenomenon of nepotism and simony, and the consequent decline in their qualifications (and age!), to internal quarrels among the rabbis and to the decline of prestige of the rabbis in the eyes of the populace. Jacob Katz tended to focus mostly (though not exclusively) on the second half of the eighteenth century in discussing these phenomena. See his classical study *Tradition and Crisis,* trans. B. Cooperman (New York, 1993), 19–199. See also Chimen Abramsky, "The Crisis of Authority within European Jewry in the Eighteenth Century," in *Studies in Jewish Religion and Intellectual History, Presented to Alexander Altmann,* ed. S. Stein and R. Loewe (Tuscaloosa, Ala., 1979), 13–28. On the other hand, Elchanan Reiner, in a series of articles, has focused on the internal intellectual changes within the Ashkenazi Rabbinate in the early modern period, and insisted on the intellectual vitality of the rabbinate, especially in Poland, down to the eighteenth century. See Reiner, "The Ashkenazi Élite at the Beginning of the Modern Era: Manuscript versus Printed Book" in *Polin: Studies in Polish Jewry* vol. 10: *Jews in Early Modern Poland,* ed. G. D. Hundert (1997): 85–98, and Reiner, "Beyond the Realm of the Haskalah—Changing Learning Patterns in Jewish Traditional Society," *Jahrbuch des Simon-Dubnow-Instituts* 6 (2007): 123–33. See an expanded version of the latter article in *Let the Old Make Way for the New: Studies in the Social and Cultural History of Eastern European Jewry: Presented to Emanuel Etkes,* ed. D. Assaf and A. Rapoport-Albert (Hebrew; Jerusalem, 2009), 2:289–311. The crucial question concerns the social ramifications of these intellectual changes. I am grateful to Professor Reiner for fruitful conversations and important references on these matters.

13. David Ruderman himself has focused on this issue in his recent book, *Early Modern Jewry,* chap. 4. See also the classical studies of Gershom Scholem, *Sabbatai Sevi: The Mystical Messiah 1626–1676,* trans. R. Z. Werblowsky (Princeton, N.J., 1976), and "Redemption through Sin" in *The Messianic Idea in Judaism* (New York, 1971), 78–141. Also, Katz, *Tradition and Crisis,* esp. chap. 20; Feiner, *The Origins of Jewish Secularization,* chap. 3; Elisheva Carlebach, *The Pursuit of Heresy: Rabbi Moses Hagiz and the Sabbatian Controversies* (New York, 1990), 36, 101.

14. Among many studies see W. Haller, *Foxe's Book of Martyrs and the Elect Nation* (London, 1963);

Shmuel Almog and Michael Heyd, eds., *Chosen People, Elect Nation and Universal Mission* (Hebrew; Jerusalem, 1991), and the vast scholarly literature on the history of millenarianism in the early modern period, referred to henceforth.

15. For the parallel between the Christian and the Jewish tendency to push the soteriological significance of history to the background, see Amnon Raz-Krakotzkin, "Jewish Memory between Exile and History," *Jewish Quarterly Review* 9.4 (2007): 530–43. See an expanded version in Hebrew in *Identities: Journal of Jewish Culture and Identity* 1 (2011): 87–99.

16. Among the numerous studies on this subject see the classical book by Norman Cohn, *The Pursuit of the Millennium* (New York, 1970); William Lamont, *Godly Rule, Politics and Religion 1603–60* (London, 1969), who stresses the entrance of millenarian expectations into mainstream religious and political discourse in the first decades of the seventeenth century; Howard Hotson, *Johann Heinrich Alsted, 1588–1638: Between Renaissance, Reformation and Universal Reform* (Oxford, 2000), who deals with an influential millenarian theologian on the continent and his academic milieu.

17. On the persistence of millenarian expectations after 1660, see, among others, William M. Lamont, *Richard Baxter and the Millennium* (London, 1979); Hillel Schwartz, *The French Prophets: The History of A Millenarian Group in Eighteenth-Century England* (Berkeley, Calif., 1980), and, of course, the repercussions of the Sabbatai Zevi affair to which we referred above.

18. For the idea of progress as a "secularized" version of messianism, see the classical study of Ernest Lee Tuveson, *Millennium and Utopia: A Study in the Background of the Idea of Progress* (Gloucester, Mass., 1972). A critique of this interpretation has been articulated most famously by Hans Blumenberg in *The Legitimacy of the Modern Age,* trans. R. M. Wallace (Cambridge, Mass., 1983). Yet, his notion of "Secularization *by* Eschatology" rather than "Secularization *of* Eschatology" (part 1, chap. 4) can suit the interpretation offered here. On "political messianism," see Jacob L. Talmon, *Political Messianism: The Romantic Phase* (London, 1960). On the secularization of history, see among others, Yehoshua Arieli, "The Modern Period and the Problem of Secularization," in Arieli, *History and Politics* (Hebrew; Tel Aviv, 1992), 135–200.

19. For a recent collection of articles on this subject see Carl R. Trueman and R. Scott Clark, eds., *Protestant Scholasticism, Essays in Reassessment* (Colorado Springs, Colo., 2005).

20. See, among many others, Michael Heyd, *Be Sober and Reasonable: The Critique of Enthusiasm in the Seventeenth and Early Eighteenth Centuries* (Leiden, 1995). For England, the classical book by Gerald R. Cragg, *From Puritanism to the Age of Reason* (London, 1950), and a host of more recent studies.

21. Whether a similar dialectic can be found in Jewish society, especially in connection with reactions to the Sabbatean movement and, later, with respect to the Hasidic movement, I leave to experts on Jewish history of the period to determine. The classical study which addresses these questions is of course Katz, *Tradition and Crisis.*

22. It should be stressed, however, that within Western Christianity the Trinity was unmistakably transcendent; only the various operations of the Godhead in its three personae were related to the world. In Eastern Christianity, on the other hand, the Trinity formed a sort of a chain in which the activity of the Father passes to the Son and hence to the Holy Spirit. See Catherine M. LaCugna, "Trinity," in *The Encyclopedia of Religion* (2nd ed.; Farmington Hills, Mich., 2005), 14:9360–64.

23. The classical survey of these movements is E. Morse Wilbur, *A History of Unitarianism,* 2 vols. (Cambridge Mass., 1948, 1952). See also: Róbert Dán and Antal Pirnát, eds. *Antitrinitarianism in the Second Half of the 16th Century* (Budapest, 1982), especially the article by John C. Godbey, "Socinus and Christ," in ibid., 57–63; H. J. McLachlan, *Socinianism in Seventeenth-Century England* (London, 1951). For a more recent discussion and detailed bibliography of Socinian writings see Daniela Bianchi, "Some Sources for a History of English Socinianism. A Bibliography of 17th Century English Socinian Writings," *Topoi* 4 (1985): 91–120. She rightly emphasizes the differences between

Sozzini's original views and those developed in England in the course of the seventeenth century. See also Martin Muslow and Jan Rohls, eds., *Socinianism and Arminianism: Antitrinitarians, Calvinists and Cultural Exchange in Seventeenth-Century Europe* (Leiden, 2005).

24. On Newton's anti-Trinitarian leanings see Frank E. Manuel, *The Religion of Isaac Newton* (Oxford, 1974), 57–62, and James E. Force, "Sir Isaac Newton, 'Gentleman of Wide Swallow': Newton and the Latitudinarians," in *Essays on the Context, Nature, and Influence of Isaac Newton's Theology,* ed. J. E. Force and R. H. Popkin, (Dordrecht, 1990), 122–28. On the attacks on Locke as "Socinian," especially by Edward Stillingfleet, see John Marshall, *John Locke: Resistance, Religion and Responsibility* (Cambridge, 1994), 342–50. On a balanced view of Locke's anti-Trinitarian views, though not necessarily strictly "Socinian" see, ibid., 414–27. For a detailed bibliography of the controversy around Locke's relationship to Socinianism, see D. Bianchi, "Some Sources for a History of English Socinianism," 106–7.

25. See on this subject, Michael Heyd, "Original Sin, the Struggle for Stability, and the Rise of Moral Individualism in Late Seventeenth-Century England," in *Early Modern Europe: From Crisis to Stability,* ed. P. Benedict and M. P. Gutmann (Newark, Del., 2006), 197–233.

26. It is not by chance, it seems to me, that Christ is presented primarily as the Messiah in Handel's famous Oratory under that title, which had been highly popular already at that time.

A JEW FROM THE EAST MEETS BOOKS FROM THE WEST

❊ ❊ ❊

Yaacob Dweck
Princeton University

החידא חידה הוא (*ha-ḥida' ḥida hu'*).[1] This three-word Hebrew phrase puns on the Hebrew word for riddle, *ḥidah*, and the acronym for the Hebrew name of Ḥayim Yosef David Azulai, *ḤIDA*. One might paraphrase Churchill and say that Azulai is an enigma wrapped in a mystery.

Born in Jerusalem in 1724, Azulai lived in Ottoman Palestine and Egypt for the first three decades of his life. For a period of four years in the 1750s he traveled throughout the Ottoman Empire and Europe as an emissary for the Jews of Palestine. He then returned to Palestine for some fifteen years before setting out on another journey of roughly the same duration in the 1770s. At the end of his second tour as an emissary, Azulai did not return to Palestine as he had formerly, but settled in Livorno, where he lived until his death in 1806.

It was as an emissary and then as a resident of Livorno that Azulai wrote the works for which he is best known: *Shem ha-gedolim*, his bio-bibliographic anthology that occupies a pivotal position between the compendia of the previous centuries by Christian Hebraists like Bartolocci and Wolf, and the monumental achievements of the Jewish bibliographers of the next century such as Steinschneider and Neubauer; *Birke Yosef,* his glosses and explanations of Joseph Karo's *Shulḥan 'arukh;* and *Ma'agal tov,* a travel notebook composed during his time as an emissary. But these three works for which he is justly known are only a fraction of his enormous literary

239

output. Azulai was a graphomaniac of nineteenth-century proportions firmly entrenched in the Sephardic diaspora of the eighteenth century. There is virtually no
area of rabbinic literature that he did not write about: biblical exegesis, talmudic
commentary, legal responsa, Kabbalah, both practical and theoretical, to name a
few.[2] He even wrote a commentary on *Sefer ḥasidim*, a work of medieval German
pietism seemingly quite far from his intellectual milieu.

Amidst this vast and overwhelming display of rabbinic erudition, *Maʿagal tov*
stands out. It is one of his few works that does not take as its starting point either
a sacred text or a legal problem. The book began as an account of his travels, as
one can easily discern from its textual history. *Sefer maʿagal tov ha-shalem*, as it was
published by Aron Freimann in 1934, brings together Azulai's account as he had
recorded it in two separate manuscripts.[3] Both manuscripts are quite small: that of
the first journey 8 x 15 cm and that of the second 9 x 12 cm.[4] The size of these manuscripts bears directly upon their function. They were small enough to be carried on
his person, either in the equivalent of a pocket or in a fold in his clothing. Internal
evidence from the work suggests that Azulai kept other manuscripts in his pockets,
as shall emerge below, and it stands to reason that while traveling he kept these
notebooks on his person and entered his thoughts at odd moments.

The accounts of the two journeys do not differ markedly in substance or style.
Each contains entries that range from a single sentence to several pages; for certain
periods, there is an individual entry for every day; for others, many weeks pass
without so much as the stroke of a pen. Throughout, the language is extraordinarily
dense and allusive: rhyming prose alternates with cascades of allusions to biblical
and rabbinic literature. But the writing is often episodic, sometimes inscrutable, and
frequently disjointed. Both notebooks include a remarkably similar introductory
paragraph, in which Azulai described them as records of his travels and the many
divine miracles performed for him on his journeys. These short statements, which
appear to have been written retrospectively, offer alluring evidence that Azulai imagined an audience for his diary, but precious little indication as to who this may have
been. Unlike *Shem ha-gedolim*, which he explicitly addressed to young Jewish men in
a self-conscious echo of Karo's *Shulḥan ʿarukh*, the work does not contain a named
addressee. The later history of the manuscripts—they remained in the possession of
his descendants well into the nineteenth century—might lead one to hypothesize
that they were addressed to his children.

Azulai was an extraordinarily prolific author who printed a number of works in
his own lifetime, keenly aware of the power of the printed word and obsessed with
writing. Azulai himself used the word *sefer*, or book, to refer to the notebook of his
second journey, which he titled *Sefer maʿagal tov*, and his other writings corroborate
that he referred to his travel diary as a *sefer*. The word *sefer* was evidently labile
enough for Azulai to encompass a text that would probably be called a *kuntres* in
rabbinic Hebrew or a *yoman* in modern Hebrew.[5] The diaries themselves offer a
wealth of information—anecdotes, reflections, and data—about the printed Hebrew

book at a crucial moment in European Jewish life. Picking up where prior scholars have left off in their study of this text, I posit that books are a crucial point of intersection between Azulai as a traveler and the different Jewish communities he visited.[6] Along the way, I look briefly at one of Azulai's near contemporaries, Israel Landau (1758–1829), before suggesting that Azulai's focus on Hebrew books offers another vantage point on the fragmentation of Jewish communal life at the end of the eighteenth century.[7]

It would be short-sighted to limit the discussion of Azulai's diaries as evidence for the fact that the printed book had become deeply engrained in European Jewish life. While this may be true, it is also banal. By the time Azulai encountered Europe in the third quarter of the eighteenth century, the printed Hebrew book, along with a new cadre of intellectuals such as editors, printers, correctors, and censors, had been active agents of Jewish culture for well over two centuries. Combined with a series of other factors, including the geographic realignment of Jewish populations, the spread of Jewish mysticism, and the development of new markets for Hebrew literature, the printed book, as well as its authors and producers, had dramatically reshaped early modern Jewish culture. It had transformed the transmission of knowledge, established a corpus of texts as a rabbinic canon, and redefined what it meant to circulate a work in manuscript. When Azulai, on his travels, described printed Hebrew books, he was describing a feature of a social world that was already firmly entrenched in Jewish life.[8]

The printed book may no longer have been new by the middle of the eighteenth century, but in Azulai's hands, and in his accounts of that handling, it could lead to a series of anecdotes and encounters that highlight the roles that it played as a marker of boundaries between seemingly distinct bodies of knowledge. In his diaries, Azulai's descriptions of books were rarely about *pesak,* the formulation of a legal ruling, nor were they usually about exegesis, the correct interpretation of a sacred text. Rather, the printed Hebrew book, along with its even more prized ancillary, the Hebrew manuscript, functioned as a means to cross and to erect boundaries between different bodies of knowledge. These different bodies of knowledge were sometimes social and personal, as in Azulai's experiences in Ashkenaz, at times institutional and geographic, as in his experiences in Royal Libraries, and at other times intellectual and cultural, as in North Africa and northern Europe. But it would be a mistake to reduce the complexity of these bodies of knowledge to one form. The point is that by following Azulai and his encounters with printed books one can catch the printed Hebrew book, already well over two centuries old and no longer new, as an agent and embodiment of knowledge. By examining Azulai's encounters with Hebrew books, a whole series of oppositions—sacred and secular, public and private, Sephardic and Ashkenazic, East and West—come under considerable pressure. Azulai's reflections on books point up the limits of these categories in the second half of the eighteenth century while simultaneously underscoring their enduring power.

I. EIGHTEENTH-CENTURY COLLECTIONS OF HEBREW BOOKS

In the spring of 1774, after an extended stay in Tunis to which I shall return, Azulai crossed the Mediterranean and arrived in Livorno. Before he could enter the city, he remained in a quarantine-station for thirty-nine days. While there, he wrote, "I began and completed *Shem ha-gedolim*," referring to his bio-bibliographic study of medieval and early modern rabbis. Upon leaving the quarantine-station, Azulai requested permission from the communal leaders of Livorno to print *Shem ha-gedolim*, and the first edition of the work appeared shortly thereafter. Two successive editions, in 1786 and 1798, would appear in his lifetime. All three editions reflect the impact of his travels. For example, in his diary he notes that while in Izmir he saw a manuscript of responsa written by Joseph Karo; in *Shem ha-gedolim*, when he listed Karo's writings, he included this manuscript of his responsa in Izmir among them. The biographies of rabbinic figures that he wrote in *Shem ha-gedolim* took the form of bibliographic descriptions of their works. Books served him as the means to write Jewish lives and to map the Jewish world.

As he traveled to collect charity, Azulai practiced a form of book tourism in the different places he visited. This practice of book tourism involved not only examining rare printed books and manuscripts and recording the data in his journal and bio-bibliographic writings, but also visiting printing presses and libraries. While in Venice he writes, in a description of the celebrated Venetian Hebrew press founded in the sixteenth century by Alvise Bragadin: "on Wednesday I went to the Bragadin press owned by Signor Gad ibn Samuel Foa, and I saw several rooms where they forged square type and Rashi type."[9] Azulai did not travel to Izmir, Livorno, and Venice in order to look for books or data about them; he traveled to collect charity, and as a result of his position as an emissary he took the opportunity to examine books and seek them out.

The book tourism practiced by Azulai relates to his repeated expressions of wonder that appear throughout his diaries. Of all the different places that excite his curiosity throughout his travels—the zoo in Florence, the *Wunderkammer* of a wealthy magnate in Amsterdam, and the doors of the Duomo in Pisa—none caused him as much excitement as the great collections of Hebraica, both Jewish and non-Jewish, that he encountered in his travels. For him, large collections of Hebrew books in both Western European libraries as well as in various Jewish communities were a source of amazement. Upon visiting the Royal Library in Paris, he exclaimed: "I saw numerous Jewish books separated from the rest. They are but a small section of the library, for there are houses filled with books of all religions and all sciences in many languages. It is a wondrous thing."[10] Azulai's sense of wonder is instructive on several counts. The large collections of books in the possession of wealthy individuals in various Jewish communities or European libraries were simultaneously foreign and familiar. In his early thirties, at the time of his first trip as an emissary, Azulai had spent most of his life either in Jerusalem, Hebron, or Egypt, immersed in the study of rabbinic literature. Upon entering the Royal Library he saw the classics of the Jewish past—nearly the entirety of his intellectual world—constitute a small fraction of a considerably larger book collection. At the same time, as an alien traveler in an alien world, these Jewish books served him as fixed points on his journey. He knew where he was when he saw a volume of Maimonides' Code; more importantly, he knew what to do with such a book. When confronted with a bewildering mass of books in a variety of scripts, Azulai could only gape with wonder; when faced with a volume of Maimonides, he could actually ask the librarian for permission to read it.

The point though is not only about curiosity and wonder, but about bodies of knowledge and the borders that separate them. Azulai was among the first Jewish scholars to recognize the importance of public or semi-public collections in Europe for the purposes of Jewish scholarship. He not only wondered at the collections of Hebrew manuscripts; he compared different editions of printed books and sought out manuscripts that had long been forgotten. He used this information in his own work, such as *Shem ha-gedolim*, and continually revised his conclusions based on the information that he obtained over the course of his journeys. One is still a far cry from the comparative philology of Leopold Zunz a generation later, but Azulai stands poised at the boundary between traditional Jewish learning and the origins of modern Jewish scholarship. In the middle of the eighteenth century, a full half-century before the advent of modern Jewish scholarship, Azulai could imagine the public library joining the study house and the synagogue as a potential site for the production of Jewish knowledge.

The experience of Israel Landau in the Royal Library in Prague two decades later offers an instructive foil to Azulai's in Paris.[11] In the preface to his reprinting of Abraham Farissol's sixteenth-century geographical work *Igeret orḥot 'olam*, Landau mentioned the scarcity of printed copies and pointed to the only extant one known to him in the Royal Library in Prague as justification for reissuing the text. Like Azulai, Landau transliterated the word for library, "Bibliothek," into Hebrew characters.[12] A few pages later, at the conclusion of the prefatory materials to his edition, Landau extolled the virtues of the Royal Libraries in Prague and Vienna. The masses were allowed to read there, and even Jews were granted admission. Unlike Azulai, Landau was not an emissary in the midst of an extended journey; he was a native of Prague describing the library in the city in which he lived. Nevertheless, his account of the library concludes on a note of striking similarity: "I was delighted and my pride surged when I saw there—in the library—the Torah of our Lord among the thousands of books, the Torah of Moses, the Words of the Prophets, the books of the sages of the Talmud, their commentaries, and other extraordinary works are all standing there in an exalted place."[13] The large royal collections of books led these two figures, Landau and Azulai—so different in so many respects—to a similar reaction: an exclamation of pride that the books of their own tradition had found a place, albeit a small one, on the shelves of a royal library, combined with a sense of wonder that such repositories of books existed at all. In Azulai's case, this led to the search for early printed editions and forgotten manuscripts. In Landau's case, this pride served as a goad for the republication of an early modern text in a new edition. Both these tasks, the comparison of editions and the republication of texts, would come to characterize much of Jewish scholarship in the next century.

II. BOOKS AND THE JEWISH COMMUNITY

Books played a number of functions in Azulai's interactions with foreign Jewish communities in the Diaspora. On his first tour as an emissary Azulai spent over half a year in the Rhine-Main region of Germany, an area he referred to as Ashkenaz.[14] Emissaries of the Jewish communities in Palestine traveled with a set of signed documents and ledgers from their home communities that served to authorize their collection of charity and prevent fraud.[15] As Azulai made his way north from Innsbruck to Amsterdam, he stopped in over forty different towns or cities. Repeatedly, he faced doubts and skepticism of his credentials as an emissary. On numerous occasions he was accused of having forged the signatures of the rabbinate in Jerusalem and Hebron. In some cities, he successfully cajoled communal leaders to accept the authenticity of his documents; in others he was less successful and did not receive the hospitality usually given to emissaries, much less any charity. His diary for this period often reads like a string of outbursts punctuated by comic misunderstandings. On his second tour as an emissary, Azulai avoided Germany entirely and traveled to the Low Countries through France.

In Azulai's visit to Hanau a Jewish book played a crucial role in his encounter with the local rabbi. "We arrived in Hanau, and the guards denied us entry. I sent a note to the rabbi but I had given up hope. Finally, I bribed the guards and they allowed us to pass. As I was walking, the beadle [of the community] confronted us in a great rage. Against his will, he brought us to his home. I said to him, 'go and get the rabbi of the community. It is disrespectful to the land of Israel for me to be here.' That day I went to the rabbi and presented him my papers and account book. He looked through it, but said he did not recognize a single one of the signatures and had no way of verifying them. While we were talking, I noticed a book on the table, a copy of the Bet Shemuel, and I began to speculate with him about the laws concerning the separation of a man and woman before marriage. When he saw that I had the aura of Torah, he turned to me with a kind countenance and holy words and his eyes lit up the room."[16]

In this exchange, a Jewish book served as a cultural bridge between Jews who inhabited different worlds and initially treated each other with a fair degree of mistrust. Azulai did not enter the rabbi's house and begin a conversation about a random aspect of Jewish law; only when he caught sight of a book, the Bet Shemuel, a commentary to Joseph Karo's Even ha-'ezer by the seventeenth-century Polish rabbi Samuel ben Uri Shraga Phoebus, did he begin to "speculate" with his host. While Azulai used his knowledge to establish his credibility, the book served as a prompt for his demonstration of erudition. This performance of erudition allowed Azulai to collapse the geographic and cultural disparities that separated him from his learned host. A month earlier, while in Fürth and confronting a host similarly skeptical of his credentials, Azulai had no opportunity to use his erudition, and his requests for both hospitality and funds were turned down. In Hanau, a book enabled Azulai to achieve insider status with great speed, as he received both gracious hospitality and personal donations from his host after this exchange. But erudition had its limits. The Hanau community did not follow the lead of its rabbi and refused to allocate the communal funds for charity to Azulai's mission.

Azulai may have avoided Ashkenaz on his second tour as emissary but his long stay there on his first tour included at least one extraordinary visit: a meeting with Rabbi Jacob Joshua Falk, author of the *Pene Yehoshua*.[17] Late in the summer of 1754, Azulai made his way to Worms with the express purpose of visiting Falk. He recounted:

> We traveled in the carriage that went each week from Frankfurt [am Main] to Worms and arrived on Wednesday at the time of the afternoon prayer. I went immediately to greet the rabbi, the aforementioned author of the *Pene Yehoshua*. His visage was that of an angel of the Lord, and he greeted me kindly. I recounted to him all that had occurred to me, and I prostrated myself before him, bringing my soul out of its prison (Ps 142:8). Among the things I recounted to him was that his radiant book was seen clearly in the lovely land [of Palestine], that all the scholars and rabbis of Jerusalem, may it be rebuilt, drew upon the radiant light of his Torah, the spirit of his understanding and the splendor of his wisdom, especially Rabbi Isaac Cohen, may his memory be for a blessing, who rejoiced in his heart, because he [Falk] had cited his [Cohen's] work *Bate kehunah* in the final section. Even I, a young man, rejoiced when I saw the second volume when I was in Hanau.[18]

In contrast to his experience in Hanau, Azulai did not need to catch sight of a work of Ashkenazi *halakhah* to begin his conversation. Nor did Falk require much further proof than the ensuing discussion to recognize that his interlocutor was worth his time. One must imagine this encounter from Falk's perspective as well Azulai's.

By the time Falk met Azulai in Worms, he was over seventy years old and had recently been deposed as the rabbi of Frankfurt due to his intense opposition to the Sabbatian tendencies of Rabbi Jonathan Eybeschütz, rabbi of the triple community in Altona-Hamburg-Wandsbeck.[19] Falk was the author of a talmudic commentary, the *Pene Yehoshua,* that revolutionized the study of Talmud in the modern era.[20] The second volume of the commentary, which was the first to appear in print, had been published in Amsterdam in 1739. The first volume, which was the second to appear in print, had been published in Frankfurt in 1752.[21] Azulai, who was less than half Falk's age, arrived at his temporary residence in Worms with the news that scholars in Jerusalem had been reading his work with great admiration and some degree of thoroughness. Isaac ha-Cohen Rapoport, author of *Bate kehunah*, had been flattered to find a reference to his work in the very final section of Falk's commentary. Falk continued his meeting with Azulai the following day and clearly perceived in him something of a kindred spirit, as he discussed the Emden-Eybeschütz controversy with him at considerable length and showed him a number of Sabbatean passages in Eybeschütz's work.

From Azulai's perspective, the meeting with Falk was an extraordinary occasion. His travels in Ashkenaz up to that point had been difficult, to say the least. Nevertheless, he went out of his way to visit Worms and to meet Falk, a scholar whose work he had evidently devoured in Jerusalem. Only a week earlier in Hanau, he had been overjoyed to see that another volume of Falk's commentary had been published. If Azulai thought he was visiting a celebrated talmudist, this was undoubtedly true. But it was not the whole story. This outstanding scholar was also deeply immersed in the battle raging across the European rabbinate known as the Emden-Eybeschütz controversy. Falk took Azulai into his confidence, and showed him a series of documents that implicated Eybeschütz as a Sabbatian, to which Azulai reacted with horror. In this exchange with Falk, Azulai did not need a physical book to collapse the boundaries of age, geography, and culture that might have separated him from his host. But it is important to underscore how Azulai's knowledge of Falk's printed book, his intellectual awareness of its contents, and his news that Rapoport had been elated to find a reference to his work, allowed him to traverse a series of boundaries and be taken into Falk's confidence.

If Jewish books during his time in Hanau and Worms functioned for Azulai as a form of international currency, they played a very different role during his stay in Tunis. In studying travel literature, Elliott Horowitz has focused upon the moment a traveler crosses the threshold from the familiar to the unfamiliar as a marker of potentially revealing historical insight.[22] Azulai's exclamations about the great collections of Hebraica in Royal Libraries demonstrate how unfamiliar Western Europe was, even on what one might assume were the most familiar grounds for an eighteenth-century rabbinic bibliophile, with Jewish books. Azulai traveled as an emissary not only in Western Europe, but also in the Ottoman Empire and North Africa. On his second journey, he traveled from Jerusalem to Livorno via Alexandria and Tunis. His diary for the six months he spent between Jerusalem and Tunis covers three pages in Freimann's edition; by contrast, his writing about Tunis, which he visited for roughly the same amount of time, is four times as long and includes some of the most captivating passages of his entire journal. In a revealing passage, Azulai described how the Jews of Tunis related to his books.[23] "But they [the Jews of Tunis] treated me with great honor and they wanted to see all of my writings and all of my books, and specifically to examine whether or not I had kabbalistic books. In my possession I had a manuscript book whose subject I shall recount presently."[24] Azulai proceeds to describe at great length his initial encounter and subsequent acquisition of a manuscript written by Hayim Vital. Azulai's entry on Vital in *Shem ha-gedolim* depends heavily upon this description and the purchase of this manuscript.

He then continued with his description of the Jews in Tunis: "I had a chest of books with me. When I said to them that I did not know any Kabbalah, I removed that manuscript [by Vital] and secretly put it in my garments. And when they came and rummaged through the books they did not find this book among them, for it certainly would have been lost.... They repeatedly urged me to open the small chest that had my writings, but I guarded the keys. At one point they forced themselves upon me, took the keys, and attempted to take the book with my writings as a keepsake, but I began to scream, invoking bans (Heb. *ḥaramot*) [against them] until they returned the keys to me." In contrast to Hanau, where a Jewish book enabled Azulai to find common ground with a skeptical rabbinic colleague, in Tunis Jewish books served as markers of difference among Jews rather than sameness. Azulai's attempt to hide a manuscript of Vital's writings, his refusal to share his own writing, his very denial—patently false—of his knowledge of Kabbalah, all point to the distance he felt between himself and the Jews of Tunis. Both Hanau and Tunis were foreign to Azulai; yet they were foreign in different ways, and he was also foreign in different ways. In Hanau he appeared to a skeptical rabbinic colleague as a beggar seeking to make a buck; only after he demonstrated his learning, by discussing a work of Ashkenazi halakhah no less, did he receive his supper. In Tunis, his erudition required no demonstration; if anything he needed to protect it, quite literally, from theft.

Scholars have long seen the second half of the eighteenth century as a point of transition in European Jewish life. Azulai's travel diaries offer a fragmentary but exceptionally articulate view of European Jewry as it was understood and experienced by someone from the outside. The Jews of Europe and Europe itself were matters of intense and enduring interest to him. One of the central means through which Azulai encountered Europe and its Jews was the printed Hebrew book. If one follows Azulai's encounters with the printed Hebrew book and through the printed Hebrew book, a whole series of categories begin to blur. In the Royal Library in Paris, Azulai experienced the state as a collector and producer of Jewish knowledge. In Worms, he encountered a revolutionary Ashkenazi scholar whose writings would transform the study of Talmud in the next century, but who had recently been deposed from his position as rabbi because of his stance in the central controversy of his day. In Livorno, where he would live for the rest of his life, Azulai wrote and printed the book that would establish his reputation. In Tunis, beyond Europe's borders, Azulai had seen his own knowledge and possession of Hebrew books emerge as a liability. The printed Hebrew book for Azulai was as much a marker of knowledge and its boundaries as it was a social object that served as a source of wonder and danger. Azulai's encounters with the printed Hebrew book offer some indication that the cultural categories that wreaked such creative havoc on Jewish society at the end of the eighteenth century—East and West, the Levant and Europe, Sepharad and Ashkenaz, public and private, rabbinic and lay—were blurring, but not quite broken.

Notes

1. "ḤIDA is a riddle." Meir Benayahu, *Rabi Ḥayim Yosef David Azulai* (Jerusalem, 1959), 1:9.

2. In addition to Benayahu's biography, see Theodore Friedman, *The Life and Work of Hayyim Joseph David Azulai: A Study in Jewish Cultural History* (Ph.D. diss.; Columbia University, 1952); *Sefer ha-HIDA,* ed. M. Benayahu (Jerusalem, 1959). On Azulai and Kabbalah see Avital Sharon, "Kabbalistic Commentary on Passages in Tractate Megillah by the HIDA in his *Petaḥ "enayim"* (Hebrew; M.A. thesis; Hebrew University, 2007).

3. *Sefer ma'agal tov ha-shalem,* ed. A. Freimann, (Jerusalem, 1934). Hereafter *Ma'agal tov.* Three translations have the merit of existing. See *The Diaries of Rabbi Ha'im Yosef David Azulai,* trans. B. Cymerman (Jerusalem, 1997). Haïm Harboun, *Les voyageurs juifs du XVIIIe siècle: Haïm Yossef David Azoulaï,* 2 vols. (Aix-en-Provence, 1997–99); *Ma'agal tov (Il buon viaggio),* trans. A. M. Somekh (Livorno, 2012).

4. New York, Jewish Theological Seminary of America, MS 5388 and MS 5389.

5. See J. H. Chajes, "Accounting for the Self: Preliminary Generic-Historical Reflections on Early Modern Jewish Egodocuments," *Jewish Quarterly Review* 95.1 (2005): 1–15.

6. Matthias B. Lehmann, "*Levantinos* and Other Jews: Reading H. Y. D. Azulai's Travel Diary," *Jewish Social Studies* n.s. 13.3 (2007): 1–34. Oded Cohen, "*Ma'agal Tov* by *HIDA*: A Meeting of Tradition and Modernity" (Hebrew; M.A. thesis; Tel-Aviv University, 2010).

7. For a concise formulation see Chimen Abramsky, "The Crisis of Authority within European Jewry in the Eighteenth Century," in *Studies in Jewish Religious and Intellectual History Presented to Alexander Altmann,* ed. S. Stein and R. Loewe (Tuscaloosa, Ala., 1979), 13–28.

8. See J. R. Hacker and A. Shear, eds., *The Hebrew Book in Early Modern Italy* (Philadelphia, 2011).

9. *Ma'agal tov,* 84.

10. Ibid., 34. On Azulai in Paris see Maurice Liber and Alexander Marx, "Le séjour d'Azoulai à Paris," *REJ* 66 (1913): 243–73.

11. See Sharon Flatto, *The Kabbalistic Culture of Eighteenth-Century Prague: Ezekiel Landau (the 'Noda Biyehudah') and His Contemporaries* (Portland, Or., 2010), 48.

12. Abraham Farissol, *Igeret Orḥot 'olam* (Prague, 1793), short preface, unpaginated. On this edition, see David B. Ruderman, *The World of a Renaissance Jew: The Life and Thought of Abraham ben Mordecai Farissol* (Cincinnati, Ohio, 1981), 164.

13. Farissol, *Igeret orḥot 'olam,* 8b.

14. On Azulai in Germany see Leo Prijs, "Das Reisetagebuch des Ch. J. D. Asulai," *Zeitschrift für Bayerische Landesgeschichte* 37 (1974): 878–916.

15. Abraham Yaari, *Sheluḥe Erets Yisrael* (Jerusalem, 1997), chap. 1.

16. *Ma'agal tov,* 20.

17. Israel M. Ta-Shma, "R. Jacob Joshua Falk and His book '*Penei Yehoshua,*'" in *Keneset meḥkarim: 'Iyunim be-sifrut ha-rabanit bi-mei ha-benayim* (Jerusalem, 2010) 4:271–82. Ta-Shma cites Azulai's description of Falk's radiant countenance on 271. For Ta-Shma's study of Falk see Elchanan Reiner, "Beyond the Realm of Haskalah: Changing Learning Patterns in Jewish Traditional Society" (Hebrew), in *Yashan mi-pne ḥadash: Shai li-Emanuel Etkes,* ed. D. Assaf and A. Rapoport-Albert (Jerusalem, 2009), 2:298, n. 18.

18. *Ma'agal tov,* 23.

19. See Sid Z. Leiman, "When a Rabbi is Accused of Heresy: The Stance of Rabbi Jacob Joshua Falk in the Emden-Eibeschuetz Controversy," in *Rabbinic Culture and Its Critics: Jewish Authority, Dissent and Heresy in Medieval and Early Modern Times,* ed. D. Frank and M. Goldish (Detroit, 2008), 435–56.

20. See Ta-Shma, cited above and Reiner, "Beyond the Realm of Haskalah," 2:289–311.

21. Ibid., 301, n. 21.

22. See his "Towards a Social History of Jewish Popular Religion: Obadiah of Bertinoro on the Jews of Palermo," *Journal of Religious History* 17.2 (1992): 138–51. See pg. 151 for Horowitz's discussion of Azulai.

23. On Azulai in Tunis see Yaron Tsur, "La culture religieuse à Tunis à la fin du XVIIIe d'après le récit de voyage de Haïm Yossef David Azoulay," in *Entre Orient et Occident: Juifs et Musulmans en Tunisie*, ed. D. Cohen-Tannoudji (Paris, 2007), 63–76.

24. *Ma'agal tov*, 58.

PRINTING, FUNDRAISING, AND JEWISH PATRONAGE IN EIGHTEENTH-CENTURY LIVORNO

✠ ✠ ✠

Francesca Bregoli
Queens College,
The City University of New York

Very Illustrious Sir, both before God and before the world, I would be ungrateful
if I thought to dedicate this small work to anybody else but Your Lordship. If it
were sheltered from such high patronage, once it arrived into common acceptance,
I would have the constant doubt that it would not be defended by the usual denigration of malignant critics, which is eliminated by such noble protection as that
of Your Lordship. I am grateful for this, because with this minuscule homage I can
reverently show you my gratitude for the most bountiful favors that your magnifi-
cence has bestowed on me.

THE minuscule homage was the *Sefer sha'ar Yosef,* a talmudic commentary on the
tractate *Horayot* that Hayim Yosef David Azulai, the HIDA (1724–1806), gave to print
during his stay in Livorno in 1756.[1] The *Sha'ar Yosef* was the first book published by
HIDA, who at that time was a young itinerant fundraiser (sing. *shaliah,* pl. *shelihim*)
on a mission for the Jewish community of Hebron. The long dedication in Spanish,
from which I have quoted the first few lines, was printed at the beginning of the
book in honor of Dr. Michael Pereira de Leon, a wealthy member of the Livornese
Jewish elite who granted financial help to defray the publication of Azulai's book
and supported him during his stay in town.[2]

It is well known that during the second half of the eighteenth century, the Tuscan
port of Livorno on the Tyrrhenian Sea became one of the main Mediterranean hubs
for the publication of Hebrew legal writings by living or recently deceased Levantine
and Maghrebi authors, and for their distribution to centers where Livornese merchants had established trading firms, such as Tunis, Smyrna, and Salonica.[3] Less
known, however, are the local conditions that enabled the success of this specific
Hebrew publishing activity. Recent studies on the Italian book trade have shown
that eighteenth-century Italian publishers tended to lack substantial capital and
usually tried to avoid any market risk. There is no evidence of a true literary mar-

ketplace and the development of capitalist-style publishing until the second half of the nineteenth century. Before then, financial backing from the nobility and the Church was crucial to the production and the diffusion of Italian books, sometimes in the form of book subscriptions.[4] In the Hebrew publishing world, traditionally conservative, we find a similar situation. Usually, the publication costs were not covered by the publishers, but rather by external patrons, donors, and frequently by the clients themselves. This was especially true for books by living authors, such as Azulai's *Sha'ar Yosef.*

To better understand the success story of Livorno as a Hebrew publishing center, as well as the success stories of those rabbis who were able to print several of their works in these circumstances, we need to account for networks of material support within which the scholars, who published their manuscripts and those of their ancestors, operated. In this essay, I would like to offer a few preliminary observations about this system from the point of view of patron-client relations. Until the mid-1970s, historians tended to portray patronage either as the context for exceptional artistic creativity, such as in Renaissance Florence, or as a troublesome leftover of feudal structures, incompatible with the advance of capitalism and "rational modernization." Today, these interpretations have been revised.[5] Recent studies have shown that patronage was not a voluntary activity, in which one could choose to engage or not, but rather an engrained and far-reaching process that shaped identities and hierarchical orders in early modern Europe.[6] Patronage was a pervasive "productive system," to use Mario Biagioli's expression, which not only drove clients up the social ladder but also defined scholarly values, structures of communication, and professional identities.[7] In this light, I will look specifically at the relationship that two itinerant rabbis, ḤIDA and Judah Ayash, both known for their legal traditionalism, forged with the patrons who sponsored their scholarly and printing activities in Livorno.

ḤIDA's older contemporary, the Algerian rabbi Judah Ayash (1690–1760), had three of his halakhic manuscripts printed in Livorno during his lifetime. For the publication of his first books, the *Leḥem Yehudah* (1745), a commentary on Maimonides' *Mishneh Torah,* and the collection of responsa *Bet Yehudah* (1746), Ayash enjoyed the financial support of benefactors in Algiers.[8] In the case of his third halakhic volume, the *Bene Yehudah* (1758), however, he was able to rely on the help of a Livornese patron, Moses Ḥayim son of Raphael Abraham Franco, who "set aside some of his money in the form of a *nedavah,*" an offer, for its publication. Franco was, like Pereira de Leon, a member of the Livornese Sephardi elite and belonged to a respected mercantile family. Not only did Franco sponsor Ayash's publication, but he also provided the rabbi with a place to stay. Before Ayash's arrival, the Francos "prepared and emptied a house for me," wrote the author in his introduction, "a nice place with nice utensils, everything was ready and appointed."

Moses Ḥayim, depicted as a pious and devoted Jew, showed liberality and love of scholarship: "He would appoint everything that I [lit., my eyes] demanded from sacred writings, both old and new. With pleasure he bought books and would lend them to me, for my sake; his heart understood by mere hints that I desired them."[9] Moses' hospitality was supplemented by the rest of his family, whom the introduction also praises at length for their generosity, devotion, and kindness—not only his father Raphael Franco, but in particular the women of the house, his mother Rachel and his wife Donha Rosa Rodrigues Miranda.

For authors, the offer of a book to a potential or current benefactor was an act pregnant with meaning, on which careers and opportunities were built. Not unlike actual gifts,[10] given in order to honor and gain the friendship of patrons, the offering of a book to a powerful sponsor could be a strategic moment in the ritualized relationship between dependent authors and their supporters, one which marked the entry into, and formalization of, a patron-client relationship.[11] Azulai's dedication to Michael Pereira de Leon thus was not a unique phenomenon. Indeed, at the beginning of his *Sefer Bene Yehudah* Judah Ayash inserted a dedication as well. This too was written in a florid Baroque Spanish, in honor of Moses Haim Franco.

Spanish was the formal language of the Livornese Sephardi elite. It is not known if Azulai and Ayash knew it (and its literary conventions) in the 1750s; it is possible that they did not personally compose the dedications and may have relied on local "ghostwriters" to pen them on their behalf.[12] Nonetheless, we must assume that these texts reflected the rabbis' concern with pleasing their sponsors. For instance, Ayash's benefactor was compared to no less than the biblical Moses. Just as God had sent manna to the people of Israel after Moses' prayers, so that their pilgrimage in the desert should not be arduous, so Moses Franco had guided Ayash's family, "a small pilgrim people, taking care of us with the manna of his kind gifts with such generosity and a truly frank and pious soul (*Franco, y Pio*)."[13]

Ayash's and Azulai's texts reflect well-known rhetorical techniques in the genre of the dedication. Both scholars not only emphasize their deep debt of gratitude, but also minimize their own role as authors; only thanks to the patron's protection will their works be safe from malignant critics.[14] "Out of gratitude," Ayash continued, "I am compelled to dedicate this small work to you. Once it is protected under your wing there will be no malignant critics who will be able to criticize it or bite it with their stubborn teeth."[15] For his part, Azulai justified his request for protection by extolling the learning and piety of Pereira de Leon. "It is furthermore right that I ask you to defend this work," Azulai wrote,

> because you are adorned with such abundant literature, perfect in the divine science, and well-read in the humane letters. You unveil the most secret dogmas [and] the most subtle systems in the Holy Law with frankness, clarity and pleasantness. In jurisprudence and medicine, your unequivocal opinion is impossible to disagree with. In erudition, you are endowed with linguistic command; in politics, you [know] morals and the art of prudence; your advices, instructions, and edification accurately testify to this. [You are] an ardent follower of the Divine Law and honor its teachers.[16]

The system of patronage ties established during one generation, thanks also to ritual gestures such as a book dedication, did not necessarily come to an end after the death of either the author or his benefactor. In this sense, we can accurately talk about a multigenerational support *network*. This is illustrated by the case of Judah Ayash's sons, who went to Livorno to publish three more of their father's works after his death in 1760. During their stays in town, Jacob Moses and Joseph Ayash enjoyed assistance from the same Livornese supporters who had helped their father. When Jacob Moses Ayash arrived in the Tuscan port twenty-three years after his father's death he received help from Franco's family, which he duly praised and thanked in his introduction to the *Sefer mateh Yehudah* (1783), a commentary on the *Shulḥan 'arukh* (*Oraḥ ḥayim*).[17]

During the same visit, Ayash the younger was also able to strike up a relationship with another Livornese supporter, Eliezer Ḥay Recanati, who already counted Azulai and the talmudist and poet Isaac Ḥayim Frosolone (at that time both living in Livorno) among his protégés.[18] Like Moses Haim Franco, Recanati was a powerful member of the Livornese Jewish mercantile elite, who belonged to the first Italian family admitted to the mostly Sephardi Mahamad (a body of sixty governors from among the most established families in town) of this Tuscan community.[19] When Ayash's youngest son Joseph arrived in Livorno ten years later to print yet another of his father's manuscripts, the *Sefer kol Yehudah* (1793), both Moses Ḥayim Franco and Eliezer Ḥay Recanati had died. The tradition of patronage however was kept alive by their relatives: Recanati's sons Isaac Ḥay and Joshua, on the one hand, and Franco's widow Donha Rosa, on the other, assisted Joseph during his Livornese stay with financial support and hospitality.[20]

Scholarly and publishing assistance was also intimately related with support in other areas. As in ḤIDA's case, several other rabbis who sought to print books in Livorno were traveling as *sheliḥim* for Jewish communities in the Holy Land.[21] A connection with an influential local patron willing to *apadrinar* (sponsor, protect) an emissary could prove particularly crucial in the case of fundraising missions, when communal funds as well as private donations were mobilized.[22]

Thus Jacob Moses Ayash, an itinerant fundraiser for the Jewish community of Jerusalem, relied on Eliezer Ḥay Recanati not only for printing support, but also for his own fundraising purposes.[23] ḤIDA too benefited from the protection of Pereira de Leon in relation to his fundraising activities. In fact, Pereira de Leon and ḤIDA had become acquainted on the occasion of Azulai's very first fundraising visit to the Tuscan port in 1753, and their relationship was strengthened during his second longer stay in the Tuscan port in 1755 and 1756.[24] This fruitful friendship was resumed again when Azulai stopped in Livorno during his second fundraising mission in 1774, and it developed into a stable affiliation with the Pereira de Leon household after the rabbi moved to the Tuscan port.

According to Azulai's recollection in his *Ma'agal tov*, he almost ruined his chances during his first fundraising mission because of some negative comments about old

Livornese *pekide erets israel* (Deputies for the Holy Land), the communal deputies in charge of the funds destined to assist foreign Jewish settlements, which were found among his papers. However, Pereira de Leon, who was acting as a deputy that year, sided with the rabbi, striving to suppress the incident, and backed him successfully when the Mahamad considered his fundraising requests. The intervention of Pereira de Leon was particularly welcome, as Azulai had originally hoped to rely on another "powerful friend" then serving as *parnas*, who, to his great dismay, could not attend the communal meeting because of an illness.[25] Again in 1774, Azulai wrote in his diary that he was unable to collect the money allocated to his mission after an altercation with the community's *pekide erets israel,* but could rely on Pereira de Leon and other local friends to raise generous funds through individual donations.[26]

It seems obvious that for itinerant Jewish authors and scholars, who had even fewer opportunities to enjoy institutional support than their gentile peers, entry into a client relationship with a powerful patron was often perceived as the only way to publish their works and advance in their endeavors. But what about the benefactors themselves? Informal support (both private and public) of Jewish spiritual leaders had been in practice since antiquity and it was certainly still a key feature of early modern Jewish culture. Examining the ties established by authors and their sponsors from the point of view of patron-client relationships illuminates further the dynamics of this partnership as well as the ambitions of members of the Jewish mercantile elite.

Patron-client relations represent a way in which society structures and regulates the flow of resources, and are based on interactions characterized by the simultaneous exchange of different types of assets and promises of solidarity.[27] Both patrons and clients tend to represent their associations as voluntary; patrons like to portray their acts as disinterested and arbitrary.[28] However, it would be a mistake to take this at face value, and we should rather emphasize the *mutual interest* of both parties in such relations. It is important to ask, therefore, not only if connection with a wealthy patron enhanced the credibility of a rabbi, or if the patrons had any influence on how the writings of their protégés developed, over what was printed, and over its consumption—but also what kind of benefit the lay sponsors themselves might have reaped.

What could have been the motivations of men like Pereira de Leon, Recanati, and Franco, busy exponents of the Livornese commercial class, in striking lasting relationships with itinerant rabbis? Both Pereira de Leon and Recanati were members of the Livornese Mahamad. Pereira de Leon was a relatively recent addition to the Livornese communal council, to which he was only appointed in 1741. From that moment on, he served keenly and continuously in a variety of public offices,[29] and also acted as *parnas* in 1756 and 1764.[30] Recanati had perhaps an even more active career, serving repeatedly as *parnas* in 1761, 1765, 1769, 1773 and 1781.[31] Franco was, on the other hand, personally distant from the political life of Livornese Jewry, though he was related to some of its protagonists, such as Joseph Franco, a powerful merchant with ties in London and one of the most distinguished leaders of the Livornese community.[32]

There is no doubt that Pereira de Leon, Recanati, and Franco were representatives of the Livornese Jewish economic and political elite. It is possible that the time-honored model offered by Rashi's interpretation of the symbiotic partnership between the tribes of Zebulun and Issachar gave them some inspiration for their patronage. The tribe of Zebulun, whom Rashi depicted as merchants, provided resources for that of Issachar to devote itself entirely to Torah study.[33] Without Zebulun, Issachar could not thrive. And just like Rashi's Zebulun, wealthy Livornese benefactors would likely have expected to share in the spiritual reward achieved by Torah scholars from entering a relationship with a rabbi. Pious Jewish merchants who were distracted by their practical concerns and businesses and were unable to devote their life fully to Torah would have found consolation in assisting a scholar. It is telling that one of the recurrent features in both Hebrew introductions and vernacular dedications are the elaborate lists of blessings inserted after the name of each donor, as if the patron could vicariously get closer to God through the help of his rabbinic protégé, who promised to pray on his behalf. Consider for instance the last lines of Ayash's dedication to Franco: "I beseech Your Lordship to please accept this small gift that my grateful affection dedicates to you, and I am praying God that he may prolong the life of Your Lordship for many years and maintain you at the peak of your utmost happiness and greatness."[34] One suspects that the length of the blessing directly reflected the generosity of the benefactor.

It is also necessary to consider the indirect intellectual prestige and cultural capital a patron would acquire through his association with a rabbinic scholar. Significantly, not every scholar received material support and help for publication— why ḤIDA and Ayash, but not others? For one thing, both ḤIDA and Ayash were already relatively well-known by the time they arrived at Livorno. Their fame preceded them and would have made them more attractive to potential sponsors. Book dedications may shed additional light on this question. As Roger Chartier has remarked, the dedication of a book to a princely sponsor was not only the "instrument of an unsymmetrical exchange," reflecting the association between a hopeful author and a powerful individual who offered his protection in a "deferred countermove." Dedications also mirrored a prince's absolute power. The patron saw himself praised as the original inspiration and author of the book, as if the writer were offering his benefactor a work that belonged to him in the first place.[35]

It is possible to consider the last paragraph of Azulai's dedication to Pereira de Leon in this light: "This entire summary of perfections makes Your Lordship a champion, so that with *your knowledge and loving intellect you* may open this door,[36] which the stubborn key of my *short experience* keeps close, so that, by showering *your wisdom*, many others may enter to drink. May God let prosper Your Lordship with a long life and blessings, which he may grant you and all your worthy family. Amen."[37] In a bold rhetorical move, ḤIDA granted his patron—whom he described as most accomplished in both Jewish and non-Jewish scholarship, including legal, medical, and political knowledge—the ability to give his own work epistemological legitimacy. Only Pereira de Leon could open the "Door of Joseph." Azulai, the young ḥakham who was establishing a reputation as a rabbinic prodigy among Jewish communities throughout the Diaspora, contrasted the knowledge, loving intellect, and wisdom of Dr. Pereira de Leon with his own "short experience." By accepting Azulai's dedication, Michael Pereira de Leon not only increased in fame and recognition, but also most significantly found himself in the extraordinary position of giving authority to his protégé's halakhic commentary.

In the early modern Christian world, princely patrons saw themselves praised as incomparable poets or scientists through the means of the dedication. Within the Jewish world, the currency of "patronage exchange" seems to have been Torah scholarship. Judah Ayash generously bestowed the honorific title of maskil on Franco in his introduction to the Bene Yehudah, and so did his son Jacob Moses for Recanati in the Mateh Yehudah; however, there is no evidence that Franco or Recanati were ever nominated as maskilim. In fact, Franco paid practically every year from 1768 to 1778 to be excluded from the honor of ḥatan Torah (bridegroom of the Torah), in which a distinguished member of the congregation is called to read the last verses of the Torah on the occasion of Simḥat Torah. So did Recanati on repeated occasions.[38] These requests for exemption were most likely due to the frequent business trips that Livornese Jewish merchants undertook, though other factors may have played a role as well.[39] We come to appreciate further the particular appeal of scholarly sponsorship in the community of Livorno, where some members of the Jewish upper classes chose not to participate in certain aspects of congregational life, but nonetheless yearned for identification with traditional Jewish knowledge and its production. Association with a respected rabbi provided the patron with intellectual and religious cachet, strengthening his image as a Torah expert within the community.[40]

In conclusion, in the second half of the eighteenth century, at least three Jewish patrons supporting itinerant rabbinic scholars were present simultaneously in Livorno. This patronage system should not only be taken into consideration to explain the development of the port as a Hebrew-printing hub during that period, but can also open up fresh avenues for research. Eighteenth-century Jewish communities of traders, such as London and Bordeaux, have been frequently depicted as pragmatically integrated into the broader society but wanting in Jewish intellectual life, as if all the energy of their members were spent in the commercial field.[41] However, Jewish patronage of foreign scholars and itinerant fundraisers may have served in certain instances as a virtuous alternative for local cultural productivity.

Similarly, wealthy Sephardi merchants are often portrayed as "secular" avant la lettre, and quite disinterested in the spiritual life of the Jewish community. Referring to the sermons that ḤIDA delivered in Livorno, which decry the lapse in observance of its Jewry, Meir Benayahu could not help but conclude that the more Livornese Jews grew wealthy, the less they cared for religion.[42] In fact, the situation of the

Livornese mercantile elites is more nuanced. In the Tuscan port we find a more conservative situation than previously suspected, of which the complex support system that some of the established exponents of the economic and political elite provided to rabbinic scholars from abroad, such as ḤIDA and Ayash, is just one example. This configuration dispels doubts about the disinterest in Jewish spirituality on the part of powerful merchants of both Sephardi and Italian background, shows that economic success did not automatically translate into assimilation or loss of Jewish values, and suggests that ostensibly "secular" behaviors could coexist with religious motivations. While the Livornese economic elite may have grown less strict in its observance of Jewish laws or less active in synagogue life, sponsorship of rabbinic scholars offered an avenue to the community's leaders to play Zebulun on behalf of itinerant Issachar, conspicuously and publicly sharing not only in the rewards, but also in the honors of Torah scholarship.

Notes

I would like to thank Omri Elisha, Ted Fram, Abigail Green, Joseph Hacker, Juan José Ponce-Vázquez, and Elli Stern for their help and suggestions.

1. Ḥayim Yosef David Azulai, *Sefer sha'ar Yosef* (Livorno, 1756), dedication (n.p.).

2. On the stay of ḤIDA in Livorno, see Meir Benayahu, *Rabi Ḥayim Yosef David Azulai* (Jerusalem, 1959), 54–80. During his time there, ḤIDA prayed in Pereira de Leon's private oratory and took care of the religious and kabbalistic education of the doctor's sons. ḤIDA's other benefactor in Livorno was Eliezer Ḥay Recanati.

3. On Livornese Hebrew in eighteenth-century printing, see Francesca Bregoli, "Hebrew Printing in Eighteenth-Century Livorno: From Government Control to a Free Market," in *The Hebrew Book in Early Modern Italy*, ed. J. Hacker and A. Shear (Philadelphia, 2011), 171–95; Bregoli, "Hebrew Printing and Communication Networks between Livorno and North Africa, 1740–1789," *Report of the Oxford Centre for Hebrew and Jewish Studies* (2007–2008): 51–59; Marvin J. Heller, "Abraham ben Raphael Meldola and the Resumption of Printing in Livorno," *International Sephardic Journal* 2 (2005): 83–94; see also the classic work of Guido Sonnino, *Storia della tipografia ebraica in Livorno* (Turin, 1912).

4. Renato Pasta, "The History of the Book and Publishing in Eighteenth-Century Italy," *Journal of Modern Italian Studies* 10 (2005): 200–18; 199–204; Françoise Waquet, "Book Subscriptions in Early Eighteenth-Century Italy," *Publishing History* 33 (1993): 77–88.

5. Ronald Weissman, "Taking Patronage Seriously: Mediterranean Values and Renaissance Society," in *Patronage, Art, and Society in Renaissance Italy*, ed. F. W. Kent and P. Simons with J. C. Eade (Canberra, 1987), 25–45.

6. I found especially helpful the reflections on patronage and court society in Mario Biagioli, *Galileo, Courtier: The Practice of Science in the Culture of Absolutism* (Chicago, 1993), 11–101. See also Gabriele Jancke, "Early Modern Scholars' Patronage Networks and Their Representation by Autobiographical Writers (16th Century)," *Net Culture Science/Netz Kultur Wissenschaft* (2004): 1–9; Peter W. Shoemaker, *Powerful Connections: The Poetics of Patronage in the Age of Louis XIII* (Newark, Del., 2007), 26–56.

7. Biagioli, *Galileo Courtier*, 16, 90.

8. Judah Ayash, *Sefer leḥem Yehudah* (Livorno, 1745), *hakdamat ha-meḥaber* (n.p.); Ayash, *Sefer bet Yehudah* (Livorno, 1746), *hakdamat ha-rav ha-meḥaber* (n.p.).

9. Judah Ayash, *Sefer bene Yehudah* (Livorno, 1758), *hakdamat ha-mehaber* (n.p.).

10. Roni Weinstein, "Gift Exchanges during Marriage Rituals among the Italian Jews in the Early Modern Period. A Historic-Anthropological Reading," *Revue des Études Juives* 165 (2006): 493–97.

11. On gift giving as part of patron-client relations, see Biagioli, *Galileo Courtier,* 36–54 and Roger Chartier, *Forms and Meanings: Texts, Performances, and Audiences from Codex to Computer* (Philadelphia, 1995), 36.

12. After he settled in Livorno, Azulai most likely preached his sermons in Spanish (see Benayahu, *Rabbi Hayim Yosef David Azulai*, 58, n. 20). However, it is not known if he already knew the language during his first stay in the city.

13. Ayash, *Bene Yehudah*, dedication (n.p.).

14. Chartier, *Forms and Meanings*, 37

15. Ayash, *Bene Yehudah*, dedication (n.p.).

16. Azulai, *Sha'ar Yosef,* dedication (n.p.).

17. Judah Ayash, *Sefer mateh Yehudah* (Livorno, 1783), *hakdamat ben ha-rav ha-mehaber* (n.p.).

18. Jacob Moses Ayash received financial support for his publication from several other members of the Livornese aristocracy: Shemaya Bassan, Moses Aghib, Jacob Aghib, Moses Hayim Rekah, Samuel Miranda and Joseph Miranda Leon, Joseph Leon, Joseph Ergas, Samuel Leon, the four brothers Samuel, Joseph, Abraham and Isaac Abudarham, the three brothers Benjamin, Jacob Elijah and Samuel Nissim, sons of David Rekah, and Joseph and Isaac Nattaf.

19. Renzo Toaff, *La Nazione Ebrea a Pisa e a Livorno (1591–1700)* (Florence, 1990), 178, 180–82; Jean Pierre Filippini, "La nazione ebrea di Livorno," in *Storia d'Italia. Annali 11. Gli ebrei in Italia*, vol. 2. *Dall'emancipazione a oggi*, ed. C. Vivanti (Turin, 1997), 1047–66: 1051–54.

20. Judah Ayash, *Sefer kol Yehudah* (Livorno, 1793), *hakdamat ben ha-rav ha-mehaber* (n.p.).

21. On the relationship between the Livornese community and traveling emissaries from the Holy Land, see Toaff, *Nazione Ebrea*, 371–76.

22. *Deliberaçoims do Governo*, volume F, 71v. I am grateful to the heirs of the late Prof. Renzo Toaff who allowed me to peruse their microfilms of the eighteenth-century "Deliberaçoims do Governo" (DdG).

23. Ayash, *Mateh Yehudah, hakdamat ben ha-rav ha-mehaber* (n.p.)

24. Benayahu, *Rabbi Hayim Yosef David Azulai*, 41–42. During mealtimes, Azulai would visit Pereira de Leon, who for fifteen months treated him "with great kindness and even greater honor." His Livornese stay ultimately led to the publication of the *Sha'ar Yosef.*

25. Hayim Yosef David Azulai, *Ma'agal tov ha-shalem*, ed. A. Freimann (Jerusalem, 1934), 4. The minutes of the Livornese Mahamad confirm that 450 *pezze* were set aside on behalf of the Jewish community of Hebron. Azulai received 50 *pezze* for his own travels (DdG, volume F, 144r–v).

26. Azulai, *Ma'agal tov*, 66–67. According to the minutes of the Livornese Mahamad, Azulai was granted 600 *pezze* on behalf of the Hebron community, together with the customary 50 *pezze* for his travels (DdG, volume I, p. 8). It is possible that Azulai deemed the sum insufficient and a disagreement ensued.

27. S. N. Eisenstadt and Louis Roninger, "Patron-Client Relations as a Model of Structuring Social Exchange," *Comparative Studies in Society and History* 22 (1980): 49–50.

28. Biagioli, *Galileo Courtier*, 85.

29. The Mahamad appointed him Deputy of the Holy Land in 1752 (DdG, volume F, 121r) and 1768 (ibid., volume H, p. 153) and Trustee of the Synagogue (an office that supervised finances connected with religious and ritual matters) in 1752 (DdG, volume F, 126v) and 1766 (ibid., volume H, p. 102). Pereira de Leon served also as a Deputy of *Sebuim* (an office in charge of funds for the liberation of Jewish captives) in 1771 (ibid., p. 204) and was elected as one of the censors in 1773 (ibid., p. 248).

30. DdG, volume G, p. 64; ibid., volume H, p. 43.

31. DdG, volume G, p. 192; volume H., pp. 71, 162, 245; book 1, p. 142. Among other offices, he also served the community as a Trustee of the Synagogue in 1762 (volume G, pp. 229–30), 1772 (volume H, p. 236), and 1784 (volume I, p. 208); as a Deputy of the *ḥevrah baʻale teshuvah* in 1779 (volume I, p. 104); and as a Deputy of *Sebuim* in 1781 (volume I, p. 131) and 1787 (volume K, p. 7).

32. One of his brothers, Abraham Ḥayim was a merchant in London, while another, David Ḥayim, was elected as a member of the Mahamad in 1771.

33. Rashi to Deut 33:18.

34. Ayash, *Bene Yehudah,* dedication (n.p.).

35. Chartier, *Forms and Meaning,* 42.

36. This is an allusion to the work's title, *Shaʻar Yosef.*

37. Azulai, *Shaʻar Yosef,* dedication [emphasis mine].

38. DdG, book H, pp. 145, 171, 194, 216; book I pp. 32, 43, 60, 78.

39. Some Livornese Jews may have wished to be excluded because of the onerous expenses that accompanied the honor of *ḥatan Torah,* as it was customary for the honoree to offer a reception after the synagogue service. It is also tempting to speculate that some merchants wished to be excluded because they did not possess the Hebrew skills necessary to recite the Torah.

40. For an important comparison with the patronage system established by wealthy Polish Jewish merchants on behalf of Hasidic masters, see Glenn Dynner, "Merchant Princes and Tsadikim: The Patronage of Polish Hasidim," *Jewish Social Studies* 12 (2005): 64–110.

41. Frances Malino, *The Sephardic Jews of Bordeaux. Assimilation and Emancipation in Revolutionary and Napoleonic France* (Tuscaloosa, Ala., 1978), 26.

42. Benayahu, *Rabbi Ḥayim Yosef David Azulai,* 59–60.

AN INTERPRETIVE TRADITION

❊ ❊ ❊

Connecting Europe and the "East" in the Eighteenth Century

Andrea Schatz
King's College London

I

THE "idea that we live in the description of a place and not in the place itself"[1] has been articulated as such in the twentieth century, but the questions and challenges, which it captures so well, are not peculiar to the modern period. Wherever belonging was not taken for granted, the meanings of a place could become the subject of intense reflection and debate, which in turn invites scholars today to raise their own questions. What did Jews mean when they mentioned "Frankfurt" or "Prague," "Amsterdam" or "Berlin," "France" or "Europe"? How did various different ways of describing a place affect the possibility of belonging to it? How could one question, subvert, and alter the description of a place? How were individual and institutional acts of defining and interpreting terrain—verbally, visually, materially—linked to various modes of inhabiting it? In the eighteenth century, when European Jews began to reject openly the assumption that they lived in their towns and villages as foreigners, when they debated among themselves about how to frame their relationship to their places of residence, and when some of them began to fight for the right to belong to their states as citizens, they did not only rethink and reshape their Jewish commitments. They also sought to change—implicitly and explicitly—the description of the places in which they lived and to ascribe to them features which would make it possible to inhabit them as both Jews and citizens.

In doing so, Jewish authors often highlighted European connections to regions that in the non-Jewish world were increasingly perceived as sites of the "other": especially to the Middle East and North Africa. David Ruderman has emphasized "connectedness" as an interpretive category which allows us to analyze the politics and cultures of a particular place while also taking into consideration transregional and even transcontinental networks, patterns, and developments. Taking up Sanjay Subrahmanyam's notion of early modern "connected histories,"[2] Ruderman has argued that, in tracing "connections, contacts, and conversations over time and across specific localities,"[3] we can analyze the global dimension of migrations and of the circulation of material goods and ideas in the early modern world without minimizing local differences or imposing comparative perspectives that are inevitably shaped by the perspectives, preferences and limitations of particular areas of study.[4]

Here, I would like to add that "connectedness" is a feature of the early modern world, which was transformed already in the eighteenth century into a useful interpretive tool. It was precisely at the moment when early modern transregional connections and networks gave way to new frameworks based on modern national boundaries and colonial systems of domination that some Jewish authors began to include early modern connectedness as a vital feature in their descriptions of a modern and profoundly inhabitable Europe. Among them was Naphtali Herz Wessely, whose treatise *Divre shalom ve-emet* (Words of Peace and Truth, Berlin 1782–85) became famous for suggesting bold reforms of Jewish culture and education. The treatise soon became part of the struggle of contemporary Jews for new descriptions of the places where they lived. When Berr Isaac Berr published his French translation of Wessely's translation in 1790, he addressed it to the Abbé Jean-Siffrein Maury, who had rejected, in a short and fiercely hostile speech, Clermont-Tonnerre's plea in Parliament for the extension of citizenship to Jews, claiming that Jews as a nation "have a large province" in Poland and, as citizens, would soon also own "half" of the Alsace.[5] Berr perfectly captures the tenor of Maury's remarks: "they not only contend that the Jewish religion presents an obstacle, which prevents those who profess it from ever becoming citizens, but also that the religion itself is somehow tarnished. Having established this principle, you are nonetheless kind enough to demand *protection* for the Jews, although your compassion, after your speech, quite resembles Monsieur de Voltaire's remark (still, one ought not to burn them)."[6] Berr then introduces Wessely's treatise into this context of contested interpretations of places: "I do not know on what proofs you rely in your assertions; but let me, a Jew . . . who knows the spirit of his own people . . . contest the opinion which you have put forward with some evidence."[7] In the footnote attached to the word "Juif," Berr asserts his naturalization as a Jewish and French citizen of Nancy: "Naturalized by virtue of the royal letters patent, registered with the Parliament of Nancy, residence of the undersigned." Finally, Berr adds the response he received from Maury: "While I will persevere in my opposition to your pretensions, I will always seek for the

Jews the protection and hospitality which mankind demands and which the French nation owes to all foreigners."[8] While Berr insists that Nancy can be described as a place where Jews can reside as French citizens, Maury is relentless in his insistence that it can only be described as a French city if Jews remain foreigners.

Wessely himself certainly perceived his efforts as geared toward the full integration of Jews into contemporary society. Here, however, I would like to read Wessely's text not so much as an exceptional, profoundly innovative text, but rather as a document that is interesting precisely because it emphasizes transnational and transregional connectedness and, in doing so, articulates approaches and attitudes that we can find much earlier as well as much later—and that are remarkably out of sync with dominant trends in the non-Jewish world. Recontextualizing several passages of his treatise and reading them against the backdrop of contemporary debates on Europe and "the East" may point to the complexity of maskilic interventions, which did not only aim at modifying the meanings of Jewishness but also at changing the descriptions of "Nancy" and "Berlin," "France" and "Europe," and, in the process, accorded an important role to early modern facets of "connectedness."

II

If we look at discussions of religions, cultures, and political systems in the eighteenth century, they seem governed by an interpretive approach which is familiar to us as the "temporalization" of difference. What is different is defined as temporally distant: it represents an earlier stage in human history. Margaret Hodgen, Anthony Pagden, and many others have examined the emergence of this method of comparison.[9] The temporalization of differences across regions, societies and cultures can be traced back, as Hodgen shows, to various beginnings, both secular and religious: to the early modern revival of historiography, to a new confidence in the achievements of the present era as expressed by the Modernists in their *querelle* with the Ancients, and to Christian theological thought. What was different belonged to an ancient stage of human history which extended erratically into the present, and what was similar pointed to the dynamics of change, progress and integration into the universal—and secular—history of mankind.[10] This conceptualization of difference had been developed as part of the Christian idea of supersession: what was different in Judaism was interpreted as a relic of particularistic resistance to the universal truth of Christianity; what was similar was understood as a promise of future conversion and unification with the, allegedly universal, Christian faith.

In the Enlightenment debates on civil rights for Jews, it became obvious that such Christian interpretations of difference remained painfully relevant. Even those who advocated equal rights for Jews did so on the basis of the assumption that emancipation and a secular political framework would ultimately lead Jews to abandon their specific "rabbinic" practices and national affiliations and persuade them to become, as individuals, undifferentiated German or French citizens.[11] Those who opposed emancipation, for instance, Johann David Michaelis, the influential theologian, Orientalist, and public intellectual from Göttingen, held that Jews would never be able to extricate themselves from their ties to the ancient rabbinic world and its history of religious and political decline.

In Michaelis's work, we encounter a further interpretive move that shaped debates on progress and difference in the eighteenth century: difference was defined as a sign of distance in terms of time, but also, increasingly, as distance in terms of space. Jews were associated with an ancient past, and simultaneously also with a foreign place: the Orient. The intellectual differentiation between Europe and the Orient had, of course, a long history. Among its most complex and powerful articulations is Montesquieu's treatise *L'esprit des lois.* The work, published in 1748, defines and discusses three different forms of government: republicanism, the monarchy, and despotism. Montesquieu's investigation of these three types allowed him to present a detailed, incisive, yet largely indirect critique of the French state under Louis XV that, in Montesquieu's view, hovered precariously between monarchism and despotism. While Montesquieu emphasized that the three forms of government are ideal types, he nevertheless linked them to specific historical and geographical places: republicanism was associated with Athens and Rome, the monarchy with England, and despotism was described as typical of "oriental" rule, whether in Turkey, Persia, Mongolia, or Morocco. About religion, Montesquieu writes: "In these [despotic] states, religion has more influence than anywhere else; it is fear added to fear. The peoples in the Mohammedan empires in part derive from their religion their extraordinary veneration for their rulers."[12]

It was here, in Montesquieu's "Spirit of the Laws" that a taxonomy which had emerged over two centuries took the form of a new master narrative.[13] The numerous differences between the various regions that were perceived as part of the Orient were largely ignored just as the contrasts and tensions among the various countries that were seen as part of Europe were disregarded. In Montesquieu's work, the new master narrative had a self-critical edge (Montesquieu was clearly more interested in Paris than in Persia), but this did not persist, and the concept of the Orient became a vehicle of imperial aspirations rather than internal transformations.

For our purposes, one particular aspect of Montesquieu's complex discussion of "Europe" and the "Orient" deserves to be highlighted. For him, the Orient is not the other, or elsewhere; it is that with which European states are entangled and from which they need be liberated: the Orient was in fact too close—Persia, in other words, could be found at the heart of Paris. It is striking that the Orient is not yet the Other (that transformation from here to there, from us to them, required the efforts of European philosophers, scholars and politicians). Montesquieu argued that France should extricate itself from the dominance of its own despotic aristocracy, and, a few years later, Michaelis, who admired Montesquieu's "The Spirit of the Laws," explained to his readers that German legislation should disentangle itself from its biblical—Oriental—roots. According to authors such as Michaelis, European states could become modern and secular only by asserting their historical, political and cultural difference and distance from the Orient.[14]

This raises obvious questions regarding Jewish politics and culture in the eighteenth century. Where would Jews situate themselves as Europe sought to disentangle itself from the Orient? And where would they be situated by others? A small, but telling, example for the casual way in which Jews could be associated with the Orient can be found in contemporary travel literature. In 1773, Johann Hermann Riedesel published his *Remarques d'un voyageur moderne au Levant* as a sequel to his successful *Reise durch Sicilien und Großgriechenland* (Zurich, 1771), a travelogue which had been printed on the initiative of his friend Johann Joachim Winckelmann. Riedesel's description of Constantinople emphasizes the strong contrast between the beauty of the city, as it presents itself from the outside, and the rather unpleasant prospect which awaits the traveller who ventures inside: "The streets, which are badly paved, dirty and lined by wooden houses, built like those of the Jews of Livorno and Frankfurt on the Main with protruding oriel windows, which render the streets even darker and narrower, are the object of disgust and displeasure, when one first looks at them."[15] The German translator of the book who, in other places, does not hesitate to express doubt or disagreement in his annotations, confirms this description in a footnote, adding that Riedesel's remarks agree with the earlier observations of Spon and Tournefort.[16]

If one compares Jacob Spon's *Voyage d'Italie, de Dalmatie, de Grece, et du Levant* (1679) and Joseph Pitton de Tournefort's *Relation d'un voyage du Levant* (1717) to Riedesel's description, one notices, however, that their accounts of the city are far more complex. It is true, they mention the contrast between the beautiful panorama and the narrow streets inside the city, but this does not prevent them from appreciating also the attractive buildings of the inner city—and nowhere do they mention the Jewish houses of Frankfurt or Livorno. Tournefort's introduction to his description of Constantinople, in particular, deserves a closer look. He writes (in the contemporary English translation): "*Constantinople*, with its Suburbs, is, beyond dispute, the largest city of *Europe*; its Situation, by consent of all Travellers, and even the ancient Historians, is the most agreeable and the most advantageous of the whole Universe. It seems as if the Canal of the *Dardanelles*, and that of the *Black Sea*, were made on purpose to bring it the Riches of the four Quarters of the World: those of the *Mogul*, the *Indies*, the remotest North, *China* and *Japan*, come by the way of the Black Sea; and by the Canal of the *White Sea*, come the Merchandizes of *Arabia, Egypt, Ethiopia*, the Coast of *Africk*, the *West-Indies*, and whatever *Europe* produces."[17] Here, the geographical situation of Constantinople and its economic role at the crossroads between "the four Quarters of the World" are placed within the sphere of the European continent: the city is depicted as a European outpost of global connectedness.

When Riedesel describes the city several decades later, the emphasis has shifted. The connections he perceives between the streets of Constantinople and those of the

Jewish quarters in Livorno and Frankfurt do not contribute to the description of the admirable features of the city, but highlight its foreign and alienating character. In this context, the reference to European Jewish houses suggests that their inhabitants are the "familiar aliens" of European cities who might more naturally be associated with politically and culturally distant places at or beyond the boundaries of Europe.[18] In light of such shifting perceptions of connectedness, it seems telling that the translator who expressed his agreement with Riedesel's account was Christian Wilhelm Dohm, who firmly supported civil rights for Jews and, in his treatise *Über die bürgerliche Verbesserung der Juden* (On the Civic Improvement of the Jews, 1782), expressed his hope that "these unfortunate Asian refugees" would eventually become European compatriots.[19] Even Dohm appears to have felt that the long history of Jews in Europe was not quite enough to consider them Europeans, and that somehow they still belonged to Asia. His remarks imply that these names—"Europe" and "Asia"—refer to mutually exclusive spheres of connectedness.

III

Among the authors of the Jewish Enlightenment who would beg to differ was Naphtali Herz Wessely. Wessely's admiration for the Sephardic community of Amsterdam, where he had lived for some time in the 1760s, is well known. What has not received quite the same attention, however, are Wessely's references to the Jews of the Ottoman Empire. For Wessely, the merchant Jews of the Middle East and North Africa could serve as models for Ashkenazic Jews who sought to refashion Jewish life in the transition from early to later modernity. Wessely already refers to them in the initial volume of the *Divre shalom ve-emet,* when he speaks about Jewish communities whose members cultivate the vernaculars of their non-Jewish surroundings. Wessely recommends the Jews of England, France, and Poland as worthy of emulation, and he also mentions the Jews of *artsot ha-mizrah* (the lands of the East), who are capable of speaking Turkish and Arabic properly.[20]

After his first treatise triggered fierce controversies, Wessely sought to clarify various points in a second volume, *Rav tuv le-Yisrael,* published just a few months after the first treatise and addressed to the Jewish community of Trieste. In this second treatise, Wessely sought to explain that he never intended to suggest that the entire Jewish nation had experienced a period of cultural decline in recent centuries. He praises the Italian Jewish communities for the cultivation of languages and excellent manners, and he links their achievements to their trade "with the great kingdoms of Europe, Asia, and Africa." A few lines later he adds:

> The same distinct quality (*yitron*) can also be found among our brethren, the sons of Israel in the lands of the East and West (*mizrah u-ma'arav*) and in the Yemen, in Anatolia, Syria and Armenia, in Erets Yisrael, Assyria and Babylonia, and in all the communities of Israel along the shores of the Mediterranean Sea, from Egypt to Tunis, Algier and the Western end, which is the kingdom of Morocco: most of them

speak Spanish or Turkish properly, and many of them also speak Italian and French. When their scholars come to our territories (*gelilot*), we enjoy their company and their conversation. They honor the people and each other; they speak correctly and act ethically. Scholars of great learning and fear [of God] have lived for generations in these lands, and they wrote many books and left a blessing in the fields of halakhah, exegesis, and in ethical and pleasant behaviour.[21]

Wessely himself may have anticipated incredulous readers who would ask themselves how he could know such things. Therefore, he confirms: "This I have seen with my own eyes among our brethren, the sons of Israel, the Sephardim of Amsterdam."[22]

If we read this passage against its contemporary background, it seems remarkable for many reasons. First of all, at a time when Europe and the Orient were subject to political, cultural, and intellectual attempts to establish a clear distance between them, Wessely makes connections and connectedness a focus of his argument. His references to Syria, Yemen, Tunisia, and Morocco clearly serve primarily an internal Jewish polemical purpose: they aim to show that the allegedly miserable state of Jews in Ashkenaz and Polin is an anomaly, and that it is desirable and possible to transcend it, as the perceived superior state of Jews in the vast territories of the Sephardic world demonstrates. However, this internal Jewish argument simultaneously addresses the Christian world. Amsterdam, this quintessential European city, is depicted as the hub of a trade network, which now also reveals its broader political and cultural relevance. Jews can belong to modern Europe not if they cut their ties to the "lands of the East," but rather if they cultivate them.

With this argument, Wessely expresses his indebtedness to an early modern geographical consciousness, which knew of the division between Europe, Asia, and Africa, but not of a dualism between East and West. Wessely's references to Amsterdam and the Ottoman Empire remind us of Tournefort's description of Constantinople as a great European city as well as of taxonomies of geographical space, as we can find them in popular early modern Hebrew and Yiddish works such as Abraham Farissol's *Igeret orḥot 'olam* (Letter on the Ways of the World, Venice, 1586) or the Yiddish *Tla'ot Moshe*, published by Moshe bar Avraham in Halle in 1711–12. Taking up Farissol's description, Moshe bar Avraham claims that "these are the lands belonging to Europe: Spain, France, and Germany in its entirety, Russia, Turkey, Hungary, Moravia and Bohemia, Poland, Macedonia, Dalmatia, Thrace, Croatia, Italy in its entirety and its islands." Here, not only Constantinople, but Turkey "in its entirety" is reclaimed for Europe, and any taxonomy which seeks to establish clear boundaries between Europe and the Orient is rendered meaningless by the many places in Eastern and Southeastern Europe that do not fit.[23]

It bears emphasis, however, that Wessely's argument is built on more than an unspecific evocation of premodern Jewish diaspora networks. It reflects a commitment to a world of early modern transregional connections, which had been created by Jewish as well as non-Jewish commercial and cultural activities, and had their specific Jewish as well as Christian and Muslim dimensions. Indeed, Wessely focuses on economics and culture and seems quite indifferent to Jewish religious practices, which helped to sustain transregional connections, as well as to political developments in the non-Jewish world, which required reorienting commitments along national boundaries. Studied against this background, Wessely's argument for the transformation of Ashkenazic culture on the basis of connectedness reveals its implications for all European identities: they are reimagined as connected identities, bound by commercial and cultural links across Europe, Asia and Africa.[24]

Related to the argument about connectedness is Wessely's emphasis on the modern relevance of the Middle East and North Africa. These regions are not depicted as "elsewhere" in terms of geographical space or historical time; rather, they are presented as part of his own world and his own times. In contrast to Christian depictions of the Orient as an archaic or ahistorical sphere, which exists outside European histories of progress, Wessely presents the Ottoman Empire as a strictly contemporary world, which can serve as a model for European Jews who seek to reshape their present and future. In Johannes Fabian's terms, Wessely's "East" is "coeval," and the time of his argument is "shared time" or "Intersubjective Time."[25]

IV

Wessely's insistence on connectedness as a feature of modern Europe, which should not be missing from any of its descriptions, harkens back to early modern interpretive traditions, as we find them in Simone Luzzatto's references to Venice and the Ottoman Empire, and it points to later maskilic explorations of connectedness, as they occur in Isaac Euchel's "Letters of Meshullam ben Uria ha-Eshtemo'i" (1786) or in Samuel Romanelli's "Travail in an Arab Land" (1792). It remains to be studied what happened to this interpretive tradition in the long nineteenth century. Here, I would like to conclude with its recurrence in the twentieth century.

In 1938, Cecil Roth spoke before the members of the Jewish Historical Society of England on "The Jew as European," and his main theme was "the fact of interdependence."[26] Roth did not hesitate to point to the contemporary relevance of his topic: "Incidentally, the very name 'Europe,' far from having an intolerant and exclusive implication, deriving from an obvious geographical distinction, was of Asiatic—nay, of Palestinian—origin; for it was derived from a Semitic damsel of that name, daughter of a Phoenician king of Tyre, who was carried captive into Crete by Zeus. It is a point, I venture to think, worthy of Herr Hitler's attention."[27] On the following pages, Roth points to the long history of connectedness between Asia, Africa, and Europe, on which "Western civilization" was built, and in doing so, he inscribes Jewish history into the history of Europe:

> The first period of Jewish history was not enacted in a remote territory of the barbaric world. It was at a focal point of the ancient polity, where Europe and Asia and Africa met, where troops and diplomats and merchants were constantly passing back-

wards and forwards, bringing fruitful ideas in their train as well as more perishable commodities. . . . There is, indeed a growing body of opinion which holds that the Hebrews were very closely associated with the enterprises and achievements of the Phoenicians—including that colonising activity which first brought the seeds of civilised life to many parts of Western Europe.[28]

Roth's short history of the intense relations between Europe, the Middle East, and North Africa ends with rather poignant reflections on his own times:

It is, indeed, only in comparatively recent times that the idea of Europe as a cultural as well as geographical entity has triumphed. . . . It is only during the past two decades, following the last Graeco-Turkish War, that the great interchanges of population have at last made it possible to draw a more or less clear-cut division in this part of the world, ethnically, religiously, and politically (except for the Muslim enclaves in Thrace and Bosnia); though simultaneously the occidentalisation of a great part of the Levant has obscured the difference.[29]

Europe can be described without reference to the "fact of interdependence" only as the result of violent historical ruptures. But even then, the history of connectedness seems to have been interrupted only temporarily: for Roth it is already possible to discern once again the beginnings of new intersections and connections.

Roth's lecture can be read as part of an interpretive tradition that seeks to conceive of Europe in other than Eurocentric terms. His words, however, alert us also to the challenges and limitations that may affect such interpretations. Wessely often relies on imprecise information and conjecture when describing the many places he evokes in support of his argument for connectedness. Thus, for instance, his account of the linguistic practices of Jews in the Ottoman Empire completely ignores the role of Ladino and idealizes the familiarity of Jews with Turkish and Arabic. This is not an expression of Orientalism, since Wessely proceeds in exactly the same way when writing in rather generalizing terms about French Jews (prompting Berr Isaac Berr to correct him in his French translation). For Wessely, it is clearly more important to rewrite Jewish and Christian descriptions of Europe than to be sufficiently attentive to the details of Jewish life in the Middle East or North Africa. This complicates and undermines his argument about connectedness. In Roth's reformulation of connectedness as an interpretive tool, we come across the colonial and imperial contexts, in which "connectedness" reveals its ambivalence. The term suggests symmetric and reciprocal relationships, while more often than not connections were shaped by asymmetric economic, cultural and political frameworks. Finally, Sanjay Subrahmanyam himself points to the question whether connectedness is an interpretive tool which ultimately favours attention to "elite" movements.[30] In analysing the interpretive tradition that focuses on connectedness as an alternative to Orientalist divisions of the world, it will be important to keep in mind where this tradition tends to remain tied to the approaches it seeks to transcend. As a critical term, however, "connectedness" may help us study the complexities of histories and identities in the the eighteenth century, when early modern traditions were mobilized for the creation of non-nationalistic and non-Eurocentric descriptions of modern Europe.

Notes

1. Wallace Stevens, letter to Henry Church, April 4, 1945, in *Letters of Wallace Stevens*, ed. H. Stevens (Berkeley, Calif., 1996), 494.

2. Sanjay Subrahmanyam, "Connected Histories: Notes towards a Reconfiguration of Early Modern Eurasia," *Modern Asian Studies* 31 (1997): 735–62.

3. David B. Ruderman, *Early Modern Jewry: A New Cultural History* (Princeton, N.J., 2010), 12.

4. Ibid., 224–25.

5. An English translation of his speech of December 23, 1789 can be found in Lynn Hunt, ed., *The French Revolution and Human Rights: A Brief Documentary History* (Boston, 1996), 88–89.

6. *Instruction salutaire adressée aux communautés juives de l'Empire par le célèbre Hartwic Weisly, juif de Berlin . . .* ([Paris], 1790), 3–4.

7. Ibid., 5.

8. Ibid., 9–10.

9. Hodgen speaks of the "temporalization of the spatially conceived series of forms"; Margaret T. Hodgen, *Early Anthropology in the Sixteenth and Seventeenth Century* (Philadelphia, 1964), 390; see also Anthony Pagden, *European Encounters with the New World from Renaissance to Romanticism* (New Haven, Conn., 1993).

10. Hodgen, *Early Anthropology*, 389–90.

11. Cf. Jonathan M. Hess, *Germans, Jews and the Claims of Modernity* (New Haven, Conn., 2002), 37; and Andrea Schatz, "Interrupted Games: Lessing and Mendelssohn on Religion, Intermarriage and Integration," *Lessing Yearbook* 39 (2010): 51–72.

12. Montesquieu, *Selected Political Writings*, ed. and trans. M. Richter (Indianapolis, Ind., 1990), 153.

13. Lucette Valensi, *The Birth of the Despot: Venice and the Sublime Port*, trans. A. Denner (Ithaca, N.Y., 1993 [1987]).

14. See Jonathan Sheehan, *The Enlightenment Bible: Translation, Scholarship, Culture* (Princeton, N.J., 2005), 214–17.

15. Johann Hermann Riedesel, *Remarques d'un voyageur moderne au Levant* (Amsterdam, 1773), 166.

16. Johann Hermann Riedesel, *Bemerkungen auf einer Reise nach der Levante*, trans. C. W. Dohm (Leipzig, 1774), 131.

17. Joseph Pitton de Tournefort, *Relation d'un voyage du Levant*, 3 vols. (Paris, 1717), 2:173 (English: *A Voyage into the Levant*, trans. J. Ozell, 2 vols. [London, 1718], 1:348).

18. It is part of a larger project to relate these shifts in the interpretation of connectedness in general and Jewish connections in particular to larger developments, which have been characterized by Ian Coller as the "gradual displacement" of an early modern "vernacular" cosmopolitanism by an Enlightenment cosmopolitanism, which was, paradoxically, shaped by national exclusiveness. This process also affected the role of Greeks and Jews: "These intermediary groups of non-Muslims in Muslim society no longer represented natural allies or even commercial rivals, as they once did; they were now presented as figures of disempowerment and of corruption, precisely because of their intermediarity." Ian Coller, "East of Enlightenment: Regulating Cosmopolitanism between Istanbul and Paris in the Eighteenth Century," *Journal of World History* 21 (2010): 467.

19. Christian Wilhelm Dohm, *Über die bürgerliche Verbesserung der Juden*, vol. 1 (Berlin, 1781), 8.

20. Naphtali Herz Wessely, *Divre shalom ve-emet* (Berlin, 1782–85), chap. 7.

21. Ibid., part II: *Rav tuv le-Yisrael*, [fol. 3b].

22. Ibid.

23. For Farissol's ancient sources, see David B. Ruderman, *The World of a Renaissance Jew: The Life and Thought of Abraham B. Mordecai Farissol* (Cincinnati, Ohio, 1981), 134–36; for *Tla'ot Moshe*, its author and its sources, see Chone Shmeruk and Israel Bartal, "'Tla'ot Moshe'—The First Yiddish Geography Book and Description of the Land of Israel by R. Moses bar Abraham the Proselyte" (Hebrew), *Cathedra* 40 (1986): 121–37.

24. This nonnationalist vision of modern Europe is confirmed when Wessely speaks of a new openness and new initiatives concerning the emancipation of Jews across Europe: the Prussian, Austrian, French, and Russian kings and emperors are equally named as proponents of emancipation as a transnational European, enlightened project; Wessely, *Rav tuv le-Yisrael*, 30b–32a.

25. Johannes Fabian, *Time and the Other: How Anthropology Makes Its Object* (New York, 2002), 30–32.

26. Cecil Roth, *The Jew as European* (London, 1938), 6.

27. Ibid., 4.

28. Ibid., 5.

29. Ibid., 7.

30. Subrahmanyam, "Connected Histories," 748.

GIBBON'S JEWS

⌗ ⌗ ⌗

Dead but Alive in Eighteenth-Century England

David S. Katz
Tel Aviv University

THE first volume of Edward Gibbon's narrative of *The History of the Decline and Fall of the Roman Empire* (1776) quite naturally comes into the final stretch with a typically stirring if somewhat conventional discussion of Constantine's conquest of Byzantium in 324 C.E. Scholars are still perplexed by Gibbon's editorial decision to conclude this first volume with a deeply controversial attack on early Christianity, knowing full well that it would be a number of years—five, as it happened—before another volume would be published, taking up the tale of Constantine where he left off. The shocking and almost vindictive irony of those two apparently anti-Christian chapters 15 and 16 makes us forget that Gibbon also had a lot to say about the Jews there, views formulated against the background of contemporary perspectives regarding Judaism and living Jews in late eighteenth-century England.

I

"We have already described the religious harmony of the ancient world," Gibbon reminded his readers towards the beginning of chapter 15, "and the facility with which the most different and even hostile nations embraced, or at least respected, each other's superstitions." Sadly, he goes on,

A single people refused to join in the common intercourse of mankind. The Jews, who, under the Assyrian and Persian monarchies, had languished for many ages the most despised portion of their slaves, emerged from obscurity under the successors of Alexander; and as they multiplied to a surprising degree in the East, and afterwards in the West, they soon excited the curiosity and wonder of other nations. The sullen obstinacy with which they maintained their peculiar rites and unsocial manners, seemed to mark them out a distinct species of men, who boldly professed, or who faintly disguised, their implacable hatred to the rest of human-kind.

Gibbon is justly famous for his footnotes, which are not merely learned, but often more ironic, sardonic, and downright nasty even than the text which they illuminate. His footnote to the last sentence quoted above leads the reader to three lines from Juvenal's fourteenth satire, regarding "all that Moses committed to his secret tome, forbidding to point out the way to any not worshipping the same rites, and conducting none but the circumcised to the desired fountain." Gibbon admits that the "letter of this law is not to be found in the present volume of Moses" but "the wise, the humane Maimonides openly teaches, that, if an idolater fall into the water, a Jew ought not to save him from instant death."[1] Gibbon's source for this rather harsh recommendation is noted as the *Histoire des juifs*, first published by the Huguenot historian Jacques Basnage (1653–1723) at The Hague in 1706.[2] (Merely a secondary source, but accurate nonetheless.) Maimonides (1135–1204) in his *Mishneh Torah* (1170–80), *Sefer nezikim, rotseaḥ u-shmirat nefesh*, chapter 4, *halakhah* 11, does indeed instruct us that with regard to "a gentile idolater with whom we are not at war," although "we should not try to cause their deaths," nevertheless, it is "forbidden to save their lives if their lives are threatened. For example, if such a person fell into the sea, one should not rescue him."[3]

This opening salvo against the Jews is emblematic of Gibbon's historical technique. Where possible, he goes to the sources, not limiting himself to purely historical documents alone, which for him consisted of printed books. In areas beyond even his reach, Gibbon used the most reliable secondary sources of his day. In the case of Maimonides, Gibbon ended up getting it right, however repugnant the philosopher's advice. "The current of zeal and devotion," wrote Gibbon of the Jews, "as it was contracted into a narrow channel, ran with the strength, and sometimes with the fury, of a torrent."[4]

Deviating somewhat from his focus on the ancient world, Gibbon then offers up some general remarks about the history of the Jews and their proclivities:

This inflexible perseverance, which appeared so odious or so ridiculous to the ancient world, assumes a more awful character, since Providence has deigned to reveal to us the mysterious history of the chosen people. But the devout and even scrupulous attachment to the Mosaic religion, so conspicuous among the Jews who lived under the second temple, becomes still more surprising, if it is compared with the stubborn incredulity of their forefathers. When the law was given in thunder from Mount Sinai; when the tides of the ocean, and the course of the planets were suspended for the convenience of the Israelites; and when temporal rewards and punishments were the immediate consequences of their piety or disobedience, they perpetually relapsed into rebellion against the visible majesty of their Divine King, placed the idols of the nations in the sanctuary of Jehovah, and imitated every fantastic ceremony that was practised in the tents of the Arabs, or in the cities of Phoenicia.[5] As the protection of Heaven was deservedly withdrawn from the ungrateful race, their faith acquired a proportionable degree of vigour and purity. The contemporaries of Moses and Joshua had beheld with careless indifference the most amazing miracles. Under the pressure of every calamity, the belief of those miracles has preserved the Jews of a later period from the universal contagion of idolatry; and in contradiction to every known principle of the human mind, that singular people seems to have yielded a stronger and more ready assent to the traditions of their remote ancestors, than to the evidence of their own senses.

In any case, Gibbon continues, the "Jewish religion was admirably fitted for defence, but it was never designed for conquest":

When the posterity of Abraham had multiplied like the sands of the sea, the Deity, from whose mouth they received a system of laws and ceremonies, declared himself the proper and as it were the national God of Israel; and with the most jealous care separated his favourite people from the rest of mankind.

As a result, "that unsocial people" was disinclined with regard to "the admission of new citizens":

The descendants of Abraham were flattered by the opinion, that they alone were the heirs of the covenant, and they were apprehensive of diminishing the value of their inheritance, by sharing it too easily with the strangers of the earth. A larger acquaintance with mankind extended their knowledge without correcting their prejudices; and whenever the God of Israel acquired any new votaries, he was much more indebted to the inconstant humour of polytheism than to the active zeal of his own missionaries.[6] The religion of Moses seems to be instituted for a particular country as well as for a single nation; and if a strict obedience had been paid to the order, that every male, three times in the year, should present himself before the Lord Jehovah, it would have been impossible that the Jews could ever have spread themselves beyond the narrow limits of the promised land. That obstacle was indeed removed by the destruction of the temple of Jerusalem; but the most considerable part of the Jewish religion was involved in its destruction; and the pagans, who had long wondered at the strange report of an empty sanctuary, were at a loss to discover what could be the object, or what could be the instruments, of a worship which was destitute of temples and of altars, of priests and of sacrifices.

The fall of the Second Temple in 70 C.E. led to a complete restructuring of the Jewish people themselves:

Yet even in their fallen state, the Jews, still asserting their lofty and exclusive privileges, shunned, instead of courting, the society of strangers. They still insisted with
inflexible rigor on those parts of the law which it was in their power to practise. Their
peculiar distinctions of days, of meats, and a variety of trivial though burdensome
observances, were so many objects of disgust and aversion for the other nations, to
whose habits and prejudices they were diametrically opposite. The painful and even
dangerous rite of circumcision was alone capable of repelling a willing proselyte from
the door of the synagogue.[7]

Gibbon summarized the Jews and their history by quoting in a footnote the Highest
Authority, from Numbers 14:11: "How long will this people provoke me? And how
long will it be ere they *believe* me, for all the *signs* which I have shewn among them?"
To which Gibbon adds: "It would be easy, but it would be unbecoming, to justify the
complaint of the Deity from the whole tenor of the Mosaic history."[8]

In brief, Edward Gibbon was not very keen on Jews, past or present. As we
have seen, he was very careful about his sources, and the chief written authority on
Jewish history often cited in his footnotes was the aforementioned Basnage. Reading
Gibbon's footnotes gives the modern reader an intellectual MRI into his academic
mind. It is for this reason that the prodigious Gibbon scholar J. G. A. Pocock has
produced five substantial volumes in a great project to place Gibbon's masterpiece in
the evidentiary and cultural context from which it grew. Pocock fleshes out names
like Basnage and helps us understand how and why Gibbon chose to rely on particular authorities in the course of writing his monumental history of the decline and
fall of the Roman Empire.[9]

Professor Pocock was surely right in tracking down and studying the foundations
of Gibbon's scholarship that support his magnificent edifice. But there was a crucial
difference between the sources available to Edward Gibbon in eighteenth-century
England with regard to the ancient Romans as opposed to first-century Jews. The
Romans were dead and gone and no one thought that contemporary Italians had
much claim on their human legacy. The Jews, on the other hand, miraculously still
survived, and one of the consequences of this apparently divinely-bestowed gift was
that most people believed that to know a Jew in eighteenth-century England was
to gain an understanding of the essential character of their forebears who—despite
having witnessed the evidence of his divinity—had rejected Christ. The very visible
Jews in Gibbon's London were living historical fossils whose public image and actual social condition reflected inevitably on their ancestors in Palestine during Roman
times. Sadly, by and large it was not a pretty sight.

II

One point of near universal agreement between Christians and Jews in eighteenth-century England was the low quality of Anglo-Jewish life and culture, especially among the Ashkenazi community. Rabbis had to be imported from abroad,

and they were generally appalled by what they found when they arrived in London: no wonder that people like Gibbon held a poor opinion of Jewish communal society. When the venerable Rabbi Aaron Hart died in the spring of 1756, the Ashkenazim of the Great Synagogue turned to the son of the recently deceased Ashkenazi rabbi in Amsterdam, who took the job. Hirschel Levin duly Anglicized his name to Hart Lyon, came to London, and served his flock between 1756 and 1764, the entire period of the Seven Years' War. Rabbi Hart Lyon wasted no time, and shortly after his arrival told the congregation exactly what he thought of them. At an intercession service ordered by King George II in June 1757, speaking in Yiddish, quoting Aristotle, and praising the English government for their liberal treatment of the Jews, R. Lyon said that he came to

> warn you against the small sins you have fallen victims to. The shaving of the beard, a non-Jewish custom, strictly and repeatedly forbidden in our Torah . . . but you regard them as minor matters, not realizing that they are the pillars on which Judaism stands. You direct a non-Jewish servant to light the fire, to make fresh tea or coffee on Sabbath. Do not forget the punishment for this sin is that fire breaks out in your houses.

Rabbi Lyon on other occasions berated his Jews for collecting their mail at the Post Office on Saturday mornings and then asking passing gentiles to open the letters for them: "Although this is not forbidden," he explained, "I have heard that it is a scandal in the eyes of Gentiles." But even worse, he lamented,

> Day by day, we can see with our own eyes the decay of our people. We sin and act against the law of God; all our endeavours are to associate with the Gentiles and to be like them. That is the chief source of all our failings. See, the women wear wigs and the young ones go even further and wear décolleté dresses open two spans low in front and back. Their whole aim is, not to appear like daughters of Israel. On the one side we claim with pride that we are as good as any of our neighbours. We see that they live happily, that their commerce dominates the world, and we want to be like them, dress as they dress, talk as they talk, and want to make everybody forget that we are Jews . . . See where these thoughts lead you to, and how we live here. We dress on non-Jewish holidays better than on our own festivals; the Christmas pudding which the Christians prepare in memory of the Apostles is more favoured than the Mazzoth. Even the children call the non-Jewish feasts "Holy" days and do not seem to know that our holy day is the Sabbath. Soon they will come to regard the "Habdalah" service [on Saturday night] . . . as a sign for the beginning of the Sabbath.

Exasperated, Rabbi Hart Lyon declared, it "were better if you would read at least secular books instead of playing cards." He was disgusted with the fact that "instead of gathering in the houses of learning, people go to operas, plays, concerts, and clubs."[10]

It will come as no surprise that R. Hart Lyon eventually threw in the tallis. He opened negotiations with the Jewish community in Halberstadt in 1763 and abandoned London the following year. It was said that when Hart Lyon was asked why he was leaving, he replied that that question was the first religious inquiry he had ever received in England.[11] Seven years later, Hart Lyon was translated to Mannheim and finally to Berlin, where he served for about eight years before his death in 1800, becoming associated with Moses Mendelssohn and other luminaries of the Haskalah. Summing up his life's work, R. Hart Lyon supposedly remarked that in London he had money but no Jews; in Mannheim, Jews but no money; but in Berlin he had no money and no Jews either.[12]

Even taking into account a certain amount of clerical hyperbole, it is clear that Anglo-Jewry was somewhat of a disappointment to learned continental rabbis. Aaron Hart, the rabbi of the Ashkenazi Great Synagogue who died in 1756, was even acquainted with William Whiston's work on miracles, which he wordlessly took off a shelf and showed to a pesky gentile who invaded his study to harangue him on the subject of the messiah.[13] No wonder that eighteenth-century rabbis in England felt so annoyed at being stuck in a distant and lowly northern outpost of Jewish civilization.

Foreign rabbis might well compare the Jews in England with Jews they had known on the Continent and find Anglo-Jewry to be wanting in the balance. The native gentile English population (chiefly in London, where Gibbon lived for many years) had the opportunity to form their own impressions about the Jews and their general character. Unfortunately, what attracted their attention was the disproportionate link between the Jews and crime. More likely than not, the average London fence might be a Jew.

"The Jews are the most notorious receivers of stolen plate, and consequently the greatest encouragers of housebreakers in this kingdom," noted the *Newgate Calendar,* a six-volume compendium of eighteenth-century crime written by William Jackson. Just leafing through the books, any reader would be struck by numerous references to Jewish fences from 1700 onwards: "which they sold to the Jews on the following day," "and sold them to their old acquaintance, the Jews," and many more. The Jewish neighbourhood of Duke's Place was a Mecca for pickpockets and housebreakers, and everyone knew that as the place to go to turn stolen goods into ready cash.[14]

A typical deal went down like this one at the beginning of 1771. Luke Cannon and John Siday, two gentile thieves, brought their loot to a certain Moses Levi, a Jewish fence whose cover was "a dealer in old cloaths." Levi bought the stolen goods, consisting of "some valuable cloaths, and 650 ounces of plate, paying for it upwards of one hundred and seventy pounds in cash and a note." Levi in turn passed on the hot gold to another Jewish dealer named Joseph Jacobs, who like his father Lazarus was a fence. When the gang was discovered, tried and convicted, the two gentiles were hanged and Moses Levi transported for fourteen years, but the other Jew was acquitted having made "very artful defences."[15]

Apart from fencing stolen goods, late eighteenth-century London Jews were so associated with a scam called "Queer Bail" that it was also commonly known as "Jew

Bail." As one contemporary crime expert reported, "Hounds-ditch and Duke's Place furnish the King's-Bench and Old-Bailey with Jewish geniuses ready for all cases." A typical Jew Bail con went like this:

> A Jew was lately examined, in order to *justify bail* in the King's-Bench. The Counsel demanded, "what street he live in, and what shop he kept?" He replied, "Houndsditch; but he kept no shop." "How was his property vested?" "In monies." "Where is it vested?" "I have it about me." He then pulled out a small pocket-book, which handing to one of the Judges, he said, "If your Lordship will take the *throubles,* (for I don't want to *throuble* your Lordship or the Court) to open dat book, you'll find I have properties enough."—His Lordship opened the pocket-book, and finding in it Bank-bills to the amount of three or four thousand pounds, ordered the Bail to be taken. Moses at his going out of Court, meets another Brother-Jew, to whom he returns the pocket-book, and so the Bail is justified; and is what is called *Jew-Bail.*[16]

Another type of swindle with which Jews were commonly associated was even more complex, as William Jackson explains:

> One of them hires a house, and appears as a merchant of great credit and importance; while his accomplices get credit of any one who is weak enough to trust them, and give bills on the supposed merchant. These bills are generally received without suspicion; for previous enquiry having been made respecting the character and circumstances of the merchant, no doubt of either remains; and these impostors proceed for a long time, undetected.

According to Jackson, among "the number of these atrocious offenders, the Jews have been principally concerned; and it is not unfrequently that a Jew merchant is the acceptor of the false bills; but the acceptor is never to be found when the day of payment arrives."[17]

Jews were not traditionally associated with violent crimes, but unquestionably the most notorious Jewish crime of eighteenth-century England was the Chelsea Murders of 1771, an armed robbery that went very wrong. The leader of the gang of eight Jews was a physician named Levi Weil, who had studied at the University of Leiden, and now, with his brother, brought over a group of Dutch Jews to assist him in crime. They began with a number of successful house-breaks, and intended to carry on with their well-tried methods at the home of Mrs. Elizabeth Hutchins in Chelsea. The robbers forced their way into the house on the evening of June 11, 1771, overpowered the maidservants and Mrs. Hutchins, and then upstairs murdered one of the manservants in his bed, while another servant who lay with him at the time made his escape through the window, pursued by bullets. The gang left the house soon afterwards, carting away a considerable quantity of plunder, and at least sixty-four guineas in cash. They were caught a few months later and hanged by the end of the year.[18]

The Chelsea murders rebounded onto the Anglo-Jewish community as a whole and reinforced an already criminal stereotype. "A Jew could scarcely pass the streets but he was upbraided with the words 'Hutchins' and 'Chelsea,'" it was said, "and many of them were pulled by the beards; while those, who ought to have taken the insulters into custody, stood calmly by, and triumphed in the insult."[19] The social activist Francis Place gives a very striking description of the public mood against the Jews immediately after the Chelsea murders:

> Every Jew was in public opinion implicated, and the prejudice, ill will and brutal con-
> duct this brought upon the Jews, even after they had been detected and punished for
> it, did not cease for many years. "Go to Chelsea" was a common exclamation when a
> Jew was seen in the streets and was often the signal of assault. I have seen many Jews
> hooted, hunted, cuffed, pulled by the beard, spit upon, and so barbarously assaulted
> in the streets, without any protection from the passers-by or the police, as seems when
> compared with present times, almost impossible to have existed at any time. Dogs
> could not be used in the streets in the manner many Jews were treated.[20]

One newspaper reported just before the trial began at the Old Bailey that within "these few days a great number of Jews have left the kingdom."[21]

That being said, any intelligent and decently-connected Englishman such as Gibbon knew that nevertheless there were some prominent Jews whose company was sought, and who could be seen in polite society. There was Samson Gideon (1699–1762), the Jewish stock-jobber who very nearly got a peerage for himself, and, by converting his son to Christianity, procured him a baronetcy at age thirteen which would evolve into a proper title as Lord Eardley thirty years later.[22] One could also point with pride to Joseph Salvador (1716–1786), who was a central figure in government finance, and very much involved with Clive and the East India Company, though he was not a director, as has sometimes been claimed. Salvador was also the main instigator behind the creation of what became the formal representative of Anglo-Jewry, the Board of Deputies of British Jews.[23] One might even make a claim for Jewish intellectual life in eighteenth-century England by praising the writings of Moses Marcus (b. 1701), who engaged in learned polemics with important scholars.[24] There was also David Levi (1742–1801), who managed to provoke a written debate with Joseph Priestley.[25] But the critical mass was too low to alter substantially the rather negative stereotype of Jews and Judaism in eighteenth-century England.

Foreign visitors to England might well understand a social system that placed Jews under heavy political and financial liabilities and even made them fear some-times for their very survival. But they were flummoxed by the English solution of giving full rights to Anglican men with landed property and excluding most anyone else, lumping together Jews and many Christians in some things and subdividing the have-nots in a nebulous hierarchy of disability. It was hard to call the English anti-Jewish when clearly they were anti so many other groups of people as well. But eighteenth-century Anglo-Jewry did not help themselves by being linked to so many negative and often well-founded images.

III

Which brings us back to Edward Gibbon. Apart from his historical writing, Gibbon was not particularly concerned about Jews. His correspondence includes references to Jews, but mostly they are fairly mild and only conventionally offensive. When selling his house in 1733, he was able to reject a churlish offer when Lord "Temple acted like a Jew, and I dare say now repents of it."[26] At the end of the same year, he was to be found retailing a witticism declared by a debtor who proclaimed that the man who had offered to pay what he owed "is a second Messiah" because he was "born for the destruction of the Jews."[27] This meager fare hardly marks Gibbon down as having an excessive interest in Jews, let alone anti-Jewish sentiments in general.

As for contacts with actual Jews, there was one he held in great respect, his step-mother's physician, Philip de la Cour (c.1710–80), MD (Leiden, 1733), licentiate of the Royal College of Physicians, 1751.[28] Dr. de la Cour lived in Bury Street, London, but spent a good deal of time living and working in Bath.[29] "Are you acquainted with Dr. Delacour?" Gibbon wrote to a friend in the spring of 1778 from Bath, "In truth there is much kindness in that Jew and much good sense likewise; he gives as good dinners as the superstition of the females of his family will permit, and has a proper contempt for all that a reasonable man ought to despise."[30] Philip de la Cour was a spa physician to the rich and famous, yet despite their social intercourse, when the doctor died, Gibbon referred to his passing as "the Jew's departure."[31] Gibbon and de la Cour might eat together, but one should not exaggerate any notion of social equality.

The equation of biblical Israelites with contemporary Jews was not peculiar to Edward Gibbon, nor did it end with him. Indeed, the belief that one could gain an insight into the world of the Bible by studying the habits and lifestyles of modern Jews only grew stronger in the following century (and in some Evangelical circles has never died). In Victorian England, Benjamin Disraeli would lump together all Semitic populations, arguing that "Arabs are only Jews upon horseback."[32] The great biblical critic William Robertson Smith (1846–94) would study Bedouin tribes to learn about the home life of the patriarchs.[33] The continuity between Israelites and Jews is still a mainstay of Jewish belief, and Gibbon for all his general historical skepticism accepted this genealogical axiom.

When the question of Jewish readmission was debated in Cromwellian England a century and a quarter previously, the noble Sephardi Jews of Amsterdam looked a lot better than the Jewish fences and house-breakers who created the negative stereotype of the Jews of Georgian England. There were good Jews too, and Gibbon was in close contact with at least one of them, his stepmother's physician. But the negative image of the Jews still prevailed, and when Gibbon came to write his famous chapters 15 and 16 of the *Decline and Fall*, he could not but extrapolate back-wards to ancient Rome his judgment of the Jews as "a distinct species of men, who boldly professed, or who faintly disguised, their implacable hatred to the rest of human-kind."[34]

Notes

1. Edward Gibbon, *The History of the Decline and Fall of the Roman Empire*, ed. D. Womersley (London, 1994), 1:447–48.

2. [Jacques] Basnage, *Histoire des Juifs* (2nd ed.; The Hague, 1716), in fifteen octavo vols., translated with Basnage's praise for its accuracy (I.iii–iv) as *The History of the Jews* (London, 1708). Gibbon's reference of I.vi.c.28 is corrected by his Everyman editor (1910) Oliphant Smeaton to I.v.c.24.

3. אבל עובדי כוכבים שאין בינינו ובינם מלחמה ורועי בהמה דקה מישראל וכיוצא בה אין מסבבים להן המיתה ואסור להצילן אם נטו למות כגון שראה אחד מהן שנפל לים אינו מעלהו שנאמר לא תעמוד על דם רעך. ואין זה רעך:

4. Gibbon, *Decline*, 1:448.

5. At this point, Gibbon adds a very curious footnote: "For the enumeration of the Syrian and Arabian deities, it may be observed that Milton has comprised in one hundred and thirty very beautiful lines, the two large and learned syntagmas, which Selden had composed on that abstruse subject."

6. Always careful to show his sources, Gibbon appends a footnote here to reiterate that "All that relates to the Jewish proselytes has been very ably treated by Basnage, *Histoire des Juifs*, I. v. c. 6, 7."

7. Gibbon, *Decline*, 1:448–51.

8. Ibid., 1:449n. Gibbon has some more unpleasant things to say at the end of chapter 37 about Jews in seventh- and eighth-century Spain.

9. J. G. A. Pocock, *Barbarism and Religion* (Cambridge, 1999–2011). Pocock looks carefully at Gibbon's fifteenth and sixteenth chapters in the fifth volume, subtitled "Religion: The First Triumph," part III. He mentions Gibbon's references to Jews on pp. 249–52.

10. Jewish Theological Seminary, New York City, MS Adler 1248, 84 fos., including most of Hart Lyon's sermons in London. I have not seen this, but relied on the translation in C. Duschinsky, "The Rabbinate of the Great Synagogue, London, from 1786–1842," *JQR* (n.s.) 9 (1918–19): 103–37, 371–408; 10 (1919–20): 445–527; 11 (1920–21): 21–81, 201–36, 345–87: here 11 (1920–21): 109–23. This long article was printed in book form as well (London, 1921) and repr. 1971.

11. Quoted, without source, by Cecil Roth, *The Great Synagogue* (London, 1950), 121.

12. Duschinsky, "Great Synagogue," *JQR* 11 (1920–21): 130–37.

13. Edward Goldney, *Epistles to Deists and Jews* (London, 1759), v, viii, 6–13, 165–76. Cf. Goldney, *A Friendly Epistle to the Deists* (London, 1760), 5–7.

14. William Jackson, *The New and Complete Newgate Calendar* (London, [1795]), 2:147, 147 n., 148, 149. Cf. 2:388, 391; 3:96, 163, 167, 168, 169; 4:81, 133. For a chapbook dramatization of Jewish avarice, see *The Northern Lord; Or, the Cruel Jew's Garland* (Hull, [c.1785]).

15. Jackson, *Newgate*, 5:15.

16. G. Parker, *A View of Society and Manners in High and Low Life* (London, 1781), 2: 21–23.

17. Jackson, *Newgate*, 3:998.

18. For the Chelsea murders, see esp. ibid., 5:17–25 and *London Chronicle*, 2335 (Nov. 28–30, 1771): 527; 2337 (Dec. 3–5, 1771): 544; 2338 (Dec. 5–7, 1771): 551–52; 2339 (Dec. 7–10, 1771): 557–59; 2340 (Dec. 10–12, 1771): 568. Other sources include *Gents. Mag.* 41 (1771), 518, 521, 566; Andrew Knapp and William Baldwin, *The New Newgate Calendar* (London, 1826), 3:282; R. Leslie-Melville, *The Life and Work of Sir John Fielding* (London, 1934), 261–64. An important primary source is PRO, State Papers 37/8. See also Todd M. Endelman, *The Jews of Georgian England* (Philadelphia, 1979), 198–202.

19. Jackson, *Newgate*, 5:23.

20. Brit. Lib., Add. MS. 27287, fols. 145–46: quoted in Mary D. George, *London Life in the Eighteenth Century* (New York, 1964), 132. Place also suggests that the appearance of Jewish boxers such as Daniel Mendoza in the 1780s helped to change this, for he "set up a school to teach the art of boxing as a science, the art soon spread among the young Jews and they became generally expert at it. The consequence was in a very few years seen and felt too. It was no longer safe to insult a Jew unless he was an old man and alone."

21. *London Chronicle* 2337 (December 3–5, 1771), 544.

22. Generally, see John Eardley Wilmot, "A Memoir of the Life of Samson Gideon," in John Nichols, *Illustrations of the Literary History of the Eighteenth Century* (London, 1817–58), 6:277–84; John Francis, *Chronicles and Characters of the Stock Exchange* (London, 1849), 88–91; L. S. Sutherland, "Samson Gideon: Eighteenth Century Jewish Financier," *Transactions* 17 (1953): 79–90; Sutherland, "Samson Gideon and the Reduction of Interest, 1749–50," *Economic History Review* 16 (1946): 15–29; Albert Montefiore Hyamson, *The Sephardim of England* (London, 1951), 128–33.

23. Generally, see Maurice Woolf, "Joseph Salvador, 1716–1786," *Transactions* 21 (1968): 104–37.

24. See most notably David B. Ruderman, *Connecting the Covenants: Judaism and the Search for Christian Identity in Eighteenth-Century England* (Philadelphia, 2007), especially chaps. 1–4.

25. See David S. Katz, *The Jews in the History of England, 1485–1850* (Oxford, 1994), 296–300; and Richard H. Popkin, "David Levi, Anglo-Jewish Theologian," *JQR* 87 (1996): 79–101.

26. Gibbon to J. D. Itolroy, June 12, 1773: *Private Letters of Edward Gibbon*, ed. R. E. Prothero (London, 1896), 1:186 = Letter 170.

27. Gibbon to J. B. Holroyd, December 16, 1773: *Private Letters*, ed. Prothero, 1:198 = Letter 181.

28. William Munk, *Roll of the Royal College of Physicians of London* (London, 1878), 2:178.

29. *Court and City Register* (London, 1760), 226; Joan Lane, "The Medical Practitioners of Provincial England in 1783," *Medical History* 28 (1984): 353–71, esp. 360.

30. Gibbon to J. B. Holroyd, April 25, 1778, from Bath: *Private Letters*, ed. Prothero, 1:336 = Letter 345. Cf. Gibbon's other references to Philip de la Cour: Gibbon to his stepmother, October 16, 1775, from Bentinck Street: *Private Letters*, ed. Prothero, 1:272–73 = Letter 267; same to same, n.d. [1778], from the House of Commons: *Private Letters*, ed. Prothero, 1:337 = Letter 346 [apparent reference].

31. Gibbon to his stepmother, May 30, 1781: *Private Letters*, ed. Prothero, 1:399 = Letter 416. Philip de la Cour is also mentioned in a letter by Thomas Gray to Horace Walpole, September 8, 1756: Horace Walpole, *Correspondence*, ed. W. S. Lewis, et al. (New Haven, Conn., 1937–83), 14:93.

32. Benjamin Disraeli, *Tancred, or, the New Crusade* (London, 1847), chap. 32.

33. W. R. Smith, *Lectures on the Religion of the Semites. First Series. The Fundamental Institutions* (2nd ed.; London, 1894).

34. Gibbon, *Decline*, ed. Womersley, 1:447–48.

THE "HAPPY TIME" OF MOSES MENDELSSOHN AND THE TRANSFORMATIVE YEAR 1782

❄ ❄ ❄

Shmuel Feiner

Bar-Ilan University

MOSES Mendelssohn (1729–86), the Jewish enlightened philosopher from Berlin, was not a particularly optimistic person. He was rather dubious about what his contemporary, Immanuel Kant, for example, regarded as a fundamental principle of the Enlightenment and the ethos of modernity, the ability of humans, as rational beings, to change, to reject prejudice and to cast off their dependence on the representatives of authority and tradition. Mendelssohn had little faith in a future in which the values of humanism, morality, and reason would guide behavior. He believed that under every stone "barbarism" was awaiting the chance to raise its head and impose on people the shackles of religious coercion and civil oppression—to rob them of their dignity and to mock the optimistic dreams of the Enlightenment project.[1]

But in the winter of 1782, this skeptical philosopher was for a short while swept up with enthusiasm. In the first week of January, Nathan, his and Fromet's youngest son, was born, and received into the family with great love and joy. Only five days earlier the Edict of Toleration, signed by the Emperor Joseph II, had been published in Vienna, arousing great hopes and expectations, and, a few weeks later, at the end of January, Naphtali Herz Wessely's far-reaching program for the transformation of Jewish education was printed in Berlin. "Thank kind Providence," Mendelssohn shared his feelings with his readers, "that I live to see yet, in my old days, the happy time (*diesen glücklichen Zeitpunkt*), when the Rights of Man are beginning to be taken to heart, in their true extent."[2] From his vantage point in the capital of Prussia, then under the rule of Frederick II, he witnessed the progress of several processes so historically significant that it seemed they might, after all, signal a revolutionary change. At this historical juncture, Mendelssohn observed with heightened curiosity:

> Both Lessing and Dohm, the former a philosophical poet, the latter a philosophical statesman, conceived the grand aim of providence, viz. the destination of man, conjointly with the rights of man. And, at the same time, an admirable monarch not only followed the same principles, but also formed a plan commensurate to his vast sphere of action, the carrying into execution of which seems to require more than human powers.... I live in a country, in which one of the wisest sovereigns that ever ruled over men made the arts and sciences flourish, and rational liberty of thinking become so universal, that the effects thereof extend to the humblest inhabitant of his realm.[3]

However, Mendelssohn's "happy time" was relatively brief. When he read Johann David Michaelis's critique doubting that Jews were capable of integrating into the state, and arguing that their religion, lowly moral character, and faithfulness to the messianic vision of a return to the Land of Israel would make it impossible to ever trust the Jews as loyal citizens, it shook Mendelssohn's confidence in the possibility of authentic change. In early February 1782, when he read the full text of the Edict of Toleration for the Jews of Vienna, he began even to doubt Joseph II's true intentions.[4]

Still, the feeling that something was happening induced him to write a boldly challenging text, which was known as the *Preface* (*Vorrede*) to the German translation of *Vindiciae Judaeorum,* the seventeenth-century apologetic work on Judaism written by the Amsterdam rabbi, Menasseh ben Israel. It would be no exaggeration to describe the *Preface* as a radical text in which, for the first time, Mendelssohn set forth a vision for a new structure for Jewish life, and called upon the rabbinical leadership to relinquish its supervisory authority. It was Dohm's revolutionary work, *Concerning the Amelioration of the Civil Status of the Jews,* that roused Mendelssohn to write the *Preface.* Dohm demanded that the state fundamentally change its attitude to the Jewish minority and take responsibility for the transformation of the Jews.[5] Dohm referred to the Jews as an individual case of a fundamental issue—to which the Enlightenment's campaign of religious tolerance applied—and in doing so broke new ground. Now, Mendelssohn proclaimed with unconcealed emotion, the problem of the anomalous existence of the Jews is becoming a test case for the viability of the ideas of the eighteenth-century Enlightenment. The discourse of religious polemics had been replaced by a discourse on human rights:

> It is not of the vindication of Judaism, or the Jews either, that he [Dohm] wants to write. He merely conducts the cause of mankind, and defends their rights. And fortunate will it be for us, if that cause becomes at once ours; if there be no such thing as urging the rights of mankind without at once claiming ours. The philosopher of the eighteenth century takes no notice of difference of dogmas and opinions, he beholds in man *man* only.[6]

Sadly, however, this optimistic text of Mendelssohn's was immediately torn to shreds. The anonymous response by August Cranz, one of the cleverest spokesmen from the second rank of the German Enlightenment, shattered even the most modest of Mendelssohn's expectations. Cranz, who found in Mendelssohn's concept of tolerance a challenge to Judaism, stated that religious tolerance clashed with the Jewish religion and its commandments. He called on the Jewish philosopher to acknowledge the contradiction and deny his religion. On June 12, the anonymous article, "The Search for Light and Right" (*Das Forschen nach Licht und Recht*), came out, and Mendelssohn learned that his advocacy of religious tolerance was wrongly understood as a step towards conversion to Christianity. Cranz countered even Dohm's main argument with the claim that the Jewish commandments, which raise high walls between Jews and non-Jews, are an obstacle in the way of granting Jews citizenship. Indeed, Cranz wrote, this is a "happy time" now that the dawn is rising on a world illuminated by the sunlight of tolerance. He described the process toward citizenship as gradual, and only realizable if Mendelssohn will lead the great revolution of annulling the commandments that stultify the Jews and make it impossible for them to be accepted as citizens. Moreover, Cranz informed the German Enlightened community that the mask had fallen off Mendelssohn's face. If until now he had hidden his true views, in his *Preface*, the real Mendelssohn, who distanced himself from the "religion of his forefathers," has been revealed.

And if this were not enough, as soon as Mendelssohn wrote his *Preface*, the persecution of his friend and collaborator, Wessely, began. In his 1782 *Divre shalom ve-emet*, Wessely had criticized traditional education and proposed that it be replaced by a modern Jewish school, a suggestion that aroused an organized protest by the rabbinical elite. Similar to the way members of the German Enlightenment began to doubt the sincerity of Mendelssohn's Jewish identity, rabbinical circles began to suspect that Wessely was trying to undermine the foundations of Judaism. On top of all this, Mendelssohn was still angered by the excommunication of Netanel Posner, a freethinking, fashionable Jew, by Raphael Kohen, the rabbi of the Altona community—a scandal that continued to reverberate from its origins in the north of Germany in the last months of 1782. Kohen, who regarded himself as the guardian of the religious powers of the rabbinical elite, attempted to dissuade members of his community from breaching religious norms and defying the rabbis.[7] Once again, the fulfillment of the Enlightenment seemed to Mendelssohn farther off then ever before. Nevertheless, it is not possible to blot out the significance of this happy period, or to ignore the sense of a historical shift that stirred his emotions.

The importance of the 1780s, including the story of Jewish modernization, has not escaped the notice of historians, and much attention has been devoted to these two great episodes of the decade: Joseph II's legislation as an introduction to the emancipation of European Jewry and Wessely's proposal to reform Jewish education as the onset of the Haskalah. Jacob Katz, in his *Tradition and Crisis*, singled out this decade as the point of the shift. Like many historians who preceded him, Katz ascribed the great change to Mendelssohn, the hero of the modern era, and to his reception in the society of German scholars who were indifferent to his religious identity. In Katz's view, that moment in the social history of the Jews was the apogee of the crisis of traditional society. The openness of the "neutral society" in Germany enabled a significant change in the relations between Jews and their environment and the overthrow of the existing barriers.[8]

David Ruderman, who has suggested a periodization that draws a line between the early modern age and the modern age, was even more precise in observing the importance of the year 1782. In this article I want to support that claim, to enrich the picture of that special year and to follow its major trends. However, that transformative year was not only a milestone on the way to the social emancipation and integration of German Jews as Katz presented it. Nor did it mark the end of one historical era (the early modern age) as Ruderman argued. Rather, it brought to fruition dramatic historical processes that had begun at the turn of the seventeenth and eighteenth centuries. Without John Toland's 1714 essay on the granting of citizenship to the Jews of Britain, Gotthold Ephraim Lessing's 1754 play *The Jews,* and the 1753 controversy in England over the Jew Bill, for example, it is difficult to understand Joseph II's edicts of toleration. And without the early Haskalah of Raphael Levi of Hanover or Israel of Zamosc and Mendelssohn's pioneering Hebrew periodical *Kohelet musar,* it would be impossible to understand Isaac Euchel, the founder of the Haskalah movement and its innovative periodical, *Hame'asef.* In general, although the processes of Jewish secularization, which also shaped profound processes of change and posed a challenge of far-reaching changes to the religiously faithful, matured both in practice and in thought at the end of the eighteenth century, these processes were in fact firmly rooted in earlier decades.[9] The events in 1782 were more complex and meaningful than the advent of the Haskalah in Germany and the reformist legislation in Austria. The most significant revolution took place less on the level of relations between the Jews and the state, and more in the rise of new trends and the emergence of modern projects within Jewish society and the drawing of boundaries between various Jewish groups. By paying a visit to this special, transformative year and closely observing it we can become familiar with the rise of cultural and social conflicts among European Jews and appreciate the intensity of the dramatic revolutionary trends that emerged at the time.

In 1782 there were no more than two million Jews in the world, about three-quarters of them in Europe, where the largest Jewish population lived in Poland (a segment of them already under the rule of Russia, Austria, and Prussia). While fewer than one hundred thousand Jews were dispersed throughout the German states, several intense processes, of significance to the coming generations, occurred there.[10] Two interesting reports can help us to look at the situation of the Jews in Europe. The first is that of Abraham Triebesch, the chronicler from Moravia who wrote in *Korot ha'itim* (1801) about the events of the 1780s with particular enthusiasm. He regarded two events as especially important: the expansion of the Jewish library, on the domestic front, and political changes in the states of Central Europe in the external sphere. Drawing a distinction between the two competing elites, that of the rabbis and that of the *maskilim*, Triebesch noted with pride that the Jewish library was enriched by erudite rabbis of the likes of Jonathan Eybeschütz, Ezekiel Landau, Pinḥas Hurwitz and Raphael Kohen, and by "great intellects" such as Naphtali Herz Wessely, Isaac Satanow, and Moses Mendelssohn. At the same time, extraordinary rulers had emerged on the stage of European politics, in particular the Emperor Joseph II.[11] However, in Triebesch's view, this decade also marked the decline of religion due to increasing state intervention in Jewish life. The demand for modern education, fluency in the language of the state, and a limitation on religious jurisdiction were all signs that "the religion was dwindling and losing its place of honor."[12]

The second vantage point is that of Wessely, whose audacious program for modern Jewish education was based on a broad view of the Jewish situation in this transformative period. In 1782 he also shared in the great expectations of the Emperor in Vienna, and believed that a historical shift was taking place before his and his contemporaries' eyes. His was a more far-reaching view than Triebesch's, and he was far more optimistic than Mendelssohn. He believed that all of humankind would in the future undergo a transformation that would remove all religious conflicts from the world and place humanity upon a path of tolerance, peace between states, and love of one's fellow man. Wessely regarded Joseph II's policy of toleration as a historical event comparable to the invention of printing and the discovery of America. The rhetoric he employed in speaking of the Emperor was no less than messianic: "In this generation you have seen that God has created a great man who helps men…, His Excellency Joseph II."[13] This was the culmination, Wessely believed, of a process that had matured over a period of at least two centuries, from the time when Holland and England opened their gates to Jews. In the countries of the Holy Roman Empire, it was the rulers of Prussia who introduced a policy of freedom and tolerance before all other states. Wessely heaped lavish praise on Friedrich II, ignoring his selective legislation that discriminated against the Jews in Prussia.[14] Convinced that considerable change was taking place in the Jews' situation, Wessely drew a distinction between those Jews in the Diaspora who were still living, as he put it, in the past, and those who were already living in the present and poised for the future. In his view, Berlin, the city where he lived, was an exception in the Ashkenazic world. Its Jewish community heralded the future, and as a resident of Berlin he was able to turn to the Jews in Europe and suggest that they construct their lives based on that model.

When we turn our gaze from Vienna and Berlin to other places in Europe, we find different trends. At the very time when faith in the supernatural was being subjected to the criticism of reason and various processes of secularization were accelerating, belief in magic was growing stronger and religious leaders were gaining influence and prestige: Kabbalah was on the ascendancy and its books were being widely distributed in numerous copies; Hasidism was on the rise in Poland-Lithuania and the polemic against it was being conducted in heated religious rhetoric. For example, when advocates of the Haskalah were crossing the border from Poland to the German states to satisfy their desire for secular knowledge and to join the Enlightenment project of the Jews, in 1781, one of these, Isaac Halevi Satanow, crossed the border in the opposite direction and returned to Poland for a short time. Satanow was an autodidact who came to Berlin from Galicia, and later managed the modern printing house (*Die orientalische Buchdruckerei*) of the German *maskilim*. He arrived in Koritz, in the Ukraine, where he established one of the great projects of kabbalistic literature in the modern era.[15] In 1782 he printed two manuscripts, *Ets hayim* and *Peri ets hayim*, by R. Hayim Vital, the disciple of R. Isaac Luria Askenazi, the Ari.[16] These works, printed with the agreement of kabbalist circles from Brody and Ostra and the participation of several close associates of the first hasidic leader, the Baal Shem Tov, fostered the spread of Kabbalah and the emergence of Hasidism. Until this time, Lurianic Kabbalah, as it was passed down to future generations by Vital, was mainly esoteric and elitist. But hereafter, these fundamental texts from sixteenth-century Safed, previously studied in manuscript by only a few, became canonical holy books accessible to many. The mission proposed by the *Ets hayim* proved inspiring to its students. Not only did the mystical language instill religious life with a spiritual significance beyond the study of the Torah and the observance of the commandments, but men were called upon to play an influential role in a fascinating dialogue conducted between the upper and lower worlds.[17]

In 1782, the Koritz press also printed *Tsafnat pa'aneah*, one of the first hasidic books and the last work of R. Yaakov Yosef of Polnoye, who died that year. The book developed the doctrine of the *tsadik*, or spiritual leader, which would become the basis for the legitimacy of the hasidic leadership. It concerns primarily the devotion (*devekut*) of the masses to the *tsadikim*, which enables even those of a low spiritual level to achieve, through the mediation of the leader, a religious experience of closeness to God. However, stress on the loftiness and mission of the *tsadik* had a negative effect on the status of the non-hasidic elite, the talmudic scholars. A polemical tone was set between the new, aspirational, religious elite and the established rabbinical leadership. For example, when R. Yaakov Yosef of Polnoye wanted to show the corruption of the rabbinical elite and how its members were pursuing wealth and departing from the true worship of God, he actually compared them to whores: "for he is like the whore who when she lies with her husband, her thoughts stray to the foolish matters of the adulterers . . . thus the students while they study commit adultery with the wealthy in their thought and the wealthy commit adultery in every one of their business negotiations, thinking those thoughts when they study Torah and pray."[18]

It is no wonder that this humiliating criticism infuriated the *mitnagdim* and that the publication of these books revived their fighting spirit which had died down somewhat in the previous decade. The Vilna Gaon was the driving force behind the persecution of the *hasidim* in 1772, and the effort to oust them from normative Judaism (as a sect that threatened the foundation of religion in general and the ethos of Torah study in particular), was largely dependent on his special status in Lithuania. In the summer of 1781, handbills were again printed, serious threats were made, and the nascent hasidic movement was persecuted as a dangerous heretical sect.[19] Voices of anxiety and frustration rose from the handbills and letters. The rhetoric was fiery, and the accusations grave. The belief of the *mitnagdim* that they were facing a great heresy increased their sense of danger, and gave rise to an urgent need to block the influence of the hasidic leadership. In their eyes, they were waging no less than an existential war. In the course of 1782, this second anti-hasidic campaign died down at last, the struggle to be revived only in the next decade.

In Berlin, however, relatively little was known about what was happening among the Jews in the communities of Ukraine and Lithuania. In fact, among the Berlin *maskilim* there was a growing tendency to cut themselves off from these communities. It was the philosopher Solomon Maimon who significantly contributed to raising a wall between the Jews of enlightened Germany and those of "backward" Poland. Maimon himself underwent several cultural conversions in his lifetime. The first was very brief, when he became enthused by what he initially heard about Hasidism; the second conversion lasted much longer and brought him to the philosophy of the Enlightenment. After he immigrated to Germany he became one of the harshest critics of Polish Jewry. In 1782 Maimon was in Berlin, and there, as he noted in his revealing autobiography, he experienced a spiritual rejuvenation. At the very same time Satanow left Berlin for the Ukraine to print books on Kabbalah, Maimon arrived there, where he read the works of Leibniz, Locke, and Spinoza and developed into a freethinker who did not hesitate to write and express his skeptical ideas. Maimon met Moses Mendelssohn, and their relationship was one of mutual respect. Mendelssohn encouraged him and "was very surprised that a Polish Jew who had had only a glimpse of Wolf's metaphysics, understood it in such depth that enabled him to question his conclusions."[20]

In Berlin and Königsberg, the two main centers of the emerging Jewish Enlightenment, a cultural revolution was then already on its way. Three formative texts, Wessely's *Divre shalom ve-emet*, printed in January of 1782, Mendelssohn's *Preface* written in March, and *Naḥal ha-besor*, which in December announced the founding of the Jewish Enlightenment movement, provide an insight into the importance of 1782 as a transformative year.

Divre shalom ve-emet was a provocative text; it was an open letter proposing that Jewish education be based on both the "teaching of God" and the "teaching of man," and calling upon the Jews to respond favorably to Joseph II's initiative. On the one hand, it gave the Haskalah a program and ideology, and, on the other, it launched the first *Kulturkampf*. Thus, it had a direct effect on the line drawn between the rabbinical leadership and modern Jewish intellectuals. It called for far more than just the establishment of modern schools; it purported to transform traditional fundamental values and called attention to flaws in the Jewish leadership in Germany and Poland and to the failure of traditional education. Wessely's steadfast faith in the dramatic historical shift being witnessed by his generation induced him to embark on a subversive path, circumventing traditional authority and attempting to mobilize Jewish public opinion to support his program. He saw himself suffering from the serious decline in the status of Jews in the world, and shared with his readers his sense of inferiority and his desire to restore respect for the Jews. This goal, which for decades had motivated the early *maskilim*, now was translated into an agenda. In his public critical treatise, Wessely employed Enlightenment rhetoric time and again to assail those responsible for the historical negligence in Jewish education: graduates of traditional Jewish schools were cut off from essential general knowledge about the world and were like "those slumbering in the intoxication of stupidity." Adopting universal knowledge would not only provide knowledge outside the boundaries of the religious culture, but would also totally change patterns of thought: "they will accustom their thoughts to think in every matter with reason and not with vain imaginings, nor will they believe the foolish prattle of women or strange, wondrous tales told to them."[21] Reactions to Wessely were extreme and major rabbis hastened to defend their status and the system of values they believed in. On March 23, Rabbi Ezekiel Landau of Prague, in a sermon on *Shabat ha-gadol*, denounced Wessely as an "evildoer who has dared to say that the Torah is worth nothing and a carcass is better than learners of Torah," identifying him as a dangerous heretic who denied the Jewish faith.[22]

On March 19, 1782, when Mendelssohn completed his *Preface* to the German translation of Menasseh ben Israel's *Vindiciae Judaeorum*, the furor over *Divre shalom ve-emet* had not yet erupted. A few days later, however, he became deeply involved in the *Kulturkampf*. The *Preface* contained Mendelssohn's position on religious toler- ance, so it is not surprising that the attack on Wessely was immediately interpreted as a serious violation of that principle. Mendelssohn had tried to persuade Dohm that he had erred in his program to rehabilitate the Jews by failing to abolish the authority of religious communal autonomy. Mendelssohn did not conceal his fear that the right to exercise religious punishment would be abused: "I can imagine no possibility of bridling false religious zeal," he wrote, "as yet there is not a clergy sufficiently enlightened that such a right (if it exists at all) may be entrusted to them without any harm." Very concerned, Mendelssohn turned then to the rabbis asking them to relinquish that authority voluntarily.[23] It seems he had never before allowed himself to speak out as bluntly as he did in early 1782. Then, in the mood of the "happy times," he condemned the behavior of rabbis like Raphael Kohen of Hamburg who persisted in persecuting Jews who deviated from the norms of the religion. "Alas! It will require ages yet, before the human race shall have recovered from the blows which those monsters inflicted on it,"[24] Mendelssohn wrote in an- ger about the domination of the religious establishments.[25] He defended his Berlin colleague, Wessely, not only behind the scenes, but he also joined the deist David Friedlander in a threatening letter sent by them and five other Berlin Jews on May 5 to the Lissa community, whose rabbi, David Tevely, was one of Wessely's most vociferous critics. In the letter, they demanded that the community punish the rabbi, and threatened, if they didn't comply, that they would be silenced by the rulers of the state.[26] Fortunately, Mendelssohn wrote in a private letter on June 11, that, while in Poland Jews were inciting against Wessely, in Germany, "the enlightened group" (*der vernünftigere Theil der Nation*) among the Jews was vigorously supporting him. He did not hesitate to point to the "bad part of the nation" (*der schlechtere Theil der Nation*), to express his identification with Wessely as a member of the German group (*deutscher Mitbrüder*), and to denounce the threats of excommunication issued against him "from all sides in Poland."[27] Mendelssohn's recognition of the deepening chasms within Jewish society between Poles and Germans, and between "fanatics" and "the enlightened," is telling. Apparently, it was at this moment he realized that a *Kulturkampf* was erupting.

The year 1782 ended with another formative document: *Naḥal ha-besor*, signed by the founders of the Jewish Enlightenment movement *Ḥevrat Dorshe Leshon 'Ever* (Society for the Promotion of the Hebrew Language), headed by Isaac Euchel, a young *maskil* from Copenhagen who was then a student of Immanuel Kant. This document was the declaration of independence of the movement, which was first founded as a local circle in Königsberg, Prussia on December 11, 1782. After two early generations of *maskilim*, the Haskalah grew to maturity, and that slim pamphlet heralded the establishment of the modern Jewish literary republic.[28] In an effort to resolutely separate the new model of the Haskalah's periodical from existing religious models a line was drawn between the religious literature for which the rabbinical elite was responsible and the modern, non-religious literature that the maskilic elite was promoting was intended to create a modern network of communication linking the *maskilim* and enhancing their ability to exert influence. *Naḥal ha-besor* was a mobilizing document that proclaimed the opening of the movement's ranks to anyone interested in joining and contributing to cultural rejuvenation. It addressed young Jews in particular, but rested on the achievements of the veteran *maskilim*. On December 26, the *Ḥevrah* (Society for the Promotion of the Hebrew Language), sent Wessely a letter informing him of its establishment and its plan to publish a Hebrew periodical. This unexpected letter imbued Wessely with a sense of success, one he badly needed at the end of that turbulent year.[29] He encouraged the initiative of the young *maskilim*, and depicted them as pioneers bringing the light of Enlightenment to Jewish society.[30]

But this was not the only perspective on the meaning of this year. In 1782, R. Judah Leib Margolioth of the Buzanow community followed all these events and texts from afar. When in Königsberg, Euchel outlined the program of the Haskalah movement, Margolioth published in Poland his book of science *Or 'olam*.[31] He was only a few years older than Euchel, and although he already tended to regard the Haskalah favorably, this book could hardly be part of the Haskalah project. Margolioth was attracted to the sciences, and, like early *maskilim* at the start of the century, was aware that the "wisdom of science" had been neglected in Jewish culture. He wanted to remedy that. But his book conveys a double message. His nearly erotic passion for science is restrained by his deep fear that the Haskalah might have destructive consequences, and he portrays the wisdom of science as inferior to the wisdom of Torah.[32] For Margolioth, too, 1782 was a transformative year, but its significance was different. He decided to halt at the entrance to contemporary Haskalah, to withdraw from the early Haskalah, and to become a resolute opponent to Mendelssohn, whom he knew and admired. Mendelssohn's *Preface* alarmed him. While Mendelssohn advocated a Judaism that eschews religious coercion, Margolioth believed that coercion was one of the fundamentals of the Jewish religion. While Mendelssohn opposed Dohm's proposal that the Jewish community should continue maintaining the right to punish those who strayed from religious norms, Margolioth supported Dohm's position. And when, in reaction to Cranz's criticism, Mendelssohn proposed that a distinction should be made between universal religious beliefs and those specific to Judaism, Margolioth argued that such a division has no basis in the Jewish religion, as it only encourages heresy and religious permissiveness. While *Naḥal ha-besor* voiced an optimistic expectation that the gates of knowledge and rejuvenation would be opened, Margolioth sensed an oncoming crisis and foresaw an utterly bleak future for talmudic learning. "Where are my brothers?" he asked, "in the past I knew them and they were the choicest young men, but the study of philosophy has turned them into haters of the Torah and its scholars… My heart mourns for those who lost their way, and [today] there is no one who can rescue them from their abandonment."[33]

If we look at the history of modern Jewish culture as a chessboard, in 1782 most of the pieces were already laid out on the board: *maskilim*, freethinkers, rabbis fearful of change, the modern school, the teachers attempting to replace the *melamed*, the followers of Hasidism and its opponents, the revivers of Kabbalah and rational philosophers, those rebelling against the authority of the community and those who demanded religious discipline and obedience. This is when the *Kulturkampf* erupted and marked the new boundaries being drawn through the heart of Jewish society. Trends that were just emerging decades earlier now matured. In 1782 the various labels—the boundaries—between the different groups and the topics that ignited controversy and struggle were clearly fixed. The *mitnagdim* were able to identify the *hasidim*, the rabbis could single out the *maskilim* and the freethinkers, and the "Germans" could spot the "Poles." Yet, evaluations at that time were not strictly predictable. When, for example, R. Hirschel Levin ran away from his home during the height of the Wessely affair, abandoning the Berlin community, he left a letter in which he identified those he held responsible for undermining the community's stability ("Some new men have arrived who have found allies to vilify their religion"). Yet his son, a rabbi in his own right, was a supporter of the Enlightenment project, defended the proposal for modernizing Jewish education, and subverted the authority of the rabbinical elite of which he and his family were an integral part.[34]

And where was Moses Mendelssohn at the end of that turbulent year? Over a period of several months, Mendelssohn, who in his *Preface* was thankful for having been privileged to see the inception of the humanist revolution led by philosophers and statesmen, now felt disillusioned by the impediments to eradicating "barbarism." On June 25, about two weeks after the great insult he had suffered from Cranz's pamphlet, *The Search for Light and Right*, he wrote to his friend August Hennings in Copenhagen that he did not believe in historical progress but rather in a process marked by digressions and retreats, which he compared to the walk of a crane (*Krahnengang*).[35] This pessimism as to the ability of the human race to make progress was expressed that summer when he began to write *Jerusalem*. Anyone observing history as it is, he argued, will easily discover that God did not plan a march of progress: "Now, as far as the human race as a whole is concerned, you will find no steady progress in its development that brings it ever closer to perfection. Rather do we see the human race in its totality slightly oscillate; it never took a few steps forward without soon afterwards, and with redoubled speed, sliding back to its previous position."[36] While individual man is capable of progressing in his life toward perfection, history fluctuates like a pendulum and the human race as a whole is like a man climbing ladders and sliding down poles. Reality only occasionally shows a change for the better, but retreat is inevitable: "Mankind continually fluctuates within fixed limits, while maintaining, on the whole, about the same degree of morality in all periods—the same amount of religion and irreligion, of virtue and vice, of felicity and misery." From the vantage point of the end of 1782, at the height of the Cranz, Wessely, and Posner affairs, Mendelssohn reviewed his "happy time" as no more than a fleeting meteor: "Now and then a dot blazes up in the midst of the great mass, becomes a glittering star, and traverses as an orbit which now after a shorter, now after a longer period, brings it back again to its starting point, or not far from it."[37]

Translated from the Hebrew by Chaya Naor.

Notes

1. On Mendelssohn, see among others: Alexander Altmann, *Moses Mendelssohn: A Biographical Study* (Philadelphia, 1973); Allan Arkush, *Moses Mendelssohn and the Enlightenment* (New York, 1994); David Sorkin, *Moses Mendelssohn and the Religious Enlightenment* (London, 1996); Shmuel Feiner, *Moses Mendelssohn: Sage of Modernity*, trans. A. Berris (New Haven, Conn., 2010); Michah Gottlieb, *Faith and Freedom: Moses Mendelssohn's Theological-Political Thought* (Oxford, 2011).

2. Moses Mendelssohn, *Vorrede, Menaseh Ben Israel Rettung der Juden*, in Mendelssohn, *Gesammelte Schriften* 8 (Stuttgart, 1983), 3; "Mendelssohn's Preface to *Vindiciae Judaeorum*," in *Writings Related to Mendelssohn's Jerusalem*, trans. M. Samuel (London, 1838), 77.

3. Mendelssohn, *Preface*, 78–79

4. Altmann, *Moses Mendelssohn*, 462–63

5. Christian Wilhelm von Dohm, *Über die bürgerliche Verbesserung der Juden*, I-II (Berlin, 1781, 1783).

6. Mendelssohn, *Preface*, 80.

7. Shmuel Feiner, *The Origins of Jewish Secularization in Eighteenth-Century Europe*, trans. C. Naor. (Philadelphia, 2011), 163–70.

8. Jacob Katz, *Tradition and Crisis, Jewish Society at the End of the Middle Ages*, trans. B. D. Cooperman (New York, 1993 [1961]), chap. 23.

9. Feiner, *Jewish Secularization.*

10. Jacob Katz, ed., *Towards Modernity: The European Jewish Model* (New Brunswick, N.J., 1987).

11. Abraham Triebesch, *Korot ha'itim* (Brünn, 1801), para. 56.

12. Ibid., para. 54, 57.

13. Naphtali Herz Wessely, *Divre shalom ve-emet* (Berlin, 1782), chap. 4.

14. Wessely, *Rav tov livne Yisrael* (Berlin, 1782), 24–25, 30–31.

15. Shmuel Werses, "Isaac Satanow and His Work, *Mishle Assaf*," in idem, *Trends and Forms in the Haskalah Literature* (Hebrew; Jerusalem, 1990), 163–86; Moshe Idel, "Perceptions of Kabbalah in the Second Half of the Eighteenth Century," *Journal of Jewish Thought and Philosophy* 1 (1991): 55–114.

16. R. Ḥayim Vital, *Sefer 'ets ḥayim* (Koritz, 1782); R. Ḥayim Vital, *Sefer peri ets ḥayim* (Koritz, 1782). See Chaim Lieberman, *Ohel Rachel* 3 (New York, 1984), 35–59.

17. *Peri 'ets ḥayim*, author's introduction.

18. Yaakov Yosef HaKohen, *Sefer Tsafnat pa'aneaḥ* (Koritz, 1782), 15:1.

19. Mordecai Wilensky, *Hasidim and Mitnaggedim: A Study of the Controversy between Them in the Years 1772–1815* (Hebrew; Jerusalem, 1970), 103–4.

20. Salomon Maimon, *An Autobiography*, trans. J. C. Murray (Chicago, 2001), 214–15.

21. Wessely, *Divre shalom ve-emet*, chap. 4.

22. Yehezkel Landau, *Derushe hatselaḥ* (Warsaw, 1886), sermon 39.

23. Mendelssohn, *Preface*, 111–15.

24. Ibid., 112.

25. Ibid., 103–4.

26. Feiner, *The Jewish Enlightenment*, trans. C. Naor (Philadelphia, 2002), chap. 6.

27. Mendelssohn, letter to Wolf Dessau, in Mendelssohn, *Gesammelte Schriften* (Stuttgart, 1977), 13:68–71.

28. *Naḥal ha-besor* (Königsberg, 1782).

29. *Naḥal ha-besor*, 4.

30. Ibid., 5–6.

31. Judah Leib Margolioth, *Sefer or 'olam* (Nowidwor, 1782).

32. Ibid.

33. Judah Leib Margolioth, *Sefer 'atse 'eden* (Frankfurt on the Oder, 1802), 16:2.

34. Saul Levin, *Sefer ketav yosher* (Berlin, 1794). See Feiner, *Jewish Secularization*, chap. 11.

35. Mendelssohn, *Gesammelte Schriften*, 13:64–66.

36. Moses Mendelssohn, *Jerusalem, or on Religious Power and Judaism*, trans. A. Arkush (Hanover, N.H., 1983), 96.

37. Ibid., 97.

A TALE OF THREE GENERATIONS

❈ ❈ ❈

Shifting Attitudes toward Haskalah, Mendelssohn, and Acculturation

Sharon Flatto
Brooklyn College,
The City University of New York

DRAMATIC changes swept over Prague's Jewish community during the last decades of the eighteenth century. State legislation transforming the political status of the community, beginning with the abolishment of its autonomy in the 1781 *Toleranzpatent,*[1] led to increasing acculturation. Concurrently, maskilic forces, which migrated from Berlin in the 1770s, challenged the traditional educational, religious, and social norms of the community.[2] The official sanction of the Absolutist Habsburg monarchy's innovations, coupled with the internal infiltration of maskilic ideas, threatened to undermine the Jewish community's most basic values.

The scholarly studies of this period have underestimated the trenchant initial response of Prague's leading rabbis to these maskilic goals and even to various state imposed changes. Consequently, they have also overlooked the striking turnabout of the second and third generation of these same Prague rabbinic families, who later embraced these very developments.[3] Yet it is precisely in the story of these Prague families' ongoing leadership where the full drama and complexity of the acculturation process during these transitional years is acutely manifest. In this regard, the experience of Prague's community differs considerably from those of other prominent Jewish communities elsewhere in Central and Western Europe, which have received the bulk of scholarly attention. In most Ashkenzic communities, the acculturation of rabbinic figures led to their diminished communal involvement. This, however, was not the case in Prague. Its principal rabbinic families underwent significant acculturation without a complete dissolution of their authority. Only the terms of their involvement changed.[4]

R. EZEKIEL LANDAU—PATRIARCH

The larger than life founder of Prague's leading rabbinic dynasty was Ezekiel Landau (1713–1793), the Noda' bi-Yehudah, a towering halakhic authority and major rabbinic figure in his time.[5] Having attained a profound mastery of the corpus of Jewish literature, his counsel in legal and communal matters was sought by a wide spectrum of scholars and laity.

Landau's astounding erudition coupled with fine diplomatic skills led him to be appointed Chief Rabbi of Prague (1754–93), one of the largest and most influential eighteenth-century Jewish communities. He served in this post and as the official head of Bohemian Jewry for nearly forty years. In these roles, he was in frequent contact with the Habsburg monarchs, Maria Theresa (1717–80) and Joseph II (1741–90), and immediately felt the larger impact of their policies. Given his prominence during this transitional period, he was one of the first rabbinic authorities to contend with the challenges posed to traditional culture by both the state and Enlightenment. Various scholars have misinterpreted Landau's accommodations of certain of these trends as a sign of endorsement, when in actuality he was critical of these innovations which he sometimes had no choice but to accept.[6]

Joseph II's legal edicts, beginning in 1781 and lasting the entire decade, aimed at the systematic Germanization of Habsburg Jewry. The most effective of these was the decree that all children receive a secular education and that large communities establish government supervised *Normalschulen* (modern elementary schools).[7] Due to his conservative stance, Landau insured that Prague's Jewish *Normalschule,* which opened in 1782, was limited in scope, offering classes only in the afternoon to children ages eleven to thirteen.[8] He further negotiated that primarily practical skills, such as German grammar, reading, and arithmetic—not Hebrew or Jewish subjects —be included in the curriculum. Landau thereby secured that the majority of a pupil's day and school years would be devoted to Jewish studies taught at the *ḥeder* and *yeshivah* controlled by the rabbis. By establishing a rigid separation between Judaic and secular studies, the *Normalschule's* influence was limited. Nevertheless, even the few hours spent there, with its scant offerings, detracted from time traditionally devoted to Torah.[9]

Exacerbating the threat to Prague's traditional curriculum was the increasing influence of Berlin's *maskilim.* During the last decades of the eighteenth century, their teachings made inroads into Prague. These *maskilim* supported the Habsburg's educational and cultural reforms, which intersected with many of their own aims, especially the promotion of secular studies and knowledge of the vernacular. One of the principal vehicles used to foster the latter goal was Mendelssohn's German Pentateuch translation, published along with the maskilic commentary, the *Biur* (Berlin, 1783).[10]

THE HASKALAH AND MENDELSSOHN

Landau's response to the Haskalah and this translation project has been widely debated. Moses Samet claimed that "Landau did not oppose the Haskalah *at all*."[11] Alexander Altmann argued that Landau did not disapprove of Mendelssohn or the use of his translation until secularization had made "serious inroads" into Prague in the "wake of Joseph II's educational reforms."[12] A Russian archival collection of Landau's writings, made public in recent years,[13] as well as numerous other sources from his era, indicate otherwise.

Although Landau never mentioned Mendelssohn in his published sermons, he referred to him in various approbations, letters, and talmudic glosses, written not long after Joseph II's reforms. In a 1782 letter to Berlin's Chief Rabbi Zevi Hirschel Levin, he responds to Mendelssohn's call to rabbis to rescind their authority to excommunicate,[14] exclaiming that "Mendelssohn is an apostate, heretic, and informer."[15] He continues that if he could verify that Mendelssohn had indeed published these ideas, he would admonish all Jews to distance themselves from Mendelssohn and his followers. Samet, and then Altmann, insisted that this letter, which they had never seen firsthand, must be a forgery since it is "not in accord" with everything else known about Landau.[16] While this letter is admittedly sharp in tone, it is in line with Landau's other caustic critiques of various *maskilim* and Mendelssohn's translation.

An account of Landau's extreme denunciation of both Mendelssohn and his translation is reported in an article by the Prague-born rabbi and historian Gutmann Klemperer (1815–1884). There, he wrote that a contemporary of Landau relayed that the latter issued a curse on Mendelssohn's translation during a *Shabat ha-Gadol* sermon, delivered just before Passover. He became so agitated while discussing the matter that his fur cap nearly fell off his head.[17] Although this and other anecdotes recorded by Klemperer are hearsay, it is possible that, living only decades later, he encountered individuals who witnessed these events. If his account is true, it would constitute the first evidence of Landau's explicit denunciation of Mendelssohn in a sermon.

Landau's published condemnations of Mendelssohn's Pentateuch project are found in other literary genres. The first appears in his talmudic commentary on *Berakhot,* written around 1783.[18] After two ensuing years of silence, he again comments on this translation, in a 1785 approbation for Sussmann Glogau's more literal German Pentateuch. He asserts that he prefers Glogau's translation since Mendelssohn's "forces the youth to spend their time reading gentile books in order to become familiar with high German." He continues that while Mendelssohn's intentions may have been good the results "are devastating."[19] This approbation was soon published and mocked on the pages of the maskilic journal *ha-Me'asef.*[20] Half a year later, he reiterated these reservations in an approbation for another work competing with Mendelssohn's translation, Solomon Dubno's Pentateuch edition. There he claimed that Mendelssohn's translation "will be an obstacle for Jewish children," leading to the "neglect of Torah study."[21] Notwithstanding these critiques,[22] he did not ban Mendelssohn's translation.[23]

With no ban in place, and with the increasing Germanization of Prague Jewry, Mendelssohn's translation gained popularity in Prague.[24] In 1783, Mendelssohn recommended to the overseer of Prague's *Normalschule*, the priest Kindermann, that his translation, which had admirers in Prague, be sold at the local bookstore supplying the primary school.[25] Standing in the way of these efforts, however, was the *Normalschule's* limited curriculum, negotiated by Landau. No maskilic texts, including Mendelssohn's, could be taught there during his tenure.[26]

In many ways, Landau's second controversy concerning maskilic projects was even stormier. It centered around the *maskil* Naphtali Herz Wessely's (1725–1805) 1782 publication of *Divre shalom ve-emet* (Words of Peace and Truth).[27] Here, Wessely famously argues that *torat ha-adam* (= teachings of humanity, an expression he uses for secular studies) is a prerequisite for studying divine law. He further suggests that only gifted pupils, who *choose* to, should advance to talmudic studies. This proposal was obviously unacceptable to most contemporary rabbis. Landau headed the opposition.

The Russian archival collection shows that Landau attacked Wessely not only in public sermons,[28] but in various letters sent to European rabbis. In the first of these, written to a rabbi in Vienna, he relates that were it not for government restrictions he would issue a ban against this heretic.[29] He further requests the assistance of nearby communities, including Pressburg and Nicholsburg, to garner support for his denunciation.

Landau, however, was not categorically opposed to all secular scholarship. In halakhic matters he was willing to consult with those knowledgeable in science, and occasionally he gave approbations for books addressing history, science, and mathematics. What drove his opposition was that, like many Ashkenazic rabbis, he believed the focus of study should be almost exclusively Talmud and *halakhah.*

Wessely's proposed educational reforms, which would give priority to secular studies, were consequently reprehensible to Landau. In a well-publicized attack he laments, in a 1782 sermon, that "an evil man" has arisen, who impudently asserts that "etiquette is more important than Torah."[30] While Landau is quick to censure Wessely's program, he takes care not to criticize Joseph II's utilitarian educational initiatives.

Landau's condemnation of maskilic projects did not end here. In the introduction to his commentary on *Berakhot* (published in 1791), he defended the *aggadah* (rabbinic legends) which he stated is harshly critiqued "by the *asafsuf* (riffraff) in our midst."[31] Although the use of the biblical term *asafsuf* seems innocent enough,[32] given the content of his remarks and the year in which they were written, he is clearly riffing on the maskilic journal, *ha-Me'asef,* and its contributors, *ha-me'asefim.*

Sensing Landau's antagonism, the *maskilim* turned him into a symbol of intransigent rabbinic opposition to cultural change. From the late 1780s until after Landau's death, numerous *maskilim,* including David Friedländer, Isaac Euchel, and Marcus

Herz, vilified Landau on ha-Me'asef's pages.[33] They especially lampooned his conservative views on early burial and Mendelssohn's translation. Samet argued that the maskilic adoption of Landau as an "anti-Haskalah" icon has biased scholarship's views of his response to Mendelssohn and the Jewish Enlightenment.[34] The sources suggest that their portrayal of Landau was no accident.

Landau's harsh view of Mendelssohn, and by extension of the Haskalah, is reflected, in an ironic manner, in a eulogy for Landau entitled *Alon Bakhut* (Prague, 1793). It was composed by the *maskil* Joseph Ha'efrati, who lived in Prague during the 1790s. The eulogy's title page contains a portrait of Landau and Mendelssohn embracing in the Garden of Eden.[35] The text's body, a lengthy description of the imaginary reconciliation between these two figures in the afterlife, suggests Ha'efrati's recognition that Mendelssohn never secured Landau's approval during his lifetime.

THE NEXT GENERATION: R. SAMUEL LANDAU

After Landau's death, his son Samuel (ca. 1750–1834), whose influential career and writings remain virtually unexamined in academic scholarship, became a preeminent leader in Prague. Beginning in 1794, he served on Prague's rabbinical court,[36] and in 1826 was appointed its *Oberjurist* (president), a post he held until his death. Since the state eliminated the Chief Rabbinate after Ezekiel's death, this position made Samuel the effective leader of Prague Jewry. Educated at his father's yeshiva, Samuel also succeeded him as its director (*rosh yeshiva*). In these posts, Samuel, like his father, responded to numerous halakhic queries, many of which appear in his *Shivat Tsiyon* (Prague, 1827). A substantial number of others are included in his father's *responsa* collection, the *Noda' bi-Yehudah.*[37]

In his youth, Samuel affiliated with the *Gesellschaft der jungen Hebräer* (Society of Young Hebrews),[38] the maskilic circle in Prague.[39] There are also reports that the *Zylinder Hut* (top hat), which symbolized progressive education, was worn at his yeshiva just as it was at the study house (*bet midrash*) of the moderate leader of Prague's Haskalah, Baruch Jeitteles.[40] In later years a few of his letters were also published in *ha-Me'asef*. Minimally, this demonstrates his interaction with *maskilim*.[41] Other writings point to his direct promotion of maskilic projects.

In contrast to his father's vehement opposition to Mendelssohn's Pentateuch translation, in the early 1780s Samuel was one of the initial subscribers to its first edition.[42] Remarkably, by 1816 Samuel advocates, in a sermon, that parents use Mendelssohn's translation to teach children both Torah and correct German. He advises that, "one should start teaching a boy Torah in the holy tongue along with a German translation, as found in the Pentateuchs published in Berlin, Vienna and Prague."[43] Samuel is almost certainly referring to Mendelssohn's translation here, which was published in Berlin (1783), Vienna (1808), and Prague (1801, 1807). Notably, this endorsement stands in stark contrast with his father's harsh condemnation, and also with the stance of one of the leading voices of his generation, the Chief Rabbi of Pressburg, R. Moses Sofer (1762–1839). In fact, the *Hatam Sofer*'s censure of Mendelssohn was so intense that he included the directive: בספרי רמ"ד על תשלחו יד (Do not touch [i.e., study] Mendelssohn's works) in his ethical will to his children.[44]

Samuel's embrace of aspects of Wessely's curricular program is also remarkable. Similarly to Wessely, he endorses changing the traditional *order* of study, recommending that at the early age of six or seven a child should already be introduced to German and secular subjects. Fathers, he implores, must "ensure that their sons succeed in both Torah and *derekh erets*" (lit. way of the land).[45] Strikingly, Samuel's use of the phrase *Torah im derekh erets* in order to designate Torah and secular studies, a later motto for Neo-Orthodox Judaism, predates Samson Raphael Hirsch's (1808–1888) use of this slogan by several decades.[46] Certainly, Samuel's advocacy of teaching young boys secular disciplines alongside Torah study is a far cry from the limited permission granted by his father for secular instruction. And even that was only begrudgingly conferred as a concession to the state.

Echoing Wessely, Samuel also radically argues that only gifted pupils pursue talmudic studies and that this significant choice be given to the student. When a child with intellectual promise reaches age twelve, he should decide "whether to devote himself to secular disciplines or Talmud."[47] In line with Wessely, Samuel tries to limit the number of adults whose full time pursuit is talmudic study. Allowing talented students to focus solely on secular disciplines would have been appalling to his father.

Samuel also supported another central maskilic goal: the study and revival of Hebrew.[48] He recommended using Mendelssohn's translation not only as a tool for teaching German but also for proper Hebrew. Along the same lines, he stresses the importance of teaching children the Pentateuch in Hebrew, the language "spoken by God," and not from the recently published abridged German Bibles.[49] Similarly, despite halakhic leniencies in this area, he insists that Jews continue praying in the Divine tongue.

To illustrate Hebrew's significance, Samuel—in maskilic fashion—refers in a sermon to a 1721 epistolary novel by Montesquieu. "The French scholar Montesquieu in his book *Lettres Persanes* (*Igeret Parsi*) makes a praiseworthy argument, explaining that the Jews' ability to survive in the Diaspora is their continued use of the holy language."[50] Notably, Samuel cites non-Jewish sources to promote his goals, a tactic used by both Wessely and other *maskilim*. Surely, Samuel knew that this method was already under rabbinic attack.[51]

In advancing Hebrew, Samuel, like various *maskilim,* also endorses the publication of secular Hebrew books. In 1824, he gave an approbation for *Shvile 'olam,* a Hebrew book on the geography, history, and culture of Africa and Asia, writing that its appealing content will foster the study of Hebrew. He laments that while the number of gentile scholars who make an effort "to elevate the holy tongue has increased . . . the opposite has occurred to the children of Israel. Among us there are people whose entire purpose is to destroy and cause the Hebrew language to be forgotten among the youth."[52] The publication of secular Hebrew works, he maintains, will help to rectify this calamity of the Jews' dwindling knowledge of Hebrew.

Notwithstanding Samuel's support of the maskilic ideals of secular study and reviving Hebrew, and that he himself had a maskilic son,[53] one cannot classify him solely as a *maskil* or modernizer. On many issues, including his attitudes toward gentiles and the use of the vernacular, he had much more conservative views than most *maskilim*. Further, in numerous areas, particularly those relating to religious reform, which he addressed during the last decades of his life, he was an arch traditionalist. Did his orientation change over the course of the years from a more open to a more conservative stance? Did the ground beneath him simply shift?[54] Or was it a combination of both?

THE THIRD GENERATION:
FROM RABBIS TO COMMUNAL LEADERS

The next generation of Prague Jewry was led by the progressive grandson and nephew of Ezekiel and Samuel Landau, Moses (1788–1852). Born a year before the French Revolution and living through the 1848 revolutions and the careers of Goethe and Schiller, Moses embodied many values of the Enlightenment and Romanticism.[55] Like his grandfather and uncle, Moses headed several Prague Jewish institutions. But he was involved in neither Prague's rabbinic court nor its rabbinic academies.

Instead, he held positions in various educational, political, religious and communal institutions. In 1823, he became the *dritte Gemeindeälteste* (third representative) of the Jewish community's board of directors, and, in 1834, its president. In many senses, this position rendered him the head of Prague's Jewish community. Ironically, considering his family history, in 1819 he was appointed the superintendent of Prague's Jewish *Normalschule*, an institution his grandfather had only reluctantly accommodated. Moreover, beginning in 1809, when Samuel was Prague's second rabbinic judge, and continuing throughout Moses' tenure as the *Normalschule* superintendent, the school broadened its curriculum to include Hebrew language and texts, changes Ezekiel Landau had explicitly opposed.[56] In 1815, the *Normalschule*'s hours were extended, another policy rejected by his grandfather. Assuming tasks which had previously been under the direction of Prague's rabbinate, Moses also established a Jewish orphanage in 1835, and remained its overseer until his death. Toward the end of his career (1849), the Jewish community chose him to serve as the *stadtverordneter* (alderman) to the city parliament, and in 1850 he was elected to the *Stadtrath* (municipal council).[57]

MOSES AND THE HASKALAH

Moses collaborated in various maskilic projects, especially through the Hebrew press he established in 1827 and ran for over twenty years. During this time, he also contributed to the maskilic Hebrew-literary annual, *Bikure ha-'itim,* which succeeded *ha-Me'asef*.[58] When it was discontinued in 1832, he published several volumes of the subsequent maskilic journal: *Kerem Ḥemed*.[59]

In another act of familial betrayal, from 1833 to 1837 Moses published a twenty-volume Bible, which included Mendelssohn's German Torah translation. This multi-volume work also contained the *Biur* and Mendelssohn's introduction to the Pentateuch. Strikingly, Moses enhanced Mendelssohn's project by providing his *own* German translation for various biblical books not originally translated by Mendelssohn, such as Joshua and Judges (1833), Isaiah (1837), and Job (1836). He also assigned a variety of *maskilim* to translate other biblical books. As if these infidelities were not enough, toward the beginning of the work the publication included an essay and poem praising Mendelssohn's Pentateuch—by his grandfather's arch nemesis, Wessely![60]

Moses also spent much of his scholarly energy studying and promoting Hebrew. Both Jewish and gentile scholars viewed him as an authority on Hebrew language and approached him with various linguistic inquiries.[61] He paid tribute to Hebrew in his book on its status during the rabbinic period. This work on Hebrew, composed —ironically, particularly given his grandfather's views—in German is entitled *Geist und Sprache der Hebräer nach dem Zweiten Tempelbau* (Prague, 1822).

Moses perpetrated grander acts of "disloyalty." He composed and published German poetry and other *belles lettres*,[62] including a short poem extolling Mendelssohn. He dramatically proclaims: "Mendelssohn! You taught immortality—the most Divine teaching. What you taught was your eternal reward" [i.e. Mendelssohn has become immortal].[63] This paean to Mendelssohn's legacy is a sharp departure from his grandfather's scathing critique of the philosopher, specifically of Mendelssohn's promotion of German for non-utilitarian purposes. In many ways, Moses' interests and writings about German literature were the embodiment of his grandfather's fear that soon Jews would study German works as ends in themselves, thereby impeding their singular focus on Torah.

Having no children of his own, Moses' numerous intellectual, communal and cultural contributions are what he bestowed to Prague Jewry as a legacy for the Landau family name.

CONCLUSION

To what can we attribute these seismic generational shifts? From the end of the eighteenth century to the beginning of the nineteenth century Prague's landscape had altered dramatically due to Habsburg legislation. Nineteenth-century leaders faced formidable challenges which hardly existed in the previous generation. In the post-*Toleranzpatent* world, Jews were given educational and cultural opportunities previously unimaginable.[64] While Ezekiel Landau was trying to stop the dam of acculturation from opening (which he perhaps mistakenly attributed more to the spread of German rather than the Habsburg state), Samuel and Moses lived during the deluge of government-endorsed changes.

Instead of just holding on, these second and third generation leaders advanced a novel conception of Judaism, which was enhanced, not weakened, by secular study and Enlightenment ideals, such as the importance of knowing high German,

Hebrew grammar, and studying secular subjects at the onset of one's schooling. Samuel advocated the motto of "Torah and *derekh erets*" from an early age, instead of simply limiting secular studies to utilitarian pursuits. Moses, too, promoted the inclusion and expansion of Jewish studies at the secular *Normalschule*, a divide his grandfather fought bitterly to maintain. By endorsing an ideology which embraced both Torah and *derekh erets*, knowledge of German and the revival of Hebrew, traditional learning and Haskalah, they succeeded in remaining powerful leaders during this era of irreversible transformation. Out of the crucible of maintaining traditional faith in an ever changing world, these Jewish leaders posited the benefits of wedding rabbinic learning with Enlightenment values. Espousing a transitional ideology enabled these second and third generation leaders to be respected and effective.

Scholarship's neglect of late eighteenth-century Prague's flourishing traditional culture and influential rabbinate caused the dramatic evolution in its leaders' reaction to acculturation and Haskalah to be overlooked. Assertions by scholars that Ezekiel Landau was somewhat open to Haskalah are inconsistent with the wide array of sources in which he strongly censures Mendelssohn, various maskilic projects, and an emphasis on secular studies. In contrast, the second and third generation members of the Landau family supported the study of German and secular disciplines, Mendelssohn's translation, and the ideals of the Haskalah, while still promoting traditional Jewish values and texts and assuming leadership positions within Prague's Jewish community. Although afforded increased opportunities to integrate into Prague's wider intellectual and cultural *milieu*, second and third generation Landaus devoted most of their efforts to guiding the Jewish community— Samuel, as the president of its prominent rabbinic court and yeshiva, and Moses, as a Hebrew book publisher and the head of the Jewish *Normalschule* and numerous administrative councils.

The acculturation of the Landau patriarchs over three generations, alongside their simultaneous retention of a strong family identity as communal leaders, presents us with a unique response to modernity.

Notes

1. On Joseph II's *Toleranzpatent* and later reforms, see, for example, T. C. W. Blanning, *Joseph II and Enlightened Despotism* (Harlow, 1970); Alfred Pribram, ed., *Urkunden und Akten zur Geschichte der Juden in Wien* (Leipzig, 1918), 1:494–500; Derek Beales, *Enlightenment and Reform in Eighteenth Century Europe* (London, 2005).

2. On the Haskalah in Berlin and elsewhere see, for example, Shmuel Feiner and Israel Bartal, eds., *The Varieties of Haskalah* (Hebrew; Jerusalem, 2005); Shmuel Feiner and David Sorkin, eds., *New Perspectives on the Haskalah* (Oxford, 2001); David Sorkin, *The Berlin Haskalah and German Religious Thought: Orphans of Knowledge* (London, 2000); Olga Litvak, *Haskalah: The Romantic Movement in Judaism* (New Brunswick, N.J., 2012). On Prague's Haskalah, see Kestenberg-Gladstein, "The National Character of the Prague Haskalah," (Hebrew) *Molad* 23 (July–August, 1965): 221–33; Louise Hecht, *Ein jüdischer Aufklärer in Böhmen: Der Pädagoge und Reformer Peter Beer* (Berlin, 2008).

3. This oversight is part of the broader phenomenon of the scant scholarship on tradition-

al eighteenth-century Prague Jewry. Even Ruth Kestenberg-Gladstein's magnum opus, *Neuere Geschichte der Juden in den böhmischen Ländern*, vol. 1 (Tübingen, 1969) and William Mccagg's more general *History of Habsburg Jews* (Bloomington, Ind., 1989) largely ignore Prague's numerous traditional leaders and writings.

4. This article is part of a larger work in progress, "Tradition and Modernization in Nineteenth-Century Prague."

5. On Landau, see my *The Kabbalistic Culture of Eighteenth-Century Prague* (Oxford, 2010). On Landau's early years in Poland, see David Katz, "A Case Study in the Formation of a Super-Rabbi" (Ph.D. diss.; University of Maryland, 2004). Several important, albeit hagiographic, studies exist; see, for example, Jekuthiel Kamelhar, *Mofet ha-dor* (Piotrków, 1934).

6. See, for example, my discussion of Moses Samet and Alexander Altmann below.

7. On *Normalschulen*, Prague's *Normalschule* and Landau, see Moses Wiener, *Nachricht von dem Ursprunge und Fortgange der deutschen jüdischen Hauptschule zu Prague* (Prague, 1785); Johann Wanniczek, *Geschichte der prager, Haupt-, Trivial- und Mädchenschule der Israeliten* (Prague, 1832); Hillel Kieval, "The Unforeseen Consequences of Cultural Resistance: *Haskalah* and State-Mandated Reform in the Bohemian Lands," *Jewish Culture and History* 13.2–3 (2012): 108–23.

8. Wanniczek, *Geschichte der prager Hauptschule*, 14–15; Kestenberg-Gladstein, *Neuere Geschichte*, 45, 50.

9. Wealthy students were often taught secular studies by tutors. See Hillel Kieval, "Caution's Progress," *Toward Modernity*, ed. J. Katz (New Brunswick, N.J., 1987), 94, 96.

10. On Mendelssohn's Bible translation, see among others, Alexander Altmann, *Moses Mendelssohn* (Philadelphia, 1973); David Sorkin, *Moses Mendelssohn and the Religious Enlightenment* (Berkeley, Calif., 1996); Edward Breuer, *The Limits of Enlightenment: Jews, Germans, and the Eighteenth-Century Study of Scripture* (Cambridge, Mass., 1996).

11. Moses Samet, "Mendelssohn, Wessely and the Rabbis of Their Time" (Hebrew), in *Mehkharim be-toledot am Yisrael ve-Erets Yisrael le-zekher Zevi Avneri*, ed. A. Gilboa, et al. (Haifa, 1970), 254, reprinted recently in Samet, *Chapters in the History of Orthodoxy* (Hebrew; Jerusalem, 2005), 89.

12. Altmann, *Moses Mendelssohn*, 398.

13. The public gained access to this collection after it was purchased by the Karlin-Stolin *hasidim* from a descendent of Landau in Russia. Much of it has been microfilmed by the Institute for Microfilmed Hebrew Manuscripts at the National Library of Israel in Jerusalem.

14. A handwritten copy penned by Landau is extant in the Russian archival material. This May–June 1782 letter was first printed in Akiva Schlesinger, *Lev ha-'ivri* (4th ed.; Jerusalem, 1924), 1:6b. It, however, was published from a copy of a copy in the collection of Landau's great-grandson, Wolf. Notably, this letter was *not* printed in *Lev ha-'ivri*'s earlier editions. More recently, a facsimile of Landau's original letter was published in *Kovets bet Aaron ve-Yisrael* 8.3 (1993 [5753]): 123–25. See also Yisrael N. Heschel's accompanying article, "The Opinions of the Rabbinic Leaders of the Generation in Their Battle against the *maskil* Naphtali Herz Wessely," 122–25 (Hebrew). In *Rav tov le-vet Yisrael* (Berlin, 1782), Wessely translated into Hebrew Mendelssohn's recent call for Jewish communities to relinquish some executive powers.

15. *Kovets Bet Aaron ve-Yisrael* 8.3 (1993): 123–25.

16. Samet, "Mendelssohn, Wessely and the Rabbis of Their Time," 252, n. 109, reprinted in Samet's *Chapters in the History of Orthodoxy*, 86, n. 110; Altmann, *Moses Mendelssohn*, 835, n. 84. Interestingly, Samet admitted that he cannot prove that this letter is a forgery from the letter itself.

17. Gutmann Klemperer, "Das Rabbinat zu Prag," *Pascheles' Illustrierter israelitischer Volkskalender* 32 (5644) [1883–1884]: 97–98.

18. Landau, *Tselah, Berakhot* 28b. While this work was published in 1791, it appears to have been completed by 1783. See Landau's comments in the epilogue of *Tselah, Pesahim* (Prague, 1783.)

19. Landau's approbation for Glogau's *Torah ve-hamesh Megilot,* dated June 21, 1785.

See also Altmann, *Moses Mendelssohn*, 382–83. Even this approbation was probably difficult for Landau given his harsh critique of biblical translations in general and particularly their proliferation during his day. See his *Petiḥah* to the *Tselaḥ, Berakhot*.

20. *ha-Me'asef* (1786): 142–44. Although *ha-Me'asef*'s editor doubted Landau's authorship of this approbation, I, as other scholars, such as Altmann, Katz, and Samet, see no reason to question it.

21. While Dubno originally collaborated on Mendelssohn's translation project, he eventually abandoned it. He never completed his plans to produce his own Pentateuch edition. Accordingly, Landau's approbation for it was only published later by Gabriel Polak in *Ben Gorni* (Amsterdam, 1851), 44. See Altmann, *Moses Mendelssohn*, 382, 402–3; Breuer, *The Limits of Enlightenment*, 24–25.

22. Landau's stance on this topic is indeed complex. There are a few sources where he calls Mendelssohn a scholar and indicates that his translation is fine for the learned elite. See the Landau sources cited in Samet, "Mendelssohn, Wessely and the Rabbis," 24; and Maoz Kahana and Michael Silber, "Deists, Sabbatians, and Kabbalists in Prague" (Hebrew), *Kabbalah* 21 (2010): 369, 384. Even in these sources, however, Landau never encourages the general use of this translation, and certainly not by students.

23. Rumors that Landau had banned the translation proved to be false. See Mendelssohn, *Gesammelte Schriften* 19 (Stuttgart, 1974), no. 248, 278–79.

24. On the rapid spread of Mendelssohn's translation to various Jewish communities, see Steven Lowenstein, "The Readership of Mendelssohn's Bible Translation," *Hebrew Union College Annual* 53 (1982): 179–213, later republished in his *The Mechanics of Change* (Atlanta, 1992), 29–64.

25. Moses Mendelssohn, *Gesammelte Schriften,* ed. G. B. Mendelssohn (Leipzig, 1843), 5:611–13. On Kindermann, see Eduard Winter, *Ferdinand Kindermann Ritter von Schulstein* (Augsburg, 1926).

26. Altmann, *Moses Mendelssohn*, 397–98, 488; Kieval, "Caution's Progress," 102, n. 40.

27. On *Divre shalom ve-emet* (Berlin, 1782), see, for example, Mordechai Eliav, *Ha-ḥinukh ha-Yehudi be-Germanyah* (Jerusalem, 1960), 39–51; Shmuel Feiner, *The Jewish Enlightenment in the Eighteenth Century* (Hebrew; Jerusalem, 2002), 113–29, 165–87, *passim,* and its English translation, *The Jewish Enlightenment,* trans. C. Naor (Philadelphia, 2002), 87–104, 139–62.

28. Landau's first public censure of *Divre shalom ve-emet* occurred on Jan. 16, 1782. See *Kovets Bet Aaron ve-Yisrael* 8.1 (1992): 163.

29. Ibid., 162–65. Landau seems to have written this letter after the above-mentioned condemnation and before his scathing denunciation on the Sabbath preceding Passover, March 23, 1782.

30. *Derushe ha-tselaḥ,* sermon 39, 53a.

31. Landau, *Tselaḥ, Berakhot,* introduction.

32. Num 11:4.

33. See, for example, Marcus Herz's censure of Landau's defense of early burial (German appendix to *ha-Me'asef,* 1787); Isaac Euchel (*ha-Me'asef,* 1787), 133; David Friedländer, *Sendschreiben an die deutschen Juden* (appendix to *ha-Me'asef,* 1788). See also Aaron Wolfsohn's, "Sicah be'erets ha-ḥayim" (*ha-Me'asef* 7 [1794–1797]: 54–67, 120–53, 203–27, 279–98). Several scholars conjecture that the anonymous rabbi mocked in this piece is Landau.

34. Samet, "Mendelssohn, Wessely and the Rabbis," 240.

35. See Michael Silber, "The Historical Experience of German Jewry and Its Impact on Haskalah and Reform in Hungary," in *Toward Modernity,* 116.

36. The high court was now comprised of three ranked jurists. After much wrangling, in 1794, Samuel was appointed the third-ranked judge.

37. Over seventy *responsa* of Samuel's are published in *Noda' bi-Yehudah,* vol. 2.

38. On this society and its journal, see Ruth Kestenberg-Gladstein, "A Voice from the Prague Enlightenment," *Leo Baeck Institute Year Book* 9 (1964): 295–304.

39. While various scholars claim that in later years Samuel also subscribed to *ha-Me'asef,* I have found no evidence for this.

40. Kestenberg-Gladstein, *Neuere Geschichte,* 360, n. 49.

41. See *ha-Me'asef* 7.1 (1794): 37–53, 177–79. These concern the controversy surrounding Landau's appointment to Prague's *bet din* in 1794. Still, it should be noted that in his addendum, Samuel writes that he regrets that *ha-Me'asef* published his first letter sent by someone else.

42. He was among the first ten *prenumeratum* (presubscribers) from Prague. See the first edition of the translation (1783).

43. Samuel Landau, *Ahavat tsiyon* (Prague, 1827; reprint Jerusalem, 1966), sermon 12, January 30, 1816, p. 19a.

44. On the *hatam sofer*'s attitude toward Haskalah, see Jacob Katz, "Towards a Biography of the Hatam Sofer," in his *Divine Law in Human Hands* (Jerusalem, 1998); Shnayer Z. Leiman, "R. Moses Schick: The Hatam Sofer's Attitude towards Mendelssohn's *Biur*," *Tradition* 24.3 (1989): 83–86; Maoz Kahana, "Continuity and Change in the *Responsa* of the Hatam Sofer" (Hebrew; M.A. thesis, Hebrew University, 2004); Kahana, "From Prague to Pressburg: Halakhic Writing in a Changing World From the Noda BeYehudah to the Hatam Sofer 1730–1839" (Hebrew; Ph.D. diss.; Hebrew University, 2010).

45. *Ahavat tsiyon,* sermon 12, p. 19a. Still, Samuel's curricular proposals, arguing that young children study secular disciplines *alongside* Torah, are somewhat more moderate than Wessely's.

46. On Samson Raphael Hirsch and his use of this phrase, see Robert Liberles, *Religious Conflict in Social Context* (Westport, Conn., 1985); Mordechai Breuer, *The "Torah im Derekh Eretz" of Samson Raphael Hirsch* (Jerusalem, 1970).

47. *Ahavat tsiyon,* sermon 12, p. 19a.

48. The *maskilim*'s attempt to promote Hebrew has not been given sufficient attention by historians. Until recently, historical works have primarily examined the Haskalah's strategies to transform traditional Judaism and not its conservative efforts to preserve its core elements. Only in the past few decades have scholars, such as David Sorkin and Shmuel Feiner, focused on these and other traditional dimensions of the Haskalah. See, for example, Feiner, "Towards a Historical Definition of the Haskalah," in *New Perspectives on the Haskalah,* 184–219. Yet, in his recent book *The Origins of Jewish Secularization in 18th-Century Europe* (Hebrew; Jerusalem, 2010), trans. C. Naor (Oxford, 2010), Feiner too, like many of his predecessors, treats the Haskalah as a secularizing movement.

49. *Ahavat tsiyon,* sermon 12, pp. 18b–19a.

50. Ibid. I have been unable to locate this idea in Montesquieu's *Lettres Persanes.*

51. See Ben Zion Katz, *Rabanut, Hasidut, Haskala* (Tel Aviv, 1956), 1: 234.

52. Samuel Landau, August 18, 1824, approbation for Shimshon Bloch, *Shvile 'olam,* part 1.

53. Samuel's son Moshe moved from Prague to Uman. On Moshe, see *Hamelitz,* "The History of Moshe Landau" (Hebrew) (1862), no. 43, 689–91, no. 44, 703–4.

54. In an 1814 sermon (*Ahavat tsiyon,* no. 10, p. 15a–b), Samuel decries the sharp decline in halakhic observance during his generation, particularly the public desecration of the Sabbath.

55. Literature on Moses Landau is scant. See *inter alia Allgemeine Zeitung des Judenthums* 23 (May 1852): 269–271; J. Brandeis, "Biographie des Dichters," in *M. I. Landau's: Hinterlassene vermischte Schriften,* ed. Senders and Brandeis (Prague, 1867), 195–200.

56. Bedřich Nosek, "Jewish Hebrew Studies in the Czech Lands in the Pre-Enlightenment and Enlightenment Period," *Judaica Bohemiae* 27 (1991): 33; Kestenberg-Gladstein, *Neuere Geschichte,* 50; Kieval, "Caution's Progress," 97. In 1810, Jewish history was also introduced.

57. Kestenberg-Gladstein, "A Voice from the Prague Enlightenment," 304.

58. For his involvement with the journal, see *Bikure ha-'itim*'s opening page, vol. 4 (1823).

59. Vols. 3–7 (out of 9 *Kerem hemed* vols.) were published in Prague. Bernhard Friedberg, *History of Hebrew Typography* (Hebrew; Antwerp, 1935), 29, states that Moses published most of *Kerem hemed.*

60. See both Wessely's essay "Mehalel rea'" (Prague, 1836), *Bereshit,* 25a–26b, and his poem, 26b–28a. Still, they are not original to Moses' edition. The poem and essay are found in *Exodus*

in the first edition of Mendelssohn's translation (Berlin, 1783), 3b–6b. Moses, however, not only includes these pieces but moves them to a more prominent place, the opening volume of his project.

61. See Brandeis, "Biographie des Dichters," 197, 200.

62. See M. I. Landau, *Amaranten* (Prague, 1825); Landau, *Almanac* (Prague, 1822); Landau, *M. I. Landau's: Hinterlassene vermischte Schriften*. He also composed a collection of morality tales, *Galerie der Lektüre* (Prague, 1813).

63. Landau, *Hinterlassene vermischte Schriften*, 50.

64. Of course, many of the older restrictions, such as those imposed by the 1726 *Familiantengesetze*, as well as prior prejudices remained.

AN UNDERCLASS IN JEWISH HISTORY?

❊ ❊ ❊

Jewish Maidservants in East European
Jewish Society, 1700–1900

Rebecca Kobrin
Columbia University

TSEMAḤ ATLAS [translated as *The Yeshiva*], Chaim Grade's epic two-volume Yiddish novel about nineteenth-century Poland, opens with the tragic tale of Stesye, a young, pregnant, Jewish maidservant who has been thrown out of her employer's home. At first, Stesye is painted (primarily by her former employer) as a temptress, not to be trusted. As the novel progresses, it becomes quickly apparent that this young girl is far from a seductress; Steyse is rather a simpleton who became entrapped by her former employer's twenty-year old son. This boy's rapacious ways were well-known to other girls, but this poor Jewish orphan did not know of his reputation. With no one to warn her of his wanton ways, she believed his promises of marriage, wealth and love in exchange for her companionship during his nightly visits to her bed. She did not realize that pregnancy would thrust her into an underclass in Jewish society— that she could be dumped in some small village by her employer, where she would know no one and have no way to escape poverty or the drudgery of domestic life.[1]

Grade, along with other writers, placed Jewish maidservants at the center of his tales, but these women rarely surface in the annals of East European Jewish history. The virtual erasure of Jewish maidservants (s. *misharetet*, pl. *mishartot*) and their non-Jewish counterparts (s. *shifḥa*, pl., *shifḥot*) from the historical record should not obscure how central these women were to daily existence, wherein they played a

307

central role nurturing and sustaining Jewish family life. To be sure, the fact that these women left essentially no accounts of their own and only intermittently appear in legal and communal sources complicates any effort to assess their lives. Nonetheless, researchers mining such sources from the Ottoman empire have managed to bring to life the critical role Jewish female slaves and servants played in Jewish family life, especially in the instances when they bore their masters' children.[2] As one moves west into Eastern Europe, historians do not deny the existence of Jewish maidservants, but few discuss their experiences or that of their illegitimate children.[3] Yet, Stesye's situation was far from exceptional in places like the Russian empire, where imperial census material found that over a third of Jewish women claimed that they worked as domestic servants. Why were so many women drawn into domestic service? How did Jewish society treat these women? What do these women tell us about social stratification, class, and East European Jewish society broadly? The following pages do not seek to offer the final word on this topic, but hope to raise questions and encourage further conversation concerning Jewish domestic servants and social class in Eastern Europe during the eighteenth and nineteenth centuries.

A study of Jewish maidservants can shed much light on the ways in which gender intersected with social stratification in East European Jewish society. Since the early modern period, the *kehile* (official Jewish community) in the Polish-Lithuanian commonwealth linked maid service to poverty relief. Orphans or the poorest girls for whom there were no other means of support were sent to live with wealthy householders for whom they worked to earn their dowry. As throughout Europe, working as a maid became a common life cycle passage for many young, single women of the lower class in East European Jewish society.[4] In the best cases, these orphans or cash-strapped young women would only have to work a few years before earning a respectable dowry. But, if during those years of service a woman became pregnant, she could forever alter her future, since marriage—the main avenue for female social mobility and stability—became less attainable for her. Jewish men also worked in their coreligionists' homes in order to obtain funds to support a family, but never had to fear falling pregnant, giving birth to an illegitimate child or compromising their marriage prospects. Jewish maidservants in particular, thus, offer a fresh perspective on how gender shaped poverty in eighteenth and nineteenth century Eastern Europe.

CLASS, "UNDERCLASS," AND THE EAST EUROPEAN JEWISH MAIDSERVANT, 1700–1900

Between 1700 and 1900, the number of Jewish women working as maids in Eastern Europe varied by region, but increased steadily throughout, particularly in the areas of the Russian empire. For example, while a 1764 census from Lublin found that only seven percent of the families had Jewish maidservants, by the time the Tsarist Imperial Census was conducted in 1897, thirty-five percent of Jewish women claimed they were employed as domestic servants.[5] What took place in this century and a half to establish domestic service as one of the most common occupations for Jewish women in East European Jewry?

While many factors, including urbanization and uneven industrialization, contributed to this shift, it is crucial to remember, as Eli Lederhendler points out, that this was the era in which the larger Jewish community underwent a general impoverishment or "declassing."[6] In contrast to the rise of working classes in non-Jewish East European society, Jews were caught in an opposite trajectory, largely owing to discriminatory state policies and social pressures. Marginalized in their economic pursuits and relegated to the Pale of Settlement, Jews, Lederhendler argues, "were forced into the procrustean bed of a truly 'ethnic economy,' dependent on their own dwindling resources for employment and credit opportunities."[7] Jewish artisans and petty merchants "were increasingly reduced to a single, caste-like status" akin to "the working poor."[8] As Jewish men struggled to find work, Jewish women were thrust into the only occupation available to them: domestic service.

Moses Berlin's nineteenth-century ethnographic source gives voice to the ways in which this process of declassing pushed Jewish women into domestic service. Berlin, born in Shklov in 1821, was appointed by the minister of the interior as adviser on Jewish affairs to the governor-general of White Russia. In 1861, he published *Ocherk Etnografii Yevreiskavo Naseleniya v Rossii* (Survey of the Ethnography of the Jewish People in Russia).[9] In this ethnography, Berlin claimed that there were not really fixed social classes (*kasty*) among Jews, because a Jew is very likely to pass through many economic situations in his lifetime. The market and communal ties are what determined one's station in life, as Berlin noted, "a man can be poor and then become rich through speculation, or be rich and then be impoverished because of his charitable and communal obligations."[10] But his discussion of Jewish female domestic servants suggests how class and the process of declassing *did* shape nineteenth-century Russian Jewish society. As Berlin wrote:

> When their parents cannot feed them, girls often go into service with more prosperous or wealthy Jewish families, earning room and board and saving for their dowries. This is not a bad life as they usually eat the same food as their masters and, on holidays, even sit at the table with them. Young wives of poor Jews who served in wealthy homes before their marriage and are not used to a modest way of life, often serve as wet nurses when their own children die, or even if they have living children, often give them to a cheap wet nurse for the day so they can serve as a wet nurse in a wealthy home. But they don't usually do this to add to their husband's income, but rather to eat better at the table of their employer and/or to guarantee themselves the kind of fancy clothing for which Jewish women have a weakness (*predan strasti roskoshno nariazhat'sia*).[11]

Berlin's account demonstrates that while the goal of acquiring funds for a dowry initially propelled young women into domestic service, the general impoverishment and downward mobility of East European Jewish society made them stay there. In contrast to maidservants who bore testament to the high status of their masters, Jewish domestic servants were treated as if they were part of the family.[12] Because they ate the same food, and sat at the same table, one can assume they were also deeply enmeshed in family dynamics. Second, in contrast to the rest of Europe, where maid service was primarily a lifecycle occupation for unmarried women, poorer Jewish women stayed in maid service even after marriage and childbirth, at the expense of their own family's well-being, for it allowed them to enjoy the benefits of a relative wealth that they could never dream of achieving themselves.

Berlin's account and denial of a fixed class structure in East European Jewish society should not obscure the ways in which these women were considered subordinates; their inferior status became abundantly clear when an unmarried maidservant became pregnant. Far from rare, pregnancies among maidservants and other single women contributed to the general rise in illegitimacy throughout Europe in the late-eighteenth and early-nineteen centuries.[13] But while Christian maidservants could always give their illegitimate children to the Church, Jewish women had no similar safety net for their unwanted children.[14] These women and their children subsisted in what I call an "underclass," operating on the periphery of the Jewish community. The notion of an underclass was deployed (and with much debate) within the context of American history in the second half of the twentiethcentury as scholars pondered why certain people became entrenched in the lowest rung of American society, dependent on support of the state, unable to achieve any substantial economic or social mobility.[15] Some scholars vociferously objected to the use of this term as it obscured the importance of racial discrimination, but all agreed that there were some larger structural forces at work creating conditions that made it hard for certain members of the urban poor to succeed. I use the term "underclass" to explore under what circumstances young Jewish women became part of a socioeconomic group in Jewish society from which they could not hope to emerge.[16]

DOWRY DILEMMAS

Ironically, the East European Jewish community initially saw domestic service as the most respectable strategy to help women raise funds so that they could marry. By the early modern period, the dowry had become a prerequisite for marriage. The Jewish community, like surrounding Christian society, employed various strategies to raise the necessary funds for dowries for poor Jewish girls, from soliciting kinsman and wealthy community members to establishing specific charitable organizations to address the challenge of dowering brides. But as the birthrate exploded in Eastern Europe, the growing needs of brides could not be met and many young Jewish women often also turned to domestic service to earn their dowries.[17] The communal statutes passed by the Lithuanian Council in 1623 testify to the acceptance of maid service in Jewish communal life for dealing with dowry inflation and the increasing number of applicants for aid. The statutes required applicants for dotal aid to submit written testimony that they had served as a maid for at least three years. An amendment to this statute passed in 1628 proclaimed that young women lacking written proof of their maid service would be assigned to the home of a leading taxpayer in order to work for their dowry.[18]

Forcing young Jewish women to work so they could earn their dowries clearly differentiated poor boys from poor girls. For example, a 1595 statute passed by the Jewish community of Cracow demanded that daughters of the poor become maid-servants at the age of ten, while providing financial aid for poor boys to attend school until the age of thirteen. While poor young men studied, employers expected these young women to take care of a wide array of tasks, from childcare to house cleaning, to food purchasing and preparation.[19]

The practice of employing poor Jewish women as maidservants became more common in late-nineteenth century Russia after the Polish Sejm and the Tsarist government banned Christians from working for Jews.[20] Illustrating the underlying fears of the Sejm and the Tsarist government that led to these legislations is the sensational murder case of Maria Drich.[21] In 1883, a Jewish merchant, Zimel Abramov Lotsov, informed police that his Christian domestic servant had disappeared from his house. Police searched for the young woman, but she was not found. Then, in 1884, a local fisherman found a woman's corpse in the river. Medical examiners identified the body as the missing domestic servant Maria Drich. Authorities apprehended Zimel and his wife when initial police investigations found several Christian female acquaintances of Drich who reported that Zimel's eldest son, Yankel, was in love with Maria and intended to convert to Catholicism to marry her.[22]

While her murder was unusual, Drich's intimate relationship with her master's son was far from extraordinary. Throughout Jewish Eastern Europe and its migrant Diaspora we find young girls enmeshed in similar situations; some met tragic fates similar to Drich.[23] Sarah Alexander, a nineteen-year-old Polish Jewish immigrant in New York, for example, similarly was found dead in the countryside. The circumstances that led to Sarah Alexander's end in a ditch also involved her love for her master's son and the fact that she was five months pregnant. Even more lurid was the fact that Alexander's master, Israel Rubinstein, was her father's first cousin; the father of her child was her second cousin, Pesach Rubinstein, a man who had a wife and son in Europe.

Maria and Sarah's ends were dramatic, but their vulnerability typified the situation of many maidservants in East European Jewish society. Rabbis across Eastern Europe had long described the sexual unions between members of a master's family and the household staff that left Jewish women in precarious positions.[24] Tsarist governmental authorities began addressing the issue of Jewish maidservant rape and illegitimate births after several reports of infanticide were lodged in the Vilna region. Tsarist authorities not only exposed the systematic murder of Jewish maidservants' illegitimate newborns at a group home established and supported by the Vilna *Kahal,* but also began to ask the mothers about the circumstances that lead to these illegitimate births. It is through these investigations that we can hear the voice of twenty-eight-year-old Rokha Itskova Baranovskaia, who testified in 1887 that she served in the home of Berka Shendels and became pregnant with her employer's child after their numerous encounters. At that time, "he gave her 80 rubles to give up the child for upbringing."[25] This was barely enough to support her and her child for a few months. Most employers were not so generous: Sora Davidova Germaize testified that while working for Abraham the tavern keeper in Vilna, "he had relations with her in the absence of his wife, after which her monthly period ceased." She attempted to have an abortion but failed and was left alone to raise her child.[26] Mikhlia Gersheva Baryshnikova reported that while she was working for Leib Svirskii on Saf'ianiki Street in Vilna in December 1886, he raped and impregnated her. The investigator noted "after a month, Svirskii fired her without even paying her salary."[27]

Jewish maidservants faced a difficult predicament: desperate for opportunities to earn money, they needed to keep their jobs as domestic servants, and some perhaps felt they could not afford to refuse their masters' romantic overtures. Others may have been unable to stop their overpowering suitors from fulfilling their wishes.[28] Such is evident in the case of Ryfka Gierszeniowna, a Jewish divorcee who worked as a maidservant in Poland. Gierszeniowna testified that she was raped by a local butcher on two separate occasions when trying to buy food for her employer's family.[29] Realizing that she had conceived from these episodes, Ryfka fled her employer's home to her hometown of Baranów until her child's birth.[30] Similarly Leia Vaismanova described in 1869, to a Russian court, how she became pregnant by a Jewish soldier who was a guest in her employer's home and who similarly saw her as exploitable. Jewish men across the class spectrum, from wealthy merchants to communal butchers, thought little of having their way with these women, as few seemed to fear the consequences of such actions. Jewish domestic servants were such a vulnerable group in Jewish society, as historian Elisheva Carlebach points out, that Jewish communal ledgers only consider these women and their illegitimate children when fighting over which community will pay to bury them.[31] These women and their overlooked progeny exemplify what economist Gunnar Myrdal defined as underclass in the 1960s: a group of people "who are more and more hopelessly set apart from" the community, whose plight is ignored, and who do not participate in the wider community's life, ambitions and achievements."[32]

By the end of the nineteenth century, the vast majority of unwed Jewish mothers in Eastern Europe, ChaeRan Freeze argues, were domestic servants.[33] While we do not have precise statistics concerning the number of children born to Jewish maidservants, it is clear that unions producing children rarely resulted in marriage since most of the men involved were already married.[34] Even in the cases where the father of the illegitimate child was single, marriage was unusual. An early eighteenth-century case recounted by R. Jacob Reischer, a rabbinic authority born in Rzeszow, Poland and head of Prague's *bet din*, revolves around a master's son who fathered a child with his family's Jewish maidservant; the master's son then ran away to another country and married a more "appropriate" woman of his social class.[35]

Since marriage was key to maintaining social status in the changing class structures of East European Jewish society, it should come as little surprise that the pregnant maidservant lurked on the periphery of society, with few options for herself or her children. Testifying to the peripheral status of Jewish maidservants and their illegitimate children is the "home" supported by late-nineteenth century Jewish leaders in Vilna. While on the surface it appeared that Jewish leaders recognized the plight of Jewish maidservants in setting up a home for their illegitimate children, their mission was not to care for these children, but rather to erase them, sanctioning the director's infanticide, as she abandoned these innocent infants in the forest.[36] Indeed, East European Jewish society did not believe these young Jewish children deserved to be treated according to the same ethics as other Jewish children, because they had fallen into the underclass of East European Jewish society.

CONCLUSION

Jewish maidservants, and their illegitimate "fatherless" children, offer a unique perspective on the economic divides within East European Jewish society during the eighteenth and nineteenth centuries. The fate met by Jewish maidservants' illegitimate children during this time bears testament to the lowly status held by their mothers. Few financial resources and the need for dowry funds initially attracted poor women to domestic service, which was then embraced by Jewish communal leaders as a form of poor relief enabling young poor girls to live within the rubric of Jewish family life. But as East European Jews' economic prospects faded, these women came to be exploited and lived at the mercy of their employers. Pregnancy vividly illustrates their vulnerability, but even those maidservants who did not become pregnant lived in a precarious situation. As one young women summed up in a nineteenth-century Russian newspaper, "As long as I was healthy and worked as hard as an ox, I was given room and board. But when I got sick for a couple weeks, even though my masters were nice, honest people, they didn't want to take care of a strange, sick girl."[37]

By looking at the places where the traditional norm of caring for the vulnerable become upended, we can gain a clearer picture of the ethics and norms of an entire society. As Cissie Fairchilds points out, "maidservants deserve more scholarly attention not only by reason of their influence on the family . . . [but also because] the occupation fulfilled many important social functions and was a mirror of the society's basic values."[38] What does the treatment of pregnant maidservants and their illegitimate offspring tell us about East European Jewish society in this era in which many descended into poverty? Indeed, nothing illustrates more vividly the collapse of the norms of social responsibility, and Jewish ethics, than the institutional response to the plight of Jewish maidservants and their children in the Vilna region. After these women were exploited, the community unceremoniously disposed of their children. Such treatment of Jewish maidservants and their illegitimate children suggests why this group constituted a hidden underclass in East European Jewish society. By expanding our focus to include these women when assessing the stark economic divides within European Jewish society, scholars of East European Jewry will not only bring to light the social reality of the time, but will also come to appreciate more fully the hopes, aspirations and fears of those whose travails were invisible in their own day and who have been forgotten by history.

Notes

1. The tale of Stesye and its impact on the main characters of the novel can be found in Hayim Grade, *Tsemaḥ atlas: Di Yeshive* (Los Angeles, 1967), 77–149.

2. Yaron Ben-Naeh, "Blond, Tall, with Honey-Colored Eyes: Jewish Ownership of Slaves in the Ottoman Empire," *Jewish History* 20.3–4 (2006): 315–32; Ben-Naeh, "Ve-hayta lecha shifḥat 'olam": Avdut ve-avadim ba-ḥevrah ha-yehudit ha-'otomanit," *Hamizraḥ he-ḥadash* 50 (2011): 66–90.

3. Domestic servants surface only briefly in general works on East European Jewish history such as Bernard Weinryb's *A Social and Economic History of the Jewish Community in Poland, 1100–1800* (Philadelphia, 1973) and Salo Baron's *The Jewish Community: Its History and Structure to the American Revolution* (Philadelphia, 1945). Several articles treat the topic in different countries. See Elliott Horowitz, "Ben adonim le-meshartot ba-ḥevra ha-yehudit ha-Europe'it ben yeme ha-benayim le-reshit ha-'et ha-ḥadashah," in *Eros, erusim ve-isurim*, ed. I. Bartal and I. Gafni (Jerusalem, 1998), 193–211; Elisheva Carlebach, "Fallen Women and Fatherless Children: Jewish Domestic Servants in Eighteenth-Century Altona," *Jewish History* 24 (2010): 295–308; ChaeRan Freeze, "Lilith's Midwives: Jewish Newborn Child Murder in Nineteenth-Century Vilna," *Jewish Social Studies* 16.2 (2010): 1–27. Rebecca Kobrin, "'The Murdered Hebrew Maid Servant of East New York,' Gender, Class, and the Jewish Household in the East European Jewish Migrant Diaspora," in *Gender and Jewish History*, ed. D. D. Moore and M. Kaplan (Bloomington, Ind., 2010), 72–87. Tamar Shimshi-Licht's wonderful unpublished dissertation "Jewish Servants and Maids in Early Modern Germany" (Ph.D. diss.; Ben Gurion University, 2006).

4. Antoinette Fauve-Chamoux, "Domestic Service and the Formation of European Identity," in *Domestic Service and the Formation of European Identity: Understanding the Globalization of Domestic Work, 16th–21st Centuries*, ed. A. Fauve-Chamoux (Bern, 2004), 103–13; Cissie Fairchilds, "Female Sexual Attitudes and the Rise of Illegitimacy: A Case Study," *Journal of Interdisciplinary History* 8.4 (1978): 636.

5. Raphael Mahler, *Toldot ha-yehudim be-Polin: 'ad ha-me'ah ha-19* (Merḥavyah, 1946), 284–85; Arcadius Kahan, "Impact of Industrialization in Tsarist Russia," in *Essays in Jewish Social and Economic History*, ed. R. Weiss (Chicago, 1986), 65, n. 14.

6. Eli Lederhendler, *Jewish Immigrants and American Capitalism: From Caste to Class* (Cambridge, 2006), 36.

7. Ibid.

8. Eli Lederhendler, "Classless: On the Social Status of Jews in Russia and Eastern Europe in the Late Nineteenth Century," *Comparative Studies in Society and History* 50.2 (2008): 515.

9. See Mosei Berlin, *Ocherk etnografii evreiskogo narodonasileniia v Rossii* (St. Petersburg, 1861). My thanks to Natan Meir for showing me this source. For more on Berlin and this ethnography, see I. Lurie and A. Zeltser, "Moses Berlin and Lubavich Hasidism: A Landmark in the Conflict between Haskalah and Hasidism," *Shvut: Studies in Russian and East European Jewish History and Culture* 5 (1997): 32–64.

10. Berlin, *Ocherk etnografii evreiskogo narodonasileniia v Rossii*, 51.

11. Ibid., 41.

12. Cissie Fairchilds, *Domestic Enemies: Servants and Masters in Old Regime France* (Baltimore, Md., 1984), 12–13, 37.

13. R. Schumacher, "Unwed Mothers in the City. Illegitimate Fertility in 19th-Century Geneva," *Journal of Family History* 12.3 (2007): 189–202; L. A. Tilly, J. W. Scott, M. Cohen, "Women's Work and European Fertility Patterns," *Journal of Interdisciplinary History* 6.3 (1976): 447–76.

14. John Boswell, *The Kindness of Strangers: The Abandonment of Children in Western Europe from Late Antiquity to the Renaissance* (New York, 1988).

15. This term was controversially deployed in the 1980s and 1990s. See Nicholas Lehman, "The Origins of the Underclass" (June, 1986) *The Atlantic Online*. Retrieved March 12, 2012. Michael Katz, ed., *The Underclass Debate* (Princeton, N.J., 1992).

16. Herbert Gans, "From 'Underclass' to 'Undercaste': Some Observations about the Future of the Post-Industrial Economy and Its Major Victims," in *Urban Poverty and the Underclass*, ed. E. Mingione (Cambridge, Mass., 1996), 141–42.

17. While there are few reliable statistics before the nineteenth century, the trends identified in this era probably were present in earlier centuries. From 1825 to 1880, the annual net increase among Jews was over 1.5 percent, their numbers rising from 1.6 to 4 million in those years, and growing to 5 million by 1897. By comparison, the non-Jewish population of Russia experienced an annual net increase of about 1.1 percent. By the end of the century, a quarter of the Jewish population was under ten years of age, and half were under twenty. See Kahan, "Impact of Industrialization," App. 50, table A2.

18. Elliott Horowitz, "The Worlds of Jewish Youth in Europe, 1300–1800," in *A History of Young People in the West*, vol. 1, ed. G. Levi and J.-C. Schmitt, trans. C. Naish (Cambridge, Mass., 1997), 85–88.

19. See Gershon Hundert, *The Jews in a Polish Private Town: The Case of Opatów in the Eighteenth Century* (Baltimore, Md., 1992), for a depiction of the various chores assigned to Jewish maidservants. Servants' involvement in serving food is evidenced in various visual sources as well. See Joseph Gutmann, *The Jewish Life Cycle* (Leiden, 1987), plate XIX. Also response literature hints at the various tasks falling upon Jewish maidservants. See Yair Bacharach, *Ḥavot Yair* (Sudlikov, 1834 [1702]), no. 48, which discusses how an employer should deal with non-kosher food with regard to Passover vegetables which were accidentally bought by his maid during the Passover holiday.

20. On the legislation concerning Jewish employment of Christian servants see Ḥayyim Hillel Ben-Sasson, "Takanot ishure shabat be-Polin u-mashma'utam ha-ḥevratit veha-kalkalit," *Zion* 21 (1957): 183–206; on non-Jewish servants in Jewish homes see Judith Kalik, "Christian Servants Employed by Jews in the Polish Lithuanian Commonwealth in the 17th and 18th Centuries," *Polin* 14 (2001): 259–70; Adam Kaźimierczyk, "The Problem of Christian Servants as Related in the Legal Codes of the Polish-Lithuanian Commonwealth during the Second Half of the Seventeenth Century and in the Saxon Period," *Gal-Ed* 15–16 (1997): 23–40.

21. "Fanatizm Evreev," *Volynskiia Eparkhial'nyia Vedomosti* 30 (1886). I would like to thank Ellie Schainker for sharing these sources on the Drich case with me.

22. "Ubiistvo evreiami khristianki," *Sankt-Peterburgskie Vedomosti* 103, 107 (1885). "Po liutsinskomu delu," *Nedel'naia Khronika Voskhoda* 23 (1885): n.p.

23. All the information on the corpse of Sarah Alexander and her activities as a maidservant for her relatives is derived from the trial transcript of her accused killer, her cousin Peysakh Rubinstein. See *The Trial of Pasach N. Rubinstein for the Murder of Sarah Alexander in the Town of New Lots . . .* (New York, 1876).

24. All rabbinic responsa were accessed at www.biu.ac.il/jh/Responsa on July 8, 2010. See S. Moses de Medina (d. 1589), *Responsa me-ha-Rashdam, Even ha-'ezer* (Lemberg, 1862), no. 233; J. Trani (d. 1639), *Responsa u-piske ha-Maharit* (Lvov, 1861), no. 26 and his *Responsa Maharit* (Prague, 1767)

part 2; no. 17; Y. Sirkes (d.1640), *Responsa ha-Bakh ha-Yeshanotu* (reprint, Jerusalem, 1959) no. 100; Y. Bacharach (1699), *Havot Yair* (reprint, New York, 1950), no. 231, which all describe different cases in which either the master himself or male members of his family were sexually involved with their female Jewish servants. For a description of cases involving either the master or a member of his household actually marrying their domestic servants, see Yair Bacharach, *Havot Yair,* nos. 60 and 176.

25. LVIA,1. 448, op. 1. D, 5228 quoted in Freeze, "Lilith's Midwives," 7.

26. LVIA,1. 228, op. 1, d. 5528, quoted in Freeze, "Lilith's Midwives," 7.

27. LVIA, f. 448, op. 1, d. 5228,11. 45–45 ob. quoted in Freeze, "Lilith's Midwives," 8.

28. Fairchilds, *Domestic Enemies*, 88–94. Using the *déclarations* of maidservants who give birth out of wedlock, the author illustrates how clearly most "seductions" were rather forms of rape.

29. Hundert, *Jews in a Polish Private Town,* 72–74.

30. Ibid., 73.

31. Elisheva Carlebach, "Fallen Women and Fatherless Children," 302–5.

32. Gunnar Myrdal, *Challenge to Affluence* (New York, 1963), 10.

33. In Russia, in general, the majority of unwed mothers were domestic servants. See David L. Ransel, *Mothers of Misery: Child Abandonment in Russia* (Princeton, N.J., 1988).

34. In general it is difficult to ascertain illegitimate births in nineteenth-century Russia, but for Jews it is even more challenging. See David Ransel, "Problems in Measuring Illegitimacy in Prerevolutionary Russia," *Journal of Social History* 16.2 (1982): 111–27.

35. Yaakov Reischer, *Responsa Shevut Yakov,* part 3, no.121 accessed at www.biu.ac.il/jh/Responsa on July 8, 2010.

36. Freeze, "Lilith's Midwives," 1–27.

37. A. Dinstmeydl, "A kleyn brivl funem gehenem in 'Kol mevaser,'" *Kol mevaser* no. 43 (1869): 294.

38. Fairchilds, *Domestic Enemies,* 19.

PART V

FROM THE EARLY MODERN TO THE LATE MODERN (AND BACK AGAIN)

❈ ❈ ❈

DID NORTH AMERICAN JEWRY HAVE
AN EARLY MODERN PERIOD?

※ ※ ※

Beth S. Wenger

University of Pennsylvania

THE phrase "early modern" rarely, if ever, appears in scholarly treatments of Jewish history in colonial North America and the early United States. In recent years, the early modern period has emerged as a defining epoch of transition in European Jewish history—one characterized by increased social and economic mobility, new religious ideas, weakening rabbinic authority, and a proliferation of Jewish knowledge sparked by the expansion of printing. Yet, the notion of an early modern period remains virtually absent as a category in the historiography of early Jewish life in the North American colonies and the United States. At first glance, the reasons for such an absence are readily apparent. The paradigm "early modern" appears irrelevant for interpreting a society that lacked any medieval Jewish past and therefore did not experience the same sort of transition to modernity that characterized Jewish life in Europe. Indeed, most scholars continue to regard the United States as a nation born on the precipice of modernity, given that expanding legal freedoms and religious voluntarism already defined Jewish experience by the late colonial period. Moreover, until recently, most scholarly treatments of American Jewish history have been structured solely through the prism of United States history, treating the North American colonies in isolation from other Atlantic Jewish settlements and offering a teleological interpretation that renders the 1654 arrival of Jews in New Amsterdam the putative origin of Jewish communal life in the United States.[1]

This tendency has been corrected only in the last twenty-five years, as Jewish historians have looked beyond political boundaries to examine colonial North America in the broader context of the Atlantic Jewish world.[2] At the same time, the scholarship on port Jews—those merchants who lived in port cities throughout the Mediterranean and Atlantic worlds—has broadened concepts of modernity by exploring how trade and mobility moved not only goods but also new ideas back and forth across the Atlantic.[3] All these developments have helped transform the study of early American Jewish life from older narratives about the mythical "Jewish Pilgrim Fathers" toward a more complex focus on networks of interconnected merchants, communities, and multiple Jewish diasporas of the New World.[4] Yet, even scholars of Atlantic and port Jewry seldom employ the category "early modern" to describe colonial North American and United States Jewry, at least not as the phrase is used in European Jewish history, namely to define an era of "mobility, communal cohesion, a knowledge explosion, rabbinical authority in crisis, and a muddling of religious identities."[5]

Jewish life in the North American colonies and in the early Republic does not neatly fit into European paradigms of early modern Jewish history. There was certainly no explosion of Jewish knowledge and no rapid increase in the printing of Jewish books to be found in these early years. In fact, most Jews of this era seemed to have possessed only a rudimentary knowledge of Hebrew. Not until the nineteenth century did American Jews begin publishing Jewish books, newspapers, and translations of Jewish texts. America's early communities also boasted no sophisticated supra-communal organizations that remotely compared to Poland's Council of Four Lands or even to less complex community structures in Europe. Yet, in other ways, early American Jews pushed the boundaries of religious and social life much further and more rapidly than their counterparts in European societies. Colonial American Jews outpaced most European Jews in rates of social and economic mobility and in their regular contact with Christian neighbors. Christian Hebraism also took on new theological and cultural dimensions on North American shores. From the start, early American communities faced serious challenges to Jewish communal authority and were forced to adjust to religious voluntarism, ultimately creating religious options for Jews at a furious pace. If early modern European Jews witnessed a crisis and a weakening of rabbinic authority, North American Jews in the colonies and early Republic operated without rabbis altogether. (The first ordained rabbi did not settle in the United States until 1840.) The complete absence of rabbinic authority and lack of state interference in internal Jewish affairs hastened the development of new forms of Jewish self-definition and made for a culture of remarkable innovation. Despite its manifest differences, examining North American Jewry as part of, rather than apart from, the early modern Jewish world, and considering it in comparative context, creates a more diverse and multifaceted portrait of Jewish experience in this transitional epoch.

Jews arrived in North America in significant numbers toward the close of the early modern period and at a moment when, according to historian Jon Butler, co-lonial America was in the process of becoming "the first modern society" in eco-nomic and political terms as well as in its unparalleled ethnic diversity and religious pluralism.[6] Before making the journey across the Atlantic, most colonial American Jews had experienced at least some of the transformations of Jewish life in early modern Europe, but they settled in a society that was inventing itself anew. In a cli-mate where established hierarchies were losing influence and power, early America witnessed unprecedented challenges to religious authority, heightened interaction between Christians and Jews, and new forms of communal organization. While some of these phenomena had emerged in early modern Europe, they reached full efflorescence in the colonies and early Republic. Although early America lacked great Jewish erudition, it nonetheless became a harbinger of new expressions of community and culture at the dawn of the modern era.

Like Jews throughout the New World, North American Jews found their lives defined by constant mobility and travel. The letters circulated in the 1730s and 1740s between members of New York's Franks family, a prominent merchant clan, document trips to and from Philadelphia, Jamaica, India, England, Holland, Georgia, and South Carolina, just to name a few of their destinations. Michael Gratz, who was born in Langendorf, in Upper Silesia, began his business endeavors in Berlin, then tried his fortunes in Amsterdam, London, and the East Indies, before finally joining his older brother Bernard in Philadelphia in 1759.[7] Geographic mobility and transient lifestyles characterized Jewish life in both the Atlantic and the early mod-ern European worlds. Yet, Jewish intellectuals and those steeped in classical Hebraic learning were not among those who made the journey to the North American fron-tier, and thus, Jewish cultural production did not follow in the wake of Jewish migra-tions, as had often been the case in Europe.[8] "It took fully 200 years from the arrival of the Jews in North America," one scholar has noted, "before the pangs of Hebraic culture produced a Hebrew book in the full sense of the term."[9] When a substantial Jewish literature did emerge in the mid-1800s, its primary language was English, and the range of books, newspapers, and translations of classic texts constituted a veritable "Atlantic Jewish republic of letters," as Arthur Kiron has suggested.[10] But the tiny population that settled in colonial North America and the early Republic possessed neither the resources nor the acumen to create the Jewish cultural produc-tion that was to emerge in the following centuries.

With some notable exceptions, most Jews who made the journey to early America practiced Judaism with a basic knowledge of Hebrew but with limited facility with rabbinic texts. Colonial Jews certainly brought their prayer books to the New World, and a sufficient number of Jewish men had the skills to lead worship services and satisfy the fundamental Jewish needs of the small communities. Tombstone inscrip-tions, surviving *ketubot*, and a handful of original Hebrew prayers, including one composed for the 1789 inauguration of George Washington, reveal that at least a few were well-versed in the Hebrew language. Nevertheless, in the 1760s, Isaac Pinto felt compelled to translate the Sabbath and High Holiday prayers into English because he observed that Hebrew was "imperfectly understood by many, by some, not at all." Colonial American Jews did want their children to acquire a basic Jewish knowledge, so, for example, New York's Congregation Shearith Israel employed private tutors and, by the 1730s, established its first formal Hebrew school. Yet regardless of their faithfulness to tradition, the majority had little desire or ability to pursue higher levels of Jewish knowledge.[11]

Ironically, many of the most extensive Judaica collections in North America were compiled by Christians. Christian Hebraism flourished on both sides of the ocean, but with some distinct features in early America. Not only did Christian interest in Jewish sources thrive in an atmosphere devoid of eminent Jewish scholarship, but it was also bolstered by notions that the New World was a place of providential destiny and by claims that Native Americans were descended from the ten lost tribes of the Israelites. Fascination with the ten tribes spread from Europe to the Americas, as both Jews and Christians, spurred in part by the publication of Menasseh Ben Israel's *Hope of Israel*, proposed a range of Jewish/Indian theories. North American Puritans interpreted the New World's Jewish origins as further proof of its divine destiny, and placed particular meaning in observations that "the rites, fashions, ceremonies, and opinions of the [native] Americans are in many ways agreeable to the custome of the Jewes."[12] As Jonathan Boyarin has observed, "the Indian (often seen as the wild man, unformed and chaotic, positioned at 'the boundaries of humanity') and the Jew (false and negative, hiding the true nature of Scripture)" both served, in different ways, to challenge and define Christian identity in the age of colonialism.[13] When it came to the Jewish "Other," Christian Hebraists on both sides of the Atlantic looked to Jewish sources to unlock the meaning of Scripture, believing that the truth of divine revelation emerged more powerfully in the original language of the Bible.

Ezra Stiles, who spent much of his life in Newport, Rhode Island, and also served as president of Yale College, maintained an abiding interest in deciphering clues to the coming of the Messiah and in understanding the fate of the ten lost tribes, though he rejected the notion that connected them to Native Americans. Like many other devout Christians, Stiles mastered the Hebrew language and gained facility with the Hebrew Bible as well as classical Jewish texts. He amassed an extensive Jewish library, read the *Zohar*, the Talmud, and a host of rabbinic commentaries, always through the prism of his Christian faith.[14] As a Newport resident, Stiles formed close personal relationships with local Jews, including Rev. Isaac Touro who taught him Hebrew, and the prominent merchant Aaron Lopez. Stiles often visited the Newport synagogue, eagerly exchanged ideas with a few rabbis who made short trips to the city, including forging a meaningful intellectual engagement with R. Haim Carigal of Hebron who spent several months in Newport in 1773.[15] Searching for Christian meaning not only in Jewish texts but also in Jewish customs and traditions, Stiles noticed in one of his visits to the congregation that Jews kissed the strings of their prayer shawls three times during the recitation of the Shema and wondered, "Did this originally denote acknowleg[t] of Trinity in Unity?"[16]

A number of pious Christians assembled extensive Jewish book collections, both privately and in the colonies' first colleges, and kept the Hebrew language alive in the New World. At the ten colleges established before the Revolution instruction in "Hebrew and the shemitish languages" comprised an integral part of the curriculum, both for theological purposes and as part of a well-rounded education in the classics.[17] As in early modern European communities, converts from Judaism often played key roles in Christian Hebraism in the North American colonies. Judah Monis, who was most likely born in Italy to a family of former conversos, arrived in New York in 1715, and began teaching Hebrew to both Jews and Christians. He corresponded with Puritan clergy about a number of religious matters, including Kabbalah. Monis moved to Cambridge, Massachusetts, in 1720, and after converting to Christianity began his long career as a Hebrew instructor at Harvard University. Scholars have disagreed about the sincerity of Monis's conversion, but whatever his beliefs or motivations, Monis maintained a fruitful dialogue with Christian scholars and clergy during his almost forty-year tenure at Harvard. Monis's *A Grammar of The Hebrew Tongue* (1735), the first Hebrew textbook published in North America, became a standard text in many colleges and, despite its many errors, a manual regularly used by Christians who desired to master the language.[18]

James Logan of Philadelphia did not use Monis's text, but he did supplement his rudimentary knowledge of Hebrew with a program of independent study, using a Hebrew lexicon published abroad and becoming an accomplished Hebrew reader.[19] A Quaker born in Ireland, James Logan was a leading figure in Philadelphia, serving as mayor and chief justice of the Supreme Court, among a host of other positions in the first half of the eighteenth century. A gifted intellectual as well as a person of abiding faith, he determined to read Jewish sources in the original language and began acquiring Jewish books as part of his extensive library. A genuine bibliophile, he amassed an extraordinary and wide-ranging 2,600 volume collection, which included an enormous amount of Judaica. He purchased Hebrew bibles and prayer books, the *Shulḥan 'arukh*, and the six-volume edition of the Mishnah with the Maimonides and Bertinoro commentaries, just to name a few. In the eighteenth century, Logan created the largest collection of Hebraica in North America, and likely the most remarkable personal library of Judaica anywhere in the colonies. Logan, too, befriended a Jewish convert to Christianity, Isaac Miranda, from whom he not only purchased Jewish books but also sought to glean what could be learned from "a Jew by Education."[20] As in Europe, Christian Hebraists operated in a "new cultural space" characterized by intersecting realms of religious knowledge, but that space took on unique dimensions in the North American colonies, where many Christians initially outpaced Jews in their knowledge of Hebrew and collections of Jewish books. Colonial Jews seemed to exhibit little concern about Christian interest in Jewish texts. They displayed greater apprehension in later years when missionary activity escalated in the nineteenth century. In the colonial period, most Jews were more preoccupied with establishing themselves as individuals and creating the rudimentary building blocks of Jewish life than worrying about Christian mastery of Jewish sources.[21]

While early American Jews possessed limited Jewish resources and knowledge, many displayed considerable secular literacy and a few contributed to the creation of some of the colonies' first educational institutions. In the absence of any system of public education, Shearith Israel's school taught not only Hebrew, but also English, reading, writing, and "Cyphering." The children of elite merchants, like New York's Franks family, received additional private schooling where they learned math, Greek, and Latin. Abigail Franks, though hardly typical of most colonial Jews in terms of status and wealth, voraciously read everything from histories of England and Poland to the literature of Alexander Pope and Joseph Addison to the British monthly *Gentleman's Magazine*. Nathan Levy of Philadelphia owned works by Locke and Plutarch, books on math, law, and poetry, as well as one of the most extensive Jewish libraries, consisting of about thirty-two Hebrew books.[22] They may have lagged behind their European counterparts in classical Jewish erudition, but many early American Jews played pivotal roles in creating the first secular libraries and educational institutions in the colonies. As early as 1757, David Franks became a member of Philadelphia's Library Company, a private subscription library that lent books only to members but allowed the public to use its reading room. Several other prominent members of the Philadelphia community, including members of the Gratz and Hays families, also joined and supported the institution.[23] Likewise, in Newport, three Jews—Abraham Hart, Moses Lopez, and Jacob Rodrigues Rivera—helped to found the city's Redwood Library. Newport Jews also contributed to the establishment of what would become Brown University. The budding educational institutions of colonial North America allowed Jews and Christians to engage one another in non-sectarian settings and to work together as founders of these nascent intellectual experiments, creating a level of Jewish-Christian dialogue and cooperation seldom seen in early modern Europe.[24]

Jews and Christians not only shared in intellectual discourse, but they also interacted socially and in the business world. Jewish men, particularly the economic elite, participated actively in Masonry. As early as 1734, in Georgia, members of the Sheftall family joined the Masons, and as many as fifteen Newport Jews belonged to St. John's Lodge by the mid-eighteenth century. In an organization that valued status above ethnicity or religion, merchant Moses Michael Hays rose to the post of Deputy Inspector General in 1769, the highest position available to a Mason in North America.[25] When Hays lived in New York, he and his father engaged in business with many of the city's most prominent non-Jewish residents, including members of the Van Wyck, Van Deussen, Beekman, and Livingston families. The small size of colonial American communities ensured that Jews and gentiles regularly did business together, and more than a few Jews joined with Christian partners in formal commercial endeavors. In the 1730s in Savannah, Jews and Christians even attended each other's worship services.[26] Members of elite Jewish families often socialized with their non-Jewish neighbors; Abigail Franks reported spending summers with some of her closest Christian friends. The novelty of the colonial enterprise, where everyone was a relative newcomer and where social boundaries were more fluid, reduced some of the barriers between Christians and Jews that existed elsewhere in the early modern world.[27]

Nevertheless, despite an unprecedented degree of interaction and acceptance in colonial America, all sorts of prejudices about Jews lingered. Rev. Thomas Barton of Lancaster, Pennsylvania, described the city's Jewish merchant Joseph Simon as "a worthy, honest Jew," but Rev. David McClure, who also conducted business with Simon, charged that Jewish traders "hesitate not to defraud when opportunity present."[28] Long-held beliefs that Jewish traders lacked moral scruples and sought profit above all else survived in the New World, as did longstanding attitudes about the inferiority of Judaism as a religion. For all his personal connections with Jews and interest in Jewish customs, Ezra Stiles believed fervently that Jews would always suffer for their rejection of Christ. When Rhode Island authorities denied the petition of Aaron Lopez and Isaac Elizer for naturalization—a notable exception to the general pattern of legal tolerance in early America—Stiles concluded that "Providence seems to make every thing to work for the mortification of the Jews, and to prevent their incorporation into any nation; that thus they may continue a distinct people." He further noted that their political failure in Rhode Island "forbodes that the Jews will never become incorporated with the People of America any more than in Europe, Asia, and Africa."[29] Enduring prejudices remained even as Jews maintained close business and social ties to non-Jews and experienced virtually unprecedented religious and legal tolerance.

The openness of colonial America presented unique challenges for Jewish religious and communal life. With no rabbis in the colonies until the nineteenth century and with synagogues entirely reliant on the voluntary support and compliance of their members, Judaism in early America operated on untested ground. Colonial Jews fashioned their communities out of whole cloth, using patterns imported from Europe, adapted by necessity to the novel circumstances of the New World. While colonial synagogues were hardly democratic, the seeds of religious voluntarism and lay authority that would define Jewish practice in the modern period were planted early. In the absence of clergy, lay leaders supervised all arenas of Jewish life. Synagogue officials made most decisions on their own, occasionally sending legal inquiries to rabbinic authorities in Europe. In colonial North America, lay control exceeded that of anywhere else in the New World. Communities throughout the Caribbean employed a ḥakham (sage) to provide leadership, but early America's congregations did not retain the services of any religious authority. Those with wealth and status led colonial synagogues; they held the best seats and they ruled autocratically. Throughout the eighteenth century, synagogues remained the central and the sole Jewish institutions in America, and, with only one in each community, they operated as monopolies. Synagogues controlled the Jewish cemetery, paid the *shochet* who provided kosher meat, offered rudimentary Jewish education to children, and supervised every Jewish lifecycle event from the cradle to the grave.[30]

New York's Shearith Israel congregation initially managed its affairs according to the European paradigm, attempting to exert supreme control over its members. The congregation exacted fines for all sorts of transgressions, both inside and outside the synagogue. Shearith Israel's leaders tried to enforce strict adherence to Jewish law, warning those who "dayly violate the principles [of] our holy religion, such as Trading on the Sab[b]ath, Eating of forbidden Meats & other Heinous Crimes" that they might lose their membership or, more seriously, be prohibited from being buried in the Jewish cemetery—one of the most severe penalties that could be exacted.[31] But six months later, facing objections from members, the *adjunta* (synagogue board) reconsidered and welcomed back the congregants that it had admonished. Fines and other disciplinary action were commonplace, but excommunication remained exceedingly rare. In fact, the repeated threats demonstrate the limited reach of early American synagogues, which, unlike most congregations in Europe or other Atlantic communities, could not rely on the government to bolster their authority. Colonial governments in North America, at least those in the comparatively pluralistic societies where Jews chose to live, gave religious communities significant autonomy and preferred not to intervene in their affairs. This set the stage for a very different brand of religious community on North American shores.

Lay officials attempted to keep tight rein on their members, but regularly complained that in contrast to European communities, "the congregation here has no power to discipline anyone." There were cases of utter defiance. In Philadelphia, Mordecai M. Mordecai objected when leaders of Mikveh Israel synagogue ruled that a Jewish merchant who had married a non-Jewish woman "should be buried in a corner of the cemetery, without ritual washing, without a shroud and without a ceremony." Mordecai chose to rebury the body, complete with a shroud and a proper ritual. On another occasion, Mordecai performed a Jewish marriage ceremony for his niece after she had married a non-Jewish man.[32] When the congregation's leaders protested his actions, Mordecai claimed that he possessed superior knowledge of rabbinic law than any of the synagogue officials. New York's Naphtali Phillips observed that although the leaders of Shearith Israel acted as if they "were masters of the life and liberty and fortunes" over all members, in reality, "there never was a time, whether it was the spirit of the new country or not, when there was that implicit obedience from the congregation to these edicts that there had been in Amsterdam."[33] Synagogue leaders used disciplinary measures and strong admonitions in an attempt to enforce standards of behavior in an environment where hierarchical religious authority proved weak and ineffective. Long before democratic process came to American congregations, it was apparent that the practice of Judaism and the structure of Jewish communal life had taken on new dimensions. While Europe was experiencing a host of challenges to rabbinic authority, Jews in the colonies and early Republic had already begun refashioning Judaism without rabbis; religious authority was not simply in crisis, it was being overhauled to fit the nascent modern world taking shape in the open frontiers.

One of the most unique characteristics of early American Jewish life was the high degree of cooperation between Ashkenazim and Sephardim. In communities throughout Europe and the West Indies, Ashkenazim and Sephardim maintained separate synagogues, cemeteries, and social lives, but in colonial America mutual collaboration quickly became the norm. Sephardic Jews certainly retained religious and cultural hegemony; Sephardic rite prevailed throughout colonial synagogues, despite the fact that Ashkenazim constituted a majority of the population in some communities as early as 1720. At Shearith Israel, prayers for the King of England were recited in Portuguese until the Revolution. Conflict between Ashkenazim and Sephardim by no means disappeared and in fact, tensions percolated regularly within colonial Jewish communities. The worst disputes occurred in Savannah during the 1730s when the two groups fought bitterly over the construction of a synagogue. Yet, despite a constant undercurrent of Sephardic claims to cultural superiority and Ashkenazic allegations that Sephardim fell short in the rigors of religious practice, the differences failed to rupture the collaborative enterprise. In 1729, when the Jewish community of Curaçao agreed to provide financial assistance to New York Jews as they set out to build their first synagogue, Curaçao's ḥakham insisted that although Ashkenazic Jews "are more in Number than Wee there," the Sephardic leaders of Shearith Israel should not allow them to "have any More Votes nor Authority than they have hitherto."[34] Nonetheless, Shearith Israel's history reveals that Sephardim and Ashkenazim worked together to build the synagogue and shared equally in its governance. Even the taboo of intermarriage between the two groups disappeared relatively quickly in early America. In 1740, when Sephardic Isaac Mendes Seixas married Ashkenazic Rachel Levy, the union provoked considerable outrage among Sephardim. Abigail Franks reported that, "The Portugeuze here are in a great ferment abouth it And think Very Ill of him."[35] But marriages between Ashkenazim and Sephardim became increasingly common in the colonies. In fact, the son of the Seixas-Levy union, Gershom Mendes Seixas, became the first native-born ḥazan at Shearith Israel and led the community into the early nineteenth century. The small size of the early American Jewish population does not completely explain the extent of the cooperative spirit, since other small communities in the New World retained a potent Ashkenazic-Sephardic divide. In the colonial religious world, as in other arenas of North American life, hierarchies did not hold sway and the notion of shared Jewish peoplehood seems to have taken root far earlier than in other nascent communities.[36]

Intermarriage between Jews and Christians proved a more vexing challenge in early America. On the one hand, intermarriages testified to the extent of Jewish acceptance and integration; on the other, they threatened the viability of the small Jewish community. With few barriers to limit social contact and a scarcity of eligible partners, Jewish intermarriage rates likely ranged from ten to fifteen percent in colonial America.[37] The most well-documented episode occurred in 1742 when Phila Franks, daughter of Abigail and Jacob Franks, secretly married Oliver DeLancey, son of a prominent non-Jewish family. Abigail Franks had gladly socialized with non-Jews and adopted their dress and cultural norms, but intermarriage remained an affront to her religious principles. Upon learning the news, she refused to leave her home and vowed never to see her daughter again, even as her husband attempted to force a reconciliation. "I am determined," she wrote to her son, "I never will see nor lett none of the family goe near her." Most Jews who intermarried eventually lost connection to Jewish life, but some retained strong ties to the Jewish community; such was the case for David Franks, also a child of Abigail and Jacob, who married a Christian woman. Jewish identity often emerged in hybrid forms in early America. Two colonial Jewish men who intermarried, whose sons would not have been considered Jews according to Jewish law, nonetheless chose to have them ritually circumcised.[38] As these examples reveal, while Jews on the European continent struggled to cope with "conspicuous boundary crossings between Judaism and Christianity" sparked by the reentry of conversos into Jewish life and the multiple challenges posed by Christian Hebraism, Jews in North America not only grappled with those issues, but also encountered far more radical expressions of mingled identities. Early America's more fluid social and religious boundaries prompted colonial Jews to confront challenges to Jewish identity that would later define modern Jewish experience. In fact, by the late eighteenth and early nineteenth centuries, North American congregations attempted to draw a line of demarcation around Jewish identity by stipulating in their by-laws and constitutions that those who intermarried would be barred from membership and excluded from religious privileges.[39]

America's Jews understood that their communities had increasingly ceased to resemble those they had left behind in Europe. After the Revolution and the ratification of the Constitution, synagogues consciously adopted new democratic procedures. New York's Shearith Israel went so far as to include a "bill of rights" in its constitution, and other congregations also began to select their leaders "by adult male suffrage." While they embraced the expansion of rights that came with the establishment of the new nation, Jewish leaders continued to be concerned about the consequences of unprecedented personal autonomy in matters of religion that allowed "each [to act] according to his own desire." America's Jews did not want their practice of Judaism to become unrecognizable to their European coreligionists. When, in 1784, Philadelphia's Mikveh Israel congregation determined to build a *mikveh* (ritual bathhouse), one of its leaders explained that the need was paramount because "should it be known in congregations abroad that we had been thus neglectful of so important a matter, they would not only pronounce heavy anathemas against us, but interdict and avoid intermarriages with us, equal as with a different nation or sect, to our great shame and mortification."[40]

Just as eighteenth-century Philadelphia Jews continued to consider themselves part of the larger Jewish world whose centers were thousands of miles away, so too, do early American Jews belong in the historiographic conversation about early modern Jewry more broadly. The experiences of colonial North American Jews were indeed distinct in many respects. Christian Hebraism took on unique dimensions in a society where few Jews were steeped in classical Jewish learning, and Jewish communities operated more fluidly without hegemonic leadership. At the same time, the undermining of religious authority and the mingling of identities that occurred in early modern Europe emerged more rapidly and more radically on the colonial frontier. Situated at the geographic and cultural outer boundaries of the early modern Jewish world, colonial North America and the early Republic of the United States served as a laboratory for testing the possibilities and redesigning the contours of Jewish life under unprecedented circumstances. In an atmosphere of expanding legal rights, fading hierarchies, and weakened established institutions, Jews who had come from Europe and settled in what would become the United States presaged the dynamics of Jewish modernity and drafted a new blueprint for Jewish community and culture that would, in time, characterize most of the Jewish world.

Notes

Thanks to members of Philadelphia's Working Group in American Jewish Studies for their helpful suggestions on this essay.

1. Arthur Kiron, "Mythologizing 1654," *JQR* 94.4 (2004): 586.

2. Paolo Bernardini and Norman Fiering, eds., *The Jews and the Expansion of Europe to the West, 1450–1800* (New York, 2001); Richard L. Kagan and Philip D. Morgan, eds., *Atlantic Diasporas: Jews, Conversos, and Crypto-Jews in the Age of Mercantilism, 1500–1800* (Baltimore, Md., 2009).

3. David Cesarani, ed., *Port Jews: Jewish Communities in Cosmopolitan Maritime Trading Centres, 1550–1950* (London, 2002); see also *Jewish History* 20.2 (2006).

4. Arnold Wiznitzer, "The Exodus from Brazil and Arrival in New Amsterdam of the Jewish Pilgrim Fathers, 1654," *Publications of the American Jewish Historical Society* 44.1 (1954): 80–97.

5. David B. Ruderman, *Early Modern Jewry: A New Cultural History* (Princeton, N.J., 2010), 192.

6. Jon Butler, *Becoming America: The Revolution Before 1776* (Cambridge, Mass., 2000), 7, 2–4.

7. Eli Faber, *A Time for Planting: The First Migration, 1654–1820* (Baltimore, Md., 1992), 44–45; Edwin Wolf 2nd and Maxwell Whiteman, *The History of the Jews of Philadelphia* (Philadelphia, 1975), 40.

8. Ruderman, *Early Modern Jewry*, 41–53.

9. Isaac Rivkind, "Early American Hebrew Documents," *Publications of the American Jewish Historical Society* 34 (1937): 53.

10. Arthur Kiron, "An Atlantic Jewish Republic of Letters?" *Jewish History* 20.2 (2006): 171–211.

11. Jacob Kabakoff, "The Use of Hebrew by American Jews During the Colonial Period," in S. Goldman, ed., *Hebrew and the Bible in America: The First Two Centuries* (Hanover, N.H., 1993), 191–97; Isaac Pinto, trans., *Prayers for Shabbath, Rosh Hashanah and Kippur* (New York, 1765–66), preface.

12. Thomas Thorowgood, *Jewes in America, Or Probabilities that the Americans are of that Race* (London, 1650), 6.

13. Jonathan Boyarin, *The Unconverted Self: Jews, Indians, and the Identity of Christian Europe* (Chicago, 2009), 27.

14. George Alexander Kohut, *Ezra Stiles and the Jews: Selected Passages from his Literary Diary* (New York, 1902), 9–12; Arthur A. Chiel, "Ezra Stiles and the Jews: A Study in Ambivalence," in Goldman, *Hebrew and the Bible*, 157.

15. Michael Hoberman, *New Israel/New England: Jews and Puritans in Early America* (Amherst, Mass., 2011), 177–96.

16. Kohut, *Ezra Stiles and the Jews*, 26.

17. Shalom Goldman, *God's Sacred Tongue: Hebrew & the American Imagination* (Chapel Hill, N.C., 2004), 29.

18. Goldman, *God's Sacred Tongue*, 31–46; Hoberman, *New Israel/New England*, 86–120; Judah Monis, *A Grammar of the Hebrew Tongue* (Boston, 1735).

19. *James Logan, 1674–1751: Bookman Extraordinary* (Philadelphia, 1971), 29–30.

20. Wolf and Whiteman, *Jews of Philadelphia*, 16–20.

21. Ruderman, *Early Modern Jewry*, 119.

22. Faber, *Time for Planting*, 71; Edith Gelles, ed., *The Letters of Abigaill Levy Franks, 1733–1748* (New Haven, Conn., 2004), xxii, xxxi; Wolf and Whiteman, *Jews of Philadelphia*, 35.

23. Wolf and Whiteman, *Jews of Philadelphia*, 314.

24. William Pencak, *Jews & Gentiles in Early America, 1654–1800* (Ann Arbor, Mich., 2005), 92; Hoberman, *New Israel/New England*, 173–75.

25. Pencak, *Jews & Gentiles in Early America*, 92; Hoberman, *New Israel/New England*, 224–232; Morris A. Gutstein, *The Story of the Jews of Newport* (New York, 1936), 168–69.

26. Holly Snyder, "A Tree with Two Different Fruits: The Jewish Encounter with German Pietists in the Eighteenth-Century Atlantic World," *The William and Mary Quarterly* 58.4 (2001): 870.

27. Hoberman, *New Israel/New England*, 207–08; Faber, *Time for Planting*, 84–87; Gelles, ed., *Letters of Abigaill Levy Franks*, xxii.

28. Faber, *Time for Planting*, 95–96.

29. Franklin B. Dexter, ed., *Extracts from the Itineraries and other Miscellanies of Ezra Stiles* (New Haven, Conn., 1916), 52–53.

30. Jonathan D. Sarna, *American Judaism: A History* (New Haven, Conn., 2004), 12–20.

31. "The Earliest Extant Minute Books of the Spanish and Portuguese Congregation Shearith Israel in New York, 1728–1786," *Publications of the American Jewish Historical Society* 21 (1913): 74–75, 36–37, 51–53.

32. Pencak, *Jews & Gentiles in Early America*, 218; Wolf and Whiteman, *Jews of Philadelphia*, 128–30; Sarna, *American Judaism*, 44–45.

33. Pencak, *Jews & Gentiles in Early America*, 53; Sarna, *American Judaism*, 15–17.

34. David De Sola Pool, *The Mill Street Synagogue (1730–1817) of the Congregation Shearith Israel* (New York, 1930), 49.

35. Leo Hershkowitz and Isidore S. Meyer, eds., *The Lee Max Friedman Collection of American Jewish Colonial Correspondence: Letters of the Franks Family (1733–1748)* (Waltham, Mass., 1968), 66–67.

36. Faber, *Time for Planting*, 52–66; Sarna, *American Judaism*, 18–20.

37. Malcolm Stern, "The Function of Genealogy in American Jewish History," in *Essays in American Jewish History to Commemorate the Tenth Anniversary of the Founding of the American Jewish Archives under the Direction of Jacob Rader Marcus* (Cincinnati, Oh., 1958), 83–86.

38. Hershkowitz and Meyer, *American Jewish Colonial Correspondence*, 116–122; Sarna, *American Judaism*, 27–28; Faber, *A Time for Planting*, 93.

39. Ruderman, *Early Modern Jewry*, 159, 159–89; Faber, *Time for Planting*, 121–22.

40. Pencak, *Jews & Gentiles in Early America*, 70–72, 15.

LANGUAGE AND PERIODIZATION

❈ ❈ ❈

Mendele Moykher Sforim and the Revival of Pre-Haskalah Style

Israel Bartal

The Hebrew University of Jerusalem

I

MENDELE Moykher Sforim (Mendele the Book Peddler, the literary pseudonym of Shalom Jacob Abramovitch, 1835–1917) has been regarded by generations of critics and literary scholars as the "inventor of the style" (*yotser ha-nosakh*). Mendele wrote in Hebrew and Yiddish, and his oeuvre in both languages occupies an important place in the Jewish literary canon in general and in the linguistic history of modern Hebrew literature in particular. Mendele's literary creation has been usually connected by both historians and literary critics with the Haskalah and its post-Enlightenment affiliations—be it nascent Jewish nationalism, social radicalism and/or Russian-style populism.[1] This bilingual writer, who was born in White Russia and lived most of his life in Ukraine, wrote and published in Hebrew and Yiddish for more than fifty years, and his use of those languages developed over the course of that long period. He rewrote a considerable number of his works, and his complete oeuvre was published only a few years before the beginning of WWI. His writings in their final version were published in honor of his seventy-fifth birthday: in Hebrew as *Kol kitve Mendele Mokher Sfarim*, 3 vols. (Kraków and Odessa, 1909–12) and in Yiddish as *Ale verk fun Mendele Moykher Sforim* (Warsaw, New York, and Vilna, 1911–13). The later editions of his writings in both languages are based, with few changes, on these editions.

The relationship between the two languages used by this great bilingual writer has occupied the attention of several generations of critics and scholars. Shmuel Werses (1915–2010), who studied the literary criticism of Ḥayim Nahman Bialik, wrote enthusiastically of that perceptive poet's ability to rise above the conflict between the partisans of Hebrew and Yiddish and to see Mendele's style as a whole. According to Werses, Bialik saw in Mendele's language a sort of "higher synthesis that Mendele was able to attain, the higher blend of the essence of all styles, which expressed the unique qualities of the language in each generation."[2] Students of modern Eastern European Jewish literature also considered the question of "priority" in the formation of a bilingual blend of Mendele's sort. Mendele's oeuvre was not the first to be written in a language that amalgamated Hebrew and Yiddish into a new "style," different from the Hebrew prose of the *maskilim*, the partisans of the Jewish Enlightenment. Dov Sadan saw earlier instances in which "the two gates of language"[3] were opened; he cited, on the one hand, the Hasidic collection of legends known as *Shivḥe ha-Besht* and, on the other, the writings of the *maskil* Mendel Lefin. Werses regarded the anti-Hasidic satires of Joseph Perl (1773–1839) as precedents for Mendele's bilingual work. He asserted that "until now, we have seen Mendele Moykher-Sforim (Sh. Y. Abramovitch) as a classic example of a bilingual writer who translated his work from Yiddish to Hebrew and created, in effect, two separate, parallel, artistic versions, each existing in its own right. But it seems as a practical matter that Joseph Perl preceded him in creating a dual oeuvre of this sort."[4] He also noted the difference between Mendele, who first wrote a substantial portion of his prose in Yiddish and then produced a different version in Hebrew, and Perl, "who was compelled . . . to translate and shape the extra-literary world, whose language was Yiddish, and provide it Hebrew garb; and only later did he restore that world—which he had initially garbed, intentionally, in parodic Hebrew calque translations—to its natural and original language."[5] Ken Frieden recently noted the part played by the *maskil* Mendel Lefin (1749–1826) and the Bratslav hasidic rabbi Nathan Sternhartz (1780–1844) in the shaping of a Hebrew writing style "in what sounds like an oral style."[6] According to Frieden, these two writers were able to create, through their early–nineteenth-century travel writings, the illusion that spoken Hebrew existed in the years 1815 to 1823—a language that, in Frieden's words, "calqued contemporary vernaculars."[7] Frieden traces a direct line from the "folk Hebrew" created by Lefin and Sternhartz, through Perl's satires, to modern Hebrew literature—a line that ties Mendele's *Masa'ot binyamin ha-shelishi* (The Travels of Benjamin the Third, 1878/1896) to these travel writings.[8]

Mendele's linguistic project can serve as a key to one of the major issues of Jewish modernity. While being a *maskil* in his ideology and politics for several decades, his use of both Hebrew and Yiddish in most of his literary career was very different from that of other Eastern European members of the Haskalah movement. His linguistic decision-making presented, in a way, a traditionalist mode that stood in stark contrast to that of his fellow *maskilim*. One could claim that Mendele had resorted to the pre-Enlightenment Ashkenazi bilingualism, going back in his Hebrew prose to an early modern linguistic phase. In ideological terms, Mendele could be described as a sworn modernist. From a linguistic point of view, however, Mendele opted in his bilingual creation for an early modern Jewish culture that continued to flourish in Eastern Europe, regardless of the contemporary maskilic project.

II

The Jews of the Ashkenazi Diaspora, which in the early modern period spread from Alsace in the west to the eastern frontiers of the Polish-Lithuanian Commonwealth, spent more than a millennium in a linguistic environment where a variety of Romance, Germanic, and Slavic languages was used. The influence of Germanic and Slavic languages on the Ashkenazi Jews' spoken and written vernaculars was applied in several historical phases. It began with the formation of a Jewish-Germanic spoken vernacular (Yiddish) in Central Europe that was used alongside the "Holy Tongue" in one of the Ashkenazi accents, which in turn was comprised of several strata of Hebrew and Aramaic. It reached its peak in the early modern period with linguistic contacts between Jews who used simultaneously Yiddish and the Holy Tongue and several dialects of German and/or Slavic languages, and it ended with the modern linguistic encounter among speakers of Yiddish, Hebrew, German, Russian and Polish in the nineteenth and early twentieth centuries.[9]

The Hebrew used by Mendele in his mature works developed within the polyglot environment in which the literatures of Eastern European Jews took shape between the eighteenth and twentieth centuries. In the multilingual environment in which Hebrew writers and poets worked, several "Jewish" languages were in use, as were at least three "state languages" (Russian, Polish, and German, their use varying with time and place), and several vernaculars of the peoples living side-by-side with the Jews of the Russian and Austrian empires. Even though Russian was the administrative language in some western provinces of the tsar's empire, Polish retained its official status in the northern reaches of the Pale of Settlement until the middle of the nineteenth century. The Jewish population conducted its administrative and economic business with its non-Jewish neighbors on two linguistic planes. In dealings with agents of the tsarist government and the Polish nobility, they used Russian, Polish, and sometimes German, but economic dealings in the towns and villages were conducted in a dialect of one of local vernaculars—Ukrainian, Belorussian, Lithuanian, Polish (where it was spoken by the peasants in the region) and others. This linguistic polysystem remained almost unchanged from the times of the Polish-Lithuanian Commonwealth and began to alter only in the second half of the nineteenth century.

The Jewish Enlightenment introduced ancient Hebrew as the literary idiom of new Ashkenazi intellectual elites. Most Haskalah writers who published their works in the years between 1780 and 1860 wrote revived (pseudo-) biblical Hebrew. But along with Haskalah literature, the period under discussion saw an uninterrupted production of halakhic and kabbalistic works, Hasidic discourses, popular stories, and business letters, all in a Hebrew whose components were quite different from those of the language of the *maskilim*. The language of these texts continued the early modern "neutral" attitude toward Jewish multilingualism of all sorts. It encompassed, on the one hand, post-biblical Hebrew strata; on the other, it was open to influences from Yiddish and from the local languages. This language had a much stronger affinity to the spoken language of Jews and non-Jews than did the form of Hebrew so valued by the *maskilim*. Moreover, the texts contained a sort of Hebrew "spoken language" that continues, in one way or another, the bilingual character of early modern Ashkenazi society. A variety of texts that were in extensive use in the seventeenth and eighteenth centuries—from communal minute-books (*pinkasim*) to moralistic books—consist of several linguistic layers, be they Hebrew, Aramaic, Yiddish and/or non-Jewish languages.[10] This linguistic pluralism found its way well into the Russian empire of the nineteenth century. For example, the Hebrew of the Hasidic hagiographic work *Shivḥe ha-Besht* (published in three Hebrew editions in 1815 and in two Yiddish editions in 1816) draws on Eastern European Yiddish influences, is open to the region's vernaculars, and cites live speech close to the spoken language of Eastern European Jews. We should recall as well that the Yiddish version of *Shivḥe ha-Besht* was one of the first works printed in Eastern European Yiddish rather than in the Western Yiddish that was quite remote from the spoken language of the Pale of Settlement. The stories in the book report in Hebrew what had been told orally in Eastern European Yiddish, in a manner similar to that used decades later by Mendele in his Hebrew works.

In what follows, I want to consider several aspects of Abramovitch-Mendele's literary output within the Jewish bilingualism and the generally polyglot culture in which the Jews of the Russian Empire lived, spoke, and wrote. This talented bilingual author sought in his writings to regain an affinity with late and contemporary linguistic strata that had been shunted aside for about a century because of the *maskilim*'s ambitious leap back to ancient layers of Hebrew. As I see it, Mendele's style, which developed over the course of decades of writing in Hebrew and in Yiddish, was not a post-Haskalah invention; rather, it was an enhancement and expansion of the pre-Haskalah written language that had prevailed in Central and Eastern Europe for centuries before the birth of modern Hebrew literature. The maskilic Hebrew that favored biblical language was displaced, in Mendele's wake, by a multilayered language that had been used earlier and that ultimately left maskilic Hebrew a short-lived episode in the history of modern Jewish culture.

III

Let me begin with the history of one word in Yiddish: *be'*.

גדולה 'בע' שהיא משמשת אצלנו היהודים בכמה וכמה לשונות ובאה במקום
תשובה על כל הקושיות שבעולם. 'בע' עולה יפה בעל עניין ודברי שיחה, היהודי
מסתייע בה בצוק העתים ובכל שעה שהוא נתפס במצודה.

[In Ted Gorelic's English translation: "[Great is "בע"] for it is a positive gem of a word, which can be made to signify most everything you want it to. And there is no construction you cannot put to it, nor situation it won't answer to its need."] [11]

Be', a one-syllable word defined by Alexander Harkavy as an "exclamation of taunt"[12] and translated by Uriel Weinrich as "pooh!"[13] provides a good example of Abramovitch's use of the multilingual materials readily available to him in the Eastern European environment. The word has numerous meanings in the spoken language of Eastern European Jews; it is a Yiddish word that is spoken, not written. In the passage referred to, the writer explicates some of its possible meanings in a way that only a native Yiddish speaker can understand. For example, only an Eastern European Jew will know that one who cries *koymemiyes* is saying to his creditor that he has gone bankrupt (in other words, that the creditor will never see his money again). A Hebrew reader unfamiliar with the language spoken by Jews in Eastern Europe will not imagine that someone derisively suggesting he can sue him in an *u-nesane toykef* court is saying that there is no chance the lawsuit will prevail. In addition, Mendele is playing on the assonance of Hebrew and Aramaic words with words in the spoken language, be it Yiddish or one of the local non-Jewish languages. Reb Alter, a leading character in *Sefer ha-kabtsanim* (The Book of Beggars), is described as *"me'va'abe'a ke-ilem u-me'na'ane'a be'yado"* [bleating like a mute and tossing up his hand].[14] In the Hebrew of the midrash, the word *me'va'abe'a* connotes the sound associated with coughing or clearing one's throat. By using it, Abramovitch blends spoken Yiddish, in which *be* stands for bleating, with the language of the written Hebrew sources. He thereby emulates Hasidic sermonizers and rebbes who, in their Yiddish discourses, played on similarities between the sounds of words in Hebrew and words in the spoken languages of Jews and non-Jews in Eastern Europe. Haskalah writers, in contrast, ridiculed these discourses, citing them as conclusive proof that the *Hasidim* were ignorant and their language substandard. They opted for the langauge of the ancient Hebrews. As a matter of fact, the *maskilim* "modernized" the pure language of Scripture, embracing a Bible that Jonathan Sheehan has described as "a project rather than an object, a project that was repeatedly undertaken in the first third of the eighteenth century."[15] Abramovitch, unlike his peers, reverted to a pre-Haskalah multilingual manner and knowingly obscured the deliberate distinction between Hebrew and Yiddish that had characterized the language of many Haskalah writers. The spoken Hebrew of his protagonists absorbed words, phrases, and syntactic structures from sources that were neither Hebrew nor Aramaic. But not only did Mendele unreservedly integrate all that material into a Hebrew textual expanse; he also produced a text that led the reader to sense that he was "hearing" the spoken language in all its melodiousness, rhythm, and special sensitivity to time and place. Beyond that, some components of Yiddish penetrated the multilayered expanse of the Hebrew (and Aramaic) language, where they were fully absorbed. Mendele's "imported" *be'* was made to conform to the Hebrew morpho-semantic system and generated a verb, but the writer went further and used a verb with the identical sound that had already existed in earlier strata of Hebrew! Reb Alter's *be'*, and other words Mendele incorporated into his work, underwent the same process as some of the Greek words that had been absorbed into rabbinic Hebrew, becoming integral parts of the Hebrew language to this day. Two verbs in Israeli spoken Hebrew—*le-kater* (to complain; a word of Slavic origin, from Yiddish *koter*,[16] a male cat, *kot* in Polish, with cognates in Russian and Ukranian) and *le-sandel* (to lock)[17](with its source in ancient Greek)—show how well Mendele's efforts at fusion paralleled what had taken place in the spontaneous development of the Hebrew language over the *longue durée*. He freed himself from the linguistic purism of the Eastern European *maskilim*, joining the Ashkenazi Hebrew of his time and the Yiddish of Eastern Europe to a tradition of openness to outside influence extending from antiquity to our own day. In *Sefer ha-kabtsanim*, Mendele integrates other monosyllabic Yiddish words into the speech of his protagonists: *na*, repeated as *na-na; et*, which Harkavy defines as "it's nothing! It's of no consequence!";[18] and *ai*. These words, like *be'*, utterly demolish the conceptual (as well as ideological) and stylistic walls between elevated and common language and between words of biblical origin and words in the daily language of beggars and servants.

IV

Let me turn now to the penetration of the Hebrew text by words from the non-Jewish, Eastern European vernaculars. In one chapter of *Sefer ha-kabtsanim*, Mendele is searching for Reb Alter, who has disappeared. He comes upon a farm garden and tastes some of the vegetables. An *Orl* (uncircumcised Ukrainian or Belorussian male), catches him red-handed and beats him; a conversation then ensues.[19]

In the Yiddish version of the passage, the non-Jew speaks in "their class language"[20]—that is, not in Russian, the official language of the state, but in the language spoken by the local farmers (Ukrainian or Belorussian), a language regarded by the Jews as inferior, simple, and vulgar. Mendele quotes the farmer's vernacular, transcribed into Yiddish. In the later Hebrew version, however, the author creates something like the spoken language of a non-Jew, imitating the syntax and using special Hebrew and Aramaic words to allude to certain words in Slavic speech. For example, *bar nash* (Aramaic for "human being" or "person") is used by the writer instead of the Slavic word *tshelovitshe* (transliterated "tselovitsche" in Hillel Halkin's English translation).[21] In *Masa'ot binyamin ha-shelishi*, a Jew addresses a Ukrainian farmer in Aramaic: *tsafra tava, emor na, barnash* [Good morning! Tell me, man].

In one of my early works, I examined all the passages in Mendele's Hebrew and Yiddish works in which the speech of non-Jews is quoted, and I found the regular use of set formulas, syntactical allusions to the non-Jewish languages, and special words that signify an encounter between Jews and non-Jews.[22] Influenced by ideological considerations, Mendele's representation of the spoken language of

Russian government officials, members of the Polish aristocracy, and Ukrainian and Belorussian farmers underwent several changes over the years. He began by idealizing the Tsarist government, as did the *maskilim*, moved on to idealization of the members of the more popular classes, and ultimately made his way, in his later Hebrew writings, to a realistic depiction of the linguistic contacts between Jews and their surroundings. The representation within the Hebrew text of Russian, Ukrainian, and Polish varied with the ideological changes.

The Hebrew version of *Masa'ot binyamin ha-shelishi* provides several examples of how Mendele was able to fashion bilingual Jewish speech within the polyglot western provinces of the Russian Empire. Let me cite one of them, a depiction of a multilingual encounter between Jews and a farmer. Wanting to go to the Land of Israel, Benjamin and Senderl set out on their journey without knowing the way. In an account that ridicules the Jews' utter disconnection from their immediate environment, Mendele leads his travelers through the villages of the Pale of Settlement. They take a road that brings them to a place called in Hebrew *Shikaron* (drunkenness), but they cannot distinguish between imagination and reality. It is the boorish Ukrainian farmer who brings them back to their true time and place; he meets them and engages them in a conversation that is part Yiddish and part Ukrainian.[23] In the Yiddish version (combined with Ukrainian):

> *Shtsho? Yaki Srul? Nye batshil ya Srul* [What? What Srul? . . . I've never seen Srul?]).[24]

Benjamin, the traveler totally lost in distant worlds, knows Yiddish, Hebrew, and Aramaic (*ha-targum loshn*)—the language of those legendary *bne Mosheh* (sons of Moses) whom he is trying to reach. He enhances his knowledge of Aramaic by reading *akdomes* (the hymn recited on the first day of Shavuot). To connect with the local populace, however, he relies on his assistant Senderl, who picked up the local vernacular when "walking in the market with his wife." Mendele is having fun here, presenting a polyglot encounter in Hebrew, but the text with all its nuances can be understood only by someone reading it with Ashkenazi pronunciation. Senderl asks about the way to the Land of Israel—*erets yisrael*, which sounds, in the South Eastern Ashkenazi pronunciation, like *Srul*, a Jewish personal name known to the local villagers. The farmer responds in his own language that he has seen no Srul, and Benjamin attributes the confusion to the farmer's boorishness and stupidity. The farmer, meanwhile—the only one whose feet are planted on the ground—goes on his way berating them and trying to show them the road as it exists, here and now. Benjamin says:

> And by the way, do you know what I was humming? It was the Akdomus for *Shavuos*, and don't think I didn't have my reasons. You see, once we arrive, God willing, in the land of the ten tribes . . . the language spoken there is the very same Chaldean that the Akdomus is written in. . . . If we were bound for Europe we could get along in German, . . . but I am quite certain that none of the ten tribes knows a word of it.[25]

In Benjamin's remarks about Aramaic and *ashkenazit* (he would have said "*ashkenaz-es*"), Mendele is alluding to a Jewish bilingualism different from that prevailing in the communities of Eastern Europe—to an environment in which one of the Aramaic dialects is used as the vernacular. His visionary hero diligently strives to learn the vernacular of "the sons of Moses" from ancient works, but he cannot speak the spoken language of his immediate non-Jewish surroundings nor does he even recognize the need to learn it. Benjamin believes his spoken language—Yiddish—equips him to speak German, something clearly evident in the Yiddish version of the story: "Here, abroad, one could get along in our language, *daytsh*, but there they, for sure, do not know German."[26]

The Hebrew of various historical periods, Aramaic (together the principal components of the "Holy Tongue" used within early modern European Jewish society), Ukrainian and Belorussian (the spoken languages of the immediate non-Jewish surroundings), Russian (referred to in *Masa'ot binyamin ha-shelishi* as "Muscovit," the language of the state, spoken by military men and agents of the government), and German (the language of high culture in Central Europe)—all of these languages are present, in one way or another, in the late Hebrew version of Mendele's works.

V

The foregoing examples allow us to see the Hebrew text of this Eastern European writer as a linguistic corpus clearly directed toward the members of the bilingual society in the eastern branch of the Ashkenazi dispersion. Sh. Y. Abramovitch envisioned a readership at home in both languages, and his ideal reader was expected to control Hebrew and Yiddish alike. But that meant, in effect, more than two languages, for Hebrew encompassed the Holy Tongue, that is, Hebrew and Aramaic in all their historical strata, extending from the biblical language to the language of the nineteenth-century halakhic, moral, and Hasidic works. Yiddish, meanwhile, encompassed not only the spoken language of the Eastern European Jews but also Western Yiddish, the literary language in which numerous works had been written and published through the beginning of that century—works read and studied by masses of women, men, and children who lived in the western reaches of the Russian Empire. But these readers, Jews living in cities and towns, were simultaneously resident in the polyglot environment described earlier, an environment where the languages of the state and the spoken languages of the western Russian Empire were all current. The *Hebrew* portion of Mendele's literary effort, then, was meant for Jewish readers whose vernacular was *Yiddish* and who could read and properly understand that vernacular's vocabulary, syntactical contexts and modes of expression (taking account of all its historical strata and sometimes of the principal differences among the various dialects of eastern Yiddish)—all as blended, with great artistic skill, in Mendele's Hebrew writings.

The history of modern written belletristic language, as reflected in Mendele's oeuvre, offers an instructive opportunity for the study of how ideas, opinions, and literary considerations influenced the development of modern Hebrew. As noted earlier, the Haskalah writers hoped, from the movement's earliest days, to create a "pure" written language, free of any influences of the Ashkenazi linguistic context. They recoiled from each branch of the diglossia that characterized for centuries the culture of Jewish communities in Central and Eastern Europe. On the one hand, they judged the vernacular, Yiddish, to be a corrupt jargon of German. On the other hand, they considered the written Hebrew of early modern Ashkenazim (occasionally a spoken language as well) a language that had to be purged of invalid elements that had infiltrated it over the years. Many of the *maskilim* blamed a substantial part of the linguistic decline among Ashkenazi Jews on the Jews of Poland, bearers of a flawed rabbinic-talmudic culture who spoke and wrote in a blighted language (or, more accurately, pair of languages—Hebrew and German). Naphtali Herz Wessely (1725–1805), the Berlin *maskil*, attributed the linguistic decline to the influence of teachers (so-called *melamdim*) from Poland. He used harsh terms to describe the linguistic situation in the Ashkenazi Diaspora: "And because the teachers were not proficient in language, they would use corrupt and broken Ashkenazi [that is, Yiddish—I. B.] words in explaining to the children the Hebrew words that they did not themselves properly understand. They made holy Scripture and its pleasing verse into something lacking taste, void of beauty or grandeur."[27] But despite the negative attitude toward early modern Ashkenazi Hebrew, and despite the harsh criticism often leveled against Yiddish, the writers of the Haskalah did not altogether shun the rejected stratum of Hebrew in the despised vernacular. The Ashkenazi Hebrew of the Haskalah period was used primarily for writing satires and parodies. The *maskilim* criticized the social order, economic life, and religious situation within the Eastern European communities and did so in language that made use of what they deemed undesirable linguistic strata. Their writings tied the elevated, the exalted, or the utopian to the pure language of Scripture, and the lowly, the inferior—and the realistic—to later strata of Hebrew. The contrast drawn between elevated Hebrew and the lowly real-world language—that is, Hebrew as written in eighteenth- and nineteenth-century Poland or Hebrew as used to represent Yiddish speech— became an integral part of the dialogue between the *maskilim* of Eastern Europe and the society they hoped to enlighten and "improve." The *maskilim* wrote in Yiddish because they wanted to reach a wide audience. That gave rise to the paradoxical phenomenon of writing in a language that was seen merely as a temporary tool for the dissemination of ideas—a tool that would be dispensed with once the character of early modern Ashkenazi society had changed.

VI

Abramovitch-Mendele began his literary career as a *maskil*. The use he initially made of the two branches of early modern Ashkenazi diglossia was substantially influenced by the tendency, noted earlier, to avoid the Ashkenazi Hebrew of his time— as evidenced by his novella *Limdu heytev* (Learn Well) and its later version, *Ha-avot ve-ha-banim* (Fathers and Sons), both written during the 1860s—and by the desire to write in the language that, though despised, was accessible to the masses of Jews within the Pale. Later, the influence on Mendele of Haskalah ideas waned. Instead of following in the path of Joseph Perl, he came to see the Ashkenazi Hebrew of his time, and the Yiddish of Eastern Europe, as two languages through which one could achieve a fuller representation of Jewish reality. Paradoxically enough, modernist ideologies joined new literary tastes to revive a premodern bilingual setting. Satire did not disappear from Mendele's writing, but language itself no longer played so central a role as an accessory of that satire. The innovation in Mendele's Hebrew style lay not so much in the linguistic components that he wove into his writings beginning in the 1880s (beginning with the story *Be-seter ra'am* [In the Secret Place of Thunder]), as in the transformation of those components into a single linguistic whole. In so doing, he resorted to a premodern cultural mode, that of the Ashkenazi corporative society. Mendele was not the first to bring back mishnaic language, rabbinic language, and later strata into Hebrew prose; he was preceded in that by Haskalah writers such as Mendel Lefin, Joseph Perl, Mordecai Aaron Guenzburg, and last, but not least, Judah Leib Gordon. But he was the first who was able to sever all of these components from their previous contexts—Hasidic hagiography, halakhic writings, business correspondence, travel literature, maskilic satires, and rabbinic biographies—and blend them into a literary language unprecedented in its wholeness and complexity.

As I understand it, Abramovitch returned to the pre-Haskalah written language that prevailed in the Ashkenazi Diaspora in general, and in Eastern Europe in particular, during the centuries that preceded the birth of modern Hebrew literature. This written language remained in use for writing in Abramovitch's day and continued to exist as the modern literature in Hebrew and Yiddish appeared. Rabbinic scholars used it when writing about halakhic matters, *Hasidim* used it for hagiographies and travel literature, and preachers used it to record in writing the sermons they had delivered in Yiddish. Nor was Abramovitch the first to produce in his literary writing the illusion of a living, spoken Hebrew. Here too he was preceded by Lefin, Perl, and others. Moreover, at the beginning of his Hebrew literary path, he had considerable difficulty in formulating, in the language of the Haskalah, images and idioms common in Yiddish speech. In the introduction to one of his first Hebrew works, published in the early 1860s, he apologized to his readers: "If he [the reader] is diligent, he will see how great an effort it takes to write of such matters in our holy language for our people Israel, and how many impediments the Hebrew writer will encounter as he pursues this path."[28] As his work developed, however, he was able to come up with a style in which the combination of linguistic strata appeared natural and flowing. He relinquished a purist ideology, the legacy of a century of Hebrew Haskalah literature, and he allowed Hebrew what was allowed to Yiddish: the spontaneous use of the greatest number of literary tools—written and spoken—

to design a written language that could reflect more fully the materials of the world he was writing about. At one point in *Sefer ha-kabtsanim* Abramovitch, the author, has Mendele, the literary protagonist, say something about his intentions in creating a Hebrew spoken language that can represent living Yiddish. Fishke, the lame beggar, is speaking in Yiddish, and Mendele, in a digression of great significance, comments on his words:

> It is worthwhile [says Mendele] to give voice to Fishke's speech in his Yiddish language to appreciate how difficult it was for me to improve his awkward speech and render it into Hebrew. The translation of his statement is as follows: "'You walk on your legs like a beggars' infantry, bound by affection and friendship,' he says. But my wife says we crawl like crabs."[29]

Fishke's Yiddish speech, as presented by the author in Hebrew (and here rendered into English), does not mock the folksy, corrupt Yiddish of a member of the lowest class in Jewish society. There is no parody here, not even satire, of the sort used by the enlightened critics of traditional society's spoken language. Mendele states that he wants to offer a Hebrew translation of a direct quote in East European Yiddish in a manner that represents the linguistic reality to the greatest extent possible. We see here as well indications of East European Yiddish being recognized as the folk language, in the spirit of the Russian populism that Abramovitch absorbed during the 1860s and 1870s.

Unlike in the case of his Hebrew works, where he opted for the pre-maskilic spontaneous discourse, his choice of the East European vernacular represented a dramatic discontinuity with early modern Western Yiddish. At the same time, and not unrelated to the change in his attitude toward spoken Yiddish, Abramovitch was able to sever his use of Ashkenazi Hebrew from the satirical anti-Hasidic context and set it as an additional stratum of the Hebrew language—a stratum similar to the language of the Mishnah and the Talmud that he incorporated into his post-Haskalah Hebrew writing. Abramovitch's most important contribution to the development of the Hebrew language was the design of an influential layer of living, *spoken*, language within a *written* literary text. That language incorporates materials from the Bible, the Mishnah, rabbinic language, and other strata of the Hebrew language, and simultaneously integrates the influence of Yiddish, as well as of other vernaculars. Removal of the linguistic barriers between Hebrew and Yiddish and broadening the linguistic base to encompass all historic strata of the Hebrew language clearly indicated the end of the period of the Haskalah in Eastern Europe. In many ways, Mendele managed to bring his Hebrew readers back to an early modern linguistic phase—one that had survived the modernist politics of language of the Haskalah and its post-enlightenment affiliations.[30]

Translated from the Hebrew by the late Joel Linsider

Notes

1. See, e.g., the remark by the Israeli historian Shmuel Ettinger in *A History of the Jewish People*, ed. H. H. Ben-Sasson (Cambridge, Mass., 1976), 841.

2. Shmuel Werses, "Mendele bi-rei ha-bikoret ha-Ivrit," in *Bikoret ha-bikoret: Ha'arakhot ve-gilgulehen* (Tel Aviv, 1982), 50.

3. Dov Sadan, "Petah davar," in *Mendele Mokher Sefarim, Reshimat ktavav ve-igrotav. Le-hakanat mahaduratam ha-akademit*, ed. S. Werses and C. Shmeruk (Jerusalem, 1965), 5.

4. Shmuel Werses, "Mi-lashon el lashon: samemaney ha-nosah, be-Yidish shel 'Megale Tmirin' me'et Yosef Perl," in Werses, *'Hakitsa Ami': sifrut ha-haskalah be-idan ha-modernizatsyah* (Jerusalem 2001), 306–7.

5. Ibid., 307.

6. Ken Frieden, "Neglected Origins of Modern Hebrew Prose: Hasidic and Maskilic Travel Narratives," *AJS Review* 33 (2009): 35.

7. Ibid.

8. Ibid.

9. On Ashkenazi multilingualism, see Israel Bartal, "From Traditional Bilingualism to National Monolingualism," in *Hebrew in Ashkenaz, A Language in Exile*, ed. L. Glinert (New York, 1993), 141–50; Benjamin Harshav, "Multilingualism," in *The YIVO Encyclopedia* (New Haven, Conn., 1998), 991–96; Samuel Niger, *Bilingualism in the History of Jewish Literature* (Lanham, Md., 1990); Max Weinreich, *History of the Yiddish Language* (Chicago, 1980), 1:247–314.

10. On early modern Hebrew in its bilingual context, see Andrea Schatz, *Sprache in der Zerstreuung: Die Saekularisierung des Hebraeischen im 18 Jahrhundert* (Goettingen, 2009), 64–73; for a discussion of the Yiddish component of Ashkenazi pre-Haskalah bilingualism, see Erika Timm, "Glikls Sprache vor ihrem sozialhistorischen und geographischen Hintergrund," in *Die Hamburger Kauffrau Glikl. Jüdische Existenz in der Frühen Neuzeit*, ed. M. Richarz (Hamburg, 2001), 49–67.

11. Shalom Jacob Abramovitch, *Kol kitve Mendele Mokher Sfarim: Sefer ha-kabtsanim* (Tel Aviv, 1954), 95. See Gorelic's translation of the 1888 Yiddish version of the following text: (S. Y. Abramovitsh, *Fishke the Lame, Tales of Mendele The Book Peddler*, ed. D. Miron and K. Frieden [New York, 1996], 40–41): "*Ba!* Now there goes Alter again. *Bleat! Bleat!* But he would say nothing more . . . Now you wouldn't maybe think it, but that whittled-down sheep bleat "Ba!" (plus pause-for-effect) makes for a fair power of a word. Least as Jewish folks will use it. Why, saying it was even plain noble, wouldn't half do it justice. . . . If you are down on your luck, say, and dead strapped (which God forbid!), a nicely judged 'Ba!'" will get you out of a tight spot every time . . . In short, "Ba!" can be taken in all kinds of senses, some of them clean odd and out-of-the-way, too—say like: "Call me nutcracker, 'cause I've just cracked your nut!" or "Go ahead, (or "Go 'head") sue me!" or "Yah, get roasted!" or "I don't value you tantamount to that!" and just no end of other such kind of meanings. Though it will take a little Jewish headwork to know where a particular *Ba!* is aiming. But once you have got the hang of it, why you will know its exact meaning every time, and what it signifies in point of the particular business in hand."

12. Alexander Harkavi, *Yiddish-English-Hebrew Dictionary* (New York, 1928), 126.

13. Uriel Weinreich, *Modern English-Yiddish, Yiddish-English Dictionary* (New York, 1968), 693.

14. Abramovitch, *Sefer ha-kabtsanim*, 85.

15. Jonathan Sheehan, *The Enlightenment Bible: Translation, Scholarship, Culture* (Princeton, N.J., 2005), 85.

16. Ruvik Rosenthal, *Dictionary of Israeli Slang* (Hebrew; Jerusalem 2005), 331–32, 338.

17. Ibid., 266.

18. Harkavy, *Yiddish-English-Hebrew Dictionary*, 347.

19. For the Hebrew original, see *Sefer ha-kabtsanim*, 103–4. In Ted Gorelick's translation: [" . . . and, assuming an expression which was innocent and bland together I addressed the same feller in the sort of rude gibberishy lingo which his kind of folk talk in these parts, saying (more or less): Say, my good fellow, didje maybe happen to see this other Jewfeller . . . and maybe's got this pairer broken-down hosses with him? . . . Well, speak up, speak up!" "But this big yokel only does what he had a mind to do, and won't listen to a word; and sometimes he's dragging me along by the coat sleeve, and sometimes shoving me forward from behind, the whiles talking rough at me, and saying: 'Now, gitter long, old feller . . . Gitter long!" (*Fishke the Lame*, 89).

20. Mendele Moykher Sforim, *Fishke der krumer* (Warsaw, 1928), 53.

21. S. Y. Abramovitsh, *Tales of Mendele the Book Peddler*, 334.

22. Israel Bartal, "Non-Jews and Gentile Society in East-European Hebrew and Yiddish Literature, 1856–1914," (Hebrew; Ph.D. diss.; Hebrew University, 1980), 136–46

23. For the original Hebrew, see *Kol kitve Mendele Mokher Sfarim, Masa'ot binyamin ha-shelishi* (Hebrew; Tel Aviv, 1954), 67.

24. *The Travels of Benjamin the Third* (Yiddish; Warsaw, 1928), 44. Hillel Halkin's translation from the Yiddish: "Good afternoon, can you tell me the way to the Land of Israel?" "What? . . . What Israel? I've never seen Israel," in Abramovitsh, *Tales of Mendele the Book Peddler*, 334.

25. *Travels of Benjamin the Third*, 67; English translation, Abramovitsh, *Tales of Mendele the Book Peddler*, 333.

26. *Travels of Benjamin the Third*, 44.

27. Naphtali Herz Wessely, *Divre shalom ve-emet* (*Words of Peace and Truth*) (Hebrew; Berlin, 1782), chap. 7.

28. Shalom Jacob Abramovitch, *Limdu heytev* (Study Well) (Hebrew; Warsaw, 1862), 4.

29. *Sefer ha-kabtsanim*, 75

30. On the literary aspects of this "linguistic survival" see Dan Miron, "S. Y. Abramovitsh's Hebrew-Yiddish Bilingualism: Three Types of Literary Diglossia" (Hebrew), *Ha'Ivrit, a Journal for the Hebrew Language* 59.3–4 (2011): 108–21.

THE END OR THE BEGINNING

❈ ❈ ❈

Jewish Modernity and the Reception of Rahel Varnhagen

Vivian Liska

University of Antwerp and
The Hebrew University of Jerusalem

Early, partly, sometimes, maybe modern, early modernity is a period for our
period's discomfort about periodization.

—Randolph Starn, "The Early Modern Muddle"

IN Franz Kafka's story "The Hunter Gracchus,"[1] a hunter from the Black Forest, after
his death caused by falling from a rock, has been wandering the earth in an old boat,
roaming restlessly without any prospect of reaching the shores of the nether world.
When he arrives at the port of Riga he is asked by the city's mayor to tell his story,
and to do this in "a coherent mode." Gracchus responds: "Ah, coherently. The old,
old stories." Instead of honoring the request, Gracchus dismisses the functionary:
"Ask the historians! They sit in their studies looking at the past with an open mouth,
and ceaselessly describe it. Go to them and then come back."[2] The historians, with
their "open mouths" are able to speak "coherently" and create a continuous narrative
of the past, while he, Gracchus, can only convey his story in disrupted fragments.
Kafka's hunter is mocking historians who believe that the past can be reconstructed
as a coherent, continuous and harmonious progression leading up to their own time.
An awareness of the problems with this belief lies at the heart of the premises underlying the approach to history displayed by historians of the early modern period.

At the core of David Ruderman's justification of the notion of early modernity
is a critique of "the flawed paradigm of modernization," a narrative that "posits the
triumphant march of civilization from the inferior condition of a traditional premodern society to a more superior modern one" and "considers the end of the eighteenth century as the turning point and a revolution shattering the old while usher-

ing in the new."[3] For Ruderman, and many other historians today, this flawed paradigm can be counteracted through the insertion of the concept of early modernity into the conventional tripartite periodization of ancient times, middle ages, and the modern era.[4] The contention that this transitional time between 1500 and about 1770 ought to be regarded as a period in its own right, rather than a mere preliminary phase of modernity proper, has considerable consequences for an understanding of modern history in general, and the beginnings of modern Jewish history in particular.[5] This paper will explore the assumptions and implications of this contention and probe its effectiveness within German-Jewish history via the reception of one its most famous heroines, the eighteenth-century epistolary writer, salonnière and convert Rahel Varnhagen.

THE SIMULTANEITY OF THE NONSIMULTANEOUS

An enigmatic statement in Kafka's notebooks captures a crucial insight that also underlies the notion of early modernity: "I am," he writes, "end or beginning."[6] In defying the very premises of a continuous chronology, Kafka's statement, which constructs a space between a *no longer* and a *not yet*, has been read as an emblem of all the transitions and interim periods of modernity. The context of Kafka's statement —a reflection on his own distance from the solutions that Christianity and Judaism have to offer in modernity[7]—no doubt invites such interpretations. As a parodying reversal of the Revelation and its apodictic claim to totality—"I am Alpha and Omega, the first and the last"[8]—Kafka's dictum indicates a place where totality and, along with it, coherence and continuity, are undermined. The reversal of beginning and end in Kafka's sentence is no simple negation, and the place at which it occurs is no empty space. It is an *or*, the announcement of an alternative, divesting the end of its finality. This structure of inconclusiveness, which characterizes so many of Kafka's texts, can be read as an expression of dismal uncertainty, but it can also be regarded as an affirmation of potentiality, the rendering of a moment in history that is pregnant with possibilities. With its inversion of beginning and end, the statement describes a time in which uncertainty or undecidability itself carries the promise of renewal. As an expression of the confusion of chronological sequence, Kafka's statement is also an instance of the power of literary language to respond to the challenge of conveying the discontinuity of modernity.

Kafka's texts, and modernist literature in general, are replete with such modalities as narrative fragmentation, chronological inconsistencies, and overlapping temporalities. Historians, by contrast, have more limited possibilities, and are often incapable of resisting the fallacy of retrospectively constructing a linear, unidirectional, and teleological storyline. One of the modalities at their disposal is a creative and self-conscious approach to periodization. Historiography has become increasingly aware that the naming of more or less distinct, delimited segments of time is defined by turning points that are not essentially factual but that reflect the criteria and values of retrospective projections inspired by the time, place and culture that introduces them into—and thereby disturbs—the flux of ever changing life-worlds and events. While it can be argued that periodization merely names sequential time spans for the sake of descriptions and explanations that support a sense of continuity, it can also be used to undermine linearity and rupture the "old story" of a progressive deployment of history. This disruption occurs where emphasis is given to transitional moments when end and beginning are not clearly distinguishable and the "simultaneity of the non-simultaneous" (*Gleichzeitigkeit des Ungleichzeitigen*)[9] becomes manifest. The construction of the early modern period is precisely such an instance. In suggesting both continuity with and a variance from the modern period, the early modern period is an end *or* a beginning, in which undecidability itself undermines petrified dichotomies and opens up alternative perspectives. In questioning sharp oppositions between the old and the new, the traditional and the modern, this construction reveals doubts about the idea and even the desirability of an ever fully accomplished modernity.

The naming and periodization of the era between the Middle Ages and the last decades of the eighteenth century has, since the 1970s, become the battleground for historians of modernity and its beginnings. This debate is carried out between those historians who consider this period as a mere—and meager—precursor of an actual, enlightened modernity, a "halfway house of the modern spirit,"[10] and those who, refusing to "accept modernity's own narratives about itself,"[11] regard it as a distinct and praiseworthy epoch in its own right and, more or less consciously and explicitly, consider it a heuristic tool in the search for alternative ways of approaching the history—and thereby necessarily also the idea—of modernity. This alternative construction involves a questioning of the former's narrative of continuous progress tending toward integration, assimilation, and homogenization inspired by the Enlightenment, and an emphasis on the preceding era's discontinuities and disparities, its mixing and mingling, its contradictions, incongruities, collisions, and the mutually inspiring simultaneity of incompatible, if not incommensurable, cultural, social, and religious entities and endeavors. What is praised by historians who affirm the early modern paradigm as a co-existence of tradition and modernity without *Aufhebung* or harmonization is disparaged by those who reject this paradigm as "debris of the collapsed breakthroughs to modernity that had not quite come about."[12]

The dispute between these two narratives is particularly weighty in the Jewish context. A story based on a clear dichotomy and radical transformation from a traditional society to a fully modern one would implicate the backwardness of religious Judaism and its dissolution into a radically secular mainstream modernity or, alternatively, a watering down of both modernity and Judaism embodied in the *maskilim*'s attempt to harmonize their faith and the attractions of modernity. From this perspective, Jewish modernity begins in the late eighteenth century, and whatever went on before is relegated to a premodern era, in which Jewish life is largely considered in terms of a closed community that has little or no participation in and interaction with the surrounding modern world. For Ruderman and likeminded historians, the insertion of the early modern period into Jewish history as a moment in its own right counteracts this narrative and undermines the inevitability of the linear and teleological process from the ghetto to modernity. As a time when elements of the premodern world mix and combine with premonitory visions of a new world, the early modern period, with its incoherencies, overlappings and "mixed identities," constitutes for these historians a revaluing of the manifestations of modernity before their stabilization in modernity proper. They see Early Modernity as the climax rather than the preliminary version of everything that is good—mobile, creative, heterogeneous and flexible—about modernity. This perspective finds in the early modern period a model for situations, figures, and constellations that affirm the possibility to be both consciously, even traditionally Jewish, yet at the same time eager to engage in the exploration of an ever expanding world and to embrace the contradictions, conflicts, and disparities that ensue from these multiple and potentially clashing life-worlds. Concomitantly, this perspective also considers the advent of the modern proper, in the final decades of the eighteenth century—primarily the development of nationalism and its spirit of chauvinistic homogenization—to be an end to the fertile incongruities that had been part and parcel of the richness of the early modern period. In sum, this view lends visibility to a period that allows for a simultaneous perception of the multifarious possibilities of Jewish modernization before both external and internal factors defined and consolidated its parameters and institutionalized it into the more starkly contoured categories characterizing modernity proper. The early modern period thereby becomes both a model and a reservoir of potentialities, inherent in Jewish existence faced with the premonitions of modernity, that harbors the memory of roads not taken and still informs the present. It is in this sense that Andrea Schatz speaks of invoking early modernity in terms of an attempt to "restore to our interpretations of modernity what was not included in modernity's own narratives about itself."[13] Taking the early modern period as a paradigm allows one to detect "the multi-layered, complex and flexible patterns that may characterize each period, and perhaps in particularly intense ways the end of the early modern period—the first decades of the eighteenth century."[14] One can argue on similar grounds that it is worthwhile to look at this period's symmetrical counterpart with regard to the divide between early modernity and modernity proper: it is in the last decades of the eighteenth century that one can recognize the possibilities that were lost by the time the early modern period came to an end.

In the German-Jewish context, contemporary assessments of the threshold between the Early Modern and the beginning of modernity proper are a particularly fertile ground for probing the assumption and consequences of the two narratives outlined above. In the first case, modernity is equated with emancipation, integration, and assimilation; in the second it is seen as a moment ending in a more clearcut but also more sterile modernity embodied by "solutions." These "solutions" are succinctly described in Deborah Hertz's study of German-Jewish life between the seventeenth and the early nineteenth century: "Whereas in the seventeenth century one could be either a Christian or a Jew" interacting in the manifold ways described by the historians of early modern Jewry, in the period explored by Hertz (the turn of the eighteenth and the first decades of the nineteenth century) Jews "faced three fundamental alternatives: they could remain traditional, commit to the harmonious modernization of Judaism, or try to escape Judaism altogether." Hertz concludes that "the choices which emerged in this era set the terms for the centuries since."[15] It is possible that, by invoking the early modern period, one described by Adam Sutcliffe as this "fascinatingly vivid episode" with "countervailing values" and without "final resolutions,"[16] one can provide an alternative to these choices and preclude the continuous and coherent story of a progress from a premodern to a fully enlightened modern world.

HEROINE OF JEWISH MODERNITY OR HERALD OF ITS END?

In the German-Jewish context, the stakes of narrating history as a coherent story of progressive modernization are particularly high because the continuities and discontinuities drawn in any periodization inevitably involve an interpretation of German Jewry's tragic end. A particularly significant case of the construction of a coherent story out of heterogeneous material is the reception of Rahel Levin Varnhagen, whose life was paradigmatic for the situation of the privileged class of German Jews at the end of the eighteenth century. Her thousands of letters are a lively testimony to the exhilarating possibilities that opened up hitherto unknown horizons for a Jewish woman, yet also to self-doubts resulting from unfulfilled aspirations and conflicts of loyalty that continued to haunt her throughout her life. Although Rahel is generally considered a representative of the beginning of modernity proper, or at best a liminal figure of the end of the early modern period, she is undoubtedly a case of what David Ruderman, characterizing early Jewish modernity, calls a "mingled identity."

Born in 1771 in Berlin as a daughter of a rich jeweler, she spent most of her life trying to escape what she considered the stigma of her Jewish origins, and finally converted in 1814 when she married the Christian diplomat Karl August Varnhagen von Ense. Her anxious attempt to leave her Jewish background behind, and her even more anxious efforts to be accepted in the high society, marked her existence until her death in 1833. Rahel's life story became an inspiration for many scholars of the history of women, minorities and intercultural relations, but has also been an object of scrutiny for those who tried to understand the evolution of German-Jewish history leading to its catastrophic end. Examples from this reception of Rahel's life and writings can shed light on the implications of the positions taken by historians in the debates about the beginnings of Jewish modernity and of the temptations, risks of, and possible alternatives to, constructing a teleological German-Jewish modernity. As these examples will show, the perspective of the regnant linear model leads to a portrait of Rahel's life in which her assimilation and conversion mark a sharp rupture between old and new. This binary opposition between a backward ghetto and an enlightened modernity is correlated with an either positive or negative judgment of her assimilation and betrayal of her Jewish origins. These judgments obliterate a comprehension of Rahel as a figure mediating between cultures, religions, and classes who both embraces and doubts her own solution.

The most famous study of Rahel is undoubtedly Hannah Arendt's monograph *Rahel Varnhagen: The Life of a Jewess*,[17] largely finished by 1933, completed in exile, and published in 1958. In this biography, Arendt introduces her famous and controversial distinction between the pariah and the parvenu, and describes Rahel's life in terms of the relative success and ultimate questioning of her long and desperate efforts to become a respectable member of the established society. Despite repeated attempts to shed her status of pariah through her marriage to Varnhagen von Ense and conversion to Christianity, Rahel nevertheless remained, in Arendt's view, a mere parvenu who had given up her freedom and had condemned herself to a life of opportunistic subservience to the powerful. What saves Rahel in Arendt's eyes are faint hints (given great emphasis in the final chapters of Arendt's biography), that Rahel retrospectively embraced and affirmed her former existence as Jew and pariah. Arendt's critique of Rahel's attempt to escape her Jewishness has often been read, and criticized, in terms of Arendt's overemphasis of Rahel's Jewishness at the expense of her challenges as a woman or her achievements as an author. More interestingly for the present context, Arendt has been taken to task for the more general rejection of Jewish assimilation to German society underlying her portrait of Rahel—a position she was accused of articulating under the impact of her youthful Zionist leanings. The main critique voiced about Arendt's portrait was that she made an ahistorical judgment formulated through the hindsight perspective of the annihilation of German Jewry. One of the harshest of these criticisms came from another German-Jewish intellectual, the important literary theorist, Käte Hamburger.

Hamburger expresses her disagreement with Arendt in her essay "Rahel und Goethe,"[18] which ends on an emphatic universalist credo: "The question whether someone is Jewish or German becomes irrelevant, and all that matters is the human being itself, without any concern for race, class, nation and religion as the Enlightenment and classicism regarded and wanted it."[19] Led by her Enlightenment ideals of homogeneity and integration, Hamburger polemically attacks Arendt's focus on Rahel's Jewishness, her scornful attitude toward Rahel's conversion, and the continuity she constructs between eighteenth-century assimilation and the catastrophe of Nazi Germany. Hamburger's argument against Arendt's projection of her own experiences onto a figure from the distant past—a critique Arendt's dissertation supervisor and friend Karl Jaspers had expressed years earlier[20]—is plausible from a historicist perspective. However, Hamburger's own depiction of Rahel is not devoid of a questionable continuity, albeit in a different sense. Although Hamburger acknowledges the "yawning abyss" that the Holocaust has created between German Jewry (*Deutsches Judentum*) and German Culture (*Deutsche Geisteskultur*),[21] her Enlightenment-inspired belief in universality and its progressive deployment from the time of Rahel until her own present remains unshaken. Hamburger's ideals of a coherent and stable self and a homogenous and integrated public sphere, as well as her view of Rahel as a classical humanist striving for "unity" and "harmony"[22] and her critique of Arendt, are echoed by numerous scholars and critics rediscovering Rahel as a model of emancipation from the seventies onwards, among them Rahel's biographer Heidi Thomann Tewarson.

Tewarson goes even further than Hamburger in her critique of Arendt's "Zionist-influenced anti-assimilationist" and "anachronistic"[23] judgment of Rahel as a traitor to her people. Rejecting Arendt's (admittedly speculative) belief in Rahel's return to Jewishness toward the end of her life, Tewarson sees in her conversion the fulfillment of her long-held desire to "join the large class of enlightened humanity."[24] Projecting her own ideas onto Rahel's final thoughts she concludes that "her life must have appeared to her as a small token of historical progress. . . . She could at least look with satisfaction upon her own case."[25] Tewarson defines the aim of her own study as a demonstration of Rahel's "prophetic understanding of the forces of history" because "eighteenth-century Jews had good reasons to be optimistic."[26] What they were right to be hopeful about becomes clear in her critique of Arendt, whom she accuses of being blind to the fact that "for Rahel and her generation history began anew with the Enlightenment."[27] Even more sweepingly, she states that "modern German Jewish history begins with Rahel's letters."[28] What for Tewarson is the beginning of a promising "Jewish modernity" to be fulfilled in assimilation is for Arendt the beginning of the end.

Arendt's and Tewarson's interpretations of Rahel's life and its significance could not be more opposed; yet, they share similar assumptions, which they evaluate in different ways. For Tewarson, Rahel is a heroine of emancipation, which she achieved through assimilation; Arendt criticizes Rahel on precisely these grounds and sees in her a social climber who had betrayed her origins and her less privileged, still backwards coreligionists "who were still present and geographically close by."[29] For Tewarson, Rahel is a forerunner of contemporary liberated moderns; for Arendt, she was a representative of the "Berlin Jew who looked upon his origins" and wrongly assumed that he was "not one of the last but one of the first."[30] For both, though, Rahel's modernity marks a sharp divide, and what lies before it is a dark and primitive place. Even as Arendt criticizes Rahel for her lack of solidarity with her still religious brethren, she describes their world as a "dark stage-set of poverty, misery and ignorance."[31] Tewarson could not agree more: for her, there is no Jewish history before Rahel's letters altogether. Despite their contrary views, Arendt and Tewarson have little doubt that there is a beginning and an end, and that the two can be clearly distinguished.

Finally, and very briefly, it is revealing to look at a more recent example with a surprising turn: in two different books written twenty years apart, Deborah Hertz places Rahel at the center of her reflections on the German-Jewish situation in the late eighteenth century. The first of Hertz's books, *Jewish High Society in Old Regime*

Berlin (1988) celebrates Rahel and her fellow salonnières as rebellious and largely successful daughters freeing themselves from a backward Jewish establishment and its patriarchal structures.[32] In her book on converts of this period, *How Jews Became Germans* (2007), Hertz is more cautious, yet still full of sympathy for Rahel and her assimilated and converted peers. But in a surprising, very personal—and dare one say incoherent—turn at the end of the book's epilogue there surfaces an alternative to Rahel, stemming directly from the early modern period. Following a final expression of empathy with Rahel's attempt to "escape her birth destiny through conversion and marriage," Hertz voices doubts and criticisms about Rahel's "craven social climbing," her disdain for her religious relatives, and her lack of self-respect. "More and more," Hertz concludes, "I contrasted her to the business wife Glückel of Hameln who had lived only a century before." Calling Glückel "so serene, so confident, so industrious and so beloved," Hertz commends this most paradigmatic early modern German-Jewish woman "as an alternative role model for contemporary woman." And Hertz closes: "Much was lost for Jewish women between Glückel's life and Rachel's life, to be weighed against what was gained."[33] Rahel—an end or a beginning?

Hertz's late awareness of earlier possibilities is a welcome counterpoint to the prevailing picture of the era preceding Rahel's times. And yet, in its nostalgic idealization of a more idyllic, simpler time, Hertz's turn to the early modern period does not fully do justice to the term's potential and still adheres to a progressive, teleological model of history. Possibly, this is difficult to avoid. However, when "early modern" is regarded not only as a period of time but, as Ruderman writes, also "a condition,"[34] a paradigm characterized by a specific state of mind and mode of being, it can be extended beyond its accepted time lines to the late eighteenth-century Rahel herself. Her affinities with the early modern paradigm become visible where she is described as "a polyphonous and not always harmonious self"[35]—as an outsider striving to be accepted in gentile society without accepting its norms and prejudices, as an author of idiosyncratic letters in which her Yiddish mother tongue is still perceptible behind her High German words,[36] or as a bridge-builder who "created a social space in which individuals of the most diverse backgrounds could "mix and mingle with each other," forging "bonds across classes, religious groups and the two sexes."[37]

As these quotes demonstrate, this other view of Rahel exists, but it is rarely perceived where she is approached in larger historical frameworks. This is particularly true for historians or biographers who try to fit her into either one of the two versions of the German-Jewish ghetto-to-modernity narrative: the demonstration of a continuity of this history and its inevitable end in Auschwitz, or the celebration of a former German-Jewish symbiosis looked upon with nostalgic rapture and the sigh of "the pity of it all."[38] Instead, it is primarily among scholars who read her texts as literature—or maybe read her life and person as a literary text—that Rahel appears in a more complex light.[39] When the attempt to construct a continuous and "coherent story" and an exclusively diachronic understanding of time is abandoned, Rahel emerges in all her multiple, unresolved facets, including her equivocal, inconsistent statements about herself. What then becomes visible is how she borrowed contradictory elements of different ideational paradigms in her reflections on her life as well as on art and society; how she cursed femininity as a personal obstacle, yet in various contexts affirmed its superiority to the ways of men; how she said of herself that she could write nothing but letters, yet considered her epistolary exchanges worthy of publication and spoke of herself as an artist equal to the greatest in the literary tradition; how she strove with all her means to be accepted in established society, yet repeatedly commented on its worthlessness; and finally, how she struggled with her Jewishness all her life, generally considering it her most painful stigma and doing what she could to escape it, yet never entirely freeing herself from it and in some ways never wanting to give it up entirely. On this last point, she greatly resembles the early modern converts Ruderman describes in his chapter on "mingled identities." Like them, Rahel, too, was "remapping the borders of Judaism and Christianity,"[40] and like them she "ultimately remained loyal" to her origins all her life.[41]

Her letters testify to the conflicts and the suffering resulting from her contradictions, but she was also highly self-conscious and affirmed these contradictions as a privilege and strength. Already in her early letters Rahel repeatedly and proudly praises her own doubleness, and sees in it a talent rather than a deficiency or a plight. In a letter to her close friend David Veit, himself a "successfully assimilated Jew,"[42] she contrasts herself with him and describes herself as *doppelt organisiert*, explaining: "I have a tremendous power to be double without confusing myself."[43] An echo of this serene lack of coherence is still found in her most famous words, which she is reported to have said on her deathbed: "What a history! A fugitive from Egypt and Palestine, here I am and find help, love, fostering in you people. With real rapture I think of these origins of mine."[44] For Arendt, who begins her book with this quote, Rahel's words referring to the depth of Jewish history signify her return to Jewishness at the end of her life. However, Tewarson has a strong case in objecting to Arendt's conclusion: as she and others have observed, Arendt omitted the continuation of this sentence in which Rahel calls Jesus her brother, empathizes with Mary, and expresses the solace she derives from these thoughts. Disagreeing with Arendt, Tewarson concludes that Rahel's "life must have appeared to herself as a small token of historical progress."[45] Possibly, her final sentences should not be read as a progressive supersession but as the simultaneity of the non-simultaneous, which characterized so much of her person, her writings and her life.

CODA

In the arguably most contestable passage of his book *Early Modern Jewry*, David Ruderman suggests that "the term *early modernity*" should "not be taken literally," lest it preserve "the false opposition between tradition and modernity and the implied teleology of a supposed progression from one to the other by simply introducing an intermediary stage between the two."[46] He instead proposes that it be considered as a "conventional and neutral label" to be cautiously employed by historians.[47] Ruderman is right to call for caution: an understanding of the term as *both* a period and a paradigm may not be so easy to harmonize. As a segment of history, the early modern period, with its "early" calling for a "late" or at least "later," cannot escape being constructed as an "old, old story"; but as a paradigm connoting the nonharmonized and unresolved, it emphasizes the plurality of possibilities and captures the potentiality contained in moments in the past, as well as—and maybe more than transpires in an all too upbeat account of this paradigm—the ghosts it leaves behind from struggles interrupted midway or battles lost. All in all, it allows for glimpses of the hesitations and contradictions, of the multiple options that presented themselves and did not materialize, of so much that is obliterated by the linear narrative. Rahel and her story have often been a victim of these narratives. Pointing out her closeness to the flourishing manifestations of modern "beginnings" in the early modern period interrupts the seeming straight line from ghetto to emancipation. But if this affinity is to be perceived, then historians of the early modern period must concede that its effects and characteristics extend into the late eighteenth century, and possibly beyond. There is not only a great deal of modernity in the preceding era, as they are eager to demonstrate, but the reverse—the persistence of the Early Modern in what follows—is true as well. And if the Early Modern can survive its own time, then something of it, which may precisely be the sense of being "end or beginning," may persist not only in every period but in every life. Kafka's restlessly erring hunter, who, as so often in the medium of literature, fell off certainties that were once hard as rock, finds himself roaming between realms. His existence gives credence to both the painful perplexities and promising potential of being either in this world or in another. Giving value to this *or* in history may be the early modern paradigm's most universal and lasting achievement.

Notes

1. Franz Kafka, *The Complete Stories* (New York, 1976), 226–34. Starn's epigram is from the *Journal of Early Modern History* 6.3 (2002): 296.

2. Kafka, *Stories*, 234.

3. David Ruderman, *Early Modern Jewry: A New Cultural History* (Princeton, N.J., 2010), 205.

4. See Rudolf Vierhaus, "Vom Nutzen und Nachteil des Begriffs 'Frühe Neuzeit': Fragen und Thesen," in *Frühe Neuzeit—Frühe Moderne? Forschungen zur Vielschichtigkeit von Übergangsprozessen,* ed. R. Vierhaus et al. (Göttingen, 1992), 13.

5. David Ruderman, "Introduction," in *Simon Dubnow Institute Yearbook* 6: *Early Modern Culture and Haskalah,* ed. D. Diner (Munich, 2007): 13.

6. Franz Kafka, *Nachgelassene Schriften und Fragmente,* II, ed. J. Schillemeit and H. G. Koch, (Frankfurt am Main, 1992), 98.

7. "I have not, like Kierkegaard, been led into life by the albeit already heavily sinking hand of Christianity and have not, like the Zionists, caught the last corner of the Jewish prayer shawl as it flies away. I am end or beginning." Kafka, *Nachgelassene Schriften und Fragmente,* 98.

8. Rev 1:10.

9. See Vierhaus's use of this term to characterize the early modern period in Vierhaus, "Vom Nutzen und Nachteil des Begriffs 'Frühe Neuzeit,'" 21.

10. Starn, "The Early Modern Muddle," 299.

11. Andrea Schatz, "'Peoples Pure of Speech': The Religious, the Secular, and Jewish Beginnings of Modernity," in *Simon Dubnow Institute Yearbook* 6, 176.

12. Starn, "The Early Modern Muddle," 299.

13. Schatz, "Peoples Pure of Speech," 177.

14. Ibid., 177.

15. Deborah Hertz, *How Jews Became Germans: The History of Conversion and Assimilation in Berlin* (New Haven, Conn., 2007), 218

16. Adam Sutcliffe, "Imagining Amsterdam: The Dutch Golden Age and the Origins of Jewish Modernity," *Simon Dubnow Institute Yearbook* 6, 96.

17. Hannah Arendt, *Rahel Varnhagen: The Life of a Jewess*, ed. L. Weissberg, trans. R. and C. Winston (Baltimore, Md., 1997).

18. The first version of Hamburger's essay was written in 1933/34. She considerably revised the essay after the war in light of the Holocaust and republished it in 1968. Käte Hamburger, "Rahel und Goethe," in *Rahel Varnhagen Gesammelte Werke,* ed. K. Feilchenfeldt, U. Schweikert and R. E. Steiner (Munich, 1983), 10:179–204

19. Hamburger, "Rahel und Goethe," 204.

20. Lotte Kohler and Hans Saner, eds., *Hannah Arendt/Karl Jaspers Correspondence, (1926–1969),* trans. R. Kimber and R. Kimber (New York, 1992), 727 (n. 134).

21. Edith Waldstein, "Identity as Conflict and Conversation in Rahel Varnhagen (1771–1833)," in *Out of Line—Ausgefallen*, ed. R. B. Joeres and M. Burkhard (Amsterdam, 1989), 105.

22. Hamburger, "Rahel und Goethe," 199.

23. Heidi T. Tewarson, *Rahel Levin Varnhagen: The Life and Work of a German-Jewish Intellectual* (Lincoln, Neb., 1998), 5.

24. Tewarson, *Rahel Levin Varnhagen*, 6.

25. Ibid., 222.

26. Ibid., 5.

27. Ibid., 5.

28. Ibid., 6.

29. Arendt, *Rahel Varnhagen*, 251.

30. Ibid.

31. Ibid., 250. On other issues, Arendt's approach is, however, very close to what is here designated as the early modern paradigm. This is especially true for her view of Berlin salons and her idea of emancipation as "an admission of Jews *as Jews* to the ranks of humanity." Hannah Arendt, *The Jew as Pariah: Jewish Identity and Politics in the Modern Age*, ed. R. H. Feldman (New York, 1978), 68.

32. Deborah Hertz, *Jewish High Society in Old Regime Berlin* (Syracuse, N.Y., 2005).

33. Hertz, *How Jews Became Germans*, 219.

34. Ruderman, referring to Andrea Schatz in his "Introduction," 18.

35. Waldstein, "Identity as Conflict and Conversation in Rahel Varnhagen," 112.

36. See Liliane Weissberg, "Schreiben als Selbstentwurf: Zu den Schriften Rahel Varnhagens und Dorothea Schlegels," *Zeitschrift für Religions- und Geistesgeschichte* 47.4 (1995): 231–53.

37. Seyla Benhabib, "The Pariah and her Shadow: Hannah Arendt's Biography of Rahel Varnhagen," *Political Theory* 23.1 (1995): 17.

38. Amos Elon, *The Pity of It All: A Portrait of Jews in Germany 1743–1933* (New York, 2002).

39. For strong examples, see Liliane Weissberg, "Stepping Out: The Writing of Difference in Rahel Varnhagen's Letters," *New German Critique* 53 (1991): 149–62; Barbara Hahn, *"Antworten Sie*

Mir": Rahel Levin Varnhagens Briefwechsel (Basel, 1990); and Edith Waldstein, "Identity as Conflict and Conversation in Rahel Varnhagen," 95–113.

40. Ruderman, *Early Modern Jewry*, 188.

41. Ruderman describes converts whose baptism had not fully erased their "allegiance and affection for the Jewish people, especially in critical moments," ibid., 186. The same is true of Rahel and has been described by all her biographers including Arendt and Tewarson.

42. Waldstein, "Identity as Conflict and Conversation in Rahel Varnhagen," 107.

43. Ibid.

44. Arendt, *The Life of a Jewess*, 85. See also Hertz, *How Jews Became Germans,* 215.

45. Tewarson, *Rahel Levin Varnhagen*, 222.

46. Ruderman, *Early Modern Jewry*, 205.

47. Ibid., 226.

BETWEEN YITZHAK BAER AND CLAUDIO SÁNCHEZ ALBORNOZ

※ ※ ※

The Rift That Never Healed

Yosef Kaplan

The Hebrew University of Jerusalem

"THERE is no anti-Semitism in Spain," declared the Spanish historian, Claudio Sánchez Albornoz, to his colleague Fritz (Yitzhak) Baer in 1929, when he greeted him cordially at the Royal Academy of History in Madrid.[1] Baer, who was forty at the time, had published, in Berlin, the first volume of his monumental documentary project, in German, on the history of the Jews of Christian Spain, a volume dedicated to the Jewry of the crown of Aragon and the kingdom of Navarre.[2] Historians of medieval Spain praised the academic quality of the book, which, upon its appearance, assured Baer a place of honor among the scholars of the history of Spain in the Middle Ages. The fact that he had been a student of the prominent German historian Heinrich Finke (Baer's dissertation on the Jews of Aragon in the Middle Ages, written under Finke's direction, was presented to the University of Freiburg in 1913), opened many doors for him in Spain.[3] Finke was regarded as one of the greatest historians of the medieval Catholic Church,[4] and was widely praised in Spain, receiving honorary doctorates from the universities of Barcelona, Valladolid, and Salamanca.[5] Without doubt his prestige facilitated access to Spanish archives for his student, Baer, who worked there with great intensity during his two visits in 1925 and 1926. Baer dedicated the first volume of his documentary project on the Jews of Spain to Finke and to his other distinguished teacher, Eugen Taübler, the well-known classical Jewish scholar.

Sánchez Albornoz was five years younger than Baer, but by then he had already attained a senior academic position and was well known in Madrid.[6] At the age of twenty-one he had received a doctorate from the University of Madrid, under the direction of Eduardo de Hinojosa, whose chair he inherited in 1920, only 7 years later. He had been appointed even earlier to chairs at the universities of Barcelona and Valladolid, and in 1922 he won the Covadonga Prize, marking the 1200th anniversary of the famous battle that began the war of Reconquista. At that time he was studying the history of Asturias, León, and Castile in the early Middle Ages, and he had published his first book, based on archival work in Lisbon, about the royal court of Portugal in the twelfth and thirteenth centuries.[7] In 1924 he established the highly influential journal, *Anuario de historia del derecho español* (The Annual of the History of Spanish Law), which immediately became a leading venue for important articles on the history of medieval Spain. Baer also published an article there on the responsa of R. Asher ben Yeḥiel, in 1929.[8] The brilliant young Sánchez Albornoz was already regarded as the leading scholar of medieval Spain, and in 1925, at the age of thirty-two, he was appointed as the youngest member of the Royal Academy of History.

Baer and Sánchez Albornoz had similar training. Both belonged to the tradition of nineteenth-century German historicism, which placed great value on archival work and on the publication of critical editions of documents. In 1927 Sánchez Albornoz studied for a year in Vienna at the Seminar for Cultural and Economic History directed by the historian Alfons Dopsch, who had published collections of documents from the Carolingian Period in meticulous editions.[9] Don Claudio was strongly influenced by him. Most of the conversation between Baer and Sánchez Albornoz in 1929 probably took place in Spanish, though it might have been seasoned with words and expressions in German.[10] They had many topics of conversation in common, and Baer was very appreciative of his host's warmth.

Thirty-three years later, in an angry letter dated March 29, 1962, which Baer sent from Jerusalem to Buenos Aires, Sánchez Albornoz's place of exile, he reminded his Spanish colleague of the positive impression left by that meeting and of the cordial welcome he had received in Spain when he was working in the archives: "With deep gratitude I remember the friendly welcome I received in your homeland, when I was there to do research in the Spanish archives." Nor did Baer neglect to mention the favorable critique that Sánchez Albornoz published, at that time, in the historical journal he had established a few years earlier.[11] But, he added bitterly, "Until recently I did not know that these relations had deteriorated."

Deteriorated? Sánchez Albornoz vigorously rejected his colleague's characterization, protesting that he did not know why he was angry with him. From his point of view, Sánchez Albornoz had reason to be surprised and injured. On the personal level, their relations had been very good. Sánchez Albornoz had contributed an article to the festschrift published by the Israel Historical Society in 1961 in honor of Baer's seventieth birthday.[12] Moreover, on August 5, 1959, he had written a cordial letter to Baer, informing him that he had received a copy of his Hebrew book, *Toldot ha-yehudim bi-sefarad ha-notsrit* (The History of the Jews in Christian Spain), of which a second, expanded edition had been published that year. Perhaps Baer had sent him the book, although he knew that Sánchez Albornoz did not read Hebrew. The Spanish historian had asked a student of his, an "Argentinian-Hebrew," as he put it, to write a long review article for the journal on the history of Spain that he had established and edited in Buenos Aires. Furthermore: he had told Baer that he intended to find a publisher for a Spanish translation of the book, adding: "I have a strong desire to use it in my research, and that it should be known to the Ibero-American Spanish speaking community."[13] A bit more than a year later, in a letter to Baer dated September 28, 1960, Sánchez Albornoz informed him with excitement that he had indeed found a publisher for a Spanish edition of the book. He had turned to IWO in Buenos Aires, which had apparently agreed to bear the expense of the translation and publication. The intended translator was a doctoral student of Sánchez Albornoz's, who had studied with Baer at the Hebrew University in Jerusalem for a short time in 1953.[14] The Spanish historian expressed inordinate pleasure at having found a publisher and an appropriate translator.[15] In a business-like manner he asked Baer to give his authorization and the conditions for the translation of the Spanish edition.[16] In the end he added: "I am very pleased to be informing you about this and I am doubly glad, because I am anxious to read your words in Spanish."[17] What else could be asked of him? He had initiated the Spanish translation of Baer's book, although he had not read the original, because of his great respect for the author, and he had invested great effort to advance that initiative. The translator's letter, which was sent a year afterward, indicates that students at the University of Buenos Aires were already using parts of her translation, even before its publication. However, at the end of her letter to Baer the translator saw fit to add a puzzling sentence: "and Professor Sánchez Albornoz's opinion on this detail [i.e. on the history of the Jews of Spain] is rather strange."[18]

In a blunt reply, sent on July 10, 1962, Sánchez Albornoz vehemently protested Baer's harsh claims against him, writing: "I repeat what I said at the Academy of History: there is no anti-Semitism among us." He repeated emphatically that he had always felt fondness and admiration for him, adding: "I would like our friendship to remain beyond the differences between us in our evaluation [of historical phenomena]."[19] He signed his letter, a copy of which he took care to send to Barcelona, to the Catalan scholar Millás Vallicrosa, with the phrase: "I extend my hand to you in friendship."

Baer did not bother to answer this letter. He found it sufficient to publish a stern response on the subject of their difference of opinion in an appendix to the second volume of the English edition of his book, *A History of the Jews in Christian Spain*, which was published in 1966. This response includes reference to the arguments advanced by the eminent scholar of Spanish literature, Américo Castro, which were similar in part to those raised by Sánchez Albornoz.[20] It should be mentioned that the translation initiated by Sánchez Albornoz was never published, and only in 1981, a year after Baer's death, was a (superb) Spanish translation executed by the late José Luis Lacave.[21]

It is only fair to give Sánchez Albornoz credit for the sincerity of his words. He truly did not understand why Baer was angry. He was also right about another point: nothing had changed between 1929 and 1962 in his attitude toward Baer or in his views on the topics that Baer mentioned in his letter. In 1929 Baer simply did not know what would be revealed to him thirty-three years later. Nor did others know—or perhaps they did not wish to know. And perhaps it was also because among some circles of historians of Spain, Sánchez Albornoz's opinions were not at all exceptional.

However, before discussing the content of the correspondence and the rift between the two historians, here is a brief account of the course of the two men's lives after their meeting in 1929, which was apparently the only time they met face to face.

Yitzhak Baer arrived in Palestine in 1930, upon receiving a teaching post at the Hebrew University in Jerusalem. He was the head of the Department of Jewish History, and between 1932 and 1945 he taught medieval history in the Department of History.[22] Along with his friend and colleague, Ben-Zion Dinur, he founded the Jewish history journal, *Zion,* editing it with him, and later with some of their students, until his death in 1980. Together with Dinur, he initiated academic projects, and both of them trained a generation of students, many of whom continued to teach at the Hebrew University after them, or in other universities in Israel. Unlike Dinur, who was very active in public affairs, Baer was entirely immersed in his historical research. He was a modest, ascetic person and is rightfully regarded as one of the greatest Jewish historians of the twentieth century. Despite changes in the times and shifts in taste and fashion, and despite the discovery of new sources that change the picture here and there, and despite the alternative interpretations that naturally have been suggested by historians in following generations, his great project on the history of the Jews of medieval Spain is still regarded as a masterpiece. In 1930 Baer left his home ground, the excellent libraries of Germany, and, under the difficult and rigid conditions that prevailed in Palestine at the time, he managed to persist in his academic labors. The second volume of documents on Spain, on the Jews of Castile, and on the Inquisition trials, was published in 1936.[23] Like other German Jews who left Germany before the Nazis took control, Baer watched the Nazi regime with helpless dread. In an anguished letter that he sent to various persons in Europe on April 1, 1933, he tried to call their attention to what he called "the expulsion of the Jews of Germany" on that very day.[24] Sánchez Albornoz was one of the recipients of that letter, and as he reminded him in the letter of 1962, he wished to make known to him "that German historians are to a great degree guilty for this tragedy, which later developed to proportions that one could not imagine at the time."[25] In the summer of 1933 Baer traveled to Germany to meet with his mother and other relatives, and the situation he encountered left a grave impression on him.

It became clear to him that quite a few of his former teachers and fellow students had joined the National Socialist Party. His teacher, Heinrich Finke, had done so and expressed explicit and public identification with the Third Reich and its leader. Indeed, on his eightieth birthday, July 13, 1935, he received the Order of the Eagle, in honor of his lifetime achievement, from Hitler's hands.[26] Impressed by these events, Baer published *Galut* [Exile] (Berlin, 1936), in German, a book in which he harshly condemned the Diaspora and a work that still raises many perplexities. In the foreword to the Hebrew edition of the book (1980), he states, "When I wrote this book I felt great anguish, though at the time I could not have imagined the events that later surged up and engulfed us—the murder of millions of our people by the Nazi Germans."[27] From August to September 1938 Baer returned to Germany to see his relatives, from whom he parted with deep concern. In the following years he worked to complete his monumental book about Spanish Jewry, which first appeared in Hebrew in 1945; the words he wrote about the Spanish expulsion were phrased in the shadow of the horrifying events of his times.

When the second, expanded edition was published in 1959, Baer had almost entirely left behind the study of Medieval Spanish Jewry. More than a decade earlier, after the establishment of Israel, he applied his classical and rabbinical education to the study of Judaism in the Second Temple and Mishnaic periods.[28] However, in 1962, when he sent the letter to Sánchez Albornoz, he was engaged in examining the English translation of the *History of the Jews of Christian Spain*, and in making certain changes and additions.

And what happened to Sánchez Albornoz after his meeting with Baer in 1929? The first years were a time of feverish activity for him, in both the academic and public spheres. In 1932, when he was appointed rector of the University of Madrid, he established the Institute for Medieval Studies, which was intended to prepare and publish a large collection of historical sources on medieval Spain under the title, *Monumenta Hispaniae Historica.* Moreover, at the same time he became active in the political arena, and a year prior to that he was elected to the Cortes, the Spanish parliament, representing the Acción Republicana party, headed by Manuel Azaña.[29] This was a decidedly republican party, with an anti-clerical orientation, which Sánchez Albornoz joined despite his deeply rooted affiliation with Catholicism. Don Claudio defined himself as a "conservative revolutionary" (*un conservador revoluciona-rio*),[30] and despite his party adhesion he was opposed to the divorce law, and during the first days of the Republic he spoke vehemently against the burning of churches. In 1933 he served as the vice-president of the parliament and as a government minister. Despite his political engagement, during one of the most complex and difficult times in the short-lived Spanish Republic, he devoted great effort to continuing his historical research.

In 1936 Albornoz was appointed Spanish Ambassador to Portugal, but was forced to abandon that post when the Portuguese government shifted its support and recognition to Francisco Franco.[31] Don Claudio fled to France and received a professorship at the University of Bordeaux, thanks to the efforts of the Hispanist Georges Cirot.[32] The conditions of exile did not slow him down, and during his sojourn in France he managed to finish his important book on the origins of feudalism in Spain, which he published two years later in Argentina.[33] After the defeat of France in 1940, he fled to the free zone, and from there to Algeria, Portugal, and finally he sailed to Argentina. At first he taught at the University of Cuyo, in Mendoza, until he received the chair for Spanish history at the University of Buenos Aires. He remained there until 1983, when he finally returned to Spain, and upon his death a year later he was buried in the cathedral of Avila, the city of his ancestors. During his more than forty years in exile he published many books and articles, founded the Institute for the History of Spain in Buenos Aires, and, in 1944, for the second time in his life, he established a journal, *Cuadernos de Historia de España*. In addition, between 1959 and 1971 he served as the president of the council of ministers of the Spanish government in exile.[34]

However, after 1948 the main thrust of Sánchez Albornoz's scholarship was the prolonged, stormy, harsh, and obsessive polemic against the philologist and scholar of Spanish literature, Américo Castro, who had also been a political exile since 1936 and had received a chair at Princeton in 1940.[35] In 1948 Castro published his well-known and influential book, *España en su Historia. Cristianos, moros y judíos* (Spain in its History: Christians, Moors, and Jews), a revised version of which was published in 1954 under the title, *La realidad histórica de España* (The Historical Reality of Spain), which was immediately translated into English among other languages.[36] According to Castro, Spain was formed as a historical-cultural entity as a result of the unique and special encounter that took place on the Iberian peninsula between Christians, Muslims, and Jews, or, as he defined it, the meeting among three castes. Before that encounter had fully taken place, the historical entity called *España* did not exist. Therefore the Roman period should not be regarded as part of Spanish history, nor should Seneca or Isidore of Seville be regarded as Spaniards. Nor does the Visigothic period belong to the Spanish past. Not until the thirteenth century, after the consolidation of the tripartite encounter, did Spain come into being. The severe way that this bundle was dismantled after the Christians cruelly removed the Jewish and Muslim presence from Iberia caused a deep crisis and tragic rift in Spanish society, culture, and consciousness.[37]

Until the publication of this book, relations between don Claudio and don Américo were collegial, even cordial, but afterward Castro became a constant target for Sánchez Albornoz's sharp barbs and incessant attacks, and of course Castro did not stand idly by. Don Claudio went out of his way to prove the inherent continuity in Spanish history from time immemorial until the modern age. He coined the phrase *herencia temperamental* (temperamental inheritance) and sought to describe the force that unified the Spanish in the past and in the present. This temperamental inheritance was expressed in the war of the Reconquista and the reality it created in the Christian kingdoms of Iberia. Spain was consolidated as a Christian entity, and the Muslims and Jews remained foreign to that heritage and could never have been an integral part of it or integrate into authentic Hispanic culture. In 1956 the first edition of don Claudio's monumental work, *España: Un enigma histórico* (Spain: A Historic Riddle), was published in Buenos Aires, in two hefty volumes almost entirely devoted to refuting Castro's thesis.[38] Sánchez Albornoz persisted in his attacks upon Castro in the following years as well, and it would be difficult to find among his voluminous writings, published between 1956 and his death in 1984, a single publication in which he neglected to attack Castro with extreme vehemence or at least to make sarcastic comments on Castro's thesis. He continued to do so even after Castro's death in 1972.[39] In the introduction to the sixth edition of his book, Sánchez Albornoz added the following sentence: "I honor the sentiments deriving from belonging to a certain race, and for that reason, I honor the love that Castro feels for the Hebrews, which is in effect a consequence of his family origins. But love of this sort is a poor counselor for evaluating the Spanish past and for facing its future."[40] It should be pointed out that Castro's Jewish past was never proved, and it is doubtful whether it *could* be proved; and of course it should not be relevant to understanding his historiographical views. However, in the view of the man who coined the concept "temperamental inheritance," things, of course, looked different.

When Baer began to check the English translation of his book on the history of medieval Jewry, he decided to consult Sánchez Albornoz's book, whose earlier historical works he greatly admired. He bought the second edition of 1962, but reading it, especially the large chapter in the second volume dedicated to the Jews (134 pages!), he was stunned.[41] Here is a brief summary of the contents: the Jews, in Sánchez Albornoz's opinion, were graciously received as guests in Christian Spain, but they responded to this hospitality with acts of deceit and oppression, which aroused the Spanish people against them. The question was not why the Jews were expelled from Spain in 1492 but rather why the expulsion was so late, compared to those of other kingdoms in Europe. Sánchez Albornoz's view of the Jews was shockingly essentialist and monolithic, based entirely on anti-Semitic stereotypes and on precarious generalizations. He was not deterred from unequivocally defining the mentality of the Jews: (1) they attribute importance to the collective rather than to the individual; (2) they show great interest in the life of this world and ignore the world to come; (3) they are obsessively concerned with the coming of the messiah; (4) they give intelligence a central place as the motivating force of human life. Motivated by the combination of these traits, the Jews mobilized everything in their possession to oppress, rob, and exploit the Christian populace, with the intention of controlling and ruling it. Moreover, the Christians were being kind to the Jews by imposing their religion on many of them. If the converts had not been baptized and had remained Jewish, what would have been their fate after the expulsion? They would have become worthless rabbis in the Jewish quarter of some city in Morocco. . . . In contrast, as Christians some of them were able to become important artists, prominent theologians, and talented authors and poets.[42] However, along with emphasizing their parasitism, their irrelevance to the creation of Spanish culture, Sánchez Albornoz saw fit to bring out the important "contribution" of the Jews to Spanish society, worth its weight in gold: the Spanish Inquisition was, in his opinion, a Jewish creation, because it was entirely based on the Jewish legal tradition and on the way Jews treated informers in their communities. In his opinion, the conversos played a central role in conveying this influence from Judaism to Christian society.[43]

It is only fair to mention here that Américo Castro, Sánchez Albornoz's bitter rival, preceded him in this matter and made a similar claim before him, even adding to this "Jewish contribution" to Spanish society another central "contribution": the laws of purity of blood (*limpiezas de sangre*), which were intended to separate Christians of purely Christian origin from New Christians of Jewish or Muslim origin. In his opinion, these regulations were based on Jewish foundations. Castro claimed that *limpiezas de sangre* arose from the idea of the chosen people, invented by the Jews. In this case as well, the intermediary of the conversos was essential in conveying this "Jewish" idea to Christian culture.[44]

In contrast to the objective and systematic tone of the response that Baer wrote in the appendix to the English edition, the response that he sent to Sánchez Albornoz, immediately after reading his words, was extremely emotional. "I read the pages that you devoted to the Jews with horror. Those pages are solely based on the reading of external sources and on books of secondary value; they do not refer properly to the Jewish religion, to the rich and deep religious literature of the Jews, and they do not have a correct grasp of our long and tragic history. Rather, they contain distorted and malicious interpretations of events, both general and specific."[45] In concluding his letter he referred to a letter he had sent to him in 1933, where he protested against the fate of the Jews of Germany: "Then," wrote Baer, "I received no answer from you. In your book of 1956 I found the answer to my letter of 1933."

Sánchez Albornoz replied after a delay of several months, explaining that when Baer's letter reached Buenos Aires he was in Paris, where he was teaching at the Sorbonne, and from there he had been forced to go to Mexico to accept the presidency of the Council of Ministers of the Spanish Republic in Exile. Between June 5 and June 8, 1962, he took part in a conference, in Munich, of more than a hundred Spanish politicians of every stripe, who had expressed opposition to the Franco regime.[46] Upon his return to Buenos Aires, he wrote, on July 10, 1962, on the official stationery of the Council of Ministers of the Republic, a blunt reply, arrogant and aggressive: "The tone of your letter did not surprise me, because the sensitivity of the Jews to any criticism regarding their past is very sharp. You have suffered very much during your history, and thus the hypersensitivity with which you are endowed is understandable. I understand, and I forgive, the injustice of your words and the lack of understanding that you demonstrate [in reading my work]."[47] According to him, he did not invent facts or rewrite documents, since most of the discussion in the chapter on the Jews in his book were taken from Baer's two volumes of documents, published in 1929 and 1936: "and if you go back and read your collection of documents, you will discover a huge quantity of documents that I left aside, because they would have blackened the history of the Spanish Hebrews, against whom I harbor no animosity." Nor did the words of the President of the Spanish Council of Ministers lack a threatening tone, as he argued with Baer as if he were the representative of the Jewish collective, which was about to launch an attack against him: "But if you and the members of your nation insist, I will publish long pages, rather sad, about the Spanish Jews, and I shall do it on the basis of the texts in your two useful volumes." Sánchez Albornoz did indeed claim that he harbored no resentment against the medieval Spanish Jews, though on the other hand he did have a very clear picture of their character and traits: "I am not to blame if the Spanish Jews dealt in usury and tax farming, and that these two miserable professions, along with their wealth, pride, and power aroused the hatred of Christians against them. I could have gone much farther in describing matters in those sections of the chapter, if indeed I did harbor the hatred toward members of your race that you attribute to me."

As for the part allegedly played by the conversos in the idea of the Inquisition, "historical reality is clear beyond any doubt, and it cannot be denied that the conversos fought more than anyone for its establishment in Castile. The systems and procedures of the Inquisition have nothing at all to do with the juridical heritage of Castile and Aragon, but rather they are marvelously consistent with the synagogal tradition with regard to the persecution of informers." And again, he returned to the threatening tone, even more emphatically, once again using the second person plural, as if an entire Jewish community stood behind Baer and accused him: "If you [plural] force me, I can blacken this sorry chapter of Spanish-Jewish history, just by citing the documents that you have published. You published dreadful evidence about the plague of informing and dreadful evidence about the hypocrisy, the pretense, and the intolerance of the conversos, to which I did not refer in my chapter, but they are available to me."

From the tone of the threatening warrior he passed over to that of the preacher: "I think, Baer, my friend, that the time has come for you to recognize that during the Middle Ages, you were the victims of the Spaniards, but that the Spaniards were also your victims, and the time has come for you to put an end to your hypersensitivity. The Jews have a great and splendid history. All the nations of the world have made mistakes, and you are not exempt from them. I did not pass over the mistakes of the Spaniards in silence, and therefore I had no reason to keep silence with respect to your mistakes."

He protested vehemently against the suspicion of anti-Semitism: "I do not have an atom of anti-Semitism. I have many Hebrew friends in every country of the world. I felt your pain in your difficult times, which are still close to us, of the recent persecutions, that you suffered from the Nazis. I feel disgust that cannot be overcome toward those who committed them. For three years in a row I have been invited to lecture in Germany, and I have not been able to overcome my resistance." He did not forget to mention his own suffering because he did not submit to the dictator who ruled in Spain, and the loss of property to which he was condemned because of his life in exile. "Thus I am incapable of understanding how the Jews, who were persecuted cruelly by Henry II, for example [i.e. Enrique de Trastamara, who rebelled against his step-brother, Pedro, in the 1360s; the war between them caused great destruction in the Jewish communities] could have approached him afterward."[48] In Sánchez Albornoz's view, Baer was to be condemned because "he was swept by nationalist fervor" and unjustly criticized his book. And he, Sánchez Albornoz, actually felt for Baer "and for all the great figures of modern Jewish thought" sympathy and great respect."[49]

Baer did not answer this letter. The connection between him and Sánchez Albornoz was severed and never renewed. The indefatigable Sánchez Albornoz continued to wage obstinate battle against Castro and to engage in bitter polemical struggles against other scholars, attacking them without restraint as well, sometimes with irony, sometimes with sarcasm, even after they had passed away.[50] He never changed his opinion about the Jews of Spain, and in some of the articles that he wrote in the 1960s and 1970s he repeated the harsh and stereotypical remarks that had aroused Baer's ire. In an article that he published in 1978, he again took umbrage against those who protested his attitudes regarding the Jews of Spain: "Why did I have to keep silence in the presence of the unchanging characteristics of the Jews, as usurers and tax-farmers? Every day new proof is discovered in this context. . . . The authentic historian must tell the truth, even when it is unpleasant. If I distorted history in order to flatter the Hebrews, I would be thought unworthy of that title. I did not conceal the faults of the Spanish either."[51] Moreover, in 1980 he explained why not many Jews settled in the poor regions of the Basque country and Galicia: the poverty that prevailed there did not attract them, because they reckoned they could not make profits there and deal in usury and tax-farming. "I want to emphasize this fact," he added, "in order to emphasize the generosity with which they were treated by the people of Castile, whom they hate today [sic/]."[52] He repeatedly mocked the idea of convivencia, the coexistence with mutual toleration between Jews and Christians: "Convivencia between the Christian nation and the killers of God, His oppressors?"[53] But in contrast to other rivals with whom he disputed with unbridled wrath and without mercy, he never mentioned Baer's name explicitly, though here and there he alluded to a deep dispute with him, and he hinted at him indirectly, with admiration and honor:

> The Hebrews devoted themselves to the same two enterprises that they had practiced in the South: they were tax collectors and usurers. I do not say this out of any anti-Semitic prejudice. These facts are corroborated by abundant documents, partly published by a great Jewish historian well versed in Spanish affairs. Whatever the spiritual creations of the Hebrews dwelling in Christian Spain may have been—no one can question them—people hated them intensely and furiously.[54]

After publishing the appendix against Sánchez Albornoz (and Castro) in the English edition of his book on the Jews of Christian Spain, Baer never confronted them again. It is doubtful that the later publications of his former Spanish colleague ever came into his hands. He probably did not read them, for he had lost interest in his work. The confrontation with the Spanish historian Sánchez Albornoz undoubtedly upset him at the time. But this was not the first occasion when he felt himself betrayed by historians, and not the first time that he was made aware that even the most learned of them are not immune to stereotypes, prejudices, and anti-Semitism.

Translated from the Hebrew by Jeffrey Green

Notes

1. This article is mainly based on a correspondence between Yitzhak Baer and Claudio Sánchez Albornoz. Of this correspondence, which was held in Spanish, four letters are preserved in the Central Archives for the History of the Jewish People, in a folder containing a few of Baer's personal documents. This correspondence took place irregularly from August 1959 to July 1962. Three of the letters of the Spanish historian were sent from Buenos Aires, the capital of Argentina, to Baer's private home in Jerusalem (31 Alfasi Street). The single letter of Baer's was sent from Jerusalem to Buenos Aires. All the letters are typewritten. In chronological order they are: (1) A letter from Sánchez Albornoz to Baer, August 5, 1959 [henceforth: SA1]; (2) a letter from Sánchez Albornoz to Baer, September 28, 1960 [henceforth: SA2]; (3) a letter from Baer to Sánchez Albornoz, March 29, 1962 [henceforth: Baer to SA]; (4) a letter from Sánchez Albornoz to Baer, July 10, 1962 [henceforth: SA3]. Several almost identical copies of the letter written by Baer are in the folder, and one of them has corrections written by hand. These corrections were entered in the final version of the letter, to which Baer added, in his handwriting, the date: 29.III.1962. There is also a letter in Hebrew, written from Buenos Aires by Bilha (Bertha) Senderey, addressed to Baer, with no date, but, judging by the cancellation mark on the envelope, it was sent on September 26, 1961. The statement made by Sánchez Albornoz in 1929, "No hay, antisemitismo en España," was quoted by Baer in the aforementioned letter.

2. Fritz (Yitzhak) Baer, *Die Juden im christlichen Spanien: Urkunden und Regesten*, Band I: Aragonien und Navarra (Berlin, 1929).

3. For a survey of Baer's life and work as a historian, see Shmuel Ettinger, "Yitzhak Baer (1888–1980)" (Hebrew), *Zion* 44 (1979): ix–xx; David N. Myers, *Re-Inventing the Jewish Past: European Jewish Intellectuals and the Zionist Return to History* (New York, 1995), 129–50. Baer's doctoral dissertation was published in Berlin: *Studien zur Geschichte der Juden im Königreich Aragonien während des 13 und 14 Jahrhunderts.*

4. Heinrich Finke, *Acta Aragonensia. Quellen zur deutschen, italienischen, französischen, spanischen, zur Kirchen und Kulturgeschichte aus der diplomatischen Korrespondenz Jaymes II*, vols. 1–3 (Berlin, 1908–23).

5. A brief survey of his activity as a historian can be found in *Badische Biographien*, Neue Folge, ed. B. Ottna (Stuttgart, 1987), 87–89, s.v. "Finke, (Johannes) Heinrich, Historiker." See also his autobiographical essay in *Die Geschichtswissenschaft der Gegenwart in Selbstdarstellungen*, vol. 1, ed. S. Steinberg (Leipzig, 1925), 91–128.

6. For an extensive survey of his life and scholarship see James F. Powers, "Claudio Sánchez-Albornoz y Menduiña (1893–1984)," *Medieval Scholarship. Biographical Studies on the Formation of a Discipline*, vol. 1: History, ed. Helen Damico and Joseph B. Zavadil (New York, 1995), 233–46; Luis G. de Valdeavellano, "Don Claudio Sánchez-Albornoz y Menduiña," *Boletín de la Real Academia de Historia* 181 (1984): 337–45.

7. Claudio Sánchez–Albornoz y Menduiña, *La curia regia portuguesa en los siglos XII y XIII* (Madrid, 1920).

8. Fritz Baer, "De las respuestas del rabí Acher de Toledo," *Anuario de historia del derecho español* 6 (1929): 197–213.

9. Thomas Buchner, "Alfons Dopsch (1868–1953). Die 'Mannigfaltigkeit der Verhältnisse,'" in *Österreichische Historiker 1900–1945. Lebensläufe und Karrieren in Österreich, Deutschland und der Tschechoslowakei in wissenschaftsgeschichtlichen Porträts*, ed. K. Hruza (Vienna, 2008), 155–90.

10. Claudio Sánchez Albornoz, *De mi anecdotario político* (Buenos Aires, 1972), 78.

11. See in *Anuario de historia del derecho español* 6 (1929): 542–45.

12. Claudio Sánchez Albornoz, "Mauregato: A Leaf from Asturian History," *Yitzhak F. Baer Jubilee Volume on the Occasion of His Seventieth Birthday*, ed. S. W. Baron et al. (Hebrew, Jerusalem, 1960), 174–85.

13. SA1.

14. The letter from Berta Sendery to Baer, in Hebrew.

15. SA2.

16. Ibid.

17. Ibid.

18. Letter of Berta Senderey to Baer, in Hebrew.

19. SA3.

20. Yitzhak Baer, *A History of the Jews in Christian Spain*, trans. L. Schoffman (Philadelphia, 1992), 2:444–56.

21. Baer, *Historia de los Judíos en la España Cristiana*, trans. J. L. Lacave, vols. 1–2 (Madrid, 1981).

22. Arielle Rein, "History and Jewish History: Together or Separate? The Definition of Historical Studies at the Hebrew University, 1925–1935," in *The History of the Hebrew University of Jerusalem: Origins and Beginnings*, vol. 1, ed. S. Katz and M. Heyd (Hebrew; Jerusalem, 1997), 516–40.

23. Fritz (Yitzhak) Baer, *Die Juden in christlichen Spanien: Urkunden und Regesten*, vol. 2 (Berlin, 1936).

24. Baer to SA.

25. Ibid.

26. He was one of forty-seven Germans who received this distinction between 1933 and 1944.

27. The original German edition was published by Schocken. In 1947 the Schocken publishing house in New York published an English edition of the book, translated by Robert Warshow. See Jizchak Fritz Baer, *Galut*, trans. I. Eldad (Hebrew; Jerusalem, 1980), 7.

28. For a fascinating explanation of this change, see Israel J. Yuval, "Yitzhak Baer and the Search for Authentic Judaism," in *The Jewish Past Revisited: Reflections on Modern Jewish Historians*, ed. D. N. Myers and D. B. Ruderman (New Haven, Conn., 1998), 77–87.

29. Santos Juliá, *Vida y tiempo de Manuel Azaña (1880–1940)* (Madrid, 2008); Sánchez Albornoz, *De mi anecdotario,* 78–79, 92.

30. Claudio Sánchez Albornoz, *Estudios Visigodos* (Rome, 1971), 93

31. Sánchez Albornoz, *De mi anecdotario,* 123.

32. Ibid., 142–43. On Spanish intellectuals in exile during the Spanish Civil War, see José María Balcells and José Antonio Pérez Bowie, eds., *El exilio cultural de la Guerra Civil (1936–1939)* (Salamanca, 2001), especially Mariano Peset, "Claudio Sánchez-Albornoz, un medievalista en el exilio," in ibid., 159–73.

33. Claudio Sánchez Albornoz, *En torno a los orígenes del feudalismo*, vols. 1–3 (Mendoza, 1942).

34. On the Spanish government in exile, see: José María Del Valle, *Las instituciones de la República española en exilio* (Paris, 1976); Sónsoles Cabeza Sánchez Albornoz, *Historia política de la Segunda República en el exilio* (Madrid, 1997); Milagrosa Romero Samper, *La oposición durante el franquismo/3. El exilio republicano* (Madrid, 2005).

35. For a short survey of his life, see Henry Kamen, *The Disinherited: The Exiles Who Created Spanish Culture* (London, 2007), 48–45; the best book about the development of his historical view is Guillermo Araya, *Evolución del pensamiento histórico de Américo Castro* (Madrid, 1969). A list of his main publications can be found in *Collected Studies in Honour of Américo Castro's 80th Year*, ed. M. P. Hornik (Oxford, 1965), 479–82. On the contradictory historiographical views of Castro and Sánchez Albornoz, see Thomas F. Glick, *Islamic and Christian Spain in the Early Middle Ages* (2nd rev. ed.; Leiden, 2005), 337–71.

36. Américo Castro, *The Structure of Spanish History*, trans. E. L. King (Princeton, N.J., 1954). The book was later published in Italian (1955), German (1957), and French (1963).

37. Américo Castro, *La realidad histórica de España* (8th ed.; México, 1982), 23–56, 113–38; Castro, *De la edad conflictiva* (3rd ed.; Madrid, 1972), iv–lxiv, 13–46.

38. Claudio Sánchez-Albornoz, *España: Un enigma histórico* (Buenos Aires, 1956). In the introduction he explains the reasons that motivated him to write the book (two volumes containing nearly 1,500 pages!), leaving no room for doubt: the entire book is a response to Castro's great work. He refers to the author as "my colleague and friend of long standing" (*mi viejo colega y amigo*). See p. 12 of the second edition, issued in 1962 by the same publishing house. Baer read this edition, and I had the privilege of receiving the two volumes that were in his private library after his death in 1980, from his son Shalom Baer. They contain a few marks and comments made in pencil.

39. Claudio Sánchez Albornoz, *El drama de la formación de España y los españoles. Otra nueva aventura polémica* (Barcelona, 1973); English translation: *The Drama of the Formation of Spain and the Spaniards* (Madrid, 1979); Sánchez Albornoz, *Estudios polémicos* (Madrid, 1979), 293–310; Sánchez Albornoz, *Confidencias* (Madrid, 1979), 115–25, 148–51; Sánchez Albornoz, *Postrimerías. Del pasado hacia el futuro* (Barcelona, 1981), 128–32.

40. Sánchez Albornoz, *Confidencias*, 65.; Sánchez Albornoz, *El drama*, 104–05:

41. Sánchez Albornoz, *España*, 2:164–297: Capítulo XIV—"Límites de la contribución judaica a la forja de lo español."

42. Sánchez Albornoz, *España*, 2:164–76, 178, 181, 190–206, 227–38, 255–59, 293–97.

43. Ibid., 288–98.

44. Castro, *La realidad histórica*, 40–46; Castro, *De la edad conflictiva*, 137–51; Sánchez Albornoz, *España*, 2:288, 290, 292. And see Benzion Netanyahu, *Toward the Inquisition: Essays on Jewish and Converso History in Late Medieval Spain* (Ithaca, N.Y., 1997), 1–42, 126–55. In the two essays published in this book, Netanyahu levels harsh criticism against the views of Castro and Sánchez Albornoz, pointing out their distorted view as a result of their clinging to anti-Semitic stereotypes and ignorance of Jewish sources.

45. Baer to SA.

46. Romero Samper, 301.

47. SA3.

48. All the quotes between here and the previous citation are drawn from SA3.

49. In response to Baer's complaint, that he had never received an answer to his letter of April 1, 1933, Sánchez Albornoz claimed that the letter never reached him. He then added: "Mi respuesta a ella no es mi libro que Vd., llevado por su pasión nacionalista, maltrata. Mi respuesta ha sido siempre la cordial simpatía y la devoción científica que he sentido por Vd. y por las grandes figuras del pensamiento hebraico moderno."

50. Some of his polemical articles have been collected in Sánchez Albornoz, *Estudios polémicos.*

51. Sánchez Albornoz, *Confidencias*, 160 (first published in *La Vanguardia Española,* April 22, 1978).

52. Sánchez Albornoz, *Postrimerías*, 120.

53. Sánchez Albornoz, *El drama*, 62.

54. Sánchez Albornoz, *The Drama*, 42.

DAVID B. RUDERMAN'S PUBLICATIONS

❈ ❈ ❈

1973

"Iggeret Orhot Olam of Abraham Farissol in Its Historical Context." *Proceedings of the Sixth World Congress of Jewish Studies* 2:169–78 [Hebrew].

1975

"Giovanni Mercurio da Correggio's Appearance in Italy as Seen through the Eyes of an Italian Jew." *Renaissance Quarterly* 28.3: 309–22.

1976

"The Founding of a Gemilut Hasadim Society in Ferrara in 1515." *AJS Review* 1: 233–67.

1977

Review of Ariel Toaff's, *Gli Ebrei a Perugia*. *The American Historical Review* 82.2: 382.

1978

"An Exemplary Sermon from the Classroom of a Jewish Teacher in Renaissance Italy." *Italia* 1.2: 7–38.

Review of Kenneth Stow's *Catholic Thought and Papal Jewry Policy*. *The American Historical Review* 83.2: 419–20.

1979

"A Jewish Apologetic Treatise from Sixteenth-Century Bologna." *Hebrew Union College Annual* 50: 253–76.

"Three Contemporary Perceptions of a Polish Wunderkind." *AJS Review* 4: 143–63.

Review of Shlomo Simonsohn's *History of the Jews in the Duchy of Mantua*. *The American Historical Review* 84.5: 1423–24.

Review of *Responsa of Rabbi Azriel Diena* [Hebrew], vol. 1, edited by Yacov Boksenboim. *AJS Newsletter* 24: 30, 33.

1980

Review of Robert Bonfil's *Rabbis and Jewish Communities in Renaissance Italy* [Hebrew]. *AJS Newsletter* 26: 9–11.

1981

The World of a Renaissance Jew: The Life and Thought of Abraham B. Mordecai Farissol. Cincinnati: Hebrew Union College Press.

1982

Review of Paul L. Rose's *Bodin and the Great God in Nature: The Moral and Religious Universe of a Judaiser. Renaissance Quarterly* 35.2: 284–87.

Review of Ivan G. Marcus's *Piety and Society: The Jewish Pietists of Medieval Germany. The American Historical Review* 87.4: 1074–75.

Review of Haim Beinart's *Trujillo: A Jewish Community in Extremadura on the Eve of the Expulsion from Spain. Religious Studies Review* 8.4: 402–15.

1983

"The Legacy of Two Ordinary Jews: Reflections on Reading Israel Abrahams's *Hebrew Ethical Wills.*" *Journal of Reform Judaism* 30.1: 58–66.

Review of Benjamin Ravid's *Economics and Tolerance in Seventeenth Century Venice: The Background and Context of the Discorso of Simone Luzzatto. Jewish Social Studies* 45.1: 89–90.

1984

"The Shaping of Traditions (First to Ninth Centuries)," "The Crucible of Europe (Ninth to Fifteenth Centuries)," and "The Search for Deliverance (1492 to 1789)." *Heritage: Civilization and the Jews: Study Guide*, edited with William W. Hallo and Michael Stanislawski: 57–160. New York: Praeger.

"The Shaping of Traditions (First to Ninth Centuries)," "The Crucible of Europe (Ninth to Fifteenth Centuries)," and "The Search for Deliverance (1492 to 1789)." *Heritage: Civilization and the Jews: Source Reader*, edited with William W. Hallo and Michael Stanislawski: 63–212. New York: Praeger.

Review of Jerome Friedman's *The Most Ancient Testimony: Sixteenth-Century Christian-Hebraica in the Age of Renaissance Nostalgia. The American Historical Review* 89.5: 1294–95.

Review of Johann Reuchlin's *On the Art of the Kabbalah*, translation by Martin and Sarah Goodman; introduction by G. Lloyd Jones. *Renaissance Quarterly* 37.3: 432–35.

Review of Yosef Kaplan's *From Christianity to Judaism* [Hebrew]. *Zion* 49: 306–13 [Hebrew].

1985

Review of Judah Messer Leon's *The Book of the Honeycomb's Flow (Sefer Nopheth Suphim)*, edited and translated by Isaac Rabinowitz. *Sixteenth Century Journal* 16.1: 147–48.

1986

"On Divine Justice, Metempsychosis, and Purgatory: Ruminations of a Sixteenth-Century Italian Jew." *Jewish History* 1.1: 9–30.

"Rabbi and Teacher." *Contemporary Jewish Religious Thought: Original Essays on Critical Concepts, Movements, and Beliefs*, edited by Arthur A. Cohen and Paul Mendes-Flohr: 741–47. New York: Scribner.

1987

"Science, Medicine, and Jewish Culture in Early Modern Europe." *Spiegel Lecture in European Jewish History* 7. Tel Aviv: Tel Aviv University.

"Unicorns, Great Beasts and the Marvelous Variety of Things in Nature in the Thought of Abraham b. Hananiah Yagel." *Jewish Thought in the Seventeenth Century*, edited by Isadore Twersky and Bernard Septimus: 343–64. Cambridge, Mass. and London: Harvard University Press.

"The Italian Renaissance and Jewish Thought." *Renaissance Humanism: Foundations, Forms, and Legacy*, edited by A. Rabil Jr., vol. 1: 382–433. Philadelphia: University of Pennsylvania Press.

"The Impact of Science on Jewish Culture and Society in Venice." *Gli Ebrei e Venezia secoli XIV–XVIII*, edited by Gaetano Cozzi. Milan, Edizioni Comunità: 417–48; 540–42. [Republished in *Essential Papers on Jewish Culture in Renaissance and Baroque Italy*, edited by David B. Ruderman (1992): 519–53.]

"Memoirs of a Jewish Gambler." *Orim, A Jewish Journal at Yale* 3: 110–24.

Review of Jonathan Israel's *European Jewry in the Age of Mercantilism: 1550–1750. Jewish Quarterly Review* 78.1/2: 154–59.

1988

Kabbalah, Magic, and Science: The Cultural Universe of a Sixteenth-Century Jewish Physician. Cambridge, Mass. and London: Harvard University Press.

"The Receptivity of Jewish Thought to the New Astronomy of the Seventeenth Century: The Case of Abraham b. Hananiah Yagel." *Jews in Italy. Studies Dedicated to the Memory of U. Cassuto*, edited by Haim Beinart: 73–93 [Hebrew]. Jerusalem: Y. L. Magnes Press.

"The Hebrew Book in a Christian World." *A Sign and a Witness: 2,000 Years of Hebrew Books and Illuminated Manuscripts*, edited by Leonard S. Gold: 101–13. Oxford and New York: Oxford University Press.

"Some Literary and Iconographic Influences of the Renaissance and Baroque on *Sefer Gei Ḥizzayon* of Abraham ben Ḥananiyah Yagel." *Tarbiz* 57.2: 271–79 [Hebrew].

1989

"At the Intersection of Cultures: The Historical Legacy of Italian Jewry," *Gardens and Ghettos: The Art of Jewish Life in Italy*, edited by Vivian B. Mann: 1–23. Berkeley and Los Angeles: University of California Press.

"The Academic Study of Judaism: A Challenge to the Reform Rabbi." *Central Conference of American Rabbis Yearbook* 99: 78–85.

1990

A Valley of Vision: The Heavenly Journey of Abraham ben Hananiah Yagel, translation from Hebrew with an introduction and commentary. Philadelphia: University of Pennsylvania Press.

"Job's Novella from *A Valley of Vision* by Abraham ben Hananiah Yagel." *Rabbinic Fantasies: Imaginative Narratives from Classical Hebrew Literature*, edited by Mark J. Mirsky and David Stern: 313–31. Philadelphia: Jewish Publication Society.

1991

"Hope against Hope: Jewish and Christian Messianic Expectations in the Late Middle Ages." *Exile and Diaspora: Studies in the History of the Jewish People Presented to Professor Haim Beinart*, edited by Avraham Grossman et al.: 185–202. Jerusalem, Ben-Zvi Institute and the Hebrew University of Jerusalem; Madrid: Consejo Superior de Investigaciones Científicas. [Reprinted in *Essential Papers on Jewish Culture in Renaissance and Baroque Italy*, edited by David B. Ruderman (1992): 299–323].

"Champion of Jewish Economic Interests." *Essential Papers on Judaism and Christianity in Conflict: From Late Antiquity to the Reformation*, edited by Jeremy Cohen: 514–35. New York: New York University Press.

Review of Lester A. Segal's *Historical Consciousness and Religious Tradition in Azariah de' Rossi's Me'or 'Einayim. The American Historical Review* 96.3: 904–5.

Review of *Menasseh ben Israel and His World*, edited by Yosef Kaplan et al. *Renaissance Quarterly* 44.3: 583–85.

1992

[Editor] *Essential Papers on Jewish Culture in Renaissance and Baroque Italy.* New York and London: New York University Press.

"Introduction." *Essential Papers on Jewish Culture in Renaissance and Baroque Italy*, edited by David B. Ruderman: 1–39. New York and London: New York University Press.

[Editor] *Preachers of the Italian Ghetto.* Los Angeles and Berkeley: University of California Press.

"Jewish Preaching and the Language of Science: The Sermons of Azariah Figo." *Preachers of the Italian Ghetto*, edited by David B. Ruderman: 89–104. Los Angeles and Berkeley: University of California Press.

"Contemporary Science and Jewish Law in the Eyes of Isaac Lampronti and Some of His Contemporaries." *The Frank Talmage Memorial Volume*, edited by Barry Walfish: 211–24. Haifa: Haifa University Press; Hanover, N.H.: Brandeis University Press.

"Jewish Thought in Newtonian England: The Career and Writings of David Nieto." *Proceedings of the American Academy for Jewish Research* 58: 193–219.

"In the Shadow of the Alhambra." *CCAR Journal: A Reform Jewish Quarterly* 39: 61–63.

Review of *Planets, Potions and Parchments: Scientific Hebraica from the Dead Sea Scrolls to the Eighteenth Century*, edited by B. Barry Levy. *British Journal of the History of Science* 25.3: 355–57.

1993

"Kabbalah and the Subversion of Traditional Jewish Society in the Renaissance and Beyond." *Yale Journal of Law and the Humanities* 5: 169–78.

"Tragedy and Transcendence: The Meaning of 1492 for Jewish History." *Central Conference of American Rabbis Yearbook* 102: 162–70.

"Philosophy, Kabbalah, and Science in the Culture of the Italian Ghetto: On the Debate between Samson Morpurgo and Aviad Sar Shalom Basilae." *Jerusalem Studies in Jewish Thought* 11: vii–xxiv.

"The Language of Science as the Language of Faith: An Aspect of Italian Jewish Thought in the Seventeenth and Eighteenth Centuries." *Shlomo Simonsohn Jubilee Volume: Studies on the History of the Jews in the Middle Ages and Renaissance Period*, edited by Daniel Carpi et al.: 177–89. Tel Aviv: Tel Aviv University.

Review of Frank E. Manuel's *The Broken Staff: Judaism through Christian Eyes. Jewish History* 7: 158–63.

Review of Ilana Zinguer's *L'Hébreu au Temps de la Renaissance. Renaissance Quarterly* 46.3: 591–93.

1994

Review of Minna Rozen's *Jewish Identity and Society in the Seventeenth Century: Reflections on the Life and Work of Refael Mordekhai Malki. AJS Review* 19.2: 265–68.

Review of *Studies on Gersonides: A Fourteenth-Century Jewish Philosopher-Scientist*, edited by Gad Freudenthal. *ISIS* 85.2: 315.

Review of Howard M. Sachar's *Farewell España: The World of the Sephardim Remembered. The Washington Post, Book World.* December 11.

1995

Jewish Thought and Scientific Discovery in Early Modern Europe. New Haven and London: Yale University Press.

"Medieval and Modern Jewish History." Section editor and Introduction, *American Historical Association Guide to Historical Literature.* New York: Oxford University Press.

1996

Review of Robert Bonfil's *Jewish Life in Renaissance Italy. Renaissance Quarterly* 49.4: 850–53.

1997

Sefer Gei Hizzayon shel Avraham ben Hananiyah Yagel: Mavo ve-Perushim. Revised Hebrew edition of *A Valley of Vision.* Jerusalem: Zalman Shazar Center for Jewish History.

"The Cultural Significance of the Ghetto in Jewish History." *From Ghetto to Emancipation: Historical and Contemporary Reconsiderations of the Jewish Community*, edited by David N. Myers and William V. Rowe: 1–16. Chicago: University of Chicago Press.

"On Defining a Jewish Stance towards Newtonianism: The Case of Eliakim Ben Abraham Hart's *Wars of the Lord." Science in Context* 10.4: 677–92.

"Was There a 'Haskalah' in England? Reconsidering an Old Question." *Zion* 62: 109–31 [Hebrew].

1998

The Jewish Past Revisited: Reflections on Modern Jewish Historians. Edited with David N.
Myers. New Haven: Yale University Press.

"Cecil Roth, Historian of Italian Jewry: A Reassessment." *The Jewish Past Revisited:
Reflections on Modern Jewish Historians,* edited with David N. Myers: 128–42. New
Haven: Yale University Press.

1999

Giudaismo tra scienza e fede: La crisi della prima età moderna. [Italian translation of *Jewish
Thought and Scientific Discovery in Early Modern Europe* (1995)]. Edizioni Culturali
Internazionali Genova: Genoa.

"Was there an English Parallel to the German Haskalah?" *Two Nations: British and German
Jews in Comparative Perspective,* edited by Michael Brenner et al.: 15–44. London: Leo
Baeck Institute.

"Jewish Medicine and Science." *The Encyclopedia of the Renaissance,* vol. 3, edited by Paul F.
Grendler: 310–12. New York: Scribner's.

2000

Jewish Enlightenment in an English Key: Anglo-Jewry's Construction of Modern Jewish Thought.
Princeton: Princeton University Press.

"Judaism to 1750." *The History of Science and Religion in the Western Tradition: An Encyclopedia,*
edited by Gary B. Ferngren et al.: 237–42. New York and London: Garland Publishing.

Review of *Jewish History and Jewish Memory: Essays in Honor of Yosef Hayim Yerushalmi,* edited
by Elisheva Carlebach et al. *Jewish History* 14.1: 109–13.

2001

Jewish Thought and Scientific Discovery in Early Modern Europe. (1st ed. 1995) Newly revised
paperback edition with new introduction. Detroit, Wayne State University Press.

"Medicine and Scientific Thought in the Ghetto: The Cultural World of Tobias Cohen."
The Jews of Early Modern Venice, edited by Robert C. Davis and Benjamin Ravid:
191–210. Baltimore: Johns Hopkins University Press.

"Was There a 'Haskalah' in England? Reconsidering an Old Question." *New Perspectives on
the Haskalah,* edited by Shmuel Feiner and David Sorkin: 64–85. London and Portland,
Oregon: Littman Library of Jewish Civilization.

Review of Anna Foa's *The Jews of Europe after the Black Death. The American Historical
Review* 106.5: 1863–64.

2002

Maḥshavah yehudit ve-tagliyot mada'iyot ba-'et ha-ḥadashah ha-mukdemet be-Eropah [Hebrew
translation of *Jewish Thought and Scientific Discovery in Early Modern Europe* (1995)].
Translated by David Luvish. Jerusalem: Zalman Shazar Center for Jewish History.

Review of John Efron's *Medicine and the German Jews: A History. Jewish Quarterly Review* 92.3/4: 638–43.

"Some Jewish Responses to Smallpox Prevention in the Late Eighteenth and Early Nineteenth Centuries: A New Perspective on the Modernization of European Jewry." *Aleph: Historical Studies in Science and Judaism* 2: 111–44.

Review of Allison P. Coudert's *The Impact of the Kabbalah in the Seventeenth Century: The Life and Thought of Francis Mercury van Helmont (1614–1698). AJS Review* 26.1: 194–96.

2003

"Reflecting on American Jewish History." *American Jewish History* 91: 371–78.

De culturele betekenis van het getto in de joodse geschiedenis. [Dutch translation of "The Cultural Significance of the Ghetto in Jewish History." (1997)] *Leeser Rosenthal/Juda Palache-lezing,* edited with Ruth Peeters and Emile Schrijver. Amsterdam: Vossiuspers UvA.

"George Levison." *Metzler Lexicon jüdischer Philosophen: Philosophisches Denken des Judentums von der Antike bis zur Gegenwart,* edited by Andreas B. Kilcher and Otfried Fraisse: 191–93. Stuttgart: Metzler.

2004

Cultural Intermediaries: Jewish Intellectuals in Early Modern Italy. Edited with Giuseppe Veltri. Philadelphia: University of Pennsylvania Press.

"Introduction." *Cultural Intermediaries: Jewish Intellectuals in Early Modern Italy,* edited with Giuseppe Veltri: 1–23. Philadelphia: University of Pennsylvania Press.

"Falk, Samuel Jacob Hayyim," "Hart, Eliakim ben Abraham," "Levison, Mordecai Gumpel Schnaber," and "Tang, Abraham ben Naphtali." *Oxford Dictionary of National Biography.* Oxford: Oxford University Press.

Review of Adam Sutcliffe's *Judaism and Enlightenment. Jewish Quarterly Review* 94.3: 523–30.

"Greenville Diary: A Northern Rabbi Confronts the Deep South, 1966–1970." *Jewish Quarterly Review* 94.4: 643–65.

2006

"Mezcla de identidades: judíos, cristianos y las cambiantes nociones del otro en la Europa de la era moderna temprana." *Europa, America y el Mundo: Tiempos Históricos,* edited by Roger Chartier and Antonio Feros: 25–39. Madrid: Marcial Pons and Fundación Rafael del Pino.

2007

Connecting the Covenants: Judaism and the Search for Christian Identity in Eighteenth-Century England. Philadelphia: University of Pennsylvania Press.

Early Modern Culture and the Haskalah: Reconsidering the Borderlines of Modern Jewish History [*Simon Dubnov Institute Yearbook* 6], edited with Shmuel Feiner.

"Introduction." *Early Modern Culture and the Haskalah: Reconsidering the Borderlines of Modern Jewish History* [*Simon Dubnov Institute Yearbook* 6], edited with Shmuel Feiner: 17–21.

"Why Periodization Matters: On Early Modern Jewish Culture and the Haskalah." *Early Modern Culture and the Haskalah: Reconsidering the Borderlines of Modern Jewish History* [*Simon Dubnov Institute Yearbook* 6], edited with Shmuel Feiner: 23–32.

"A History of Jewish Engagement: Doctors/Healers in the Jewish Tradition." *Healing and the Jewish Imagination: Spiritual and Practical Perspectives on Judaism and Health*, edited by William Cutter: 195–206; 218–19. Woodstock: Jewish Lights Publication.

"The Impact of Early Modern Jewish Thought on the Eighteenth Century: A Challenge to the Notion of the Sephardic Mystique." *Sepharad in Ashkenaz: Medieval Knowledge and Eighteenth-Century Enlightened Discourse*, edited by Resianne Fontaine et al.:11–22. Amsterdam: Koninklijke Nederlandse Akademie van Wetenschappen.

"Le ghetto et les débuts de l'Europe nouvelle: Vers une nouvelle interpretation." *Les Cahiers du Judaïsme* 22: 14–23.

"Three Anglo-Jewish Portraits and Their Legacy for Today: Moses Marcus, the Convert; Abraham Tang, the Radical Maskil; David Levi, the Defender of Judaism." *Report of the Oxford Centre for Hebrew and Jewish Studies (2007–2008):* 23–28. Oxford: Centre for Hebrew and Jewish Studies.

"The History of Invention: Doctors, Medicine, and Jewish Culture." *Healing and the Jewish Imagination: Spiritual and Practical Perspectives on Judaism and Health*, edited by William Cutter: 195–206. Woodstock: Jewish Lights Publication.

2008

"Michael A. Meyer's Periodization of Modern Jewish History: Revisiting a Seminal Essay." *Mediating Modernity: Challenges and Trends in the Jewish Encounter with the Modern World: Essays in Honor of Michael A. Meyer*, edited by Michael Brenner and Lauren Strauss: 27–42. Detroit: Wayne State University Press.

"The Ghetto and Jewish Cultural Formation in Early Modern Europe: Towards a New Interpretation." [English version of "Le ghetto et les débuts de l'Europe nouvelle: vers une nouvelle interpretation" (2007)]. *Jewish Literatures and Cultures: Context and Intertext*, edited by Anita Norich and Shahar Pinsker: 117–27. Providence: Brown Judaic Studies.

"The Study of the Mishnah and the Quest for Christian Identity in Early Eighteenth-Century England: Completing a Narrative Initiated by Richard Popkin." *The Legacies of Richard H. Popkin*, edited by Jeremy Popkin: 123–42. Dordrecht: Springer.

2009

"Jewish Culture in Early Modern Europe: An Agenda for Future Study." *Rethinking European Jewish History*, edited by Jeremy Cohen and Moshe Rosman: 95–111. Oxford; Portland, Or.: Littman Library of Jewish Civilization.

"Buchdruck und jüdische Kultur in der Frühen Neuzeit Europas." *Münchner Beiträge zur Jüdischen Geschichte und Kultur* 2: 8–22.

"Verschmolzene Identitäten: Juden, Christen und die veränderte Wahrnehmung der Anderen in der europäischen Frühen Neuzeit." *"Wie schön sind deine Zelte, Jakob, deine Wohnungen, Israel!" (Num 24:5): Beiträge zur Geschichte jüdisch-europäischer Kultur, Apeliotes.* [German translation of "Mezcla de identidades: judíos, cristianos y las cambiantes nociones del otro en la Europa de la era moderna temprana" (2006)], edited by Rainer Kampling: 115–31. Frankfurt am Main: Peter Lang.

2010

Early Modern Jewry: A New Cultural History. Princeton: Princeton University Press.

"Revisiting the Notion of Crisis in Early Modern Jewish History." *Jacob Katz Memorial Lecture 2.* Leo Baeck Institute: Jerusalem.

"Three Reviewers and the Academic Style of the *Jewish Quarterly Review* at Midcentury." *Jewish Quarterly Review* 100.4: 556–71.

"The Book of Covenant: How to Become a Prophet." *Der Tagesspiegel*, Supplement of the American Academy of Berlin. http://www.tagesspiegel.de/zeitung/how-to-become -a-prophet/1930348.html

2011

"Behind the Best Sellers." *The Jewish Week*, http://www.thejewishweek.com/ special_sections/text_context/behind_best_sellers.

"Reuven Bonfil: An Appreciation." *Tov Elem: Memory, Community, and Gender in Medieval and Early Modern Jewish Societies: Essays in Honor of Robert Bonfil*, edited by Elisheva Baumgarten et al.: 9–11. Jerusalem: The Bialik Institute.

2012

"Das Ghetto und die Entstehung einer jüdischen Kultur in Europa der Frühen Neuzeit: Betrachtungen zur Geschichtsschreibung." [German translation of "The Ghetto and Jewish Cultural Formation in Early Modern Europe: Towards a New Interpretation." (2008)]. *Frühneuzeitliche Ghettos in Europa in Vergleich*, edited by Fritz Backhaus et al.: 39–51. Berlin: Trafo.

"Early Modern Jewish History." *Oxford Bibliographies Online: Jewish Studies.*

2013

Erken Modern Dönem Yahudi Tarihi [Turkish translation of *Early Modern Jewry* (2010)]. İstanbul: İnkılâp Kitabevi.

"The Hague Dialogue: A Conversation that Almost Took Place between Two Jewish Intellectuals at the End of the Eighteenth Century." *Mapping Jewish Amsterdam: The Early Modern Perspective, Dedicated to Yosef Kaplan on the Occasion of His Retirement*, edited by Shlomo Berger et al. *Studia Rosenthaliana* 44: 221–39.

FORTHCOMING

A Best-Selling Hebrew Book of the Modern Era: The Book of the Covenant of Pinḥas Hurwitz and Its Remarkable Legacy. Seattle and London: University of Washington Press.

Jewish Thought and Scientific Discovery in Early Modern Europe [Russian translation]. Moscow: Knizhniki Publishing House.

"The People and the Book: Print and the Transformation of Jewish Culture in Early Modern Europe." *Faithful Narratives: Historians, Religion, and the Challenge of Objectivity,* edited by Andrea Sterk and Nina Caputo. Ithaca: Cornell University Press.

"Looking Backward and Forward: Rethinking Modernity in the Light of Early Modernity." *The Cambridge History of Judaism VII: 1500–1815,* edited by Jonathan Karp and Adam Sutcliffe. Cambridge: Cambridge University Press.

"The Transformations of Judaism." *Oxford Handbook of Early Modern History,* vol. 1. Oxford; New York: Oxford University Press.

Compiled by Yechiel Y. Schur